The Papers of
George Washington

The Papers of
George Washington

Dorothy Twohig, *Editor*

Philander D. Chase, *Senior Associate Editor*

Beverly H. Runge, *Associate Editor*

Frank E. Grizzard, Jr.,
Mark A. Mastromarino, Elizabeth B. Mercer, and
Jack D. Warren, *Assistant Editors*

Confederation Series
5

February–December 1787

W. W. Abbot, *Editor*

UNIVERSITY PRESS OF VIRGINIA

CHARLOTTESVILLE AND LONDON

This edition has been prepared by the staff of
The Papers of George Washington
sponsored by
The Mount Vernon Ladies' Association of the Union
and the University of Virginia
with the support of
the National Endowment for the Humanities,
the National Historical Publications and Records Commission,
and the Packard Humanities Institute.

THE UNIVERSITY PRESS OF VIRGINIA
Copyright © 1997 by the Rector and Visitors
of the University of Virginia

First published 1997

Library of Congress Cataloging-in-Publication Data
Washington, George, 1732–1799.
    The papers of George Washington. Confederation
series.
    Includes bibliographical references and indexes.
    Contents: 1. January–July 1784—[etc.]—5. Feb-
ruary–December 1787.
    1. Washington, George, 1732–1799—Archives. 2.
Presidents—United States—Archives. 3. United
States—History—Confederation, 1783–1789. I.
Abbot, W. W. (William Wright), 1922– II.
Twohig, Dorothy. III. Confederation series. IV.
Title.
E312.7 1992 973.4'1'092   91-3171
ISBN 0-8139-1348-9 (v. 1)
ISBN 0-8139-1672-0 (v. 5)

Contents

NOTE: Volume numbers refer to the *Confederation Series*.

Editorial Apparatus

Transcription of the documents in the volumes of *The Papers of George Washington* has remained as close to a literal reproduction of the manuscript as possible. Punctuation, capitalization, paragraphing, and spelling of all words are retained as they appear in the original document. Dashes used as punctuation have been retained except when a dash and another mark of punctuation appear together. The appropriate marks of punctuation have always been added at the end of a paragraph. When a tilde is used in the manuscript to indicate a double letter, the letter has been doubled. Washington and some of his correspondents occasionally used a tilde above an incorrectly spelled word to indicate an error in orthography. When this device is used the editors have corrected the word. In cases where a tilde has been inserted above an abbreviation or contraction, usually in letter-book copies, the word has been expanded. Otherwise, contractions and abbreviations have been retained as written except that a period has been inserted after an abbreviation when needed. Superscripts have been lowered. Editorial insertions or corrections in the text appear in square brackets. Angle brackets ⟨ ⟩ are used to indicate illegible or mutilated material. A space left blank in a manuscript by the writer is indicated by a square-bracketed gap in the text [   ]. Deletion of material by the author in a manuscript is ignored unless it contains substantive material, and then it appears in a footnote. If the intended location of marginal notations is clear from the text, they are inserted without comment; otherwise they are recorded in the notes. The ampersand has been retained and the thorn transcribed as "th." The symbol for per ℔ is used when it appears in the manuscript. The dateline has been placed at the head of a document regardless of where it occurs in the manuscript.

Since GW read no language other than English, incoming letters written to him in foreign languages generally were translated for his information. Where this contemporary translation has survived, it has been used as the text of the document and the original version has been included either in the notes or in the CD-ROM edition of the Papers. If there is no contemporary translation, the document in its original language has been used as the text. All of the documents printed in this volume, as well as other ancillary material (usually cited in the notes), may be found in the CD-ROM edition of Washington's Papers (CD-ROM:GW).

Individuals usually are identified only at the first appearance of their names. The index to each volume of the Confederation Series indicates where an identification may be found in earlier volumes.

A number of letters to and from Washington have been printed, in whole or in part, out of their chronological sequence, usually in footnotes. All of these letters are listed in the table of contents with an indication where they may be found in this or another volume.

Symbols Designating Documents

AD	Autograph Document
ADS	Autograph Document Signed
ADf	Autograph Draft
ADfS	Autograph Draft Signed
AL	Autograph Letter
ALS	Autograph Letter Signed
D	Document
DS	Document Signed
Df	Draft
DfS	Draft Signed
L	Letter
LS	Letter Signed
LB	Letter-Book Copy
[S]	Signature clipped (used with other symbols: e.g., AL[S], Df[S]

Repository Symbols

A-Ar	Alabama Department of Archives and History, Montgomery
CD-ROM:GW	*see* Editorial Apparatus
CSmH	Henry E. Huntington Library, San Marino, Calif.
CtY	Yale University, New Haven
DLC	Library of Congress
DLC:GW	George Washington Papers, Library of Congress
DNA	National Archives
DNA:PCC	Papers of the Continental Congress, National Archives
DSoCi	Society of the Cincinnati, Washington, D.C.
LNCD	National Society of Colonial Dames of America in the State of Louisiana—the New Orleans Committee Collection, New Orleans
MA	Amherst College, Amherst, Mass.
MFD	Dean Junior College, Franklin, Mass.
MH	Harvard University, Cambridge, Mass.
MHi	Massachusetts Historical Society, Boston

MiDbGr	Greenfield Village and the Henry Ford Museum, Dearborn, Mich.
MiU-C	William L. Clements Library, University of Michigan, Ann Arbor
MnHi	Minnesota Historical Society, St. Paul
Nc-Ar	North Carolina State Department of Archives and History, Raleigh
NcD	Duke University, Durham, N.C.
NHi	New York Historical Society, New York
NhSB	Strawbery Banke Inc., Portsmouth, N.H.
NIC	Cornell University, Ithaca, N.Y.
NjHi	New Jersey Historical Society, Newark
NjMoNP	Washington Headquarters Library, Morristown, N.J.
NjP	Princeton University, Princeton, N.J.
NN	New York Public Library, New York
NNC	Columbia University, New York
NNGL	Gilder-Lehrman Collection, on deposit at the Pierpont Morgan Library, New York
PEL	Lafayette College, Easton, Pa.
PHi	Historical Society of Pennsylvania, Philadelphia
PPAmP	American Philosophical Society, Philadelphia
PPRF	Rosenbach Foundation, Philadelphia
PWacD	David Library of the American Revolution, Sol Feinstone Collection, on deposit at PPAmP
RG	Record Group (designating the location of documents in the National Archives)
ViLGU	Gunston Hall, Lorton, Va.
ViLxW	Washington and Lee University, Lexington, Va.
ViMtV	Mount Vernon Ladies' Association of the Union
ViStCH	Augusta County Courthouse, Staunton, Va.
ViU	University of Virginia, Charlottesville
WHi	State Historical Society of Wisconsin, Madison

Short Title List

Albert, *Westmoreland County.*   George Dallas Albert, ed. *History of the County of Westmoreland, Pennsylvania.* Philadelphia, 1882.

Alden, *Sayre.*   John R. Alden. *Stephen Sayre: American Revolutionary Adventurer.* Baton Rouge, La., 1983.

Annals of Congress.   Joseph Gales, Sr., comp. *The Debates and Proceedings in the Congress of the United States; with an Appendix, Containing Im-*

portant State Papers and Public Documents, and All the Laws of a Public Nature. 42 vols. Washington, D.C., 1834–56.

Beltzhoover, *Rumsey.*   George M. Beltzhoover, Jr. *James Rumsey, the Inventor of the Steamboat.* West Virginia Historical and Antiquarian Society's Publication, Charleston, W.Va., 1900.

Biographical Dictionary of the Maryland Legislature.   Edward C. Papenfuse et al., eds. *A Biographical Dictionary of the Maryland Legislature, 1634–1789.* 2 vols. Baltimore, 1979–85.

Bowie, *Prince George's County.*   Effie Gwynn Bowie. *Across the Years in Prince George's County: A Genealogical and Biographical History of Some Prince George's County, Maryland and Allied Families.* Richmond, 1947.

Boyd, *Jefferson Papers.*   Julian P. Boyd et al., eds. *The Papers of Thomas Jefferson.* 25 vols. to date. Princeton, N.J., 1950—.

Contenson, *La Société des Cincinnati de France.*   Baron Ludovic Guy Marie du Bessey de Contenson. *La Société des Cincinnati de France et la guerre d'Amérique, 1778–1783.* Paris, 1934.

Diaries.   Donald Jackson and Dorothy Twohig, eds. *The Diaries of George Washington.* 6 vols. Charlottesville, Va., 1976–79.

Farrand, *Records of the Federal Convention.*   Max Farrand, ed. *Records of the Federal Convention of 1787.* 3 vols. New Haven, 1966.

Fitzpatrick, *Writings of Washington.*   John C. Fitzpatrick, ed. *The Writings of George Washington from the Original Manuscript Sources, 1745–1799.* 39 vols. Washington, D.C., 1931–44.

Griffin, *Boston Athenæum Collection.*   Appleton P. C. Griffin, comp. *A Catalogue of the Washington Collection in the Boston Athenæum.* Cambridge, Mass., 1897.

Harrison, *Virginia Carys.*   Fairfax Harrison. *The Virginia Carys.* New York, 1919.

Hening.   William Waller Hening, ed. *The Statutes at Large: Being a Collection of All the Laws of Virginia from the First Session of the Legislature, in the Year 1619.* 13 vols. 1819–23. Reprint. Charlottesville, Va., 1969.

House of Delegates Journal, 1786–1790.   *Journal of the House of Delegates of the Commonwealth of Virginia; Begun and Holden in the City of Richmond, in the County of Henrico, on Monday the Sixteenth Day of October, in the Year of Our Lord One Thousand Seven Hundred and Eighty-Six.* Richmond, 1828.

Hume, *Papers of Virginia Cincinnati.*   Edgar Erskine Hume. *Papers of the Society of the Cincinnati in the State of Virginia, 1783–1824.* Richmond, 1938.

Hume, *Society of the Cincinnati.*   Edgar Erskine Hume, ed. *General Washington's Correspondence concerning the Society of the Cincinnati.* Baltimore, 1941.

JCC. Worthington C. Ford et al., eds. *Journals of the Continental Congress.* 34 vols. Washington, D.C., 1904–37.

Kaminski and Saladino, *Documentary History of the Ratification of the Constitution.* John P. Kaminski, Gaspare J. Saladino, et al., eds. *The Documentary History of the Ratification of the Constitution.* 16 vols. to date. Madison, Wis., 1976—.

Ledger B. Manuscript Ledger in George Washington Papers, Library of Congress.

Marshall Papers. Herbert A. Johnson, Charles T. Cullen, Charles F. Hobson, et al., eds. *The Papers of John Marshall.* 7 vols. to date. Chapel Hill, N.C., 1974.

Memoir of Richard Henry Lee. Richard H. Lee. *Memoir of Richard Henry Lee.* 2 vols. Philadelphia, 1825.

Miller, *Peale Papers.* Lillian B. Miller, ed. *The Selected Papers of Charles Willson Peale and His Family.* 3 vols. New Haven, 1983–88.

Myers, *Liberty without Anarchy.* Minor Myers, Jr. *Liberty without Anarchy: A History of the Society of the Cincinnati.* Charlottesville, Va., 1983.

New York Journal of Assembly, 1787. Journal of the Assembly of the State of New-York at Their Tenth Session, Begun and Holden in the City of New-York, the Twelfth Day of January, 1787. New York, 1787.

Papers, Colonial Series. W. W. Abbot et al., eds. *The Papers of George Washington. Colonial Series.* 10 vols. Charlottesville, Va., 1983–95.

Papers, Confederation Series. W. W. Abbot et al., eds. *The Papers of George Washington. Confederation Series.* 4 vols. to date. Charlottesville, Va., 1992—.

Parsons, *Extracts from the Diary of Jacob Hiltzheimer.* Jacob Cox Parsons, ed. *Extracts from the Diary of Jacob Hiltzheimer, of Philadelphia, 1765–1798.* Philadelphia, 1893.

Polishook, *Rhode Island and the Union.* Irwin H. Polishook. *Rhode Island and the Union, 1774–1795.* Evanston, Ill., 1969.

Rutland, *Mason Papers.* Robert A. Rutland, ed. *The Papers of George Mason, 1725–1792.* 3 vols. Chapel Hill, N.C., 1970.

Rutland and Rachal, *Madison Papers.* Robert A. Rutland, William M. E. Rachal, et al., eds. *The Papers of James Madison.* [1st series, vol. 9]. Chicago and Charlottesville, Va., 1975.

Rutland and Hobson, *Madison Papers.* Robert A. Rutland, Charles E. Hobson, et al., eds. *The Papers of James Madison.* [1st series, vol. 10]. Chicago and Charlottesville, Va., 1977.

Seilhamer, *American Theatre.* George O. Seilhamer. *History of the American Theatre.* 3 vols. Philadelphia, 1888–91.

Syrett, *Hamilton Papers.* Harold C. Syrett et al., eds. *The Papers of Alexander Hamilton.* 27 vols. New York, 1961–87.

Va. Mag.   *Virginia Magazine of History and Biography.*

Wayland, *Washingtons.*   John Walter Wayland. *The Washingtons and Their Homes.* Staunton, Va., 1944.

Wick, *Graphic Portraits of Washington.*   Wendy C. Wick. *George Washington: An American Icon. The Eighteenth-Century Graphic Portraits.* Washington, D.C., 1982.

WMQ.   *William and Mary Quarterly.*

Wolf and Whiteman, *Jews of Philadelphia.*   Edwin Wolf and Maxwell Whiteman. *The History of the Jews of Philadelphia from Colonial Times to the Age of Jackson.* Philadelphia, 1957.

Zagarri, *Humphreys' Life.*   Rosemarie Zagarri. *David Humphreys' "Life of General Washington" with George Washington's "Remarks."* Athens, Ga., 1991.

The Papers of George Washington
Confederation Series
Volume 5
February–December 1787

From James Hill

Sir   1st Febry 1787

Inclosed is my Accot which I hope will meet with your approbation.[1] in Answer to your Letter handed me by Major Washington, I do not remember anything respectg the charge of the £100 by Mr Newton paid to me the 12th Sepr 1776.[2] if it was I judge I must have paid it to Col. F. Lewis, this I suppose may be seen by applyg to that Gentlemans Books. I have been so long out of possession of the Books & the length of time it happened, that every thing I knew of it has slipt my Memory.

The Accots of Mrs Dandridge & Mr Frazer I will send ⟨by⟩ the next post.[3] excuse my short Epistle as the post is ⟨mutilated⟩ waiting. I am with due respect Sir Your Mo. Obdt Serv.

James Hill

ALS, DLC:GW.

1. Hill enclosed in this letter three accounts with GW, copied from his books by James Quarles. There is a one-page account dated July–November 1772; a three-page account dated May 1775–Nov. 1779; and a three-page account dated Nov. 1772–Aug. 1778. These accounts appear in CD-ROM:GW. Another account, entitled "Memorandm of Cash receive'd from Jams Hill & Joseph Devenport On acct of Geo. Washington Esqr.," dated 3 July–30 Oct. 1779 (DLC:GW), is also in CD-ROM:GW.

2. GW's letter is dated 12 January.

3. The 1779 "Memorandm" (see note 1) shows the receipt on 23 Aug. of £872.2.6 "from William Frazer for por'k ⟨Setd⟩ by Hill." In Hill's enclosed account for Nov. 1772 to Aug. 1778 is recorded on 12 Aug. 1777 a payment of £50 "pd Mrs Frances Dandridge Order to Mr Custis."

From Henry Knox

My dear Sir   New York 1 February 1787

Notwithstanding my expectations of receiving particular accounts of the operations against the insurgents in Massachusetts yet I am disapointed by those people who are in some degree obliged by their official connection with me to communicate with me. The two enclosed letters will convey to you the most distinct ideas of the situation of affairs up to the 28th ultimo.[1] I shall continue to keep you informed of the progress of this affair. I am dear Sir Your affectionate Humble Servant

H. Knox

ALS, DLC:GW.

1. Copies of two letters from Hartford, both dated 28 Jan. with the writer not identified, give reports of Gen. William Shepard's rout of Daniel Shays' forces on 25 Jan. and of Gen. Benjamin Lincoln's arrival at Springfield on 27 January. The first of these letters, which were probably written by Jeremiah Wadsworth, quotes a letter from Shepard describing the engagement of 25 January. See Benjamin Lincoln to GW, 4 Dec. 1786–4 Mar. 1787.

To John Francis Mercer

Sir,   Mount Vernon Febuary 1st 1787

I am perfectly satisfied with your determination respecting the Negroes—The money will be infinitely more agreeable to me than property of that sort. I[1] will too, if I should want any of those people, procure them on more advantageous terms than I offered.

I beg that the Certificates may be no longer delayed—I have already sunk one hundred pounds specie by consenting to take them at 4 for 1—at the moment I did this, as appeared by the Richmond Gazette which came to my hands a day or two afterwards the price of them was 4½ and five Now Doctr Stuart tells me the latter is with difficulty obtained—I wish therefore to do some thing with these before my loss becomes greater.[2]

The money sent by Mr Diggs came safe.[3] I am Sir your most Obed. Humble Servant

G. Washington

LB, DLC:GW. Between 1793 and 1794 GW's letters, beginning with this one and continuing through that of 3 Oct. 1790, were copied in his letter book by his young nephew Howell Lewis. The mistaken impression shared by some that the mature GW was a bad speller and careless writer derives in large part from the defects of Lewis and other copyists. Lewis's misspelled words, misreadings, omissions, and bizarre punctuation disfigure and even distort the letter-book copies of many of GW's letters during these years.

In the spring of 1792 GW wrote his sister Betty Lewis to ask if her young son Howell would wish "to spend a few months with me, as a writer in my office (if he is fit for it)," working "from breakfast until [early afternoon] dinner—Sundays excepted." He was wanted for "recording letters, and other papers." Betty Lewis expressed her misgivings to her "Dear Brother," explaining that her son was "a Boy of very Slender Education." Howell Lewis when accepting the offer lamented that he had "not been more attentive to the improvement of my writing." After Lewis arrived in Philadelphia in May 1792, GW explained his appointment in these terms: "understanding that he was spending his time rather idly, and at the same time very slenderly provided for by his father, I thought for the few months which remained to be accomplished of my own servitude, by taking him under my care, I might impress him with ideas, and give him a turn to some pursuit or other that might be serviceable to him hereafter" (GW to Betty Lewis, 8 April 1792; Betty Lewis to GW, 19 April 1792; Howell Lewis to GW, 24 April 1792; GW to Charles Carter, 19 May 1792). In May 1792 Lewis joined GW's family in Philadelphia, where his brother Robert had been since May 1789. When Anthony Whitting, the manager of the plantation at Mount Vernon, died in June 1793, GW sent Howell Lewis down to act as temporary manager and to send GW weekly farm reports until a qualified farm manager could be found. In early January 1794 William Pearce took over as manager at Mount Vernon.

1. The copyist wrote "It" instead of "I."

2. For Mercer's negotiations with GW for repaying the long-term debt of John Mercer's estate with slaves and military certificates, see GW to John Francis Mercer, 9 Sept. 1786, nn.2 and 3.

3. GW recorded on 2 Feb. having received £6.10 from Mercer (Ledger B, 242).

From Arthur Young

Bradfield Hall near Bury Suffolk [England]
Sr   feb. 1. 1787.

I recd both the letters wch you did me the honour of writing, & the duplicate of one of them.[1]

It gives me a satisfaction not easily expressed to find that the liberty I took so much against common forms in writing to you, met with so favourable an interpretation; & the testimony you are so kind as to give in favour of my exertions in the Annals is the most flattering applause I could receive; from him on whom the eyes of all the world have been, & are still fixed. To acquire your approbation Sir, will be my warmest wish: To deserve it, my unceasing endeavour.

Annexed to this you receive a list of the things I have been able to get in time for the ship wch Mr Welch advises me will sail this month.[2]

The ploughs are excellent; I have had them both tried; & ploughed some furrows with them myself & find that they do their business perfectly to my wish. In regard to the mould by which the shares are made & wch you seem to lay some stress upon; I do not perfectly comprehend you; as they are not wrought, or cast on any. but I have taken every possible precaution that you should find no difficulty in their reparation, having sent three shares & three coulters to each plough, In order that you may keep one of each as a pattern to work them by; and that you may know whether they are made properly & put on so, I also send the measures of each plough by wch you may examine them;[3] for if they do not at any time go well (that is quite easy in hand & for small distances almost without holding: I should add that I saw them both go without being touched, for several seconds) you have only to alter them till they agree with the measures & then you are sure of their performing. I should add that they are made for a 9 inch furrow, & from 4 to 6 or 8 inches deep; & to be drawn by two stout oxen or horses: the depth of 8 inches only in loose easy friable soils. The horses are to go abreast & without a driver. I have sent one pair of whippletrees. Should you afterwards approve better of Wooden ploughs I would with great pleasure send you one; but they admit scarcely any alteration; if once twisted or drawn out of the right line, new ones must be made. Whereas you will see on examining these ploughs that they are to be taken entirely to pieces by the screws in half an hour.

In regard to the seeds, yr order came at a time when I could not send you my own Velvit wheat wch is perfectly free from any other sort: this now sent has a small mixture of red. I have sent 2 bushels of a wheat called Harrissons of wch I hear an extraordinary character; also 2 bushels of spring wheat of the sort the King had from the Empress of Russia & gave to Mr Ducket.[4] These two articles tho not in yr order will I hope not be disagreeable to you. I have likewise added grass seeds enough for an acre of ground exclusive of the hopclover and ray grass you ordered. From the description of your soil, wch you have given most intelligibly I have little doubt of those seeds answering. Of Sainfoine I have not sent so much as you ordered, for I cannot conceive that it will succeed at all with you. But I may be mistaken.

The ground plan of a barn &c. I have calculated for a farm of 500 acres well managed; but the mode of conducting it will make great variations necessary. It is sketched on the idea of all cattle being tied up: If on the contrary they are kept loose in yards the difference is nothing more than an inclosure of walls or pales, for the sheds and leantoos should be the same.[5]

A ploughman I beleive I cd get (but am not certain) at very high wages £30 or £40 a year for instance; wch single circumstance would make him good for nothing. It is amazing how rarely it answers: I have sent them to all parts of Europe, & hardly one that turned out well. I however think that a very little attention to these ploughs will supersede the want of him, since they go with such ease that the holder has no labour at all; the *difficulty* of holding a plough well is a proof it is good for nothing.

When I have the honour of another letter from you, to wch I look forward, as with the expectation of certain pleasure, I should be much obliged to you to let me the general arrangement of farms in your neighbourhood. The courses of crops & the system if there is one of connecting cattle with arable crops: Or is the land so new & rich that manure is not necessary? In England husbandry never prospers but in proportion to the attention to cattle. I put no faith in your bailiff; & have formed a most erroneous idea of the compass of your mind if you are not able to instruct him. Might I take the liberty of requesting the prices of products & labour: including in the former cattle, sheep, wool &c.

As you have written for beans I should recommend your making them a preparation for wheat, & keeping them quite clean during their growth. They should either be dibbled, or drilled in rows fro. 14 to 18 inches asunder; except it be a lay; & then a row on every furrow.

I am informed that there is an agriculture Society at Philadelphia, will you allow me to beg the favour of you to transmit to them the set of the Annals I now send: I do not know how to direct to them, or would not take this liberty; but going thro' yr hands Sir, will make the present acceptable. If I can be of any service to their laudable exertions, They may freely command me.

I send also the sixth Volume of the same work of which I beg the honour of your acceptance.[6]

It would give me great & real concern If I thought Sir that you would not with the utmost freedom favour me with yr commands: nothing I assure you will give me more pleasure than executing them to the best of my power. You must allow me to consider myself as your agent for everything that concerns

agriculture. I have the honour to remain with the greatest respect Sir, Your much obliged & most devoted Servt

Arthur Young

ALS, DLC:GW.
1. GW first wrote Young on 6 Aug. 1786, an amended copy of which he
sent with his letter of 15 Nov. 1786.
2. The list has not been found.
3. Young enclosed the dimensions of one of the plows, and the transcription
of this is in CD-ROM:GW. Young's sketch of the plow is in DLC:GW.
4. William Ducket (died c.1802) of Petersham was a leading agriculturalist
of Britain, known particularly for his invention of the skim-coulter plow.
5. Young's plans for a barn were enclosed. The directions accompanying
Young's sketch of the barn have been transcribed for CD-ROM:GW.
6. GW presented the six volumes of Young's *Annals* to the Philadelphia
Agricultural Society in June while attending the Federal Convention (GW to
Samuel Powel, 30 June 1787).

From William Peacey

Hond Sir   Northbeach [England] Feby 2d 1787
   Your favor of the 5th August and that of the 16th of novembr
came safe to hand the former on the 6th of Decemr the latter
on the 12th Jany last It was great Joy to me to hear that my Old
Servant (James Bloxham) was with your Excellency—I sincerely
hope he may answer Your Expeactation as he was throw me rec-
omended to Your Excellency by The Honle G. W. Fairfax[.]
James Bloxham's first Letter (in august) was ritten in Bad Spirits
on acount of Being at so great a distance from his fammily—his
Last of November the 12 was Vearry Plaseing[1] he have Ritten
for his wife and Two Daughters to come over to him, his two
Sons to be left hear to have some Learning—according to Your
Desire I have Opend a Corrispondence with Wakelin Welch
Esqr. who have beene Verry kinde in procuering a Passage for
Mrs Bloxham and hur two Daughters—I have Inclosed you a
bill of the Seeds I have Sent—am Sorry it is not in my Power
to Send the plows by this convayance—the plows we use have
Wheel's, and Bloxham have written for Plows without a Wheel
I have had Plows made but am doutfoll of thair answering so
well as some I have Seene in the Ragland Parts of Worcester-
shire, I have written to a frend to Send me two but thay will be

too Late for this convayance. Mr Welch in forms me that thare is a Vessel that will Sail Soon.[2] Your Excellency may Depend on the plows Coming by the next Vessel—Caleb Hall have not made up his Mind to Leve this Kingdom. I have had three Blacksmiths who have a great Desire to Embark for America if Your Excellency should have Ocasion of one of that Trade.[3]

I have no Dought but I could Send a Wheelright if Your Excellency wold wish to have one from England. I shall be Verry happy in doing any thing in the Farming way for Your Excellency in England. I am Hon. Sir Your Most Oblig'd and Duty foll Sarvant

　　　　　　　　　　　　　　　　　　William Peacey

ALS, DLC:GW.

1. James Bloxham's letter to Peacey of 23 July 1786 is printed as an enclosure in GW's letter to Peacey of 5 Aug. 1786; Bloxham's letter to Peacey of 12 Nov. 1786 is referred to above in GW's letter to Peacey of 16 November.

2. Wakelin Welch wrote to William Peacey on 17 Jan. informing him that "a fine Vessel," *Mary*, John Andrews, master, would depart from London in February and asked Peacey if he should engage passage for Mrs. Bloxham and her children. Peacey replied in the affirmative sometime before 23 Jan. when Welch again wrote, saying that he had reserved a cabin for Mrs. Bloxham and her two children at a price of thirty guineas which included "found with fresh Provision & Wine during the Voyage." The ship was "Brittish & one of the first Characters" and Captain Andrews "a very good Man." Welch advised Mrs. Bloxham to bring extra bedding for the cabin and plenty of clothing and goods from England with her since they were "very dear" in Virginia. The packages of seeds that GW had ordered were also to be sent on the same ship. Both letters are at ViMtV.

3. See GW to Peacey, 16 Nov. 1786, n.3.

To Henry Knox

My dear Sir,　　　　　　　　　　Mount Vernon 3d Feby 1787

I feel my self exceedingly obliged to you for the full, & friendly communications in your letters of the 14th 21st & 25th ult.; and shall (critically as matters are described in the latter) be extremely anxious to know the issue of the movements of the forces that were assembling, the one to support, the other to oppose the constitutional rights of Massachusetts. The moment is, indeed, important! If government shrinks, or is unable to enforce its laws; fresh manœuvres will be displayed by the insur-

gents—anarchy & confusion must prevail—and every thing will
be turned topsy turvey in that State; where it is not probable the
mischiefs will terminate.

In your letter of the 14th you express a wish to know my intention respecting the Convention, proposed to be held at Philada in May next. In *confidence* I inform you, that it is not, at this
time, my purpose to attend it. When this matter was first moved
in the Assembly of this State, some of the principal characters of
it wrote to me, requesting to be permitted to put my name in
the delegation. To this I objected—They again pressed, and I
again refused; assigning among other reasons my having declined meeting the Society of the Cincinnati at that place, about
the same time; & that I thought it would be disrespectfull to that
body (to whom I ow'd much) to be there on any other occasion.
Notwithstanding these intimations, my name was inserted in the
Act; and an official communication thereof made by the Executive to me; to whom, at the same time that I expressed my sense
of the confidence reposed in me, I declared, that as I saw no
prospect of my attending, it was my wish that my name might
not remain in the delegation, to the exclusion of another. To
this I have been requested, in emphatical terms, not to decide
absolutely, as no inconvenience would result from the non-
appointment of another, at least for some time. Thus the matter
stands, which is the reason of my saying to you in *confidence* that
at present I retain my first intention—not to go. In the mean-
while as I have the fullest conviction of your friendship for, and
attachment to me; know your abilities to judge; and your means
of information, I shall receive any communications from you,
respecting this business, with thankfulness. My first wish is, to
do for the best, and to act with propriety; and you know me too
well, to believe that reserve or concealment of any circumstance
or opinion, would be at all pleasing to me.

The legallity of this Convention I do not mean to discuss—
nor how problematical the issue of it may be. That powers are
wanting, none can deny. Through what medium they are to be
derived, will, like other matters, engage public attention. That
which takes the shortest course to obtain them, will, in my opinion, under present circumstances, be found best. Otherwise, like
a house on fire, whilst the most regular mode of extinguishing
it is contending for, the building is reduced to ashes. My opinion

of the energetic wants of the federal government are well known—publickly & privately, I have declared it; and however constitutionally it may be for Congress to point out the defects of the fœderal System, I am strongly inclined to believe that it would not be found the most efficatious channel for the recommendation, more especially the alterations, to flow—for reasons too obvious to enumerate.

The System on which you seem disposed to build a national government is certainly more energetic, and I dare say, in every point of view is more desirable than the present one; which, from experience, we find is not only slow—debilitated—and liable to be thwarted by every breath, but is defective in that secrecy, which for the accomplishment of many of the most important national purposes, is indispensably necessary; and besides, having the Legislative, Executive & Judiciary departments concentered, is exceptionable. But at the same time I give this opinion, I believe that the political machine will yet be much tumbled & tossed, and possibly be wrecked altogether, before such a system as you have defined, will be adopted. The darling Sovereignties of the States individually, The Governors elected & elect. The Legislators—with a long train of etcetra whose political consequence will be lessened, if not anihilated, would give their weight of opposition to such a revolution. But I may be speaking without book, for scarcely ever going off my own farms I see few people who do not call upon me; & am very little acquainted with the Sentiments of the great world; indeed, after what I have seen, or rather after what I have heard, I shall be surprized at nothing; for if three years ago, any person had told me that at this day, I should see such a formidable rebellion against the laws & constitutions of our own making as now appears I should have thought him a bedlamite—a fit subject for a mad house. Adieu, you know how much, and how sincerely I am, ever, Yr Affecte & most Obedt Servant

Go: Washington

Mrs Washington joins me in every good wish for yourself—Mrs Knox and the family.

ALS, NNGL: Knox Papers; LB, DLC:GW. It should be noted that Howell Lewis's letter-book copy of this particular document is a remarkably accurate one.

From Thomas Peters

Sir   Baltim[or]e Feby 3. 87.

I must beg your pardon for my having been so remiss in not answering your favour of Decem. 4 but I assure you I suppos'd I had done it,[1] And I am very sorry I have not at present the Barley you write for to send, but as I informd you before I think I shall not disappoint you, my Partner is going to Phila: next Week and will exert himself to procure the Quantity you want. I likewise shall have by the first Vessell, (or at least I expect it) from new England a Quantity of Spring Barley where it is to be had of the best quallity, the first that comes to hand I will Immediately send you, as I wish to encourage the raising of Barley to the Southd I have exerted myself to have Seed provided for me in time.

I can not find any other person in this Town that has Clover Seed but the person named in the enclosd which I have sent you with his own Account of it & his Prices.[2] should it be such as you wish pray inform me & what Quantity and the way it is to be sent you, which shall be done with Pleasure by Your Most Obedt Hume Servt

                                                       Thos Peters

ALS, DLC:GW.

1. See GW to Peters, 20 January.

2. The enclosure, a communication from Amos Leney to Peters, this date, states: "I have about 13 busl of good clean Clover seed of the last crop which I sell @ 75/ p. busl or 15 p. lb. by the smaller quantity." Leney added the postscript: "It is Red Clover-Seed."

To Henry Lee, Jr.

My dear Sir,   Mount Vernon February 4th 1787

I thank you for asking my commands to Fredericksburg. It is not my wish to be your competitor in the purchase of any of Mr Hunters tradesmen: especially as I am in a great degree principled against increasing my number of Slaves by purchase and suppose moreover that Negros sold on creadit will go high. yet if you are not disposed to buy the Bricklayer which is advertized for Sale, for your own use—find him in the vigour of life—from report a good work man & of tolerable character and his price does not exceed one hundred, or a few more pounds, I should be glad if you would buy him for me. I have much work in this way to do this Summer. If he has a family, with which he is to be sold; or from whom he would reluctantly part I decline the purchase—his feelings I would not be the means of hurting in the latter case, nor *at any rate* be incumbered with the former.[1] I am &c.

G. Washington

LB, DLC:GW.

1. This may be the slave Neptune who in March 1787 was owned by John Lawson of Dumfries and, apparently, was bought by him from a Mr. Hunter. See Lawson to GW, 17 Mar., n.1, and 2 April, and *Diaries*, 5:131. Mr. Hunter was probably James Hunter, Jr. (1746–1788), merchant and planter, formerly of Fredericksburg who by this time had moved his mercantile operations to Portsmouth. He still, however, had some business interests in Fredericksburg. James Hunter, Jr., was a younger cousin and formerly the ward of James Hunter, Sr. (d. 1785), iron manufacturer, of Fredericksburg and King George County. The two James Hunters are often confused. See Coakley, "The Two James Hunters," *Va. Mag.*, 56 (1948), 3–21.

From Battaile Muse

Honourable Sir,   February 4th 1787
   Your Letters dated the 3rd & 24th of Last month I received & have done Every thing in my Power To Accommodate you with money—I now Send by Mr A. Morton fifty pounds Should Mr Wales Fail To Take up my order please To Inform me, that I may provide; I have wrote of this date to Mr Wales To Pay it at the day apointed or sooner if Possable, my money is their in His hands on Interest at my pleasure, and I am in hopes He will Pay Punctually; I have not Collected near that Sum, I wish To be always Forward in my accts, If Mr Wales Fails, I think I shall not altho I have not money in hand, yet I will Furnish what Ever I Promise. by that Time I expect To have as much as that amount Fall into my hands of yours. I do not Expect To Trancemit any more untill about the 18th or 20th of april, at which Time I Shall waite on you my Self, unless some unforeseen accident prevents It—I shall raise Every Shillings in my Power by that Time—I was Last week with Every Tenant, and I Shall Visit

them again next week—the bad roads has prevented Some of them geting down their Tobacco Mr Airess Promises To Pay by the first of april but I doubt it, as he depends on Collecting Standing Debts which is next To an Impossible To obtain in this County. I have Told Him of the Necessity and how Necessary it is For Him To Pay, He is of the same opinion, He made but a Very Small Crop Last year.[1] I Expect all, but Him, on this Side the Ridge will Pay up by the 1st of april, if not those that Fail Will be Caled To acct—the Fauquier Tenants accts will Take Some Time To bring up altho many has paid by runing a way.

I Obtained Six Judgements in Fauquier Court Last may—I Issued one Execution agt Jacob Rector For £131—out of which Sum I have only received £35. when I am To get the Ballance is uncertain, as the sheriff Plays off—I shall Endeavour To Bring Him Too. Last week I Took out another Execution by way of a spurr To the others—as in april the whole must Issue, if Judgement Stands over Twelve months I can not Issue Execution without another hearing, and that will be Too Troublesome & Expensive To All Parties all the Tenants I Put on the Land Last year But Harrel run away—one I attached, the Others I Shall Sue the Securities for Payment—their is Two Lots now Vacant I expect To rent them next week when I am on the Spot for the present year, Some of the Lots are rented for one year & Some for Ten years. I attached Horses from one that was runing away the Trial does not Come on untill march Court the 4th monday where I must attend—their is a Pooer Tenant in Fauquier on Lot No. 3 that owes much rent, He has a good waggone Horse for Sale at £22. Several other Tenants wants To Sell Horses— whether you are in great want or not I wish you To buy— as Horses are their Chief dependance To Pay rents with, and at Sheriffs Sales for Horses their will be no bidders therefore the Payment will be Tedious and put of with Trouble and Expence—If you want Plow Horses I wish you To Send and Express To Inform me at Leesburg next Monday or Tuesday I shall be at that place and on my way To Plan matters as well as I can with the Fauquier Tenants altho I Left them Last week. I have a distress & attachment out agt Jacob Recter for Last years rent & the present years rent, as I was Told He was about To remove—I must go & See whether that Business is done as well many other things to do—the Tenants in Fauquier do as they please with the Leases—one place has Sold three Times Last year altho the Lease Expresses that it shall not be Sold without Consent—I have Sued Thompson I Expect I could get a Horse from Him and no more altho His debt is £50[2]—Charles Rector & Capn Kennady I Fear is not able To Pay the Cost of a suit.[3]

John Marshall Esqr. attorney at Law in Richmond give me a Letter To Thornton Washington—when I got Home Thornton was gone Below To See His Friends and not Expected To return Soon As I new the Letter Contained Papers respecting your Lands I Broke it open—one of which papers I Send you as I am unacquainted with any witness respecting that Business[4]—I am with Every Sentiment of Regard & attention your Obedient Humble Servant

Battaile Muse

ALS, DLC:GW.

1. John Ariss was leasing 700 acres of GW's land on Bullskin Run in Berkeley County. See Ariss to GW, 5 Aug. 1784, n.2.

2. For Muse's dealings with those of GW's tenants referred to in this letter, see the notes in Lists of Tenants, 18 Sept. 1785, and Muse to GW, 28 Nov. 1785, and notes.

3. For Muse's dealings with David Kennedy, see GW to Muse, 8 Mar. 1786, n.3.

4. The editors of the *Marshall Papers* did not find the letter from Marshall to Thornton Washington. The letter undoubtedly related to what claims the Hites might have on Thornton Washington's land in Berkeley County. See Thornton Washington to GW, 6 June 1786, n.2.

From Lafayette

My dear General   Paris february the 7th 1787
The last letter I Had from You is dated November the 19th, and Announces the Safe Arrival of the Asses who I Hope Will Be less frigid than those of His Catholick Majesty—Whatever Be their intrinsic Value, I Have found it Encreased in a Maryland Paper to a degree Which does Not indeed do justice to the Maltheze Merchants—and as the Estimate of the three Animals is truly Extravagant, I must tell you, altho' it is not Very Usual for people Who Make a present to Give the Receiver a Peep into

the Bill, that the trium Asinanat's Cost in Maltha does Not Much Exceed fifty Guineas, and Yet the jack Ass is the Best that Could Be found on the island.[1]

I have Given You an Account of the Assembly of Notables, Wicked People say *not able*[,] which would Have Already Begun Had Not three of the Ministers, the Count de Vergennes, M. de Calonne, and the Keeper of the Seals fallen Sick Very importunately.[2] I am Sanguine in the Hope that this Assembly will Be productive of Good Consequences. I flatter Myself We May Get a Kind of House of Representatives in Each province, Not to fix, it is true, But to divide the taxes, and an abolition of Several duties on the Commercial intercourse Within the Kingdom. it is not probable that the affair of the protestants Will Come Before the House. As the Reclamations of the Clergy and a Bigoted party Might Hurt the Business, We shall, I Hope, Have it done Before long one Way or other, and Nothing Hinders the King deciding at once on that important affair, provided He does not Mind too much the opponent party Whose only Means are to intrigue or Complain, and Since We Have the inconveniences of power, let us in this instance Have the Benefits of it. The Easier so, as the Greater Part of the Clergy, if Unconsulted, Will Not throw obstacles in the Way, and the people at large wish for a More liberal system.

My journey to Krimée Will not of Course take place, and Nothing Can Be determined Upon While the length of our Session is Not Known. I Will Acquaint You With Every thing that is Worth Crossing the Atlantic. This letter is Carried By Col. franks Who Has Particularly well Behaved in His Mission to Marocco and By Mr Banister Who is Going Home. this Young Man is Very clever.[3] france Has just Made a treaty of Commerce With Russia Wich does Honour to Count de Segur. The Health of Count de Vergennes is Rather in an Alarming Situation. Nothing Settled as yet in Holland. the New King of prussia Seems Averse to the idea of imitating His predecessor, and does not, as You Easely Guess, shine the more for it.

We are told that the disturbances in New England are Subsiding. God Grant it! the people of America ought to Be Made Sensible that Any MisConduct lowers them the More in the opinions of Europe as they Have Been So Highly and So deservedly Admired, and they are Most Seriously interested in preserving their Happiness at Home, and their Consequence Abroad.

Adieu, My Most Beloved General, Be pleased to present My Best Respects to Mrs Washington, Mrs Stuart, Your Respected Mother, all your family. Remember me to George, the Young ones, and all friends. let your Affectionate Recollecton, and fatherly Blessing often Attend Your absent, Your dearest, and Most devoted friend, and let your Heart judge What I so Warmly feel, and Cannot Sufficiently Express, that With Every Sentiment of Affection, Respect, and Gratitude I am My Great and Good General till the last throb of My Heart Your Loving friend and affet. Servt

lafayette

Mde de lafayette and the Young family Beg their Best Respects to You and Mrs Washington

ALS, PEL.

1. See GW to James McHenry, 29 Nov. 1786, n.2.

2. See Lafayette to GW, 13 Jan., n.2.

3. Thomas Jefferson wrote James Madison on this day: "I do not know whether you are acquainted with young Bannister who goes by the packet. He is of good understanding and of infinite worth" (Boyd, *Jefferson Papers*, 11:125). John Banister, Jr., whose father Col. John Banister (1734–1788) of Battersea in Dinwiddie County was a delegate to Congress in 1778, died in 1789.

From Ezra Stiles

Sir   Yale College [Conn.] Febry 7. 1787.

As I know by your Letters to Col. Humphreys, that you are sollicitous for the Events of the Tumults in the State of Massachusetts; and as I have authentic Intelligence by two of my Pupils this day arrived here from beyond Northampton, one of whom had been captivated at Petersham by the Insurgts and was there released Ldsdy 4th Instant; I thought it might not be unacceptable to communicate to you immediately what you will soon have more particularly authenticated from Head Quarters.[1]

Gen. Lincoln with about 3000 men having arrived at Worcester settled the sitting of the Court there January 23 without Opposition; ⟨& pro⟩ceeded for Springfd, where the Continental Stores were guarded by Genl Shephard for Government. Capt. Shays & Wheeler with about 1200 Insurgents findg themselves unequal to a Resistce at Worcester made for Springfd; and there on thursdy 25 January about IV h. P. M. marched up within 250 yds of the Arsenal, & approachg still 100 yds nearer was fired upon by Gen. Shepherd. Three Men of the Insurgents were instantly killed & one mortally wounded who is since dead. This checked & routed the Insurgents, who immedy retreated & retired to Checopee 6 m[iles] no. of Springfd. Day with about 500 lay across the River at W. Springfd. On the 27th Gen. Lincoln arrived at Springfield and joyned G. Shepd with 4 Regts & 5 Compas. About Noon, followed by 2 or 3 Regts in the Eveng. The same day 27th III ½ h. P. M. Gen. Lincoln marched in Force & crossed Connectt River & dispersed Day & his Corps without Resistance about half of which left him & fled to their homes. Day with 250 fled for No. Hampton which he reach'd XI h. at Night. The same Night Shays left his post at Checkopee & passed thro' So. Hadly to Amherst 6 Miles due East fr. Northampton, where he was joyned by Day & others, which made the united Corps 2000 or 2500, not more.

On monday 28th January Gen. Lincolns Army marched fr. Springfd for Amherst. But findg Shays had retired with his Corps to Pelham 8 M. further East, G. Lincoln turned off & took up Quarters in Hadly two Miles fr. No. Hampton. On 30th G. Lincoln sent a Letter of Mon⟨illegible⟩ to Shays and his Army, now sensibly diminishing, for they had flatterd themselves it would never have come to Blood. The two Armies thus lay posted at Hadly & Pelham 14 M. apart till Saturday. On Saturday 3d Inst. near sunset advice arrived at Hadly that Shays decampt & left Pelham the middle of that afternoon & put himself in march for Petersham. Gen. Lincoln instantly put his Army in Motion, marched all night, overtook & surprized Shay's Army next Morng being 4th Inst. took about 100, released a Number of Prisoners & dispersed many. Shays retreated with Precipitation to Warwick with about 1200. Warwick joyns on Hampshire State Line.

One of my Pupils, a young Gentleman of Solidity and good Information, was taken into Custody by Shays Party, and was with him at Petersham. He tells me he judges that Shays Corp⟨s⟩

when overtaken at Petersham did not exceed 2500 at most & probably was much less. Thus have they fled hitherto before the Governments Army. The Body of the People friends to the Insurgents, but not in Arms, are rather still and astonished. And it is probable their Camp has received an unrecoverable Shock. They did not expect such a spirited & firm Resistance. Just before the Action at Springfie[l]d 190 Slieghs full of armed Volunteer Friends crossed to Springfd & in one afternoon they with others joyning strengthend G. Shephds Corps to above 900 phps above 1000 Forgive the Inacuracy of the hasty Draft Subjoyned.[2] Your Maps will correct the Geography. I have the Honor to be, Sir Your most hble servant

Ezra Stiles

ALS, DLC:GW.

1. GW wrote to Stiles on 23 Feb. from Mount Vernon: "Sir, I have the pleasure to acknowledge the receipt of your letter of the 7th inst. and likewise one of the 9th of Novr handed to me by the Revd Mr [Jedediah] Morse together with your election Sermon, for which I beg you will accept of my best thanks.

"I am much obliged to you for the account which you gave me of the situation of affairs in Massachusetts. I sincerely rejoice to find by that, and other late advices, that the tumults in that State are likely to be soon suppressed, that Government will again be established, and peace & tranquility prevail. It must afford the greatest satisfaction to every humane & feeling mind to see that so little blood has been spilt in a contest which, a few weeks ago, threatened to drench the State of Massachusetts. I am Sir, with respect & esteem, yr most Obedt He Servt Go: Washington" (LS, CtY: Stiles Papers; LB, DLC:GW).

2. The enclosed map is in DLC:GW. For Gen. Benjamin Lincoln's own account of his campaign against Shays' forces, see Lincoln to GW, 4 Dec. 1786–4 Mar. 1787.

From Henry Knox

My dear Sir   New York 8 Feby 1787.

My last to you was of the 1st instant since which I have received your favor of the 25 Jany.[1] You will probably have received mine long before this time of the 14th ultimo which will satisfy you that I received duly your favor of the 26th December.

I now enclose you (*in confidence*) three Copies of letters written by our friend Lincoln to Govr Bowdoin which will shew you in a more connectd State his proceedings than you will find elswhere—I also enclose you a printed copy of two of his letters, one to Shays, and to another person, of the 30th ultimo[2]—The last statement of the business appears to be nearly as follows, but No precise information was received by the post last evening— Genl Lincoln must have with him at Hadley 15 or 16 miles North of Springfield 3500 Men—The insurgents were on the 2d instant at Pelham, above 20 Miles North east of Springfield with a force perhaps of 2500—Some parley seems to have taken place and it is not improbable that the business may issue in a compromise no way tending to strengthnen government. These Limited powers, adequate I am persuaded he would terminate the affair on proper principles—That he would bring the principal leaders to merited punishment, and let the mass of the insurgents return to their respective homes, taking the oaths of allegiance. But it is probable that the legislature which is in session may interfere and direct a general act of indemnity. If this should be the case it will not only affect That particular government, but prostrate the general principle of government throughout the United States.

I presume the affair will be so far advanced, as that we shall be able to judge of its issue by the next post which will arrive on the 10th or 11th—By the post which will depart from this City on the 12th I shall do myself the pleasure of informing you further. With the most respectful compliments to Mrs Washington I am my Dear Sir Your Affectionate humble Servant

H. Knox

ALS, DLC:GW.

1. GW's letter of 25 Jan. has not been found.

2. The enclosed copies of letters from Gen. Benjamin Lincoln to Gov. James Bowdoin reporting on developments are dated at Worcester on 24–25 January. The Library of Congress has also identified a number of other enclosures, including copies of Lincoln's letters to Bowdoin, 27, 28 Jan., and to Henry Knox, 28 Jan., a copy of a letter from Gen. William Shepard's aide-de-camp Abel Whitney to Knox, 2 Feb., and a copy of an intercepted letter from Luke Day to Daniel Shays, dated at Springfield on 25 January.

To Thomas Peters

Sir,   Mount Vernon February 9th 1787
As your last letter of the 3d insta. places me on better ground with respect to seed Barley your former one of the 18th of No-

vember did—and as will be inconveniant and injurious to me to withhold some of my best grownd from Oats till it may be too late to put this grane in to advantage from the uncertain expectation of Barley.

This letter is to pray that you will decline all further trouble in enquiring for the latter, on my account. as I have wrote to the same Gentlemen who procured me 50 Bushels (and could then have got an 100) to add 50 more if now to be had.[1] If your Barley from the Eastward should arrive in Season to be sown—is of the spring sort, and good in quality—and you can spare a few bushels to put me in Seed against another year I shall be obliged by it; a dozen bushels may suffice.

Clover Seed I have supplied myself with long ago. I hope you will have the goodness to excuse me for the trouble I have given you in making these inquiries. I am Sir, yr most obed. Servant

G. Washington.

LB, DLC:GW. If the first two sentences of the copyist's version of this letter were converted to one and a number of missing words were supplied, the sense, if not the precise wording, of the letter that GW sent to Peters perhaps could be recaptured. See the letter from Peters of 3 Feb. and the editors' note on the copyist in GW to John Francis Mercer, 1 February.

1. See GW to Clement Biddle, 11 February.

From Thomas Clagett & Co.

Sir   London 10 February 1787

Having established a House in this City with a view of transacting business on Consignment we beg leave to make you a tender of Our Services, and to Solicit a share of your confidence and favours.

Being determined to enter into no Engagements which might deprive us of the means of executing on the very best terms the Business entrusted to our care, We mean, therefore, cautiously to avoid Shipping Goods but for Property actually in hand.

We shall pay ready Money for every article we purchase and give our Correspondents Credit for the Discounts and Drawbacks at the foot of each bill of parcels. On Tobacco we charge the same Commission as the first Houses in London have done for the two last years, and on Goods 2½ ⅌ Ct & ½ ⅌ Ct for making Insurance.

We sincerely hope these Terms will meet your Approbation, and as we apprehend they will confine our Business to narrow limits, we shall, of course, be the better able to attend to that which may fall into our hands. We are very respectfully Sir Your most Obedt Servts

Tho: Clagett & Co.

L, DLC:GW.

This may be Thomas Clagett (1741–1792), a merchant in Piscataway, Prince Georges County, Md., whose brother Horatio became a successful merchant in London after the Revolution (*Biographical Dictionary of the Maryland Legislature*, 1:220–21; Bowie, *Prince George's County*, 126–27).

Letter not found: John Francis Mercer to GW, 10 Feb. 1787. On 1 April GW wrote Mercer: "Enclosed I return the letter which you forwarded to me the 10th of Feby."

To Clement Biddle

Dear Sir,   Mount Vernon February 11th 1787

As we are now on the verge of the middle of Feby and the season is fast approaching when the ground should be in readiness to receive spring grain, permit me to remind you of the Barley you were so obliging as to procure for me—and beg (as I have been disappointed in another expectation) that the 50 bushels may be encreased to one hundred, if in your power to do it conveniently.[1] At any rate write me decidedly, what I have to expect, that I may not, in expectation of Barley, with-hold my best grounds from oats till it is too late to sow them, to advantage, Ascertain the freight, in the Bill of Lading that I am to pay for the Barley and Clover Seed: without this is previously done, impositions are but too commonly met with.

Since writing to you last, I have met with, and obtained the quantity wanted, of Jerusalem Artichoke.[2] What price would well cured Herrings sell for with you, by the barrel? Are they in demand? and what would be the freight from this River to Philadelphia? I have about 50 Barrels that I am told are good. with great esteem I am—Dear Sir, Yr Obed. Humble Servt

G. Washington

P.S. If the Vessel by which you send the Barley and should not have sailed, pray send me two good and Strong linnen Wheels.

I would thank you for paying Mesr Sidden and Co. for the Columbien Magazenes which they have sent me. G.W.[3]

LB, DLC:GW.
1. See Biddle to GW, 2 January.
2. GW wrote Biddle on 5 Dec. 1786.
3. See GW to Thomas Seddon & Co., 9 January.

To Benjamin Franklin

Dear Sir,   Mount Vernon 11th Feby 1787
On the 3d of Novr I had the honr of addressing your Excelly a letter, of which the enclosed is a copy. Having heard nothing from you since, I am led to apprehend a miscarriage of it, and therefore give you the trouble of a duplicate: not knowing what reply to make to Sir Edward Newe[n]ham, or what more to do in this business untill I am favoured with your answer.[1] With the greatest respect & regard I have the honor to be Yr Excellency's Most Obedt Hble Servt

                                        Go: Washington

ALS, owned (1988) by Dr. and Mrs. C. Phillip Miller, Chicago, Ill.; LB, DLC:GW.
1. GW wrote Edward Newenham on 10 Mar. enclosing Franklin's response, which has not been found.

From David Humphreys

My dear General.   Hartford [Conn.] Feby 11th 1787
I had the honour to receive, last evening by the Post, your letter of the 23d of Jany, and am happy to relieve you from your apprehension, by informing that your confidential favor of the 26th of Decr with its enclosures had long since been safely received; & duly acknowledged in a private letter which was forwarded more than a fortnight since, by Colo. Wadsworth. But as he has business at New York & in Philadelphia, and travels like Mr Morse at his leisure, this may probably reach you, before his arrival at Mount Vernon.[1]

In my last, I fully accorded with you, my dear General, on the inexpediency of your attending the Convention in May next: and gave you my reasons pretty fully on the subject.

It now gives me pleasure to advise you, that affairs have taken as favorable a turn in Massachusetts, as could be expected. The official letters (which are published) will inform you of the manner in which the mob from Hampshire, Berkshire & Worcester Counties assembled at Springfield; how they attempted (under Shays) to take possession of the Stores & Barracks; and finally how Sheppard by firing his *Field Peices* killed four Men & dispersed the rest. No small arms were discharged on either side. The next day Lincoln arrived from Boston with about 2500 Men, and routed a part of the Mob at West Springfield, without bloodshed. Shays soon after collected the different parties, who were in arms against government, at Pelham—Genl Lincoln advancing to Hadley, the Insurgents scattered, some retiring home, others coming in & taking the oath of allegiance. Shays, thus abandoned, fled with about 100 of the principals to the Hampshire Grants; as is supposed, either with a design of making their way to Canada, or of waiting to see whether the General Court (now sitting) will not pass an Act of oblivion in their favour. The plans of the Insurgents do not appear to have been devised, or managed, with system, or even with common ability. At an earlier period it was obviously in their power to have seized the public Magazine. The suppression of this crude essay, I am in hopes, will give a firmer tone to our governments in the East.[2]

I beg you will make me to be remembered to Mrs Washington & the family with every token of essteem, and that you will believe me to be with sentiments of the highest veneration & respect Your sincere friend & Hble Servant

D. Humphreys

ALS, DLC:GW.

1. Humphreys is referring to his letter to GW of 20 January. Jeremiah Wadsworth was at Mount Vernon on 17 and 18 February.

2. See Benjamin Lincoln to GW, 4 Dec. 1786–4 Mar. 1787.

To Thomas Newton, Jr.

Mount Vernon. February 11th 1787.

It is now two or three months since I requested, in very explicit terms, that if my flour was not then sold, that it might be disposed of for what ever it would fetch, & the money remitted to me by Doctr Stuart who was then attending the Assembly, or some other safe conveyance. As I have heard nothing from you since, it is probable the letter may have miscarried—I therefore beg that no further delay may arise in transmitting me the proceeds, as I want the money.[1]

In the letter alluded to above, to the best of my recollection I asked if well cured Herrings commanded a ready sale at Norfolk and what pr Barrel.[2] I am Sir, yr most obed. Servt

G. Washington

LB, DLC:GW.

1. On 4 May 1787 GW noted receiving a bill for £70 Virginia currency drawn by Newton on Colin McIver of Alexandria (Ledger B, 245).

2. GW's letter has not been found, but see GW to Newton, 19 Aug. 1786.

From Mauduit du Plessis

Sir, Savannah 12th Feby 1787.

I have not forgot the attention with which your Excellency treated me when I was at Mount Vernon, nor the polite reception which Madam Washington gave me; I beg you both to accept of my warmest acknowledgements.[1]

From the moment I left you, my General, I have had reason to complain of the lot which has persecuted me, for, a few days after, I was thrown, my horse, Chair & myself, into a Gully 18 feet deep. A little beyond Monforts's mill, passing over a bridge, it broke down under my horse; providence preserved me, for if the top of my Chair had been down I should have crushed my head in a thousand peices, but its being up, saved me from the disaster; my horse was not so fortunate as myself, for he was dangerously wounded so that I was obliged to leave him at Halifax. After having travelled this far, finding the bridges broken, & the rivers very high, I was obliged to embark, with my horses for

Charleston; this passage which is commonly made in 24 hours, I was 19 days in performg & suffered greatly from hungar & thirst—6 days of the passage we were in imminent danger of perishing, & finally, 3 hours after I landed, the vessel was lost upon the bar.[2]

I proceeded on to Georgia as soon as possible, & eight days after my arrival at Savannah I fell sick, & was three times brought to the door of death, but it pleased God to let me escape & I have been three months in a very low state.

I have lost my Surgeon by a fever, and likewise every European domestic which I brought with me from France. I arrived alone at my Mills, but was extreemly surprised upon findg only a part of the mills which I purchased in France of Mr John McQueen; they say it is not the fault of him, but of his Agent who disposed of them during his Absence—this I am willing to beleive but it is as true that I have found but a part of what I purchased.[3]

I hope that by industry, perseverance & attention, this settlement will, in time be pretty considerable; I shall employ myself to make it useful, & in some degree, agreeable, since it is to be the place of my residence in preference to Savannah, as I am determined to have every thing carried on under my own inspection, for the eye of the Master makes the horse fat.

While I lay sick I sent for Genl McIntosh & gave him the letter which you wrote to him, as well as that of the Count de Estaing—in consequence, an extraordinary meeting was called in which I was admitted into the Society of the Cincinnati; General McIntosh showed me every attention imaginable. Think what obligations I am under to your Excellency for the honor which I have received by my admission![4]

Colo. Washington, who lives in Charleston, has been so kind as to charge himself with the conveyance of a small package which contains 6 India fans; I beg you to present them, for me, to Madam Washington; they have no merit in themselves but as a mark of gratitude.[5]

I wish I could be so happy as for my affairs to permit me to go & breath that pure & agreeable air which is inseperable from, & which every one enjoys who inhabits, the place where General & Madam Washington reside. I beseech your Excellency to be persuaded of the truth of this, & of my profound respect.

Duplessis
Brigadier of the Armies of the King

Translation, DLC:GW; ALS, in French, DLC:GW, transcribed for CD-ROM:GW.

1. See Mauduit du Plessis to GW, 20 July 1786.

2. Du Plessis left Mount Vernon on 19 August. Halifax, the county seat of Halifax in northeastern North Carolina, is on the Roanoke River.

3. See Mauduit du Plessis to GW, 20 July 1786, n.3.

4. For the testimonial letter that d'Estaing wrote for du Plessis on 9 May 1786, see Mauduit du Plessis to GW, 20 July 1786, n.2. GW's letter to Lachlan McIntosh has not been found.

5. The fans were from "Chinne," not India. The translator provided: "but as a mark of gratitude"; du Plessis wrote instead: "que parce qu'ils viennent de loin."

From Henry Knox

My dear Sir   New York 12 February 1787

In my last to you of the 8th instant I enclosed you a number of General Lincolns letters to Govr Bowdoin, in order to give you a connected statement of the rebellion in Massachusetts. I have now the great satisfaction of informing you, that this ugly affair, is in a train of being speedily and effectually suppressed—pursuing my former plan, I enclose you (in confidence) 4 copies of letters from Genl Lincoln, to Govr Bowdoin which brings the affairs to the 5th instant inclusively.[1]

The legislature of Massachusetts convened in Boston on Saturday evening, the 4th instant. The Governors speech detailed to them the progress of the insurrection—A Committee was immediately appointed to consider it—who reported the existence of a rebellion, in the State, an approbation of the Conduct of the executive, and an assurance of the utmost support to Government. The two houses mct on Sunday for the consideration of the report, and there were no doubts that they would adopt it. This conduct must have been produced by the imminent danger, but happily the business was the same day terminated.

Several Gentlemen in the legislature of Massachusetts to

whom I wrote on the subject assure me of their hearty concurrence in the proposed convention to be held next May, and that they shall urge the matter in the Legislature with all their might—I am persuaded that they will appoint delegates, but as I mentioned to you in my letter of the 14th ultimo, they will be the only state from New England—and as the Convention will be able *only to propose* perhaps it may answer all the purposes as if the others were to choose.

Congress will this day have nine states represented which is for the first time, since the existence of the new Congress, that is, since the first monday in Novr last. With sincere and affectionate Compliments to Mrs Washington I am my dear Sir Your most obedient humble Servant

H. Knox

ALS, DLC:GW.

1. The enclosed copies of letters from Gen. Benjamin Lincoln to Gov. James Bowdoin are dated at Hadley on 30 Jan. and 1 Feb. and at Petersham on 4 and 5 February. Also enclosed was a copy of Lincoln's order of 4 February. Knox wrote Lincoln on 14 Feb.: "I have communicated at the request of our Old friend General Washington the history of your movements from time to time" (NNGL: Knox Papers).

To David Stuart

Dear Sir,   Mount Vernon Feb. 12th 1787.

At length I have received the sheriffs acct against me for Taxes—a copy of which I enclose you. Mr Ratcliff supposes I am well acquainted with the manner of discharging it, but in truth I am not—nor whether his charges are right, or not; I shall thank you therefore for your Inspection, & comparison of it with the revenue Acts; and then, for providing me with the means for discharging it to the best advantage; according to your offer.[1]

At Christmas, when Peter, his Wife, & others of the family informed me his time was up, I sent him home, but he returned; informing me that as there was no place provided for him, Mrs Stuart desired him to remain here till your return from the Assembly. It did not occur to me, either of the times you were here, to inform you, that as he may be called away before the covering season comes on, and the time of the Mares dropping their young, at which alone he would be essentially serviceable to me, that I derive no advantage from his stay; as feeding & dressing can be performed as well by any other person as himself; consequently that I have no desire to keep him, if you find a use for him.[2] I am, Dear Sir Yr most Obedt & Affe. Servt

Go: Washington

This letter was sent to Alexandria on Monday, by Mr Lear, who not seeing you in Town brought it back.[3]

ALS, PWacD: Sol Feinstone collection, on deposit PPAmP.

1. Richard Ratcliff (Ratcliffe; c.1750–1825) was commissioner of the tax in Fairfax County. At one time or another he also was a justice of the peace, a deputy sheriff, and coroner of the county. The enclosed account of the taxes owed by GW has not been found. George Gilpin had been elected sheriff in November 1786. A controversy ensued over Ratcliff's collection of GW's taxes. See Ratcliff to GW, 10 April 1788.

2. Stuart wrote GW on 15 Feb. that Peter was to continue at Mount Vernon through the year, and apparently he was still working for GW as late as April 1788 (Ledger B, 265).

3. GW recorded in his diary on Monday, 12 Feb., that "Mr. [Tobias] Lear went to an Assembly at Alexandria to be held this evening" (*Diaries*, 5:104).

To Clement Biddle

DEAR SIR: MOUNT VERNON, 14th Feb., 1787

I forgot, in the letter I wrote to you the day before yesterday,[1] to request the favour of you to send 6 *Screw* Augers, that will bore holes 2½ inches.—I want them for Posting and railing—If this size is not sufficiently large they may be made bigger—for this, or indeed any kind of work I am informed that Screw Augers are much preferred. I am, Dear Sir, Yr. Most Obedt. Servt.,

G. WASHINGTON.

William J. Campbell Catalog, no. 45, n.d., n.p.

1. GW is referring to his letter of 11 February. See Biddle to GW, 20 February.

To Charles Washington

Dear Charles,   Mount Vernon February 14. 1787

When the enclosed was written, I knew nothing of Georges intention of visiting Berkeley.[1] The safe conveyance offorded by him, is very favourable and gladly embraced it.

Having seen Bushrod and Corben Washington on their way from Berkeley their information is the subject of this letter and is exceedingly distressing to me in as much as I have not the means of affording immediate relief. By them I learn that the remaning Negros of my deceased Brother Samuels Estate are under an execution and a momentary Sale of them may be expected and this too by the extraordinary conduct of Mr White in applying moneyes received towards the discharge of a Bond *not in Suit* when they ought to have given it in payment of Mr Alexander's Claim on which judgment had been, or was on the point of being, obtained. How in the name of Heaven came Mr White to be vested with powers to dispose of the Money he should recover unaccompanied with instructions respect to the disposal. will not Mr Alexander when he sees every exertion making to pay him have mercy on the Orphan. Can he as a Father and man of feeling see the Fatherless reduced from Competency to distress untouched. If there was an unwillingness to pay him. If property had not been sold for the express purpose of doing it, and if there was not a prospect of being done in a very short time it would be right in Mr Alexander to push matters to extremity. but when (as I am informed) every exertion is making to satisfy him, to cause perhaps three pounds worth of property to be sold to raise 20/ Cash would be inconsistant with that benevolence which should be characteristic of every man and to which from what I have heard of the Gentlemen he is justly entitled. I therefore think that as Executor to the Will and guardian to the boys you should before the dye is cast apply by fair & candid representation to Mr Alexander on this subject— not in the cold mode of letter but by personally to see if this evil can not be averted.[2] Vain would it be for me to offer Mr Alexander any assurances of the money at a short given day—I have it not. I cannot get it from those who owe me without suit and I hate to sue them. I have offered Lands for sale at very moderate prices but have not, been able to sell them—otherwise, or if I could raise the money by any other means I would relieve my Nephews without hisitation from the impending evil. Indeed I would essay any thing to save the Estate for if the negros are sold for ready money they will go for a song. to add aught to this is unnessary. with the most affe⟨t⟩e regard. I am ever yours

G. Washington.

P.S. My love in which Mrs Washington Joins to my Sister and the family.

LB, DLC:GW. When preparing his edition of GW's letters in the late 1820s, Jared Sparks understandably entered changes in this and other letters copied very imperfectly by Howell Lewis in GW's letter book. Sparks's emendations have been ignored. See the source note in GW to John Francis Mercer, 1 Feb. 1787.

1. The enclosure has not been identified. According to GW's diary George Augustine Washington left Mount Vernon for Berkeley County on 16 Feb. (*Diaries*, 5:105).

2. The "evil" may indeed have been averted at this time, for two years later, on 19 Feb. 1789, George Steptoe Washington, Samuel Washington's son, wrote GW about "the embarrassment under which our estates labour at present upon account of that debt which it owes to Mr Alexander." Mr White is probably the Frederick County attorney Alexander White with whom GW had had dealings with regard to Gen. Charles Lee's estate. Alexander has not been identified.

From Henry Knox

New York 15 February 1787

I thank you my dear Sir for your kind favor of the 3d instant which I received yesterday. I beg leave to make an observation once for all which is, that you would not consider yourself as under obligation to answer any of my letters, (unless I should particularly request the favor) untill you should find sufficient leisure and inclination for the purpose. It would pain me[1] exceedingly were I in the least to add to your embarrasment which I am persuaded must be occasioned by your numerous correspondents.

I received nothing from Genl Lincoln last evening. But I enclose you a Boston paper which will show you the proceedings of the Legislature on his success—Instead of marching the 2600 men as a reinforcement to Lincoln which is mentioned in the papers they will enlist 1000 men for six months, and station them in the upper counties. The legislature will disfranchise all who were in rebellion of, and under the rank of non commissioned officers for a given time. The persons who acted as officers will have to undergo a judicial trial. I am my dear Sir with perfect respect & affection Your humble servant

H. Knox

ALS, DLC:GW.
   1. Knox wrote "be."

Letter not found: Richard Henry Lee to GW, 15 Feb. 1787. GW wrote Lee on 20 Feb.: "Your favour of the 15th . . . came safe to hand."

To Battaile Muse

Sir   Mount Vernon Feby 15. 1787.
   I have just received your letter of the 4th inst. and the 50 pounds sent by Mr A. Morton.
   Mr Wales accepted the order upon him, and says he will *endeavour* to pay it when it becomes due, but as the time of payment has not yet arrived I cannot say anything decided upon it. It is not in my power to send a person to meet you at Leesburg as the time which you mentioned to be there is already elapsed. Tho' I am not in want of horses at present, yet, as it may prevent my tenants from being distressed, & perhaps be the only chance I may have to secure my rent, I will consent to take a few, at a reasonable price, provided they are young, strong & serviceable, I should prefer good breeding Mares; but old horses I will not receive at any rate. The cut money which you sent me in the above 50 pounds fell short, by weight, 10/6—I do not regard the present deficiency, but only mention it that in future you may receive it by weight, as it is the only way in which it will pass here. I am Sir yr Obdt Hble Servt

Go: Washington

LS, in the hand of Tobias Lear, A-Ar: Jabez L. M. Curry Collection; LB, DLC:GW.

From David Stuart

Dear Sir, Abingdon 15th Feby 1787

I shall take steps immediately for discharging your taxes on the best terms—I have written to Mr Henley to dispose of the tobacco directly—From some conversation the other day with Mr Wilson, I expect Certificates and indents may be had as cheap from him, as in Richd—I shall know this tomorrow: and if they cannot, I shall write to Mr Donald in Richmond for them.[1]

With respect to Peter, it will be very agreeable to me that he should continue out the year—Mrs Stuart informed me of his having been here, but as I concluded his successor could not be so well acquainted with the management of a horse in the covering season; I intended when last at Mt Vernon, to have informed you that I should not expect him this year.[2] I am Dear sir with great regard Your Obt Servt

David Stuart

ALS, DLC:GW.

1. For GW's inquiry about the payment of his taxes, see GW to Stuart, 12 Feb., and note 1. For the annual payment due from John Parke Custis, see GW to Stuart, 5 Nov. 1786, n.3. David Henley was manager of the Custis plantations. William and James Wilson were Scottish merchants in Alexandria. For the arrangements with regard to payments made with Alexander Donald, Robert Morris's representative in Richmond, see Donald to GW, 22 May.

2. See GW to Stuart, 12 February.

From James Tilton

Dr Sir, Dover [Del.] 15 Feby 1787.

I had the honor to receive your circular letter of the 31 Octr 1786 together with your private favour dated the 7th Novr following.[1] Contrary to my opinion & inclination, the state society have hitherto continued to elect me their president. I should therefore have thought it my duty to have answered you on the subject of your circular letter before now, had I not been delayed in the oportunity by which I intended to write.

At the last meeting of the society, Captn McKennan was appointed, on behalf of all the members, to wait on the President General and obtain his signature to their Diplomas. The wound he received in his arm at German Town, broke out soon after, &

has hitherto delayed his Journey. He now entertains the pleasing hope of prosecuting his Jaunt to Mount Vernon very soon, and promises to deliver this letter with his own hands.[2]

I shall not fail to lay your letter before the society at their meeting in April next. They will regret, I know, that any thing should deprive them of your name & influence, at the head of the association. That degeneracy of health, which threatens an abatement of your usefulness as well as happiness will, and ought to be, particularly afflicting. The same affectionate regard, which would make the Delaware Society very reluctant to any change of the President General, will, probably, induce them to conform, in that respect, to whatever they shall be persuaded is most agreeable to your wishes.

Captn McKennan will be able to explain the particular business on which he is sent, and to give every information relative to this state society. I will only observe generally, that at the first state meeting, after the last general meeting, the delegates from this state society communicated to their brethren the transactions of the general meeting. These transactions were referred to a committee to report thereon, particularly with respect to an application to the legislature, for an incorporation. The committee from time to time, at the respective meetings of the society, requested further time, until the last meeting: when they reported, that no state society in the union had been able to procure an incorporation 'tho some had attempted it; and that they were well convinced, it would be very inexpedient to propose such a thing in Delaware. The society thereupon declined the measure, and resolved to instruct their delegates to the next General meeting.[3] I have reason to think the principal objects of these instructions will be the security of their funds & perpetuity of the society. This will be the principal business of our meeting in April next, when we hope to have every information to be obtained previous to the general meeting. We do not despair of an establishment, upon so unexceptionable a footing, as not to excite the Jealosy of the good people of America: and then, a little time will evince, that our association is not only harmless, but of public utility.

I sincerely wish you a perfect restoration of health; and that you may be equally happy in the success of your future endeavours for the public good, as in the great event of your past labours! With the greatest respect, I have the honor to be Dear Sir, your most obt Servt

James Tilton

ALS, DLC:GW.

1. The letter of 7 Nov. 1786 has not been found.

2. GW recorded in his diary the visit on 26 April of "a Captn. McCannon" who arrived at Mount Vernon "and got 40 Diplomas signed for the Delaware line" (*Diaries*, 5:144). William McKennan served as an officer throughout the Revolution and was at this time secretary of the Delaware Society of the Cincinnati.

3. One of the amendments to the Institution, or constitution, of the Society of the Cincinnati adopted at its meeting in Philadelphia in 1784 was the provision that the state societies should seek incorporation in their respective states. See Winthrop Sargent's Journal, n.34, in General Meeting of the Society of the Cincinnati, 4–18 May 1784, printed above.

To Mary Ball Washington

Hond Madam,   Mount Vernon February 15 1787

In consequence of your communication to George Washington, of your want of money, I take the (first safe) conveyance by Mr John Dandridge to send you 15 Guineas which believe me is all I have and which indeed ought to have been paid many days ago to another agreeable to my own assurances.[1] I have now demands upon me for more than 500£ three hundred and forty odd of which is due for the tax of 1786; and I know not where, or when I shall receive one shilling with which to pay it.[2] In the last two years I made no Crops. In the first I was obliged to buy Corn and this year have none to sell, and my wheat is so bad I cannot neither eat it myself nor sell it to others, and Tobaca I make none. Those who owe me money cannot or will not pay it without Suits and to sue is like doing nothing, whilst my expences, not from any extravagance, or an inclination on my part to live splendidly but for the absolute support of my family and the visitors who are constantly here are exceedingly high; higher indeed than I can support, without selling part of my estate which I am disposed to do rather than run in debt or continue to be so but this I cannot do, without taking much less than the lands I have offered for sale are worth. This is really and truely my situation—I do not however offer it as any excuse for not paying you what may really be due—for let this be little or much I am willing; however unable to pay to the utmost farthing; but it is really hard upon me when you have taken every thing you wanted from the Plantation by which money could be raised—When I have not received one farthing, directly nor indirectly from the place for more than twelve years if ever— and when, in that time I have paid, as appears by Mr Lund Washingtons account against me (during my absence) Two hundred and Sixty odd pounds, and by my own account Fifty odd pounds out of my own Pocket to you. besides (if I am rightly informed) every thing that has been raised by the Crops on the Plantation. who to blame, or whether any body is to blame for these things I know not, but these are facts. and as the purposes for which I took the Estate are not answered nor likely to be so but dissatisfa[c]tion on all sides have taken place, I do not mean to have any thing more to say to your Plantation or Negros since the first of January except the fellow who is here, and who will not, as he has formed connections in this neighbourhood leave it as experience has proved him I will hire. of this my intention I informed my brothe[r] John some time ago, whoes death I sincerely lament on many Accounts and on this painful event condole with you most sincerely. I do not mean by this declaration to with hold any aid or support I can give from you; for whilst I have a shilling left you shall have part, if it is wanted, whatever my own distresses may be. what I shall then give I shall have creadit for. now I have not for tho' I have received nothing from your Quarter, and am told that every farthing goes to you, and have moreover paid between 3 & 4 hundred pounds besides out of my own pocket I am viewed as a delinquent. & considered perhaps by the world as unjust and undutiful Son. My advice to you therefore, is, to do one of two things with the Plantation—either let your grandson Bushrod Washington, to whom the land is given by his Father have the whole interest there, that is lands and negros, at a reasonable rent—or, next year (for I presume it is too late this, as the overseer may be engaged) to let him have the land at a certain yearly rent during your life; and hire out the negros—this would ease you of all care and trouble—make your income certain—and your support ample.[3] Further, my sincere, and pressing advice to you is, to break up housekeeping, hire out all the rest of your servants except a man and a maid and live with one of your Children. This would relieve you entirely from the cares of this world, and leave your mind at ease to reflect, undisturbedly on that which aught to come. On this subject I have been full with my Brother John and it was determined he should endeavor to get you to live with him—He alas is no more & three only of us remain— My House is at your service, & would press you most sincerely & most devoutly to accept it, but I am sure and candour requires me to say it will never answer your purposes, in any shape whatsoever—for in truth it may be compared to a well resorted tavern, as scarcely any strangers who are going from north to south, or from south to north do not spend a day or two at it— This would, were you to be an inhabitant of it, oblige you to do one of 3 things, 1st to be always dressing to appear in company, 2d to come into in a dishabille or 3d to be as it were a prisoner in your own chamber The first yould not like, indeed for a person at your time of life it would be too fateiguing. The 2d I should not like because those who resort here are as I observed before strangers and people of the first distinction. and the 3d, more than probably, would not be pleasing to either of us—nor indeed could you be retired in any room in my house; for what with the sitting up of Company; the noise and bustle of servants—and many other things you would not be able to enjoy that calmness and serenity of mind, which in my opinion you ought now to prefer to every other consideration in life. If you incline to follow this advice the House and lotts on which you now live you may rent, and enjoy the benefit of the money arising there from as long as you live—this with the rent of the land at the little falls & the hire of your negros would bring you in an income which would be much more than sufficient to answer all your wants and make ample amends to the child you live with; for myself I should desire nothing, if it did not, I would, most chearfully contribute more. a man, a maid, The Phæten and two horses, are all you would want—to lay in a sufficiency for the support of these would not require ¼ of your income, the rest would purchase every necessary you could possibly want, and place it in your power to be serviceable to those wth whom you may live, which no doubt, would be agreeable to all parties.

There are such powerful reasons in my mind for giving this

advice, that I cannot help urging it with a degree of earnestness which is uncommon for me to do. It is I am convinced, the only means by which you can be happy. the cares of a family without any body to assist you—The charge of an estate the proft of which depend upon wind weather—a good Overseer—an honest man—and a thousand other circumstance, cannot be right, or proper at your advanced age & for me, who am absolutely prevented from attending to my own plantations which are almost within call of me to attempt the care of yours would be folly in the extreme; but the mode I have pointed out, you may reduce your income to a certainty, be eased of all trouble—and, if you are so disposed, may be perfectly happy—for happiness depends more upon the internal frame of a persons own mind—than on the externals in the world. of the last if you will pursue the plan here recommended I am sure you can want nothing that is essential—the other depends wholy upon your self, for the riches of the Indies cannot purchase it.

Mrs Washington, George & Fanny Join me in every good wish for you and I am honored Madam, Yr most dutiful & affe. Son

G. Washington

LB, DLC:GW.

1. John Dandridge, Martha Washington's nephew, had dinner at Mount Vernon on 2 February.

Mary Washington wrote to her son John Augustine Washington before his death in January 1787: "it be time I am borring a Little corn no corn in the corn hous I Never Lived soe pore in my Life was it not for Mrs french [probably Anne Brayne Benger French of Fredericksburg] & your sister [Betty Washington] Lewis I should be almost starvd butt I am Like an old almanack quit out of date" (ViMtV).

2. See GW to David Stuart, 12 Feb., and Stuart to GW, 15 February.

3. The "Plantation" GW is referring to here is the Little Falls quarter on the Rappahannock River which was owned by Mary Washington but had been rented to GW, along with most of her slaves, ever since she moved to Fredericksburg in late 1771 or early 1772. See Account with Mary Washington, 27 April 1775, source note, printed above. Although GW was paying her £30 annual rent for the plantation and a total of £92 annual rent for her slaves, his mother or her overseer was evidently receiving all the profits and forwarding none of them to him (see GW to John Augustine Washington, 16 Jan. 1783). Over the years GW frequently lent his mother money, usually indicating that he did so in the presence of some family member. Mary Washington's account in GW's Ledger B, 124, shows unpaid loans made to her during the period 1 Dec. 1774 to 15 Feb. 1787 totaling more than £300. Despite all this, Mary Washington seems to have frequently complained to neighbors and

friends about her poverty and hinted that GW and her other children were not supporting her. In 1781 GW was shocked to find that the Virginia legislature was considering voting a pension for her relief, a measure to which GW quickly put an end (see Benjamin Harrison to GW, 25 Feb. 1781, GW to Harrison, 21 Mar. 1781, and GW to John Augustine Washington, 16 June 1783).

GW's brother John Augustine Washington, who died in January, willed to his son Bushrod Washington "my Land in Stafford County conveyed to me by my Mother Mrs. Mary Washington . . . containing 400 Acres" (Wayland, *Washingtons*, 122–23). Mary Washington had evidently conveyed Little Falls quarter to her younger son during the Revolution or shortly thereafter but had retained rights to the land during her lifetime. John Augustine Washington had taken over general management of the quarter in 1783 at GW's request (see GW to John Augustine Washington, 16 Jan., 15 June 1783).

The "fellow" that GW decided to keep at Mount Vernon was probably the "Negroe Boy George" who was left to GW in his mother's will (Wayland, *Washingtons*, 79–81).

To Charles Willson Peale

Sir,   Mount Vernon Feb. 16th 1787.

You will receive by the Stage the body of my Gold Pheasant, packed up in wool agreeable to your directions. He made his Exit yesterday, which enables me to comply with your request much sooner than I wished to do.[1] I am afraid the others will follow him but too soon, as they all appear to be drooping; whether it is owing to their being confined, or to the Climate, I am not able to say: I am very desirous of giving them Liberty, but the danger of their being taken by Hawks prevents me. I am Sir Yr most Obedt Hble Servt

Go: Washington

LS, in the hand of Tobias Lear, PWacD: Sol Feinstone Collection, on deposit PPAmP; LB, DLC:GW.

1. Peale wrote on 31 Dec. 1786 asking GW to send to him in Philadelphia the carcass of any of the pheasants, presents from Lafayette, that might die. GW agreed to do this on 9 January.

To Thomas Stone

Dear Sir,   Mount Vernon February 16 1787

Your favor of the 30th Ulto came duly to hand. To give an opinion in a caus of so much importance as that which has warmly agitated two branches of your legislature, and which, from the appeal that is made, is likely to create great, and perhaps dangerous divisions, is rather a delicate matter; but as this diversity[1] of opinion is on a subject which has, I beleive, occupied the minds of most men; and as my sentiments thereon have been fully and decidedly expressed long before the Assembly either of Maryland or this State were convened; I do not scruple to declare that, if I had a voice in your Legislature, it would have been given decidedly against a paper emission Upon the general principles of its utility as a representative, and the necessity of it as a medium. and as, far as I have been able to understand its advocates (for the two papers you sent me were the same, and contained no reasons of the House of Delegates for the local want of it in your State, though I have seen, and given them a cursory reading, elsewhere) I should have been very little less opposed to it.

To assign reasons for this opinion would be as unnecessary as tedious. The ground has been so often trod that a place hardly remains untouched. But, in a word, the necessity, arising from a want of specie greater than it really is, I contend that it is by the substance, not with the shadow of a thing, we are to be benefited. The wisdom of man, in my humble opinion, cannot at this time devise a plan by which the credit of Paper money would be long supported; consequently depreciation keeps pace with the quantum of the emission; and articles for which it is exchanged rise in a greater ratio than the sinking value of the money. wherein then is the Farmer, the Planter, the Artizan benefitted? The debtor may be, because, as I have observed, he gives the shadow in lieu of the substance, and in proportion to his gain, the creditor, or the body politic suffer: for whether it be a legal tender or not, it will, as hath been observed very truly, leave no alternative—it must be that or nothing. An evil equally great is, the door it immediately opens for speculation; by which the least designing, & perhaps most valuable part of the community, are preyed upon by the more knowing and crafty speculators. But contrary to my intention & declaration, I am offering reasons in support of my opinion—reasons too, which of all others, are least pleasing to the advocates for Paper money I shall therefore only observe, generally, that so many people have suffered by former emissions, that, like a burnt child who dreads the fire, no person will touch it who can possibly avoid it. The natural consequence of which will be, that the specie which remains un-exported, will be instantly locked up. With my great esteem and regard—I am Dr Sir your most obed. Servant

G. Washington

LB, DLC:GW.

1. Sparks may have corrected Lewis's spelling of "diversity." See GW to Charles Washington, 14 Feb., source note.

From Philip Marsteller

Honord Sir,   Alex[andri]a, Febr. 17th [1787].

Agreeable to request I send the remainder of the Blankets purchased for you agreeable to Bill enclosed (your Nephew hav-ing taken with him 15 Blankets, the best of the Purchase) the Bill of the whole amounting to £6.0.9 I gave to your Nephew—Linnen of the goodness you mention none has yet come to Hand but make no doubt Shall get some soon—Checks there is none at present on reasonable Terms. Grass & other Scythes are now in my possession, but not yet ripe for market but soon will be—Therefore must only wish you to belleve that I Watch not only the Sale but the Season in your behalf[1]—With respect I subscribe my self your Hum. Servt

P. Marsteller

ALS, DLC:GW. Marsteller misdated the letter 1786. See note 1.

1. In late 1786 GW and Marsteller entered into an agreement whereby Marsteller would purchase goods and supplies for GW at public sales in Alex-andria. See GW to Marsteller, 15 Dec. 1786.

From Thomas Smith

Sir   Carlisle [Pa.] 17th February 1787

Mr McCrea, who informed me that he kept the Post-office in Alexandria, was up at the Supreme Court at Bedford, in No-vember last, & was to return immediately; I embraced the op-pertunity to inform you that we had Tried and gained all the Ejectments which I had the honour of bringing for you in Wash-ington County: I took the liberty of mentioning that it would be necessary that you should appoint some Person to receive the Possession from the Sheriff, unless you and the Defendants should come upon Terms that would supersede the necessity of Issuing writs of Possession. On my return from the Circuit Courts, unexpected business called me suddenly to the City, in which I arrived a Day before the Judges—I was detained there so long, that for the first Time, I could not attend the County Courts over the Mountains; this absence has prevented me from knowing whether such Terms have been made or proposed, and therefore I take the liberty (although perhaps unnecessarily) to remind you that the Agent should be appointed & the writs of Possession executed, before Harvest; unless the Defendants have solicited, and obtained, the favour, at which I took the liberty to hint, in the Letter to which I allude: if their solicitations shall have obtained the gift of their crops, they will have a proper sense of the obligation; but if the suit of Possession should be delayed to be executed so long that they may, without solicitation, reap the benefit, they will not esteem it any favour at all.[1]

When I was in Philadelphia, I left provisional orders with the Prothonotary, to be executed when I should think it proper— for there being now four Terms in the year in the Supreme Court, it would be of no use to order the writs of Possession, until nearly about the Time that your Agent could attend to receive the Possession; therefore, in order to avoid unnecessary Expence, & that the writs may be sent up to the Sheriff at such Time as may be convenient to you, I inclose a Præcipe to the Prothonotary, who will send the writs to you, to send to the Sheriff by the Person whom you may appoint to receive Possession; unless you should order Mr Bend to send them, as he can, to the Sheriffs: you will perceive that I have ordered him to Issue them at such Time Returnable as you shall direct—If the Sheriff Should receive the Writs when I am at Washington County Court, I shall of course, give him directions, if any should be necessary, respecting the execution of them—if I should be absent, Mr Ross will give any assistance that my be requisite.[2]

It gave me, as it must give every good citizen of the united States, very sincere pleasure, to observe that you will probably be in Philadelphia in May—I most ardently Pray that you may be as sucessful in the Cabinet, in giving energy, permanency & happiness to the United States, as you was in the Field, in establishing them as a Nation.

Attendance of the Courts of Nisi Prius at that Time of the year will prevent me from being in the City, but as soon as I shall hear of your arrival, I will transmit your Papers by a safe conveyance.

If you should have come on terms with the Defendants in the Ejectments, I am convinced that you will excuse this Letter, which I should not have taken the liberty of writing, had I any certainty as to that fact. I have the honour to be with great respect, Sir, your most obedient & very humble Servant

Thomas Smith

ALS, DLC:GW.

1. See Smith to GW, 7 Nov. 1786, and notes, for the conduct of GW's cases by Smith and James Ross in the trial of GW's Millers Run ejectment suits.

2. The enclosed *præcipe*, or order, directed by Smith to Edward Bend, prothonotary of the Pennsylvania Supreme Court, dated 19 Feb. 1787, calls for him to issue writs of *habere facias possessionem* (writs of execution) to Washington County, Pa., against GW's lessees "James Scott, the younger," and "Samuel McBride & others." Smith's instructions to the prothonotary reads: "You will Please to Issue those writs Returnable at the April or June Term, & transmit them, as the Plaintiff, should direct, & Issue a fi. fa. in each, if not already done" (DLC:GW).

To David Humphreys

My Dear Humphreys,   Mount Vernon February 18th 1787

Colo. Wadsworth has handed me your obliging and much esteemed favor of the 20th ulto for which I offer you my sincere thanks.

The tranquil state, in which the people of this commonwealth are affords me nothing to offer you in return for the interesting communications in your letter of the above date the House of Delegates, in maryland, have adjourned in high dudgeon. As you are neare the theatre of more important transactions—and have the wheels of the political machine much more in view then I have, I hope you will not find it incompatible with your military duties to allot a few moments for the purpose of keeping me adviced of their revolutions, my anxiety for the welfare of this Country encreases with the attempts to destroy its peace, what is to be done is in every ones mouth, yet none can answer. which is conviction to my mind, that matters must get worse before they will be better. You have the good wishes of every one in this family and the warmest affection of your sincere friend.

G. Washington

LB, DLC:GW.

From Clement Biddle

Feby 20 1787

I had engaged the Freight & was preparing to Ship the Articles you had ordered in the Sloop Dolphin Capn Steward (the first Vessel that had offered this Spring for Potowmack) when I received your favour of 11th inst., Mr Haines had Kept 50 bushels of Barley for me but could share no more[1]—what I send is New England Summer Barley which is much the best. I should have applied to another Brewer to make up the 100 Bushels, but Mr Haines who has taken much pains to introduce & improve the Culture of Barley in this State, informs me that the Summer barley does not answer here so well as in New England & after many trials they now generally raise the Winter Barley here—the Summer Barley comes foward too fast in this Climate & he thinks will be more apt to do it in Virginia. I have made no Engagements for the Produce of it.

I have procured some Grass seed which I think is extraordinary good & much Cheaper than it has been sold. You have also the Spinning Wheels, all of which Articles are Shipped on board the Sloop Dolphin Aaron Steward Master for alexandria & you have the Bill of Loading & Invoice inclosed—the Sloop will leave this about Sunday next, & I hope will be with you in Good time for seeding—the Captain could not deliver the Goods before he reached Alexandria as he must first enter there. I have paid Mr Seddon & Co. for the magazine for Six months. Well Cured Herrings have sold @ 22/6 or three dollars ⅌ Barrell—they ask 3/9 this Currency ⅌ Barrel freight—the freight from hence is inserted in the Bill of Loading.

Mrs Biddle begs leave to present her best respects to Mrs Washington & am &ca

C. Biddle

See sd Invoice over leaf[2]

ADfS, ViMtV: Clement Biddle Letter Book.

1. Biddle wrote GW on 5 Nov. 1786 about securing barley from the Philadelphia brewer Reuben Haines.

2. Biddle's invoice, as appears in his letter book and transcribed in CD-
ROM:GW, shows charges of £15 for 50 bushels of seed barley, £15 for 300 lbs.
of red clover seed, £2.5 for two spinning wheels, and 10 shillings paid to
Thomas Seddon & Co. for the *Columbian Magazine.* Charges for containers,
handling, and shipping, in addition to Biddle's commission, bring the total
to £36.4.6.

To Bridget Kirk

Madam,   Mount Vernon February 20 1787
I must beg the favor of you to give the bearer (Mr Lear a
young Gentlemen who lives with me) a decided answer with respect to the money which is due to me from the Estate of Mr
Kirk your late husband,[1] I wish it may not be forgotten that the
Flour for which this money is due ought to have been paid on
the delivery of it notwithstanding I have been kept out of it so
long.

I beg leave to add that it is from the real want of it I make
such frequent, and pressing applications. I am Madam your
most obed. Servant

G. Washington

LB, DLC:GW.

1. On 29 Oct. 1788 GW collected £7.18.5 due him from the estate of James
Kirk (Ledger B, 275), a wheat merchant originally from England who kept an
office and store in Alexandria but lived across the Potomac in Maryland. Kirk,
a former mayor of Alexandria, died in April 1786. See references to Mrs.
Kirk's bond in William Deakins to GW, 2 Nov. 1787, and GW to Deakins, 8
Mar. 1788. In 1797 Archibald McClean (McLean) acted to settle the account
of the estate of Bridget Kirk with GW (McClean to GW, 4 Aug. 1797).

To Richard Henry Lee

MOUNT VERNON, February 20, 1787.
DEAR SIR—Your favour of the 15th, with the seed of the
honey locust came safe to hand, and claims my particular
thanks.[1] I have but one doubt of its forming the best hedge in

the world; and that is, whether it can be sufficiently dwarfed. If this cannot be effected, the other purpose mentioned in your letter, and a valuable one too, of subserving stock, is alone sufficient to induce the cultivation of the tree.

Mrs. Washington offers respectful compliments to Mrs. Lee, to whom, though I have not the honour of being known, I beg leave to tender mine;[2] we both join in best wishes for you, and the young ladies, and with great esteem and respect, I have the honour to be, dear sir, Your most obedient and affectionate servant.

GEO: WASHINGTON.

Memoir of Richard Henry Lee, 2:34–35.

1. Letter not found. GW had seeds of the honey locust sowed on 23 April "behind the Stables" (*Diaries*, 5:142).

2. Lee's second wife was Anne Gaskins Pinckard Lee, to whom he had been married since 1769.

Letter not found: to Jeremiah Wadsworth, 20 Feb. 1787. In the *Collector,* September–October 1956, GW is quoted as writing: "The Post of this day, brought similar information of yours." Goodspeed's catalog (1918), no. 125, item 2761, indicates that GW referred to Henry Knox and is quoted as having written: "the gentleman at whose house I am." The "gentleman" is identified as "Mr. Fendal." GW and Mrs. Washington on 20 Feb. had dinner in Alexandria at the house of Philip Richard Fendall and his wife Elizabeth Steptoe Lee Fendall, with Henry Lee, Jr., and his wife Matilda Lee Lee (*Diaries*, 5:107). Lee, who had been reelected to Congress, did not attend Congress in New York until 19 April.

From James Madison

Dear Sir   New York Feby 21. 1787

Some little time before my arrival here a quorum of the States was made up and Genl Sinclair put in the Chair. We have at present nine States on the ground, but shall lose South Carolina today. Other States are daily expected. What business of moment may be done by the present or a fuller meeting is uncertain.[1] The objects now depending and most immediately in prospect, are 1. The Treaty of peace. The Secretary of foreign Affairs has very ably reported a view of the infractions on both sides, his exposition of the contested articles, and the steps proper to be taken by congress. I find what I was not before apprized of that more than one infraction on our part, preceded even the violation on the other Side in the instance of the Negroes. Some of the reasoning on the subject of the debts would be rather grating to Virginia. A full compliance with the Treaty according to judicial constructions, and as a ground for insisting on a reciprocal compliance, is the proposition in which the Report terminates.[2] 2. a Recommendation of the proposed Convention in May. Cong[res]s have been much divided and embarrassed on the question whether their taking an interest in the measure would impede or promote it. On one side it has been urged that some of the backward States have scruples *agst* acceding to it without some constitutional sanction: On the other that other States will consider any interference of Congs as proceeding from the same views which have hitherto excited their jealousies. A vote of the Legislature here entered into yesterday will give some relief in the case. They have instructed their delegates in Congs to move for the recomendation in question. The vote was carried by a majority of one only in the Senate, and there is room to suspect that the minority were actuated by a dislike to the substance rather than by any objections agst the form of the business. A large Majority in the other branch a few days ago put a definitive veto on the Impost. It would seem as if the politics of this State are directed by individual interests and plans, which might be incommoded by the controul of an efficient federal Government.[3] The four States North of it are still to make their decision on the subject of the Convention. I am told by one of the Mass[achuset]ts delegates that the Legislature of that State which is now sitting will certainly accede and appoint deputies if Congs declare their approbation of the measure. I have similar information that Connecticut will probably come in, though it is said that the interference of Congress will rather have a contrary tendency there. It is expected that S. Carolina will not fail to adopt the plan, and that Georgia is equally well disposed. All the intermediate States between the former and N. York have already appointed deputies except Maryland which it is said means to do it, and has entered into some vote which declares as much. Nothing has yet been done in the New Congs with regard to the Missisippi. Our last information from Massts gives hopes that the mutiny or as the Legislature there now style it, the Rebellion is nearly extinct. If the measures however on foot for *disarming* and *disfranchising*, those concerned in it should be carried into effect, a new crisis may be brought on.[4] I have not been here long enough to gather the general sentiments of leading characters touching our affairs & prospects. I am inclined to hope that they will gradually be concentered in the plan of a thorough reform of the existing system. Those who may lean towards a monarchical Govt and who I suspect are swayed by very indigested ideas, will of course abandon an unattainable object whenever a prospect opens of rendering the Republican form competent to its purposes. Those who remain attached to the latter form must soon perceive that it can not be preserved at all under any modification which does not redress the ills experienced from our present establishments. Virginia is the only State which has made any provision for the late moderate but essential requisition of Congs and her provision is a partial one only.

This would have been of earlier date, but I have waited for more interesting subjects for it. I shall do myself the pleasure of repeating the liberty of dropping you a few lines as often as proper occasions arise, on no other condition however than your waving the trouble of regular answers or acknowledgments on your part. With the greatest respect and Affection I am Dr Sir Yr Obedt friend & Servt

Js Madison Jr

ALS, DLC:GW; Copy, DLC: Madison Papers.

1. Arthur St. Clair was elected president of Congress on 2 Feb. 1787. The South Carolina delegates were to serve only until 21 Feb. (*JCC*, 32:11, 31).

2. For John Jay's report of 13 Oct. 1786 on violations of the terms of the Treaty of Peace of 1783 by individual American states, see Jay to GW, 27 June 1786, n.2.

3. The New York legislature on 15 Feb. rejected the impost amendment to the Articles of Confederation and on 20 Feb. voted to recommend a convention to revise the Articles (*New York Journal of Assembly, 1787*, 52, 55, 59–60; Madison's Notes on Debates, 21 Feb., in Rutland and Rachal, *Madison Papers*, 9:290–92).

4. See the notes that Madison made on the speech that Rufus King delivered to Congress on 19 Feb. regarding to the dangers of the situation in Massachusetts after the defeat of the insurgents by government forces (ibid., 276–79).

From Henry Knox

My dear Sir   New York 22 February 1787.

The storm in Massachusetts is subsiding for the present. But what effects the disfranchisement of a great body of people will create is not easy to say. a numerous body of high spirited men, conceiving themselves oppressed by the government composed of their equals, will reguard the oppression more than the causes which gave birth to it—They will be probably plotting perpetually, to releive themselves from burdens, which they will think intolerable. This will manifest itself variously, and perhaps in some cases in open hostility—Although the insurgents are fled, and dispersed, yet the government conceives itself unsafe without a force. accordingly 1500 men, are raised for five months. This force is to be posted by detachments throughout the disafected Counties—Neither discipline or prudence, will restrain the troops to such conduct, as to avoid offence—The people will think themselves curbed and tyrannized over. The troops will consider the least symptom of discontent, as a step to open hostility—one or the other must be masters—The operation will require force, and hence probably springs a standing army, for the support of government—my conjectures may be erroneous, but it is not impossible but something like this will result from the commotions of Massachusetts.

Congress will probably adopt the idea of a convention for the revision of the Confederation to assemble in May at Philadelphia—This will take away the objections against the legality of the proposed convention. and meet the ideas of the eastern States—I hope it will be effected in Congress & a general attendance of the states be the consequence—I am my dear Sir Your truly respectful and affectionate

H. Knox

ALS, DLC:GW.

Letter not found: to Alexander Spotswood, 22 Feb. 1787. On 5 Mar. Spotswood wrote: "Your Favr of the 22d February . . . never came to my hands until this day."

From William Moultrie

Sir   Charleston [S.C.] February 23rd 1787

Your Excellency's Circular Letter, addressed to me, as President of the Society of the Cincinnati of this State, wherein you were pleased to express your desire of not being re-elected President of the Order on their next general Meeting—I did myself the Honor of laying before the Society at an extra meeting held the 12th instant.[1]

At the same time that we return your Excellency our Sincere thanks for the Honor you have conferred on us during your Presidency, and the Sentiments of attachment which you have expressed for the Society—we must lament the Causes you have assigned for declining being again elected at the next General Meeting, as they appear to be almost insuperable bars, to any hopes of prevailing on you, once again, to accept of being President.

Yet Sir, Since the date of your Letter, an Event has happened which may prove more favourable to our hopes and wishes— Your Country Still holding you in View, when her first Characters are required to come forward and Act for her good—have made choice of your Excellency in her Delegation to the Convention of the States which is to meet at Philadelphia in May next—a Serious and truly important Call! and which your Excellency's regard for the general Interests of America, has Occasioned you to forego all other considerations, and quitting the desireable Sweets of retirement, accept the appointment—Thus then shall we hope that, as the general triennial Meeting of the Society will be convened at the same time and at the same place, Your Excellency will find less difficulty in complying with the ardent wish of this State's Society—and that you will again be President.

We have once more to Offer to you, Sir, our Sincere thanks for the Honor the Society has gained by your Patronage—and to offer to Heaven unfeigned prayers that your Excellency's health, happiness and prosperity may be continued, and that you may long be spared—for the benefit of your Country and Mankind. I have the Honor to be, Your Excellency's Most Obedient Humble Servant

Willm Moultrie

LS, DLC:GW.
1. GW's circular letter to the Society of the Cincinnati, printed above, is dated 31 Oct. 1786.

From Philip Pendleton

Sir.   Berkeley Co. Feby 23rd 1787.

The late decision between the Hites Grantees & the late Lord Fairfax, has occasioned great uneasiness in this County. among many others, a few of us who are interested in lands adjoining a Tract you hold on Bulskin are a little alarmed; It appears by the proceedings in that suit that a survey had been made for Joist Hite on both sides that run. So much thereof as lay on the So. side they acknowledge to have been sold to one Lewis Thomas under whom you hold, as well as by a Patent from Lord Fairfax granted either to Thomas, George Johnson from whom we are informed you were the immediate purchaser or to yourself since your purchase.

in making the survey on which this Patent Issued we find no regard was paid to the Original made for Hite but in this as in many other Cases of a similar nature, some parts were intentionally left out & other lands of greater value taken in as best suited the purchase. the lands thus left out, were considered as Vacant Lands & have without any kind of molestation been Patented held & enjoyed ever since by other persons. I am told that about four acres of the original Survey is possessed by Mr Robt Throckmorton about Seven by John McCormack & a few, I do not know how many by Thornton Washington who holds thro' me of Owen Thomas who was the Eldest son & Heir at Law of Lewis, under whom you claim the Lands you hold there. We are well assured that shoud you have all the rights of Lewis Thomas to that survey you are perfectly satisfied with the survey on which your Patent Issued and do not wish or expect to recover one acre more, yet a Copy of the decree has been served upon us, which makes it necessary for us to State our Claims to the Court—the equity of which your Excellency will at once percieve arises from the Conduct of those claiming under Hite who Carved out their own lands & left the ballance to the next adventurers[1]—However we think it woud save us a great deal of expence & Trouble, woud your Excellency relinquish to us & those claiming under us your right in such parts of the Original survey as we are respectively possessed off. we have requested the bearer hereof John McCormack to wait on you for that purpose. this we the more readily expect as your Excellency never has heretofore put in any claims to these lands. I will only beg leave to add that it will perhaps render us essential service & for which we shall ever retain the most gratefull sentiments. I have the Honour to be yr Excellency's Mo. Obt Servt

Phil. Pendleton

ALS, PHi: Gratz Collection; Sprague transcript, DLC:GW.

1. For a discussion of the disputed claims of the Hites to land in Berkeley County and GW's title to his Bullskin lands, see Thornton Washington to GW, 6 June 1786, and notes. For GW's sale of this tract of land to Pendleton who sold it to Charles Washington, GW's brother and Thornton Washington's father, see Bond to Philip Pendleton, 7 Dec. 1771, printed above.

To Jaques Campion

Sir,   Mount Vernon February 24th 1787
    Your letter of the 26th of Jany came duly to hand.[1] I am much obliged to you for your good wishes, and interest which you take in my welfare—The Asses are in very good order, but I am sorry to inform you that the Gold cock and the Silver hen pheasant are ded; the others appear to be drooping, and I am afraid that all the care and attention which is paid to them will not be able to preserve them.[2] I am Sir yr Humble Servant

G. Washington

LB, DLC:GW.

1. Letter not found.

2. GW wrote in his diary for 29 Nov. 1786: "Mr. [Jaques] Campion (who brought the Asses and Pheasants here from the Marqs. de la fayette) [left] for Alexa. to proceed in the Stage for Baltimore. Gave him 30 Louis dores for his trouble" (*Diaries*, 5:73). See also GW to James McHenry, 11 Nov. 1786.

To Robert Carter

Sir,   Mount Vernon 24th Feb: 1787
    The Gentleman who does me the honor of presenting this letter to you, is the Reverend Mr Griffith, with whom I have had

a long acquaintance. As he has some business to transact with you, or proposion to make, I beg leave to introduce him to your civilities, and to yr attention as a Gentleman of worth and of very respectable character.[1]

My Compliments if you please to Mrs Carter. I am Sir yr most Obedt Hble Se⟨vt⟩

Go: Washington

ALS, PHi: Dreer Collection.

The letter is addressed to "Robt Carter Esqr. Nomeny." Robert Carter, a grandson of Robert "King" Carter (1663–1732), lived at Nomini Hall in Westmoreland County. He served on the governor's council from 1758 to 1775 and had extensive landholdings in Virginia.

1. It has not been determined what business the Rev. David Griffith wished to conduct with Carter, but it would appear that he took with him a letter from GW to members of the Dismal Swamp Company regarding Henry Emanuel Lutterloh's proposal to import into Virginia several hundred German laborers, which GW thought might be used by the company in building the proposed canal in the swamp. See Lutterloh to GW, 3 Jan. 1787, GW to Lutterloh, 8 April 1787, and John Page to GW, 9 Mar. 1787. See also the letter GW wrote to Samuel Powel of Philadelphia on behalf of Griffith on 5 April 1786, in which he refers to Griffith's business interests in Alexandria.

To Benjamin Lincoln, Jr.

Sir, Mount Vernon Feby 24th 1787.

I have recd your letter of the 24th Ulto & the receipt for Messrs Josiah Watson & Co. bill of exchange which was enclosed in it. I am much obliged to you for the Acct of the political situation of your State which you gave me, and am very happy to find, by later advices, that matters are soon likely to terminate entirely in favor of Government by the suppression of the insurgents, and it adds much to the satisfaction which these accounts give that it may be effected with so little blood-shed. I hope some good may come out of so much evil, by giving energy & respectability to the Government.

General Lincoln's situation must have been very painful, to be obliged to march against those men whom he had heretofore looked upon as his fellow citizens, and some of whom had, perhaps, been his Companions in the field; but as they had, by their repeated outrages, forfeited all the rights of Citizenship, his duty & patriotism must have got the better of every other consideration & led him with alacrity to support the Government. I am Sir.

L[S], MH; LB, DLC:GW. The signature on the receiver's copy at MH, in the hand of Tobias Lear, has been cut off.

To Henry Knox

Mount Vernon 25th Feb. 1787

Accept, my dear General Knox my affectionate thanks for your obliging favors of the 29th, 30th, & 31st of Jany and 1st 8th & 12th of the present month.

They were indeed, exceedingly satisfactory, and relieving to my mind which has been filled with great & anxious uneasiness for the issue of General Lincoln's operations, and the dignity of Government.

On the prospect of the happy termination of this insurrection I sincerely congratulate you; hoping that good may result from the cloud of evils which threatned not only the hemisphere of Massachusetts but by spreading its baneful influence, the tranquillity of the Union. Surely Shays must be either a weak man— the dupe of some characters who are yet behind the curtain— or has been deceived by his followers. Or which may yet be more likely, he did not conceive that there was energy enough in the Government to bring matters to the crisis to which they have been pushed. It is to be hoped the General Court of that State concurred in the report of the Committee, that a rebellion did actually exist. This woud be decisive, and the most likely means of putting the finishing stroke to the business.

We have nothing new in this quarter except the dissentions which prevailed in, and occasioned the adjournment of, the Assembly of Maryland; that an appeal might be made to the people for their sentiments on the conduct of their representatives in the Senate & Delegates respecting a paper emission; which was warmly advocated by the latter and opposed by the former— and which may be productive of great, and perhaps dangerous divisions. Our Affairs, generally, seem really, to be approaching to some awful crisis. God only knows what the result will be. It shall be my part to hope for the best; as to see this Country happy whilst I am gliding down the stream of life in tranquil retirement is so much the wish of my Soul, that nothing on this side Elysium can be placed in competition with it.

I hope the postponement of your journey to this State does not amount to a relinquishment of it—and that it is unnecessary to assure you of the sincere pleasure I should have at seeing you under this roof. Mrs Washington unites with me in every good wish for Mrs Knox yourself and family. With sentiments of the warmest friendship I am—Yrs most Affectionately

Go: Washington

P.S. I had wrote this letter & was on the point of sending it with others to the Post Office when your favor of the 15th instt was handed to me. The spirit & decision of the Court is very pleasing & I hope will be attended with happy consequences. G.W.

ALS, NNGL: Knox Papers; LB, DLC:GW.

From Nicholas Simon van Winter and Lucretia Wilhelmina van Winter

Monseigneur, [Amsterdam] de⟨r⟩ 26 fevrier 1787

Vos Lettres, que nous avons eu l'honneur de recevoir l'Année passée, par la main de Monsieur le Marquis de la Fayette, par les quelles vous avez eú la bonté d'agréer les Vers de ma chere Compagne, (hommage dû a votre magnanimité et a Votre Vertu,) nous donnent ⟨assèz⟩ de ⟨pardiesse⟩ pour vous presenter à prèsent Germanicus, Nous nous flattons, que votre admiration poúr le meilleur Héros de l'Antique Rome, (l'Objet du Poëme dont nous avons l'honneur de vous offir úne Tradúction Françoise) n'est-pas moindre que la nôtre.[1] Peutêtre l'Amerique, delivrée par vous, reconnoîtra-t-elle Son Libérateur dans ce Tableaú. Peutêtre donne-t-il un jour occasion à un Poëte de l'Amerique de chanter le Germanicus de la Patrië. Permettez que deux Epoux Hollandois, qui aiment leúr Patrië, tâ⟨c⟩hent de soutenir sa réputation Litéraire, trop peu connúë chez l'Etranger. Daignez donc recevoir l'Ouvrage d'une Citoyenne des Pays Bas Unis; accordéz lui l'honneur d'y fixer votre attention quelques instans; et quoi qu'il semble, que l'infirmité de Son Autheur ne lui promette pas une longue carriere, elle rémit ses voeúx sinceres a ce un de Son Epoux pour votre prosperité &

votre gloire. Acceptéz les temoignages du profond respect, avec lequel nous avons l'honneur d'être.

ADf, Amsterdam: Collectie Six.

1. Lucretia Wilhelmina van Winter published in 1787 the poem *Germanicus, poëme, en seize chants.* The book was in GW's library at the time of his death.

From Clement Biddle

Feby 27. 1787.

I reced your favour of 14th in time to procure five Augers—they are made in the Country & I could not get a sixth at the Shops which sell them. they Cost 6/ is £1.10.0. to your Debit I have sent them by Capt. Steward by whom I shipped the Barley &c. & inserted them in the Bill of Loading which remained here—he Sails this Day for Alexandria & returns here immediately—I consulted the Iron Mongers who Supply the Fence Maker & by their advice have sent two Inch Augers which my Father also informs me are quite large Enough for Post Holes—the Sort sent are deemed much best for any Kind of work. The Barley is Rhode Island Barley which is much the best & Colo. Wadsworth tells me he always gets his Seed from thence—the Clover seed is very good & I hope they will be with you in Season & am your Excellencys &ca.

Clement Biddle

ADfS, ViMtV: Clement Biddle Letter Book.

From Henry Knox

My dear Sir   New-York 27th February 1787

My last to you was on the 22d instant, in which I stated my apprehensions respecting the proposed disfranchisement in Massachusetts. I did not mean to find fault with the measure. I am persuaded circumstances have rendered it necessary, and proper. But any rigorous chastisement of the rebels, will enflame them and render it right and expedient for the government to provide for its own safety against the sudden attempts of men, who have already flown to Arms, in order to redress ideal grievances. The assembly have voted £40000 to pay the expences, which have been & will be incurred by the rebellion. This circumstance will exceedingly embarrass them, because, they must Mortgage their only efficient fund, which has been invariably hitherto applied to the payment of the debts due to the late Army, who now must go without their interest.

I have received a letter from General Lincoln dated at Pittsfield in the County of Berkshire, in which he says, that Shays and some of his officers have fled to Canada—and that the rest of the insurgents have dispersed—that his parties were busily engaged in receiving the submissions and apprehendg desafected characters.[1]

I enclose a newspaper, containing the act of the legislature for disfranchisement.

You will have observed that Congress has passed an Act approving the idea of a convention, so worded, as to include all appointments already made—This circumstance will remove all objections to the convention on account of its legality. With Mrs Knoxs and my very affectionate respects to Mrs Washington I am my dear Sir Your sincere and most Obedient humble Sert

H. Knox

ALS, DLC:GW.
1. See Benjamin Lincoln to GW, 4 Dec. 1786–4 Mar. 1787.

Letter not found: from Edward Newenham, 27 Feb. 1787. On 25 Dec. 1787 GW wrote Newenham that he had received his letter of "27th of Feby."

From Charles Willson Peale

Dr Sir   Phila[delphi]a Feby 27. 1787
Your obliging favor of the Body of the Golden Pheasant, I have received in good condition, although by a stage two Days after the receipt of your Letter. The delay was vexatious, yet I am richly paid in being able to preserve so much beauty.[1] Before this time I had thought those Birds which I have seen in the Chinease paintings were only works of fancy, but now I find them to be only aukcrd Portraits.

I am sorry that thier lives cannot be preserved. I did not find the body very lean, the musels of the Thighs were strong, which with smallness of the Wings, makes me think that they run fast and fly but little. When you have the misfortune of loosing the others, if the weather should be warm, be pleased to order the Bowels to be taken out and some Pepper put into the Body, but no Salt which would spoil the Feathers. and if you please to have some directions put on the box which would prevent delay on the Passage of them. Another labour which I have lately undertaken I hope will give you Pleasure, I mean the making of Prints in Mezzotinto from my Portraits of Illustrous Personages. I am fully confident amongst the number are many dear to you. From the experience I have lately had, I feel my powers to execute in this way the most faithful Liknesses, as I hope to prove by the next Plates that I publish. I have finished a Plate of Doctr Franklin, which I give to the Public as a specimen of the Size and manner of my intended series of Prints, yet I do myself injustice, as this Print is much coarser than the others will be.[2] Please to present my most respectful Compliments to Mrs Washington, and believe me with much respect Dr Sir your very Humble Servant

C.W. Peale

ALS, DLC:GW; ADfS, PPAmP: Charles Willson Peale Papers.
    1. See GW to Peale, 16 February.
    2. During the Constitutional Convention, GW sat for Peale who wished to make a mezzotint of him (Peale to GW, 29 May, June 1787; see also Wick, *Graphic Portraits of Washington*, 15–16).

Letter not found: to George Steptoe Washington, 27 Feb. 1787. On 2 Mar. George Steptoe Washington wrote GW: "I receiv'd your letter dated 27th Feby."

From Samuel Hanson

Sir   Alexandria 28th Feby 1787
    At the request of Mr George Fitzhugh I do myself the pleasure to forward to you Dr Youngs 1st 3d & 4th Vols. of his Tour. The 2d Vol: being missing (& never sent to me by him) I have detained the others some time, with the hope of procuring it in the Neighbourhood, in order to send you the Set compleat. Having as yet been unsuccessful, & being informed that the 2d Volume is not material to the Sense of the rest, I think it best to

keep them no longer. I shall, however, continue my pursuit after the missing Volume.[1]

Mr Fitzhugh also requested me to inform you that another Work on Agriculture, of considerable reputation, is entirely at your Service. It is entitled Museum Rusticum, and is now in my Hands. Should you have an Inclination to peruse it, I will immediately send it.[2]

I beg leave to inform you that I have several Treatises on Husbandry of great Character, with which it would give me great pleasure to accomodate you; as well because I am informed you are engaged in a course of Experimental Agriculture, as to testify that profound respect with which I have the Honour to remain Sir Your most obedt Servt

S. Hanson of Saml

ALS, DLC:GW.

1. George Lee Mason Fitzhugh (1748–1836) was the son of Col. William Fitzhugh of Maryland. For GW's acquisition in 1786 of Arthur Young's books on his tours through Northern England and Ireland, see GW to Biddle, 10 Feb. 1786, n.3.

2. GW bought volumes 1 through 6 of *Museum Rusticum et Commerciale: or, Select Papers on Agriculture, Commerce, Arts, and Manufactures* (London, 1764–66) through Robert Cary & Co. in 1766. See Enclosure: Invoice to Robert Cary & Co., 23 June 1766, n. 3. The work remained in the Mount Vernon library until after GW's death.

From David Humphreys

My dear General,   Springfield [Mass.] Feby 28th 1787.

Since I had the pleasure of writing you last, I have received Orders to march the part of my Regt which is raised in Connecticut to this place. Two compleat Companies arrived on saturday last. They occupy the Barracks & take the guard of the Arsenal & Magazines. I intend to return to Hartford in a few days, & shall remain there probably for some time.[1]

As I conceived you would be anxious to know what is the actual situation of affairs in this part of the Country, which has been the scene of tumult & confusion; I take up the pen to inform you, in brief, that after the Insurrection was quelled in this County, General Lincoln marched into Berkshire. In which County Genl Patterson is Majr Genl of Militia, his conduct is variously reported—upon the whole it is said not to reflect much credit upon him. As Lincoln approached, the Insurgents, who were collected in bodies of from 100 to 150 & 200, fled. Some of these are still undispersed, & lurk on the frontiers of N. York & Vermont. The time of Service of the men who were raised for the first expedition, is expired. Government are proceeding to raise 1000 more for four months. Lincoln with a handful of Recruits is at Pittsfield, & will continue to command the new Levies. Tho' the spirit of Rebellion does not seem to be absolutely broken, yet it is to be presumed, with prudence and perseverance it may be utterly subdued.

You will see in the public Papers the Proceedings of the Legislature of this State, which carry much stronger marks of energy & decision, than have been exhibited on any former occasion.

I am just informed, that in consequence of the refusal of the Legislature of New York to comply, satisfactorily, with the Requisition of *Congress* respecting the five pr Cent impost; the last mentioned Body have recommended to all the States to send a Representation to the Convention which is to be holden at Philadelphia in May next. This may give a new Complexion to that Businesss—Requesting to be remembered to Mrs Washington & the family I have the honour to be with the sincerest esteem & affection your friend & humble Servt

> D. Humphreys.

ALS, DLC:GW.

1. Humphreys wrote on 11 February. After receiving Henry Knox's orders of 9 Feb., Humphreys, "dress'd in all the extra ellegance of Paris," marched with his men to Springfield, where he remained for a short time until relieved by Henry Jackson (James Swan to Henry Knox, 26 Feb. 1787, NNGL: Knox Papers; Knox to Henry Jackson, 9 Feb. 1787, DNA:PCC, item 150).

From Fielding Lewis, Jr.

Dr Sir　　　　　　Bloomsbery Frederick County Fabry 28th—87

I am grately Obliged to you for the timber you was pleased to give me Neare Recter town[1]—am Sorrey that it never has been in my power to Come to See you Since peace Owing to the Distressd Situation I have been in ever Since—(til now) Your Mentioning my being in Fairfax and never going to Se you is Very

Right, but when there, I was Obliged to be evry day indevoring to make up Money to discharge my debts—and Should not have injoyed my Self in Seing you when in Such a Situation—but now being Cleare of debt I hope to Spend two or three weakes with you in Some Satisfaction.[2]

My Son will hand you this—and Inclosed I have Sent you a fue lines of[3] his riteing as perhaps you may want him in Some busniss or Other, Should it be the Case he may Continue with you till of Age which will not be for this fore Years to Come[4]— With my love to My Aunt—I remain yrs with Evrey Esteem and Regarde.

Fielding Lewis

N.B. Should you not want him you will oblige me In geting him into busniss—his temper is Smooth and Easey—and I can Say I am hapy in his behavior if it Continues & I at preasent have no room to believe to the Contrarey but what it will. F.L.[5]

ALS, ViMtV.

1. See GW to Lewis, 4 Dec. 1786.

2. Lewis's freedom from debt probably did not last long. On 25 Sept. 1792 Betty Lewis wrote GW that she had "at this time three of my Grandchildren to support, and god knows from every Account but I may expect as many more shortly. Fieldings is so distrest that his Children would go naked if it was not for the assistance I give him" (ViMtV).

3. Lewis wrote "if."

4. Lewis's son George Warner Lewis reached Mount Vernon on 6 Mar. and left the following morning (*Diaries*, 5:113–14).

5. GW's response to this request has not been found.

From John Armstrong

Dear General   Carlisle [Pa.] March 2d 1787—

Amongst many others, I consider myself your Excellencys debtor—and that the small Annuity of a letter is the least discharge I can offer. how this acknowledgment has been made in the two preceding years, memory is now too weak to inform me, and having enuff to do with the trivial Originals, I do not pretend to keep Coppys—but whether my last reached you or not, will be known by the liberty I took of expressing three or four *particular wishes,* in detail, at the close of it.[1]

That our political affairs at present possess but a sable aspect, and are ground of serious concern to every worthy American, I know must be Obvious to you—the early refusal of some of the States, to admit the *Impost* (and 'tis again refused by New-York the other day) I fear will bring on ruine—Congress is & has been, but a Council of advice, whose influence daily grows less. amongst all our diseases as far as I can observe, *distrust*, or the want of confidence, is not the least. it is hard to tell how we shall be governed, when we cannot trust ourselves, or which is the same thing, the men of our own choice! We seem to require more time, & perhaps discipline too, before we gain that knowledge of Government in general and of that species we have adopted in particular, that can quallify us for proper & rational Subjection, even to laws of our own making. and whosoever expects more than this from the splendid word liberty—perverts the only true meaning of it. Our happy transition from the former State, is neither well understood nor properly improved—too many think they are wise—too many selfwilled—jealous of the advantages of a Sister-State, or partial to their own; forgetting practically at least, that the Federal interest is *one & but one*. as to incidental advantages that are merely local, natural & inevitable, they may happen to all in their turn, they belong to the body, and should never be grudged; as well may we envy our feet, because our Shoes may happen to be better than our Hatt. On the other hand, Congress too, may probably need a reform—patience—*Economy* in the whole circle of their business, with frequent & explicit accounts of the disbursments of the peoples money—encouragement of honesty, industry & frugality. from what we have heard, we must be ready to concieve that Congress have Set out in the Arrangments of their federal government, on a large & expensive Scale: a written display of them would indeed be pompous enough, and might induce strangers to believe us to be a well established & wealthy nation. a number of great *departments, Boards & Tables*—Rented Houses, & a group of Clerks—Capital Officers, with three & some of them four thousand dollars ℔ annum: and all this without moral certainty or high probability, that their finances were equal to a gradual discharge of the national debt at least, as well as to this projected expence of the Federal Government. but what services may have resulted from this well Organized System, these three years past, are not so obvious as might be wished—my meaning in these hints is far from standing opposed to method; and am also sensible that some considerable Polititions have laid it down as a Maxim, that a republican Government requires *more Servants* than a Monarchial—this may be so, (or rather problematical) but we know no human maxim how generalsoever, that does not vary in it's use according to the circumstances under which it is to be applyed. An economical reformation, would appear well, as coming from the *head,* and likely to produce good effects—the Civil list perhaps with safety might be curtailed, & the Salaries of the absolutely necessary lessened—this would contribute much to conciliate the people & restore confidence to that body—and altho it be true in the general, that in the time of *Peace* we ought to prepare against *War,* I cannot readily admit that such preparation should lead us to infringe the rules of justice, or risque our national faith & credit—I confess dear General, I should rather See the rulers of our country in the present situation, trust the protection of God, in their weak State—than attempt to be either wise, pompous, or strong, at the expence of honor & justice; apprehending more immediately as I do from intestine difficulties, than from foreign invasion.

Most men are ready to say that Congress should have more power, as much as will answer the end of government—but what degree of power will serve this great purpose, is the question—and not easy to ascertain; this difficulty great enuff in itself, is enhansed, by the strange spirit we see too ready to prevail amongst different classes of men, every man or his neighbour, is now wise eno.—or jealous eno.—in their own conceit, or at least every State is likely to have their own Oracle. by disease & otherwise Superannuated as I now am, as you will see in the sequel of this letter, I have put my brain to the rack of late, in quest of some permanent or probable ground short of a *plenary or Coercive power,* and confess (tho' with fear & trembling) I can find none—the power & ability of execution, is the very essence of power, this must be lodged somewhere, otherwise legislation is to no effect. but will this be yielded, and where shall it be placed? It must be yielded sooner or later, or we must be a much better people than at present. however evident this may be to some men, it is very questionable whether it will yet be concured in, or whether at this Crisis, or in the first instance it ought to be adopted. there are some measures or things, wrong in themselves, that when gone into, cannot be altered for the better: so there may also be measures the most proper & salutary in themselves, that must for a time be waved & give way to the force of prejudice, which probably may happen in the question above. In a former letter I ventured to say you were not likely to have altogether done with publick appointments—and therfore mention the satisfaction of many, to see your nomination for the Convention in May next. the States will probably all send delegates, but with what restrictions we cannot tell, the late conduct of New-York relative to the Impost, is not promising—the meeting appears to be of great importance, may God Vouchsafe his blessing to it—however gloomy & unsettled the present state of things may be, there is still this Solid consolation left behind, that as God has lately favoured this country with a deliverance so remarkable & worthy of himself, we may humbly hope he has something farther in store for his Church amongst us, than to leave this people to division, anarchy & ruine! and for this hope in the favourable superintendence of the deity, we have the highest assurance interspersed thro' his word, provided we do not, or have not already *forfieted it*. Our attention as a people or nation to the Gospel of jesus, (the only ground of pleasing God) and his institutions, is very far from what it ought to be, a comparative Supineness, or neglect, is too apparent, even among those we have esteemed as the best—Other Classes either verging to deism, or grossly ignorant & profane—these things & their fruits, are what we have to fear—⟨&⟩ notwithstanding, a merciful God may not yet take these forfietures at our hands; so as to leave us to ourselves—I am glad to find your Legislature supporting the morallity of the Sabbath day. If the rumour be true that the people of Kaintucky have Seized a Spanish Sloop with goods & money coming near to, or amongst them it has at this distance the aspect of very bad policy—more especially as it's said the Governor of New-Orleance, has been rather favourable to them, and in several cases winked at his masters orders in their favour! there are various apprehensions to be infered from the forward & untutored spirit of our western people.

The allarming flame in Massachusetts seems nearly extinguished, but if the subsequent measures of that State respecting the insurgents should be severe, amounting to *death,* Confiscation, or disfranchisement, the consequences may be bad, as tending to rekindle the flame. Shall I tell you in *confidence,* I have now twice heard, nor from low authority, some principal men of that State begin to talk of wishing one general *Head* to the Union, in the room of Congress!

Whether I mentioned my present disorders in a former letter to you I disremember, therefore take the liberty of doing it now. near two years ago, I was instantaniously seized with a vertigo or dizziness, attended with great Stomach sickness for a few hours, which frequently returned for about ten days, when it left me, but the *Swiming or dizziness* of my head remains, greatly affecting my memory & hearing tho' without any acute pain. It is of the paralytic kind, and at my age not to be removed, but rather to look for a farther Stroak of the same kind—In this situation it is some consolation to Mrs Armstrong & myself that our Sons are Spared—the D[octo]r after a long contest with a pulmonary complaint, is pretty well recovered, but has not yet attempted his practice. The other yet remains in Philadelphia, on a mere subsistance, but I hope at once improving his mind, and outgrowing the Sallies of youth—he is said to have many friends, perhaps too many in his situation.[2] I cannot dear General conclude this letter already too long, without a farther tresspass on your time—In Our New College began at this place, the professors are punctual, men of regularity & good Scholars, I often secretly wish you acquainted with our Principal Dr Nisbet, from Montrose in Scotland—he is a man of plain manner, a kind of walking library—speaks several of the modern, as well as the dead languages—of quick disernment & sound judgment—a great republican, but decidedly in favor of Coercive power in the Executive body, more especially as ours are elective.[3]

I have for some time given over the thoughts of ever seeing Philada again but the funds of this institution being very weak I am often pressed by the Board of Trustees to endeavour to go down with the Principal in order to collect something for the institution—I confess the prospect of seeing you again will be a great inducement, to my undertaking this disagreeable effort hower small the effect may be, the generous & wealthy having been called on already. as I wish your name to be enrolled amongst the benefactors of this institution, I hope you may be so fortunate as to have a few Extra guineas in your pocket for this laudible purpose. I shall when in town, send you the Doctors discourse on the advantages of human learning, & his introductory address to the Scholars.[4] I have dear General, with great truth, the honor to be your Excellencys faithful friend & most humble Servant

John Armstrong

ALS, DLC:GW.

John Armstrong (1717–1795) as colonel of the Pennsylvania Regiment was GW's counterpart in the Forbes expedition in the fall of 1758.

1. Armstrong is referring to his letter of 25 Jan. 1785.

2. For Armstrong's earlier reference to the illness of his elder son, Dr. James Armstrong, see his letter to GW of 25 Jan. 1785. Dr. Armstrong had at one time practiced medicine in Virginia (see Armstrong to GW, 24 Dec. 1773). The younger son, John (1758–1843), was the author of the Newburg Addresses.

3. Charles Nisbet (1736–1804), a Presbyterian clergyman, came to Carlisle from Scotland in 1785 to become principal of Dickinson College, a position he held until his death.

4. On 5 June 1787 Armstrong sent Nisbet's *The Usefulness and Importance of Human Learning, a Sermon Preached before the Trustees of Dickinson College. Met at Carlisle, May 11, 1786; and Published at Their Desire* and *An Address to the Students of Dickinson College, by the Rev. Charles Nisbet, D.D. on His Re-election to the Office of Principal of Said College,* both of the works printed in Carlisle in 1786 and bound together. The volume was in the library at Mount Vernon when GW died in 1799.

To William Hartshorne

Sir   Mount Vernon Mar. 2d 1787.

Whatever sum Colonels Gilpin and Fitzgerald think proper to order, or the state of the treasury will enable you to pay, the Contractor for supplying the Workmen for the Potomack Company—the same being due to him—will be agreed to[1] by Sir Yr Most Obedt Hble Ser⟨vt⟩

Go: Washington

ALS, Gallery of History, Las Vegas, Nevada.

1. George Gilpin wrote below GW's signature: "Considering the state of the Treasury and other matters relative to the business of the Potomack Compy it is my opinion that more than three Hundred pounds Cannot be Conveniently paid at this time." On the reverse of the page John Fitzgerald wrote to Hartshorne: "Please pay the within Sum of Three Hundred Pounds to Captn

Westfall." This is followed by Abel Westfall's acknowledgment that he had "Received of Mr Hartshorne Treasurer of the Potowmac Company Three Hundred pounds in consequence of the within order." All are dated 2 March. On 7 Mar. 1787 Hartshorne gave the company's manager, Richardson Stewart, £252.9.6 to pay the wages of 103 men and 2 women who had worked as many as sixty-four days and as little as one day between 20 Dec. 1786 and 4 Mar. 1787 at the Great Falls (DLC: Misc. Manuscript Collection Potomac Company). Westfall, who lived in Berkeley County, had entered into a contract with the Potomac River Company in April 1786 to supply the company's workers with rations for one year (*Diaries*, 4:311).

From John Minter

Jacobs Crick [Pa.] the 2 day of March 1787
Sir I am informed you have a Conveyance of three tracts of Land from Vallentine Crawford one of which I as administrator sold to the widow Stephenson to rais money to pay the debts of Mr Crawford not knowing their was any inthrolment on it I have sum reason to believe the Lands was Conveyd to you as a security for a sum of Money that he owed to you if this is the Case you will Let Mr Wells know the amount of your demand as he is know impowerd to settle Crawfors Estate[1]—I refer you to Mr Wells for the situation I am in and hope you will give up the Land on gitting a Crtainty for what Crawford is indebted to you—from yours—

John Minter
ADMinSt.

ALS, DLC:GW. The letter was sent "Pr Favior Ben⟨j⟩. Wells."
    John Minter served as a captain of the Yohogania County militia during the Revolution. In 1776 Valentine Crawford sold Minter "a certain negro woman named Sall" (Albert, *Westmoreland County*, 60).
    1. For Valentine Crawford's debt, see GW to Thomas Smith, 8 May 1786, n.1.

Letter not found: from Edward Newenham, 2 Mar. 1787. On 25 Dec. 1787 GW wrote Newenham that he had received his letter of "2d of march 1787."

From George Steptoe Washington

Dear Uncle	Alexandria March 2d 1787

I receiv'd your letter dated 27th Feby the contents of which give me great concern,[1] sensible of the usefullness of a good education and the many advantages which result from it I have always made it a primary consideration nor have I allowed a thought of dress and plasure to engross my attention prejudicial to it. I believe I am rather defective in the spelling and writeing of english as I always paid more attention to my lattin but I shall make it my particular study, with every other peice of advice you shall be kind enough to give me. Your letter seems to insinuate that I make my brother Ferdinand the object of my immitation I am very sensible of his unbecoming conduct and altogether disapprove of it:[2] I have other relations who have afforded me a better example and which would be more agreeable to me to follow.

The letters I have sent to you were wrote in a hurry and without much attention I shall here after be more particular. Your affectionate et dutifull Nephew

Geoe S. Washington

ALS, ViMtV.

1. Letter not found.

2. Ferdinand Washington (1767–1788), son of Samuel and Anne Steptoe Washington, was five or six years older than his brother George Steptoe who with the youngest of the three brothers, Lawrence Augustine Washington, was being kept in school in Alexandria by GW. After Ferdinand died of consumption in 1788, GW made clear that he had "totally disapproved of" the extravagant conduct of his nephew (GW to Robert Chambers, 28 Jan. 1789). GW later in this year was to receive complaints about George Steptoe Washington's conduct from Samuel Hanson of Samuel, into whose house at Alexandria he and his brother had moved in January 1787 (see Hanson to GW, 23 Sept. and 18 Nov. 1787).

Letter not found: James Mercer to GW, 10 Mar. 1787. On 15 Mar. GW wrote Mercer: "Your favor of the 10th came duely to hand."

From Alexander Spotswood

Dear Sir   Nottingham March 3d 1787

By the Stage you will receive 3 bushle of my oats—One Busshle of Siberian Barly—Half of my Stock of the Bunch Homony Bean—& half d[itt]o of the English white Feild pea.[1]

The oats are the best kind that I ever propagated, but unfortunately, and in order to make out my crop—I saved two years ago some of the Black oat, which has occasioned a mixture—those I now send, are out of a parcel made from picked Seed, but Still I discover a few Black grains; therefore, wou'd advise, before you sow—to have them run over by hand.

The quantity sent, sowed about the 25th of this month, on one Acre of High manured land well prepared, and the seed put in with a light Harrow—will if no accident happens, Yeild you 70 bs.

The Barley is a Spring grain, & may be Sowed at the Same time of the Oats on half an acre, Harrowed in.

The Bunch homony beans I can Say Nothing off as to my own knowledge, I am Told they are Superior to the Other kind—& I presume may be Planted about the time of planting yr last corn.

The Feild pea, are usually Planted in England from the 20 february to the 20 of March—but here, where our vegetation is more Rapid; I presume about the first week in April will be in good time—The oats are what are called the Dutch Whites; if my Stilliards are good, they weigh 42 lbs. to the bushle—and I believe the crop before wd have Weighed 50 at *least* Betsy Joins me in the most afft. Manner to the Family. I am dr Sr with afft. regd yr most ob. H. Sert

Alexr Spotswood

ALS, DLC:GW.

1. See Spotswood to GW, 5 March.

From Henry Knox

My dear sir   New York 5 March 1787.

I wrote you on the 22d ultimo, that the affairs of Massachusetts were quietly settling down to peace and good order. But by recent advice from General Lincoln, it appears that the Insurgents who fled from Massachusetts, have received encouragement from the Inhabitants of this State bordering on the Line—and that embracing the time when the greatest part of his force were disbanded on the 23 ultimo, and before his force for four months were enlisted in any considerable numbers, the insurgents to the amount of three hundred headed by one Hamlin, made an irruption to Stockbridge and great Barrington on the 27th ultimo—Genl Lincoln on the 27th sent an express to Govr Clinton on this subject which was laid before the legislature now in session—In consequence of some resolutions he set out from this City on Sunday, in order to expell the Massachusetts Insurgents from this State.

Since his departure, a letter has been received from Kenderhook, dated the 1st instant mentioning that an action had taken place near great Barrington on the 27th between a party of Massachusetts troops & the insurgents, in which four were killed on each side and 40 wounded—The government kept the ground and the insurgents retreated into this State with their wounded and some prisoners—I beleive this account may be true although it is not official General Lincoln in his letter states that he had sent parties in pursuit of the Insurgents, and that they were at great Barrington.[1]

The legislature have this day made choice of delegates to represent this State who are, Colo. Hamilton, Judge Yates, and a Mr Lansing.[2]

Colonel Wadsworth arrived here last evening and begs his respects may be presented to you. I am my dear Sir Your affectionate & respectful humble Servt

					H. Knox

ALS, DLC:GW.

1. For an overview of the sequence of events in Massachusetts during Shays' Rebellion, see Benjamin Lincoln to GW, 4 Dec. 1786–4 Mar. 1787, and notes.

2. Robert Yates (1738–1801), a member of the New York Supreme Court, and John Lansing (1754–c.1829), mayor of Albany, were supporters of George Clinton and antinationalists. They attended the convention in Philadelphia but withdrew on 5 July in opposition to the convention's acceptance of what they conceived to be a plan for a consolidated government.

From John Peck

Sir   Richmond County 5th March 1787.
Enclosed are duplicates of two letters which I have had the honor to address to you but have not hitherto been favored with any answer. The former together with the Diplomas alluded to therein were delivered to Capt. Clagget in Piscataway who engaged to present them to you in a few days. The other was sent by a certain John Elwood master of a sloop that trades from Philadelphia to Alexandria.[1] Mr Collins the young gentleman who bears this will wait on you.[2] If the Diplomas have received your Signature, would wish that they might be transmitted by him. I have the honor to be With the greatest esteem Your most Humb. servt

Jno. Peck

ALS, DLC:GW. The enclosed copies of Peck's letters of 16 Aug. and 4 Sept. 1786 are in DLC:GW and the originals are printed above.
1. See notes in Peck's letters of 16 Aug. and 4 Sept. 1786. See also GW to Elias Dayton, 6 Nov. 1786.
2. GW does not record in his diaries a visit from a Mr. Collins. Collins may be a son of Christopher Collins of Richmond County, a neighbor and friend of Peck's father-in-law, Robert Carter.

From Israel Shreve

Burlington County State of New Jersey
Dear Sir,   5th March 1787
Some time ago I receivd your Letter in Answer to mine respecting your Lands on the Great Kanhaway.[1]
Since which I have Several times heard you have about Sixteen Hundred Acres of Land at or near Redstone In Pennsylvania called Washingtons Bottoms, which you Incline to Sell. I have not Seen the Lands But am Pretty well informed of the Situation Quality and Improvements thereon, by persons of my Acquaintance that Live near the Premises—If you do Incline to Sell the sd tract of Land altogether with the Improvements thereon, and Willing to take final Settlement Notes for pay, I should be glad to Purchase of you, said Notes are on Interest which Interest I am told will pay Tax in Virginia Eaqual to Cash, If So I hope you will oblige me In takeing them &c.—If my

proposals are agreeable Please as soon as Convenient, to let me know your price, And If any ways reasonable I will Immediately come to your Seat and Confirm the Bargan, I hold no other Notes But those Originally given to me for my Services and Supplies, (I am no speculator) And wish to purchace a tract of Land to Sit down upon, and one with Improvements on might suit a man of my Age Better than to Settle altogether in the woods, I am informed that Land at Redstone Rents for But little—Occationed by there being no Market near.[2]

However I think I could with Industry Get a Comfortable Liveing and be Improveing the Land.[3] I am Sir with Great Respect your Most Obedt Servt

Israel Shreve

ALS, DLC:GW.

1. Shreve's letter is dated 22 June 1785 and GW's, 15 July 1785.

2. Shreve eventually purchased Washington's Bottom in Pennsylvania from GW. For a summary of GW's dealings with Shreve, see the source note in Shreve to GW, 22 June 1785.

3. Shreve sent GW a copy of this letter, dated it 12 Mar., and added: "So far is a Duplicate of a Letter Dated the 5th Inst. put in the post office.

"Dear Gen. Since Writeing the first Letter dated the 5th Inst. I have had further Information respecting your Determination to Sell the Said Land. I hope I can Bring about a Bargan with you. I am Destitute of a Suitable farm in this State to Live Comfortable upon—and most of my Property is in final Settlement Notes, If you are Desirous to Sell Said Land, I could give a Sum in Such property the Interest of which woud be Considerable more than the Rents ariseing from the Lands. I have been Bred a farmer and prefer that way of Life to any other, and can with a good Conscince Leave a State so ungrateful as New Jersey is to her Officers and Soldiers, However this I Leave, and must wate to hear from you, You will forgive my freedom in Writeing to you in this manner, I expect showing my Anxiety to purchase of you will not make any Difference in one whom I can so much rely on. I am Dear Gen: with great Respect Your most Obedt Servt Israel Shreve" (DLC:GW).

From Alexander Spotswood

Dear Sir   Nottingham March 5th 1787

Your Favr of the 22d February pr Majr Barret, never came to my hands until this day.[1]

The Seeds I promised you, were Sent of by the Stage this day to Alexandria; to the Care of the Clerk of the Stage office at that place, & every precaution mentioned in yr lettcr, has been attended to by me—Sent 3 bus. of oats—1 bus. Barley—the Bunch homony bean, and a Small quantity of the White Feild pea—which I find Subject to the bug—The oats weigh 42 lbs. and are the best Sort I ever Saw, but notwithstanding the precaution I used in picking the Seed which produced them, I find Still a few black grains among them—Therefore wd advise you to have them run over by hand—The Charge of Stage Carraige, will make them come Sufficiently High, without an additional one—You are exceeding Welcome to them—and if you like the Oat—will if I make a good crop this Year (haveing prepared much ground) will Furnish you next yr; and I hope with as much as will sow you a Full crop—of this will advise you of in time.[2]

Will you be so obligeing, as to Communicate Yr Several Experiments in Corn to me—and what distance, yeilds the best crops—have you any of the green Top Turnip—any of the large yorkshire red—if you have none & wish to have some, I shall be able to Send you some of the Seed of each—having put out about 200—Mrs Spotswood Joins me in best Wishes for the health & Happiness of all about you. I am dr Sr with much Esteem & aff. Regard Yr obt

A. Spotswood

ALS, DLC:GW.

1. Letter not found. Major Barrett may be William Barrett (d. 1815) of North Carolina who had served as a lieutenant and captain in the 3d Continental Regiment of Dragoons from 1778 until the end of the war.

2. In his cash accounts for 8 Mar., GW enters the payment of £1.5 for "Freight of 2 Bags Oats in the Stage from Gl Spotswood" (Ledger B, 242). See also Spotswood to GW, 3 March.

From Thomas McKean, William Jackson, and Francis Mentges

Dear General,   Philadelphia March 6th 1787

In obedience to a resolve of the Standing-Committee of the Pennsylvania Society of the Cincinnati, we do ourselves the honor to inform your Excellency that your circular letter of the 31st of October last, addressed to the President of our State-Society, was laid before the Committee at their last meeting.

They desire to communicate their respectful thanks for the early information which you have been pleased to give of the triennial general-meeting—and to express, with heartfelt concern, their regret at the necessity, which induces your desire not to be re-elected to the Presidency.

While they admit the cogency of those reasons which are assigned for your determination—they lament, with the sorrow of sincere affection, that impaired health should be numbered among them—and they profer the prayer of grateful regard for its speedy restoration.

Your Excellency's wishes will be intimated to our Delegates to the general-meeting—and your letter will be laid before a Meeting of the State-Society which is called on the 26th instant. With profound respect and attachment, We have the honor to be Your Excellency's Most obedient, humble Servants

Thos McKean
W. Jackson
F. Mentges

LS, DLC:GW.

Letter not found: from Wakelin Welch & Son, 7 Mar. 1787. On 8 Jan. 1788 GW wrote Welch & Son: "I have recd your letter of the 7th of March."

To David Humphreys

My Dear Humphreys,   Mount Vernon March 8th 1787
    Colo. Wadsworth, as I informed you in my last, presented me your obliging favor of the 30th of January and the Post since has handed me the subsequent one of the 11th Ulto.[1]
    My sentiments, respecting the inexpediency of my attending the proposed Convention of the States in Philadelphia remain the same as when I wrote you last, tho' Congress I am informed are about to remove one of the objections by their recommendation of this Convention[.] I am still indirectly, and delicately pressed by many to attend this meeting; and a thought has run thro' my mind of late attended with more embarrassment than any former one. It is whether my not doing it will not be con-

sidered as an implied derelection to Republicansm. nay more, whether (however injurious the imputation) it may not be ascribed to other motives. my wish is I confess to see this convention tried;[2] after which if the present form is not made efficient, conviction of the propriety of a change will pervade all ranks and many be effected by peace. till then, however necessary it may appear to the more descerning part of the community, my opinion is, that it cannot be accomplished without great Contention and much confusion for reasons too obvious to ennumarate. It is one of evils perhaps not the smallest, of democratical Governments that the People must feel before they will see or act under this view of matters, and not doubting but you have heard the sentiments of many respectable charractors since the date of your letter of the 20th of Jany on this subject & perhaps since the business has been moved in Congress of the propriety or impropriety of my attendance let me pray you my dear Sir, to give me Confidentially the public opinion & expectation as fair as it has come to your knowledge of what it is supposed. I will or ought to do on this occasion. you will readily see the necessity of my receiving it soon, if it is to have an operation contrary to the former because my communications to the Executive of this State are not considered as definitive I must make these so shortly.[3]

I congratulate you on the favourable Issue to the exertions of the Government of Massachusetts to quell the insurrection which at one period assumed an appearance of being formidable. you have the best wishes of everyone in this family; possess the sincere regard and Friendship of Dr Sir, yr affect. Hble Servant

G. Washington.

LB, DLC:GW.

1. GW wrote Humphreys on 18 Feb. and thanked him for his letter of 20 (not 30) Jan., given to him by Jeremiah Wadsworth, which is printed above.

2. The copyist wrote "tied."

3. It would appear that the copyist botched this passage worse than most; for perhaps a closer approximation of what GW actually wrote to Humphreys, see GW to Knox, this date.

To Henry Knox

My dear Sir,   Mount Vernon 8th Mar. 1787
    Will you permit me to give you the trouble of making an indi-
rect, but precise enquiry, into the alligations of the enclosed letters. I flatter myself that from the vicinity of Elizabeth Town to
New York, and the constant intercourse between the two, you
will be able to do it without much trouble. It is but little in my
power to afford the pecuniary aids required by the letter writer;
but if the facts as set forth be true, I should feel very happy in
offering my mite, and rendering any services in my power on
the occasion. Be so good, when you write to me on this subject,
to return the letters & translations.[1]
    The observations contained in your letter of the 22d Ulto
(which came duly to hand) respecting the disfranchisement of
a number of the Citizens of Massachusetts for their rebellious
conduct, may be just; and yet, without exemplary punishment,
similar disorders may be excited by other ambitious and discon-
tented characters. Punishment however ought to light on the
principals.
    I am glad to hear that Congress are about to remove some
of the stumbling blocks which lay in the way of the proposed
Convention. A Convention I wish to see tried—after which, if
the present government is not efficient, conviction of the propriety of a change will dessiminate through every rank, and class of
people and may be brought about in peace—till which, however
necessary it may appear in the eyes of the more discerning, my
opinion is, that it cannot be effected without great contention,
and much confusion. It is among the evils, and perhaps is not
the smallest, of democratical governments, that the people must
feel, before they will *see*. When this happens, they are roused to
action—hence it is that this form of government is so slow. I
am indirectly, and delicately pressed to attend this convention.
Several reasons are opposed to it in my mind, and not the least
my having declined attending the General Meeting of the Cincinnati, which is to be holden in Philadelphia at the same time,
on account of the disrespect it might *seem* to offer to that Society,
to be there on another occasion. A thought however has lately
run through my mind, which is attended with embarrassment.
It is, whether my non-attendance in this Convention will not

be considered as a dereliction to republicanism—nay more—whether other motives may not (however injuriously) be ascribed to me for not exerting myself on this occasion in support of it. Under these circumstances let me pray you, my dear Sir, to inform me confidentially, what the public expectation is on this head—that is, whether I will, or ought to be there? You are much in the way of obtaining this knowledge. and I can depend upon your friendship—candour—and judgment in the communication of it, as far as it shall appear to you—My final determination (if what I have already given to the Executive of this State is not considered in that light) cannot be delayed beyond the time necessary for your reply.[2] With great truth I am yrs most Affectly

Go: Washington

ALS (photocopy), DLC:GW; LB, DLC:GW.

1. GW is referring to the letters from the comtesse d'Anterroche on behalf of her son who was living in New Jersey. See Comtesse d'Anterroche to GW, 18 Sept. 1786, and notes. See also Knox's response of 26 Mar. to GW's letter.

2. Knox's reply of 19 Mar. was one of the most forceful arguments made in writing to GW for his attendance at the convention to be held in Philadelphia.

From Battaile Muse

Honourable Sir,   Berkeley Cty March 8th 1787

Your Favour By Major George Washington I received and shall attend To it[1]—I set out this day To the Tenaments in Fauquier they are so Very Poor in General that I Fear but Little is To be Expected From them—I am obliged To attend that Court To obtain Justice From some of them—I Fear not more than one or Two of their Horses will answer your Purpose—if I Find it necessary To Take a Horse or Two, I shall Endeavour To get them down before the 20th of april—about that Time I shall be down my Self and will raise all the money I can by that Time—Suppose £100 but that Cannot be Ensured as I have none in hand—I am happy To hear by Mr Wales that He Paid the £100. I receive all money—but half Dollars by weight—Gunies Pass at 5 Penney weight Five Grains—half Dollars not weighed—the Money I sent I was Very Carefull in weighing all but the half Dollars in which money I suppose Lost the 10/6 I shall be Very

Carefull To attend To your directions. Your acct at this Time Stands Indebted To me about £25. I have the Promises from the People of about £180 if I receive £100 it will be as much as I can Expect From Promises in these days. I am Sir with Every Sentiment of Respect—your Obedient Humble Servant

Battaile Muse

ALS, DLC:GW.
   1. GW's letter is dated 15 February.

From William Deakins, Jr.

Sir.   George Town [Md.] March 9th 1787.
   I have sent by your Boat 200 Bushels Oats, tho the price is higher than I could have Wished but at this season they Generally Advance in price, I think you will find them Very good, & I am sorry I could not supply the full Quantity you want.[1] I am with the highest Respect Your Excellency's Obt hble Servt

Will. Deakins Junr

ALS, DLC:GW.
   1. Deakins added this invoice:

115 Bushels Oats @ 3/6	£20: 2:6
24 Bushels Poland Oats @ 3/9	4:10:0
61 Bushels 3/	9: 3:0
200 dollars at 7/6	£33:15:6

GW does not record in his cash accounts this purchase from Deakins. For the oats that GW bought in March from various people, see Ledger B, 242.

From John Page

Dear Sir   Rosewell March the 9th 1787
   The little Time Mr Griffith has to spend with me, & my present State of Mind must be my Apology for this short Scrawl.[1]
   The Directors of the Dismal Co. I am certain will be perfectly satisfied with any Plan which you would adopt. The one you hint at in your Letter, is I think the only one which suits the Finances & Disposition of the Company.[2] The Members are too Lukewarm to advance Money if they had it, & too indolent to attend to the Execution of any Plan which requires any Attention on their Part. I have no Hopes of deriving any Advantage

from any other Scheme than that which you have suggested. I therefore wish you to encourage Col. Lutterlohs Plan as far as you may think proper—& I am of Opinion that we had better give ⅓d. or even ½ for reclaiming the whole than keep it upon the Terms we now hold it—I think the Col. might dispose of 100 Tradesmen & Farmers besides the Labourers which the Compy would take, immediately & on good Terms. I am dear Sir with the highest Respect & Esteem your most obedient Servant

John Page

ALS, DLC:GW.
    1. For reference to the Rev. David Griffith's trip to tidewater Virginia, see GW to Robert Carter, 24 Feb., n.1.
    2. GW's letter has not been found, but its likely contents are revealed in GW to Henry E. Lutterloh, 8 April. See also Lutterloh to GW, 3 Jan. 1787.

To Thomas Cushing

Sir   Mount Vernon March 10th 1787
    By your letter & Acct of the 22d of Feby 1786, there appears a balance in my favor of fifteen pounds thirteen shillings Lawful Money, which I take the liberty to draw a bill for in favor of Mr Thomas Porter of Alexandria, payable ten days after sight.[1]
    I am happy to find by the last Accounts from the Northward that the disturbances in your State were almost totally suppressed, & I hope before this that peace & good order are again restored. Mrs Washington joins me in my best wishes for Mrs Cushing & yourself. I am Sir, With esteem & regard Yr most Obedt Hble Servt

Go: Washington

LS, in the hand of Tobias Lear, NjMoNP; LB, DLC:GW.
    1. Letter not found, but see GW to Cushing, 5 April 1786.

To Samuel Haven

Revd Sir,   Mount Vernon Mar. 10th 1787
    Although I gave the greatest credence to your acct of the talents & good behaviour of Mr Lear, yet before I subscribed to them, I was desirous of a little time to form my own judgment

of both. To this, and this only, you will be pleased to attribute my not acknowledging the receipt of your favor of the 6th of May, at an earlier period.[1]

It is with pleasure I now inform you, that the deportment of this young Gentleman since he has been a member of my family, has been so perfectly proper and pleasing, as to render him highly esteemed. Sensible that saying this to a gentleman who has discovered an interest in his welfare, could not be unpleasing, is the cause of my giving you the trouble of this letter, at the same time that it affords me an opportunity of thanking you for the polite and affectionate wishes with which your letter is replete, & to assure you of the respect with which I am—Revd Sir Yr Most Obedt Hble Ser⟨vt⟩

Go: Washington

ALS (photocopy), MHi; LB, DLC:GW.

1. GW also wrote on this date thanking John Langdon and Joseph Willard for their letters written in May 1786 recommending Tobias Lear for the position of secretary in GW's household. He wrote Langdon: "Sir, I pray you to attribute my long silence in not acknowledging the receipt of your favor of the 5th of May, by Mr Lear, to any cause rather than the want of esteem or respect.

"Although I might perhaps, with as much truth as many others, assign business as the cause; yet this was not my principal motive for the delay. I wished for a little time and opportunity, to form my own judgment of Mr Lear before I gave testimony to his merits; and it is now with pleasure I can assure you that, I entertain the highest opinion of his worth. His deportment since he became a member of this family has been so perfectly proper and pleasing, in every point of view, as to render him the favourite of every one, and it is much our wish that his own contentment in it, may be equal to our satisfaction. I have the honor to be Sir Yr Most Obd. Hbe Se⟨rvt⟩ Go: Washington" (ALS, NhSB: John Langdon Collection; LB, DLC:GW).

In similar vein he wrote Joseph Willard: "Revd Sir, Let me entreat that my long silence, in not acknowledging the receipt of your polite letter of the 15th of May last, may be ascribed to any cause rather than want of respect for your character and gratitude for the favourable sentiments you have therein expressed of me. As the letter was introductory of Mr Lear, I found myself inclined, though disposed at the sametime to give full credence to your account of the talants and good disposition of this young Gentlemen to take time, and seek occasions, to form my own judgement of him; and it is with pleasure I now assure you that, his deportment since he came into this family has been such as to [LB, DLC:GW] obtain the esteem, confidence, and love of every individual in it.

"As (from the interest you have taken in his welfare) I persuade my self this testimony of my approbation of his conduct will not be displeasing to you, I could no longer with-hold it; especially as it affords an occasion of assuring you of my good wishes for the University over wch you preside, and of the esteem & respect with which I have the honor to be, Revd Sir Yr Most Obedt Hble Ser⟨vt⟩ Go: Washington" (ALS [photocopy], Alvin Schener Catalog 2 [1926]). The letters written to GW in May 1786 by Haven, Langdon, and Willard are all printed in Lear to GW, 7 May 1786, n.1.

Langdon acknowledged GW's letter from Portsmouth, N.H., on 6 April: "I was honord a few days since with your Excellencys kind favor of the 10th Ult. in which you are pleased to acknowledge the merits of Mr Lear this testimony which you have given of him will be considered both by himself and friends as a mark of the highest honor and I hope he'll embrace every opportunity of shewing his gratitude for this and all other favors" (DLC:GW).

To John Jay

Dear Sir,   Mount Vernon Mar: 10th 1787

I am indebted to you for two letters: The first, introductory of Mr Anstey needed no apology—nor will any be necessary on future occasions.[1] The other, of the 7th of Jany is on a very interesting subject, deserving very particular attention.

How far the revision of the fœderal system, and giving more adequate powers to Congress may be productive of an efficient government, I will not, under my present view of the matter, presume to decide. That many inconveniencies result from the present form, none can deny. Those enumerated in your letter are so obvious, & sensibly felt that no logick can controvert, nor is it probable that any change of conduct will remove them. And that all attempts to alter or amend it will be like the propping of a house which is ready to fall, and which no shoars can support (as many seem to think) may also be true.

But, is the public mind matured for such an important change as the one you have suggested? What would be the consequences of a premature attempt?

My opinion is, that this Country have yet to *feel*, and *see* a little more, before it can be accomplished. A thirst for power, and the bantling—I had like to have said monster—sovereignty, which have taken such fast hold of the States individually, will, when joined by the many whose personal consequence in the line of State politics will in a manner be annihilated, form a strong phalanx against it; and when to these the few who can hold posts of honor or profit in the National government are compared with the many who will see but little prospect of being noticed, and the discontents of others who may look for appointments the opposition would be altogether irrisistable till the mass as well as the more discerning part of the Community shall see the Necessity.

Among men of reflection few will be found I believe, who are not *beginning* to think that our system is better in theory than practice—and that, notwithstanding the boasted virtue of America it is more than probable we shall exhibit the last melancholy proof that Mankind are not competent to their own government without the means of coercion in the Sovereign.

Yet, I would try what the wisdom of the proposed Convention will suggest; and what can be effected by their Councils. It may be the last peaceable mode of essaying the practicability of the pres[en]t form, without a greater lapse of time than the exigency of our Affairs will admit. In strict propriety a Convention so holden may not be legal—Congress however may give it a colouring by recommendation, which would fit it more to the taste, without proceeding to a definition of powers. This, however Constitutionally it might be done, would not, in my opinion, be expedient; for delicacy on the one hand, and Jealousy on the other would produce a mere nihil.

My name is in the delegation to this Convention; but it was put there contrary to my desire, and remains there contrary to my request. Several reasons at the time of this appointment and which yet exist combined to make my attendance inconvenient, perhaps improper tho. a good deal urged to it—With sentiments of great regard & friendship I have the honor to be—Dr Sir Yr Most Obedt and Affecte Hble Servt

Go: Washington

P.S. Since writing this letter I have seen the resolution of Congress recommendatory of the Convention proposed to be held in Philadel[phi]a the 2d Monday in May.

ALS, NNC; LB, DLC:GW.

1. Jay's letter of 20 Oct. 1786 introducing John Anstey is printed in note 1, George William Fairfax to GW, 25 Jan. 1786.

From Matthew McConnell

Sir   Philad[elphi]a 10th March 1787
I have taken the liberty to send for your perusal the inclosed
Pamphlet, which I beg you will accept of.[1] And have the honour
to be, with great esteem & respect Sir Your most Obedient &
very humble Servt

Mat. McConnell

ALS, DLC:GW.

1. Matthew McConnell's 90-page pamphlet, printed in Philadelphia in 1787
by Robert Aitken, is entitled *An Essay on the Domestic Debts of the United States of
America. Giving an Account of the Various Kinds of Public Securities, and, Generally in
What Manner the Debts Arose: with the Provision Made and Proposed for Payment of the
Interest and Principal Thereof by Fœderal Measures, and of Those Adopted by Individual
States*. . . . GW thanked McConnell for the pamphlet on 23 Mar.: "Sir, you will
please to accept of my best thanks for your polite attention in sending me your
Essay on the Domestic Debets of the United States which together with your
letter of the 10th instant, I have rcd. I have not yet had opportunity to peruse
your work but I think from the contents that it must be a useful and valuable
performance. I am Sir Yr most Obed. Hbe Servt G. Washington" (LB,
DLC:GW).

Letter not found: from James Mercer, 10 Mar. 1787. On 15 Mar. GW
wrote Mercer: "Your favor of the 10th came duely to hand."

To Edward Newenham

Dear Sir,   Mount Vernon March 10th 1787
I shall not wonder if you should be surprized at my not acknowledging the receipt of your esteemed favor of the 12th of
last August at an earlier period. Immediately after it came to my
hands—not knowing what you had written to Doct. Franklin or
to Mr Jay, or what steps might have been taken on the subject
matter thereof by either or both of those Gentlemen I wrote to
the former for information; giving assurances of my disposition
to carry your wishes into full effect if there were not impedi-
ments in the way which coud not, consistently, be surmounted.
I waited from that period (early in November) till February in
daily expectation of an answer; but receiving none, I addressed

(supposing my first letter must have miscarried) a duplicate to the Doctrs and receiving the answer which is enclosed.[1]

Though I had heard of the resolution alluded to in Mr Jay's Letter to the Doctors preveous to my writing to him yet I was willing to know the truth, and to see how far Congress would think it right to adhere to the policy of their resolution.

I beg leave to make a tender of my best wishes to Lady Newenham, in which Mrs Washington Joins, and assurances of the respect and esteem with which I have the honor to be Dr Sir Yr most Obed. and very Humble Servant

G. Washington

LB, DLC:GW.

1. GW first wrote to Benjamin Franklin on 3 Nov. 1786 about Newenham's request that his son be made a United States consul in France, and he then sent Franklin a copy of the letter on 11 Feb. 1787. Franklin's enclosed reply has not been found. See also Newenham to GW, 12 Aug. 1786.

From John Rawlins

Honored Sir   Baltimore March 10th 1787

I have sent you, pr Capn Man's Packet the freizes for doors and windows, which I hope will please you, Mr Tharp informed me he ad Agreed with you for the Composition work, in your Salloon room, at £43.12s.od. Virginia currency the lowest I can afford to do it for is £45.os.od. Maryland currency which I hope your Excellency will not think too much, if its Conveinient should be Glad, you could send the money by the Bearer Capn Man or A Draft on any Gentleman in this Town, would answer the same,[1] your Compliance with the above request will at this time greatly serve and Oblige Yr Most Obdt Hble Svt &c.

John Rawlins

ALS, DLC:GW.

1. GW acknowledged Rawlins's letter on 13 April and explained why he "did not think proper to comply with the contents of it at this time." See note 2 of that document.

To Lord Dunmore

Sir,   Mount Vernon in Virginia March 11th 1787.
With your Excellency's permission—though I have not the honor of being known to you—I will take the liberty introducing the bearer Mr Fendall, his Lady & Miss Lee, to your civilities.[1]

They are much esteemed and deservedly respected in this Country. Ill health of Mrs Fendall, has induced her Physicians to recommend the Air of the Sea to her; and the Bahama Islands seem to be the object of their Voyage.

I am persuaded these worthy people will do Justice to my recommendation. That a philanthropic attention to them will be as pleasing to your Excellency as to them—and that the interest I take in their welfare is the best apology I can offer for this freedom—I have the honr to be—Sir Yr Most Obedt Hble Ser.

Go: Washington

ALS, owned (1978) by Mr. Bruce Betzel, Alexandria, Va.; LB, DLC:GW.

1. Philip Richard Fendall and his wife Elizabeth Steptoe Lee Fendall lived in Alexandria. Mrs. Fendall was the widow of Philip Ludwell Lee of Stratford and the mother-in-law of Henry Lee, Jr., of Stratford. Her younger daughter was named Flora Lee. Mrs. Fendall died within the next two years. GW addressed the letter to the governor of the Bahama Islands, unaware that his old opponent, Lord Dunmore (John Murray, fourth earl of Dunmore [1732–1809]), had recently been made governor, a post Dunmore held from 1787 to 1796.

From Edmund Randolph

Dear sir   Richmond March 11. 1787
I must call upon your friendship to excuse me for again mentioning the convention at Philadelphia. Your determination having been fixed on a thorough review of your situation, I feel, like an intruder, when I again hint a wish, that you would join the delegation. But every day brings forth some new crisis, and the confederation is, I fear, the last anchor of our hope. Congress have taken up the subject, and appointed the second Monday in May next, as the day of meeting. Indeed from my private correspondence I doubt, whether the existence of that body even thro' this year may not be questionable under our pres-

ent circumstances. Believe me to be my dear sir yr affectionate
friend & servant

Edm: Randolph

ALS, DLC:GW.

Letter not found: to William Goddard, 12 Mar. 1787. In item E 667, the
Collector of June 1944 cites this quotation from a letter that GW wrote
to Goddard: "You will please to insert the enclosed Advertisement in
your paper and continue it three weeks."

From Gilles de Lavallée

New York 13 March 1787.

I did myself the honor to write to your Excellency upon the
subject of manufactures, & enclosed a Copy of a recommendation from Mr Jefferson; you was pleased to return me an answer
by which your Excellency informed me that you had forwarded
my memorial to the Legislature of Virginia to know their determination upon the matter, which you would do me the favor to
send to me.[1] I have waited until this time & have recd no news
respecting it; in consequence I have made an engagement with
Spain, for which place I shall take my departure this day. I thank
your Excellency for your attention; but no establishment of European manufacture can succeed here—America is not suitable
for the business on account of the scarsity of money—the deficiency of power in the Government—the personal interest of
every member—the want of the confidence of the people in
their Rulers—the fluctuation of the Legislature. You have given
liberty to America—she has abused it—her manners are cor-
rupted—Craft & subtlety have taken place of good faith—labour is despised—the innocence & modesty of the females is
succeeded by effrontry & impudence—the facility of obtaining
a divorce has dissolved the sanctity of marriage—the early independence of children has disturbed the peace of families—your
Laws have neither energy nor firmness—the disunion of the
States facilitates & encourages disobedience &c. &c. I quit
America sick of its Liberty, its manners & its laws. I respect &
admire its great men, particularly your Excellency—It gives me
pain to see that so much is done for a people unworthy of the

benefits—My soul is peirced to see such abuse of Liberty—I am
well acquainted with the Laws of the Ancients & moderns—
I have travailed through Europe—I am a friend to humanity,
I would sacrifice my life for it, but here, my wishes, my desires,
my knowledge, my talents are superfluous, useless & even prejudicial—I depart therefore filled with respect & admiration for
the great Characters, & with pity for the People. I am with the
most profound respect Yr Excllency's Very Hble Servt

Delavallée.

Translation, DLC:GW; ALS, in French, DLC:GW. The ALS, dated 12 Mar., has
been transcribed for CD-ROM:GW.

1. Lavallée's letter to GW has not been found, but see GW to Lavallée, 23
Dec. 1786, and note 1 of that document.

To Charles Willson Peale

Sir,   Mount Vernon March 13th 1787.
I have received your letter of the 27th Ulto acknowleding the
reception of the body of the Golden Pheasant. I have sent by
the Dolphin Captn Steward the body of a French hen Pheasant
which died this day. I chose this mode of conveying it rather
than by the Stage, as the Packet calls here to receive some things
for Philadelphia; & I think, all circumstances considered, that it
will meet with as quick & safe a conveyance as if it went by land.
I wish you great success in the Mezzotinto Prints which you
have undertaken, & have no doubt but your abilities in works of
Genius will ensure it. I am Sir Yr most Obedt Hbe Servt

Go: Washington

LS, in the hand of Tobias Lear, owned (1992) by Mr. Gary Hendershott, Little
Rock, Ark.; LB, DLC:GW. Written in GW's hand on the cover: "By the Dolphin
Cap: [Aaron] Steward with a Small Box."

To Clement Biddle

Dear Sir,   Mount Vernon March 14th 1787
Your letters of the 20th and 27th Ulto are both before me.
The Barley & other things by the Dolphin are arrived—and by
the return of this Vessel I consign you, as per bill enclosed, 45

Barrls of Herrings, which you will be pleased to dispose of to the best advantage, and place the proceeds to my credit. It is hardly necessary to add that, the sooner these fish are disposed of the higher the sale of them probably will be, as the season for the new is near at hand. They are very good, I am told, having been lately examined.

As I beleive the half yearly interest of my Certificate is nearly due, and a small balance was in my favor previous to the purchasing the Articles by the Dolphin, I will wait for the Sale of the Fish to know how the Accts between us will then be. In the interim, please to send me one dozn of the best corn Scythes of a proper length, and strength at the heel, and in the backs, and the same number of the best Grass Scythes—two strong bramble Scythes, & two flax spinning wheels. The Dolphin returns to this Port in the course of next month, and will afford a good Conveyance. What does the best Hyson Tea, and dble refined Sugar sell at with you? And how are linnens now?—particularly those of the finer sort. With great esteem I am Dear Sir Yr very Hble Servt

Go: Washington

P.S. How does White & red Lead, ground in Oil sell? Are not these things often bought cheap at the public Vendues?

G. W——n.

LS, PHi: Washington-Biddle Correspondence; LB, DLC:GW. The postscript is in GW's hand.

From Benjamin Fitzhugh Grymes

Dear Genl   Eagles Nest March 14th [17]87

It affords me the highest satisfaction to have it in my power to oblige you by sending of you five bushels of Jerusalem Artichokes, and had it not been for an [un]luckey experiment I shd have been able to have spared you a large quantity, but I have sent you the better half. In order to increase my crop, I cut off the tops three different times breast high, and by that means, made not a bushel from near 500 hills in my garden, the few I have I collected from a few hills not more than twenty in number, where the hogs could not get to them, they are very fond of them, and from experience, I find that there is nothing we can raise so cheap and that hogs are fonder of: 500 bushels at least may be made from an acre of good Tobo g[roun]d which are at least equal to 100 bls of Corn.[1] Col. S[t]ith will deliver you this, with a dish of the best fish I have by me.[2] I have lately met with some of the Guinea grass seed, some of which I intended to have sent you but my Uncle tells me you have tried it and do not like it I will thank you for your sentiments on that, and the Magoty bay Pea, so much extolled of late.[3] I have by me some Irish potatoe Seed, and expect to have some Cotton in the Seed, shd you be in want of either please to inform me, and I shall be happy in obliging of you. I am sir with the greatest respect to you & yrs yr Mt ob. fd & Sert

B. Grymes

ALS, DLC:GW.

1. GW also corresponded with George Weedon about the cultivation of Jerusalem artichokes (*Helianthus tuberosus*). See GW to Weedon, 25 March. For GW's description of how he on 11, 12, and 13 April prepared the ground for the artichoke tubers and then planted them, see *Diaries*, 5:132–33.

2. GW does not record a visit at this time from John Stith (1755–1808).

3. Grymes probably is referring to his mother's brother William Fitzhugh of Chatham.

To James Mercer

Dear Sir,   Mount Vernon 15th March 1787

Your favor of the 10th came duely to hand,[1] and with very sincere concern I read the acct of your ill health; but if your other complaints have left you, the Asthma, though troublesome & distressing, is not a dangerous one; I will hope therefore that the agreeable Season which is fast approaching, will perfectly restore you good health.

Under cover with this, you will receive the original Deed for the Lands on four miles run; which you will please to return when your purposes are answered by the reference to it, for drawing the deed of confirmation: for your justice in offering which, and kindness in drawing it, I pray you to accept my warmest acknowledgments.

The mode suggested by you to obtain the bond which I passed to Messrs McCoull & Blair, is, in my judgment, the *only* proper one; so far as it respects you, or the Representatives of your fa- ther (if the credit is to be applied to their acct) it is precisely the same whether you acct with me, or them, for the principal & interest of the sum which was to have been paid for the Land under the circumstances of your claim; because if the right is determined to be in you, so much will have been discounted from my demand on the Estate—If in them, it is only paying to them, as Attorneys of Lindo & Cozenove what otherwise would have been demanded of me. The case with me would be widely different, for if I allow this sum with the Interest in a final settle- ment and my bond remains unretired, I am open to a prosecu- tion thereon; and may be greatly distressed by the actual pay- ment after having allowed it in a discount before I can have any redress, which would very illy accord with the present state of my finances. Should Mr McCoull refuse to accede to your pro- posal, it would imply strongly, his intention of resorting to me for payment.[2]

However desirous I am, & always shall be, to comply with any commands of my Country, I do not conceive that I can, with consistent conduct, attend the proposed Convention to be holden in Philadelphia in May next. For besides the declaration which I made in a very solemn manner when I was about to retire, of bidding adieu to all public employment; I had just be- fore the appointment of delegates to this Convention written and dispatched circular letters to the several State Societies of the Cincinnati informing them of my intention not to attend the General Meeting which was to take place about the same time and in the same City—and assigned reasons which apply as forc- ibly in the one case as the other. Under these circumstances, to attend the Convention might be considered disrespectful to a worthy set of men for whose attachment and support on many trying occasions, I shall ever feel the highest gratitude & af- fection.

It is unnecessary I hope to assure you of the pleasure I shall always receive at seeing you here, whenever business or your health will permit. The latter, possibly, might be benefitted by the change of Air. With sincere esteem & Regd I am Dear Sir Yr Most Obt Ser.

Go: Washington

Copy, DLC:GW; LB, DLC:GW. The copy has this notation: "(A.L.S. in possession of Major-General Preston Brown, U.S. Army, Ret⟨d⟩ Vineyard Haven, Mass. Copied 2 December 1935)." Because the twentieth-century copy appears to follow more closely the original text, it is printed here rather than the letter-book copy made for GW by Howell Lewis.

1. Letter not found. Very few of the numerous letters to GW in the 1780s from John Francis Mercer or from his half brother, James Mercer, regarding the Mercer debt to GW have been found.

2. For further information about what was at issue in 1787 with regard to the Four Mile Run tract in Fairfax County, acquired by GW in 1774 from George and James Mercer, see GW to James Mercer, 19 Nov. 1786, n.1.

From Hannah Crawford

Dear Genl   Fayette County Pennsa March 16th 1787

I make no Doubt but you have heard of the Resolution of the Legeslative Body of your State, passed in my favour which will Enable me to make you satisfaction for your great kindness to me.[1] you may Depend on having the bond paid up as soon as I Draw the first years Allowance, money being So Scarce here and so Dificult to come at, that it will not be in my power to do any thing sooner. the first years Allowance becoms Due the 9th Day of Jany Next—I purpose making application to congress for the five years pay Allow'd to Offrs of the Continental Army, & if I Obtain a Certificate for it, it will be in my Power to Discharge a great part of the Debts Due the Creditors of my Deceased Husbands Estate. please present my Compliments to your Lady— I am withe much Real Esteem my Dear friend Your most Obliged & very Hume Sert

Hannah Crawford

ALS, DLC:GW.

1. For GW's dealings with Hannah Crawford, see Hannah Crawford to GW, 4 June 1784, GW to Thomas Freeman, 8 May 1786, and John Minter to GW, 2 Mar. 1787. On 2 Dec. 1786 the Virginia house of delegates read Mrs. Crawford's petition "that her late husband, Col. William Crawford, was killed [by Indians] in the service of his country during the late war, leaving his family in very indigent circumstances; and praying relief." The petition was referred to a committee, and on 9 Jan. 1787 the House accepted the committee's recommendation "that the same allowance ought to be made [to Hannah Crawford] . . . as is allowed by law to the widows of officers of equal rank killed in the late war" (*House of Delegates Journal, 1786–1790*, 83, 150). William Crawford, his

son-in-law William Harrison, and his brother Valentine Crawford's only son, William, were tortured to death at Upper Sandusky in 1782.

To Benjamin Fitzhugh Grymes

Dear Sir,   Mount Vernon 16th Mar: 1787

I am very much obliged to you for the Jerusalem Artichoke and fish, which you were so obliging as to send me by Colo. Stith; and if opportunity serves, Mrs Washington will be equally thankful to you for a little Cotton Seed. Of the Irish Potatoes I believe I have enough to seed the ground I intend for this Crop; but as the quantity will be large, I may be mistaken; and if you raise for Market I may be a customer.[1]

The Guinea grass will not stand our frosts—otherwise I should esteem it the most productive, and most valuable of any we could raise: The growth is rapid—drought has no effect on it—and the quantity it yields is astonishing. Mine (not having the Seed in time) was not sown till the middle of June and produced no seed; otherwise even as an annual plant I think it would be worth cultivating for Hay & should have tried it in this way if I had saved a single Seed—If you sow yours as soon as the danger of frost is past there may be time for the seed to ripen—It does not vegitate quick—nor does it spring fast till the root begins to feel the ground, or the blade to shade it—then you may almost see it grow.[2] With respect to the Magoty bay Pea—or Bean as they are (improperly I think called) I can say nothing experimentally of the valuable qualities that are ascribed to it. I have received letters from some Gentlemn on the Eastern shore, and lately have seen one a Mr Custis who attribute surprizing property's to this Pea as a fertilizer of the soil (his acct & mode of managing it I enclose you) but I confess I have no great opinion of it notwithstanding—and much less since I find, on comparison, that it is now growing spontaneously all over my fields, without perceiving any of those benificial effects which are talked of.[3] How long it has been in th⟨em⟩ I cannot undertake to say, for till I got a few of the Seeds and planted them in my garden, and being struck with the similarity of the two was lead to a close investigation, they never had attracted my notice, more than any other of the common herbage of the field had done. Now I am satisfied they are the same, tho' the Gentleman with whom I have lately conversed on the subject informs me, that there are two sorts and that the right one has a small stem abt ½ an inch long which joins the pod to the stalk of the plant & its branches. I am Dear Sir Yr most Obedt Servt

Go: Washington

P.S. What time do you plant the J: Artichoke? Do they succeed best in hills, or drills—and what culture do they require? What kind of Land—light or stiff suits best.

ALS, MiDbGr.
    1. See Grymes to GW, 14 March.
    2. GW experimented with the cultivation of guinea grass (*Panicum maximum*) in 1785 and 1786 (*Diaries*, 4:118, 127, 135, 154, 161, 185, 186, 217, 223, 304, 322, 5:129, 137).
    3. On 5 Mar. "a Mr. Custis of the Eastern sh[o]r[e] came in—dined and stayed all Night" at Mount Vernon (ibid., 5:113). Custis's enclosed account of the mode of raising peas has not been found.

From John Lawson

Sir   Dumfries March 17th 1787
    I am sorry it has not been in my power to comply with my promise to you by sending up the Negro Fellow we talked about at Mr Fendall's before this time.
    I gave directions to the Overseer with whom he now lives to send him up about ten days ago & having been from home since expected he had been sent accordingly; but on my return I find that he had the misfortune, the very day before he was to have set off, to cut his leg so badly that he has not been able to walk since & I am affraid will not soon—As soon as he recovers I shall send him to you unless I have your directions otherwise, & if he suits you upon examination you may have him on the same terms I purchased.[1] I am very respectfully Sir Your mo: obt Servt

Jno. Lawson

ALS, DLC:GW. Written on the cover: "Honor'd by Mr [Thomas William] Ballendine."
    1. The slave, named Neptune, came up to Mount Vernon from Dumfries on 8 April but returned to Dumfries on 25 April, not wishing to be "Sold at

So great a distance from his Wife" (Lawson to GW, 25 April). He did agree, however, to become a hired hand at Mount Vernon. See Lawson to GW, 2, 18 April, and GW to Lawson, 10 April. See also GW to Henry Lee, Jr., 4 Feb. 1787.

From James Madison

Dear Sir,   New York March 18th 1787

Recollecting to have heard you mention a plan formed by the Empress of Russia for a comparative view of the aborigines of the New Continent, and of the N.E. parts of the old, through the medium of their respective tongues, and that her wishes had been conveyed to you for your aid in obtaining the American vocabularies, I have availed myself of an opportunity offered by the Kindness of Mr Hawkins, of taking a copy of such a sample of the Cherokee & Chactaw dialects as his late commission to treat with them enabled him to obtain, and do myself the honor now of inclosing it. I do not know how far the list of words made use of by Mr Hawkins may correspond with the standard of the Empress, nor how far nations so remote as the Cherokees & Chactaws from the N.W. shores of America, may fall within her scheme of comparison. I presume however that a great proportion at least of the words will answer, and that the laudable curiosity which suggests investigations of this sort will be pleased with every enlargement of the field for indulging it. Not finding it convenient to retain a copy of the inclosed as I wished to do for myself, I musk ask the favor of your amanuensis to perform that task for me.[1]

The appointments for the Convention go on very successfully. Since the date of my last, Georgia, S. Carolina, N. York, Massts & N. Hamshire have come into the measure. Georgia & N. Hampshire have constituted their Delegates in Congs their representatives in the Convention. S. Carolina has appointed Mr J. Rutledge, Genl Pinkney, Mr Laurens, Major Butler, and Mr Chs Pinkney late a member of Congs. The deputies of Massts are Mr Dana, Mr King, Mr Ghoram, Mr Gerry, Mr Strong. I am told that a Resolution of the Legislature of this State which originated with their Senate lays its deputies under the fetter of not departing from the 5th of the present articles of Confederation. As this Resolution passed before the Recommendatory act of

Congress was known, it is conjectured that it may be rescinded; but its having passed at all denotes a much greater prevalence of political jealousy in that quarter than had been imagined. The deputation of N. York consists of Col. Hamilton, Judge Yates and a Mr Lansing. The two last are said to be pretty much linked to the antifederal party here, and are likely of course to be a clog on their colleague. It is not doubted now that Connecticut & R. Island will avoid the singularity of being unrepresented in the Convention.[2]

The thinness of Congs has been an obstacle to all the important business before them. At present there are nine States on the ground but this number, though adequate to every object when unanimous, makes a very slow progress in business that requires seven States only. And I see little prospect of the number being increased.

By our latest and most authentic information from Massts it would seem that a calm has been restored by the expedition of Genl Lincoln. The precautions taking by the State however betray a great distrust of its continuance. Besides their act disqualifying the malcontents from voting in the election of members for the Legislature &c. another has been passed for raising a corps of 1000 or 15,000 men, and appropriating the choicest revenues of the Country, to its support. It is said that at least half of the insurgents decline accepting the terms annexed to the amnesty, and that this defiance of the law agst Treason, is countenanced not only by the impunity with which they shew themselves on public occasions, even with insolent badges of their character, but by marks of popular favor conferred on them in various instances in the election to local offices.[3]

A proposition has been introduced & discussed in the Legislature of this State, for relinquishing its claim to Vermont, and urging the admission of it into the Confederacy. As far as I can learn difficulties will arise only in settling the form, the substance of the measures being not disliked by any of the parties. It is wished by those who are not interested in claims to lands within that district to guard agst any responsibility in the State for compensation. On the other side it will at least be insisted that they shall not be barred of the privilege of carrying their claims before a federal Court, in case Vermont shall become a party to the Union. I think it probable if she should not decline becoming such altogether, that she will make two conditions if not more. 1. that neither her boundaries, nor the rights of her citizens shall be impeachable under the 9th art. of Confederation. 2[.] that no share of the public debt already contracted shall be allotted to her.[4]

I have a letter from Col. Jno. Campbel dated at Pittsburg, from wch I gather that the people of that quarter are thrown into great agitation by the reported intention of Congs Concerning the Mississippi, and that measures are on foot, for uniting the minds of all the different settlements which have a common interest at stake. Should this policy take effect I think there is much ground to apprehend that the ambition of individuals will quickly mix itself with the first impulses of resentment and interest, that by degrees the people may be led to set up for themselves, that they will slide like Vermont insensibly into a communication and latent connection with their British Neighbours, and in pursuance of the same example, make such a disposition of the Western territory as will entice into it most effectually emigrants from all parts of the Union. If these apprehensions be not imaginary they suggest many observations extremely interesting to Spain as well as to the United States.[5]

I hear from Richmond with much concern that Mr Henry has positively declined his mission to Philada. Besides the loss of his services on that theatre, there is danger I fear that this step has proceeded from a wish to leave his conduct unfettered on another theatre where the result of the Convention will receive its destiny from his omnipotence. With every sentiment of esteem & affection I remain Dear Sir Your Obedt and very hble servt

Js Madison Jr

ALS, DLC:GW.

1. GW copied Madison's list of Indian words and then returned the list to him (GW to Madison, 31 March). Neither copy has been found. For GW's role in securing Indian vocabularies for Catherine I of Russia, see Richard Butler to GW, 30 Nov. 1787, and the enclosures and notes in that document. On 10 Jan. 1788 GW forwarded to Lafayette the Cherokee and Choctaw vocabulary that Madison had sent him. Benjamin Hawkins (1754–1818) of North Carolina was one of the five commissioners appointed in 1785 by Congress to treat with the Cherokee and other southern Indians.

2. From South Carolina, John Rutledge, Charles Cotesworth Pinckney,

Pierce Butler, and Charles Pinckney attended the Convention; Henry Laurens did not. From Massachusetts, Elbridge Gerry, Nathaniel Gorham, Rufus King, and Caleb Strong attended; Francis Dana did not. Alexander Hamilton, Robert Yates, and John Lansing, Jr., from New York all attended the Convention but each only for a part of the time.

3. For a general description of Benjamin Lincoln's suppression of Shays' Rebellion, see Lincoln to GW, 4 Dec. 1786–4 Mar. 1787, and notes.

4. Alexander Hamilton's bill to acknowledge the independence of Vermont was introduced in the New York legislature on 15 March. It passed the house on 11 April, but the senate rejected it. See Syrett, *Hamilton Papers*, 4:112–18, 126–41.

5. John Campbell (d. 1799), the owner of large tracts of land in the area of the falls of the Ohio River, represented Jefferson County in the Virginia general assembly and favored the separation of the Kentucky district from Virginia.

From Henry Knox

My dear Sir   New York 19 March 1787

The disturbances by the Massachusetts insurgents on the frontiers of this State, were quieted by an action which happened, on the 28th ultimo near great Barrington in which a number of them were taken prisoners. Govr Clinton therefore on his arrival, at the borders of Massachusetts finding no business, congratulated Genl Lincoln and returned to this City.

The leaders of the rebellion are undoubtedly in Canada. What countenance they will receive is uncertain. They were stopped some time at the Isle aux noix untill permission was received for their admission into the province, when they proceeded to Quebec. The insurgents of less note have taken refuge in Vermont, the government of which have too much favored them. some difficulty is likely to arise on this head.

Instead of 1500 Men for four months General Lincoln has concluded one thousand a sufficient number. He is to command them, at the special request of the Legislature—and also any militia which may be occasionally necessary[.] He has deservedly obtained great credit by the prudent manner of conducting the business and bringing it to its present favorable state.

I have the satisfaction of acknowledging the receipt of your favor of the 8th which I received on the 17th instant.

I will as soon as possible, make the necessary enquiries in a suitable manner, respecting the person at Elizabeth-Town, and when I inform you of the result, I will return the letters and translations on the subject.[1]

The opinion of Congress respecting the proposed convention has had good effects. It is now highly probable that the convention will be general. All the States have already chosen delegates to attend it, excepting[2] Rhode-Island and connecticut, and there can be but little doubt of their making a seasonable choice.

Your observations in favor of the experiment of a convention are conclusive—Our present federal government is indeed a name, a shadow without power, or effect. We must either have a government, of the same materials, differently constructed, or we must have a government of events.

But should the convention possess the magnanimity to propose a wise modification of a national government, without regarding the present local, and contracted views, that the mass of the people in the respective States entertain of the subject leaving to time, better information, and events to ripen their judgements much, much might be hoped But if only propositions be obtained for bracing up the present radically defective thing, so as [to] enable us to drag on with pain and labor, for a few years, then better had it been, that the idea of the convention had never been conceived.

As you have thought proper my dear Sir, to request my opinion respecting your attendance at the convention, I shall give it with the utmost sincerity and frankness.

I imagine that your own satisfaction or chagrin and that of your friends will depend entirely on the result of the convention—For I take it for granted that however reluctantly you may acquiesce, that you will be constrained to accept of the presidents chair. Hence the proceedings of the convention will more immediately be appropriated to you than to any other person.

Were the convention to propose only amendments, and patch work to the present defective confederation, your reputation would in a degree suffer—But were an energetic, and judicious system to be proposed with Your signature, it would be a circumstance highly honorable to your fame, in the judgement of the present and future ages; and doubly entitle you to the glorious republican epithet—The Father of Your Country.

But the men generally chosen, being of the first information, great reliance may be placed on the wisdom and vigor of their Councils and judgements and therefore the balance of my opinion preponderates greatly in favor of your attendance.

I am persuaded that your name has had already great influence to induce the States to come into the measure—That your attendance will be grateful, and your absence chagrining—That your presence would confer on the assembly a national complexion, and that it would more than any other circumstance induce a compliance to the propositions of the convention.

I have never written to you concerning your intention of declining to accept again the presidency of the Cincinnati—I can only say that the idea afflicts me exceedingly.

That the society was formed with pure motives you well know. In the only instance in which it has had the least political operation, the effects have been truly noble. I mean in Massachusetts where the officers are still unpaid and extremely depressed in their private circumstances, but notwithstanding which the moment the government was in danger, they unanimously pledged themselves for its support—While the few wretched officers who were against government were not of the Cincinnati. The clamor and prejudice which existed against it, are no more—The men who have been most against it say, that the society is the only bar to lawless ambition and dreadful anarchy to which the imbecillity of government, renders us so liable, and the same men express their apprehensions of your resignation.

Could I have the happiness of a private conversation with you, I think I could offer you such reasons, as to induce you to suspend your decision for another period of three years. Suffer me then my dear Sir, to entreat that you would come to Philadelphia one week earlier, than you would do in order to attend the convention, and to chear the hearts of your old military friends with your presence—This would rivet their affections and entirely remove your embarrassment in this respect of attending the convention.

God who knows my heart, knows that I would not solicit this step, were I of opinion that your reputation would suffer the least injury by it—I fully beleive that it would not—But I beleive that Should you attend the convention and not meet the cincinnati, that it would sorely wound your sincere friends and please those who dare not avow themselves your enemies. With affectionate respects to Mrs Washington I am my dear Sir your respectfully affectionate

H. Knox

ALS, DLC:GW.
  1. See GW to Knox, 8 March.
  2. Knox wrote "expecting."

From John Hopkins

Sir.   Richmond March 20 1787.

Mr Buchanan applied to me some time since for a further payment on your subscription to the James River Company, and as there were several pressing demands on it, and you at a distance I have taken the liberty of paying to the Treasurer the sum of Fifty pounds, on your account, for which I herewith transmit you a Receipt. This sum you will be pleased to pay into the hands of Mr Charles Lee of Alexandria, who will take the trouble of bringing it to me in April next. I have the honor to be with very Great Respect Sir Your Most Obedient humble servant

Jno. Hopkins

ALS, DLC:GW.
  1. GW has this entry in his cash accounts for 24 Mar.: "By the James River Company pd the Treasurer [James Buchanan] 50.0.0" (Ledger B, 242). See GW to Hopkins, 25 March.

From Louis de Pontière

My General,   St Etienne [France] 20th March 1787.

Permit me to offer myself to your remembrance, and to lay open to you my embarrassed situation since I quitted the service of the United States; You may recollect that I recd, at my departure in 1784, what was due to me for my services in Notes, amounting, in French Money to 27000 livres, of which I was to receive the interest annually until the principal shd be discharged. This was the only resource wh. I had to reimburse my friends for the monies wh. they had advanced me during the war. I returned to France in full confidence of receiving my interest annually, notwithstanding which more than two years have elapsed and I have not recd anything, which has deprived me of the means of support.

I beseech your Excellency to take my case under your consideration, and lend me your good offices towards obtaining the payment of the principal, or at least of the interest wh. is due, and to point out to me what steps are necessary to be taken in this matter, for I find myself in a most deplorable situation.

I sollicited, and obtained in the year 1785, an employment in the legion of the Count de Mailleboies in the service of Holland, but you know what arrangments took place in the following year, since which I have been out of employ; there is not a day passes in which I do not think of the time which I spent in America, & shd think myself exceeding happy if I could yet be employed under your Orders, and have an opportunity of shewing new zeal for your service & that of the United States. I am, with sentiments of the most profound respect, my General, Your very Hbe & Obedt Servt

Depontiere

formerly A.D.C. to the Baron Stuben

P.S. If you do me the favor to honor me with an answer I beg you to address your letter as follows

Monsr Depontiere at Monsr Delatuillerie at the Royal Manufactory of Arms St Etienne in Forest.

Translation, in the hand of Tobias Lear, DLC:GW; ALS, in French, PHi: Gratz Collection.

Louis de Pontière arrived in the United States in 1777 with Steuben and served as his aide-de-camp. He was brevetted a major on his retirement in 1783. No response to this letter has been found.

From Buckner Stith

Sir   March 22d 1787

I have seriously had thoughts of troubling you with an Epistle these four Years, but my Mind has all the way fallen under the task; 'till just know, after smoking three full Pipes, which you know inebriates a good deal if the Tobacco be strong, and a little Man here informing me he lived within three miles of your

House, zounds said I, I will this minute write to the General. I will tell him, that I am the same Man who marched with him and old Laurence from Chotanck to Fredericksburg, how Laurence and him laughed at me for holding the wine glass in the full hand, but as I was five Years older than either of them, I thought I might hold the wine glass as I pleased; that we lost a Horse or two in the Trip, and were obliged to walk honestly in turn clear to Chotank again; and moreover I will tell him, that although Laurence and I might notice him on the Road when in turn to walk, a sound looking, modest, large boned young Man, still I would not defend the matter for a round sum, that were Laurence and I put to the oath, that we thought at the same time, we had each of us an equal chance at least with him, for a Generalship.

Now as the giving you an account of the many good things said of you in this part of the World, might be disagreeable to you, shall be totally silent; knowing (if I be but a piece of a Connisieur,[1] and Satan tells me at times, I am the hundredth pard of one) that the good Mind wants not adulation. To speak in my own way it would be thus, I had rather see you in sound health bending over bushes and mire in full Chace with twenty four Hounds, than to hear the most difficult point discussed of the most difficult RETREAT ever made, between your Honour and the old King of Prussia's ghost.

The force of the three full pipes being for some moments evaporated into open air, and my Mind reduced into its primitive littleness again, must sincerely proceed to ask pardon for the trouble (sure enough) I have given you in reading the above stuff, and ask also to subscribe myself Your most obedient humble Servt

Buckner Stith Senr

ALS, DLC:GW.

This letter from Buckner Stith (1722–1791), originally of the Chotank area of the Northern Neck of Virginia, is unique in that it is the only known letter from a companion of GW's childhood recalling the days of their youth. Stith, who was living at this time at his home Rock Spring in Brunswick County, was a justice of the county and a captain in the Brunswick militia. His sons John (1755–1808) and Robert Stith were married to Ann (d. 1824) and Mary Townshend Washington respectively, daughters of GW's cousin and childhood friend Lawrence Washington of Chotank, the "old Laurence" mentioned in this letter. In July 1764 Buckner Stith paid £32 to Joseph Royle to have printed 1,000 copies of his detailed tract on tobacco which was reprinted in Richmond in 1824 (Virginia Gazette Daybook, 1764–66, ViU; Christopher Johnston, "The Stith Family," *WMQ*, 1st ser., 21 [1912–13], 181–93). *Buckner Stith's Opinion on the Cultivation of Tobacco* was advertised in Royle's *Virginia Gazette* (Williamsburg), 6 July 1764.

1. Stith drew an asterisk here and noted at the side of the page: "not in my Dictionary."

To Benjamin Lincoln

My dear Sir,   Mount Vernon 23d Mar: 1787

Ever since the disorders in your State began to grow serious I have been particularly anxious to hear from that quarter; Genl Knox has, from time to time transmitted to me the state of affairs as they came to his hands; but nothing has given such full & satisfactory information as the particular detail of events which you have been so good as to favor me with, and for which you will please to accept my warmest and most grateful acknowledgments.[1]

Permit me also, my dear Sir, to offer you my sincerest congratulations upon your success. The suppression of those tumults & insurrections with so little blood shed, is an event as happy as it was unexpected; it must have been peculiarly agreeable to you, being placed in so delicate & critical a situation.

I am extremely happy to find that your sentiments upon the disfranchising act are such as they are; Upon my first seeing it I formed an opinion perfectly coincident with yours—viz.—that measures more *generally* lenient might have produced equally as good an effect without entirely alienating the affections of the people from the government. As it now stands, it affects a large body of men, some of them, perhaps, it deprives of the means of gaining a livelihood. The friends and connections of those people will feel themselves wounded in a degree, and I think it will rob the State of a number of its inhabitants if it produces nothing worse.

It gives me great pleasure to hear that your Eastern settlement succeeds so well. The sincere regard which I have for you will always make your prosperity a part of my happiness. I am—

My dear Sir, with sentiments of the Most perfect esteem & regard Yr Most Obedient and Affecte Hble Servt

Go: Washington

ALS, MH; LB, DLC:GW.
    1. See Lincoln to GW, 4 Dec. 1786–4 Mar. 1787.

To John Parke

Sir,   Mount Vernon March 23d 1787
    I have receeved the 2 Vol. of your poetical works which you
were so polite as to send me and for which I beg you to accept
of my best thanks⟨.⟩ The Honor which you have done me in
dedicating your book to me merits my grateful acknowledgements; altho' I have refused many applications which have been
made to dedicate litterary performances to me—yet I always
wish to give every possible encouragement to those works of Genius which are the production of an American. Had I know[n]
of your intention to publish your work I would with pleasure
have become a subscriber. I am Sir Yr Most Obed. Hble Servt

G. Washington

LB, DLC:GW.
    John Parke (1754–1789), of Poplar Grove, Kent County, Del., served as a
lieutenant colonel in the Continental army until 1778. He had Eleazar Oswald
of Philadelphia print for him in 1786 his *The Lyric Works of Horace, Translated
into English Verse: To Which Are Added a Number of Original Poems*. Included in the
volume is a pastoral play set at Mount Vernon with Washington as Daphnis
surrounded by singing shepherds and shepherdesses, hunters and huntresses.
The poem is entitled: *Virginia: A Pastoral Drama, on the Birth-Day of an Illustrious
Personage and the Return of Peace, February 11th, 1784*. Parke dedicated the volume "To his excellency, George Washington, Esq. L.L.D. late General and
Commander in Chief of the Armies of the United States of America, Marechal
of France, &c. &c. &c." (Griffin, *Boston Athenæum Collection*, 159–60).

From David Humphreys

My dear General   New Haven [Conn.] March 24th 1787
    I have but just had the pleasure to receive your two favours
of the 18th of Feby and 8th instant—Nor will I delay a moment
giving my sentiments on the subject of the latter, for the sake of

throwing them into a more elegant dress or methodical arrangement. I need hardly preface my observations by saying, that I feel myself superlatively happy in your confidential communications, and in opportunities of proving that I do not write for the purpose of acquiring a reputation for fine composition, but for the sake of justifying the favourable opinion you have been pleased to form of my attachment & sincerity.

I may then with justice assert that so far from having seen any reason to change my opinion respecting the inexpediency of your attending the Convention in May next, additional arguments have occurred to confirm me in the sentiment. The probability, which existed when I wrote before, that nothing general or effectual would be done by the Convention, amounts now almost to a certainty. For the Assembly of Rhode Island (as I am lately given to understand) have decided against sending any Representation. Connecticut is under the influence of a few such miserable, narrow-minded & I may say wicked Politicians, that I question very much whether the Legislature will chuse Members to appear in the Convention; and if they do, my apprehension is still greater that they will be sent on purpose to impede any salutary measures that might be proposed. This, there is little doubt, is actually the case with N. York, as it is asserted, two out of their three Delegates are directly antifœderal. What chance is there, then, that entire unanimity will prevail? Should this be the fact, however, would not the several Members, as it were, pledge themselves for the execution of their system? And would not this inevitably launch you again on a sea of Politics? As you justly observe matters must probably grow worse before they will be better.

Since I had the honour of addressing you last on this subject, I have been in the way of hearing the speculations of many different Characters on the proposed Convention, and their conjectures on the part you would act in consequence of your appointment to it. I have heard few express any sanguine expectations concerning the successful issue of the Meeting, & I think not one has judged it elegible for you to attend.

In this part of the Union, your not attending will not be considered either by the fœderal, or antifœderal party, as a dereliction of Republicanism. The former believe it unimportant, or perhaps, injurious, to the national Interests for you to come forward at present—the latter look upon the Convention as rather intended to subvert than support Republicanism: and will readily excuse your non-attendance.

Notwithstanding your circular letter to the Cincinnati, I think it probable the General Meeting will re-elect you President—I hope they will—for matters, I am confident, will in some way or another work right before all is over.

Congress appear to be in a state of mortal stupefaction or lethargy. It seems probable the Troops will be disbanded.[1] I shall go to N. York next week but shall return in a few days, & your letters addressed to me at Hartford will still continue to be regularly received.

I wish all my friends at Mount Vernon to be persuaded that something more heartfelt than common Complts is offered them on my part; while, you my dear General, should do me the justice to believe, that there is no one, in your numerous circle of acquaintance, more sincerely attached to you than your affectionate friend

D. Humphreys

ALS, DLC:GW.

1. Humphreys is referring to the troops raised for Congress by Henry Knox as secretary of the army in response to Shays' Rebellion. Humphreys had been made commander of the Connecticut contingent of Congress's forces.

To John Hopkins

Sir,   Mount Vernon Mar. 25th 1787

The last post brought me your favor of the 20th.

At the same time that I pray you to accept my thanks for the advance you were so obliging as to make, on my Acct to Mr Buchanan (as treasurer for the James river Company) I cannot help expressing my surprise at the application to you. Sure I am that nothing ever dropped from me that could induce him to make it; & I now beg that if it should ever be made on any similar occasion, that you would be pleased to refer him to me; for I should feel very unhappy if it should so happen that I might not have it in my power to answer a similer call. Your letter, with Mr Buchanons rect, is the first intimation I have had of the Company's call on the Members for a dividend of their subscription. In the present instance I happen to be provided, and send the money with my sincere acknowledgments to you for the advance of it, by Mr Ch. Lee. begging you to receive the assurances of my esteem & regard I am Sir Yr Most Obedt Servt

Go: Washington

P.S. Your favor did not get to my hands till last Night, and I was about dispatching this letter to day to Mr Lee when a Gent. from Alexandria coming in, informs me that he was to set off this morning for Richmond—I nevertheless send the money up to take the first safe conveyance down to that place. As this renders the matter more precarious I would thank you for acknowledging the receipt of this letter and the money by the Post. Yrs &ca G.W.

ALS, owned (1990) by Mr. H. Bart Cox. On the cover GW wrote: "If by Post, free Go: Washington."

To Lafayette

My Dear Marquis,   Mount Vernon March 25th 1787

Since writing you a hasty letter in November last, by a vessel which was then passing my door, I have been honored with your kind and obliging favor of the 26th of October; for the affectionate sentiments with whch it is replite I pray you to accept my warmest and most grateful acknowledgments and the strongest assurances of everlasting Friendship.[1] I am writing to you my Dear Sir but where will the letter find you? In Crimea, Constantinople, or the Archepelago? or will it await your return to Paris? About this time you must according to your account be setting out for the first, to make the tour of the latter. If it should get to your hands before, or during the interview you will [have] with her imperial majesty it will afford you an opportunity of informing her personally, that the request she made to you of obtaining an Indian Vocabulary is in a proper train for execution. I have the strongest assurances from both General Butler who is now superintendant of Indian affairs and residing on the Ohio, and Mr Hutchins the Geographer who is also employed in that Country that they will delay no time nor spare any pains to make it as perfect as they can. As soon as I receive, I will forward it to you.[2]

I fear this long trip will be a means of postponing your visit to this Country to the very great regret of all your friends and particularly so to me who would wish to see you once more before I go in search of Elisseum. you will long ere this have heard of the Insurrections in the State of Massachusetts—to trace the causes of them would be difficult, and to detail their progress would be unnecessary as the steps taken by that government and the proceedings generally are very minutily related in the public gazettes with which I am informed you are regularly supplied. I shall therefore proceed to the more pleasing part of the business and inform you that the tumults are at an end [and] the principals fled to Canada—It is apprehended however that an act of the Legislature disfranchising [those] who were aiding or abetting, is pregnant with as much evil as good, as the operation is too extenciv.

These disorders are evident marks of a defective government; indeed the thinking part of the people of this Country are now so well satisfied of this fact that most of the Legislatures have appointed, & the rest it is said will appoint, delegates to meet at Philadelphia the second monday in may next in general Convention of the States to revise, and correct the defects of the federal System. Congress have also recognized, & recommended the measure. What may be the result of this meeting is hardly within the scan of human wisdom to predict—It is considered however as the last essay to support the present form.

Your endeavors my dear Marquis to serve this Country are unremitted, the letter from the Minister to Mr Jefferson (who I am happy to find is so much respected and esteemd at the Court of France) which you had the goodness to send me, is a recent instance of it. & I wish the conduct of the States may entitle them to a continuation of your good offices as I also do that the Protestants may be grateful for the reliefs you have afforded them.

The dutch though a Phlegmatic people have been too long quarrelling to come now to blows and if matters there can be settled without it the probability is that the tranquellity of Europe may be of some continuance unless the disagreement betwen the Russians and Turks should become more serious. It seems almost Nugatory to dispute about the best mode of dealing with the Algarines when we have neither money to buy their friendship nor the means of punishing them for their depredations upon our people & trade. If we could command the latter I should be clearly in sentiment with you and Mr Jefferson, that chastisement would be more honorouble, and much to be prefered to the purchased friendship of these Barbarians—By me, who perhaps do not understand the policy by which the Maritime powers are actuated it has ever been considered as reflecting the highest disgrace on them to become tributary to such a banditti who might for half the sum that is paid them be exterminated from the Earth. This want must turn our faces from the Western Ports, even it should be found that we have not been the first infractors of the Treaty. To investigate this matter, as their have been crimination on both sides, the Secretary for Foreign affairs is now employed.

General Greene's death is an event which has given such genl concern and is so much regretted by his numerous friends that I can scarce persuade myself to touch upon it even so far as to say that in him you lost a man who affectionately regarded & was a sincere admirer of you.

Tho' last mentioned, it is among my uppermost thought to thank you once more, my dear Marquis for the valuable animals you sent me under the care of Mr Campion and to request my dear friend that you will let me know the cost of them that I may remit the amount for be assured I have had it in contemplation to give you more than the trouble of procuring them.

I have lately lost a Brother (Colo. John Auge Washington which I mention to account for the black Seal of this letter) the rest of my friends, and every individual in this Family are tolerably well and join most cordeally in every vow that can contribute to the health and happiness of Madam La Fayette your self and family—Esqr. Tab[3] will soon be able to offer you his own homage as he begins to write very prettily—I have no expression that can convey to you the warmth of my friendship and the affectionate attachment I have to you. Adieu believe me ever yr

G. Washington.

P.S. Mr Campion observing that red birds were not among the feathered tribe of France—and the wood or summer duck were very rare their I send you too pair of the latter & several of the former which the Capt. Atkinson who is bound for Havre de gras has promised his care of.

LB, DLC:GW.

1. GW wrote Lafayette on 19 Nov. 1786.

2. Richard Butler enclosed the Indian vocabulary in his letter to GW of 30 Nov. 1787.

3. Howell Lewis, the copyist, should have written "Tub," the nickname given to little George Washington Parke Custis. As he sometimes did, Jared Sparks made a number of corrections in this document, all of which have been ignored as elsewhere.

To George Weedon

Mount Vernon, March 25, 1787.

I have received your favor of the 19th. and thank you for the trouble you have taken to procure for me the Jerusalem Arti-choke, but as Captn. Grymes has been so obliging as to send me five Bushels of them which I expect are enough to plant an acre of ground (which will be sufficient to make the experiment I had in contemplation) as there is no way of getting them but by the Stage or sending on purpose for them and as it might have been inconvenient to Mr. Page to have spared what he furnished you with for my use, I pray you to return them to him with my thanks for the kind intention.[1]

I shall follow the directions contained in your letter unless upon further inquiry of him or others a better can be suggested, but I shall be glad to know whether in hills, or in drills, is the usual mode of planting, and at what distance. I am, etc.

Fitzpatrick, *Writings of Washington*, 29:182–83. The ALS was advertised in the Henkels Catalog no. 660, item 83, 11 Feb. 1891.

1. Letter not found. Mr. Page was probably Mann Page, Jr., who lived at Mannsfield near Fredericksburg. For references to the Jerusalem artichoke, see Benjamin Fitzhugh Grymes to GW, 14 Mar., and GW to Grymes, 16 March.

From James Gibbon

Dr sir   Petersburgh Virga March 26th 1787

I am very sorry at this late period of time to trouble you par-ticularly as all your officiall business has ceas'd so long; Your opinion will nevertheless avail sufficiently.

A Demand, I long since made to the commissioner of accts

for the army, for what I consider'd my due (the commutation) has remaind undetermind till now, owing chiefly to my business confining me at this place so as to prevent a personall application at N. York—The nature of my demand is briefly this, which I submitt to yr justice & altho you can now, be furnish'd with no other than my own assertions as testimony I flatter myself, as they are founded in propriety, they will have some weight[.] at the time of the revolt of the Penna line I was on furlough in Phila. labouring under the appearances of a consumption so much as to render my doing duty impracticable. The design of my furlough was, to seek an oppt. of Going to the W. Indies which I was advis'd to by Dr Rush to whom I had apply'd and whose certificate, descriptive of my situation, Genl Knox or Mr Pierce are now posses'd of[1]—Previous to my effecting my purpose, the revolt took place—I imediatly joind the troops at Prince Town where I remaind till turn'd out by order of theeir board of Sergeants and then join'd my brother officers at Penny town partaking in the kind of Duty there perform'd for our mutual saf'ty in which time my disorder increas'd so as to oblige my returning to Phila. tho ⟨there⟩, with a piece of duty assign'd me by the late Govr Reeid which was perform'd: my disorder still increasing an immediate change of climate was advis'd as absolutly indispensable and an oppt. offering of going to martinique I embrac'd it, having abt the time of my departure sent the resignation of a regimentall commission, as I then held it and a brevett tho acting solely under the latter—my holding the former I consider'd as of little avail as a rearangment was abt to & did take place by which I shou'd have been put on the Supernumery list—The act of Congress accompanying the brevett is in the opinion of Mr Pierce to whom Congress referr'd the claim competent to the admission of it—he, however as a public officer wishing to eir on the Safe side has recommended my obtaining yr opinion on the Subject—this sir, as I consider my claim strictly just, I flatter myself you will take the trouble to give me by letter[2]—I'm far from wishing to take advantage of the publick nor is my claim founded upon precedents which have pass'd, of less propriety. Im sir with great respect & esteem Yr Most Obt

J. Gibbon

⟨It⟩ is hardly necessary to observe sir, that exte⟨nded⟩ furloughs were seldon denied at Head Quarters under circumstances of this kind and that the trouble I put you to wou'd not have been necessary had it been in my power, previous to departure, for the W. Indies, to have made the application.

ALS, DLC:GW.

James Gibbon (1758–1835) of Petersburg was brevetted captain after the capture of Stony Point, N.Y., in July 1779.

1. John Pierce (d. 1788) was the commissioner of army accounts to settle military claims against Congress.

2. GW responded from Mount Vernon on 15 April: "Sir, I have recd your letter of the 26th Ulto wherein you request my opinion with respect to your obtaining the benefit of the Commutation—I am sorry that I cannot, with propriety comply with your request; as I have never interfered with, nor had any knowledge of the settlement of those Accts I can have no grounds whereon to form an opinion—Mr Pierse, to whom you say Congress has referred your Case, is undoubtedly better qualified from the documents which he has, to judge of the propriety or impropriety of it than I can possible be—With respect to extensive furloughs, I can only say that I never considered myself authorized to grant them to officers to go off the Continent, but when application was made for that purport I referred them to Congress. I am Sir Yr Most Obedt Hbl. Sert G. Washington" (LB, DLC:GW). Gibbon wrote GW again on 16 July 1788, to which GW replied on 1 Aug. that "upon a recurrence to the General Orders, I find y⟨ou⟩r Brevet promotion announced to the Army in the words of the resolve of Congress; and, that, by farther researches among the memorandums of resignations, I can discover nothing more on the Subject." For subsequent correspondence between the two on this and other matters, see Gibbon to GW, 12 Feb. 1789, and notes 1 and 2 of that document.

From Henry Knox

New-York 26th March 1787

I have attended my dear Sir to your request respecting the Chevalier D'anterroches, and the following sketch is the result.

He is the son of a general officer in the french service old and infirm; His uncle is the bishop of Condon, rich, and miserly; besides which he is a relation of the Marquis de la Fayette—In the early part of his Life his father designed him for the church, and forced him to enter on studies necessary for the profession—As this business was his horror, he fled to England and enlisted as a soldier, but afterwards became an officer, by what means does, not appear, but he came out to Canada with Genl

Burgoyne in the year 1776 or 1777, and was taken prisoner at Saratoga. On information that France had decidedly espoused the Cause of America he left the Service of England—whether he refused to be exchanged, resigned, or the precise means of leaving the british Service I cannot ascertain.

Some four or five years ago, he was at chatham, Morris County, in the house of a Mr Pool, where he fell sick—Mr Pool is a shoemaker, his daughter was extremely attentive to the sick chevalier, who testified his gratitude on his recovery by marrying her—Two or three children are the fruits of the Marriage. He lives on a small farm near Elizabeth Town, and is in great distress but is in constant expectation of being releived by his relations. His character is unexceptionable, and he is spoken of as a deserving man.

My own opinion is that nothing would more effectually please him than placing him in the french service—But his Wife and children seems to be an insuperable bar to that idea—perhaps were you to write to the Marquis de la Fayette a letter calculated for him to show to the persons of influence, the poor chevalier might obtain some office in the customs, in the islands, or vice consul of some of these states by which he might maintain his family—I know of nothing in the gift of the United States at present which would releive him—were it practicable for him to enter the service in a military line, the payments are so defective that his family would starve.[1]

The Courts of justice are sitting in Massachusetts for the trial of the rebels—Commissioners are appointed to accompany the Courts to pardon any they may think proper, probably before trial. I am my dear Sir Your respectfully affectionate friend and very humble Servt

H. Knox

ALS, DLC:GW.
    1. See GW to Knox, 8 Mar., n.1.

Letter not found: to John Lawson, 26 Mar. 1787. On 2 April Lawson wrote GW: "I am this day favor'd with yours of the 26th Ulto."

From Mauduit du Plessis

My General,   Charleston [S.C.] 26th March. 1787
My health, and the air of Georgia have determined me to give
up all to Mr McQueen, & return to France, if my disorder will
permit me ever to see it again. I hope in a few days to embark on
board an English Vessel. I cannot express to you the joy which I
feel, at the idea of having it in my power, in about 2 months, to
embrace my wife, children, relations & friends.

I shall never forget the attention & kindness which Your Excell[e]ncy & Madam Washington shewed me. I shall do myself
the pleasure of letting you hear from me in France; & shall be
always happy to receive your commands there.

I beg your Excellency to receive the assurances of my most
sincere attachment & perfect Respect,

Duplessis

Translation, DLC:GW; ALS, in French, PHi: Gratz Collection.

Letter not found: Benjamin Fitzhugh Grymes to GW, 27 Mar. 1787. GW
wrote Grymes on 10 April: "Your favor of the 27th ult. was put into
my hands the 7th instt."

To Edmund Randolph

Dear Sir,   Mount Vernon 28th Mar. 1787
Your favor of the 11th did not come to my hand till the 24th;
and since then, till now, I have been too much indisposed to
acknowledge the receipt of it. To what cause to ascribe the detention of the [letter] I know not, as I never omit sending once,
and oftener twice a week to the Post Office—In Alexandria.

It was the decided intention of the letter I had the honor of
writing to your Excellency the 21st of December last, to inform
you, that it would not be convenient for me to attend the Convention proposed to be holden in Philadelphia in May next; and
I had entertained hopes that another had been, or soon would
be, appointed in my place; inasmuch as it is not only inconvenient for me to leave home, but because there will be, I apprehend, too much cause to charge my conduct with inconsistency,

in again appearing on a public theatre after a public declaration to the contrary; and because it will, I fear, have a tendency to sweep me back into the tide of public affairs, when retirement and ease is so essentially necessary for, and is so much desired by me.

However, as my friends, with a degree of sollicitude which is unusual, seem to wish my attendance on this occasion, I have come to a resolution to go if my health will permit, provided, from the lapse of time between the date of your Excellencys letter and this reply, the Executive may not—the reverse of which wd be highly pleasing to me—have turned its thoughts to some other character—for independantly of all other considerations, I have, of late, been so much afflicted with a rheumatic complaint in my shoulder that at times I am hardly able to raise my hand to my head, or turn myself in bed. This, consequently, might prevent my attendance, and eventually a representation of the State; which wd afflict me more sensibly than the disorder which occasioned it.

If after the expression of these sentiments, the Executive should consider me as one of the Delegates, I would thank your Excellency for the earliest advice of it; because if I am able, and should go to Philadelpa, I shall have some previous arrangements to make, and would set of for that place the first, or second day of May, that I may be there in time to account, personally, for my conduct to the General Meeting of the Cincinnati which is to convene on the first Monday of that month—My feelings would be much hurt if that body should otherwise, ascribe my attendance on the one, and not on the other occasion, to a disrespectful inattention to the Society; when the fact is, that I shall ever retain the most lively and affectionate regard for the members of which it is composed, on acct of their attachment to, and uniform support of me, upon many trying occasions; as well as on acct of their public virtues, patriotism, and sufferings.

I hope your Excellency will be found among the *attending* delegates. I should be glad to be informed who the others are—and cannot conclude without once more, and in emphatical terms, praying that if there is not a *decided* representation in *prospect*, without me, that another, for the reason I have assigned, may be chosen in my room without ceremony and without delay; for it would be unfortunate indeed if the State which was the mover of this Convention, should be unrepresented in it. With great respect I have the honor to be Yr Excellys Most Obedt Ser.

Go: Washington

ALS, PHi: Dreer Collection; LB, DLC:GW.

To James Madison

My dear Sir,   Mount Vernon 31st Mar. 1787

At the sametime that I acknowledge the receipt of your obliging favor of the 21st Ult. from New York, I promise to avail myself of your indulgence of writing only when it is convenient to me. If this should not occasion a relaxation on your part, I shall become very much your debtor—and possibly like others in similar circumstances (when the debt is burthensome) may feel a disposition to apply the spunge—or, what is nearly a-kin to it—pay you off in depreciated paper, which being a legal tender, or what is tantamount, being *that* or *nothing*, you cannot refuse. You will receive the nominal value, & that you know quiets the conscience, and makes all things easy—with the debt⟨ors⟩.

I am glad to find that Congress have recommended to the States to appear in the Convention proposed to be holden in Philadelphia in May. I think the reasons in favor, have the preponderancy of those against the measure. It is idle in my opinion to suppose that the Sovereign can be insensible of the inadequacy of the powers under which it acts—and that seeing, it should not recommend a revision of the Fœderal system, when it is considered by many as the *only* Constitutional mode by which the defects can be remedied. Had Congress proceeded to a delineation of the Powers, it might have sounded an Alarm; but as the case is, I do not conceive that it will have that effect.

From the acknowledged abilities of the Secretary for Foreign Affairs, I could have had no doubt of his having ably investigated the infractions of the Treaty on both sides—Much is it to be regretted however, that there should have been any on ours. We seem to have forgotten, or never to have learnt, the policy of placing ones enemy in the wrong. Had we observed good faith on our part, we might have told our tale to the world with a good grace; but compl[ain]ts illy become those who are found to be the first agressors.

I am fully of opinion that those who lean to a Monarchical governmt have either not consulted the public mind, or that they live in a region where the levelling principles in which they were bred, being entirely irradicated, is much more productive of Monarchical ideas than are to be found in the Southern States, where from the habitual distinctions which have always existed among the people, one would have expected the first generation, and the most rapid growth of them. I also am clear, that even admitting the utility; nay necessity of the form—yet that the period is not arrived for adopting the change without shaking the Peace of this Country to its foundation.

That a thorough reform of the present system is indispensable, none who have capacities to judge will deny—and with hand and heart I hope the business will be essayed in a full Convention—After which, if more powers, and more decision is not found in the existing form—If it still wants energy and that secresy and dispatch (either from the non-attendance, or the local views of its members) which is characteristick of good Government—And if it shall be found (the contrary of which however I have always been more affrd of, than of the abuse of them) that Congress will upon all proper occasions exercise the powers with a firm and steady hand, instead of frittering them back to the Individual States where the members in place of viewing themselves in their national character, are too apt to be looking. I say after this essay is made if the system proves inefficient, conviction of the necessity of a change will be dissiminated among all classes of the People—Then, and not till then, in my opinion can it be attempted without involving all the evils of civil discord.

I confess however that my opinion of public virtue is so far changed that I have my doubts whether any system without the means of coercion in the Sovereign, will enforce obedience to the Ordinances of a Genl Government; without which, every thing else fails. Laws or Ordinances unobserved, or partially attended to, had better never have been made; because the first is a mere nihil—and the 2d is productive of much jealousy & discontent. But the kind of coercion you may ask?—This indeed will require thought; though the non-compliance of the States with the late requisition, is an evidence of the necessity.

It is somewhat singular that a State (New York) which used to be foremost in all fœderal measures, should now turn her face against them in almost every instance.

I fear the State of Massachusetts have exceeded the bounds of good policy in its disfranchisement⟨s⟩—punishment is certainly due to the disturbers of a government, but the operations of this act is too extensive. It embraces too much—& probably may give birth to new, instead of destroying the old leven.

Some Acts passed at the last Session of our Assembly respecting the trade of this Country, has given great, and general discontent to the Merchants of it. An application from the whole body of those at Norfolk has been made, I am told, to conven⟨e⟩ the Assembly.

* * * * *

I had written thus far, and was on the point of telling you how much I am your obliged Servant, when your favor of the 18th calls upon me for additional acknowledgments.

I thank you for the Indian Vocabalary which I dare say will be very acceptable in a general comparison.[1] Having taken a copy, I return you the original with thanks.

It gives me pleasure to hear that there is a probability of a full Representation of the States in Convention; but if the delegates come to it under fetters, the salutary ends proposed will in my opinion be greatly embarrassed & retarded, if not altogether defeated. I am anxious to know how this matter really is, as my wish is, that the Convention may adopt no temporising expedient, but probe the defects of the Constitution to the bottom, and provide radical cures, whether they are agreed to or not—a conduct like this, will stamp wisdom and dignity on the proceedings, and be looked to as a luminary, which sooner or later will shed its influence.[2]

I should feel pleasure, I confess in hearing that Vermont is received into the Union upon terms agreeable to all parties—I took the liberty years ago to tell some of the first characters in the State of New York, that sooner or later it would come to that. That the longer it was delayed the terms on their part, would, probably be more difficult—and that the general interest was suffering by the suspence in which the business was held; as the asylum wch it afforded, was a constant drain from the Army in place of an aid which it offered to afford. and lastly, considering the proximity of it to Canada if they were not with us, they might become a sore thorn in our sides, wch I verily believe would have been the case if the War had continued. The Western Settlements without good & wise management of them, may be equally troublesome. With sentimts of the sincerest friendship I am—Dear Sir Yr Affecte Servt

Go: Washington

Be so good as to forward the enclosed Mrs Washington intended to have sent it by Colo. Carrington, but he did not call here.[3]

ALS, NN: Emmet Collection; LB, DLC:GW.
    1. Madison sent the Indian vocabulary with his letter of 18 March.
    2. It perhaps should be noted that in all of this discussion of the work to be done by the Convention, GW gives no hint that three days before he had written Gov. Edmund Randolph to agree, in effect, to attend as a delegate from Virginia. Randolph wrote Madison on 4 April: "Genl. Washington is prevailed upon to agree to go to Phila. if his health will permit" (Rutland and Rachal, *Madison Papers,* 9:364–66).
    3. Edward Carrington was a member of Congress from Virginia.

From Charles Willson Peale

Dr Sir   Phila[delphi]a March 31. 1787
    Your obliging favor of the 13th I received on the 28th[.] The Pepper I beleive preserved the body from being thrown over board. My Anticeptic Powders I hope will preserve the remains, yet not so perfect as I could wish as many of the feathers fall off.
    I believe the conveyance by the stage waggon with a particular direction will be the most certain.
    If you wish to possess any bird, or Annimals, which you may at any time send to preserve the form, please to inform me, and I will most chearfully do my best to serve you. I am with much regard your obliged Hble Servant.

C. W. Peale

ALS, DLC:GW; LB, PPAmP: Charles Willson Peale Papers. The letter-book copy, entered between letters of 27 Mar. and 20 April 1787, is misdated "Decr 31, 1787."

To John Francis Mercer

Sir,   Mount Vernon April 1st 1787
Enclosed I return the letter which you forwarded to me the 10th of Feby.[1] For particular reasons and purposes, whatever money you may incline to pay me consequent of your promises would come very opportunely before 25 of this month. To this period, sufficient time is allowed to obtain the Certificates you have at Richmond—after which I shall hold myself discharged from any obligation to receive them.[2]

The detention has already deprived me of every advantage I could have made of them in the payment of Taxes whilst I am sustaining the loss by their depreciation in the hands of others. My Compliments if you please to Mrs Mercer. I am Sir yr most obedient Humble Servant

                                          G. Washington

LB, DLC:GW.
    1. No letter of 10 Feb. from Mercer has been found.
    2. See GW to Mercer, 1 Feb. 1787, and the references in note 2 of that document.

To Richard Sprigg

Dear Sir,   Mount Vernon Aprl 1st 1787
It is, I believe, beyond a doubt that your Jenny is with foal by my Spaniard. As I have two imported female Asses (very fine) which will be put to my Jacks this Season, & from which I may expect the pure breed; you are very welcome to the produce of your own, & the sooner you send for her the better, and less risk will be run in removing her. At present she is in very fine order having been well fed & attended through the Winter[1]—With compliments to Mrs Sprig I am—Dear Sir Yr Obedt Hble Servt

                                          Go: Washington

ALS, PWacD: Sol Feinstone Collection, on deposit PPAmP.
    1. One or more of Sprigg's jennies were at Mount Vernon before the end of June 1786, and the arrangements for the return of two of them to Maryland were not completed until the end of September 1787 (GW to Sprigg, 28 June 1786, 28 Sept. 1787). GW is referring to the jennies that Lafayette gave him in 1786 (see James McHenry to GW, 5 Nov. 1786, and the references in note 1 of that document).

To Henry Knox

My dear Sir,   Mount Vernon 2d Aprl 1787

The early attention which you were so obliging as to pay to my letter of the 8th ulto is highly pleasing and flattering to me.[1] Were you to continue to give me information on the same point, you would add to the favor; as I see, or think I see, reasons for and against my attendance in Convention so near an equilibrium, as will cause me to Determine upon either, with diffidence. One of the reasons against it, is, an apprehension that all the States will not appear; and that some of them, being unwillingly drawn into the measure, will send their Delegates so fettered as to embarrass, & perhaps render nugatory, the whole proceedings. In either of these circumstances—that is—a partial representation—or cramped powers, I should not like to be a sharer in this business. If the Delegates come with such powers as will enable the Convention to probe the defects of the Constitution to the bottom, and point out radical cures—it would be an honorable employment—but otherwise it is desireable to avoid it —and these are matters you may possibly come at by means of your acquaintances among the Delegates in Congress; who, undoubtedly know what powers are given by their respective States. You also can inform me what the prevailing opinion with respect to my attendance, or non-attendance, is; and I would sincerely thank you for the confidential communication of it.

If I should attend the Convention, I will be in Philadelphia previous to the meeting of the Cincinnati, where I shall hope, & expect to meet you and some others of my particular friends the day before; in order that I may have a free & unreserved conference with you on the subject of it; for I assure you this is in my estimation, a business of a delicate nature—That the design of the Institution was pure I have not a particle of doubt. That it may be so still, is perhaps equally unquestionable. But, quære, are not the subsidence of the Jealousies of it, to be ascribed to the modification which took place at the last Genl Meeting? Are not these rejected in toto by some of the State Societies, and partially acceded to by others? Has any State so far overcome its prejudices as to grant a Charter? Will the modifications & alterations be insisted on, or given up, in the next Meeting? If the first, will it not occasion warmths & divisions? If the latter, and I should remain at the head of this order, in what light would my signature appear in contradictory recommendations? In what light would the versatility appear to the Foreign members, who perhaps are acting agreeably to the recommendations of the last General Meeting?[2] These, and other matters which may be agitated, will, I fear, place me in a disagreeable predicament if I should preside, and were among the causes which induced me to decline the honor of it, previously to the meeting. Indeed my health is[3] become very precarious—a Rheumatic complaint which has followed me more than Six months is frequently so bad, that it is with difficulty I can, at times, raise my hand to my head, or turn myself in bed. This, however smooth & agreeable other matters might be, might almost in the moment of my departure, prevent my attendance on either occasion.

I will not at present touch on any other parts of your letter, but would wish you to ponder on all these matters, & write to me as soon as you can. With the most sincere friendship I am My dear Sir Yr affecte Servt

Go: Washington

ALS, NNGL: Knox Papers; LB, DLC:GW.

1. Knox answered GW's letter of 8 Mar. on 19 March.

2. GW was soon to receive further confirmation that the reforms in the Society of the Cincinnati which he had persuaded the delegates to the General Meeting in 1784 to adopt were being rejected by the state societies. On 16 April Jeremiah Fogg, secretary of the society of New Hampshire, forwarded him a copy of resolutions adopted by the New Hampshire Cincinnati at a meeting on 3 Feb. 1787: "1st This society object to the plan proposed by the last general Meeting to submit the appropriation of funds to the Legislatures of the respective States, or to leave the existence of the Society to the regulation of charters which may never be obtained, and in failure of which the society must cease to exist.

"⟨2nd⟩ That the abolition of hereditary succession adopted by said general meeting is so repugnant to the design of the institution and so destructive of the Principles upon which it was originally founded that it ought not to be agreed to.

"3ly Liberty of correspondence being the right of free men of every denomination in America, this Society can never consent to relinquish that right and thereby degrade themselves below every other class of Citizens.

"4ly The Society propose that the descendants of new-elected Members be intituled to the privilege of admittance upon the death of an Ancestor in the same manner as the descendants of ancient Members.

"And that upon the death of any new elected or ancient Member it shall be the business of the society in the state where such deceased Member dwelt to nominate and appoint such of his sons (if any he have) as will be most likely to fill the place of his Ancestor with credit and notify him of his appointment, upon which he shall upon appearing and subscribing to the institution be considered as a Member and entituled to all the privileges of other Members" (DSoCi).

3. GW put a correction mark over "is."

From John Lawson

Sir   Dumfries April 2d 1787
I am this day favor'd with yours of the 26th Ulto[1] & I am inform'd by the Overseer with whom my Negro Fellow lives that his leg is now nearly well—I have therefore directed him to send Neptune (who will deliver this) to Mount Vernon the moment he thinks him able to travel without injuring himself.

I shall esteem it a favor if you will let me be inform'd when he arrives, & should you keep him your acknowledgement for the value will be sufficient as I have settled with Mr Hunter for the amount.[2] I am Sir Your very hble Servt

J. Lawson

ALS, DLC:GW.
    1. Letter not found.
    2. See Lawson to GW, 17 Mar., n.1.

From Edmund Randolph

Dear sir   Richmond April 2. 1787.
Your favor of the 27th Ulto was handed to me this moment.

Solicitous as I am for your aid at Philadelphia, I could not prevail upon myself to wish you to go, unless your health would fully permit. But indeed, my dear sir, every thing travels so fast to confusion, that I trust one grand effort will be made by the friends of the united states.

There is a decided prospect of a representation: and the board have peremptorily determined not to fill up another vacancy. The members, now in nomination are, besides yourself, Mr Madison, Mr Mason, Mr Wythe, Mr Blair, Mr R. H. Lee and myself.

You will oblige me by saying how I shall forward the money to be advanced from the treasury.

You recollect, that congress have altered the day of meeting to the 14th of may: at which time it is my purpose to take you by the hand. I am dear sir yr affte friend

Edm: Randolph

ALS, DLC:GW.

From Benjamin Franklin

Dear Sir,   Philad[elphi]a April 3. 1787

I have often thought that the Number of People, who by Curiosity and the Admiration of your Character are drawn to call at Mt Vernon, must be very troublesome to you, and have therefore generally declin'd giving any introductory Letters. But my Nephew Mr Jonathan Williams, who was a faithful and active Agent of the United States during the whole War, in shipping Stores, Arms, Ammunition &c. for the Army, being on his Way to Richmond, and desirous of paying his Respects to you, I hope you will excuse my giving this Line of Information concerning him, which at the same time may express my best Wishes for your Health and Happiness, and Hopes of seeing you here at the Convention, being persuaded that your Presence will be of the greatest Importance to the Success of the Measure.[1] With sincere Esteem and Respect, I am, Dear Sir, Your most obedt & most hum. Servt

B. Franklin

ALS, anonymous donor.

1. Jonathan Williams (1750–1815) served as his uncle's private secretary in France during the Revolution. In 1790 he became judge of the court of common pleas in Pennsylvania, and in 1802 he was made the first superintendent of the U.S. Military Academy at West Point.

Letter not found: from David Stuart, 30 April 1787. On 5 May GW wrote "I have received your favor of the 30th."

From Edward Moyston

Sir   Philadelphia 4th April 1787

As the Convention of the States is expected to meet in this City in the next Month, I make bold to request your influence with such Gentlemen of your acquaintance as may want Accommodations. I have fitted up Chambers in the most convenient manner, and am certain that they will find it more agreeable than any private Lodging House in Town, as they will always have more Attendants, should their own be out of the way, than are commonly to be found in private Houses, and as I have altered the House they may be as private as in any other. On my arrival in Philadelphia, I found the Cheese which I promised to send, entirely spoiled with the Heat. I sent two by the Sloop Dolphin Captain Steward, of the best quality I could find.[1] Mr Drayton's Negro having given himself to me, I have transmitted him home to his Master, he says he left some Cloaths at Mount Vernon, and if they are worth the Trouble, you will please to order some of your Servants to forward them to me, I shall send them home by the next Packet.[2] Should you please to make use of any Tavern to Lodge at, I hope for the preference, and could I know that you would, before your Arrival, every thing in my power should be particularly fitted to suit your convenience. In the Philadelphia Paper of this Date is an Advertisement of mine, which I should be glad to have inserted in the Alexandria News Paper for three or four Months and hope you will take the trouble to order some of your People to acquaint the printer of it.[3] Should you have any Commands that I can execute you will please at any time to send your orders to me and they shall be paid the strictest attention to. I am Sir With the greatest Respect Your most Obedient Servant

                                        Edward Moyston

ALS, DLC:GW.

1. Edward Moyston had been the proprietor of the City Tavern on Second Street in Philadelphia since 1779. He consulted GW at Mount Vernon in July 1786 about the possibility of his opening a tavern in Alexandria (*Diaries*, 5:16).

2. See GW to James McHenry, 11 Nov. 1786, n.1.

3. Moyston's advertisement does not appear in the Alexandria newspaper, but it is to be found in the *Pennsylvania Packet, and Daily Advertiser,* 4 April 1787. Moyston assured those who would "use his house" that he had, among other

things, "provided himself with cooks of experience, both in the French and English taste" and had "laid in a fresh supply of liquors of the very first quality."

From James Brindley

Sir   Havre de Grace [Md.] April 5th 1787
I was detained in Charleston untill the 17th of March and returned for expedition, by the Philadelphia Packet—therefore had not time to return by Land. If You have any occasion for me on Potomac Please let me know and I will attend. have some expectation of Visiting James River Canal, but not Yet certain. I recd a Letter and a small Packet for You from Coll Washington which comes with this. He and Family was well when I left Charleston. I am Sir, Your very Humbe Servt

Jas Brindley

ALS, NjMoNP.
1. The letter from William Washington of South Carolina has not been found.

From George Turner

Sir,   New York, April 5th 1787
At the Request of the Cincinnati of South-Carolina, I have the honour to forward herewith, for the Favour of your Excellency's Signature, an Hundred and two Diplomas. The Box containing them, encloses, also, a Return of the Members for whom they are intended: The additional Diplomas are meant for those who may chuse to have Duplicates; excepting one, which is designed for Lieutenant-Colonel Langborn, now abroad.[1]

As the Society of that State have expressed an anxious Desire to be honoured with your Name, Sir, as their President, I feel equally anxious to lay these Diplomas before your Excellency in due Time to obtain it.

May I request to have them returned to me here by some safe Conveyance, addressed to *George Turner in New-York* (and, least I may be absent) *To the Care of the honorable William Grayson in Con-*

gress.[2] With the greatest Respect, Sir, I have the honour to be Your Excellency's most obedient humble Servant

G. Turner

P.S. The Box goes to the Care of Doctor Craig at Alexandria.

ALS, DLC:GW.

George Turner, who attended the General Meeting of the Society of the Cincinnati in May 1784 as a delegate from South Carolina, was made the assistant secretary general of the society in May 1787.

1. For William Langborn's sojourn in Europe, see Lafayette to GW, 6 Feb. 1786, n.13.

2. GW wrote to Turner on 26 April from Mount Vernon: "Sir, Your letter of the 5th inst., and the box containing the diplomas for the officers of the State of So. Carolina, came duly to hand. I have signe[d] the diplomas and sent the box to Doctr Craik in Alexandria to be forwarded by a safe conveyance and have directed it to the care of Colo. Grayson as you requested—The enclosed list I have returned agree[a]ble to your desire. I am Sir Yr most Obed. Hble Servt G. Washington" (LB, DLC:GW).

To John Rumney, Jr.

Sir,   Mount Vernon April 6th 1787
However desirous I may be of accomodating the wishes of so deserving a Lady as you represent Mrs Wilson to be, yet Mrs Washington concurs in sentiment with me that my family already is, and soon will be too large to admit of an increase.[1]

I can say little more at this time, respecting the Estate of the deceased Colo. Thos Colvill than what is contained in my account of it to Major Swan (resited in one of the letters which you put into my hands) except that I have used every means in my power lately to Collect materials (and very defective indeed they are) for a final settlement of the Administration.

What the surplus of the [e]state will be, when the debts and Legacies are all paid, is more than I can inform you—the Testator himself, as will appear by his will, had a doubt of their being *any*—and what will be done with *it*, if there should, must be a matter for future determination. when the Administration is closed, which it is my sincere wish to do so as fast as the nature of the case will admit; I shall for my own Justification, and security, take Council with respect to the application of the surplus, if any, under the existing Laws of this Country.[2] The auther of the letters of Instruction to you is mistaken I conceive when he says the claim of one Clawson was admitted—unless by admission he m⟨e⟩ans that it was received.[3] If this was not his idea, it will give him no pleasure to be informed that near twenty others, I believe, have been admitted in the same way under the indefinite, and I might add, indegested clause of the will which has stirred up so many pretenders as to render it a matter of difficult investigation to determine rightly in the case. With great esteem & regard I am Sir yr most Obed. Servant

G. Washington.

LB, DLC:GW. ALS offered for sale in McKay catalog no. 988, item 991.

1. Rumney dined at Mount Vernon on Sunday, 1 April, when he may have spoken of Mrs. Wilson, who has not been identified. See *Diaries*, 5:126.

2. For references to the protracted efforts to settle Thomas Colvill's estate, see GW to John Swan, 23 May 1785, and note 2 of that document. See also Rumney to GW, 22 Jan. 1788, and GW to Rumney, 24 Jan. 1788. After the estate was finally settled in 1797, GW wrote George Pearson on 15 Sept. 1797 that the residue of Colvill's estate came to "nine hundred and thirty two pound⟨s,⟩ seventeen shillings an[d] seven pence three farthings."

3. "One Clawson" has not been identified.

From Israel Shreve

Burlington County
State New Jersey 7th Apl 1787

Dear General

I wrote two Letters to you Dated Last month But the Conveyance is So uncertain, I once more Trouble you with this which I Expect will be handed to you by my Brother William, who is going to Alexander.[1]

The Subject of all my Letters wrote to you this Spring Is respecting a Tract of Land of about 1600 Acres Laying in Pennsylvania Near Redstone Called Washingtons Bottoms, which I have freequantly been Informed You Incline to Sell, which If True, I shod be Exceeding glad to Purchace, If Such pay as I can make will Answer your Purpose, Real Cash I cannot Command, But have Final Settlement Notes, which I am told Answers in Virginia As well as Money at Interest—I am No Speculator, only hold my own Original Notes for my Services and Some Supplies

that I furnished &c., of this Property I Should be wil⟨lg⟩ to Give
a generous Price, So that the Interest would Exceed the rent of
Said Lands—I have not Seen the Land but am pretty well informed of the Situation Quality and Improvements thereon, I
want Land to Settle upon my Self, being bred a farmer Prefer
that Calling to any other, and Wish to Leave Jersey and Settle
where I can Purchace Good Land, I Suppose the Neighbourhood where this Tract Lies for want of a Market at Present is not
very good to make Money or raise it from Sale of Produce, But
I think a Comfortable Liveing may be had there, My Brother
the Bearer of this Letter has Lived Near Devores ferry in the
forks of Youghagania within 10 or 12 miles of Your Land, Near
Two years Past, he is what may be Called in Jersey A Neat
Farmer and a Good Judge of Lands and every thing respecting
a farm, I have requested him to Waite on you And Inquire
whether, this Tract as before mentned is for Sale or Not, If it is,
to know the Terms paid Down in the aforesaid Notes, If I can
Presuade you to oblige me So much as to receive Such Property
for Pay. There has been No facillities Drawn on Said Notes for
Back Interest, I have receivd two years Interest on about one
third part, the others No Interest hath been paid on, I Shall
Authorise My Brother to bargan for me, and If favourable I will
come and pay the Notes. I am Dear General your Most Obedt
Servt

Israel Shreve

ALS, DLC:GW. The letter was "favoured by Colo. William Shreve."
 1. Shreve wrote GW on 5 and 12 Mar.; the part of Shreve's letter of 12 Mar.
that is not a repetition of what he wrote on 5 Mar. is printed in note 3 of his
letter of 5 March.

From Jean Le Mayeur

Sir   Peterbirg april 8. 1787
    Since I left the seet of his Excellency, I met with several misfor-
tunes the first I have been burried almost in the mod at dunfries
and near falmouth since that time to much devotion Carried me
in to another, two weelks ago in amelia Cunty on my way to
church (in compagny with a number of ladies on horse back) to
hcard a sermon to be preached by a foreign clergyman one of

their horses made a kick at mine, which unfortunetly miss him and I received it so violently that the heel of his shou Cot my boot double and stocking througt to the bone which confined me to my bed for Eleven days.[1]

I hope his Excellency and Lady Washington to whom I present my profond Respect is in better health then when I left Mount Vernon and think by this time I may venture to pay my Compliment of felicitation and his Lady. I have no doubt but that his Excellency has knowledge of the death of Col. Carry who has left his children almost without any fortune, and has sold to his son in law, Tom Randolph (wedower[)] a Tract of land for seventeen thousand pounds which has been paid him in *Cash* and since his death it has been found the whole was morgaged and Col. Tom Randolph at Tuckhoe is security for twenty five thousand pounds for which Col. Carry gave him—his dweling place, Mill and dependancys for his security a dett he had Contracted prior to the Commencement of the war, as well as a seizure of ninety negros which was made before his death, and since two action have been brought of three thousands pounds Each (I have forgot wether currency or sterling) besides a number of smaller sums.[2]

Miss Lucy Randolph is Married to Mr Latile three weeks ago at wilton.[3] I have the honour to be with the highest Respect and veneration your Excellency most obedient and most humble Servant

John Le Mayeur

ALS, DLC:GW.

1. Le Mayeur's departure from Mount Vernon was not auspicious: he left on 9 Feb. "but meeting with some accident to his Chaise returned again"; not until the next day "After breakfast" did he "again set out" (*Diaries*, 5:103).

2. Archibald Cary (1721–1787) of Ampthill in Chesterfield County, president of the Virginia senate, though in straitened circumstances, at the time of his death held 2,180 acres and 36 slaves in Chesterfield County, 4,992 acres and 189 slaves in Cumberland County, and 7,000 acres and 41 slaves in Buckingham County. His daughter Jane (1751–1774) at the time of her death was married to Thomas Isham Randolph of Ben Lomond in Goochland County, the "wedower" mentioned here. Another daughter, Anne (1745–1789), was married to Col. Thomas Mann Randolph (1741–1794) of Tuckahoe in Goochland County. According to his will, proved 3 Mar. 1787, Cary divided his estate equally between his three surviving daughters and the eldest sons of his two deceased daughters (Harrison, *Virginia Carys*, 91–93, 177).

3. Joseph Latil, a Frenchman who was pressing for payments to Beaumarchais from the state of Virginia, married Lucy Randolph, daughter of the late Peyton Randolph of Wilton and Lucy Harrison Randolph. Lucy Latil died in 1790.

To Henry Emanuel Lutterloh

Sir,   Mount Vernon April 8th 1787

I have received your letter of the 3d of Jany containing a proposition of the delivery of several hundred German families to settle some of those large tracts of unimproved Land in this State.

I cannot, as an individual, do any thing, at present, towards promoting your d[e]sign, having no occasion for people of the decription mentioned in your letter except a few Mechanics, which I should be glad to procure; upon advantageous terms but as a member of a Company owning a tract of land known by the name of the Great Dismal Swamp, I can inform you thus I know it is their wish & desire to have it settled. It lies in the Neighbourhood of Norfolk, contains of that which is patented besides Entires[1] about 40,000 Acres, & is capable of being made as valuable a tract of Land as any in the Country, as well on account of its vicinity to Norfolk Pourtsmouth and Suffolk and the State of North Carolina as its lying in such a situation as to have the Canal, which it is in contemplation to open between Albemarle sound & Elizabeth R: run directly through it and which will greatly facilitate the draning of it. But the Company are so dispersed and, in a manner, inattentive to the business, that I am pretty certain they would not be brought to advance any money or incur any expence in settling it further than to give such a proportion of the Land as shall be to the mutual satisfaction of the parties—what this proportion would be I am not able to say, tho I have no reason to doubt but that it would be highly advantageous to the Settlers. I should think however, if you incline to enter upon this business, it would be best for you to veiw the land, that you might form an opinion of the proportion which it would be proper to give, and make your proposals accordingly—I would in that case use every endeaver to convince the Company that an agreement might be entered into. I conceive a proper introduction of those industrious people would be highly beneficial to this Country, & shall be happy to give you any assistance in my power towards the effecting of your plan[2]—With very great esteem and regard I am Sir yr most Obed. Servant

G. Washington

LB, DLC:GW.

1. GW may have written in the letter sent to Lutterloh "entireties," meaning portions of the land in the undivided possession of individual estates.

2. GW had already written to at least one member of the Dismal Swamp Company about Lutterloh's proposal. See John Page to GW, 9 March.

From Leven Powell

Dear Sir,   Loudoun April 8th 1787.

The Bearer will now deliver the residue of the Buck-wheat purchased for you, which would have been down sooner, but for the Hurry we were in to get Tobacco down & I knew it could be sent in time for your purpose. Being but an indifferent Farmer & never having made Crop of Buck-Wheat obliged me to consult some of our Farmers with respect to the information you require.[1]

The ground should be well broke up early in June, Plow'd again in July & the Seed put in with an Harrow by the last of that Month, this is said to be the proper way, but I have offen observed the farmers to give their ground but one plowing & Harrow twice, once before & again after sowing.

Good land properly managed Will produce from 30 to 40 bushels ℔ acre & half a bushel of seed is Sufficient. Mean land produces less & requires more seed, say three Pecks to the Acre; from my own observations I think as much depends upon the Season as the Soil & more for the growth of this Crop than any other & which I have found more frequently to fail. It is generally esteem'd & I believe is the best feed for Milch Cows, ground into Meal & Mix'd with Cut straw or Chaff It is given in the same manner to Horses not much used. Made into a Slosh, it fattens hoggs Quick but it is necessary to give them ten or twelve days feed of Indian Corn to give the meat a firmness which it will otherwise want. I shall always be happy to serve you when in my power & am with very great regard Dear Sir Yr ob: Hble Servt

Leven Powell

ALS, DLC:GW.

1. Leven Powell wrote from Loudoun a letter to GW on 18 Dec. 1786, which was inadvertently omitted from volume 4 and will be printed in full at the end of volume 6. In the letter Powell wrote that he was having trouble getting a wagon to send down "the residue of the Buck Wheat" and that he hoped GW could wait "'till a more Leisure time." See also GW to Powell, 21 Dec. 1786, and *Diaries*, 5:74.

From David Humphreys

(Private)

My dear General.   Fairfield [Conn.] April 9th 1787

Since I did myself the honor to address you on the 24th Ulto I have been in New York, & find such a variety of opinions prevailing with respect to the Convention, that I think it expedient to write to you again on the subject.

General Knox has shewn to me, in confidence, his last letter to you. tho' I cannot concur in sentiments altogether, yet, I think with him, should you decide to be present at the Convention, it will be indispensable to arrive in Philadelphia the preceding week, in order to attend the Genl Meeting of the Cincinnati. This may palliate, perhaps, obviate one of my former objections.[1]

I mentioned in my last that I had not conversed with a single character of consideration, who judged it proper for you to attend the Convention, I have now seen several who think it highly interesting that you should be there. Gouverneur Morris & some others have wished me to use whatever influence I might have to induce you to come. I could not have promised this without counteracting my own judgment. I will not, however, hesitate to say, that I do not conceive your attendance can hazzard such personal ill consequences as were to be apprehended, before the proposed Meeting had been legitimated by the sanction of Congress.

If the difference of opinions amongst the Members of this national Assembly should be as great as the variety of sentiments concerning the result; the progress of business before it, will be attended with infinite perplexity & embarrassment. Besides the two primary objects of discussion, viz. 1st whether the old Constitution can be supported, or 2nd whether a new one must be established: I expect a serious proposal will be made for dividing the Continent into two or three seperate Governments. Local politics & diversity of interests will undoubtedly find their way into the Convention. Nor need it be a matter of surprize to find there, as subjects of disagreement the whole western Country, as well as the navigation of the Mississipi.

Should you think proper to attend, you will indisputably be elected President. This would give the measures a degree of national consequence in Europe & with Posterity. But how far (under some supposable case) your personal influence, unattended with other authority, may compose the jarring interests of a great number of discordant Individuals, & controul events, I will not take upon me to determine. We cannot augur any thing very favorable, if we are to judge of future dispositions by those exhibited since the War. The United States at large, with a sovereign contempt, (as if it was the only mark of Sovereignty they could boast) have neglected your most earnest recommendations for doing justice to the Army. Congress continues to sport with your feelings, by refusing, for a course of years, a compliance with their explicit promises respecting the confidentential Persons, who were recommended in your farewell address to their notice. The declaration on that occasion was void of ambiguity, nor could circumstance or language add to its solemnity. But hear oh Heavens! & be astonished oh Earth! Congress, as an acknowledgment of your influence, a proof of their gratitude, and a reward for your services, have (not to say pertinaciously) but with a series of consistencies not always discoverable in their proceedings, denied to accord the last & only favor you ever asked at their hands. It is true, Heaven was mocked by their engagements—your friends Cobb & Trumbull can testify the infraction of them.[2] I only mention this as one instance of national infamy to prove how much lighter than the least of all conceivable triffles are the faith & honour of the United States: & to shew how little credit their future promises ought to obtain. Should a candid History survive the turbulence & rascality of the times on which we are fallen, Posterity will doubtless stand amazed, while they appreciate the conduct of the age!

I imagine there will be no representation from this State at the Genl Meeting of the Cincinnati unless I attend myself. Should I be disengaged from military affairs in season, I shall probably come on, & may pass the summer at Mt Vernon But every thing depends upon contingencies.

I am sick of public men & public measures—Tranquility & elegant speculations would accord best with my dispositions. It begins to be time for me to think of domestic life if ever I intend it. Indeed, could I find an amiable Lady, with a property which would put one at his ease, & who could like a man circumstanced as I am, I would marry tomorrow.[3]

My best & most respectful Complts attend Mrs Washington & every Soul at Mount Vernon. With sentiments of the sincerest friendship & esteem I have the honor to be my dear General Yours affectionately

D. Humphreys

ALS, DLC:GW. Humphreys marks the letter "(Private)."

1. Humphreys is referring to Henry Knox's letter of 19 March.

2. For GW's "address to Congress, respecting the Gentlemen who had composed my Family" (GW to Knox, 2 June 1784), see note 3 of that document.

3. Humphreys did not find his "amiable Lady" with a sufficient fortune for nearly ten years. On 1 Jan. 1797 he wrote GW from Lisbon: "I have now to disclose to you a prospect of domestic happiness which is just opening for myself. . . . I propose very soon to connect myself for life with a Young Lady of this City. She is the daughter of a Mr John Bulkeley, an eminent Merchant" (DLC:GW). Ann Frances Bulkeley Humphreys remained his wife until his death in 1818.

From Henry Knox

My dear Sir   New York 9 April 1787

I thank you for your kind favor of the second instant which I received by the last post.

Since my last to you, the legislature of Rhode-Island who seem to be unworthy of the rank of freemen, have rejected the proposition of the convention. But this may not be conclusive— The people themselves in that State may take the matter up, of which there is some probability, and send delegates—Connecticut will most probably come into the measure, their legislature being called with that intention—Maryland have resolved to send delegates.

I cannot learn that the delegates of any of the states are fettered with instructions excepting the state of Massachusetts, and the delegates do not I am persuaded consider their instructions of any moment. The present appearances are favorable to a general attendance—and that the delegates will have ample powers to point out radical cures for the present political evils.

It is the general wish that you should attend. It is conceived to be highly important to the success of the propositions of the convention.

The Mass of the people feel the inconveniences of the present government, and ardently wish for such alterations as would remedy them. The alterations must be effected by wisdom and agreement, or by force—this convention appears the only mean to effect the alterations peaceably—If that should be unattended by a proper weight of wisdom and character, so as to carry into execution its propositions, we are to look to events, and force, for arms. were you not then to attend the convention slander and malice might suggest that force would be the most agreable mode of reform to you—When civil commotion rages, no purity of character nor services however exalted, can entirely sheild from the shafts of calumny.

On the other hand the unbounded confidence the people have of Your tried patriotism, and wisdom, would exceedingly facilitate the adoption of any important alterations that might be proposed by a convention of which you were a member, (& as I before hinted) and president.

Your ideas respecting the proceedings of some of the state societies of the Cincinnati are but too just—I will most chearfully meet You in Philadelphia, at any time previous to the meeting that you may think proper, in order to discuss and fully consider this subject.

The french packet has just arrived, by which I have a letter from the Marquis de la Fayette of the 7th of Februa⟨ry⟩.

The Count de Vergennes is dead, and will probably be succeeded by the Duke de Vauguyon.[1]

The Marquis looks forward to military employment in this Country for the reduction of the Western posts, and Canada[,] But one might venture to predict that no such operations will be undertaken, untill the government shall be radically amended. At present we are all imbecillity. I am my dear Sir with the most perfect respect Yr affectionate

H. Knox

ALS, DLC:GW.

1. Vergennes died on 13 Feb. 1787. Paul-François de Quélen, duc de La Vauguyon (1746–1828), French minister in Madrid, was not recalled from Spain and made foreign minister by Louis XVI until 1789.

To Edmund Randolph

My dear Sir,   Mount Vernon April 9th 1787
In reply to your favor of the 2d I have to request that you will not be at the trouble of forwarding any money to me from the treasury.

If I should attend the Service, it will suit me as well to receive it from you in Philadelphia as at this place. If I should not, I have no business with it at all.

It gives me pleasure to find by your letter that there will be so full a representation from this State. If the case had been otherwise I would in emphatical terms have urged again that, rather then depend upon my going, another might be chosen in my place; for as a friend, and in confidence, I declare to you that my assent is given contrary to my judgment; because the act will, I apprehend, be considered as inconsistent with my public declaration dilivered in a solemn manner at an interesting Æra if my life, never more to intermeddle in public matters. This declaration not only stands on the files of Congress, but is I believe registered in almost all the Gazettes and magazines that are published—and what adds to the embarrassment is, I had previous to my appointment, informed by circular letter the several State Societies of the Cincinnati of my intention to decline the Presidency of that order & excused myself from attending the next General meeting at Philadelphia on the first Monday in May—assigning reasons for so doing which apply as well in the one case as the other. Add to these, I very much fear that all the States will not appear in Convention, and that some of them will come fettered so as to impede rather than accelerate the great ends of their calling which, under the peculiar circumstances of my case, would place me in a disagreeable Situation which no other member present would stand in. As I have yielded however to what appeared to be the earnest wishes of my friends, I will hope for the best; and can assure you of the sincere and Affect. regard with which I am Dr Sir yr Obed. Servant

G. Washington

LB, DLC:GW.

To William Gordon

Dear Sir,   Mount Vernon April 10th 1787
I have received your favor of the 13th of July and 28th of Septr.

I am pleased to hear of your safe arrival in London and of the happy meeting with your friends. I wish you success in the publication of your work and that your future establishment (which you say was not then fixed) may be agreeable to your wishes.

The bill which was sent to Rhode Island had the good fortune to come back protested—Mr Watson the drawer immediately gave me another (including interest) upon a Gentlemen in Salem for £43.3.8 ⟨this⟩ Currency, which was forwarded to your friend Mr Mason of Boston and paid.[1]

It is not in my power to give you such accurate information of our Settlements in the Western Country as might answer the purposes of a publication—my own knowlege of it being more general than particular—and information you know is not always to be relied upon—The idea however, of it being made up of ["]the scum and refuse of the Continent, that the people are opposed to Congress—and attached to the British government" is of a piece with other doctrines and consequent publications which have recoiled upon the authors, and which one would think was enough to discourage such unfounded and short sighted reports.

Mrs Washington having of late been much less troubled with the billious cholick than formerly has made no use of the precription you were so obliging as to transmit but is not less thankful on that account for your kind attention to her in this instance and joins me, as does the rest of the family in every good wish for yourself and Mrs Gordon. With great esteem & respect I am Revd Sir yr most Obedt Hble Servt

G. Washington

LB, DLC:GW.
  1. See Benjamin Lincoln, Jr., to GW, 24 Sept. 1786, n.1.

To Benjamin Fitzhugh Grymes

Dear Sir   Mount Vernon Aprl 10th 1787.

Your favor of the 27th ult. was put into my hands the 7th instt; and the same day I sowed, in drills, the Guinea grass you had the goodness to send me.[1] I beg you to accept my thanks for the offer of Potatoes; but fortunately, meeting with a Rhode Island Vessel in pursuit of Fish, I have bartered for a hundred and odd bushels of them, of a very fine kind. The Soil best adapted for Carrots is sandy, or a light loam—If your meadow is of either of these, and not too wet, there can be no question of its yielding this root in grt abundance; and I wish it was in my power to supply you with seed for it; but except a very little which my Gardener saved—the rest (and trifling it is altogether) has been procured by spoonfuls from one or another, as I could beg it. The tryal I made last year of this root was on a very small Scale—& the Season, perhaps, as unfreindly as could have happened; yet I am convinced that in a proper Soil, the culture of Carrots will be found very advantageous for feeding the farm horses, and every species of Stock. By an unlucky mistake of my People, I shall not be able to save Seed against another year, for in topping them (after they were taken up) they cut the head so low, as to prevent their sprouting—I have, consequently, set out but a very small proportion of what I intended for Seed.

In such land as you describe your Meadow to be, 7 feet by 1 may not be too near, otherwise I should be more inclind to a greater width between the Rows, where an intermediate crop is introduced. Upon a large Scale, Carrot Seed from the form of it, will be found tedious & troublesome to drill, unless some mode out of the usual way can be devised, to do it. The Seed ought to be very slightly covered, and the plts not to stand nearer than 8 or 9 Inches in the rows. Thus managed, with the same working the Corn receives, & one hoeing, I am inclined to think that the rows of Carrots will yield five, 8, or I do not know but 10, bushels of Carrots for every one of Corn. I am—Dear Sir Yr Most Obedt Servt

Go: Washington

ALS (photocopy), DLC:GW.
    1. Letter not found, but see Grymes to GW, 14 Mar., and GW to Grymes, 16 March.

To John Lawson

Sir,   Mount Vernon April 10th 1787
    On the 8th Instant Neptune delivered me your letter of the 2d Instant. Although he does not profess to be a workman, yet as he has some little knowledge of Bricklaying—seems willing to learn—and is with a man who understands the business, I will keep him—and this shall be my obligation to pay you the sum for which he sold, at the time and agreeably to the terms of Mr Hunters Sale. I am Sir yr most Obed. Servant

G. Washington.

P.S. Since writing the above, and informing Neptune of my determination to buy him he seems a good deal disconcerted on acct of a wife which he says he has at Mrs Garrards[1] from whom he is unwilling to be so far removed this also embarrasses me as I am unwilling to hurt the feelings of any one—I shall therefore if agreeable to you keep him a while to see if I can reconcile him to the seperation (seeing her now and then) in which case I will purchase him—if not I will send him back, and pay what hire you shall think fit and is reasonable to charge for the time he is here. G.W.

LB, DLC:GW.
    1. Mrs. Garrard may have been the widow of William Garrard of Stafford County who died in 1787.

From William Lee

Dear Sir   Green Spring April 11th 1787
    I have had the honour of receiveing your very obligeing favor of last month, informing me of the very unlucky accident that

befell the Jenny; which I regret exceedingly, not on my own Account, but because it May be a small disappointment to your wishes which I shall ever think myself happy if I can in any manner be the means of promoting.[1]

I feel very sensibly your goodness in offering to accomodate me with the use of one of your Jacks, if I had a Jenny to send to him; unfortunately my stock of those Animals is now reduc'd to one pitifull Jack who may possibly be the means of procureing me some shaby Mules; the one which you are please'd to say shoud be taken care of for me if any Convenient and agreeable Opportunity shoud offer, before it is sent for, may be forwarded to my Brother at Menokin.[2] with the sincerest esteem & highest respect, I have the honor to remain your Mo. obt hble Servant

W. Lee

LS, DLC:GW.

William Lee (1739–1795) of Stratford Hall in 1769 married Hannah Philippa Ludwell of Greenspring in James City County, where they lived until his death.

1. GW's letter to Lee has not been found.

2. Francis Lightfoot Lee (1734–1797) lived at his place, Menokin, in Richmond County.

To John Cannon

Sir,   Mount Vernon April 13th 1787

I have recd your letter of 22d of Jany and as I wish to dispose of my Land near you (as well as the tract in Fayette County) I will with pleasure mention my terms to you, that you may make them known and give assurances of the title upon their being complied with.[1] The Land in Washington County will sell @ 30/ Pensylvania Currency pr Acre (payable in Specie)—one fourth down, and the other ¾ in Annual payments with interest from the date of the Bonds—perhaps a longer time may be granted for the ¾ if the interest is paid punctually. I had much rather sell the whole tract together than to have it divided into Lots— but if a division would facilitate the sale I have no objection, provided the Lots do not interfere with, nor injure the sale of each other & if they sell one with another so as to average the above price for the whole.

As it is my primary object to sell all my lands in that part of the Country, I should not wish to have them leased for any long time, least it should obstruct the sale of them.

I am much obliged to you for your goodness in offering to manage my Land for me in Fayette County; and as Majr Freeman is about to leave that part of the Country I will accept of your kind offer—My terms for that tract are 40/ Pensa Currency pr Acre the payments to be made as above[2]—I have lately had an application for this tract from a Gentlemen in Jersey—and am in daily expectation of his final answer to my terms[3]—this however need not prevent the application of others as I am under no obligation to give the preference to any one, but shall close with the first that comes to my terms—I recd a letter from Mr Smith in Feby mentioning that unless I came upon terms with the defendts it would be best to have the Sherriff execute writs of possession to my Agent before Harvest, that those who had put seed in the Ground might consider it as an obligation confered upon them, to be permitted to take off their Crops—whereas, if writs of possession were not executed, they would take them of course as their right—but, I suppose, as they have become tenants the immediate necessity of this measure is superceded[4]—I know nothing of any promise which Colo. Crawford made of leaving out any part of the land when he surveyed it—the patent was taken out agreeable to his return and cannot now be altered—However, if the Land is sold I will consider Mr Hillis as a preferable purchaser of that piece which runs along his line so as to include his improvements; provided it does not affect the sale of the rest.[5] With great esteem I am Sir yr most Obed: Hbl. Sert

G. Washington

P.S. Inclosed is the form of the writs of Possession as forwarded to me by Mr Smith—if it should be necessary to execute them.[6]

LB, DLC:GW.

1. Cannon's letter of 22 Jan. 1787, in answer to GW's letter of 28 Nov. 1786, has not been found.

2. See GW to Freeman, 28 Nov. 1786, and Freeman to GW, 18 Dec. 1786.

3. See Israel Shreve to GW, 7 April.

4. See Thomas Smith's letter of 17 Feb. 1787 advising GW how he should proceed after winning his Millers Run ejectment suit.

5. William Hillis was one of those who had occupied part of GW's Millers Run tract.

6. See Thomas Smith to GW, 17 Feb., n.2.

To John Rawlins

Sir,   Mount Vernon April 13th 1787.

I have received the freizes for the doors and windows which I think are very pretty together with your letter sent by Capt. Man, but I did not think proper to comply with the contents of it at this time.[1] Altho' it is not my desire to enter into any dispute respecting the payment of the money, yet before I do it I wish you to view the work, that you may, yourself judge of the execution—My sole motive for employing Mr Tharp to execute the common plaster work, and giving a higher price than what I could have had it done for by others, was the expectation, that, agreeable to promise, it would have been done in a masterly manner; but this is not the case—and you would think so yourself, was you to see it—the Stucco work in the Parlour is much cracked and Stained—the plain work in the New Room and in every other part of the House, is in fact but little better than the plaster which was pulled down. Mr Tharp said something should be done to hide the Stains and blemishes, but that it was not proper to do it when he was here—this I expect will be performed. There is likewise wanting to compleat the New Room 6 doz. large hollows—3 doz. dble F.O.G. and 6 feet of fluting—some person was to have been sent by you to decorate the pilasters, which has not yet been done. When the work is compleated and your engagement properly fulfil your will find on my part no inclination to withhold the pay.[2] I am Sir Yr Humble Servant

G. Washington

LB, DLC:GW.

1. Rawlins's letter is dated 10 March.

2. The required work on the New Room was completed during GW's absence at the Federal Convention, and George Augustine Washington paid £45 to Hammond on John Rawlins's order in July. See GW to George Augustine Washington, 1 July, 29 July 1787, n.3, and GW to Johnzee Sellman, 25 Sept. 1787. See also GW to Rawlins, 29 Aug. 1785, n.1.

From Gilliss Polk

Sir   Somerset County [Md.] Apl 14th 1787
   George Digges Esqr. of Prince George's County, Applyed to
me to procure for you, one thousand feet of flooring plank, to
be precisely 24 feet long when dressed, and to be clear of Knots
and Sap,[1] A hard Saying this, however I undertook it, and with
difficulty have procured it, nearly Answering the description,
(after Sawing about twice that quantity) it is Not Perfectly clear
of Knots, but believe Your Carpenter may find one Side of Each
plank to answer Very well, the thickness was not mentioned
to me, I have thought proper to have it Sawed Inch and half,
apprehending that to be Sufficiently thick.
   Mr Digges and I did not agree on any price, as I was Unacquainted with the difficulty of Geting Such Stuff, but can Now
Say I had Rather get four times the quantity of common plank,
the price of common plank of that thickness and quartered is
8/9 clear of freight, the freight is in proportion with Inch plank
at 2/ ℔Ct. The price may appear extravagant as common plank
is at this time Remarcably low, but as I Shou'd be sorry to be
thought Mercenary, Shall be perfectly Satisfyed with Your Setting the price, at What you think Reasonable; the Money you'll
please pay to Capt. Nutter.[2] I am Sir With Singular Esteem yours
to Command.

                                         Gilliss Polk

ALS, DLC:GW.
   1. See George Digges to GW, 5 Jan. 1787, n.1.
   2. GW's reply to Polk's letter has not been found, but see Polk to GW,
20 May.

From Richard Henry Lee

Dear Sir,   Chantilly April 16. 1787
   I have the honor to send you by this opportunity the Act of
Assembly passed in 1772, by which yourself, with me and others,
were appointed Trustees to manage the sale of the Land held in
Tail by Mr Wm Booth and his Lady, and to purchase and settle
other lands to descend as those in Tail would have done. Mr
Booth did long since sell the Intailed Land to Squire Lee of

Maryland, and purchased other land of Colo. Thruston, out of which, I understand, he proposes to settle on his Son a satisfaction for the Land that was intailed.

You will please to observe Sir, that this Act has a suspending Clause, and if it was never assented to, then our right to act in this business has never existed, but Mr Booth the younger (as heir to his Mother) having the Fee simple under the Act of Assembly passed in 1776 for destroying Intails; possesses now the only power to make a conveyance to the purchaser. As these Acts for docking Intails were of a private nature, the persons concerned did formerly interest themselves in such matters, and their Agents in London usually transmitted to them the Assent authenticated. On this plan, Mr Booth may perhaps be in possession of this document, by which alone, it appears, that we can have any right to make a conveyance—If such shall be your opinion, and the Assent be shewn to you; I will most readily, and so undoubtedly will Mr Lee the other surviving Trustee join you in a conveyance whensoever the parties shall desire it, and produce to you a proper assurance from Mr Booth the younger that his father has sufficiently assured him of a full equivalent for the Land the intail of which was dockt.[1]

Mrs Lee & myself join with our daughters in presenting our best respects to Mount Vernon. I have the honor to be dear Sir, with singular respect & esteem your affectionate and obedient servant

Richard Henry Lee

ALS, DLC:GW; copy, DNA: RG 76, Great Britain, Claims under Treaty of Ghent, claim 590.

1. In 1772 William Booth and his wife, Elizabeth Aylett Booth, obtained the passage of an act by the Virginia assembly docking the entail of a 500-acre tract of land at the mouth of Nomini River in Westmoreland County, which had been left to Elizabeth Booth by her grandfather Henry Ashton. The act provided that title to this plantation, called Nominy, would be vested in four trustees, Richard Henry Lee, Richard Lee of Lee Hall, Westmoreland County, GW, and GW's brother John Augustine Washington. The trustees were to sell the land and convey the proceeds to the Booths so that they could buy other land which would go to Elizabeth Booth's heirs at her death. The act was not to go into effect until approved by the king (8 Hening 640–41).

On the same day that Richard Henry Lee wrote to GW, Elizabeth Aylett Booth's heir, William Aylett Booth of Frederick County, Md., wrote the trustees GW and Richard Henry Lee: "Gentlemen I have this day received from my Father Mr William Booth a deed for 350 Acres of land Whereon he now lives in li[e]u of the entailed Land I have therefore to request that you will Make a deed or Conveyence Agreeable to Law to Mr Richard Lee or to his representative, for the land purchesed by him of my Father being the land the entaile of which is docked by Act of Assembly the Said Mr Lee or his representative Satisfying the Payment of the Money to my Father his heirs or Assigns" (DLC:GW). Below Booth's letter Samuel Beall wrote: "Gentlemen I have Lodged Mr Lees Bond with Mr Brooke Beall of George Town. it is assigned to me by Mr Booth on Miss Lee's making payment to my Brother Brooke. his Letter, or Receipt, for the Balance due on said Bond will entitle Mr Lee to a Deed which I shall take as aperticular favour to you to execute agreeable to Act of Assembly." Beall's letter is followed by this notation, in another hand: "Miss Alice Lee is informed that it is doubtful whether the Royal assent was ever grtd to the Act of Assembly here alluded to, in case it was not the right of conveyance is in Mr Booth junr[,] if it was given it is in the trustees. Mr Beall can easily have this resolved & Miss Lee is ready to receive the conveyance from either (as the right shall appear) in behalf of her Brother Richard Lee."

The purchaser of the entailed Booth land, known as Squire Lee, was Richard Lee (c.1707–1787) of Blenheim, Charles County, Maryland. Alice Lee (1748–1789) and Richard Lee, Jr. (d. 1834), were two of his children. Samuel and Brooke Beall were sons of Samuel Beall (c.1713–1788) of Frederick County, Md., who had been a partner of David Ross and Richard Henderson in the Frederick, or Antietam, ironworks. Richard Henry Lee wrote again to GW on 8 July 1788 enclosing a letter from William Aylett Booth (which has not been found) requesting the trustees to convey the Nominy plantation to Richard Lee, Jr. However, since "circumstances" unknown to Booth "renders this improper" (Richard Lee, Jr., had moved to England), Richard Henry Lee reported, the attorney Charles Lee had suggested that Booth give directions for the trustees to convey the property instead to Eleanor Ann Lee (d. 1806), another of Richard Lee, Jr.'s sisters. It was left that the trustees should convey the deed to Eleanor as soon as Booth had given his assent and Brooke Beall had certified "his receipt of the ballance due on this purchase."

From James Madison

Dear Sir   New York April 16 1787

I have been honoured with your letter of the 31 of March, and find with much pleasure that your views of the reform which ought to be pursued by the Convention, give a sanction to those which I have entertained. Temporising applications will dishonor the Councils which propose them, and may foment the internal malignity of the disease, at the same time that they produce an ostensible palliation of it. Radical attempts, although unsuccessful, will at least justify the authors of them.

Having been lately led to revolve the subject which is to undergo the discussion of the Convention, and formed in my mind *some* outlines of a new system, I take the liberty of submitting them without apology, to your eye.[1]

Conceiving that an individual independence of the States is utterly irreconcileable with their aggregate sovereignty: and that a consolidation of the whole into one simple republic would be as inexpedient as it is unattainable, I have sought for some middle ground, which may at once support a due supremacy of the national authority, and not exclude the local authorities wherever they can be subordinately useful.

I would propose as the ground-work that a change be made in the principle of representation. According to the present form of the Union in which the intervention of the States is in all great cases necessary to effectuate the measures of Congress, an equality of suffrage, does not destroy the inequality of importance, in the several members. No one will deny that Virginia and Massts have more weight and influence both within & without Congress than Delaware or Rho. Island. Under a system which would operate in many essential points without the intervention of the State Legislatures, the case would be materially altered. A vote in the national Councils from Delaware, would then have the same effect and value as one from the largest State in the Union. I am ready to believe that such a change will not be attended with much difficulty. A majority of the States, and those of greatest influence, will regard it as favorable to them. To the Northern States it will be recommended by their present populousness; to the Southern by their expected advantage in this respect. The lesser States must in every event yield to the predominant will. But the consideration which particularly urges a change in the representation is that it will obviate the principal objections of the larger States to the necessary concessions of power.

I would propose next that in addition to the present federal powers, the national Government should be armed with positive and compleat authority in all cases which require uniformity; such as the regulation of trade, including the right of taxing both exports & imports, the fixing the terms and forms of naturalization &c. &c.

Over and above this positive power, a negative *in all cases, whatsoever* on the legislative acts of the States, as heretofore exercised by the Kingly prerogative, appears to me to be absolutely necessary, and to be the least possible encroachment on the State jurisdictions. Without this defensive power, every positive power that can be given on paper will be evaded & defeated. The States will continue to invade the national jurisdiction, to violate treaties and the law of nations & to harrass each other with rival and spiteful measures dictated by mistaken views of interest. Another happy effect of this prerogative would be its controul on the internal vicisitudes of State policy; and the aggressions of interested majorities on the rights of minorities and of individuals. The great desideratum which has not yet been found for Republican Governments, seems to be some disinterested & dispassionate umpire in disputes between different passions & interests in the State. The majority who alone have the right of decision, have frequently an interest real or supposed in abusing it. In Monarchies the sovereign is more neutral to the interests and views of different parties; but unfortunately he too often forms interests of his own repugnant to those of the whole. Might not the national prerogative here suggested be found sufficiently disinterested for the decision of local questions of policy, whilst it would itself be sufficiently restrained from the pursuit of interests adverse to those of the whole Society? There has not been any moment since the peace at which the representatives of the Union would have given an assent to paper money or any other measure of a kindred nature.

The national supremacy ought also to be extended as I conceive to the Judiciary departments. If those who are to expound & apply the laws, are connected by their interests & their oaths with the particular States wholly, and not with the Union, the participation of the Union in the making of the laws may be possibly rendered unavailing. It seems at least necessary that the oaths of the Judges should include a fidelity to the general as well as local constitution, and that an appeal should lie to some national tribunals in all cases to which foreigners or inhabitants of other States may be parties. The admiralty jurisdiction seems to fall entirely within the purview of the national Government.

The national supremacy in the Executive departments is liable to some difficulty, unless the officers administering them could be made appointable by the supreme Government. The Militia ought certainly to be placed in some form or other under the authority which is intrusted with the general protection and defence.

A Government composed of such extensive powers should be well organized and balanced. The Legislative department might be divided into two branches; one of them chosen every [   ] years by the people at large, or by the legislatures; the other to consist of fewer members, to hold their places for a longer term, and to go out in such a rotation as always to leave in office a large majority of old members. Perhaps the negative on the laws might be most conveniently exercised by this branch. As a further check, a council of revision including the great ministerial officers might be superadded.

A national Executive must also be provided. I have scarcely ventured as yet to form my own opinion either of the manner in which it ought to be constituted or of the authorities with which it ought to be cloathed.

An article should be inserted expressly guarantying the tranquility of the States against internal as well as external dangers.

In like manner the right of coercion should be expressly declared. With the resources of Commerce in hand, the national administration might always find means of exerting it either by sea or land; But the difficulty & awkwardness of operating by force on the collective will of a State, render it particularly desireable that the necessity of it might be precluded. Perhaps the negative on the laws might create such a mutuality of dependence between the general and particular authorities, as to answer this purpose. Or perhaps some defined objects of taxation might be submitted along with commerce, to the general authority.

To give a new System its proper validity and energy, a ratification must be obtained from the people, and not merely from the ordinary authority of the Legislatures. This will be the more essential as inroads on the *existing Constitutions* of the States will be unavoidable.

The inclosed address to the States on the subject of the Treaty of peace has been agreed to by Congress, & forwarded to the several Executives. We foresee the irritation which it will excite in many of our Countrymen; but could not withold our approbation of the measure. Both, the resolutions and the address, passed without a dissenting voice.[2]

Congress continue to be thin, and of course to do little business of importance. The settlement of the public accounts—the disposition of the public lands, and arrangements with Spain, are subjects which claim their particular attention. As a step towards the first, the treasury board are charged with the task of reporting a plan by which the final decision on the claims of the States will be handed over from Congress, to a select sett of men bound by the oaths, and cloathed with the powers, of Chancellors. As to the Second article, Congress have it themselves under consideration. Between 6 & 700 thousand acres have been surveyed and are ready for sale. The mode of sale however will probably be a source of different opinions; as will the mode of disposing of the unsurveyed residue. The Eastern gentlemen remain attached to the scheme of townships. Many others are equally strenuous for indiscriminate locations. The States which have lands of their own for sale, are *suspected* of not being hearty in bringing the federal lands to market—The business with Spain is becoming extremely delicate, and the information from the Western settlements truly alarming.

A motion was made some days ago for an adjornment of Congress for a short period, and an appointment of Philada for their reassembling. The excentricity of this place as well with regard to E. and West as to N. & South has I find been for a considerable time a thorn in the minds of many of the Southern members. Suspicion too has charged some important votes on the weight thrown by the present position of Congress into the Eastern Scale, and predicts that the Eastern members will never concur in any substantial provision or movement for a proper permanent seat for the national Government whilst they remain so much gratified in its temporary residence. These seem to have been the operative motives with those on one side who were not locally interested in the removal. On the other side the motives are obvious. Those of real weight were drawn from the apparent caprice with which Congress might be reproached, and particularly from the peculiarity of the existing moment. I own that I think so much regard due to these considerations, that notwithstanding the powerful ones on the other side, I should have assented with great repugnance to the motion, and would even have voted against it if any probability had existed that by waiting for a proper time, a proper measure might not be lost for a very long time. The plan which I shd have judged most eligible would have been to fix on the removal whenever a vote could be obtained but so as that it should not take effect until the commencement of the ensuing federal year. And if an immediate removal had been resolved on, I had intended to propose such a change in the plan. No final question was taken in the case. Some preliminary questions shewed that six States were in favor of the motion. Rho. Island the 7th was at first on the same side, and Mr Varnum one of her delegates continues so. His colleague was overcome by the solicitations of his Eastern brethren. As neither Maryland nor South Carolina were on the floor, it seems pretty evident that N. York has a very precarious tenure of the advantages derived from the abode of Congress.

We understand that the discontents in Massts which lately produced an appeal to the sword, are now producing a trial of strength in the field of electioneering. The Governor will be displaced. The Senate is said to be already of a popular complexion, and it is expected the other branch will be still more so. Paper money it is surmized will be the engine to be played off agst creditors both public and private. As the event of the Elections however is not yet decided, this information must be too much blended with conjecture to be regarded as matter of certainty.

I do not learn that the proposed act relating to Vermont has yet gone through all the stages of legislation here; nor can I say whether it will finally pass or not. In truth, it having not been a subject of conversation for some time, I am unable to say what has been done or is likely to be done with it. With the sincerest affection & the highest esteem I have the honor to be Dear Sir Your devoted Servt

Js Madison Jr

ALS, DLC:GW; copy, DLC: Madison Papers.

1. Madison had already given to Gov. Edmund Randolph on 8 April these propositions regarding a new system of government for the United States. Before the Convention GW abstracted Madison's proposals when he made his compilation of the views of Madison, John Jay, and Henry Knox on forming

a new constitution for the country. GW's Notes on the Sentiments on the Government of John Jay, Henry Knox, and James Madison, April 1787, is printed below.

2. Acting on John Jay's report of 13 Oct. 1786 as secretary of foreign affairs in which he conceded the truth of the British foreign minister's charges that individual states had prevented the enforcement of the terms of the Treaty of 1783 regarding the treatment of Loyalists and the collection of British debts, the Congress on 21 Mar. 1787 adopted a series of resolutions condemning such actions by the states and asserting its authority to make treaties "binding on the whole nation" (*JCC*, 31:781–874, 32:124–25). On 13 April Congress ordered the forwarding to the states of an address, or letter, drafted by Jay incorporating the sense of its resolutions of 21 Mar. (ibid., 32:177–84). See also William Grayson to GW, 27 May 1786, n.3.

From John Lawson

Sir   Dumfries April 18th 1787

By yesterdays post I received your favor of the 10th inst., and observe the contents.

Neptune came to me before he set off & made the same objections you mention, which I thought I had fully obviated by informing him that if I sold him to you (which was then uncertain) I had no doubt of your permitting him to visit his Wife at proper times, & that he would with you be employed in work which was much more agreeable to him than the labor I should be obliged to put him to if he remained with me—He then seemed to be perfectly satisfied—Indeed if I were to keep him I might probably be under a necessity of sending him much farther from his Wife than where he now is—I am therefore in hopes he will reconcile himself to his situation & that he will prove useful to you. I am with much Esteem Sir Your most obedient Servt

Jno. Lawson

ALS, DLC:GW.

From William Jackson

My dear General,   [c.20 April 1787]

Flattered by the opinions of some of my friends, who have expressed a wish that I would offer myself a Candidate for the

Office of Secretary to the fœderal Convention—I presume to communicate to you my intention—and to request (so far as you shall deem it consonant with the more important interests of the Public) your influence in procuring me the honor of that appointment.[1]

To say more on this subject would be to offend against that generous friendship, which I am persuaded, if held compatible with the service of our Country, will prompt an active goodness in my favor. With the most respectful affection I am, my dear General, Your obedient Servant

W. Jackson

ALS, DLC:GW. GW docketed the undated letter: "recd 24th Apr. 1787."

1. Jackson was elected secretary of the Convention when it was organized on 25 May. For a description of Jackson's unsatisfactory journal, or minutes, of the Federal Convention, see Farrand, *Records of the Federal Convention*, 1:xi–xiv.

To Edward Newenham

Dear Sir,   Mount Vernon April 20th 1787

Not till Within these few days have I been honoured with your favours of the 13th and 25th of November last I should if they had come to hand sooner been earlier in my acknowledgment of them.[1]

I sincerely wish that this letter may find Miss Newenham in a perfectly recovered State of health, and Lady Newenham and yourself relieved from those anxious cares and sollicitudes which her indisposition must natterally have created. I hope also that neither this, nor any thing else, will prevent you from fulfilling your long intended voyage to America. should this event take place at so early a period as your last letters indicated any information on the points you have referred to me will hardly arrive in season. yet, as there is a possibility of it, the enclosed, which I have obtained from a well informed Gentleman in Alexandria—(more conversant in matters of this kind than I am)—will answer your queries with respect to the sorts of linnens which are most saleable in our Markets[2]—The prices of provisions is governed by the Seasons, and quality—generally—Beef and Mutton from the month of January till June fluctuates from 4d. to 6d.—from June till January from 2½d. to 4d.—Veal and

Lamb are commonly sold by the Quarter the latter from 2/6 to 4/ the other in proportion to the age and quality of the Meat. These prices you will please to observe are in the Currency of *this* State which by the *legal* exchange is 33⅓ worse than Sterling. Bills however are negotiated at 40 pr Ct and have been so for sometime, which will enable you to determine whether money, or letters of creadit, will answer your purposes best. the former would give least trouble, tho' there is some risk—Bills on London are in more general demand, and consequently command the best prices.

The manner in which you employ your time at Bell champ[3] (in rasing nurseries of fruit, forest trees, and shrubs) must not only contributes to your health & amusement, but it is certainly among the most rational avocations of life for what can be more pleasing, than to see the work of ones own hands, fostered by care and attention, rising to maturity in a beautiful display of those advantages and ornaments which by the Combination of Nature and taste of the projector in the disposal of them is always regaling to the eye at the sametime in their seasons they are a grateful to the palate.

I should have much pleasure in admiring your skill in the propogation and desposal of these things in a visit to Bell Champ. but declining health and an anxious wish to spend the remainder of my days in retirement will fix me to Mount Vernon and a small circle round it whilst I tread on this Theatre.

I will not give you the trouble of receiving a long letter from me at this time because the probability, I think is, that you will have left Ireland before it can get thither—I shall only add therefore that it was with pain I gave the information containing in my last respecting the application for the Consulship at Marsaillis the Inclosures which I transmitted would account for the disappointment and though to be regretted in the present case the principle deserves more to be applauded than condemned for few things being in the gift of Congress it was thought that such as could dispose of ought to be given to those who had suffered in the service of their Country during the late contest and a resolution to that effect having taken place that body which for the sake of consistency was obleged to adhear to it.[4] I beg to be presented in respectful terms to Lady Newingham—

and have the honor to be with great esteem and regard. Dr Sir yr most Obed. Hble Servt

G. Washington

LB, DLC:GW. ALS listed in *American Book Prices Current,* 71 (1985), 985.

1. Neither letter has been found.

2. The enclosure has not been found.

3. Bell Champ was Newenham's seat outside Dublin.

4. See Newenham to GW, 12 Aug. 1786, and GW to Newenham, 10 Mar. 1787.

From Robert Morris

Dear Sir   Philad[elphi]a April 23d 1787

The Public Papers have announced Your consent to serve as a Member of the Convention to be held in this City.[1] this is what I ardently wished for & I am truely rejoiced at it—I was only restrained from writing to you by Motives of delicacy, thinking that your own judgement rather than the perswasion of Friends ought to determine. I hope Mrs Washington will come with you & Mrs Morris joins me in requesting that you will on your arrival come to our House & make it your Home during your Stay in this City. We will give You as little trouble as possible and endeavour to make it agreable, it will be a charming season for Travelling, and Mrs Washington as well as yourself will find benefit from the Journey Change of Air &c. As I hope soon for the pleasure of seeing you I will only add that you must not refuse our request & the honor you confer by acceptance shall ever be considered as a great favour.[2]

Our New Bishop brought the enclosed letter from England, He desired me to forward it & to present his most respectfull Compts.[3] I am Dear Sir Your most obedt & humble Servant

Robt Morris

ALS, DLC:GW.

1. On Saturday, 21 April 1787, the *Pennsylvania Packet, and Daily Advertiser* (Philadelphia) printed a dispatch from Richmond, Va., dated 11 April: "It is with peculiar satisfaction we inform the public, that our illustrious fellow citizen, GEORGE WASHINGTON, Esq. has consented to serve on the ensuing federal convention to be held in Philadelphia the second Monday in May next: and that his Excellency Edmund Randolph, Esq. proposes leaving this City early in that month, on the same business."

2. GW on 5 May refused Morris's invitation, but upon his arrival in Phila-delphia on Sunday, 13 May, he was persuaded by the Morrises "to lodge with them" (*Diaries*, 5:155). He continued to live in the Morrises' house on the south side of Market Street below Sixth Street throughout his stay in Philadelphia.

3. The letter from England has not been identified. The "new Bishop" was William White (1748–1836), the brother of Morris's wife, Mary.

From David Humphreys

My dear General   Hartford [Conn.] April 25th 1787
Mr Rogers, who will have the honor of delivering this letter, is an American Gentleman with whom I became acquainted in London. Being of Massachusetts he was introduced to me by Mr Adams, and appeared to be upon terms of intimacy with that Minister. Afterwards I had the pleasure of being a fellow Passen-ger from Europe with Mr & Mrs Rogers: & considered myself under many obligations for their courtesy & politeness in allevi-ating the tediousness of confinement at Sea.

Mr Rogers proposes, in passing thro' Virginia, to wait upon your Excellency at Mount Vernon. In that case, I beg leave to commend him to your attention and hospitality.[1] My best & most affectionate regards attend the whole family. I hope to be with them in all the month of May—in the mean time. I have the honor to be Your sincere friend & Hble Servant

D. Humphreys

ALS, owned (1971) by Mr. John Rogers, New Canaan, Connecticut.

1. Daniel Denison Rogers (1751–1825) of Exeter, N. H., became a successful Boston merchant. In 1781 he married Abigail Bromfield (d. 1791), the daugh-ter of another Boston merchant, and in 1782 took his wife abroad for her health. After they returned from England to Boston in 1787, Rogers's business affairs often led him south to Virginia and the Carolinas.

From John Lawson

Sir   ⟨Dumfr⟩ies 25th April 1787
Your favor of the 17th is now before me, & this day only Nep-tune made his appearance he says his only reason for coming away in the manner he did was to avoid being Sold at So great a distance from his Wife; at the Same time he says he is very

willing to be hired to you—I have therefore Sent him up again that you may, if it Suits you, keep him or hire by the Month or Year as you may chuse & on Such wages as are reasonable of which you will be a better judge than myself. I am respectfully Sir Your mo: obt Servt

Jno. Lawson

ALS, DLC:GW. The letter was sent "By Neptune."

From Clement Biddle

Phil[adelphia] April 26. 87.

By the Sloop Dolphin Capt. Steward who sailed last week for Alexandria I have shipp'd the scythes & Spinning wheels of which acct & bill of loading are inclosed the Scythe Maker could get only one of the Briar Scythes finished in time[1]—I gave Capt. Steward the necessary Certificate of these articles being the Manufacture of this State to save the duties—very few vessels loading for the west Indies occasioned but little demand for the Herrings & I was obliged to put them in Store & as new Herrings were plenty & I could get no more than 20/ ℔ Barrel I have sold them at that price but being just deliver'd I have not time to make up & inclose the amount of Sales—I received £3.16.5 paper money for Interest in your Certificate which is to your Credit.

Your favour Covering a Letter for Col. Ste. Bayard at Pittsburg came to hand just as a Mr Parker was seting off for there who took it in Charge & promised to deliver it with Care[2]—But few Linens have arrived lately & they cannot be had low but I should expect rather lower than with you—one of our China vessels having arrived at new york & 3 others expected there, & here in a few days we may on their arrival probably get the best Fresh Hyson Tea @ 10 ℔ lb. & that which is called Gun Powder at about 12/ or 13/ Indeed we may Count on all Kinds of China Goods being low as the Accounts of the success of the vessels in this Trade are very Promising Double refined sugar is @ 17d. ℔ lb. by the Cwt—there is but little white & redd lead for Sale in the spring vessels from London[.] Bristol & Holland have only two arrived and several are Hourly Expected—Mrs Biddle begs to present her Compliments to you & Mrs Washington—I am Dr Genl &c.

C. Biddle

ADfS, ViMtV: Clement Biddle Letter Book.

1. Biddle's copy of his "Invoice of Sundries shipp'd on board Sloop Dolphin Capt. Steward for Alexandr. for His Excy Genl Washington Mt Vernon" reads:

1 dozen Cradling Scythes	4.12. 0
1 doz. Grass Scythes	3.10. 0
1 Briar Scythe	0. 5.10
2 Spinning wheells	2. 5. 0
	10.12.10
Commission 2½ Cet	0. 5. 4
	£10.18. 2

2. GW's letter to Stephen Bayard has not been found, but see GW to John Cannon, 16 Sept. 1787. Mr. Parker is the Alexandria merchant Josiah Parker. Stephen Bayard, who served as an officer in the Pennsylvania forces during the Revolution and was brevetted colonel in 1783, formed a partnership after the war with Isaac Craig to carry on a mercantile business in Pittsburgh.

From David Griffith

Dear Sir,   Fairfax Glebe 26th Apl 1787
Being under the necessity of immediately discharging some claims against me, I am obliged to call upon my friends for their subscriptions to enable me to avoid a threatning difficulty—My Son waits on you for yours due for the last year, and you will oblige me greatly in discharging it. The Gallery being not yet compleated, no demand has hitherto been made of Pew rent— It has been determined that the Ministers support should remain upon the former footing until that event takes place, which I flatter myself will happen in the course of a very few weeks.[1] With respectful compliments to Mrs Washington, I am Dr Sir, Your most obedt & very huble Servant

David Griffith

ALS, DLC:GW.

1. The subscription, which was the annual payment parishioners made for the minister's support, was soon to be replaced by pew rent. See Griffith to GW, 31 Mar. 1788, n.1. Griffith had sons named David and Richard.

From Battaile Muse

Andrew Wales's Alexandria

Honourable Sir, april 26th 1787

I have at this place three Casks of good Salt Butter weight, 55 lb. 55 do 56 do amount 166 lb. @ 10d. ℔ lb. If you are in want Please To Send me word by Eight oclock Tomorrow at this place whether you will Take it—it's the Property of Colo. Fairfaxes and made at my House To Prove it's Quality I have this day had It Inspected by Mr Thorn & others who assert that it's good[1]— I am disapointed in receiveing money at this place therefore I shall not have it in my Power To Let You have but a small Sum if any before I return, I shall wait on you next week. I am your obedient Humble Servt

Battaile M. Muse

ALS, DLC:GW.

1. Battaile Muse was also rental agent for George William Fairfax's Shenandoah Valley lands. "Mr Thorn" is probably the Alexandria merchant Michael Thorn.

To Henry Knox

My dear Sir, Mount Vernon 27th Aprl 1787.

After every consideration my judgment was able to give the subject, I had determined to yield to the wishes of many of my friends who seemed extremely anxious for my attending the Convention, which is proposed to be holden in Philadelphia the second Monday of May. And tho' so much afflicted with a rheumatic complaint (of which I have not been entirely free for Six months) as to be under the necessity of carrying my arm in a sling for the last ten days, I had fixed on Monday next for my departure, and had made every necessary arrangement for the purpose when (within this hour) I am summoned by an express who assures me not a moment is to be lost, to see a mother, and *only* Sister (who are supposed to be in the agonies of death) expire; and I am hastening to obey this melancholy call, after having just bid an eternal farewell to a much loved Brother who was the intimate companion of my youth and the most affectionate friend of my ripened age.

This journey (of more than one hundred miles) in the disordered State of my body will, I am persuaded, unfit me for the intended trip to Philadelphia, & assuredly prevent me from offering that tribute of respect to my compatriots in arms which result from affection and gratitude for their attachment to, and support of me upon so many trying occasions.

For this purpose it was, as I had, tho' with a good deal of reluctance, consented (from a conviction that our affairs were verging fast to ruin, to depart from the resolution I had taken, of never more stepping out of the walks of private life) to serve in this Convention that I determined to shew my respect to the Genl meeting of the Society, by coming to Philadelphia during its sitting—As the latter is prevented, and the highest probability the other will not take place, I send such papers as have, from time to time come to my hands, and may require inspection and the consideration of the Cincinnati, to your care.

An apology for the order in whh they are sent is highly necessary, and my present situation is the best I can offer. Tomorrow I had determined to set a part for the inspection & arrangement of them, that such only, or the parts as were fitting, might be laid before the Society; for unless I had time to go over them again with a person who understands the French language, I am not even certain that all of what I send may relate to the affairs of the Cincinnati, and certain I am that some are too personal—the sending of which will not, I hope, be ascribed to improper motives, when the *only* one I had (as I am in the moment of my departure from home, and uncertainty with respect to the time of returning to it) is, that nothing which has been referred to me may be with-held—In the jumbled order you receive these papers I send them to Doctr Craik in Alexandria, to be forwarded by a safe hand in the Stage to Philadelphia.[1]

I make a tender of my affectionate regards for the members who may constitute the General meeting of the Society, and with sentiments of the highest esteem I am—My dear Sir Yr Obedt Hble Servt

Go: Washington

ALS, DSoCi; LB, DLC:GW.

1. GW went down to Fredericksburg on this day. The tutor William Fogg wrote from Fredericksburg: "Genl Washington has been here to see his Mother who has been ill . . . the Genl is much altered in his person one arm

swung with Rheumatism—his whole Conversation is upon Agriculture" (type-script of a letter, misdated 12 April 1787, to an unidentified person, at one time in the possession of Mr. Robert Lull, Newburyport, Massachusetts). Finding both Mary Washington and Betty Lewis "better than I expected," GW returned home on 30 April. He did not set out for Philadelphia until 10 May. The Society of the Cincinnati began its General Meeting on 7 May in Philadelphia. GW did not attend any of its sessions after his arrival in the city on 13 May. He did, however, dine on 15 May with the members of the society who were attending and on 18 May accepted reelection to its presidency, with the proviso that the duties of the office would "be executed by the Vice President" (*Diaries*, 5:144, 157; GW to d'Annemours, 20 Feb. 1789). See also Myers, *Liberty without Anarchy*, 95–97 and 116, n.22.

To Henry Knox

My dear Sir　　　　　　　　　　Mount Vernon 27th Aprl 1787

Hurried as I am I cannot (not expecting to see you in Philadelpa) withhold the copy of a Paragraph in a letter which came to my hands yesterday from Mr Jefferson, and a translation of the article "Cincinnati" from the Encyclopedie Methodique; forwarded to me by the same Gentleman as they relate to the Society & serve to shew the light in wch it is viewed in France.

I do not know what the Article from the Encyclopedie Methodique contains as it is in French further than from the purport of Mr Jeffersons letter—and being received but yesterday it could not be translated previous to my departure but have desired a Gentleman who lives in my family to do it and have left this letter to be sent with it.[1]

In my present state of mind I can hardly form an opinion whether it will be best to lay the matter before the Society as coming from Mr Jefferson or as from a person of as good information as any in France—I must therefore leave it wholly with you to do as you may think most proper. You know my sentiments from the proceedings of the last General meeting and from my Circular letter. In haste I am yr Affecte Servt

Go: Washington

ALS, NNGL: Knox Papers; LB, DLC:GW.

1. Presumably GW copied for Knox all of the very long second paragraph in Thomas Jefferson's letter to GW of 14 Nov. 1786. In this passage Jefferson describes his role in the writing of the article highly critical of the Society of the Cincinnati for Démeunier's *Encyclopédie Méthodique* and writes to GW of

"the mass of evil which flows from this fatal source," "a curse," "this germ of destruction." The "translation" of the encyclopedia article which was to be made at Mount Vernon by Tobias Lear and enclosed in this letter has not been found.

From George Lee

Sir, Poplar Hill [Md.] 28th April [17]87
By Mr T. Hanson I have sent you a small quantity of the great longsided scots cabbage seed[1]—It shd be sown so as to have your plants about the middle, or latter end of June, to transplt in rows of rather more than the common distance in gardens—for if the ground is duly & properly prepared, they will (propitious seasons following) grow much larger & of course occupy a much large[r] space than any other plant of the same species. These cabbages are intended cheifly for the feed of Cattle in the Winter season, when all kinds of green food are become scarce—& if the Climate shou'd suit them—as I hope it may—I am satisfied great advantages may be derived from the culture of them. I am Sir Your obedt Servt

Geo. Lee

P.S. Mrs Lee joins me in Compts to your Lady—Major Washington & his Lady—G. Lee

ALS, DLC:GW.
George Lee (1736–1807), a planter of Prince Georges and Charles counties in Maryland, was a son of Philip Lee (c.1681–1744) of Prince Georges County. He was married to Chloe Hanson Lee (1743–c.1807), daughter of Samuel Hanson (1716–1794) of Charles County, Maryland.
1. Thomas Hawkins Hanson Lee (1750–1810) of Prince Georges County, Md., was the brother of Samuel Hanson of Samuel, who lived in Alexandria, and also of George Lee's wife Chloe.

From Henry Lee

Dear Sir Leesylvania April 28th 1787
I have Sent you by my Servant One bushel of Italian forward black eyed Peas they were first brought into this Country by Mr Madza on James river they are the best Sort of Pea of the kind.[1] I am Sorry to hear you have an Attack of the Rheumatizm I have

been Severely afflicted with it, this Winter & Spring tho' I am now able to ride out—otherwise I should have paid my respects to you at Mount Vernon before this—with my best respects to Mrs Washington I am Most respectfully Yr Excellencys Most Obt hble servt

H. Lee

ALS, DLC:GW.

Henry Lee of Prince William County died later in this year.

1. "Mr Madza" was Philip Mazzei.

From La Luzerne

Sir, [c. April 1787]

The hopes which I have entertained for this year past of revisiting America has prevented me from writing to your Excellency of late. An ill state of health obliged me to postpone my return to America which was to have been in the spring of 1786. The Physicians advised me to take the Spa waters for the reestablishment of my health, & I find it has benefitted me. I flatter myself I shall be able to pay my respects to you at Mt Vernon the approaching summer.

Here follows a sentence the writing of which is so blind that I cannot give it a literal translation, but the import of it is—*he should be very happy to see Genl Washington in France where he might enjoy the esteem of the prince & the affections of the people.*[1]

We have learnt with great satisfaction that the convention which met at Annapolis passed resolutions to enable Congress to pay the interest of the debt, & to gave stability & regularity to your commercial concerns: it is much to be wished that the deputies, who are to meet at Philadelphia in the month of may, would give a finishing stroke to this important business. It is really painful to the friends of America, and especially to those who have been witnesses to the courage & fortitude which united so extensive a people in the defence of their liberty, to see a nation which justly merits the esteem & veneration of the Universe, lose the good opinion of the world by not complying with engagements which the smalest nation would consider as easy to be fulfilled. I entertain too good an opinion of the disposition of the people and the probity of the representatives not to be convinced, that one day or other, we shall see them decide justly & firmly upon this important point; but I fear that these resolutions may come too late to prevent those prejudices which the principle nations in Europe will imbibe & which will not be easily eradicated.

It appears that your negotiations with the Emperor of Moroco have been brought to a favorable close by Mr Berkley; it is said that the Americans are to be treated in all the ports of that Empire upon the same footing with the most favored nations. The Barbarians are now the only nation in a state of war—all the rest are in a profound peace. Russia & the Turks are very much opposed in their interests with respect to the Crimée,[2] but they seem to content themselves with frequent threatenings. The dispute between Holland and the Emperor is finally decided; but the intestine divisions which agitiate that republick are more dangerous to them than any thing else. The spirit of party has been carried to such a pitch that it is feared these republicans cannot long be at peace, each party wishes to raise themselves & oppress their opponents. I earnestly pray that you may never see parties of a similar nature in America; the Americans have too much good sense & discernment not to perceive that their safety & happiness depends upon their Union. It seems to me that you must be the means of cementing the Union of a great people, to whom your virtues, more than any other cause, have procured liberty.

It is a part of my constant prayer that that life which has been exerted in the cause of humanity may be long & happy, & that I may have frequent opportunities to prove to your Excellency the perfect esteem & respect with which I have the honor to be Sir Your most obedt & Hble Servt

de la luzerne

Permit me to take this opportunity of presenting my respects to Madam Washington.

Translation, DLC:GW; translation, DLC:GW; ALS, in French, DLC:GW. The second translation appears to be in Elizabeth Powel's hand. The ALS has been transcribed for CD-ROM:GW. GW docketed both translations; the more accurate of the two is printed here.

1. La Luzerne wrote: "jeusse été bien plus heureux de vous voir en france jouir de l'estime et de la consideration d'un prince, & d'une nation a la qu'elle vous etes cher a tout de titres, et qui auroit fait un bonheur de vous possêder.

mais il faut respecter les raisons de votre excellence, et se borner au bonheur de le revoir en amerique."

2. After "Crimée," La Luzerne wrote "et au Cubán." Kuban is the area near the Sea of Azov annexed by Catherine in 1783.

Notes on the Sentiments on the Government of John Jay, Henry Knox, and James Madison

[c. April 1787]

Mr Jay

Does not think the giving any further powers to Congress will answer our purposes. for among reasons,

Because some of the members will have partial & personal purposes in View; which, and ignorance—prejudice and interested views of others will always embarrass those who are well disposed.

Because Secrecy and dispatch will be too uncommon—and foreign as well as local interests will frequently oppose, and sometimes frustrate the wisest measures.

Because large assemblies often misunderstand, or neglect, the obligations of character, honor & dignity; and will collectively do, or omit things which an Individual Gentleman in his private capacity would not approve—reasons &ca.

The Executive business of Sovereignty depending on so many Wills, and those Wills moved by such a variety of contradictory motives & inducements will in general be but feebly done—and

Such a Sovereign, however theoretically responsible cannot be effectually so in its departments & Officers, without adequate Judicatories.

He therefore—

Does not promise himself any thing very desirable from any change which does not divide the Sovereignty into its proper departments—Let Congress Legislate—let others execute—Let others judge.

Proposes—

A Govr Genl limited in his prerogatives and duration. That Congress should be divided into an upper & lower house. The former appointed for life—The latter annually—That the Govr General (to preserve the Ball[anc]e) with the advice of a Council formed for that *only* purpose of the great judicial Officers, have a negative on their acts.

What powers should be granted to the Government so constituted is a question which deserves much thought—The more however, he thinks the better—The *States* retaining only so much as may be necessary for domestic purposes—And all their principal Officers Civil and Military being Commissioned and removal by the National Government.

Questions the policy of the Convention because it ought to have originated with, & the proceedings be confirmed by the People—the only source of Just authority.

General Knox

It is out of all question that the foundation of the Government must be of republican principles—but so modified & wrought together that whatever shall be erected thereon should be durable & efficient—He speaks entirely of the federal Government— or what would be better—one *government* instead of an association of Governments.

Were it possible to effect, a government of this kind—It might [be] constituted of an assembly or lower house chosen for one, 2 or three years—A Senate chosen for 5, Six or Seven years— and the Executive under the title of Governor General, chosen by the Assembly & Senate for the term of Seven years but liable to an impeachment of the lower house and triable by the Senate.

A judicial to be appointed by the Governor General during good behaviour, but impeachable by the lower house and triable by the Senate.

The Laws passed by the General Government to be obeyed by the local governments and if necessary to be enforced by a body of armed men.

All national objects to be designed and executed by the Genl Government without reference to the local governments.

This is considered as a government of the least possible powers to preserve that federated government—To attempt to establish less will be to hazard the existence of republicanism, and to subject us to division of the European powers or to a despotism arising from high handed Commotions.

Mr Madison

Thinks an individual independence of the States utterly irreconcilable with their aggregate Sovereignty. And that a consolidation of the whole into one simple republic would be as inexpedient as it is unattainable. He therefore proposes a middle ground, which may at once support a due supremacy of the national authority, & not exclude the local authorities whenever they can be subordinately useful.

As the ground work, he proposes that a change be mad[e] in the principle of representation—and thinks there would be no great difficulty in effecting it.

Next, that in addition to the present federal power the national governmt should be armed with positive & compleat authority in all cases which require uniformity; such as the regulation of trade, including the right of taxing both exports & imports, the fixing the terms & forms of naturalization &ca &ca.

Over and above this positive power, a negative *in all cases* whatever on the legislative acts of the states as heretofore exercised by the Kingly prerogative appears to him absolutely necessary ⟨&⟩ to be the least possible encroachment on the state Jurisdictions—without this defensive power he Conceives that every positive [power] which can be given on Paper will be evaded. reasons, see them.

The Controul over the Laws would prevent the internal viscissitudes of State policy and the aggressions of interested Majorities.

The national supremacy ought also to be extended he thinks to the Judiciary departments—the oaths of the Judges should at least, include a fidelity to the General as well as local constitution—and that an appeal should be to some national tribunals in all cases to which foreigners or Inhabitants of other States may be parties. The Admiralty Jurisdictions, to fall entirely within the purview of the Natl governmt.

The National Supremacy in the Executive departments is liable to some difficulty, unless the Officers administering them could be made appointable by the Supreme Government. The Militia ought entirely to be placed in some form or other under the authority which is entrusted with the general protection and defence.

A government composed of such extensive powers should be well organized and ballanced.

The Legislative department might be divided into two branches, one of them chosen every [   ] years, by the People at large, or by the Legislatures; the other to consist of fewer Members, to hold their places for a longer term, and to go out on such a rotation as always to leave in office a large Majority of old Members.

Perhaps the Negative on the Laws might be most conveniently exercised by this branch.

As a further check, a Council of revision including the great Ministerial Officers might be super added.

A National Executive must also be provided. He has scarcely ventured as yet to form his own opinion either of the manner in which it ought to be constituted, or of the authorities with which it ought to be cloathed.

An article should be inserted expressly guarantying the tranquility of the States against internal as well as external dangers.

In like manner the right of Coercion should be expressly declared, with the resources of Comm⟨erce in hand⟩, the national administration might always find means of exerting it either by Sea or land; But the difficulty and awkwardness of operating by force on the Collective will of a State, render it particularly desireable that the necessity of it might be precluded—Perhaps the Negative on the Laws will create such a mutuality of dependance—between General & particular authorities, as to answer or perhaps some defined objects of taxation might be submitted along with Commerce to the genl authority.

To give a new system its proper validity and energy ratification must be obtained from the people and not merely from the ordinary authority of the Legislatures. This will be the more essential as inroads on the *existing Constitutions* of the States will be unavoidable.

AD, DLC:GW. On the cover GW labels this: "⟨Sentiments⟩ of Mr Jay—Genl Knox and Mr Madison on a form of Governmt previous to the General Convention held at Philadelphia in May 1787."

GW wrote this memorandum after receiving James Madison's letter of 16 April and probably before leaving Mount Vernon on 9 May, certainly before the opening of the Convention on 25 May. His "Notes" on the ideas of the three men about a reformed government for the American Union are in fact précis, or summaries, of letters that he received from each: from John Jay, 7 Jan. 1787, from Henry Knox, 14 Jan. 1787, and from Madison, 16 April 1787.

From Essarts

May 1st 1787.

It is well known to all the world that your Excellency, after having fought for the liberty of the thirteen States, like a true Fabius, supported with an indefatigable zeal those laws & establishments which might tend to advance the happiness of your Country. Admiring your virtues, I am persuaded that the inclinations of a great man will not be averse to the reading of the works of one of the best of Citizens, a citizen who consecrated his life & fortune to the purposes of humanity & to the establishment of pure & refined manners.

My attachment to this tender parent & virtuous man induces me to promote his views as much as is in my power by collecting & publishing his different memoirs. Your Excellency will permit me to present you a copy as a tribute due to your patriotic virtues.[1] I have the honor to be respectfully Yr most Hble & obedt Servt

La Comptess des Essarts

Translation, in the hand of Tobias Lear, DLC:GW; ALS, in French, NN: Washington Collection. The ALS has been transcribed for CD-ROM:GW.

1. GW wrote the comtesse des Essarts on 8 Jan. 1788 acknowledging her gift: "Madam, I have received your letter of the first of may and the books accompanying it which you did me the honor to send me.

"The works of those men who have dedicated their time and fortunes to the purposes of humanity will always be read with pleasure by the good and virtuous citizens of every country, as they contain the pure sentiments of a noble mind divested of local prejudices & particular attachments. I must therefore beg, Madam, that you will accept of my warmest acknowledgments for the favor you have conferred by sending me the works of M. de Chamousset. I have the Honor to be Madam Yr Most Obedt Hble Servant. G. Washington" (LB, DLC:GW). The chevalier Claude-Humbert Piarron de Chamousset (1717–1773), who turned his house in Paris into a charity hospital, was a reformer with a particular interest in public health and child welfare. The two-volume *Œuvres Complètes* which his daughter edited and published in Paris in early 1787 was in GW's library at the time of his death (Griffin, *Boston Athenæum Collection*, 483). On 5 April 1787 Madame des Essarts's husband, Pierre Poinsot des Essarts, comte de Bouville, wrote Thomas Jefferson saying that he wished to send a copy of a relative's writings to GW and asking for GW's coat of arms (Boyd, *Jefferson Papers*, 11:270).

Letter not found: to Gilliss Polk, 2 May 1787. Polk wrote GW on 20 May: "I Received your letter of the 2d May."

From Lafayette

My dear General   Paris May the 5th 1787

Altho' I Cannot omit an opportunity of writing to You, my letter will not Be so long and Minuted as I would like to make it, Because of the Constant Hurry of Business occasioned By the Assembly—every day, Sundays excepted, is taken up with General Meetings, Committee's, and smaller Boards—it is a pretty extraordinary sight at Versailles, the more so as great deal of patriotism and firmness Has Been displayed.

From the time of this King's Arrival to the throne, the expences of the treasury Have Been encreased of about two Hundred french Millions a Year—But it went at such a Rate Under M. de Calonne, that, Having Got a Monstrious deficiency, and knowing not How to fill it up, He persuaded the King to assemble Notable persons of each order, to please them with a plan of assemblies in each province which was much desired, and to get their Approbation for New taxes, with which He durst not By Himself saddle the Nation.

The Assembly was very properly choosen, Both for Honesty abilities, and personal Consequence—But M. de Calonne's much depended on His own powers of speaking, and intriguing, as well as on the King's Blind Confidence in Him, and all His plans—we were not the Representatives of the Nation—But Have Been supported By their partiality to us.

Calonne's plan of a provincial assembly Has Been Amended By us—His plan of a tax in kind was Rejected—it Has Been the Case with several other projects—some others were altered for the Better, and sometimes new ones substituted—and we declared that, altho' we Had no Right to impede, it was our Right not to advise unless we thought the measures were proper—and that we Could not think of New taxes unless we Knew the Returns of expenditure and the plans of Œconomy.[1]

The More we entered into the Business, the less possible it was for the Ministry to do without us—to the Assembly the public looked up, and Had the Assembly Been dismissed the Credit was gone—as we were going to separate for the easter days, I made a motion to inquire into Bargains By which, Under pretence of exchanges, millions Had Been lavished upon princes and favourites—the Bishop of langres seconded my Motion—it was thought proper to intimidate Us, and the King's Brother told in His Majesty's name that such motions ought to Be signed—upon which I signed the inclosed.[2]

M. de Calonne went up to the King to ask I should Be Confined to the Bastille—an oratory Battle was Announced Betwen us for the next Meeting, and I was getting the proofs of what I Had advanced—When Calonne was Overthrown from His post, and so our dispute ended—except that the King and family, and the Great Men about Court, some friends excepted, don't forgive me for the liberties I Have taken, and the success it Had Among the other Classes of the people.

M. de Calonne's successor was M. de fourqueux an old man who lasted But a fortnight—and now we Have Got the Arch-Bishop of toulouse at the Head of affairs—a Man of the Most UpRight Honesty and shining Abilities—M. de villedeuil, a Clever man, will act Under Him, and we may Consider the Arch Bishop as a prime Minister.[3]

We are going to Have good Houses of Representatives in each province, not to vote the taxes, But to divide them—we Have got the King to make Reductions and improvements to the Amount of forty millions of livres a year—we are proposing the means to insure a Better, and more public method of Administration—But will Be obliged in the end to make loans and lay taxes—the Assembly Have acted with firmness and patriotism— the walls of Versailles Had never Heard so many Good things— and our meeting, particularly in the alarming situation of affairs, when the kingdom was driving a way like phaëton's Cart, will Have proved very Beneficial.

I Have Been much Hurt to Hear that the unpaid interest of the American debt was Considered as a very uncertain Revenue—I said every thing that was proper on the subject—But Could not prevent that Being Considered as a fact which Hitherto Has proved But too true—full justice Has Been done to the security of the Capital—But the ponctuality of the interest Has Been Animadverted upon.

M. de Calonne's letter Has met with some difficulties from the farmers which are going to be settled—so that the Merchants Need not Be Uneasy[4]—the Cloud that was gathering on the Turks and Russians is for the moment clearing up.

My Health Has Been deranged During the assembly—So far

as to endanger a little my Breast—But a good Regimen, and a little patience, without interrupting public Business, Have got me in a very fair way—inclosed is a Copy of my signed motion which I find in a newspaper—I would Have translated it, But you will very easely Have it done—when the opinions of the several Committees will Be printed, I shall send them to America.

My most affectionate Respects and those of madame delafayette and family wait on Mrs Washington and you my dear general—Remember me to the whole family and all friends—Most Respectfully, and tenderly I Have the Honour to Be my Beloved General, Your most devoted and grateful friend

lafayette

M. de St john de Crevecoeur the french Consul at Newyork Has requested my recommendation for some informations He wishes to Have—I assured Him you would Have no objections—Tarleton Has printed a journal of the Campaigns He Has made, wherein He treats Lord Cornwallis very severly.[5]

ALS, PEL.

1. The Assembly of Notables met at Versailles on 22 Feb. 1787 and was dissolved on 25 May.

2. The bishop of Langres was César-Guillaume de La Luzerne (1738–1821). The "inclosed" has not been found.

3. Charles-Alexandre de Calonne (1734–1802) was forced to resign in April 1787. M. de Fourqueux was Michel Bouvard de Fourqueux; Etienne-Charles de Loménie de Brienne (1727–1794) was the archbishop of Toulouse; and M. de Villedeuil was Larent de Villedeuil.

4. Calonne's letter of 22 Oct. 1786 gave the ministry's approval to the agreement reached in May 1786 liberalizing the management of the French tobacco trade by the farmers-general. See Lafayette to GW, 9 Oct. 1787, n.6.

5. Hector St. Jean de Crèvecoeur (1735–1813) served under Montcalm in Canada and settled in the colony of New York. He returned to France in 1780, but he was back in New York from 1783 to 1785 and, as French consul, from 1787 to 1790. For the various forms his name has taken, see the editor's note in Crèvecoeur to Thomas Jefferson, 23 Jan. 1784 (Boyd, *Jefferson Papers*, 6:508–9). Banastre Tarleton (1754–1833) published in London in 1787 his self-serving *History of the Campaigns of 1780 and 1781 in the Southern Provinces of North America.*

Letter not found: to Jean Le Mayeur, 5 May 1787. On 23 May Jean Le Mayeur wrote that he did not receive GW's "favour of the fifth instant till yesterday."

To Robert Morris

Dear Sir,   Mount Vernon May 5th 1787.

When your favor of the 23d Ult. was sent here from the Post Office, I was at Fredericksburg (to which place I had been called, suddenly, by Express) to bid, as I was prepared to expect, the last adieu to an honoured parent, and an affectionate Sister whose watchful attention to my Mother during her illness had brought to deaths door. The latter I hope is now out of danger, but the former cannot long Survive the disorder which has reduced her to a Skeleton, tho' she is some what amended.[1]

I do not know how, sufficiently, to express my thankfulness to Mrs Morris and you for your kind invitation to lodge at your house, and though I could not be more happy any where, yet as there is great reason to apprehend that the business of the Convention (from the tardiness of some States, and the discordant opinions of others) will not be brought to a speedy conclusion, I cannot prevail on my self to give so much trouble to a private family as such a length of time must do—I hope therefore that Mrs Morris and you will not take it a miss that I decline the polite and obliging offer you have made me.[2]

Mrs Washington is become too Domestick, and too attentive to two little Grand Children to leave home, and I can assure you, Sir, that it was not until after a long struggle I could obtain my own consent to appear again in a public theatre. My first remaining wish being, to glide gently down the stream of life in tranquil retirement till I shall arrive at the world of Sperits.

Mrs Morris yourself and family, have every good wish that Mrs Washington and I can offer—and with the sincerest esteem and regard I am Dear Sir, Yr Most Obedt Servt

G. Washington

LB, DLC:GW.

1. Mary Ball Washington died in August 1789, from "the Cancer on her Breast" (Burgess Ball to GW, 25 Aug. 1789).

2. See Morris to GW, 23 April, n.2.

To David Stuart

Dear Sir,   Mount Vernon May 5th 1787.

I have received your favor of the 30th and thank you for the ennumerations contained in it.[1] They are all clear and selfevidt and in some instances may be enlarged. Did you communicate the Plan to Colonels Fitzgerald and Hooe? And how far did you give either, or both, reason to believe they would be recommended to Mr Jefferson? (to whom I shall write as soon as I get to Philada). I wish to be fully informed of this that I may govern myself accordingly.[2]

On Monday after an early dinner, or on Tuesday Morning, I shall (my rheumatic complaint having got better) commence my Journey (I believe by the way of Annapolis) to Philadelphia. It would therefore suit me very well to receive the Sum mentioned when you were here last, at that place; and probably, as you are going to Richmond, it may be so ordered. Alexanders Bills on Mr Morris would answer well—doubtfull Bills, or Bills which would be accompanied with delay, would by no means suit me, because the money would be applied 1st towards paying a debt there—and 2d in the purchase of some Goods for the family, if I can get them cheap there.[3] If I can render you, or Mrs Stuart any services while there I shall be happy in the execution of your commands—With compliments & good wishes for the family I am—Dear Sir Yr Obedt & Affecte Ser.

Go: Washington

ALS, MFD. Stuart wrote on the cover of GW's letter: "This letter relates to some observations I had drawn up at the Genls request respecting the fitness of the Potomac as a place of deposit for the fur trade."

1. Letter not found. See source note.

2. GW wrote to Thomas Jefferson from Philadelphia recommending that either John Fitzgerald or Robert Townsend Hooe be made the U.S. agent for the Couteulx Company in Alexandria. The French company was proposing to develop a large-scale fur trade in America (GW to Jefferson, 30 May). See also Lafayette to GW, 8 Oct. 1786, n.1., and Jefferson to GW, 14 Nov. 1786.

3. See Alexander Donald to GW, 22 May, and 20 June, and note 2 of each.

To Lund Washington

Dear Lund,   Mount Vernon May 7th 1787.

Company, and several other matters which pressed upon me yesterday, and which has obliged me to postpone my gourney a day longer is the reason why I did not acknowledge the receipt of your letter by Ned.[1]

I need not tell you, because a moments recurrance to your own accounts will evince the fact, that there is no source from which I derive more then a sufficienty for the daily calls of my family except what flows from the Collection of old debts—and scanty and precarious enough, God knows this is. My estate for the last 11 years have not been able to make both ends meet—I am encumbered now with the deficiency—I mention this for no other purpose than to shew that however willing, I am not able to pay debts unless I could sell Land which I have publicly advertized without finding bidders.[2]

The enclosed Bond I have had the most pointed assurances would be paid by the first of June. & for that reason if it will answer your purpose you may collect and apply the money to the use for which you want it. If this will not do, there is some flour and wheat (if there be water to grind it) in the Mill which you may dispose of for the same end because I would not wish you to be disappointed.[3] I am Yr Sincere Friend.

G. Washington.

LB, DLC:GW.

1. Letter not found. A slave named Ned was a laborer on GW's River Farm.

2. The copyist wrote "bedders."

3. The bond that GW enclosed was that of Peter Dow. Dow had been renting a tract of land on Hunting Creek since he sold it to GW in 1782. Unable to collect from Dow, Lund Washington sold some of GW's flour. GW settled his account with Lund on 2 Mar. 1789 by giving him a bond for £1,220. See Dow to GW, 20 June 1786, GW to George Augustine Washington, 8 July 1787, and Ledger B, 228.

Philadelphia Cash Accounts

[9 May–22 September 1787]

Money recd by me from sundry persons while in Philadelphia between May 27th & Septr 18th

Cash

May 27—To Mr Mathew Whiting for Mr William Hunter Junr's Draft on Robt Morris Esqr.[1]		50. 0. 0
To The Estate of Jno. Parke Custis Esqr. recd from Doctr Stuart by Alexr Donnald Esqr. for his draft on Robt Morris Esqr. 894^{85}/$_{90}$ Dolls. & Mr Morris's Note for 200 Dollars[2]		410.12. 0
June 8—To the State of Virginia for the Governor's draft on Henderson & Co. for[3]		125. 0. 0
13—To Thomas Smith Esqr. recd of him a Suit agt Cunningham in Washington Cty[4]		12.10. 0
To interest on the above Sum		1.10. 0
16—To Robt Morris Esqr. drew out of his hands[5]		315. 0. 0
27—To the Estate of John P. Custis Esqr. recd from Doctr Stuart[6]		115. 0. 0
26—To Robt Morris Esqr. drew out of his hds		100. 0. 0
July 5—To ditto ditto[7]		105. 0. 0
Augt 10—To Ditto recd of him in full of the Money lodged in his hands		180.12. 6
24—To the State of Virga recd at the Bank of Phila.		125. 0. 0
Septr 1—To Majr Junifer [Daniel of St. Thomas Jenifer] recd from him for his dividend due to the Potomack Cy £6 Sterlg		10. 0. 0
15—To the State of Virga recd from Jno. Blair Esqr.[8]		67.10. 0
18—To Robt Morris Esqr. for a Bill drawn by me on Wakelin Welch Esqr. & Son in London for £100 Sterling[9]		175. 0. 0
Amount brought over Pensya Curry £1792.14.6 eql to		1434. 3. 7¼

Contra

My Expences to & from Philadelphia & money pd by me on Sundry
Accts while there viz. from the 9th of May to the 22d of September inclusively.

May 9th—By Servants 2/4   Expences at Bla-
        densbg 14/   0.16. 4

    10—By Ferriages at Elk Ridge 2/10   Exps.
        at Balto. 51/8   2.13. 6[10]

    11—By Exps. at Skerritts[11] 9/9   Servants 1/   0.10. 9

    12—By Exps. at Havre de Grass 49/3   Fer-
        rymen 3/9   2.13. 0

    12—By Breakfast 6/6   Dinner at the head
        of Elk 12/   0.18. 6

    13—By Exps. @ Willmington 33/10   Do at
        Chester & Servts 26/7   3. 0. 5

    14—By a Barber 7/6   mendg my Coat 1/   0. 8. 6

        By a pr Silk stockings 25/   5 yds hair
        Ribbon 5/   1.10. 0

        By Ferriages @ Schuylkill   0. 3. 9

    15—By Soap Powder-Puff & a blk Silk
        Handkf for Will[12]   1. 4. 6

        By Charity—or rather to beggars   0. 8. 6

    18—By Club at the Schuylkill[13]   0.17. 6

        By Mr Barlow pd into the hds of Colo.
        Humphreys my Subs[criptio]n for
        20 Vols. of his Poem entitled the Vi-
        sions of Columbus @ 1⅓ Dol.
        each[14]   10. 0. 0

    23—By Ferriages in an Excursn up the
        Schuylkill[15]   0.11. 0

    26—By Servts 11/8   Charity 7/6   0.19. 2

    27—By 6 ps. Nankeen 54/   3 pr Nankeen
        breechs 37/6   4.11. 6

        By Charity 35/   A Ticket to the Con-
        cert 7/6[16]   2. 2. 6

June 8—By Robt Morris Esqr. put into his hds
        to be drawn for occasionally   410.12. 0

        By Robt Morris Esqr. put into his hds
        as above[17]   125. 0. 0

    9—By Washing 17/6   Ferriages & Servts
        21/3   1.18. 9

        By Sundries pd by Will   0.12. 0

        By Powder puff, Spung, soap, ⟨setting⟩
        Razors &c.   0.14. 6

    13—By 3 Concert Tickets[18]   1. 2. 6

        By Mr Craig pd him on Acct of Servts
        board[19]   8.15. 0

	By 2 pr Stockings for Will	0.13. 0
	16—By Washing	0.16. 8
	By Govr Clinton pd him by an order on Robt Morris Esqr. 840 Dollars[20]	315. 0. 0
June	17—By Charity 8/4 Ferriages 3/9 mendg my Coat 1/	0.13. 1
	By Paper 4/6—23d. Washing 17/6 Club @ Grays 6/[21]	1. 8. 0
	26—By Colonel Biddle pd him on acct	100. 0. 0
	By a Saddle for Washington Custis[22]	5.17. 6
	27—By Robt Morris Esqr. put into his hands	115. 0. 0
	By Charity 5/6 Washing 11/ 4 pr screw Hinges 30/	2. 6. 6
	By a pair of Breeches for Will	1. 2. 6
July	7—By Washing 20/5 Sundries 11/8	1.12. 1
	9—By Colonel Biddle pd him in full of Accts	35.19. 4½
	By a Play Ticket 7/6[23] Sundries 7/6	0.15. 0
	16—By Mr Craig pd him my Servts board[24]	13. 2. 6
	By Washing 17/6 17th Club @ the Tea-party 9/6[25]	1. 7. 0
	20—By Servants 3/9 21[s]t Play Ticket 7/6[26]	0.11. 3
	21—By Ferriages[27] & Servts 5/ Washing 35/	2. 0. 0
	23—By A pr leathr breeches for Paris 15/ Paper 2/	0.17. 0
	27—By Josh Cook & Co. Jewellers pd them[28]	39.15. 0
	By [John] Wagener pd him for a ps. Linen 25 yds [@] 5/9[29]	7. 3. 9
	By 4 Vols. Hudibrass 25/[30] Sundries 15/	2. 0. 0
	28—By Washing 17/6 Sundries 15/	1.12. 6
August	2—By Exps. of my horses & Servts	0.17. 6
	3—By a Seal 30/[31] Black Smith's Acct 28/ Sunds 7/6	3. 5. 6
	4—By Exps. @ Trenton 17/6[32] Sundries 7/6	1. 5. 0
	8—By a Winble Bitt 52/6[33] 1 pr Screw Hinges 7/6	3. 0. 0

By the Marquis Chastelleux travels in Engd[34]	1.10. 0
By Sadler's Acct 16/10[35] a Fan-Chair 32/6[36]	2. 9. 4
By Will gave him 17/6 10th two Mortise Locks 40/	2.17. 6
10—By Jno. Wagner for 2 ps. linen 50 yds @ 6/2	15. 8. 4
By Thos Billingston, Taylor his Acct pd[37]	9. 1.10
By Josh Rackestraw for self & others for the top of my Cupola[38]	24. 7. 5
By Colo. Biddle pd him	11. 5. 0
11—By Nelson & Wiedman for 14 Bls Plaster of Paris & the cask containing it[39]	14. 8. 0
12—By Washing 15/ Cash given away 4/	0.19. 0
By Cutting a Cypher on my Seal	0.15. 0
14—By Sundries 10/4 a Dog 15/[40]	1. 5. 4
By Thos Palmer for shoes for Mrs Washington[41]	3. 5. 6
16—By Jno. Helm for 25 Yds blk Sattin[42]	21.17. 6
August 18—By Washing 15/ gave away 15/	1.10. 0
By Josh Cook & Co. for a Gold watch-Chain	9. 7. 3
19—By Exps. in a trip to White Marsh[43]	1. 3. 9
By Sundries 7/6 1 pce Cambrick £10.5	10.12. 6
25—By Washing 16/8 Sundries 24/	2. 0. 8
By Accts pd at the City Tavern £8.14 Sunds 7/6	9. 1. 6
31—By Colo. Biddle put into his hands to pay for Sundries 50 Dollars	18.15. 0
Septr 3—By 10½ Yds Cross-barred Muslin @ 11/3	5.18. 1½
By 9¾ yds flowered ditto @ 6/6	3. 3. 4
By 6 yds Sash Ribbon 15/ a pr Gloves 7/6	1. 2. 6
4—By Mathew Cary pd him my subscription for his 2d Vol. of the Museum[44]	0. 9. 0
By Dinner & other Exps. in the Country[45]	0.17. 6
5—By a pr Sattin breeches	2.18. 9

By Lord Chesterfield's Letters to his Son 4 Vols.[46]	1. 4. 0	
7—By Mr Craig pd him board of my Servts	11. 5. 0	
8—By Washing 17/6　mending &c. 11/3	1. 8. 9	
12—By two velvet Jocky Caps	2.10. 0	
By Beaties Evidence of Religion[47]	0. 4. 0	
By Baron Haller's Letters[48]	0. 8. 4	
By Exps. Crossing the Schuylkill &c.	0. 7. 6	
14—By Jacanot Muslin @ 12/6 pr Yd[49]	3. 2. 6	
15—By a Pocket Looking Glass	0. 5. 0	
By a pr Hinges 7/　Washing 13/4	1. 0. 4	
17—By 4 Vols. of Don Quixote 22/6[50]　2 do Jno. Buncle 24/[51]	2. 6. 6	
By the Coach Maker's Acct pd[52]	51.13. 6	
By the Black Smith's do pd	1.15. 6	
18—By Mr Craig pd him in full for my Servts board	4.17. 0	
By Will gave him	0.15. 0	
By Mr Helkzimer's acct of Stablage pd him[53]	79. 6. 6	
By a brown Mare	20. 0. 0	
By Mr Morris's Servts gave them 28 Dols.	11.10. 0	
By Doctr Shippen pd him for attendg Giles	3. 0. 0	
By Doctr Jones pd him for attendg Paris[54]	1.15. 0	
By Ferriages 6/　19th Exps. at Chester 42/	2. 8. 0	
19—By do at Chester 3/　Exps. at Willmington 8/3[55]	0.11. 3	
By Exps. at Christiana 10/6　Hd Elk 29/2	1.19. 8	
20—By mendg Harness	0. 7. 6	
By Ferriages at Susquehana 18/　Exps. @ Havre de Grass 17/9	1.15. 9	
21—By Exps. @ Skerritts 34/3　Brekft a Balto. 18/6	2.12. 9	
By Ferriage at Elk Ridge landing	0. 2. 6	
By Servants	0. 3. 9	
22—By Breakfast at Bladensburg	0.14. 0	
By Ferriage at George Town	0. 7. 6	

By Dinner &c. in Alexandria amtg to   1.   5.11
    £1.0.9 Virga currency equal to
      [Pa. Currency] 1627.17.9 eql to   1302.   6.   2½
      [Va. Currency]

D, Ledger B, 253–56.

1. See William Hunter, Jr., to GW, 11 May.

2. See Alexander Donald to GW, 22 May.

3. Thomas Henderson & Co. were merchants on Second Street in Philadelphia. GW placed this payment by the state of Virginia for his expenses in the hands of Robert Morris "to be drawn for occasionally" (see Contra, this date). At the end of his Philadelphia cash accounts GW himself inserted "June 9—By Colo. Biddle pd him on acct 24.7."

4. See GW to Thomas Smith, 16 Sept. 1787.

5. GW wrote George Clinton on 9 June that Robert Morris's correspondent in New York would pay Clinton £325 to discharge GW's debt to Clinton. See note 1 in GW's letter to Clinton.

6. See Alexander Donald to GW, 20 June.

7. GW does not record receiving payment from the state of Virginia during July, but GW wrote this order, dated "Philadelphia 28th July 1787": "Sir, Please to pay to Messrs Francis and John West on order, the sum of One hundred pounds Virginia Currency, and place it to acct of Yr most Obedt Hble Servt Go: Washington." GW directed the order to "Beverley Randolph Lt Govr of Virginia." Below GW's signature is written "Philadelphia August 2. 1787. This bill will be paid on sight," signed "Edm: Randolph" (ADS, owned in 1976 by Mr. W. R. Coleman, San Bernardino, Calif.; ADS [photocopy], *Virginia Cavalcade*, Winter 1951, 43). GW left the place blank where someone, probably Edmund Randolph, inserted the names of John and Francis West.

8. On 16 Sept. GW signed a receipt: "Recd. from the Honble. John Blair One hundred and Eighty dollars [£67.10] on Acct of allowance by the State of Virga. to me as a delegate to the fœderal Convention" (photocopy in W. Edwin Hemphill, "Virginia to George Washington, Debtor," *Virginia Cavalcade*, Winter 1951, 43).

9. On 18 Sept. GW wrote Wakelin Welch from Philadelphia: "Sir's, I have this day drawn upon you in favor of Robert Morris Esqr. for one hundred pounds Sterling payable at thirty days sight—which place to Account of Sir— Your most Obed. Servant G. Washington" (LB, DLC:GW).

10. The correct amount is £2.14.6.

11. Skerrett's tavern was at the head of Bird River in Baltimore County. For GW's itinerary to Philadelphia, 9–13 May, see *Diaries*, 5:153–55.

12. Will (Billy; William Lee), GW's mulatto body servant, had been with him since 1768.

13. On Friday, 18 May, GW "Dined at Greys ferry" on the Schuylkill (*Diaries*, 5:158).

14. See David Humphreys to GW, 16 Nov. 1786, and GW to Elizabeth Powel, 6 June 1787.

15. The Convention still not having been formed, on 23 May GW had

breakfast at Thomas Mifflin's, "after which in Company with him Mr. [James] Madison, Mr. [John] Rutledge and others" he "crossed the Schuylkill" to visit Richard Peters, John Penn, and William Hamilton (*Diaries*, 5:160).

16. On Tuesday, 29 May, GW accompanied his hostess, Mary White Morris, to a concert presented by James Juhan (ibid., 163–64).

17. See note 3.

18. On 12 June GW attended a concert at City Tavern presented by Alexander Reinagle (*Diaries*, 5:169). See GW to Elizabeth Powel, c.12 June.

19. GW had three servants with him in Philadelphia, his manservant Will (Billy), his groom Giles, and his postilion Paris. See note 24.

20. See note 5.

21. On Tuesday, 26 June, GW "made one of a party to drink Tea at Grays ferry" (*Diaries*, 5:171).

22. Washington Custis is Mrs. Washington's grandson, George Washington Parke Custis.

23. GW attended the play, *High Life below the Stairs*, at the Southwark Theater on Tuesday, 10 July (ibid., 175).

24. Thomas Craig's bill and the receipt for payment on 16 July of what was owed by GW for Craig's boarding of GW's "2 Servts @ 25s." a week at his inn on Market Street is in ViMtV. See note 19.

25. On 17 July GW made "an excursion with a party for Tea to Grays Ferry" (*Diaries*, 5:176).

26. On Saturday, 21 July, GW attended James Thomson's tragedy *Edward and Eleanora* (ibid., 176).

27. On Sunday, 22 July, GW left the city before 5 o'clock in the morning and rode with others up to Spring Mill on the Schuylkill (ibid., 177).

28. Cooke & Co. were jewelers and goldsmiths on Second Street between Market and Chestnut streets in Philadelphia.

29. This may be John Conrad Waggener (Wagener, Wagner) who had a tailor shop on New Street and later on Front Street.

30. GW's copy of volume 1 of Samuel Butler's *Hudibras* was sold in 1876 (Griffin, *Boston Athenæum Collection*, 482).

31. On 12 Aug. GW records paying 15 shillings for "Cutting a Cypher on my Seal."

32. The Convention adjourned on 27 July until 6 August. One of the outings that GW took during the recess was with Robert Morris and his wife and Gouverneur Morris to Trenton "on another Fishing party" (*Diaries*, 5:180).

33. GW wrote Clement Biddle on 7 Aug. and asked him to secure a wimble bit for him and send to it to Mount Vernon for his mill.

34. After its publication in Paris in 1786 Chastellux presented GW with a copy of his two-volume *Voyages dans L'Amérique Septentrionale dans les années 1780, 1781 & 1782*. GW bought the translation *Travels in North America in the Years 1780, 1781, and 1782*, published in London in 1787. Thomas Seddon's bill for the two volumes is dated 4 Aug. (Birch's catalog 663, item 81, p.10).

35. A receipted bill dated 8 Aug. from John Stephens includes charges for "A pad to a Sadle—0.10.0[,] 2 girth straps & mending a bridle—0.1.10 [and]

left unpaid of the New Sadle—0.5.0" (NjMoNP). In 1790 John Stephens, saddler, lived on the south side of Chestnut Street in Philadelphia.

36. In his letter to Clement Biddle of 7 Aug., GW refers to the shipping of the "Chair" to Mount Vernon, and Biddle notes its purchase for 32/6 on the cover of GW's letter.

37. Thomas Billington was a merchant tailor at 96–97 High Street.

38. See GW to Joseph Rakestraw, 20 July.

39. In 1785 George Nelson, a protégé of Jacob Hiltzheimer, had a store on New Street between Second and Third. Wiedman has not been identified.

40. GW bought a coach dog on instructions from Mrs. Washington. See GW to George Augustine Washington, 12 August.

41. Thomas Palmer was a silk and stuff shoemaker on Chestnut Street between Second and Third.

42. In 1785 John Helm was a shopkeeper at 86 Sassafras Street.

43. On Sunday, 19 Aug., GW went with Samuel Powel out to White Marsh, northwest of Philadelphia, where he "Traversed my old Incampment, and contemplated on the dangers which threatned the American Army at that place" in November and December 1777 (*Diaries*, 5:181).

44. Mathew Carey (1760–1839) began publishing his magazine *American Museum* in 1786.

45. GW rode out to William Bartram's botanical garden "and other places in the Country" on Sunday, 2 Sept. (*Diaries*, 5:183).

46. The four volumes of Lord Chesterfield's *Letters to His Son* (New York, 1775) were in GW's library at his death.

47. This was James Beattie's two-volume *Evidences of the Christian Religion Briefly and Plainly Stated* (London, 1786).

48. Albrecht von Haller's *Letters from Baron Haller to His Daughter on the Truth of the Christian Religion* (London, 1783) was a translation from the German.

49. Jaconet was a cotton fabric made in India.

50. Thomas Smollet's four-volume translation of Cervantes' *The History and Adventures of the Renowned Don Quixote* (London, 1786) was at Mount Vernon at the time of GW's death.

51. GW's copy of *The Life of John Buncle, Esq.* (London, 1766) is in the Boston Athenaeum.

52. See GW to Samuel Powel, 25 July, n.1.

53. Jacob Hiltzheimer (d. 1798), a native of Mannheim, Germany, was a successful businessman in Philadelphia and at this time represented the city in the state assembly. His livery stable was on Seventh Street between Market and Chestnut.

54. Dr. John Jones (d. 1791) was practicing medicine in 1785 on Market Street between Second and Third.

55. GW left Philadelphia in his carriage on Tuesday, 18 Sept., after an early dinner, and spent his first night at Chester. For GW's return journey to Mount Vernon, see *Diaries*, 5:186–87.

From William Hunter, Jr.

Sir   Alexandria 11th May 1787
   Mathew Whiting, Esqr. was here yesterday, and was very uneasy he had not seen you, to pay some money, before you sett
out for Philadelphia,[1] I told him I could easily contrive it, if he
would give me the Cash or Tobo, Accordingly he put into my
hands £40.0.0 Virga Curry, for which I now send a dra[f]t on
Robert Morris Esqr. @ 1od. pr which doubt not will be duly
honour'd[2]—I am just from Fredericksburgh, where I understood Mrs Washington was continuing better—And am with
Respect—your Excellency's very hble Servt
                                        Will. Hunter Jr

ALS, DLC:GW.
   1. See Matthew Whiting to GW, 10 Aug. 1786, n.1.
   2. GW, who left for Philadelphia on 9 May, records the receipt on 27 May
of a £50 draft drawn on Robert Morris by William Hunter, Jr., for Whiting
(Philadelphia Cash Accounts, 9 May–22 Sept. 1787).

From Rochambeau

My dear General   Paris may the 12th 1787.
   it is dreadful to live So far that we do from one another. I
receive but in this moment the letter wherewith you have honoured me on the 31th July ultimate, that you put abord of an
English Ship, which after he had made its trade has, at last Send
it to *havre* this last days. But whatever was the cause of the tardy
news I receive from you, I am always charmed to See that my
Dear General and my good friend is enjoying of his glorious and
Philosophical retreat, where he has known fixed his glory and
his happiness.
   We are here in a terrible crisis of finances which has occa-
sionned an assembly of chief men that last yet. you heard Speak
of the ministry of M. Neker and of the flourishing Stat where he
had left our finances.[1] A devil of fool, named *Calonne* Minister
of finances Since four years, has believed to be bound to take
contrary Sense of his predecessor, and has made Succeed to an
œconomical administration, a prodigality and a devastation
which has no example. being at the end of last year without

means, he has imagined an assembly of chief men in which discovering, in his quality of quack, a part of the wound, he did propose all the remedies of an Empiric. The assembly of chief men at last has unmasked him to our Virtuous King that he had the Skill to deceive as well as a part of his council. he has been latily dismissed, and his office is given to the archbishop de toulouse, the knowledge, probity, arder and talents of which give the greatest hopes to the nation.[2] you know enough my caracter to think that it would not sympathize with that of M. de Calonne, and consequently he did not put me in that assembly, that I have been very glad of. he had also forgot the marquis de La fayette. I should have desired he had taken the Same course, but his ardour did not permitt him to be quiet.[3] We are Still in the midle of this crisis which tends to its End. but to comfort us of this misfortune, I will tell you a word of the late King of prussia, which Said to the count D'Esterno our minister, "I have been brougt up in the midle of the unhappiness of france, my cradle was Surrounded with refugees protestants that about the End of the Reign of Louis XIV, and at the beguining of the Regency of the Duc D'orleans told me that the france was at the agony and could not exist three years. I known in the course of my Reign, that the france has Such a temper, that there is no bad minister, nor bad generals which be able to Kill it, and that constitution has made rise it again of all its crisis with Strength and Vigour. it want no other remedy but time and Keep a Strict course of diet."[4] it is to the archbishop de toulouse to make use of this two means under a King born virtuous and without passions.

I have been very Sory, my dear général, of the general Green's death. I know him by reputation and correspondance, and I loved very much all his relations.[5] my consolation, my dear general, is that with Sobriety and philosophy you live under a pur skie and in good air, and that mout vernon will conserve a longtime to the america its heros and my friend.

My respects to Mad. Washington, to all your family and to all my ancients camarades and friends. I am with a respectful attachment my Dear general Your most obedient and Very humble Servant,

Le comte de Rochambeau

ALS, DLC:GW.

1. Jacques Necker (1732–1804) had been the French minister of finance before being replaced by Charles-Alexandre de Calonne in 1781.

2. Loménie de Brienne, archbishop of Toulouse, was president of the Assembly of Notables and had just replaced Calonne as director of finance.

3. See Lafayette to GW, 5 May.

4. Antoine-Joseph-Philippe-Régis (1741–1790), comte d'Esterno, was named minister plenipotentiary to Prussia in 1782.

5. Rochambeau became acquainted with Nathanael Greene's wife, Catharine Littlefield Greene, in Rhode Island in 1780.

Letter not found: from George Augustine Washington, 12 May 1787. On 17 May GW wrote George Augustine Washington: "Your letter of the 12th is this instt put into my hands."

From Christopher Gadsden

Dr Sir   Charleston [S.C.] 13th May 1787

I cannot let my worthy Friend Genl Pinckney leave us in order to join You on so important a Business for America without embracing the Opportunity of paying you my respects,[1] I hope Heaven will favor the joint Endeavors of the Convention & make their Establishments effectually useful. We are all sure of your utmost Exertions to that Purpose. That Congress ought to be well supported & render'd respectable has ever been the Opinion of the firmest Friends to the Revolution & 'tis to be hoped the unreasonable (I am afraid too often insidious) Jealousies of her abusing the Powers entrusted to her are by this Time subsided.

I am now altogether retired from public Business & return'd to the Care of my private Concerns, not only because their deranged Situation makes it necessary but also to set what little Example I can to promote an industrious Turn amongst our choice Spirits, the best means, in my Opinion, to banish old Animosities & to restore Harmony & good Neighborhood amongst them.

Our Assembly the last Setting past a Law to prohibit the Importation of Slaves for three years, & by a very large Majority rejected a proposal of making any more paper Currency These are no bad Symptoms of our coming to our Senses, & wishing to pay our Debts & keep up Public Credit, God Grant some farther

Tendencies that Way may be thought of & carried at their next meeting to the Satisfaction of their Constituents.

That all the World Dr general admire & respect your Character can be no flattery to tell you so, nor that all the United States love & esteem you, & permit me the Honor my Dr Sir to assure you that not an Individual in any one State of the thirteen does so more sincerely than your affectionate & most Obedt humble Servt

Christ. Gadsden

ALS, PHi: Gratz Collection.
    1. Charles Cotesworth Pinckney was at the Convention by 25 May.

From Arthur Lee

Dear Sir   Newyork May 13th 1787
    I have receivd private information, that it is the intention of the meeting of the Cincinnati to re-elect you as their President, notwithstanding your letter. They think you are so plegd to them, by some of your letters that you cannot refuse the Presidency.[1]
    The expected removal of Congress to Philadelphia, has again faild by one vote.[2] I am inclind to think, that the more this step is considerd, the fewer Advocates it will find. The commercial Cities of our State, are struggling against the vast superiority which Philadelphia acquird during the war. So great an addition of money & influence, as the residence of Congress woud give, to the Merchants of that place; woud I apprehend give them a decided controul over our Commerce, if not an entire monopoly. Our native Merchants woud not be able to stand against their factors & all the profits of our trade woud center in Philadelphia. The british Packet brings no news of consequence. The impeachment of Governor Hastings is determind by a great majority in the Commons.[3] The national justice of that kingdom is much interested in arresting the progress of that excessive cruelty & injustice, which have been practisd in India, in order to extort immense wealth from its wretched Natives. I hope, Sir, that your rheumatic pains are entirely removd, tho the weather, as we have it here, is more calculated to give than to releive such maladies.

Be pleasd to make my most respectful Compliments accept-able to your Lady. I have the honor to be with very great re-spect & esteem, dear Sir, Yr most obedt Servt

Arthur Lee

ALS, DLC:GW.

1. GW's announcement on 31 Nov. 1786 that he would not accept reelection to the presidency of the Society of the Cincinnati was rooted in his sense that the state societies were rejecting the reforms in the society's Institution, or constitution, which he had secured at the General Meeting in 1784. See Winthrop Sargent's Journal, 4–18 May 1784, and note 16. It became clear when the General Meeting got under way in Philadelphia that GW was correct in his assessment. "We are," wrote Maj. George Turner to Samuel Blachley Webb, "apparently, all hot for a Renewal of the old Institution. . . . General Washington will be among us in few Hours more—But, entre nous, I could almost wish for the Absence of the Illustrious Chief,—whose extreme Prudence & Circumspection (having himself much Fame to lose) may cool our laudable and necessary Ebullition with a few Drops, if not a Torrent, of Cold Water" (quoted in Myers, *Liberty without Anarchy*, 96). GW, who arrived in Philadelphia on 13 May, did not attend any of the meetings of the Cincinnati but accepted reelection to the presidency on 18 May. See Henry Knox's defense of the Society of the Cincinnati in his letter to GW of 19 March.

2. On 21 April, Massachusetts, Connecticut, and New York voted against the move. South Carolina and Maryland did not vote (*JCC*, 32:226–27).

3. Warren Hastings's impeachment was voted in the House of Commons on 3 April 1787 by a vote of nearly three to one.

From James Bowdoin

Sir   Boston May 14. 1787

It must give the highest satisfaction to every friend of the Union, that the same Gentleman, who bore so distinguished, so capital a part, in emancipating the United States, is appointed a Delegate in the intended Convention, for perfecting their federal government. It is with great earnestness hoped, that the plan of Confederation, to which that respectable body may agree, will be well formed for efficient government; and that it will be so far unobjectionable, as to be approved by Congress, and adopted by the several States. The Union may then answer the purpose of its institution, not only in regard to the internal government, and mutual interests of the States themselves; but also in regard to foreign nations. Among the latter the Union might then again appear in a reputable light; and be of importance enough to secure to itself such commercial advantages, as the situation and products of the several united States do entitle it to expect.

Major Erving, a Brother of Mrs Bowdoin, will have the pleasure of delivering you this letter. He was formerly an officer in the british army; and has seen a great deal of service. He was particularly at the reduction of the Havannah, Louisburg, Quebec &c. &c., and distinguished himself in all those Campaigns: but quitted the service some years before the british ministry invaded their then colonies.

I have the pleasure to assure you, he has always been a firm and zealous friend to the rights and liberties of America; and in that character, a character always acceptable to General Washington, I beg leave to introduce him to your Excellency.[1] I have the honour to be with the most perfect regard, Dear Sir, yr Excellency's most obedt & very hble Servt.

L (copy), MHi: Bowdoin-Temple Papers. The copy was enclosed in a letter of the same date from Bowdoin to Benjamin Franklin.

James Bowdoin (1726–1790), who was governor of Massachusetts throughout Daniel Shays' Rebellion, left office on 26 April after being defeated by John Hancock in the spring elections.

1. William Erving (1734–1791), a graduate of Harvard College in 1753, was a bachelor living in a fine house on Marlborough Street in Boston. He founded the Erving Professorship of Chemistry at his alma mater. Bowdoin also provided Erving with a letter of introduction to Benjamin Franklin.

From George Fox

Sir   Third street [Philadelphia] May 14th 1787
In conformity to an unanimous Vote of the Society for Political Inquiries, I have the honor to signify to your Excellency their request, that you would permit them to enrol your name in the list of their Honorary Members. For your information with respect to the views which gave rise to this institution, I hand you a copy of its laws, and can not but add, that the Society flatter themselves, from your continued endeavours to advance the interests, as well as promote the Liberty & happiness of your fellow citizens, that you will not decline uniting with them in an undertaking dictated by the purest motives.[1]

It is with particular pleasure, Sir, that I comply with the directions of the Society, as it affords me an opportunity of assuring you of the sentiments of profound respect with which I have the honor to be Your Excellency's most obedient and very humble Servant

Geo: Fox

LS, DLC:GW.

George Fox (1759–1828) of Philadelphia received his degree from the college at Philadelphia in 1780 and then sailed for Europe, where he remained until 1783. In 1784 he was elected a member of the American Philosophical Society. At the death of his friend William Temple Franklin, Fox inherited the greater part of Benjamin Franklin's papers, most of which were deposited at the American Philosophical Society in 1840.

1. On 9 Feb. 1787 a group of Philadelphians calling itself the Society for Political Enquiries began meeting weekly in the library of Benjamin Franklin, who was made president. The meetings discontinued after the formation of the new federal government.

From Charles Willson Peale

Dr Sir   May 16. 1787

Several Gentlemen of the Society of the Cincinati having desired to see my perspective Views with changeable effects, gives me an opportunity of asking the favor of your Company at the Exhibition this afternoon at ½ past 4 Oclock.[1] I am with much respect your Hble Servant

C.W. Peale

LB, PPAmP: Charles Willson Peale Papers.

1. On 20 May 1785 Peale opened at one end of his portrait gallery an exhibition of artfully mounted and lighted series of painted scenes which he called "Exhibition of Perspective Views with Changeable Effects." For a full description of Peale's "Moving Pictures," see Miller, *Peale Papers,* 1:428–33. George Turner, who was elected assistant secretary general at the Cincinnati's meeting of May 1787, had asked Peale to put on this special showing (ibid., 478, n.3). GW, having the day before "Dined with the Members . . . of the Society of the Cincinnati," on 16 May "Dined at the President Doctr. Franklins and drank Tea, and spent the evening at Mr. Jno. Penns" (*Diaries,* 5:157).

To George Augustine Washington

Dear George,   Philadelphia May 17th 1787.

After short stages and easy driving, I reached this City on Sunday afternoon.[1] Only 4 states—viz. Virginia, South Carolina, New York and the one we are in, are as yet, represented; which is highly vexatious to those who are idly, & expensively spending their time here.

I hope the fine rains which have watered this part of the Country were not confined to it; or rather, that the Clouds which produced them, were not unproductive as they hovered over you. All nature seems alive from the effe⟨ct⟩ of them, about this City; and the Grain appears very differently from ours.

As we have not commenced the business yet, it is impossible to say when it will end. I have not even a hope, that it will meet with dispatch. for which reason I shall be anxious for the weekly remarks—These you will have time to transcribe between Saturday and Monday Night; by which time your letter should be in the Post Office, in order that it may come off with the Mail on Tuesday Morning & be here on Friday—If any thing should occur I shall write to you by return of it.[2]

If you or Fanny should want any thing here, or think of any thing in which I can be of service it would give me pleasure to oblige you—My best wishes attend her. and remembrances to Mr Lear. I am Yr Affectly

                              Go: Washington

P.S. Your letter of the 12th is this instt put into my hands and I am hurried to get this to the Post office in time.[3]

ALS, NjMoNP.

1. For GW's record of his journey to Philadelphia from 9 to 13 May, see *Diaries*, 5:152–56, and Philadelphia Cash Accounts, 9 May–22 Sept., printed above.

2. None of George Augustine Washington's letters to GW in Philadelphia has been found, but GW's letters to his nephew confirm that George Augustine followed the instructions to make weekly reports. GW's surviving letters to George Augustine during the summer of 1787 are dated 17, 27 May, 3, 10, 15 June, 1, 8, 15, 24, 29 July, 12, 26 Aug., and 2, 9 September. Information about what George Augustine wrote not only comes from GW's letters but also can be found in the weekly farm reports that he prepared for GW (see Farm Reports, 26 Nov. 1785–16 April 1786, editorial note).

3. Letter not found.

From Gardoqui

Sir   New york 19th May 1787.

Nothing but absolute impossibility wou'd have prevented me from doing myself the honor of waiting on your Excellency upon the first good news of your Excellency's arrivall at Philadelphia, but unluckly for me I had then two Packetts upon my hands, one of which is already at Sea, so that I was depriv'd of the so much wish'd for honor of visiting your Excellency as soon as I expectted, however the hopes of doing it immidiatly after I have dispatch'd the present business releaves part of my disapointment, & for the mean time give me leave to congratulate your Excellency on your safe arrivall, & to wish with a sincere heart that the presence of so respectable a character & of the other worthy Delegates to the Convention may succeed in arranging such meassures as may produce the happiest effects to the United States.

Beleive me Sir that such is my unfeign'd wish & that no Foreigner will feel a greater satisfaction in seeing it realiz'd than myself.

I reserve the pleasure of converssing on the subjects of your Excellency's favor of the 1st Decre for the happy moment of waitting on your Excellency, observing by the by that you wou'd make yourself eassy on the she Ass, as my request was made to a Brother of mine who has some Interest at Court to gett permission & no doubt he will have done as a private affair of his own or mine.[1]

I agree perfectly in what I understand of your Excellency's letter regarding Treaties, but I wish most heartly that some resolutions of your Excellency's State had not been taken as I fear they must have made an unhappy impression on the other side of the watter.[2]

Give me leave to repeatt that I long for the honor of a personal acquaintance with your Excellency & that in the mean time I am with the greatest respectt & consideration Your Excellency's most obedt & very humble Servt

James Gardoqui

ALS, DLC:GW.

1. GW replied to Diego de Gardoqui from Philadelphia on 31 May: "Sir, The letter with which your Excellency was pleased to honor me (under cover

to General Knox) did not get to my hands till yesterday, altho' dated the 19th—occasioned by that Gentlemans having left the City before it arrived, and its following him back to New York.

"As I look with much pleasure to the moment which promises me the honor of a personal acquaintance with your Excellency—and you have assured me that this is not far distant, I will not, now, take up your time in professions of that esteem, regard and respect with which I have the honor to be Sir, Yr Excellencys Most Obet Humble Servant G. Washington" (LB, DLC:GW). See Henry Knox to GW, 29 May. On 9 Sept. GW recorded that he dined at Robert Morris's "after making a visit to Mr. Gardoqui who as he says came from New York on a visit to me" (*Diaries*, 5:184). Under the dateline "Philadelphia, Sept. 14," the *Virginia Gazette, and Weekly Advertiser* (Richmond) reported on 27 Sept.: "On Saturday night last arrived in this city from New-York, his excellency Don Diego de Gardoqui, minister from his Catholic Majesty to the Honorable Congress of the United States, on a visit to his excellency general Washington, previous to his departure for his seat at Mount Vernon."

2. See Gardoqui to GW, 29 Oct. 1787, n.1.

To Arthur Lee

Dear Sir, Philad[elphi]a May 20th 1787.

I have been honored with your favor of the 13th, since my arrival at this place.

My Rheumatic complaint having very much abated (after I had the pleasure of seeing you at Mount Vernon) I have yielded to what appeared to be the wishes of many of my friends, and am now here as a delegate to the Convention.[1] Not more than four states were represented yesterday. If any are come in since it is unknown to me. These delays greatly impede public measures, and serve to sour the temper of the punctual members who do not like to idle away their time, Mrs Washington intended to have given you the trouble of the enclosed, had it been prepared in time—As the case is, I take the liberty of committing it to your care.[2] I have the honor to be Sir, Your Most Obedt Servt

Go: Washington

ALS (photocopy), DLC:GW.

1. Lee spent the night of 20 April at Mount Vernon.
2. The enclosure has not been identified.

From Henry Lee, Jr.

Dear General,   N. York May 20th [17]87

It is with reluctance that I trouble you on any matter of a private nature, but the peculiar hardship of Mr Heards case I hope will fully apologize for this interruption.

Mr Heard was an officer in my regiment—in the year 1780 I received an order from the Quartermaster General to impress a Number of horses in Monmouth county in obedience to an order from you on the subject, it being probable from the contiguity of that county to this town that the enemy might possess themselves of the horses there & your army being then in want of this article. Mr Heard was employed by me among other officers to execute this business.

Since the peace he has been sued by the owner of one of the impressed horses, & may probably suffer considerably. In this situation he is induced to wait on you, trusting from this explanation, that you will chearfully give him every aid in your power. With the same propriety may every officer in the late army be called on for retribution for articles impressed by military order, as the present gentleman, yet it seems not improbable, but the court may decree against him, unless he can produce a let. from you on the subject.[1] I am my dear Genl with unceasing affection & respect

Henry Lee Jur

ALS, DLC:GW.

1. Between 1779 and 1782 James Heard rose in rank from cornet to captain in Light-Horse Harry Lee's legion. On 30 July 1782 GW wrote Gov. William Livingston of New Jersey informing him of a suit instituted against Heard by a Mr. Anderson of Monmouth County, N.J., and reporting that Heard contended that he was following Henry Lee's orders which were founded on GW's instructions. No letter written by GW in 1787 on Heard's behalf has been found.

From Gilliss Polk

Sir,   Annapolis May 20th 1787

I Received your letter of the 2d May Informing me of the Receipt of the plank by Capt. Nutter and am glad to find it an-

swers your wishes.[1] You express Sorrow, that I did not fix Upon
a price for the plank. The Reason why I did not was plainly this,
it had given me So much more trouble to procure it than common plank, that I was Unwilling to fix on a price Until I had
Made myself Acquainted how Such plank had been Sold, I was
Well acquainted with the difficulty of geting plank of Such
lengths, but not of that quality. However I have Since had an
opportunity of conversing on that Subject with Charles Wallace
esquire of this town whoes knowledge in them Matters may be
Relyed on, he informs me that when he built the State-House
in this City, he Made a contract for plank of that thickness and
quality, tho not so long (which makes a Material difference) for
that he was to give 17/6 ⅌Ct he Received the plank and all that
See it looked upon it to be the best they ever see, however upon
Making Use of it, he found, that Not more than one forth was
clear of Sap and Knots—and concludes, that from the discription I gave him of the plank Sent you (And I think I gave a Just
State of it) it was Worth 35/ ⅌Ct but as that Sum is So far above
what Capt. Nutter thought Reasonable I cannot think of Charging you with that Sum, I shall be content with 25/ ⅌Ct.[2] I am Sir
Yours with Esteem

Gilliss Polk

ALS, DLC:GW.
  1. Letter not found, but see Polk to GW, 14 April 1787.
  2. Charles Wallace (1727–1812) of Annapolis entered the tobacco consignment trade before the Revolution, and in 1771 he contracted for the construction of the third State House in Annapolis, more or less completed by 1776.
Wallace was a member of the Maryland Executive Council from 1783 to 1785.
The prices that Polk quotes are for one hundred feet of planking.

Letter not found: from George Augustine Washington, 20 May 1787. On
27 May GW acknowledged the receipt of George Augustine Washington's letter "of the 20th instt."

From Alexander Donald

Sir   Richmond 22d May 1787
    At the desire of Docr Stewart,[1] I have the Honour of enclosing
you Mr Morris's note for 200 Dollars, And the first of Messrs
William Alexander & Co's. bill on same Gentleman for

894.⁸⁵/₉₀ths payable at ten days sight—Both which I hope will get safe to hand.[2]

I beg you will do me the favour to acknowledge receipt of the above money. I will not trouble you with the second Copy of the bill, if I find the first gets to your hands.[3]

It would give me very great pleasure if I could be of any service to you here; & my House in London, carried on under the Firm of Donald & Burton, would have equal pleasure in rendering you any service there. I beg you will beleive me to be with very great respect and Esteem Sir Your mo: obt Sert

A. Donald

ALS, DLC:GW. This may be in the hand of Donald's clerk.

Alexander Donald, an import-export merchant in Richmond, acted as Robert Morris's business agent in Virginia.

1. See GW to David Stuart, 5 May.

2. See the entry for 27 May in Philadelphia Cash Accounts, 9 May–22 Sept., printed above. See also GW to David Stuart, 1 July.

3. GW acknowledged the receipt of the money on 2 June (see Donald to GW, 20 June), but GW's letter of 2 June has not been found. See also GW to David Stuart, 1 July.

Letter not found: from Thomas Smith, 22 May 1787. On 22 Feb. 1788 GW wrote Smith: "I have, at this late period, to acknowledge the rect of your letter of the 22d of may last."

From George Turner

Sir   Philadelphia 22d May [17]87

I have the Honour to enclose an Extract from the Minutes of the late General Meeting, which immediately concerns the Office of President-Genl—whenever the whole of the Minutes can be fairly transcribed the Copy will be forwarded to your Excellency[1] by, Sir, Your most obedient and mo: humble Servant

G. Turner
Assist: Secy Genl

ALS, DLC:GW.

1. No minutes of the General Meeting of the Society of the Cincinnati in May 1787 have been found. Edward Carrington of Virginia wrote George Weedon, 18 June 1787, that the General Meeting had "avoided the publication of any part of these proceedings except the election of Officers—publications answer no useful purposes to the Order, and are often the Means of

bringing into Public speculation things that are not matured and of course liable to misconstruction" (Hume, *Papers of Virginia Cincinnati,* 168–71).

From Jean Le Mayeur

Sir   Richmond May 23 1787
   owing to a months absence of this place, I did not received your Excellencys favour of the fifth instant till yesterday by which i am sorry to find the Majors son died.[1]
   In consequence of your Excellencys Good conseil i shall ⟨renew⟩ my devotion I intend the 8th of next month to Go from Petesburg to the sweet springs and remaine till September from there to Charlestown and next january Embark for havanah and stay till june following then return.
   If it might not be Conceived indiscressionately, I would solicit the favour of your Excellency to obtaine me a testimonial letter (from the Spanish minister) as surgeon dentist and I have no doubt that he will mention it is at your request which will promote my reputation.
   I assure your Excellency I feel myself much at a loss when I wish to apologize for the repeated obligations i have been favour'd with, particularly that in promoting my Cavaliery.[2] you will I trust accept of my unfeigned thanks. and in case you should think proper to honour me with an answer addressed to Col. Banister (at Petesburg) i shall receive it if Even i should be Gone before its arrival as his son will be at sweet springs in july. I have the honour to remaine with the most profond Respect and veneration your Excellencys most obedient and most humble servant

                                             John Le Mayeur

ALS, DLC:GW.
   1. Letter not found. The son of George Augustine and Fanny Bassett Washington fell ill on Sunday, 22 April, and died on Wednesday, 25 April, after being baptized at Mount Vernon the day before (*Diaries,* 5:142–43).
   2. Some of Le Mayeur's mares were left at Mount Vernon, and GW volunteered the services of his stallion Magnolio (Le Mayeur to GW, 10 April 1786).

Letter not found: from Annis Boudinot Stockton, 26 May 1787. On 30 June GW wrote Mrs. Stockton to thank her "for the obliging letter with which you honored me on the 26th Ulto."

To George Augustine Washington

Dear George,   Philadelphia 27th May 1787

In my last I acknowledged the receipt of your first letter; and I have now to do that of the 20th instt.[1] And once for all I will desire that you will not let your anxiety to carry on my business well, or fatigue in the accomplishment of it, go too far. This would not serve me, and may injure yourself. By attempting too much you may get sick, and do nothing effectual for me or yourself.

It gave me concern to find from your last letter that you were still in want of rain; the Country hereabouts is deluged; and the farmers are complaining of the extra: quantity. In truth scarcely a day passes with out some—On Friday last an immense quantity fell and as it had the appearance of a settled rain, I hope it extended to us. If not, patience is the best substitute—indeed the only remedy.

Hearing that Leather is to be had on better terms at Boston than in this City; and Mr Ingraham being on a journey thither I requested him to buy as much as would make 50 or 60 pair of Shoes; if this is not enough, the difficiency can be made up here, or in Alexandria. I also requested him to enquire into the price of Corn, but this need not prevent your buying if it is to be met with, as the quantity I want is too small, of itself, to engage a vessel; and I have neither money, or inclination to speculate in a larger purchase.[2]

If you tried both fresh, and Salt fish as a manure, the different effect of them should be attended to. I have no objection to putting the ground at Frenchs in Buckwheat, if the Farmer shall think it best. This Crop, Potatoes, Pease, & Turnips, were, if I recollect rightly, what I had designed for the gr[oun]d—The quantities of each, or the omission of any, may be governed by circumstances; & weather; for in this, any more than in other things, and at other plantations, there is no contending against the Seasons. Nor should the Crops which are in the ground be neglected for those that may be put there; if therefore, that part of Timberlanding field, intended for Buck Wheat, cannot be plowed before harvest without letting what you call Robins field go unplowed, it must be postponed;[3] for the working of that Corn before harvest is indispensably necessary—In a word, the good attendance of Corn in the early growth of it; and till it has tassled, and put forth Shoots, is, in my opinion, all in all, to the Crop. After this period, I do not beleive it is *much* to be hurt, either by weeds or the ground becoming hard.

How does the grass Seeds which were Sown with the grain, & flax, seem to come on? How does those which were sown in my little garden advance? And how does the Crops which are planted in drills between the Corn, come up, & progress? Also those in my experimental squares at Muddy hole; particularly the Carrots and J: Artichok—the Seeds of which I had most cause to distrust. Is there a prospect of a good deal of orchard grass Seed? let none be lost. Inform me particularly of the appearances of Barley and Oats. The latter, because it composes a principal part of my Crop, and the other because I am anxious for its success, that it may constitute a part of my course of Crops hereafter.

I send by this conveyance some Pecon nuts; which plant as soon as you can. With respect to the quantity of Shells which are, or may be wanted, it is hardly possible for me to say—for which reason, buy always when you can get them good, and Cheap—16/8 I was informed they might be had for—if not at this, get them on the best terms you can. When you go about the repository for the compost, at the mouth of the drain by the Stable, if the bottom should not be of good clay, put clay there and ram it well before you pave it, to prevent the liquid manure from sinking, and thereby being lost—this should also be done on the New sides whch are to be walled up. Cornelius when he knows for what purpose this is required will, I presume, know how to do it.

I hope the stray doe will not be lost; does any of them appear to be with young? Has any Mares been sent to the Jacks, and to Magnolio, and how many to each? If the state of the Mill run, and other circumstances will admit of it the opening, and thoroughly repairing of the race, will be an important object, because it cannot be done but in warm weather, and not to advantage but when the Water is low.

Have you made no mistake in your acct of the pease that were drilled at Muddy hole? In your report of this (May 15th) you note that 1 Bushel from Colo. Lees, and two of the large yellow (made at home) were sowed; & that of the first there were 16 rows, and of the latter 15 only; I should hardly have thought that the same quantity of Lees Pease,[4] would have seeded double the ground the others had done—And is the whole field, that is every 8th row from one end to the other sown? the quantity seems small for this also—as it does indeed in all the cuts at the different places; for if 3 Bushels were sufficient to sow the whole field at Muddy hole you must have a surplusage of seed, which might have been tried in broadcast, whilst I was apprehensive of a scarcity for the drill cultivation of them between the Corn rows.

Desire Mathew to furnish me with a Memo. of the Hinges wanted for the New-room, and to which hand they are to rise, that I may endeavor to provide them whilst I am in this place. As I see no prospect of a Speedy return (for contrary to my wish, I am made, by a unanimous vote, President of the Convention)[5] I will, in due time furnish you with a plan for conducting your harvest—In the meantime, send me my last diary, which, by mistake, I left behind me—It will be found, I presume, on my writing Table. put it under a good strong paper cover, sealed up as a letter.[6] Speaking of a Diary, it would be better in your report of the Occurrances, and the work done at the Plantations, to allow a paragraph to each. That is—when you change from one plantation to another, to begin a New line; for sometimes, without this, and perhaps not properly attending, I do not in the moment perceive the change; nor when I want to recur to it, is it so easily come at, as if in the daily report, all that related to each plantation was in paragraphs—as abovementioned.[7] Give my love to Fanny, and best wishes to Mr Lear.[8] With best Affectn I am sincerely Yrs

Go: Washington

P.S. Is the Seeds of the honey locust come up? They shd be kept clean—as every thing else in drills ought to be. Colo. Rogers of Baltimore was to have sent by the Baltimore packet to Alexandria for me a quantity of the English (imported) white thorn[9]— If they are at hand let the Farmer manage them as he thinks proper—If I did not mention it in my last, a Plow was to have been sent by Majr Snowden to Mr Hartshorn for me.[10] Endeavor to keep the willow in the Serpentine walks upright by means of the Stakes, and tow yarn or grass, or something else to tye them thereto that will not rub, or fret the bark—the small, as well as the large trees in these walks should be staked up to give them a proper elevation.

ALS, CSmH.

1. GW's "last," dated 17 May, is printed above. Neither of George Augustine Washington's letters has been found.

2. See Nathaniel Ingraham to GW, 31 May, and GW to George Augustine Washington, 10 June, 2 September.

3. Both Timber Landing field and Robin's field were parts of River farm at Mount Vernon.

4. For "Lees Pease," see Henry Lee to GW, 28 April.

5. GW was elected president when the Convention formed itself on 25 May. After Edmund Randolph presented the Virginia Plan on 29 May, the Convention went into the committee of the whole house until 19 June, during which time Nathaniel Gorham was in the chair. Thereafter GW presided.

6. GW kept a journal in a separate booklet while in Philadelphia, and after his return to Mount Vernon in the fall he entered an expanded version of his Philadelphia journal in his Mount Vernon diary. The editors of the *Diaries* give a full description of the journal and diaries (*Diaries*, 5:152–53).

7. See Farm Reports, 26 Nov. 1785–16 April 1786, printed above.

8. Allusions that GW made in the letters that he wrote to George Augustine from Philadelphia suggest that he routinely sent letters to Mrs. Washington at the same time that he wrote to George Augustine, none of which has survived.

9. Nicholas Rogers (1753–1822) of Druid Hill, a prominent merchant in Baltimore, visited Mount Vernon in August 1786 (*Diaries*, 5:31, 32).

10. GW wrote to Thomas Snowden on 7 Oct. 1786.

From David Humphreys

My dear General   New Haven [Conn.] May 28th 1787

I intended fully, when I left Philadelphia, to have written to you from New York, but on my arrival there my Servant (who was a German) ran away, & I was so occupied in procuring another, that I have not been able to take up the pen until the present moment.[1]

Recollecting imperfectly, as I do, the purport of Mr Jefferson's letter, as well as of the Extract from the Encyclopedia; I have found myself embarrassed in attempting to say any thing on so delicate a subject—especially considering it a subject on whose merits Posterity is to judge, & concerning which every word that may be drawn from you, will probably hereafter be brought into question & scrutinised—Under this view I have thought, the less that could with decency be said, the better.[2] With sentiments of perfect friendship & consideration I have the honor to be my dear General Your Most Obedt hble Servt

D. Humphreys

ALS, DLC:GW.

1. David Humphreys was among the party of former officers who went out to Chester on Sunday, 13 May, to conduct GW into Philadelphia (*Diaries*, 5:155).

2. Humphreys provided GW with a draft to be used to answer Thomas Jefferson's letter of 14 Nov. 1786 in which Jefferson had criticized the Society of the Cincinnati and had enclosed an encyclopedia article attacking it. When writing his reply to Jefferson on 30 May, GW simply copied Humphreys' draft for the part of his letter that related to the Cincinnati. See also GW to Henry Knox (second letter), 27 April 1787. Humphreys' draft has been transcribed for CD-ROM:GW.

Letter not found: from George Augustine Washington, 28 May 1787. On 3 June GW wrote George Augustine Washington: "I am sorry to find by your letter of the 28th Ulto . . ."

From Henry Knox

My dear Sir   New York 29 May 1787

I enclose you a letter from Don Diego de Gardoqui, which he transmitted to me by the post to Philadelphia after my departure, and which I received by the return post.[1]

I was happy on my return to find my daughter Lucys eye so much better, as to remove all fears of being obliged to apply the surgeons instruments to it.

As you will have states sufficient to proceed to business, we hope to hear by the post of this day that you are completely organized—Mr Peirce, & Mr Houston from Georgia set off from this place for Philadelphia yesterday. Mr Sherman & Doctor Johnson will be in Philadelphia in the course of the week. I have not heard any thing from New Hampshire, but I am persuaded, from circumstances, that the delegates from that state will be with you by the 10th of June. I am indeed happy that the convention will be so full, as to feel a confidence that they represent the great majority of the people of the United States.[2]

The grumblings in Massachusetts still continue and the insurgents on the border appear to be collecting with hostile intentions⟨.⟩ There can be no doubt that a trifling success on their part, and a prospect of subsistence woud induce great numbers to join their Standard. events are fast ripening to birth—anarchy threatens—a few hains being spung[3] we shall find ourselves without system or government—so impressed is my mind with the evils about to happen, which will naturally arise from the construction and imbecillities of the States & general constitutions of this country, that I have no hope of a free government but from the convention—If that fails us we shall find ourselves afloat on an ocean of uncertainty, uncertain as to the shore on which we shall land but most certain as to the storms we shall have to encounter.

I hope to be able so to arrange my business as to accompany Mrs Knox to Trenton in the course of next week, and thence to Philadelphia for a few days, at which some public business requires me to be present.

I have received a letter from the Isle of France from Colonel Fleuri, who requests his most affectionate respects to be transmitted to you—He is second in the command of the troops in the Isles of France and Bourbon.[4] I am my dear Sir with the highest respect and affection Your most Obedient humble Servant

H. Knox

ALS, DLC:GW.

1. Gardoqui's letter is dated 19 May; GW's response of 31 May is printed in note 1 of that document. Knox met GW at Chester on 13 May and accompanied him into Philadelphia (David Humphreys to GW, 28 May, n.1).

2. William Pierce attended the Convention on 31 May and William Houstoun on 1 June. Roger Sherman was at the Convention on 30 May, and William Samuel Johnson arrived on 2 June. The two New Hampshire delegates who did attend, John Langdon and Nicholas Gilman, did not arrive until 23 July.

3. It is not clear what Knox intended to say here.

4. This was François-Louis Teisseydre, vicomte de Fleury, whom Lafayette listed in March 1784 as one of the men in France wearing the badge of the Society of the Cincinnati (Lafayette to GW, 9 Mar. 1784 [first letter], n.6).

From Charles Willson Peale

Dr Sir   May 29, 1787
   With the utmost reluctance I undertake to ask you take the trouble of setting for another portrait, it gives me pain to make the request, but the great desire I have to make a good mezzo-tinto print, that your numerous friends may be gratified with a faithful likeness (several of whom I find is not satisfied with any of the portraits they have seen). My particular intrest alone in this business would not have induced me to be thus trouble-some, but if you can indulge me so far I will do evry thing in my power to make it convenient & easey to you,[1] as I am with the highest respect your Excellencys most obliged Hbl. Servant

                                        C.W. Peale

LB, PPAmP: Charles Willson Peale Papers.
   1. See Peale to GW, c. June 1787, and note 1 of that document.

The Virginia Plan

[Philadelphia, c. 29 May 1787]. GW's Copy of the Original Plan for a New Government as Given into Convention by the State of Virginia appears in CD-ROM:GW.

AD, DLC:GW. It is not known when GW made his copy of the document, but as a member of the Virginia delegation, he probably made it before Edmund Randolph presented the Virginia Plan to the Convention on 29 May.

   Randolph's copy of the fifteen resolutions that he offered to the Convention on 29 May has never been found. GW's copy of the Virginia Plan is almost identical to the one Madison made as printed in Rutland and Hobson, *Madison Papers,* 10:12–18. There are slight variations between the two in spelling, punctuation, and capitalization. The wording also differs in several instances: in resolution 4, GW inserted "years" after each of the last two blank spaces; in resolution 6, he wrote "legislative powers" instead of "Legislative Rights"; in resolution 9, he inserted "a" before "fixed compensation" and wrote "peace or harmony" instead of "peace and harmony"; in resolution 11, he inadvertently omitted "of Government &" after "junction"; and in resolution 13, he wrote the words "and that the assent of the National legislature" twice. For a description of the other surviving copies made by delegates of Randolph's resolutions, see Farrand, *Records of the Federal Convention,* 1:20–22.

To Thomas Jefferson

Dear Sir,   Philadelphia 30th May 1787.

It has so happened, that the letter which you did me the honor of writing to me the 14th of November last, did not come to my hands till the first of the present month; and at a time when I was about to set off for the Convention of the States, appointed to be holden in this City the 14th Instt. Consequently, it has not been in my power, at an earlier period, to reply to the important matters wch are the subjects thereof. This, possibly, may be to be regretted if the house of de Coulteaux should, in the meantime, have directed its enquiries to Philadelphia, Baltimore or New York without having had the advantages which are to be derived from the extension of the inland Navigations of the Rivers Potomack & James, delineated to them. Silence on this head may be construed into inferiority, when the fact (in my judgment) is, that Alexandria or Richmond, provided the communication with the latter can be conducted by the Greenbrier & Great Kanhawa (as some aver & others doubt) has infinite advantages over either of the Towns just mentioned. With respect to James River, I am not able to speak with so much precision as of the former, with which (having had oppertunities to be so) I am much better acquainted. To this therefore I shall chiefly confine my observations.

In investigating the advantages of Alexandria as the most proper place for a principal deposit in the Fur Trade, I have thought it necessary to leave as little room for partiality and prejudice to operate as possible, by concealing, as far as may be, the object of the investigation. Tho' the result has been favourable to Alexandria, I trust it will be found to have arisen from such weighty considerations, as must be felt by every mind; particularly that of the Merchant whose interests on this subject must alone determine the scale—With A very superficial knowledge of the relative Geography of the places (Alexanda Baltimore, Philada New York) in contemplation by Monsr Coulteaux to establish a concern in the Fur Trade to the Country yielding this article—a meer glance at the Map must decide Alexandria in point of distance to be the most convenient spot. Hence, a considerable saving would accrue in the article of Landcarriage; an object of so much importance in the communication between places seperated by immense wildernesses, and rugged roads, as to render any comment on it to a Merchant, superfluous. But the difficulty arising from this source (tho' already less) will soon, in a great measure, be obviated with respect to Alexandria, by the extension of the Navigation of Potomack. The progress already made in this great National work, Not only justifies this opinion, but the most sanguine expectations wch have been formed of its success. Granting therefore that the advantages of a greater proximity to the Fur Country, was not on the side of Alexandria, still the immense superiority which a communication almost by water, would give it, must be obvious to all who consider the ease with which the distant produce of the different, and opposite parts of the earth are mutually exchanged, by means of this element. As neither of the other places can ever enjoy this singular benefit to so great a degree, Alexandria must, of course, be the place to which the Inhabitants of the Western Country must resort with all their Commodities (unless by the other channel mentioned, Richmond should be found equal to it); and from whence they will take back their returns in foreign products with the least expence—The Act for opening a road from the highest point to which the Navigation of Potomack can be extended, to the Cheat river, must also be considered as an important circumstance in favour of Alexandria; and in the same light the act of the last Session for opening a road to the mouth of the little Kanhawa, from the road last mentioned, must be considered. Besides these, leave has been obtained from Pensylvania by the States of Virginia & Maryld, to open another road from Wills' Creek to the Yohiogani, by the nearest and best rout. By these Acts, great part of the Trade which has been accustomed to flow through Pittsburgh to Philadelphia must be derived in rich streams to the Potomack: for I believe it to be as true in commerce as in every thing else, that nature, however she may be opposed for a while, will soon resume her regular course—neither therefore the attractive power of wealth, nor the exertions of industry, will long, it is presumed, with hold from Alexandria the advantages which nature has bestowed on her.

If the great extent of territory adjacent to the Fur Country, which Virginia possesses, in comparison with the States to wch the other Towns belong, be viewed; Alexandria must still be con-sindered as the most proper place—The Country about the Illi-nois and wabash (Rivers which nearly reach the Lakes in their Course) has been long considered as the most abundant in Furs; and the completion of the Navigation of James River must, with-out doubt, render Richmond the most convenient for *these* of any others; if, as I have once or twice before observed, the Navi-gation of the Kanhawa can be improved to any good account. By those however who are not acquainted with the nature of the western waters, and the short portages between them, it may be objected that the Rivers abovementioned are too far South to meet with good Furs; but it may not be amiss to observe here, that the Rivers of lake Erie &ca communicate so nearly, and with such ease, with those of the Ohio, as to afford the short-est and best transportation from Detroit; by which all the Furs of the upper lakes must pass; whether they go to Canada—New York—Philadelphia—Baltimore—Alexandria or Rich-mond; and that the routs from thence to the two latter are thro' the territory of the United States; whereas the one to New York passes along the line, and is, besides, Subject to interruptions by Ice when these are entirely free from it. These objections, particularly the latter, apply in a degree both to Philadelphia & Baltimore; because if either can avail itself of water transporta-tion, it must be by the more Northerly stream⟨s⟩ of the Ohio, with the waters of the Susquehanna, considerably above the Mo-nongahela—and still more so above the Great Kanhawa—the first of which communicates with the River Potomack, and the latter with that of James.

The last advantage which occurs to me in favor of Alexandria, is, that the business would be carried on there without any com-petition: No one having yet engaged so deeply in it, as to hold out any encouragement—I have even been informed that Wag-gons loaded with Furs, have sometimes passed through Alexan-dria to Baltimore in search of a Market; and from Winchester it is their common practice to go there with this Commodity; tho' Alexandria is much more convenient to them. On the side of New York, the most eligable Posts for this trade are in the pos-session of the British; and whenever they are ceded it will, I expect, be found, that the Merchants of that Nation, from their

Wealth, long establishment, and consequent knowledge of the Country, will be such formidable competitors, as to draw the greater part of the Furs into Canada.

I shall now proceed to mention a person in whose skill and integrity Monsr Coulteaux may, I think, have the fullest confidence; and tho' I am precluded in some measure from so doing by being told that it is required that he should be an American born; I shall still venture to name a Gentleman who is a native of Ireland—Colo. John Fitzgerald. The active Services of this Gentleman during the War—his long residence in the Country—and intermarriage in it (with one of the most respectable families—Digges of Maryland) all entitle him to be considered as an American.[1] The laws of this Country know no difference between him and a native of America. He has besides been bred to trade—is esteemed a man of property & is at present engaged in the former in Alexandria. Lest however this should be considered as an insuperable obstacle, I shall name a second—Robert Townshend Hooe Esqr., who has every desired requisite—I shall just observe, that if the business is carried on extensively, it would probably require the various acquaintance and combined activity of each of those Gentlemen.

I come now to the other part of your letter, which concerns the Cincinnati—and here indeed I scarcely know what to say.[2] It is a delicate, it is a perplexing subject. Not having the extract from the Encyclopedia before me, I cannot now undertake to enter into the merits of the publication. It may therefore perhaps be as much as will be expected from me, to observe that the Author appears in general to have detailed very candidly & ingenuously the motives, and inducements wch gave birth to the Society. Some of the subsequent facts, which I cannot, however, from memory pretend to discuss with precision, are thought by Gentlemen who have seen the publication to be mistated; in so much that it is commonly said, truth & falsehood are so intimately blended, that it will be difficult to sever them. For my self, I only recollect two or three circumstances, in the narration, of which palpable mistakes seem to have insinuated themselves. Majr L'Enfant did not arrive and bring the Eagles during the Session of the General meeting, but sometime before that Convention. The Legislature of Rhode-Island never passed any act whatever on the subject (that ever came to my knowledge) notwithstanding what Mirabeau & others had previously advanced. Nothing can be more ridiculous than the supposition of the author that the Society was instituted partly because the Country could not then pay the Army, except the assertion that the United States have now made full & compleat provision for paying not only the arrearages due to the Officers, but the half pay or commutation, at thier option. From whence the Author deduces an argument for its dissolution. Though I conceive, this never had any thing to do with the Institution; yet, the Officers, in most of the States, who never have, nor I believe ever expect to receive one farthing of the principal or interest on their final settlement securities, would doubtless be much obliged to the Author to convince them how, and when they received a compensation for their Services. No foreigner, nor American who has been absent some time, will easily comprehend how tender those concerned are on this point. I am sorry to say a great many of the Officers consider me as having in a degree committed myself by inducing them to trust too much in the Justice of their Country. They heartily wish no settlement had been made, because it has rendered them obnoxious to their fellow Citizens, without affording the least emolument.

For the reason I have mentioned, I cannot think it expedient for me to go into an investigation of the writers deductions. I shall accordingly content myself with giving you some idea of the part I have acted, posterior to the first formation of the Association.

When I found that you and many of the most respectable characters in the Country would entirely acquiesce with the Institution as altered and amended in the first General Meeting of 1784, and that the objections against the obnoxious parts were wholly done away, I was prevailed upon to accept the Presidency. Happy in finding (so far as I could learn by assiduous enquiries) that all the clamours and jealousies, which had been excited against the original association, had ceased; I judged it a proper time in the last Autumn, to withdraw myself from any farther Agency in the business, and to make my retirement compleat agreeably to my original plan—I wrote circular letters to all the State Societies, announcing my wishes, informing that I did not propose to be at the triennial meeting, and requesting not to be re-elected President. This was the last step of a public nature I expected ever to have taken. But having since been appointed by my Native State to attend the National Convention, & having been pressed to a compliance in a manner which it hardly becomes me to describe; I have in a measure, been obliged to sacrafice my own Sentiments, and to be present in Philadelpa at the very time of the General meeting of the Cincinnati. after which I was not at liberty to decline the Presidency without placing my self in an extremely disagreeable situation with relation to that brave and faithful class of men, whose persevering friendship I had experienced on so many trying occasions.

The business of this Convention is as yet too much in embryo to form any opinion of the result. Much is expected from it by some—but little by others—and nothing by a few—That something is necessary, all will agree; for the situation of the General Governmt (if it can be called a governmt) is shaken to its foundation—and liable to be overset by every blast. In a word, it is at an end, and unless a remedy is soon applied, anarchy & confusion will inevitably ensue. But having greatly exceeded the bounds of a letter already I will only add assurances of that esteem, regard, & respect with which I have the honor to be Dear Sir Yr Most Obedt & Very Hble Ser⟨vt⟩

Go: Washington

ALS, DLC: Jefferson Papers; LB, DLC:GW; Df (fragment), DLC:GW.

1. John Fitzgerald of Ireland who settled in Alexandria before the Revolution was married to Jane (Jenny) Digges Fitzgerald (c.1754–1826), the daughter of William and Ann Digges of Warburton.

2. Except for the final paragraph, this letter repeats what Humphreys suggested in a draft that he sent to GW on 28 May.

From Roger Alden

Office of Secy of Congress [New York]

Sir　　　　　　　　　　　　　　　　　　　　　　　May 31st 1787

I have the honor to enclose to Your Excellency the news papers of this day, published in the city of New York—and I am directed by the Members of Congress present to transmit them daily[1]—with the greatest respect I have the honor to be Your Excellency's Most Obedt & most Humble servt.

Copy, DNA:PCC, item 49.

Roger Alden (d. 1836) of Connecticut, major and aide-de-camp to Jedediah Huntington during the Revolution, in 1781 became the assistant to Charles Thomson, secretary of Congress.

1. GW acknowledged Alden's letter on 8 June from Philadelphia: "Sir, I have been honored with your favor of the 31st Ult., enclosg the Gazettes of New York. Let me entreat you to make my acknowledgments to the Honble Members of Congress who were so obliging as to direct them to be sent to me; and that you would be pleased to accept, yourself, my thanks for the regularity with which they have been forwarded. I am Sir Yr most Obedt Hble Serv⟨t⟩ Go: Washington" (ALS, owned [1974] by First Convestors, Inc., Albertson, New York).

From Nathaniel Ingraham

Dear Sir   Boston 31st May 1787

I have the honor to acquaint you of my arival in this place yesterday, I have made Enquiery respecting Corn & find the price here 3/4 & the freight would be 6d. which I (presume) would not answer, the Leather I shall purchase the price is 1/2½ ℙCt & Shall Ship it to Mr Porter by a Vessell which Sails from this place to Alexandria in a few Days.[1] Should you have Occasion for any thing further by writing me a Line it Shall be attended to, & am Dr Sir with much Respect your friend & very humble Servant

            Nathl Ingraham

ALS, DLC:GW.

Nathaniel Ingraham was a merchant in Alexandria and a partner of Thomas Porter with whom GW had frequent dealings.

1. See GW to George Augustine Washington, 27 May, 10 June, and 2 September.

To Henry Knox

My dear Sir,   Philadelphia 31st May 1787.

It gave me great pleasure to find by your letter of the 29th that you were freed from all apprehension on acct of Miss Lucys eye—and that we might flatter ourselves with the expectation of seeing Mrs Knox & you at this place. It was not untill Friday last that Seven States assembled in Convention. By these I was, much against my wish, unanimously placed in the Chair—Ten States are now represented, and Maryland probably will be so in the course of a few days. Should New Hampshire come forward, Rhode-Island will then stand very *singularly* alone.

As it is not even certain that this letter will get to New York before you shall have left it I will only add Compliments to Mrs Knox and assurances of the sincerest friendship of Yr Affecte

Go: Washington

ALS, DLC: Breckinridge Long Papers; copy, NNGL: Knox Papers.

From "The Author" [Robert Goldsborough]

Sir,   Cambridge, in Maryland [1 June 1787]
If I had the honour of an Acquaintance with your Excellency, I wou'd respectfully subscribe my name to this address: But in communicating the sentiments which appear in the paper in-closed, I am not governed by a Motive of vanity in personally claiming your attention, but by a warm desire to see our political Union more perfectly established. Whether the ideas it contains can have any tendency to promote an object so ardently wished for by every patriot, is submitted to your superior Judgment. I am, sir, Like the rest of mankind, Your sincere Admirer and most obedient servant,

The Author.

ALS, DLC:GW. The letter is addressed to "His Excellency George Washington President of the Convention in Philadelphia." Eric Papenfuse has determined that the author of the enclosed proposal for the form of new government being constructed by the Federal Convention probably was Robert Golds-borough (1733–1788), a native of Cambridge, Dorchester County, Maryland. A distinguished lawyer who was at the Inns of Court in the 1750s and took a degree from the college in Philadelphia in 1760, Goldsborough was one of the drafters of Maryland's constitution in 1776. He was elected to the Annapolis Ratifying Convention in 1788 as a staunch Federalist but was too ill to attend, dying soon after it had adjourned.

Enclosure

Cambridge, in Maryland: June 1st 1787
America is like a distempered Patient, whose recovery de-pends upon the skill of the Physician: Her situation is not des-

perate; but the nicest applications will be necessary to effect her cure; The remedy is certainly in the power of the present Convention; and it is sanguinely expected that their united Wisdom will find out the healing balm and restore her to health and happiness.

It is the duty of every Citizen to bestow his Attention on her subject and to employ what talents Nature may have kindly granted, in assisting to accomplish the great business under public consideration: and I trust so confidently in the good sense and honest intentions of the members of the Philadelphia Convention, that every Man, who has any hint or information to give on an occasion so truly important, will be patiently heard. Under this idea of their candour, I presume to mention my opinion respecting the federal Government and to suggest such notions as may be found worthy of attention and improvement.

I understand then that the object desired is a review and alteration of the Articles of Confederation and the perfect establishment of *The Federal Constitution of the United States.*

In considering this Business, I wou'd keep before me the forms of government belonging to the several States; and observing the different principles applicable to *each individually* and to the *whole collectively.* I wou'd endeavor to raise the Fabric upon general and federal grounds. I wou'd positively suffer each State to retain its own sovereignty and independance—to preserve its own form of government—and to exercise within its own limits that general Jurisdiction which it now possesses. I wou'd remark (and this particular shou'd engage my keenest attention) that there exists in each Republic a *State-interest,* and in the United States *a federal* or *continental Interest*—that the State-interest is secured, protected and preserved in *each* government by a watchful constitution, which has provided, on principles of universal Necessity, a *legislative, an executive* and a *judicial* power for this essential purpose in all cases which concern her own internal regulation—and that therefore on similar principles The Federal Constitution must provide a legislative, an executive and a judicial power to secure, protect and preserve the Federal interest in every instance arising out the policy of the United States.

I wou'd not vest the *legislative* department in the hands of *Congress* upon its present establishment; that is, their form, the mode of their election and the duration of their appointments shou'd remain upon the present system; for a safer one cannot be devised: But their powers in this capacity shou'd be more enlarged and made as ample as the federal interest shou'd require; and, when ascertained, shou'd be as supreme, as absolute and obligatory upon *all continental concerns*, as the powers of legislation are in each republic. Congress shou'd consequently be authorized to enact Laws, *Statutes* or Ordinances in all Cases comprised within their Jurisdiction—whether relating to War, peace, Commerce, Navigation, Armies, Navies, Piracies, Treaties, Alliances, public Debts, Coinage, &ca &ca &ca.

But the Enaction of Statutes wou'd be fruitless, unless a force shou'd be granted to compel an obedience, and a power exist to exercise that force and put the Laws in execution. I wou'd therfore vest the *executive* department in the hands of *a Governor* assisted by thirteen *Councillors,* who shou'd be appointed and chosen by Congress annually; being neither members of their own body nor capable of a seat therein during their continuance in office. This is that department, which, when once made safe by the mode of its appointment, will be found essentially useful, by the Vigour it will add to the Statutes of Congress and the dispatch it will communicate to every public measure. It shou'd be their Business to collect the common force upon proper emergencies—to superintend the Collection of the federal Revenue—to direct arrangements in the military or naval departments—to appoint and commission proper persons to act under their direction—to sign and seal the public Statutes—and in short to exercise the powers of a supreme Magistrate and Council in all cases respecting which they shou'd derive an Authority from the hands of Congress or the Federal Constitution.

But disputes may arise between the different States or questions of importance be created on various accounts, for the termination of which a proper power shou'd be also established. I wou'd therefore vest the *judicial* Department in the hands of five able persons, to be appointed and commissioned by the supreme Governor and Council during good Behaviour; being neither members of their own body, nor of congress, nor capable of a Seat in either of those departments. It shou'd be their Business, at stated quarterly Terms, to hear and determine all disputes and Controversies arising between different States, whether on account of territory, boundary⟨s⟩ Jurisdiction or other Cause—to hear and determine all Violations of the Statutes of Congress and to adjust the penalty or punishments prescribed—to settle and decide on all admiralty-Causes either originally or by way of appeal—and in a word to take Jurisdiction of all such Matters and Cases as shou'd be committed to their Care, either directly by the Constitution or derivatively by Congress. This federal Court shou'd determine its Judgments by the Law of Nations—the Civil Law—the Statutes of Congress—or such other Authorities as may be applicable to the Nature of the Cause; and shou'd observe such forms and Course of procedure as shou'd be deemed expedient for the trial of Facts, and keep regular Entries of their Transactions by the assistance of a proper officer or Recorder.

I wou'd define the powers of each respective department as accurately as possible and leave little or nothing to discretion: There is an irresistable propensity to power in the mind of Man; and where he is permitted to exercise a Judgement of his own, the error is more commonly on the side of ambition than on the side of modesty. It is true the Nature of their several appointments in a great measure secures from danger; but still in every possible instance the less there is of doubt the less there is also of confusion.

The supreme Magistrate or *Governor-General* shou'd act in no instance but with the Assistance or Concurrence of the federal Council, or such a number of them as shou'd form a quorum for the dispatch of business: and to give each State a peculiar interest in their Deliberations, it wou'd be proper to consider whether the Council shou'd be wholly elected by *Congress,* or one of them by the Legislature of the respective States at their annual appointment of officers. They shou'd be intrusted with Authority to appoint and commission all continental officers, such as the Treasurers, the Secretaries, the Surveyors, Ministers, Ambassadors, Collectors, Judges, Admirals, Generals &ca &ca &ca whose continuance in commission shou'd be for one, three or more years according to the nature of the office and at the discretion of the Conventioners, who shou'd ascertain all these particulars. They shou'd have no controul, either of an affirmative or negative kind, over the Statutes of Congress—nor have power to direct the appropriation of public Monies, but where particularly authorized by the legislative department; and in such cases they shou'd be obliged to render Accounts.

Upon the whole, the hints above mentioned are sufficiently plain to be well understood: The very Idea of *Government* comprehends unavoidably a *power of making Laws—a power to enforce an obedience to those Laws—and a power to settle and determine* all disputes, controversies and Causes, the decision of which requires the sanction of those Laws. In other words, a *legislative,* an *executive* and a *judicial* power are essentially necessary to Government: The disposal of these powers, their definition, the judicious applicaton of them to their peculiar department, and the necessary interference of perfect Barriers between the province of each, are to make up the substantial parts of the federal Constitution and shou'd now compose the important Business of the present Convention. I need not remark that it has always been deemed essential to Liberty, that in every Government these three great powers shou'd be lodged in the hands of *different* Bodies and be kept independant of each other. That a federal Government *must exist* is universally acknowledged: This was attempted by the Articles of Confederation, and at this time makes up the object in convention to which every hope is ardently pointed. If it exist, it must contain these *three* powers; and they must be vested in *separate Hands,* or our Liberties, so dearly purchased, must be set in danger. No apprehension, it is true, has been entertained of Congress, in whom all these powers have been awkwardly blended: but it is chiefly because their Authority has been hitherto so limitted and confined to a few particular heads as to make them so little an Object of terror that they are every where treated with indifference. It is submitted to the Wisdom of those conspicuous Characters, who are engaged in this arduous Inquiry, whether this address contain such out-lines as deserve their Attention, and whether the *express* description and separation of the legislative, the executive and the judicial Departments are not essential to a perfect form of Government.

D, DLC:GW.

To Bouillé

Philadelphia June 1st 1787.

Under this cover you will do me the honor to receive a letter directed to the President, or Senior Officer of the Society of the Cincinnati in France; enclosing a resolve of the General Meeting of that Society in these United States, holden in this City, last month.[1]

If any thing, Sir, could add to the pleasure I feel in obeying the orders of this Society, it is the favourable opportunity that is afforded me of expressing to you the Sentiments of admiration and respect with which your character has inspired me; and to assure you of the esteem and consideration with which I have the honor to be Sir Yr Most Obedt and Most Humble Servt

Go: Washington

ALS (facsimile), Contenson, *La Société des Cincinnati de France*, following p. 279; LB, DLC:GW.

François-Claude-Amour de Bouillé, marquis de Bouillé (1739–1800), served as a general in the French army in the West Indies during the American Revolution. He was elected an honorary member of the French Society of the Cincinnati.

1. The enclosed letter from GW to d'Estaing as president of the French Society of the Cincinnati, also dated 1 June from Philadelphia, reads: "Sir, The enclosed resolution of the General Meeting of the Society of the Cincinnati, which I have the honor to transmit to Your Excellency, is the best apology I can make for the trouble I am now about to give you.

"Persuaded I am that, Your Excellency will derive as much pleasure from offering to, and investing the Marquis de Bouillé with the Order of the Cincinnati, as it gives me to communicate for these purposes the Sentiments of the Society. With the greatest Consideration & respect I have the honor to be Your Excellencys Most obedt & most H. Ser. Go: Washington" (ALS [photocopy], Contenson, *La Société des Cincinnati de France*, 256; LB, DLC:GW). The resolution enclosed in this letter to d'Estaing is dated 17 May 1787 and is photocopied between pp. 272 and 273, ibid.

From James McHenry

Sir   Philadelphia 1st [June] 1787

I have just received an express from Baltimore informing me that my brother lays dangerously ill, in consequence of which I set out immediately for that place. I wish to communicate this circumstance to your Excellency that it may be mentioned to the convention should my absence without leave be taken any notice of.[1] With the greatest respect I have the honor to be your Excellency's ob. st

James McHenry

ALS, DNA: RG 360, Records of the Federal Convention. McHenry misdated the letter 1 May.

1. McHenry returned to the Convention on 6 Aug. and remained until the end. His brother John, with whom McHenry was in business in Baltimore, died in 1790 at the age of 35.

Letter not found: to Alexander Donald, 2 June 1787. Donald wrote GW on 20 June: "I had the honour of receiveing your letter of the 2d Current."

From Pierre, chevalier de Gimat

La Rochelle le 2 Juin 1787

on me mande de paris, Monsieur, que Mr Le Mis de Lafayette, y est malade, et qui ne pourru peut etre pas de quelque tems, m'envoyer La Lettre de recommandation que Je lui ai demandé pour les Etats unis de L'amerique. Je vous envoye toujours mon Memoire, avec deux Lettres de le General, et deux Certificats. Je vous prie, de vouloir bien presenter le tout, à M. M. Les Membres Supperieurs de La Societé de Cincinnatus,[1] Je vous aurai toutes les obligations possibles, Monsieur, Si Je puis obtenir Cette Grace par vos Sollicitations, Si en revanche Je puis vous étre de quelque utilité Disposéz Je vous prie, de celui qui à l'honneur d'étre avec des Sentimens d'estimé et de consideration. Monsieur Votre tres humble trés obeissant Serviteur

le che. de Gimat

LS, DLC:GW. This is one of the very few letters written in French to GW at Mount Vernon in the 1780s for which a translation made for GW has not been found.

Pierre, chevalier de Gimat, colonel of the French royal artillery, was sent to Santo Domingo in command of a battalion in 1777 and remained there until 1783.

1. In the enclosed mémoire (DLC:GW), Gimat recounts his services in Santo Domingo and asks for election to the Cincinnati. Lafayette's two letters attest to Gimat's worth, and the certificate from the commanding general of Santo Domingo attests to his service on the island. Gimat's brother Jean-Joseph, che-

valier de Gimat, who while serving as Lafayette's aide de camp was wounded at Yorktown, was one of the original members of the French Society of the Cincinnati (see Gimat to GW, 12 July 1784).

To George Augustine Washington

Dear George, Philadelphia June 3d 1787.

I am sorry to find by your letter of the 28th Ulto that you have had a return of your old complaint[1]—my last caution'd you against too great exertions, & I now repeat it; because there is no occasion for it. To direct the Overseers how to apply the labour to advantage, is all that can be expected. To see to the execution, except in a ki⟨nd⟩ of rotine, is impracticable—moderate exercise will accomplish this & be of service to you, whilst by attempting too much you will do nothing, as you do not appear to have a constitution fitted for violent exertions.

It is painful to hear that the fine rains which are constantly watering this Country, & which has given a vigour and verdure to the grain & grass about this City which is hardly to be described, should not have extended to you—The coolness of the weather is common to both, and the complaint of too much rain here, is now accompanied with apprehensions, and indeed reports of damage from frost.

As there is not the smallest prospect of my returning before harvest—and God knows how long it may be after it—I enclose you the observations I made at last harvest, to be practiced on the ensuing one; because I think it will be found better than the old—at any rate it may be tried.[2] Inform me in your next how your Grain—particularly the Barley and Oats—stand on the ground—that is, the height of them, whether thick or thin—how branched—how headed—and what the farmer (who ought to be a judge) thinks of their yield, provided no accident happens—I wish also to be particularly informed of the various kinds of grass-seeds which have been sown, as well in the fields as the smaller spots. & what prospect their is, of their coming to any thing.

All the grass that is fit for Hay should be cut, or my horses &ca will be in a bad box next winter—the apparent dificiency of this article, is an argument of weight for cutting the grain whilst there is nutriment in the Straw, in the manner mentioned in the enclosed observations—this also makes it necessary to give particular attention to the Corn Crop—more especially if the Oats are likely to be short.

I am really sorry to hear that the Carro⟨ts⟩ & Parsnips are so thinly come up. Does this appear to be the effect of bad Seed, unfavourable Seasons, improper ground, or want of proper Culture? Where does this dificiency of Carrots appear greatest for on this information I shall be able to tell whether it proceeds from the first cause or not, that is bad Seed, because I have ⟨an⟩ acct with me, I think, of the places in which the different kinds were sown. I could wish, as well for the sake of the experiments I had in view, as for the profit to be derived that these, the Potatoes, Pease, &ca were up well and w⟨d⟩ stand. The Farmer should endeavor (as it appears from your Acct that there will be Seed enough for it) to put the ground which has been, & now is, plowing at French's in Pease & Potatoes—without these, or Buck Wheat, the Crop there, especially if the spring grain fails, may be very trifling indeed—I have no choice that preponderates much in favor of any one of thes⟨e⟩ Crops; for which circumstances may govern in favor of one more than the other, or of all equally—It would be a pitty not to put the Potatoes and Pease in the ground if it be practicable as the first were bought, and the other reserved, for this purpose.

In making Bricks let the Mortar be well neaded—much I believe depends upon it. Desire Cornelius or Mathew, to give me the exact dimensions of the Chimney in the New room that I may get neat castings for the back & sides, of the precise size; in doing this mention the height of it also, that the castings may be proportioned thereto, for they do not go all the way up[3]—direct Mathew also to give me the circumference of th⟨e⟩ upper piece of wood of the Cupulo on the House through which the iron spire for fastening the finishing part goes that I may get it executed and sent round from this place. the dimensions, with some kind of draft of it I conceive must be necessary for the government of the workman here—perhaps Mr Lear or yourself can give a better draught of it (on paper) than Mathew.[4]

Did no letter from Mr Young, accompany the plows & Seeds? I do not know what Seeds, or what kind of Plows he sent, but wish to be informed.[5] Mr P[e]aceys Acct you have sent. Pay Mrs

French the Sum of £87 on acct of my assumsit in favor of Robinson.[6]

The enclosed letters for Mr Lear came under cover to me. request him to translate and return to me, the French letters under this cover—I would have written to him myself but it is now 11 Oclock at Night and I am tired—the Post goes off at 6 in the Morning. My love to Fanny and best regards for Mr Lear. I am Sincerely & Affectionately Yrs

Go: Washington

P.S. As the proceedings of the Convention are not intended to be made known till the business is finished I can give you no information on this score except that the sentiments of the different members seem to accord more than I expected they would, as far as we have yet gone. There are now 11 States represented and not much hope of another as Rhode Island refused to send and New Hampshire seems unable by some means or another to come on.[7]

ALS, CSmH.

1. Letter not found.

2. GW's extensive "Notes and Observations" on his farming operations at the Mount Vernon plantation in 1785 and 1786 in DLC:GW deal with the planting and cultivation of crops rather than their harvesting. The notes and observations that he made on harvesting have not been found.

3. GW decided to have firebacks made by Charles Pettit for other fireplaces in the house as well. See particularly GW to George Augustine Washington, 26 Aug., and GW to Pettit, 7 September. Mathew Baldridge was an English joiner in GW's employ.

4. GW had Joseph Rakestraw of Philadelphia make the weathervane that is atop the cupola at Mount Vernon and arranged to have it shipped for installation before his return from Philadelphia. See GW to Joseph Rakestraw, 20 July, GW to Clement Biddle, 7 Aug., and GW to George Augustine Washington, 12, 26 Aug., 9 September.

5. See Arthur Young to GW, 1 Feb. 1787.

6. For GW's dealings with Penelope Manley French, see Charles Lee to GW, 13 Sept. 1786, and notes 1 and 4 of that document.

7. After attending the Convention the next morning, Monday, 4 June, GW "reviewed (at the importunity of Genl. [Thomas] Mifflin and the officers) the Light Infantry—Cavalry—and part of the Artillery, of the City" (*Diaries*, 5:165). Jacob Hiltzheimer reported that "in the evening [of 4 June] my wife and I went to Market Street gate, to see that great and good man, General Washington. We had a full view of him, and Major Jackson, who walked with him, but the number of people who followed him on all sides was astonishing" (Parsons, *Extracts from the Diary of Jacob Hiltzheimer*, 127).

From John Armstrong

Dear General   Carlisle [Pa.] 5th June 1787

My last letter addressed to your Excellency at Mount Vernon, intimated some expectation as well as desire, of being in Philada about this time[1]—being frequently urged by the Trustees of Dickinson College, to make a farther attempt to obtain benifactions in the City—together with this, the prospect of seeing you once more, had greatly induced me to go; but on the receit of several letters from Gentn there, I am obliged to wave the design; the Scarcity of money being almost the common text throughout this State. but a few years since, I should have thought but little of the journey with no other view than the pleasure of seeing old friends—but even laudible gratifications & business itself, must now yeild to the frailty of nature.

Let me begg your acceptance of the Copy of Doctor Nesbits discourse on the advantage of learning—with an address to the Students, herewith sent by Mr Duncan.[2] I'm sorry the delay of the Press prevents my Sending you a late address to the youth of this College, which at least affords, an agreeable amusement.

With respect to your present deliberations I dare not say either more or less, but desire to recommend them collectively, to the superintendence of God, who can give harmony & keep you from error; at this critical conjuncture of our affairs. And am dear General with great truth, Your Excellencys Affectionate humbe Servt

John Armstrong

ALS, DLC:GW. "Favoured by Mr Duncan" is written on the cover.

1. Armstrong wrote GW on 2 March.

2. See Armstrong to GW, 2 Mar., n.3. Stephen Duncan of Carlisle, Pa., was a trustee of Dickinson College.

To Chastellux

My dear Sir,   Philadelphia June 6th 1787

This letter will be handed to you by Mr Rutledge, Son to Govr Rutledge of So. Carolina—a young Gentleman of merit who is about to visit France.[1]

It is so long since a letter has passed between us, that I am not at this moment, able to determin which of us is the Debtor,[2] nor is it essential as the only purpose of the present trouble is to introduce Mr Rutledge to your Civilities[3] and to present you with a poetical work of an American Bard, (which I have not yet read it) is said to have some merit.[4] With much truth and Affectn I am my dear Marqs Yr &c.

G. Washington

LB, DLC:GW.

1. John Rutledge, Jr. (1766–1819), traveled in Europe until mid-1790. See d'Estaing to GW, 8 June 1789, n.5.

2. GW wrote Chastellux on 18 Aug. 1786 thanking him for his letter of 22 May 1786, which is missing.

3. On this day GW also wrote on behalf of Rutledge to d'Estaing, Rochambeau, and Lafayette. His letter to d'Estaing reads: "Sir, The merits of Mr Rutlidge who will do me the honor of presenting this letter to you, is the best apology I can offer for the liberty of introducing him to your politeness and attention. He is the Sone of the Honbl. Mr Rutlidge of South Carolina formerly Governor of that State he is about to make a visit to France &c.

"At the sametime that Mr Rutlidge affords me the opportunity of acknowledging the receipt of the letter which you did me the honor of writing to me by Genl Duplissis (if my former should not have got to hand) a fresh occasion is given of assuring you of the respect and regard with which I have honor to be Sir Yr Most Obedt & most Hble Servant G. Washington" (LB, DLC:GW). To Rochambeau, he wrote: "My dear Count, Permit me to introduce to your civilities Mr Rutledge the bearer of this—Son of Govr Rutledge of South Carolina—and a young Gentleman of merit, who is about to travel, and will make his first visit to France.

"I shall make no apology for this liberty, because it gives me an opportunity of repeating to you the assurances of that esteem, regard, and Affection with which I have the honor to be Yr &c. G. Washington" (LB, DLC:GW). The letter to Lafayette is printed below.

4. While in Philadelphia GW received twenty copies of Joel Barlow's *The Vision of Columbus*, a poem in nine books. See GW to Elizabeth Powel, this date.

To Lafayette

My dear Marqs   Philadelphia June 6th 1787.

Not till within this hour was I informed of the intention of Mr Rutledge (son to the Governor Rutledge of South Carolina whom I believe you know) to embark in the Packet for France, or that he was to set out in the morning for New York, to take shipping the day after. Tho' totally unprepared (immersed as I am in the business of the Convention) I cannot let this Gentleman depart without a remembrance of my friendship for you.[1] It was, when I came here, and still is, my intention, to write you a long letter from this place before I leave it, but the hour is not yet come when I can do it to my own Satisfaction or for your information. I therefore shall wait till the result of the present meeting is more matured, and till the members who constitute it are at liberty to communicate the proceedings more freely before I attempt it.

You will I dare say, be surprized my dear Marquis to receive a letter from me at this place, you will probably, be more so, when you hear that I am again brought, contrary to my public declaration, and intention, on a public theatre—such is the viscissitude of human affairs, and such the frailty of human nature that no man I conceive can well answer for the resolutions he enters into.

The pressure of the public voice was so loud, I could not resist the call to a convention of the States which is to determine whether we are to have a Government of respectability under which life—liberty, and property secured to us, or whether we are to submit to one which may be the result of chance or the moment, springing perhaps from anarch⟨ie⟩ Confusion, and dictated perhaps by some aspiring demagogue who will not consult the interest of his Country so much as his own ambitious views. What m[a]y be the result of the present deliberations is more than I am able, at present, if I was at liberty, to inform & therefore I will make this letter short, and even assurance of being more particular when I can be more satisfactory—to this period also I refer more than to acknowledge the receipt of your obliging favours of the ⟨7⟩ of February inst.

Every good wish that can flow from a warm and sincere heart, much attached to you, and every one connected with you, is presented to Madam de la Fayette and your little flock; and with sentiments of encreasing friendship and love I am my dear Marquis Yr Most obliged, and Affecte Servant

G. Washington.

LB, DLC:GW.

1. See GW to Chastellux, this date.

To Elizabeth Powel

Wednesday June 6 [1787]

Gen. Washington presents respectful compliments to Mrs Powell, & prays her acceptance of the Vision of Columbus which he promised some days ago, the Copies thereof, for which he subscribed some years since, having just come to hand.[1]

AL, ViMtV.

1. GW had subscribed to twenty copies of Joel Barlow's *The Vision of Columbus,* several of which he gave away in Philadelphia. See the entry for 18 May in Philadelphia Cash Accounts, 9 May–22 Sept. 1787, printed above. During his stay in Philadelphia, GW was frequently in the company of Elizabeth Willing Powel as well as of her husband, Samuel Powel.

To George Clinton

My dear Sir,   Philadelphia 9th June 1787

At length, I have obtained the means for discharging the balle I am owing you. Mr Morris will direct his corrispondent in New York to pay you the sum of Eight hundred and forty dollars, which will be about the amount of £325.6.0 (the balle of your Acct as rendered to Jany last) with intt thereon of Seven prCt till the middle of this month.[1]

As this is intended as a letter of advice only, I shall add nothing more at present, than my best and respectful Complimts to Mrs Clinton and the rest of your family, and that I am with sentiments of very great esteem and regard My dear Sir Yr most Obedt, and Affecte Hble Servt,

Go: Washington

ALS, ViMtV; LB, DLC:GW.

1. GW enters this payment to Clinton on 16 June in his Philadelphia Cash Accounts, 9 May–22 September. It was to pay off what he owed for the joint purchase by him and Clinton in 1784 of a 6,000-acre tract of land in Montgomery County, N. Y. (see particularly GW to Clinton, 25 Nov. 1784, n.2; see also GW to Clinton, 5 Nov. 1786). George Clinton's account with GW (NjMoNP), dated 5 Feb. 1787, shows GW's payments in 1784 and 1785 on the principal and interest of the £2,500 that he owed for his moiety of the land, leaving the balance of £325.6 due. Clinton wrote on the bottom of this letter: "Recd £836 Dollars of Mr Wm Constable to whom gave a Rect in full Dated 12th June."

To George Augustine Washington

Dear George, Philadelp[hi]a June 10th 1787.

I am very sorry to find by the last letters from Mount Vernon that you continue indisposed[1]—My wish is, that you would not, in order to facilitate my business, expose yourself to what you have not a Constitution to bear. If a person is not able to undergo the heat of the Sun, or the fatiegue of exercise in warm weather, no good, but real evil, will result from the attempt; and therefore no more should be undertaken than you can execute with ease & safety. This too, is the most effectual mode of rendering me Service.

I have received a letter from Mr Ingraham since his arrival at Boston, informing me that he had purchased, and was about to ship for Alexandria, for my use, the leather he had been requested to procure for me; consequently, you may soon expect it; with this aid you cannot be at a loss in procuring the dificency, whatever it may be.[2] Nor can you have any doubt of the Corn, if it was purchased from Mr Hunter.[3] Speaking of Corn, it leads me to caution you against turning the furrow from the drilled Corn, especially after it has got to any size. I think the drilled Corn at Morris's last year was injured thereby—and to this it was, that I inclined so strongly to the harrows; as I expected they would both weed, and stir the ground without throwing it ei⟨ther⟩ from, or to the Corn; the latter, two furrows (one on each side) if necessary, could always effect. The Corn that is manured with Fish, though it does not appear to promise much at first, may nevertheless be fine. This should be attended to, and particularly noted. For, in my conception it is not only possible, but highly probable. Delay no more time than necessity obliges, in *commencing* your turnip sowing, that the whole may be put in before the season is too far advanced, and the prospect of a Crop thereby diminished. It gives me concern to hear that the prospect of obtaining a Crop of Carrots & parsnips is so unpromising—To ascertain the value of these articles, & their product, was my grand object; in which I must be disappointed if they do not come up. Both of these, as well drilled as in broad cast, should be thinned as soon as they appear to be well established in the ground. If your Oats are heading at not more than 6 or 8 Inches high, I do not, any more than the Farmer does, see any mode by which they can be cut; consequently the next best thing must be done with them, and this I suppose he can point out. Let your Summer plowing (or fallows) for wheat, be well performed—desire the Farmer to attend particularly to this; not only at French's but wheresoever this work is going on. I would have you avoid using Mr Youngs Plows till I return, at least the one he has proved. the other may be tried by his directions, & if found superior to any other, have some more made by it, exactly agreeable to his plans—measurement—&ca—But quere, is his plow *all* Iron, or *part* Iron & *part* wood? from his letter I am in the dark on this head.[4]

Be particularly carefull of all the Seeds sent by him, & Mr Pacey.[5] Sow some of each, to try whether their vegitative properties are good, or are destroyed; and be particularly careful that they do not get mixed. The Seeds, especially those which will be to be sown soon, should not only be tried, but attention had where each sort (of the same species) is put; that no mistakes may happen, and the different kinds preserved pure & unmixed. This is very essential with respect to the Wheat. But as I observed before, the first thing necessary to be done is to ascertain the goodness of them—otherwise I may incur an expence in preparing for the reception of them unnecessarily. If the Turnip Seed should on trial (as we did the Clover Seed) prove good—do not fail to sow it in due Season—as I had rather depend upon that than the adulterated kind we have. I know not at what Season the different kind of Cabbage seeds sent me should be sown, or I would direct about them.

The Books intended for the Philadelphia Agricultural Society, I desire you will send to me, first taking out the Volume (the 6th I think) which is intended for me.[6] At the same time (possibly the same package may do) send me my Blew Coat with the Crimson collar and one of those made of the Cloth sent me by the Spanish Minister—to wit that without lapels, & lined with white Silk—as I see no end to my staying here. get the Stage Master at Alexandria to take charge of it, or Mr Porter, or some Gentleman of that place, to embrace the opportunity of a passenger (on whom dependance can be placed) coming quite through, to bring it to me.[7]

If I understand rightly the report of the ditchers, they made a miserable hand of Ditching in Easter week. It appears I think by this report that Lawson worked 3 days—Daniel 1—Boat-swain 2—and Paschall, Robbin, Bath & Charles 4 days each—In all 22 days—and in this time that they only dug 31 rods of a 4 feet ditch 21 Inches deep, & foot wide at bottom. If this Statement be true, Lawson ought to be spoken to; because it is not by any means, (unless there is something in the way of which I am not apprized) what ought to have been done.[8]

I did not know that Knowles professed, or in any degree understood Brick making—and if this is the case, he will spoil all the Bks he attempts to Burn; & I shall, in consequence, be disappointed in my work[9]—What work is Cornelius about? Who is at work with him? let this be brought into the weekly report as it is necessary I should know how he advances that I may provide for him accordingly, if I can, at this distance. What progress is made on the Green House?[10] Desire Matthew to give me the exact dimension of the Windows (one will do) of the dining room; within the casement (in the room) that I may get a Venetian blind, such as draws up & closes, and expands made here, that others may be made by it, at home. the height from the bottom to top, and width is all that is necessary within the casement.[11]

The Miller must continue, though I do not think he understands the Manufacture of Wheat equal to Roberts. It is of great importance to widen, repair, & cleanse the Race of the Mill; but whether you can do it before, or after harvest, or at all, must depend upon Circumstances; for it is impossible for me, at this distance, to determine—nor shall I pretend to give any opinion thereon.

Let Mr Lear know that I have Franked & forwarded his letter to Mr Lincoln[12]—and now send him two which came under cover to me. also that I will chearfully do the same with any others that may come to my hands from, or to him. As the Convention do not publish their proceedings I have nothing more to communicate than what you will find in the Papers, which I have ordered to be forwarded to Mount Vernon. Give my love to Fanny—and best wishes to Mr Lear.

With sincere Affection, and between ten & 11 Oclock at Night, the Post going off at 6 in the Morning I am Yrs

Go: Washington

ALS, ViMtV.

1. George Augustine's letter, which was written at some time after 28 May, has not been found. See GW to George Augustine Washington, 3 June.

2. Nathaniel Ingraham's letter is dated 31 May.

3. The Mount Vernon cash accounts for 20 June show the payment of £32 to "Willm Hunter Junr Esqr. for 40 barls Corn @ 16/" (Ledger B, 246).

4. See Arthur Young to GW, 1 Feb. 1787.

5. See William Peacey to GW, 2 Feb. 1787.

6. See GW to Samuel Powel, 30 June.

7. Gardoqui, the Spanish minister to the United States, gave GW vicuña cloth in the summer of 1786 (see Gardoqui to GW, 12 June 1786, and Henry Lee, Jr., to GW, 7, 12 Aug. 1786). GW seems at the same time to have written to Mrs. Washington asking her to have shirts made for him, for on 17 June Tobias Lear wrote Gideon Snow of the firm of Porter & Ingraham in Alexandria: "I intended to have had the Shirts made here but the General has ordered a new recruit to be made for him—I therefore told Mrs Washington that I could not get any linnen which I liked—that was a lie Snow, but yet it did not hurt me to tell it so much as it would have to have delayed anything which was doing for the Genl" (ViMtV).

8. No ditching report matching this information has been found. "Easter week" was in early April, a month before GW left Mount Vernon. James Lawson was under contract to serve as a ditcher at Mount Vernon (see *Diaries*, 5:25).

9. John Knowles, hired as a common laborer in May 1786, entered into an agreement with GW on 7 July 1789 to serve as a bricklayer for one year (DLC:GW).

10. GW began in 1784 planning for the greenhouse at Mount Vernon, which was completed in 1787. See GW to Tench Tilghman, 11 Aug. 1784, and Tilghman to GW, 18 Aug. 1784.

11. For other references to the venetian blind made in Philadelphia and sent to Mount Vernon to serve as a pattern, see GW to Clement Biddle, 12 July, 7 Aug., and GW to George Augustine Washington, 15 July, 12 August. According to his cash accounts, GW paid Ephraim Evans £3.17 in June 1788 and £1.3 in July 1788 "for paintg Venetian blinds" (Ledger B, 269).

12. Lear wrote to Benjamin Lincoln, Jr., on 4 June (MHi: Benjamin Lincoln Papers).

Letters not found: from George Augustine Washington, 10 or 11 June 1787. On 15 June GW wrote George Augustine Washington "to acknowledge the receipt of the letters from Mount Vernon of the 10th & 11th," one of which may have been from Mrs. Washington.

To Elizabeth Powel

Tuesday [c.12 June 1787]
Genl Washington presents his Compliments to Mrs. Powell & begs to know at what hour she would choose to have the Carriage—at 7 Oclock it is to go to Mr & Mrs Lloyd.

AL, ViMtV. GW's carriage was not available to him in Philadelphia after the end of July, and he was otherwise engaged on the last three Tuesday nights in July, suggesting that this missive to Mrs. Powel must have been dated no later than 10 July (GW to Samuel Powel, 25 July; *Diaries*, 5:176, 178, 179). The only Tuesdays after his arrival in Philadelphia until 11 July not otherwise accounted for in his diaries are those of 10 July, when he went to the theater outside the city to see the farce *High Life below the Stairs*, and the night of 12 June when he attended Alexander Reinagle's concert at the City Tavern, which began at 7:45. It is perhaps only giving GW the benefit of the doubt to assume that he conducted Mrs. Powel and the Lloyds to the concert on 12 June and not to the farce on 10 July. Mr. and Mrs. Lloyd may be James Lloyd (c.1756–1830) of Kent County, Md., and his wife Elizabeth, the daughter of GW's old friend James Tilghman and sister of Tench and James Tilghman, Jr.

From Henry Emanuel Lutterloh

North C[arolina] Wilmington at
Sir.   Prince Georges Creek. June 13th 1787
    Your Excellences Letter of the 8th of Aprill I had the Honour to receive but yesterday. (owing to my living at present 6 miles from Town, upon a Plantation I lately purchased.) By Your Excells. answer to my Proposalls—I find that it would be difficult to persuade the Gentlemen; in Virginia to enter into a Contract or Subscribtion to bring over a large Number of Germans which was My object when I took the liberty to propose Such an Undertaking. Not only for the Sole Benefitt of the few Subscribers; but allso to the State at large; as an Increase of Usefull Inhabitants certainly are Supporters to the Revenue and lessen to others the Taxes; and which through an Increase of White Settlers can only be done. As the Government of Virginia has lately forbid the Importation of Negrow's—I thought good Workers & Manufactures would be at this periode acceptable—I hear the back-Lands are equal to any in all the States. and that Clymath would Suet the Germans. The Number of Subscribers who would undertake Such a Plan would certainly be Promoters to

the Public best & Their advance can not only be repaid, but with a certain Surplus; which my Plan should convince the Subscribers of. I am well convinced that my being a Stranger to the Gentlemen is a great objection, to forwardg the necessary Steps in the business. Yet I flatter myself, that having the Honour to be Known to Your Excell. would alter that objection, and to prevent any Susspition—about the Receiptals of the Subscribtion. I rather wish to have Nothing to do with that—but the Subscribers could appoint a proper Persons for to Keep them Accounts. I only would fixe for myself & troubles to others abroad, a Certain Share; & the travel Expences to carry the delivery into Execution—It would give me an Opportunity to be Usefull to that State, which I wish to be—The orders for any number of Manufacto⟨res⟩ could be executed.

The Proprietors of large Tracts must be sensible That Settlin their Lands quick increases Their Revenues. That great Swamp with its Intented Canall can certainly in No other way be made Usefull Than through White Settlers. Which at the same time Might in the beginning earnt a lively hood by Working on the Channall—The Manufactores could form the Town &c. when Gentlemen can Parcele out Their Estates to White Men. The great Expences of Negrow's will be lessened; & The real Revenue be certainly paid by the said Tennants without risque or troubles. & the Government recieve more Supporters—The white should be bound by me abroad Through proper Deeds for a certain Number of years. which Nobody can do, but he who is well acq[u]ainted in the different principalities—should there be any hopes of Success in this Plan I would do myself the Honour to come & explain it more fully. The Detail of any future Execuetion of the Plan would be No object for Your Excell. to be troubled with, but Your Recomentation to a Person with whom I could converse would be the favour I beg for.[1] Having the Honour to be with the greatest Respect Your Excellency's Most obedient & Most hble Sert

Henry Emanuel Lutterloh

ALS, DLC:GW.

1. No answering letter from GW has been found.

The New Jersey Plan

[Philadelphia, 15 June 1787]. GW made and retained a copy of Propositions from the Delegates of New Jersey to the Convention which William Paterson presented on 15 June.

AD, DLC:GW. GW probably made his copy of the New Jersey plan of government on the day that William Paterson presented it to the Convention. On 15 June Madison reports: "Mr. Patterson, laid before the Convention the plan which he said several of the deputations wished to be substituted in place of that proposed by Mr. Randolp[h]. After some little discussion of the most proper mode of giving it a fair deliberation it was agreed that it should be referred to a Committee of the Whole, and that in order to place the two plans in due comparison, the other should be recommitted. At the earnest desire of Mr. [John] Lansing & some other gentlemen, it was also agreed that the Convention should not go into Committee of the whole on the subject till tomorrow, by which delay the friends of the plan proposed by Mr. Patterson wd. be better prepared to explain & support it, and all would have an opportuy of taking copies" (Farrand, *Records of the Federal Convention,* 1:242).

Paterson's own final copy of the New Jersey plan has not been found (see Appendix E, ibid., 3:611–16). The copies made by GW and James Madison, printed ibid., 1:242–45, are almost identical. The differences between Madison's version and GW's are: in article 2, GW wrote "Goods & Merchandize" instead of "goods or merchandizes," "Vellum & parchment" instead of "vellum or parchment," "rules & regulations shall be committed" instead of "rules & regulations shall have been committed," and "Suits or prosecutions" instead of "suits & prosecutions"; and at the end of the paragraph GW and Madison place "to an appeal" in different places, conveying the same meaning; in article 4, GW has "the Services by them rendered" rather than "their services," and he inserts "military" before "enterprise" in the last line; finally, in article 5, GW omits "& felonies" after "all cases of piracies." There are in addition a number of differences in spelling and punctuation.

To George Augustine Washington

Dear George   Philadelphia 15th June 1787.

The only design of this letter is to acknowledge the receipt of the letters from Mount Vernon of the 10th & 11th; and to let you or your Aunt know that the Buckles and knives mentioned in my last as having been sent, were not forwarded—I expected when I was writing those letters that Mr Porter would have been the bearer of them, but he is yet in this City. By him I mean to send the Buckles and Knives if I should think of them; when I will also write again, more fully.[1]

The letters which come from Alexandria on Tuesday Morning, do not arrive at this place till thursday evening, sometimes as late as 8 Oclock, & the Post goe[in]g off again next morning by 7 Oclock leaves so little time for writing that unless it is in cases which are pressing, I shall delay doing it till next Post day; which is on the Monday following; and which will be in Alexandria on the Wednesdays after, which I mention that in case my Letters do not reach you by the Post on Monday, they will probably be in Alexandria on the Wednesday.

When you send the two Coats wrote for in my last—accompany them with my Umbrella—I have a New one in my Study. Remember me Affectionately to all at home. I am sincerely Yrs

Go: Washington

ALS, CSmH.

1. Neither of "the letters from Mount Vernon" has been found. One undoubtedly was from George Augustine; the other may have been from Martha Washington. The "Buckles and knives mentioned in my last" were not referred to in GW's previous letter to George Augustine, dated 10 June; perhaps they were "mentioned" in a missing letter to Mrs. Washington.

Letter not found: from David Stuart, 17 June 1787. On 1 July GW wrote Stuart: "I have been favoured with your letter of the 17th Ulto."

From James Varnum

Sir   Newport [R.I.] June 18th 1787.

The inclosed address, of which I presume your Excellency has received a duplicate, was returned to me from New [York] after my arrival in this State.[1] I flattered myself that our Legislature, which convened on Monday last, would have receded from the Resolution therein referred to, and have complied with the recommendation of Congress in sending delegates to the federal Convention. The upper House, or Governor and Council, embraced the measure; but it was negatived in the House of Assembly by a large majority, notwithstanding that the greatest exertions were made to support it.[2]

Being disappointed in their expectations, the minority in the administration, and all the worthy Citizens of this State, whose minds are well informed, regretting the peculiarities of their situation, place their fullest confidence in the wisdom and moderation of the National Council, and indulge the warmest hopes of being favorably considered in their deliberations. From these deliberations they anticipate a political System, which must finally be adopted, and from which will result the safety, the honour and the happiness of the United States.

Permit me, Sir, to observe that the measures of our present legislature do not exhibit the real character of the State. They are equally reprobated & abhorred by Gentlemen of the learned professions, by the whole mercantile body, and by most of the respectable farmers and mechanics. The Majority of the administration is composed of a licentious number of men, destitute of education, and many of them, void of principle. From anarchy and confusion they derive their temporary consequence, and this they endeavour to prolong by debauching the minds of the common people, whose attention is wholly directed to the abolition of debts public & private. With these are associated the disaffected of every description, particularly those who were unfriendly during the war. Their paper-money system, founded in oppression and fraud, they are determined to support at every hazard. And rather than relinquish their favorite pursuit, they trample upon the most sacred obligations. As a proof of this they refused to comply with a requisition of Congress for repealing all laws repugnant to the Treaty of peace with Great Britain, and urged as their principal reason, that it would be calling in question the propriety of their former measures.

These may be attributed partly to the extreme freedom of our Constitution, and partly to the want of energy in the federal Union; and it is greatly to be apprehended that they cannot speedily be removed, but by uncommon and very serious exertions. It is fortunate however that the wealth and resources of this State are chiefly in possession of the well affected, and that they are entirely devoted to the public good. I have the honor of being, Sir with the greatest veneration & esteem Your Excellency's very obedient & most humble servant.

Copy, in James Madison's hand, DLC: Madison Papers. There is a second copy in the Madison Papers.

1. The enclosed address, dated 11 May, to the Federal Convention was "to be delivered to you [GW] by the Honorable James M. Varnum, Esq. who will communicate (with your permission) in person our sentiments on the subject

matter of our address." Thirteen men, headed by John Brown and Jabez Bowen, signed the address, in which they attempt to explain why Rhode Island unfortunately would not be represented in the Convention and to express their support for such reforms "as have a tendency to strengthen the union, promote the commerce, increase the power, and establish the credit, of the United States." A copy of the address in the Madison Papers (DLC) has been transcribed for CD-ROM:GW.

2. In March the Rhode Island house of delegates, by a majority of 23, voted not to send delegates to Philadelphia; in May they decided by 2 votes to send delegates but were blocked by the upper house; and in June the delegates reversed themselves again and rejected the proposal of the other house to send delegates (Polishook, *Rhode Island and the Union*, 184–85).

From Alexander Donald

Sir   Richmond 20th June 1787
I had the honour of receiveing your letter of the 2d Current—By which, I saw that the former remittance which I made you, at Docr Stewart's desire, had got safe to hand,[1] I now beg leave to trouble you with a further remittance of 306⁶⁵/₉₀th of a dollar, at the request of same Gentleman, which I hope will also reach you.[2] I am with undissembled respect—Sir your mo: obt Sert

A. Donald

ALS, DLC:GW. See source line, Donald to GW, 22 May.

1. GW's letter has not been found, but see Donald to GW, 22 May, and note 3 of that document.

2. In his Philadelphia Cash Accounts, 9 May–22 Sept. 1787, GW entered under the date 27 June the amount of £115, "To the Estate of John P. Custis Esqr. recd from Doctr Stuart."

From George Turner

                                    Lombard Street [Philadelphia]
Sir,   Saturday [c.23 June 1787]
The seventy two Diplomas left herewith, are part of those intended for the Gentlemen in France. The Remainder will be ready in a few Days.[1]

The General-Meeting directed me to obtain the President's Signature to each—and I have now the Honour to lay them before your Excellency for that Purpose. With perfect Respect,

Sir, I have the honour to be your most obedient and most humble Servt

G. Turner
A.S.G.

ALS, DLC:GW.

1. Turner wrote on 27 June: "Sir, The Bearer will deliver your Excellency an Addition of seventy eight parchment Diplomas, and five on Paper, for Framing. If the others are signed the Bearer will receive them for me" (DLC:GW).

Letter not found: to Charles Pettit, 24 June 1787. *Profiles in History,* catalog 12, item 7, gives the date 24 June 1787 for a reproduced overleaf reading: "On public Service To Charles Pettit Esqr. Assistant Q.M.G. Philadelphia." Washington's signature appears to the left of "Philadelphia."

Letter not found: from George Augustine Washington, 24 June 1787. On 1 July GW wrote George Augustine: "Your letter of the 24th . . . is before me."

Letter not found: from Alexander Spotswood, 25 June 1787. On 26 Aug. GW wrote Spotswood and referred to "yours of the 25th of June."

To Clement Biddle

Dear Sir   [Philadelphia] Friday Morng 28th June 1787

By the Post of Yesterday, I received the enclosed Memo.—If you can comply with them in time, for the Alexandria Packet it wd oblige me.[1]

If the Hatt is already got for Washington, it will be unnecessary to exchange it; If not, he prefers a black one, with such ornaments as would suit a boy of his age & the colour of the hat.[2]

I beg leave to remind you of the Linnen—two pieces—from Mr Hazlehursts;[3] and of the two pieces of finer than those you have purchased at 4/6 . For the purposes they are wanted indeed, they should be a good deal finer. I am—Dr Sir Yr Obedt Servt

Go: Washington

ALS, PHi: Washington-Biddle Correspondence.

1. The memorandum has not been identified.

2. The hat was for Martha Washington's grandson, George Washington Parke Custis.

3. In 1791 Isaac Hazlehurst & Co., merchants, were at 61 South Water Street in Philadelphia.

To Thomas McKean

[Philadelphia] Friday—29th June [1787]
Gen: Washington presents his Complts to The honbl. The Vice Presidt of the Pensa State Society of Cincinnati, and will do himself the honor of dining with the Society on the 4th of July agreeably to Invitation.[1]

AL, PHi: McKean Papers.
1. GW wrote in his diary for 4 July: ". . . went to hear an Oration on the anniversary of Independance delivered by a Mr. Mitchell, a student of Law— After which I dined with the State Society of the Cincinnati at Epplees Tavern" (*Diaries*, 5:174). Thomas McKean (1734–1817) was chief justice of the Pennsylvania Supreme Court. McKean served briefly in 1776 in New Jersey as the colonel of a battalion of Philadelphia associators.

From William Grayson

Dr Sir   New York June 30th 1787
I do myself the honor of introducing Doctor Johnson of Connecticut, a gentleman of great abilities and worth, who has been lately appointed one of the Convention:[1] I am very happy to hear you have recovered your health & remain with great respect yr Affectionate friend & most Obed. Serv.
                                                    Willm Grayson

ALS, DLC:GW.
1. William Samuel Johnson, a delegate from Connecticut, arrived at the Convention on 2 June.

To Lucy Flucker Knox

[Philadelphia] Saturday.
near 11 Oclock [30 June 1787]
Genl Washington presents his Compliments and best wishes to Mrs Knox. Business in the earlier part of the Morning, and

company since, having deprived him of the pleasure of taking a personal leave of her begs leave, before he goes to the Convention; to wish Mrs Knox a pleasent Journey, and happy meeting with her family in New York.[1]

LB, DLC:GW.
  1. Henry Knox left Philadelphia for New York in late May after attending the General Meeting of the Society of the Cincinnati but returned with Mrs. Knox in June. See Henry Knox to GW, 29 May and 14 August.

To Lafayette

My dear Marqs,   Philadelphia June 30th 1787
  The Gentleman who will do the honor of presenting this letter to you is Mr Shipping—Son of your old acquaintance Doctr Shipping of this City who having been at the Temple proposes to visit Paris, and of course to offer homage to you—He is a very sensible young man and as far as opportunities are offorded me to judge—possesses a well cultivated mind which unduces me without hesitation or apology to introduce him to your countenance and Civilities.[1] To repeat to you the assurances of that Friendship with which I am warmed would not add ought to your conviction of it because you are already persuaded of the sincere regard and affection sentiments with which I always am Yr &c.

                                        Go: Washington

LB, DLC:GW.
  1. Thomas Lee Shippen (1765–1798) was the son of the distinguished Philadelphia doctor William Shippen, Jr. (1736–1808), and of Alice Lee Shippen, sister of Arthur, William, Francis Lightfoot, and Richard Henry Lee. Young Shippen traveled in Europe until 1789 (see William Shippen, Jr., to GW, 6 April 1789). On this day, 30 June 1787, GW also wrote to Rochambeau: "My dear Count, Give me leave to introduce Mr Shippen a young Gentleman of this City, just from the Temple, to your Civilities—He is a man of Education information, and good character; and one with whom I am persuaded you will be made pleased. He proposes to visit Paris, and I believe other parts of the Continent which is the reason of my giving you the trouble of this introduction of him, at the same time that it affords an occasion of renewing those assurances of Friendship and regard, with which I have the honor to be—My dear Genl Yr Most Obedt & Affe. Servant G. Washington" (LB, DLC:GW).
  The letter that GW wrote to Thomas Jefferson introducing Shippen, which

the copyist misdated in GW's letter book, "Phila. Sept. 26th—87," a week after GW had left Philadelphia, in fact was written at about this time. It reads: "My dear Sir, The merits of Mr Shippen, Son of Doctr Shippen of this City, will be the best apology I can offer for introducing him to your attention and civilities whilst he is in Paris. He is a young Gentleman of Talents and improvement— these I am sure you love, I shall only add therefore how much and how sincerely I am—yours &. G. Washington" (DLC:GW).

To Samuel Powel

Sir,   Philadelphia June 30th 1787
In a letter which I have lately had the honor to receive from Arthur Young Esqr. Author of the Tours, and many other useful publications on practical farming in the following paragraphs.
"I am informed &c.[1]
The annals alluded to accompany this letter, and I have particular pleasure in being the mideum thro' which they are convd to the agricultural Society of this City, for the success of whose laudable endeavors to promote Agricultur, my best wishes are offered.[2] I have the honor to be Sir Yrs &c.

                              G. Washington

LB, DLC:GW. In the letter book the letter is to "The President of the Agricultural Society Philadelphia."

1. Arthur Young's letter to GW is dated 1 Feb. 1787.

2. *The Minutes of the Philadelphia Society for the Promotion of Agriculture* (Philadelphia, 1854) has this entry for 3 July 1787: "The President presented to the Society a letter from General Washington, of the 30th Ult., which was read. It was accompanied with 6 volumes of the Annals of Agriculture, by Arthur Young, Esq., who desired the General to present the same to the Society, to whom Mr. Young tenders his service" (32). Samuel Powel responded to GW's letter on this date: "Sir I am much obliged to you for your Letter of this Day, & the acceptable present of Mr Youngs Works which accompanied it I shall take the first Opportunity of presenting them to the Society, to whom the Medium of presenting them, from Mr Young, cannot fail of being particularly acceptable. Will you, Sir, add to the Favor now conferred on the Society, the Honor of being present at their next Meeting which will be held at the Carpenters Hall on Tuesday Evening next about half an Hour after Seven?" (DLC:GW). In his diary entry for Tuesday, 3 July, GW wrote: "Dined at Mr. [Robert] Morris's and drank Tea at Mr. Powells—after which, in Company with him, I attended the Agricultural Society at Carpenters Hall" (*Diaries*, 5:173).

To Annis Boudinot Stockton

Madam,   Philadelphia June 30th 1787.

At the same time that I pray you to accept my sincere thanks for the obliging letter with which you honored me on the 26th Ulto (accompaned by a poetical performance[)] for which I am more indebted to your partiality than to any merits I possess, by which your muse could have been inspir'd.[1] I have to entreat that you will ascribe my silence to any cause rather than to a want of respect or friendship for you, the truth really is—that what with my attendance in Convention—morning business, receiving, and returning visits—and Dining late with the numberless &ca—which are not to be avoided in so large a City as Philadelphia, I have Scarcely a moment in which I can enjoy the pleasures which result from the recognition on the many instances of your attention to me or to express a due sense of them,[2] I feel more however than I can easily communicate for the last testimony of your flattering recollection of me. The friendship you are so good as to assure me you feel for me, claims all my gratitude sensibility, & meets the most cordial return. with compliments to your good family I have the honor to be Madam Yrs &c.

G. Washington

LB, DLC:GW.
    1. Letter not found.
    2. See GW to Annis Boudinot Stockton, 18 Feb. 1784, and notes.

From Charles Willson Peale

Dr Sir   [c. June 1787]

Your obliging consent to set is confering a most singular favor on me, for which I hope I shall always be found grateful, on the success of this undertaking depends much of my happiness. if I am so fortunate as to make a good, and faithful Portrait, I shall be enabled to gratifie many of your warm friends by excuting a good Print and the practice I lately had in this line is only bringing in my hand to execute something I hope more Excellent. my next solicitude is to make the bussiness as convenient to you as possible. I thought by bringing my Pallette & Pensils to Mr

Morris's that you might sett at your leisure and if any Interruptions by Visitors or bussiness should take place that I would wait or attend any time convenient to you[1] and esteem every labour light in a work of so much Consequence to your much Obliged Friend and very Humble Servt

C.W. Peale

LB, PPAmP: Charles Willson Peale Papers.

1. See Peale to GW, 29 May. According to his diary GW sat for Peale before attending the Convention on the mornings of 3, 6, and 9 July (*Diaries*, 5:173, 174, 175). Peale advertised the mezzotint of GW in August (Miller, *Peale Papers*, 1:481, n.2).

To Samuel Powel

[c. June 1787]

Genl Washington presents his Compliments to Mr Powell and would, with much pleasure, dine with him on Thursday next, had he not been previously engaged to Mr Rutledge.

AL, ViMtV.

GW indicates in his diary while in Philadelphia the person or persons with whom he had dinner on every Thursday except one, and John Rutledge is not named. On the one Thursday, 7 June, that GW did not have his dinner at someone's house, he "Dined with a Club of Convention Members at the Indian Queen" (*Diaries*, 5:166).

To David Stuart

Dear Sir,   Philadelphia July 1st 1787.

I have been favoured with your letter of the 17th Ulto.[1]

In May, Mr Alexr Donald made me a remittance in Bills on Robert Morris Esqr. of this City to the amount of 1094⁸⁵⁄₉₀ Dollrs; and a few days since I received another drought on the same Gentleman for 306⁶⁵⁄₉₀ Dollars making together 1401⁶⁰⁄₉₀ Dollrs or Four hundred and twenty pounds ten Shillings Virginia Currency—which I have placed to the Credit of Mr Custis's Estate.[2]

Rhode Island, from our last Accts s[t]ill persevere in that impolitic—unjust—and one might add without much impropriety scandalous conduct, which seems to have marked all her public

Councils of late; Consequently, no Representation is yet here from thence. New Hampshire, tho' Delegates have been appointed, is also unrepresented—various causes have been assigned—whether well, or ill founded I shall not take upon me to decide—The fact however is that they are not here. Political contests, and want of Money, are amidst the reasons assigned for the non attendance of the members.

As the rules of the Convention prevent me from relating any of the proceedings of it, and the gazettes contain more fully than I could detail other occurrances of public nature, I have little to communicate to you on the article of News. Happy indeed would it be if the Convention shall be able to recommend such a firm and permanent Government for this Union, as all who live under it may be Secure in their lives, liberty and property, and thrice happy would it be, if such a recommendation should obtain. Every body wishes—every body expects some thing from the Convention—but what will be the final result of its delibration, the book of fate must disclose—Persuaded I am that the primary cause of all our disorders lies in the different State Governments, and in the tenacity of that power which pervades the whole of their systems. Whilst independent sovereignty is so ardently contended for, whilst the local views of each State and seperate interests by which they are too much govern'd will not yield to a more enlarged scale of politicks; incompatibility in the laws of different States, and disrespect to those of the general government must render the situation of this great Country weak, inefficient and disgraceful. It has already done so, almost to the final dissolution of it—weak at home and disregarded abroad is our present condition, and contemptible enough it is.

Entirely unnecessary was it, to offer any apology for the sentiments you ware so obliging as to offer me—I have had no wish more ardent (thro' the whole progress of this business) than that of knowing what kind of Government is best calculated for us to live under. No doubt there will be a diversity of sentiment on this important subject; and to inform the Judgment, it is necessary to hear all arguments that can be advanced. To please all is impossible, and to attempt it would be vain; the only way therefore is, under all the views in which it can be placed—and with a due consideration to circumstances—habits &ca—&ca—to form such a government as will bear the scrutinizing eye of criticism and trust it to the good sense and patriotism of the people to carry it into effect. Demagogues—men who are unwilling to lose any of their state consequence—and interested characters in each, will oppose any general government but ought these not to be regarded right, and Justice it is to be hoped will at length prevail.

My best[3] wishes attend Mrs Stuart, yourself and the girls—If I can render any Service whist I remain here, I shall be happy in doing it, being Dear Sir, &ca.

G. Washington

LB, DLC:GW.
1. Letter not found.
2. See Alexander Donald to GW, 22 May, 20 June, and cash entry, 27 May, in Philadelphia Cash Accounts, 9 May–22 September. See also GW's account with John Parke Custis's estate in Ledger B, 226.
3. The copyist wrote "last," and Jared Sparks changed the word to "best."

To George Augustine Washington

Dear George   Philadelphia 1st July 1787.
Your letter of the 24th, with the report, is before me; & such observations as occur, shall be handed to you.[1]

In plowing the drilled Corn, it is to be remembered, that throwing the furrow always to the plant, will leave the land in high ridges; and make it more liable to wash, & run into Gullies; to avoid wch, was one of my principal motives for introducing the Hoe & common Iron toothed Harrows, because, had these succeeded, the Grain would have been wed, & the Earth pulverized at the sametime that the land would have been left smooth & even. As these (owing to the uncommonly dry Season) cannot be used to any good purpose, the other evil should, as far as it is practicable, without injury to the Corn, be avoided.

I am glad to find that your prospect for Carrots at Dogue run & Muddy hole is not quite so gloomy as it at first appeared. If all these things are equally unproductive with the Spring grain, I shall have a melancholy prospect before me. As the first Potatoes at Market will probably sell high, examine now and then your forwardest; and when they are of sufficient size, dispose of them (if the price is more than equivalent to the loss which will probably be sustained by digging them prematurely) to those who may incline to purchase, in Alexandria—keeping an acct of the quantity, that I may form some estimate of the yield, & proportionate value of them to other Crops.

If the ground designed for fallowing, for wheat in the Autumn, is more than can be prepared *well*, the quantity should be reduced; as it is a folly to do things by halves; but before it is given up, Oxen, & every thing should be attempted in the *Plow*, to accomplish it; as my whole System will be deranged, and my next years Crop become nothing, without I again return back to Indian Corn, which I am aiming to get rid off. If however it is unavoidable, and the quantity *must* be reduced, let that field at Dogue run adjoining the upper meadow (& divided by the row of Stakes) be the first prepared, because it can be most conveniently inclosed; and will leave the rest in one common pasture. In fixing Youngs plow, go exactly by the directions he gives.

I am very glad to hear that all the imported Seeds have come up (except the rib grass, which in my opinion is the least valuable of any)—The Season for Sowing the Cabbage Seed for this years Crop, is no doubt over, and must be preserved for the next.

You may inform Thos Greene that if Drunkeness, or idleness constitutes any part of his conduct, that I have directed you to discharge him. practices of this sort are violations of the agreement, & I will keep no person in my Service who is addicted to them. Should he go, Mahony may be employed. In every place where I have been, there are *many* workmen, & *little* work, which will bring these people to their Senses again.[2]

I dare say the distribution of the Cradlers is good; if otherwise, you can easily alter it when harvest is fairly entered upon, & the defect at one place, or surplusage at another, is discovered.

If the Jacks do not perform what is expected from them, the Mares, unquestionably, must be sent to Magnolio, rather than let them go over.

Gerard Alexander, as an additional Security, I should think would be good; but I question much whether he will enter himself as such, for Bob; and should this be the case, it will exhibit a fresh proof of the necessity of bringing matters to a close with the latter, before it is too late.[3]

Endeavor, not only for the sake of the Corn, but for cleansing the ground, to till the New ground in front of the House well; as I wish very much to destroy all the Succours, sprouts, roots, &ca in it most effectually, that I may lay it down in grass as soon as this can be accomplished perfectly.

The Jerusalem Artichokes ought not to be any more ploughed; or the roots will be all turned out of the ground. The only directions I have for their management was, I believe, left with you.

As you cannot do without a Fan for your grain, I ordered one of the best kind to be made; & expect you will receive it by a Vessel which has some things on board for me, and which, it is said, will Sail from this on Tuesday; tho' it will probably be later, as it was to have gone last friday, and then to day, &ca.

By the letter you sent me from Mr Polk, he seems to understand the art of charging for his Plank, perfectly well; the payment however may be delayed till I return, and can enquire a little into matters.[4]

I understand by Mrs Washington's letter, that there is some part of the mouldings, or decorations with the plaister of Paris, that Mathew cannot put up; and says Mr Rawlins was to send a hand to do it. If this is the case it would be well to write to Rawlins about it. I do not recollect that circumstance myself but do perfectly remember, that the stains, & other blemishes in the Stucco, was to be removed; when, as he said, the Walls were sufficiently seasoned: when he left the work, he added, it was not, at that time, in a proper state for these attempts.[5] I have desired Colo. Biddle to send glass for the New room and suppose it will go (cut to the proper size) with the other things. I have directed 48 instead of 36 lights. The Wood part of the New room may be painted of any tolerably fashionable colour—so as to serve present purposes; and this might be a buff. 'Tis more than probable it will receive a *finishing* colour hereafter. The buff should be of the lightest kind, inclining to white.[6]

Give my love to Fanny, and best wishes to Mr Lear. I am Dear George Yr affecte

Go: Washington

ALS, CSmH.

1. Letter not found.

2. On 6 Dec. 1786 GW had renewed his contract with Thomas Green (George Augustine Washington agreement with Green, DLC:GW), who had been overseeing the work of the carpenters at Mount Vernon since before GW's return from the army. Green remained at Mount Vernon for six more years but not out of trouble (see, for instance, Green to GW, 15 May 1788). Thomas Mahony at this time was working as a carpenter at Mount Vernon under the terms of a contract entered into with GW on 1 Aug. 1786, printed above. Before he made the contract with GW, Mahony had served for two years as an indentured servant at Mount Vernon (List of Servants & Redemptions that has been Freed & Redeemed, 2–5 Aug. 1784, ViMtV).

3. For GW's suit against Robert Alexander to collect a prewar debt, see GW to Alexander, 14 Nov. 1786, n.1.

4. See Gilliss Polk to GW, 20 May.

5. See GW to John Rawlins, 13 April. See also GW to George Augustine Washington, 29 July, n.3.

6. GW wrote George Augustine on 2 Sept. that he "was sorry to find that the Green paint which was got to give the dining [New] room another Coat, should have turned out so bad."

Letter not found: from George Augustine Washington. GW wrote George Augustine on 8 July: "I have your letter of the first before me."

From Alexander Hamilton

Dr Sir.   [New York] July 3d '87

In my passage through the Jerseys and since my arrival here I have taken particular pains to discover the public sentiment and I am more and more convinced that this is the critical opportunity for establishing the prosperity of this country on a solid foundation—I have conversed with men of information not only of this City but from different parts of the state; and they agree that there has been an astonishing revolution for the better in the minds of the people. The prevailing apprehension among thinking men is that the Convention, from a fear of shocking the popular opinion, will not go far enough—They seem to be convinced that a strong well mounted government will better suit the popular palate than one of a different complexion. Men in office are indeed taking all possible pains to give an unfavourable impression of the Convention; but the current seems to be running strongly the other way.

A plain but sensible man, in a conversation I had with him yesterday, expressed himself nearly in this manner—The people begin to be convinced that their "excellent form of government" as they have been used to call it, will not answer their purpose; and that they must substitute something not very remote from that which they have lately quitted.

These appearances though they will not warrant a conclusion that the people are yet ripe for such a plan as I advocate, yet serve to prove that there is no reason to despair of their adopting one equally energetic, if the Convention should think proper to propose it. They serve to prove that we ought not to allow too much weight to objections drawn from the supposed repugnancy of the people to an efficient constitution. I confess I am more and more inclined to believe that former habits of thinking are regaining their influence with more rapidity than is generally imagined.

Not having compared ideas with you, Sir, I cannot judge how far our sentiments agree; but as I persuade myself the genuineness of my representations will receive credit with you, my anxiety for the event of the deliberations of the Convention induces me to make this communication of what appears to be the tendency of the public mind. I own to you Sir that I am seriously and deeply distressed at the aspect of the Councils which prevailed when I left Philadelphia—I fear that we shall let slip the golden opportunity of rescuing the American empire from disunion anarchy and misery—No motley or feeble measure can answer the end or will finally receive the public support. Decision is true wisdom and will be not less reputable to the Convention than salutary to the community.

I shall of necessity remain here ten or twelve days; if I have reason to believe that my attendance at Philadelphia will not be mere waste of time, I shall after that period rejoin the Convention.[1] I remain with sincere esteem Dr Sir Yr Obed. serv.

A. Hamilton

ALS, DLC:GW.

1. Hamilton arrived at the Convention on 18 May and left on 29 June. He is known to have attended again on 13 Aug., but he probably returned to Philadelphia earlier in the month.

From Samuel Meredith

Sr   July 4, 1787.

In complyance with a promise made you, to give a short accot of the method I practised before the Warr of Sowing & plowing in Buck Wheat with a View of inriching the Land, & destroying in some degree a large Quantity of Garlic; I now take up my Pen, & will first mention that the land was a poor light sand, that had been under Cultivation for a great many Years & was exceedingly impoverished.

The first Plowing was performed in the Spring, the second just before seeding which was (to the best of my knowledge) the 25th April, the grain grew very well, & at a time when it was supposed there was a sufficiency of seed ripe to sow it again it was plowed in & produced a crop that was little if any inferior to the former, this was afterwards plowed in, & part of the Ground had a slight dressing of dung, which had been made in the Winter, & was frequently turned & well rotted[.] After the second turning in of the Buck Wheat the Ground became a perfect Ash Heap, & in this state it was sown with White, & red Chaff Wheat, & produced according to the best information 15 Bushels an acre, & had hardly any Garlic in it.

In order to turn in more effectually the Buck Wheat, about midway from the ⟨Coulter &⟩ the head of the Plow was fixed a With or rope to which was fastened a Wedge of Hickory Wood about one foot long & Six Inches diameter sharpened almost to a point at one end, into which a hole was bored large enough to take the with or rope, so that the Wedge reached the extremity of the mould board, & of consequence drew most of the Heads of the buck Wheat in parallel lines to the plow, & was covered by the Earth formed by the Mould Board before it had escaped the pressure of the Wedge—I dont pretend to take any merit to myself in this process, as it was entirely under the direction of an English Farmer.

I mention the Wedge ought to be hickory only because when green its very heavy, & of course requires less bulk & perhaps a ⟨*illegible*⟩ chain doubled might answer the purpose near as well —In Ground full of Garlic I should think the Land being plowed in the Fall would answer a much better purpose than in the Spring.

My Neighbours supposed the Land sown in the above Method would not produce more than the seed, & perswaded me against sowing it with Wheat.

It will afford me great pleasure to think I could give a moments satisfaction to one I so much esteem, & to whom I wish every happiness being with Respect Sr Your most humble Servt

Saml Meredith

ALS, DLC:GW.

GW had dined on 20 June with Samuel Meredith (1741–1817), a Philadelphia merchant who served as a brigadier general under GW during the Revolution. Meredith at this time was a member of Congress.

From William Rawle

Sir.   Third Street [Philadelphia] 6th July 1787

I have the honor to transmit to you as President of the Convention, a resolve of the directors of the Library Company in this City.[1] I am Sir with perfect respect your most obedient humble servant

W: Rawle

LS, DNA: RG 360, Records of the Federal Convention.

William Rawle (1759–1836), who returned to Philadelphia from London in 1782 and was admitted to the Pennsylvania bar in 1783, became a member of the American Philosophical Society in 1786. In 1791 GW appointed him U.S. attorney for Pennsylvania.

1. The enclosed resolution of the Library Company reads: "At a meeting of the directors of the Library company of Philadelphia on Thursday the 5th July 1787 Resolved. That the librarian furnish the gentlemen who compose the Convention now sitting with such books as they may desire during their continuance at Philadelphia, taking receipts for the same. By order of the directors, W: Rawle secretary."

From Chartier de Lotbinière

Sir   [New York, 8 July 1787]

Having been informed on my Arrival in this City (the 26 of June) that your Excellency was hourly expected I have waited to deliver the Letter sent herewith which the Marquis de la fayette sent to me from Versailles to Paris the Day preceding my Departure for Havre.[1] But General Knox having assured me

Yesterday, at Dinner with him, that I must forego the infinite Pleasure of I expected from seeing you here and at the same time told me that the Heat of Philadelphia was at least double that which I with great Difficulty support in this Season at New York that Moreover it was very Doubtful whether you could grant me a few Moments Conversation at a time in which you are so much occupied I determined Sir to send you thro his Assistance the Letter of your very good friend and wait your orders for my Approach.[2]

It was With the greatest Satisfaction that I had frequently the Opportunity of conversing about your Excellency with the Marquis and I dare flatter myself that being recommended by one so strongly attached to you You will be pleased to give me some Share of the Kindness Esteem & friendship betwowed on him. I have the Honor to be with infinite Respect & Attachment Sir your Excellency's most obedt & humble Servt
The Marquis of Chartier de Lotbiniere

Translation, in the hand of Gouverneur Morris, DLC:GW; ALS, in French, DLC:GW.

Michel Chartier de Lotbinière (1723–1798) before 1763 was a French army officer and engineer in Canada and was now the owner of large tracts of land on Lake Champlain. See Chartier de Lotbinière to GW, 2 Jan. 1789, source note.

1. Lafayette's letter to "My dear General," dated 1 May and written from Versailles, reads: "This letter will Be forwarded By Mr le M[arqu]is de lotbinieres a french Gentleman who Had a Considerable property in Canada, and Now finds Himself within the limits of the State of Newyork—He Has Claims which, the Unconstitutional part Being set aside, Appear to me well grounded—and Altho I told Him You Had nothing to do in the Business, I was Requested By Himself, and By intimate friends of Mine to give Him this ⟨Re⟩Commandation. As I write By the same opportunity and My letter will Reach Mount Vernon Before this, I shall only Add the Affectionate and filial Respect of Your devoted and Grateful friend and Humble Servant lafayette" (PEL). Lafayette wrote again on 5 May.

2. GW replied to Chartier de Lotbinière on 15 July: "Sir, The letter which you did me the honor of writing to me the 8th Instt accompanied by one from my very good friend the Marquis de la Fayette, came duly to hand.

"The business which brough⟨t⟩ me to this City, necessarily keeps me so much confined to it, that I dare not flatter myself with the honor of paying my respects to you in New York, but if there is any matter in which I can, consistently, serve you, to obey your commands would afford me the greatest pleasure. I have the honor to be Sir yr most Obedt & most Hble Ser⟨vt⟩ Go: Washington" (ALS, CtY: Beck Collection; LB, DLC:GW, mistakenly dated 8 July).

Chartier de Lotbinière acknowledged GW's letter, from New York, on 29 July: "I did not receive untill the Evening of the 16th the Letter you honored me with on the 15th of this Month—I cannot too highly express my lively Gratitude for the Kindness & Offers of Service which you make and I will apply to you with entire Confidence whenever I find myself in want of your Protection to obtain from Congress that Justice which I have every Reason to expect. As you are detained, at Philadelphia by such numerous & important Affairs that your Excellency cannot gratify the ardent Desire which prevails here to see you I shall certainly wait on you as soon as I receive the Answers I expect from my family or when I know the Time in which any one ⟨of⟩ them will come to see me. It is ⟨so⟩ long Sir that I burn with the Desire to see you and know you more intimately that I shall profit of the Opportunity of waiting on you as soon as may be without deranging my Affairs by a longer Journey. And being with you I flatter myself it will not be long before I assure you that I am not unworthy of the Goodwill you express And that I equally deserve it by my Attachment to the United States and you their Saviour & titular Deity And by—the infinite Respect with which I am &ca" (translation, DLC:GW). Chartier de Lotbinière did visit GW before he left Philadelphia (see Chartier de Lotbinière to GW, 27 Jan. 1788).

From Charles Willson Peale

Dr Sir   [Philadelphia] July 8th 1787
   The Drapery and back ground of your Portrait is painted and if it is convenient to your Excellency to favor me with a setting to morrow morning, I will have my pallet sett with fresh ground Colours.[1] I hope and believe this setting will make it equal to any ⟨Picture⟩ from the Pensil of your very much obliged friend & Hble Servt

                                          C.W. Peale

LB, PPAmP: Charles Willson Peale Papers.
   1. See Peale to GW, c. June 1787, n.1.

To George Augustine Washington

Dear George,   Philadelphia 8th July 1787
   I have your letter of the first before me.[1] In a late one, you have said, that application had been made to Dow, without effect, for the amount of his Bond; and therefore, Flour was sold for the use of Mr L. Washington.[2] Does the latter mean to receive the proceeds of the flour & keep the Bond (for it was put

into his hands) too? If he does not, and the Bond is returned to you; I wish Mr Lear or yourself, would make a pointed demand of the payment, and if not received, to place it without delay in the hands of Colo. Simms—there is no other way of dealing with such Men—I shall be perfectly satisfied, if he does not pay immediately, that his only object has been that of procrastination. The Security, Major Little, might as well be spoken to first.[3]

I did not mean that you should make any offers to Branagan, such as I mentioned, unless application first came from him—I did not expect that it was such terms as he would embrace as long at least as his money lasted; for with this I conceive he will be constantly drunk; if he possessed prudence therefore he should leave this as deposit in your hands, even if he goes elsewhere in pursuit of work; for sure I am if he takes it into keeping he will not work whilst it lasts; or if he works *at all*, it will be under such circumstances as to bring discredit on himself.[4]

I did not mean to express an idea that my instructions, by not being fully complied with, proceeded from any inattention or neglect. I well know that unfavourable Seasons will disconcert any plan, however wisely laid, or judiciously calculated on; all that can be done in such cases is to come as near as possible to the original intention. What made me anxious about the Summer fallows was, that it was intended to introduce a rotation which will be defeated if I fail in the accomplishment—and for this reason it was that I recommended in my last that all the force of Oxen &ca should be given to the Plows, as well to establish this System, as to aid me in my next years Crop; without which, I must again return to Indian Corn, or some kind of Spring Crop neither of which would answer my purpose. Is there any prospect of your doing any thing to the Mill race whilst the drought continues? This you know can not be touched to advantage under any other circumstances.

How does your Pompkin Vines look? and what figure does the pease—Potatoes—Carrots & Parsnips make? Does your Turnips come up well, and do they escape the Fly? How does the Clover, and the other grass seeds which were sown this Spring look? Did you perceive any difference in the lay Wheat at Morris's? if so which had the preference? How was it, compared with the other Wheat when they were ripe, and cut? How is the cape wheat likely to yield, & how did the latter sowed Wheat at Morris's (that was harrowed) come on? Did the Rye adjoining, which was so very thin when I left home, come to any thing—and how has the Spelts & flax turned out? I should suppose that all the Potatoes planted in the Pen (according to Grymes's directions) must be rotten except the upper layer—but attend to it notwithstanding—What was the general height of your Barley and Oats particularly the former? and what is the Farmers opinion of them especially the first?

I am sorry to hear that the honey locust Seeds came up badly—pray keep them, and all these kind of things clean—and I had rather you should delay sowing the Turnip Seed than put it in grd that is not *well* prepared—without this my labour is lost, and I shall in vain expect a Crop.

I would not have you buy shells faster than to secure lime for Cornelius work—they will rather fall than rise—it is a natural consequence of decrease of building—What quantity of orchard grass Seed are you likely to save—and what are your prospects of Timothy seed? Give my love to Fanny and best wishes to Mr Lear. I am very sincerely and Affectly Yrs

Go: Washington

P.S. Keep the Shrubberies clean. What have you done to the Gravel Walks—or rather what remains to be done to them.

ALS, CSmH.
 1. Letter not found.
 2. Letter not found, but see GW to Lund Washington, 7 May 1787, n.3.
 3. Charles Little (c.1744–1813) lived at Cleesh with his wife Mary Manley Little. Little was an officer in the Fairfax County militia.
 4. George Augustine gave Thomas Branagan (Brannagin, Bradikin) £4.10 on 3 Aug., "at the expiration of his indentures" (Ledger B, 248). Branagan was a joiner (see numerous entries in the Mount Vernon farm reports, 18 Nov. 1786–28 April 1787, ViMtV).

To Crèvecoeur

Sir   Philadelphia July 9th 1787
 The letter which you did me the honor of writing to me by Commodore Paul Jones, came safe; as did the 3 Volumes of the Farmers letters. For both, particularly the compliment of the latter, I pray you to accept my best thanks.[1]

Let me express my gratitude to you at the sametime, Sir, for the obliging offer of transmitting any communications I may have occasion to make to my good and much esteemed friend the Marqs de la Fayette, whose Services & zeal in the cause of his Country, merits as much applause from his fellow Citizens, as it meets admiration from the rest of mankind.

I congratulate you on your safe arrival in this Country—and with sentiments of esteem & regard I have the honor to be Sir— Yr most Obedt Servt

Go: Washington

ALS, DLC: Crèvecoeur Papers; LB, DLC:GW.

Crèvecoeur had recently returned from France to become the French consul in New York.

1. Letter not found. See GW to John Paul Jones, 22 July 1787. Crèvecoeur sent GW a copy of the new three-volume French edition of his *Letters from an American Farmer* (1782), entitled *Lettres d'un cultivateur Américain . . . depuis l'année 1770 jusqu'en 1786* (Paris, 1787). GW, who had read Crèvecoeur's *Letters*, thought highly of the work (see GW to Richard Henderson, 19 June 1788).

From Chavannes de La Giraudière

Sir,   Charleston [S.C.] July 10th 1787.

Altho' I am not personally known to your Excellency I hope that a summary acct of my situation and that of an ancient & illustrious family who are, at this time, overwhelmed with miseries, will be sufficient to excite your attention, and draw down your beneficience upon the father & the children. A particular detail of my misfortunes would be too long & tedious for your Excellency's perusal; a number of respectable Characters by whom you are surrounded can attest to the truth of them.

A dispute with the late Count de Maurepas respectg a sum of Money for which the Royal treasurey was indebted to my father, (a sum which would have been thought considerable even for persons of the first rank) was the cause of my coming to America.[1] Threatened with the Bastille, but entrusted with the conducting 60 invalids to the Château de Ham in Piccardy, I went to Amsterdam with my family, intending, after the peace, to retire to Virginia with Mr Mayo, my particular friend, with whom I was very intimate at Paris, & to whom I had lent a sum of money which might be considered as a handsome fortune.

From the 4th of Jany 1782 to the 8th of October 1784 I was engaged in writing *"America delivered"*, a work in 2 Vols. in which I sung the triumph of the 13 States, that of your Excellency & all those heroes who partook of the laurels which crowned you with immortal Glory. Mr Govr Morris has a copy of it.[2]

Scarce had the Marquis de la Fayette returned to Paris when my friend & particular patron M. the Count de Segur, recommended me to this hero. I have a number of Letters from him which Mr Robert Morris & Genl Pinkney have seen, your Excellency can satisfy yourself from them. In his last, the Marquis de la Fayette advised me to go to America, promised me as many letters of recommendation, as I wished, to his friends in any part of the United States which I should chuze to go, & informed me that he should be there himself in a short time. It was then that I sat out on my voyage (after an accident which detained me more than 3 months)—After a passage of 4 Months I arrived at Philadelphia on the 24th of feby 1785. The Marquis de la Fayette had left us & I found myself possessed of two bills of exchange which were protested because there were no letters of advice recd respecting them: sick, embarassed & without friends, to compleat my misfortunes Mr Mayo had died two days before the vessel, in which he was, arrived at Boston, his loss, under my present circumstances, was like a thunder stroke to my children & myself.[3]

In this extremity I had recourse to Mr Robt Morris, who, without any knowledge of me, upon shewg him the Marquis de la Fayette's letters, generously lent me 100 florins, with which I repaired to Charleston where I had two acquaintances which I had formerly made in Paris: they could do but very little for me.

Before my departure from Philadelphia I addressed myself to a very rich Mercht of St Eustatius; whose sister one of my family had married in Guadaloup. I recd his letter of the 10th of May 1785; he promised me large sums which he had in the hands of Mr Van Bibber at Baltimore, & in the treasurey at Charleston. I immediately applied for the latter myself, & Mr Robt Morris had the goodness to seek after that in Baltimore, & instead of 80,000 livres drew but 83 Dollars. For my support in Charleston I was compelled to sell 1000, of 3000 Acres of land which I possessed in the Cty of Cambden.[4]

I am now, with my Children, upon my land; after having drawn 30 Guineas instead of 60,000 livres deposited in the publick funds by M. Van Croffen,[5] (the merchant whom I mentioned before,) I have built me a cottage in which my son, (the last sprig of his family, who has, circulating in his body, the blood of the house of Bourbon, & 3 Royal families,) with his unhappy father, lives, and we are obliged to cut down the trees to clear a small spot whereon we may raise something to subsist us & his two sisters.

I leave your Excellency to judge of the horrors of our situation; and as an addition to these calamities; I ship'd from Philadelphia, in feby last, 3 free German families, which I transpo[r]ted here at a great expence, where they quitted me. But so far are we from accepting any offers which are made us from the Spanish Colonies, that we are determined to die, if we must, in the woods of a free country, if we cannot subsist by the labour of our hands, & if we do not meet with succour in our miserable state.

I want nothing to make me happy but 3 Negroes or 200 Guineas, I could obtain the latter from Europe, but it would be two years perhaps before I could receive them, & in that time myself & children would perish with hunger & a complication of miseries.

I have not written to the Marqus de la Fayette since I have been in America, expecting his return to this Country every year, & more particularly this year, always hoping to be able to extricate myself from my difficulties, but I now find it is impossible unless I have assistance.

In the absence of the Marquis de la Fayette (who, I am certain, would not abandon me if he was in this country) I must have recourse to the benevolence of your Excellency for present aid, or we shall perish. Mr Govr Morris, who has read my genealogy, Mr Robt Morris, to whom I am under great obligations, & Genl Pinkney, to whom I am known, can attest to the truth of a part of what I have had the honor to inform you.

It is not the gift of 200 Guineas which I dare to ask of you, it is a loan of them for 5 years upon a mortgage of my lands, which men here, who are competent judges, estimate at 24,000 livres of France, with interest, at 7 pr Cent, there is no person who has any claim upon them as Genl Pinkney can inform you, & without this aid we are lost, entirely lost!

A recommendation from your Excellency, but such an one as is worthy of you, Sir, to Generals Waine & Sumpter would certainly have great influence with these illustrious men. My only hope, at this moment, is in your humanity. A subscription which you might propose yourself among so many illustrious & rich citizens as are now around you wou'd, perhaps, be a happy relief to me. But if all these means are inadmissible, I close by beseeching you to procure me a retreat on one of your plantations. In this last case, it is necessary Sir that you should be at the expence of transporting us, for except my house & our tattered Clothes, I do not possess one dollar exclusive of my 2000 acres of land. My only brother was killed at Savannah under Count D'Estaing.[6] I am the first man of letters who has sung, in verse, the glory of the American Empire, and if the first family in Europe, except a prince, whom the love of liberty has brot into the united States, should perish here, without succour, what ought the Countries of Europe to think of your Republick?

My family & myself do not blush at our situation; we have deserved better; Ambition did not bring us here, but the desire of living & dying in a free country. The storm which threatened me in Europe cannot continue long. M. de Maurepas was dead before my departure from Holland. The justice & goodness of Louis XVIth is perfectly known to me—I have written proofs of the esteem & friendship of the Count de Vergennes. M. D'Estaing was so attentive as to visit me before I left Paris; thus I have reason to hope for their protection & support. But here there is no one but your Excellency to whom I can address myself in this day of difficulty & distress.

I trust that you will not be insensible to this faithful picture of my misfortunes: I assure myself that your feeling heart, (the sensibility of which I have so fully described in every part of *"America delivered"*) will not be indifferent to this letter, & that you soon give that aid to myself & family which will entitle you to the rank of our first deliverer. In this hope, founded upon your Virtues, I dare to subscribe myself, with the most profound respect Sir Your Excellency's Most Hble & Obedt Servt

De Chavannes de la Giraudiere

As I shall tomorrow set out for my land, I beg your Excellency to address your answer to M. D. C. d. l. G. Citizen of South Carolina at his plantn on Black River; County of Cambden, recommended to Mr Vernapper Mercht Charleston:[7] & if it is favourable to me, desire it to be sent to me by express.[8]

Translation, by Tobias Lear, DLC:GW; ALS, in French, DLC:GW.

1. Jean-Frédéric Phélypeaux, comte de Maurepas (1701–1781), at the time of his death was Louis XVI's chief minister.

2. On 25 Aug. 1783 A. J. Crajenschot sent to GW de Chavannes de La Giraudière's two-volume poetic work *L'Amérique delivré*, which Crajenschot had published. See David Stuart to GW, c. April 1784.

3. Joseph Mayo of Powhatan in Henrico County was relatively young when he died early in 1785 "on his passage from Lisbon to Boston." James Currie wrote Thomas Jefferson on 5 Aug. 1785 that Mayo "has enriched some of his relations by his Legacies and has astonished some of our acquaintances by his will giving liberty to all his slaves, their number from 150 to 170" (Boyd, *Jefferson Papers*, 8:342–46). Boyd quotes from Mayo's will, drawn up in 1780, and from the act of the Virginia legislature in 1787 appointing trustees to deal with the emancipation of the slaves and setting restrictions on the process (ibid., 346, 14:494).

4. James Van Bibber married Betty Dorsey of Baltimore County, daughter of Edward Dorsey and granddaughter of Ezekiel Gilliss (Gillis). Camden, S.C., is in Kershaw County, about thirty miles north of Columbia.

5. The ALS reads "Vaucrosson." A wealthy merchant named Vaucrusson had the most palatial house in the Lower Town of Oranjestad in St. Eustatius. "The rooms were richly upholstered and from the upper gallery a bridge spanned the street to a garden laid out on the roof of a warehouse" (Johannes Hartog, *History of St. Eustatius* [Aruba, Dutch West Indies, 1976], 44).

6. No officer by the name of Chavannes de La Giraudière can be found listed as killed or wounded at Savannah.

7. The ALS reads "M. Des Verneys pere." A Francis Desverneys (Deverneys) died in Charleston in 1800. He was 68 years old and had lived in the city for twenty years (*City-Gazette, and Daily Advertiser* [Charleston], 6 May 1800). Francis Desverneys is probably the Pierre Francois Deverneys who died in Charleston at about this same time.

8. Chavannes de La Giraudière wrote GW again on 4 Mar. 1788 (DLC:GW), but the letter is so faded as to be mostly illegible. What can be read of that letter indicates that it was largely a repetition of this one, to which GW seems not to have given a reply.

To Alexander Hamilton

Dear Sir,   Philadelphia 10th July [17]87.
I thank you for your Communication of the 3d. When I refer
you to the State of the Councils which prevailed at the period
you left this City—and add, that they are now, if possible, in a
worse train than ever; you will find but little ground on which
the hope of a good establishment, can be formed. In a word, I
almost dispair of seeing a favourable issue to the proceedings of
the Convention, and do therefore repent having had any agency
in the business.[1]
The Men who oppose a strong & energetic government are,
in my opinion, narrow minded politicians, or are under the influence of local views. The apprehension expressed by them that
the *people* will not accede to the form proposed is the *ostensible*,
not the *real* cause of the opposition—but admitting that the
present sentiment is as they prognosticate, the question ought
nevertheless to be, is it or is it not the best form? If the former,
recommend it, and it will assuredly obtain mauger opposition.
I am sorry you went away—I wish you were back. The crisis is
equally important and alarming, and no opposition under such
circumstances should discourage exertions till the signature is
fixed. I will not, at this time trouble you with more than my best
wishes and sincere regards. I am Dear Sir Yr obedt Servt
                                        Go: Washington

ALS, DLC: Alexander Hamilton Papers; LB, DLC:GW.
1. Three days after Hamilton left the Convention on 29 June the delegates
found themselves in a deadlock over the question of representation in Congress and were forced to refer the matter to a "grand committee" composed
of one member from each state. When GW wrote Hamilton this letter, the
delegates were engaged in a heated debate over the distribution among the
states of seats in the lower house.

To George Clinton

Dear Sir,   Philadelpa July 11th 1787
The bearer Mr Timothy Tuttle has been with me to obtain on
some terms—I did not enquire into them—part of the lands we
have a joint interest in up the Mohawk River. The answer I have
given him is, that whatever you shall do concerning them I will

abide by.[1] With great esteem & regd I am—My dear Sir—Yr most Obedt and Affecte Hble Sert

Go: Washington

ALS, NjHi; LB, DLC:GW.
    1. For the New York land held jointly by GW and Clinton, see GW to Clinton, 9 June 1787, n.1.

To Clement Biddle

[Philadelphia] Thursday [12 July 1787]
    Genl Washington's Complimts to Colo. Biddle and would thank him for sending the Upholsterer—Davis—to him as he is desirous of having one of the Venetian blinds made as soon as may be.[1]

AL, PHi: Washington-Biddle Correspondence. Written after "Thursday," in another hand, is the date "July 12. 1787."
    1. On 15 July GW wrote George Augustine Washington that he was having a venetian blind made to serve as a pattern for making others, and on 12 Aug. he wrote that the blind had been sent. See also GW to George Augustine Washington, 10 June 1787, n.11. In 1791 John Davis, upholsterer, lived at 81 South Second Street.

Letter not found: from Wakelin Welch & Son, 14 July 1787. On 8 Jan. 1788 GW wrote Welch & Son: "I have recd your letter of the . . . 14th of July."

From Richard Henry Lee

Dear Sir,   New York July 15. 1787
    I have the honor to enclose to you an Ordinance that we have just passed in Congress for establishing a temporary government beyond the Ohio, as a measure preparatory to the sale of the Lands.[1] It seemed necessary, for the security of property among uninformed, and perhaps licentious people, as the greater part of those who go there are, that a strong toned government should exist, and the rights of property be clearly defined. Our next object, is to consider of a proposition made for the purchase of 5 or 6 millions of Acres, in order to lessen the domestic debt. An object of much consequence this, since the

extinguishment of this part of the public debt would not only relieve from a very heavy burthen, but by demolishing the Ocean of public Securities, we should stop that mischievous deluge of speculation that now hurts our morals, and extremely injures the public affairs.

Our Gazettes continue to be filled with publications against the Spanish Treaty and for opening the Mississippi, some of them plausible, but generally weak and indecent. This seems to be contending for an Object unatainable for many years, and probably never without War not only with Spain, but most likely with the Bourbon Alliance—And by such contention exposing the Government of the United States to a dishonorable acquiescence under the Captivity of its Citizens and Confiscation of their effects by Spain on the Mississippi, or entering prematurely into a destructive war in resentment for such doings. At the same time discarding the friendship for the enmity of a powerful Monarch and thereby probably loose what we may possess, our Share of a Commerce that yields annually 4 or 5 millions of dollars for Cod fish only, independant of the Flour & many valuable articles of American production used in Spain & not interfering with their own products. To say nothing of a most lucrative contraband Trade from the Ocean & on the Mississippi which a friend might wink at, but which a vigilant and powerful enemy will prevent. It seems to me that N. America is going, if we are prudent, to be the Entrepôt between the East Indies and Spanish America—If to these we could join the settlement of a disputed boundary and obtain a powerful Guarantee therefor, surely such considerations greatly outweigh the far sought apprehension of an Alliance of the Kentuckians with the British, and especially when we consider that a conduct which will procure the enmity of Spain, will probably force her into the open arms of G. Britain much to our Commercial and political injury. And after all, if this navigation could be opened and the benefits be such as are chemerically supposed, it must in its consequences depopulate & ruin the old States.

The argument may shortly thus be stated—Spain will not agree to the Navigation within her limits—Can we force it in 25 years—if we cannot, why risk, for an unatainable Object, the loss of valuable objects, and the incurring pernicious consequences. A Candid and impartial consideration of this subject, must, I think determine the question without difficulty—But I beg your pardon Sir for writing so much on this question, which I doubt not but you have fully considered before. I have the honor to be with the truest respect and esteem, dear Sir, Your affectionate and most obedient servant

Richard Henry Lee

ALS, DLC:GW.
  1. This was the famous Northwest Ordinance.

To George Augustine Washington

Dear George,   Philadelphia July 15th 1787
   Your letter and report came to hand in the ordinary course of the Post. I do not recollect how I expressed myself with respect to the painting of the New room, that is whether, when speaking of this business, you would understand that it was to be done by a proper, & good painter. This was my meaning; and therefore, having no high opinion of the skill, though a favourable one of the Industry, of the one who was there last; I advise you to try Peales Nephew, or some one more knowing, both in the mixtures, & laying on of Paint, than Morrison (I think his name was)—It will require small brushes, and considerable attention to paint the carved mouldings, to prevent their filling too much with the paint. None but the wood work, & the ornaments annexed to them, are to be painted. I mean by this that the Stucco walls are not to be touched.[1]
   I am getting a Venetian blind made to send round; that others may be made at home, by it. Tell Mathew to have poplar sawed for this purpose, as thin as it can be, that it may Season against the Pattern arrives. When dressed the pieces will be about the length that the Window is wide; not more than the ⅛ of an Inch thick—and about 5 Inches wide each piece.[2]
   I only mentioned plowing with Oxen to shew my anxiety to get the ground, which was intended for Wheat, broke up for it; that I might, if possible, pursue my course; but if Carting, and other things are opposed to it, as I believe they are; the disappointment must be submitted to.
   I would have you, as soon as possible, begin to Sow Wheat in Corn ground. I do not think that Corn receives any benefit from

working after it begins to Tassle & shoot—but sure I am, that
nine years out of ten, early sown Wheat will be best. It was not
my intention (could I have pursued my newly adopted course
of cropping) to have sown wheat among the drilled Corn except
at the Ferry and in the Neck; therefore, as necessity only will
drive me to do it, I would let it be the *last* sown at the other
place⟨s⟩. At the Ferry, there will be the Stoney field, besides the
drilled and other Corn, for Wheat; as also the ground that was
intended to be fallowed: but it is to be remembered that Rye
must be sown in the poorest parts of these grounds. The like in
the poorest part of the fallowed grd at French's. The like also at
Dogue run—(if you should be able to get it in order)—and the
like at Muddy hole. In the Neck *all* the ground now in Corn will
be laid down in Wheat and Rye. Robins field wholly in the first.
The other (now in drilled Corn on the River) partly in both. The
Rye going into the weakest, & sandiest land. It was also intended, if it could be effected, to put the Orchard Inclosure
(now in Oats) into Wheat. Having mentioned these matters, circumstances must govern in the ordering of them. I must again
repeat however, that the sooner your Seeding commences in
Corn land, the better it will be for the Wheat; and none the
worse I conceive for the Corn; as I do not believe the latter is
benefitted by working after it Shoots and Tassles. The clearer
however the ground is, when the grain is sown, the better.

The mode you propose to adopt, of following the Plows in the
drilled Corn with the Harrows, to prevent high ridges, is very
proper, & will be essential for the Wheat. If time would permit,
I am of opinion, if the harrows were to follow the plows—the
sowing follow the harrows—and then the harrows to cover the
Seed, that it would be best. But experience has fully proved
the efficacy of early sowing of wheat—to get it into the ground
therefore soon, is of all others the most interesting consideration—next to it, is that of preparing the ground *well* for its
reception.

What does the Farmer *guess*, the Barley and Oats will yield to
the acre? to come at it with exactness, is not to be expected; but
now it is cut, a Man acquainted with these matters can form
a tolerable conjecture—at least of the fields he particularly attends to. Do not suffer the different kinds of Oats to get mixed—
especially those of Spotswood⟨s⟩ with any other.[3] Sprinkling

Brine with your Cut Oats, is very proper; but as soon as you can chop the Rye at the Mill, your work horses should be fed with it, and cut Straw; the cut Oats to be used for the Saddle Horses.

The ground on which the Flax grew, is as good as any to rot it on. I cannot find out by the Ditchers report, where they are at Work. Branagans staying—even on the terms I have proposed—is perfectly indifferent to me—on his, totally inadmissible. Mr Lear's letter is franked and sent on. My love to Fanny, and good wishes to him. I am Sincerely & Affectly Yrs

Go: Washington

P.S. Have you thinned the Carrots which were too thick?

ALS, CSmH.

1. GW may have been referring to one of the children of Rachel Brewer Peale's deceased twin brother, Joseph Brewer. The painter of the new room may have been Joseph Dudley, who was paid £1.10 on 25 Aug. "in full for painting" (Ledger B, 248).

2. See GW to George Augustine, 10 June 1787, n.11.

3. For the oats sent by Alexander Spotswood, see Spotswood to GW, 3 and 5 March.

To Richard Henry Lee

Dear Sir,　　　　　　　　　　　　　Philadelphia 19th July 1787

I have had the honor to receive your favor of the 15th Instt and thank you for the ordinance which was enclosed in it.

My sentiments with respect to the Navigation of the Mississipi have been long fixed, and are not dissimilar to those which are expressed in your letter; I have ever been of opinion that the true policy of the Atlantic States would be, instead of contending, prematurely, for the free Navigation of that River (which eventually, and perhaps as soon as it shall be our true interest to obtain it) must happen, to open and improve the natural communications with the Western Country through which the produce of it might be transported with convenience & ease to our Markets.

'Till you get low down the Ohio I conceive (considering the length of the voyage to New Orleans—the strength of the currt—and the time required to perform the voyage) that it would be the interest of the Inhabitants thereof to bring their produce to our ports; and sure I am there is no other tie by which they will long form a link in the chain of fœderal union. I believe however, from the temper in which those people appear to be, and from the ambitious, and turbulent Spirit of some of their demagogues that it has become a moot point to decide (when every circumstance which attends this business is taken into view) what is best to be done. The state of Virginia having entered so warmly into the matter is not among the least embarrassing, & disagreeable parts of the difficulty.

Will you permit me to put the enclosed letter under cover to you. From the Gentleman to whom it is addressed, I have lately received a letter of which this is an acknowledgment.[1] With very great esteem and regard, I have the honor to be Dear Sir Yr Most Obedt & Affe. Ser.

Go: Washington

ALS, PPAmP; LB, DLC:GW.
1. The enclosed letter, to Chartier de Lotbinière, 15 July, is printed in note 2, Chartier de Lotbinière to GW, 8 July.

From Samuel Athawes

Gentlemen   London 20th July 1787.

It is with sincere & very heartfelt Concern that I communicate to you an Event, which will excite the same sentiments of Sorrow in your Breasts; a long & uninterrupted Attachment to & Friendship with the Object of it, has convinced me that where he was barely known he was honoured; where he was well known he was valued & venerated; & where Friendship had knot the Tie he was unreservedly beloved. You, Gentlemen, stand with me in this last predicament, & what I have felt will be communicated to your Breasts when I tell you that our most worthy & invaluable Friend George William Fairfax Esqr. departed this Life on the 3d of April last. His Health for several years past had been slender & precarious. I met him at Weymouth in the Autumn, & the Sea Air & bathing seemed to agree exceedingly well with him; he increased both in his Spirits & Appetite, & after his Return to Bath I received several Letters from him wrote in such a Strain of Chearfulness & even Hilarity as he had not been accustomed to, so that I flattered myself he had laid in a good Stock of Health for the Winter. But this pleasing Prospect Soon shut in, & about Christmas he was attacked with a Fever which with Difficulty yielded to the power of Medicine; & while he was yet weak & languid from the Effects of the Fever, he was seized with a spitting of Blood. Alarmed at this Appearance, his Physician ordered him to the Hot-well at Bristol, & there were at first some weak Symptoms in his favour; but his Fever which had never been subdued, but only weakened, gathered fresh Force, & he gradually declined till at Length he fell under the inevitable Stroke. I paid him a melancholy Visit while at Bristol, & was Witness to the Firmness of Mind & christian patience with which he sustained his Malady; they continued with him to the last, & the Remembrance of them to those of his Friends who were admitted to the Scene will serve as an Example & Admonition, & to those who were not the Reflection upon them may alleviate their Sorrow for his Departure.

The Notification of this melancholy Event would have reached you sooner if the proving of the Will here had not necessarily taken up much Time from the Residence of the Executors in different parts of the Kingdom, & till they were all sworn it could not be deposited in the Registry of our prerogative Court, nor of Course an official Copy of it be obtained to send to you, who are appointed by the Testator, his Executors & Trustees for his Estates & Effects in Virginia. It is now herewith transmitted to you, & as it is unnecessary for me to enter into the particulars of it, I will only take Occasion to say that during the Visit I paid our departed Friend at Bristol he called for & opened his Will, & desired as he had appointed me one of his Executors, that I would peruse it. I did so, & the Impropriety of joining his Executors & Trustees here with those in Virginia for the Transaction of his Affairs in either or in both Countries & the Impracticability of acting with any Effect under a Trust so constituted, struck me very forcibly; & he was so well convinced of the Truth of my Remarks that his Attorney was sent for, & by a Codicil he appointed Executors & Trustees in each Country for his Estates & Affairs in each, separately & distinctly & without Dependance on each other for the performance of discretionary or legal Acts; & I flatter myself that this Alteration by simplifying the Trusts & rendering the Execution of them as easy as possible will be fully approved by you.[1]

Heartily wishing that the Event we now deplore may be respectively removed to a great Distance from each of you, & that you may enjoy an uninterrupted Series of Health & Prosperity, I remain, very respectfully Gentlemen Your very obedient humble Servant

Saml Athawes.

P.S. There being no Opportunity at present directly to Potomack I have put the papers in a Case addressed to you & consigned it by James River Ship to my Friend Colo. Burwell near Williamsburg, whom I have requested to forward it to you, by an Express, the Expence of which you will please to pay & charge to the Estate. In the Case there is also inclosed a Gold Watch, Chain & Seals, bequeathed to Mr Ferdinando Fairfax on which I have insured £25 and two Letters from Mrs Fairfax, which you will have the Goodness to send to their respective Addresses.[2]

LS, DLC:GW. At the bottom of the letter the clerk wrote "(Triplicate) Copy. To His Excellency General Washington Wilson Miles Cary & George Nicholas Esqrs.—Executors of Geo. W. Fairfax Esqr. deceased—in Virginia." The postscript, in the same hand as the rest of the letter, was directed only to GW.

Wilson Miles Cary was Sarah Cary Fairfax's brother; George Nicholas managed Fairfax's affairs in Virginia.

1. GW refused to serve as an executor of George William Fairfax's estate. See GW to Wilson Miles Cary and George Nicholas, 15 Nov. 1787, and GW to Athawes, 8 Jan. 1788.

2. Nathaniel Burwell (1750–1814) lived at Carter's Grove in James City County outside Williamsburg. Ferdinando (Fernando) Fairfax, a son of Bryan Fairfax, was the heir to George William Fairfax's property in America. See Bryan Fairfax to GW, 16 Nov. 1787.

From Mauduit du Plessis

My dear General, Paris St Mark's Street 20th July 1787.

Previous to my departure from Georgia I had the honor of writing to your Excellency a particular account of the difficulties which I had encountered during 4 months, the disasters[1] which I had met with by sickness & otherwise, and the necessity I was under of returning to France for the reestablishment of my health.[2]

I embarked at Charleston on the 9th of April on board of an English Vessel, & arrived in France the first of June. I presume that your Excellency is so well convinced of my attachment as to beleive that I felt a sincere regret at being so far distant from Mount Vernon & its respectable inhabitants. I assure you, my dear General, that I respect & revere Madam Washington with all my soul; I beg you would tell her so, & I hope she will have the goodness to beleive it.

The Count de Rochambeau, upon my arrival, made the most particular inquiries about you, and told me that he had written to you some time in the month of may last, by the way of Holland.[3]

The Marquis de la Fayette is well. When I arrived I gave him the freshest accounts I was able of Mt Vernon in which he is warmly interested. The Count d'Estaing, who is exceeding attached to your Virtue⟨,⟩ has a great desire to see you. He received, not long since, a letter from you by the hands of Mr Rutledge; Your recommendation has the greatest weight with him, he has sought all occasions of rendering himself useful & paying attention to this young American.[4]

I beseech you, my dear General, to let me hear of your & Madam Washington's welfare often; by putting your letters under cover to the minister of France or to Mr Jefferson they will find a ready conveyance to me and I request that you will honor me with any commissions which you may have to execute in France.

I shall feel myself under a great obligation to you if you will send me an engraved copy of your portrait, such as I saw at your house. I shall hang it up in my room where I may have it always in view that it may inspire me with sentiments of benevolence, greatness, & Virtue; I ask it of you as a favor which will be peculiarly dear to me.

I send you, my dear General, some Ribband for the Cincinnati, because I observed it was scarce in America.

I beg that you would be so good as to address to me a diploma of the order of the Cincinnati, signed by yourself, as I have not received one. We all wear the decoration in France & look upon it as very honorary.[5]

I beseech you, my dear General, to accept the tribute of my sincere attachment & the profound respect with which I am yr Excellency's most Hble & Obedt servt

Duplessis

Translation, DLC:GW; ALS, in French, DLC:GW.

1. The translator wrote "disatters."
2. Mauduit du Plessis's letter is dated 26 Mar. 1787.
3. Rochambeau wrote on 12 May.
4. GW's letter introducing John Rutledge, Jr., to Lafayette is dated 6 June.
5. See GW's response regarding the engraving done by Joseph Brown and the diploma of the Society of the Cincinnati, 8 Jan. 1788.

To Joseph Rakestraw

Sir,   [Philadelphia] 20th July. 1787.
Perceiving a Vessell advertized for Alexandria, you would oblige me much in hastening the work you have undertaken for me, that I may send it by her.

I should like to have a bird (in place of the Vain) with an olive branch in its Mouth—The bird need not be large (for I do not expect that it will traverse with the wind & therefore may receive the real shape of a bird, with spread wings)—the point of the spire not to appear above the bird[1]—If this, that is the bird thus described, is in the execution, likely to meet any difficulty, or to be attended with much expence, I should wish to be informed thereof previous to the undertaking of it. I am Sir Yr very Hble Sert

Go: Washington

ALS, PPRF.

1. For GW's correspondence about the weathervane, see GW to George Augustine Washington, 3 June 1787, n.4.

To Lafayette

My dear Marqs,   Philadelphia July 21st 1787
This letter will be presented to you by Mr Rucker, Partner in the House of Constable Rucker & Co. of New York and agent for Robert Morris Esqr. in France; on whose business he now is and whose instance I take the liberty of introducing him to your Civilities & to countenance if in the course of his transactions he shall stand in need of the latter.

Mr Rucker is represented to me as a Gentleman of character and worth—one who will merit your friendship—and may be obliged by your advice—I have in charge Mr Morris's Compliments to you[1]—To add how much, and how sincerily I regard you, would be unnecessary because you are already convinced of the Affection of Your Obedt & Obliged

G. Washington

LB, DLC:GW.

1. For Robert Morris's earlier correspondence regarding John Rucker and William Constable of New York, see Morris to GW, 15 June 1784.

To John Paul Jones

Sir,   Philadelphia 22d July 1787.
I avail myself of the liberty you have been so obliging as to give me, to trouble you with the care of the enclosed packet.[1] It was my intention to have added to this trouble by encreasing the number of my letters, but business has prevented; let me pray therefore that you will do me the honor to present me, in affectionate terms to the Marqs de la Fayette, and assure him, that though hurried, I should not have slipped so favourable an opportunity of writing to him, if the business of the Convention (for I have nothing else new, to offer him) could have been communicated in the present unfinished state of it. To the Count de Rochambeau, Marqs de Chastellux & others, with whom I have the honor of a particular acquaintance, I tender my best regards—I wish you a pleast Voyage, & the attainment of the objects of it.[2] I have the honor to be Sir Yr Most Obedt Hble Servt

Go: Washington

ALS (photocopy), Maggs Bros. Catalog no. 565 (Autumn 1931); LB, DLC:GW.

1. The letters for France were held up by Jones's delays in sailing. See Jones to GW, 25 July and 9 September. On 9 Nov. Jones wrote from New York: "I shall embark to morrow . . . . I shall go directly to Paris, and deliver the two Packets you sent to my care immediately on my arrival, with two others from you that have been since put into my Hands for Mr Jefferson and the Marquis de la Fayette." GW wrote to Lafayette on 15 Aug. and sent the letter to Jones on 2 September. He wrote to Lafayette again on 18 Sept. and to Thomas Jefferson on 18 and 26 Sept., enclosing for each a copy of the new Constitution.

2. This was sent under cover of his letter to John Jay, dated "July 1787": "Will you permit me to give you the trouble of the inclosed for Commodore Jones—It is at his request I do it—I offer best wish to Mrs Jay and with every sentiments of esteem and regard. I have the honor to be Dr Sir Yr very Affe. Serva[n]t G. Washington" (LB, DLC:GW).

Letter not found: from George Augustine Washington, 22 July 1787. GW wrote George Augustine on 29 July: "Your letter of the 22d is before me."

To Elizabeth Powel

[Philadelphia] Monday Morng [23 July 1787]
Genl Washington presents his respectful Compliments to Mrs Powell and will do himself the honor of calling upon her at, or before 5 oclock (in his Carriage) in hopes of the pleasure of conducting her to Lansdown this Evening.[1]

AL, ViMtV.
1. GW's diary entry for Monday, 23 July, was: "In Convention as usual. Dined at Mr. [Robert] Morris's and drank Tea at Lansdown (the Seat of Mr. [John] Penn)" (*Diaries*, 5:177).

To George Augustine Washington

Dear George,   Philadelphia July 24th 1787.
For the benefit of exercise, I left the City at 5 Oclock on Sunday Morning, and did not return in time to write by the Post on Monday. I now acknowledge the receipt of your letter and report of the 15th & shall observe upon such parts of them as may require it.[1]
I would not wish you to ask Mr Lund Washington for Dows Bond—but when you see him you may tell him that I had directed you (if it was returned) to put it *without delay* in suit; this, no doubt will bring on an explanation of his intentions respecting it.[2]
Notwithstanding the idea which I gave to you in my last, respecting fallowing, my wish now is, that the ground, be it little or much that is got into Wheat, may be *well prepared* (the Farmer no doubt can judge of this) and sowed in *good time*. I am now determined to sow no more Wheat in the *Fallow* ground than what can be put in in this manner—hoping that a smaller quantity sown in time, in well dressed Land, will yield as much as a larger qty put in late, and in a slovenly manner whilst the residue of the ground intended for fallow may be preparing (after the Winter grain is in) for Barley and Oats in the Spring.

I am in hopes you are mistaken with respect to the injury the Wheat has sustained by rust, if it only siezed it a few days previous to harvest. The grain never can be damaged by this malady if it has got hard before it appears—If the case, in the present instance is otherwise, mine is peculiarly a hard one not only to have a very thin crop, but that injured also when our accts from all parts of Virginia are, that a better Crop both as to quantity & quality has not been in that State for many years. If however the Rye, next adjoining the latter sowed Wheat at Morris's has turned out well, it will make *some* amends;[3] for in truth I did not expect, when I saw it last, that a Scythe would ever be put into that part which bordered on the lay Wheat.

If the Farmer disapproves of the Barley he grew last year, and will describe a better sort, I will make enquiry for, and if to be obtained, procure & send some home—but quæry, has not Mr Young sent the right sort? Three pecks is, from the best information I can procure, the quantity of Buck Wheat usually sown to an Acre; and may regulate your conduct in future.

Be careful to thresh the Oats wch grew in the experimental grounds by themselves, and in the manner directed, that the result may be precisely known. What kind (I mean as to their quality) of oats, grew in front of the house—and what prospect is there of that grounds being covered with clover and orchard grass?

How is the Corn in the New ground fronting the house likely to turn out? and what are your present prospects for that grain? I will enquire into the price of Timothy seed in this City; but the sooner you can, conveniently, ascertain the quantity you have, or will be able to save yourself, the better; that on advice thereof, I may know what quantity to provide.

Such parts of the Mill race (if the whole cannot be done) as is attempted, *do well,* agreeably to the direction I left. I beg that the Shrubberies on both sides of the Serpentine walks, between them & the Walls, may be spaded up, and the ground made not only clean but light. In doing this care must be taken not to injure any of the young plants.

It is indispensably necessary to lay Cills, & good heavy ones, well morticed together, on the brick work of the Stercorary— without it, the Walls will soon be down[4]—You do very right in cutting every thing that will make Hay—The Pea vines I expect will yield a good deal of food—especially for Sheep—for this reason, I conceive they ought to be cut in that State, when the Pease appear to be *generally* ripe, and before those which first ripen begin to open, or shatter with a stroke of the Scythe.

After finishing the part of No. 6, at the Ferry, in which the Plows were when you wrote, they may proceed next to the Part of it which was in wheat. And then, if I should not return home before, to the part that was in rye, provided the latter does not appear to be well taken with Timothy; in which case I would not break it up; but bestow more culture on the other parts of that field, No. 6. What kind of Oats did the New meadow at that place produce—and how does the ground appear to be taken with Timothy?

Remember me affectionately to Fanny, and offer my best wishes to Mr Lear. I am Yr sincere friend and Affecte Uncle

Go: Washington

ALS, CSmH.

1. Letter not found. After his early morning ride, GW "breakfasted at Genl. [Thomas] Mifflins." He then rode with Mifflin and four other members of the Convention out to Spring Mill in Montgomery County (*Diaries*, 5:177). GW did not always record in his diary his early morning rides: Jacob Hiltzheimer reported on 3 July that "on returning ["Before breakfast"] we met his Excellency General Washington taking a ride on horseback, only his coachman Giles with him" (Parsons, *Extracts from the Diary of Jacob Hiltzheimer*, 128).

2. See GW to George Augustine Washington, 8 July, and note 2 of that document.

3. Morris was slave overseer at Dogue Run farm.

4. The stercorary was being built to hold the dung of the livestock for manure.

From John Jay

Dear Sir   New York 25 July 1787

I was this morning honored with your Excellency's Favor of the 22d Inst: & immediately delivered the Letter it enclosed to Commodore Jones, who being detained by Business, did not go in the french Packet, which sailed Yesterday.

Permit me to hint, whether it would not be wise & seasonable to provide a strong check to the admission of Foreigners into the administration of our national Government, and to declare expressly that the Command in chief of the american army shall not be given to, nor devolved on, any but a natural *born* Citizen.

Mrs Jay is obliged by your attention, and assures You of her perfect Esteem & Regard—with similar Sentiments the most cordial and sincere I remain Dear Sir Your faithful Friend & Servt

John Jay

ALS, DLC:GW; ADf, NNC.

From John Paul Jones

Sir,   New York July 25th 1787.

Mr Jonathan Nesbitt, the bearer of this Letter, will deliver to your order the Bust you do me the Honor to accept. I am impressed with a deep sense of the favor you thereby confer on me, and it will be my ambition through the remainder of my Life to merit that mark of your esteem.[1]

As Congress has not yet determined some things that regard my return to Europe, I am prevented from embarking in the Packet that sails this day. I expect to embark in the next Vessel, and shall be happy to be charged with your dispatches for France. On my arrival here I sent your Letter to Mr St John, who is at Boston.[2]

I apprehend it will be difficult if not impossible for the Captains Edward Stack and Eugene Maccarthy to get themselves admitted members of the Cincinnati in France. And as I am very desirous to gratify them (especially Stack, who commanded the Party in the Bon-Homme-Richards Main-top, which was of singular service in the engagement with the Serapis) I must beg the favor of you to lay the Certificates I sent you in their favor before the Society, when you Preside at the next general Convention.[3] I am, Sir, with profound veneration for your Virtues & Talents Your most obliged & most humble Servant

Paul Jones

ALS, DLC:GW.

1. Jonathan Nesbitt may have been a relative of the Philadelphia merchants Alexander and John Maxwell Nesbitt, whose father was named Jonathan. Houdon's bust of Jones remains at Mount Vernon.

2. GW's letter to St. John Crèvecoeur is dated 9 July. For GW's dispatches, see GW to Jones, 22 July, n.1.

3. Jones wrote to GW about Edward Stack and Eugene McCarthy (MacCarthy) on 18 July 1785. See note 1 of that document.

To Philip Marsteller

Sir,   Philadelphia July 25th 1787

You would oblige me by letting me know whether there is a prospect of your purchasing, on the terms specified in my letter of Instructions, any of the Articles mentioned in the list handed to you therewith—particularly Blankets—as the Season in which these will be wanted, is now fast approaching, and against which they must be provided for the accomodation of my Negros.[1] If there is a moral certainty of obtaining them through your means, I will depend thereon. if not, I must look out in time, and therefore give you the trouble of this Enquiry. I am Sir Yr most Obedt Servant

G. Washington

LB, DLC:GW.

1. For GW's business arrangement with Marsteller, see GW to Marsteller, 15 Dec. 1786, and note 2 of that document.   .

From Samuel Powel

Dear Sir   [Philadelphia] Wednesday 25 July 1787

I have just seen the Coach-painter, whose prices are as follows

chariot Ground	that is painting the Body	£ 5.
Solid Gilding	that is the whole Moulding	5. 5.
Full do	that is in all the Hollows	3.15.
Half do	that is only round the Pannels	2.10.
Ornaments	that is Arms &c.	3.
Painting the Carriage		2.10.
Gilding the Springs		2.10.

At the above prices, the Chariot Body is to be painted in Varnish, the Surface polished & reduced to a perfect Smoothness— In this Case no Varnish is put on after the painting is perfected.

There is another Mode of doing the Work, which is by painting first & varnishing after the painting is perfected, which looks very well but is not equally durable. This last Mode lessens the Expence £2.10.

The Painter informs me that it will take from four to five Weeks, according to the Weather, to perfect his Work. I have not made any Sort of Contract or mentioned any Name to him but, simply, demanded Price & Time. The Coachmaker is from Home so that I do not yet know the Price of Lining, but ⟨sh⟩all know it to Day. I am, with great Respect Dear Sir, Your most obedt humble Servt

Samuel Powel

The price for lining is £3 exclusive of the Cloth & Lace. A tolerable Cloth may be had, as the Coachmaker tells me, for 32/ ℔ Yard—It will take about Five Yards—Lace from 15d. to 2/ ℔ Yard—about 20 Yards of Lace—One Week will be required for lining a Chariot.[1]

ALS, ViMtV.
  1. See GW to Powel, this date.

To Samuel Powel

                                    Market Street [Philadelphia]
Dear Sir,   Wednesday Afternoon 25th July [1787]
  I pray you to accept my thanks, for the trouble of your enquiries into the prices for Painting, and lining Carriages. Your letter coming to me whilst I was at Dinner, prevented an immediate acknowledgment of it, & previous thereto having heard a Mr Clarke (Coachmaker in this Square) well spoken of—having seen some of his work—and having received the strongest assurances of fidelity and diligence in the execution of mine, I have committed my Chariot to him—induced thereto by the further consideration of seeing every day as I pass his workshop the progress he makes[1]—My obligation to you, my good Sir, is not lessened thereby but with sentiments of great esteem and regard I am Dear Sir Yr most Obedt & obliged

Go: Washington

ALS, ViMtV.

1. David & Francis Clark presented on 14 Sept. its itemized bill for £51.13.5½ for refurbishing GW's "Chariot," and on 17 Sept. David & Francis Clark certified that the company had "Received the Contents in full." GW also entered this amount paid on 17 Sept. in his Philadelphia Cash Accounts, 9 May–22 September. Clark's bill included these charges:

For taking off boath Chariot Axels linning them in all the Armes
 with iron & steel setting them hoping up. boxing the wheels
 axels screwed in the ends and 4 new nutts Cutting & walding
 the bands of hubbs 4 new washers fixed on shoulders of axels
 fasning the loose bolts of Carraige   £ 3.
anew pole with new ringe for Do   1.
apaire of new pole pices   .17.6
1 new Spoke putt in awheel   . 4.
2 new pannels and 2 Sadle Cloaths   1. 8.
2 pair of new Safe Colars with brass buckles neet ⟨Straps⟩ and
 belley bands   2. 5.
repairing Glass frames with 2 new St⟨*mutilated*⟩ile and brass
 Cornar plates   . 7.6
For 6¾ Yards of yellow Super fine Cloath at 37/6 pr   12.13.1½
laces hand strings Glass Do and foot man holders   5.15.1
6 lb. of Currald hair for stuffing Cusion at 2/8   .16.
¾ of a yard of Rusia Sheetting for bottom to the Cusion   . 2.9
making and putting in the Linning & nails pistole-holsters
 stuffing & nails   4. 5.
anew Wilton Carpet for the cotton bound round the ends   .18.
making up the foot man holders with 2 new brass bucke   . 2.
Painting ground Coular & varnishing Chariot boady   2.10.
Mantlings and Coats of Armes   3.
⟨*mutilated*⟩   4.10.
⟨*mutilated*⟩per pannels ⟨Ruff⟩ and butte   3.
⟨*mutilated*⟩aige and wheels   2.10.
Repairing the harnes with 8 new trace berars & 6 new Do to the
 pades.   12 new back band straps 4 breast plate Do   1. 0.
mending atrace with 4 inches leather anew taile to abreching 10
 inches long 11 new billets to bridles & rains picing arain—2
 feet longe picing tow Chuck braces with 8 inches leather   .10.
4 new ends to the Chick of bridles 6 inches longe each one new
 Crupper & 2 new Crupper straps putt to the Sadle   . 7.
2 new Gurthes for the Sadles with 8 buckles   . 5.
2 new brass adges putt round 2 winkers & 1 torrit for the pade   7.6
                                                                  ─────────
                                                                  £51.13.5½

The bill is in the possession of the New London (Conn.) County Historical Society.

To George Augustine Washington

Dear George,   Philadelphia 29th July 1787.

Your letter of the 22d is before me.[1] If the outer doors of the New room are adapted to receive Mortice locks, it will make the room more uniform; and I can get them here of good quality from Seven Inches downwards—I shall decline sending any kind 'till I hear from you again thinking it best that the whole should be of this kind if any are.[2]

Perceiving you have little chance of sowing much Wheat in Fallow land this Fall (as the plowing of it at some of the Plantations is not yet begun) and little prospect of Plowing *any* ground well; it is indispensably necessary (in order that I may have something to depend upon next year) that *all* the Corn ground at *all* the Plantations, should be laid down in either Wheat or Rye, as shall be best suited to the land; and I request it may be done accordingly; and with as little delay as possible. The Season for it is now come—and putting it in, gives the last stirring to the Corn. A Bushel, or what my Seedsmen usually bestows to the Acre, of Wheat, is, I conceive sufficient; but where there is an exact similarity of Soil, it may not, for the sake of experiment, be amiss to try different quantities from two, to eight pecks, to the acre. and of Rye from two to Six pecks. If the Barley should turn out 16 Bushels to the Acre, I shall be very well satisfied; and according to your Acct of the drought, it is more than could be expected. Should the Oats turn out in that proportion, my case will not be quite so desperate as I expected.

I am glad you settled with Rawlin⟨s⟩ as I do not like to be in debt to workmen,[3] & could you, if there is means, pay Elizabeth Alton part of her demand, it would also be pleasing; as her frequent applications are disagreeable.[4]

Priming the roof of the Greenhouse may be delayed till I return, or till you hear from me again, on the subject. in the mean while inform me what the Alexandria prices of white & red lead ground in oil, and yellow Oaker unground, are. I desire that the honey suckles against the Houses & brick Walls, may be nailed up; and made to spread regularly over them. Should those near the Pillars of the Colonades, or covered ways, be dead, their places should be supplied with others; as I want them to run up, and Spread over the parts which are painted green.

I am glad to hear that Mr Youngs Plow answers in practice, and approved of by the Farmer; who should take care to keep it in order. Is *all* that field at French's the fallowing of which was begun before I left home (I mean the one which you enter after crossing the ford, between Manley's houses & the south side of the Swamp) sowed, or Planted? and with what?

How does the grain which you have got out, yield, in quantity & quality? What has Morris been doing to his carts to require a new one to be made—& another repaired? I am certain he had a New one this spring or rather Past Winter & the old one repaired—his wants of these so soon again, is inconceivable upon fair ground.

If Hezh Fairfax is going to leave the Ferry, and John Fairfax is desirous of going there on the same terms his brother now is; I have no objection to it. but I shall not employ him at that place on standing wages; neither shall I encrease his present lay at the Home House; nor exempt him, if he lives with me, from looking after the Fishery, provided I keep it in my own hands—which is uncertain—as a good rent would induce me to let it, that I might have no trouble or perplexity about it. As to giving a Man standing wages who looks after a Plantation, & has the hands to himself, and engaged in cropping, I have no idea of it—about a home house where there is no settled work, from the profit of which an Overlooker can derive a proportionate benefit, there is a necessity for it. And whatever John Fairfax may think, he or I is a good deal mistaken if there is any business he can fall into, by which he can (Clothes excepted) clear £40 a yr; when it is next to impossible to get money on any terms. Like others however he is never to be satisfied; and strange it is to me, that so soon as a man, by doing his duty, becomes useful; and without it, would be turned away disgracefully; and perhaps have his wages stopped—that he immediately thinks his Services can never be sufficiently rewarded; & without considering what others *really* make, when all expences are paid, or what he himself could raise under like circumstances, is forever demanding what, from the Nature of the thing, cannot be given. I like John Fairfax very well, & have no inclination to change, but shall make no alteration in his lay; and had rather he should remain about the house than go to the Ferry, as he has a better knowledge than a new hand would have, of what is required of such a character.[5]

As to Cornelius's brother, it is scarcely possible to decide any thing—In the first place he may not come. In the next place, his appearance may be very much against him; and he may have no testimonials that can be relied on: he may be too young, or he may not possess those qualities which Cornelius's partiallity has bestowed on him. and lastly, I can hardly believe that a raw Irishman can be well qualified to manage Negros. If I could employ him to any advantage, I should have no objection to it, but I must see the man, and have something to judge by, before this can happen. or some body on my behalf must do it for me.[6] Give my love to Fanny and good wishes to Mr Lear. Let him know that Mr Langdon is here, and very well—as is Mr Gilman (who used to be in the Adjutant Generals department) as Deligates from New Hampshire. request Mr Lear to translate the enclosed Letters.[7] With great esteem & regard I remain Yr affecte Uncle

Go: Washington

ALS, CSmH.

1. Letter not found.

2. For further references to the locks for the New Room, see GW to George Augustine Washington, 12 Aug., 9 September.

3. The entry in the Mount Vernon cash accounts for 23 July shows the payment of £45 to John Rawlins by "his order in favr of Thos Hammond for friezes & mouldings for the New Rooms" (Ledger B, 247). See GW to George Augustine Washington, 1 July.

4. GW's cash accounts for 15 Aug. 1787 show George Augustine paying Elizabeth Alton, the widow of GW's old servant John Alton, who died in 1785, £6 "on acct" (Ledger B, 248).

5. Although John Fairfax's expected departure continued to be referred to (see GW to George Augustine Washington, 12, 26 Aug., and 2 Sept.), the overseer remained at Mount Vernon until the end of 1790, when he resigned and settled in Monongalia County. He visited Mount Vernon in the month before GW's death in 1799 (*Diaries*, 6:373).

6. On 10 Dec. 1787 GW hired the two brothers of Cornelius McDermott Roe, Edward and Timothy, as ditchers. Cornelius entered an agreement on 1 Aug. 1786 to work for a year for GW as a bricklayer and stone mason (*Diaries*, 4:191, 5:227). Before that he had served GW for two years as an indentured servant (List of Servants & Redemptions that has been Freed & Redeemed, 2–5 Aug. 1784, ViMtV). Cornelius was later employed on the building of the

U.S. Capitol and the White House (Michael J. O'Brien, *George Washington's Associations with the Irish* [New York, 1937], 187).

7. The letters may have been those of 1 May from Madame des Essarts and 10 July from Chavannes de La Giraudière, both of which were translated by Lear.

From James Maury

Sir,   Liverpool [England] 30th July 1787

I am much obliged & highly honored by your kind Letter of the 25th February[1]—& beg Leave to repeat my wishes to be useful to you.

For the News of the day I inclose your Excellency some News papers, observing to you that altho' this Country, France & prussia are hovering over the United provinces with large Fleets & Armies, yet we hope, from the generally prevailing disposition of Europe for peace, that all Matters will be adjusted without Violence.

I am happy to add that Mr Jefferson's Amendment to Mr Morris's Contract with France for Tobaccoe has not only had a favor[a]ble Effect on the price both here & in America, but has also—in many Instances, of which this present Conveyance is one, obtained from British Merchants a preference to the American Flag.[2] I have the Honor to be with the highest Respect your excellency's most obt & most hble St

James Maury

ALS, DLC:GW.

1. GW's letter to Maury, which is dated 24 Feb. in GW's letter book, is printed in note 1, Maury to GW, 3 Dec. 1786.

2. For the successful attempt by Thomas Jefferson and the American Committee to secure some alteration in the contract between Robert Morris and the farmers-general providing for a monopoly of the tobacco trade with France, see the editor's note in Simon Bérard to Jefferson, 6 May 1786, in Boyd, *Jefferson Papers*, 9:457–61.

To Elizabeth Powel

[Philadelphia] Monday Morning [30 July 1787]

Genl Washington presents his respectful compliments to Mrs Powell, and would, with great pleasure, have made one of a party for the *School* for *Scandall* this evening; had not every thing been arranged, & Mr Govr Morris and himself on the point of stepping into the Carriage for a fishing expedition at Jenny Moores; at which place Mr & Mrs Robt Morris are to be to morrow, to partake of the successes, of Mr Govr Morris & himself this day.[1]

The Genl can but regret that matters have turned out so unluckily, after waiting so long to receive a lesson in the School for Scandal.

AL, ViMtV.

1. The Convention adjourned from 26 July to 6 August. GW wrote in his diary for 30 July: "In company with Mr Govr [Gouverneur] Morris, and in his Phaeton with my horses; went up to one Jane Moores in the vicinity of Valleyforge to get Trout." The next day, "Whilst Mr. Morris was fishing," GW "rid over the old Cantonment of the American [army] of the Winter of 1777, & 8. Visited all the Works, wch. were in Ruins" (*Diaries*, 5:178–79).

From Lafayette

My dear General   Paris *August* the 3d 1787

I Have Received Your first favour from Philadelphia with the Greater Satisfaction, as it promises me the pleasure to Hear Again from you Before long[1]—a pleasure, My Beloved General, which Your friend's filial Heart wants to Anticipate, and Enjoys most Affectionately—I Have not Been surprised to Hear of Your Attendance at the Convention, and would indeed Have wondered at a denial—on the success of this Meeting the very Existence of the United states may depend—and You well know that Your Name will add a Great weight to its proceedings—I am sorry to say, But am Much More Unhappy to observe that the Name of America is declining—it Gives pleasure to Her Ennemies—it Hurts Her interest Even with Her Allies—it furnishes the opponents to liberty with Anti Republican Arguments—Her dignity is lowering—Her Credit vanishing, Her Good intentions Questionned By some, Her future prosperity doubted—Good God! Will the people of America, so Enlightned, so wise so Generous, after they Have so gloriously Climbed up the Rugged Hill, now stumble in the Easy path? I the more Heartly wish well to Your Meeting as I feel that the Happiness of My life would not with[s]tand a disappointement in my fond Hopes for the prosperity of our good United states.

I thank you, my dear General, for the fine Birds, and excel-lent Beacons you Have sent to me[2]—the poor ducks died at the Havre on their Arrival—I Beg you will send me some Again—and Beg leave to add a petition for an envoice of Mocking Birds.

The spirit of liberty is prevailing in this Country at a Great Rate—liberal ideas are Cantering about from one end of the Kingdom to the other—our assembly of Notables was a fine thing, But for those who imagined it—you know of the personal quarell I had respecting some Gifts Made to favourites at the expense of the public—it Has Given me a Great Number of powerfull and inveterate Ennemies—But was very well come to the Nation—I Have since that period presented some opinions of mine in very plain terms—I Can't say I am on a very favour-able footing at Court, if By Court You Understand the King, Queen, and and King's Brothers—But am very friendly with the present Administration—the Arch Bishop of toulouse is a man equally great By His Abilities and up Rightness—and the King's Council is Better Composed than it Has ever Been.

At the same time the parliaments, warmed by the example of the Notables, make a great Resistance Against the New taxes—they will Be forced to Register the Edicts—But it is well that they Have asked for a general assembly of the Nation, and altho' it will not take place now, I anticipate the Event, when the As-sembly of Representatives now settling in each province will Have taken a proper weight, and felt their own strength—I Hope the affair of the protestants will soon Be settled agreable to the motion I Had made the day Before our dismission.

it is not known wether the Emperor will make terms with the flemish deputies or Risk the sending of an Army from His aus-trian dominions to that Remote part of His empire—I Rather think He will Negociate—But would not Be surprised if He acted the Contrary way—prussia and Great Britain are support-ing the state Holder—france interests Herself for the Republi-can party—preparations are Making on Both sides—But I Be-lieve that this too, will take a Negociating turn, and Be Reduced to some skirmishes Among the dutch—unless the King's of prussia's partiality to His sister leads Him into Hasty Measures which would involve them all farther than they now expect.

Adieu, My dear and Respected General—My Best Respects wait on Mrs Washington the family and all friends—mde de lafayette is in Auvergne where I am Going to Meet Her and Attend the first session of the provincial Assembly—with every sentiment of filial love and Respect I Have the Honour to Be my Dear General Your Respectfull and affectionate friend

lafayette

ALS, PEL.
    1. GW wrote Lafayette on 6 June 1787.
    2. The "Beacons" are the barrel of hams that Mrs. Washington had GW send to the marquise de Lafayette in 1786 (GW to Lafayette, 8 June 1786).

Letter not found: from George Augustine Washington, 5 Aug. 1787. On 12 Aug. GW wrote George Augustine: "This letter is in acknowledgement of yours of the 5th Instt."

Draft of the Federal Constitution: Report of Committee of Detail

6 August 1787. On 6 Aug. John Rutledge delivered the report of the "Committee of detail" in the form of a printed draft of the proposed federal constitution and provided copies for the members. GW and the secretary of the Convention, William Jackson, entered on one printed copy those deletions and additions that were adopted by the Convention between 6 Aug. and 3 Sept. and were included in the draft referred to the committee of five elected on 8 Sept. "to revise the stile of and arrange the articles which had been agreed to by the House" (Madison's Notes in Farrand, *Records of the Federal Convention,* 2:177, 553).

D, DNA: RG 36, Records of the Federal Convention.
    On 23 July the Convention voted that "the proceedings of the Convention for the establishing of a Natl. Govt. (except the part relating to the Executive), be referred to a Committee to prepare & report a Constitution conformable thereto" (Madison's Notes in Farrand, *Records of the Federal Convention,* 2:95). Not only did the part of the Constitution "relating to the Executive" not appear in the committee draft of the Constitution of 6 Aug., it and most of the provisions regarding the Senate as well as several other important sections of the Constitution did not receive final approval of the Convention until after GW and Jackson had discontinued entering the changes that were being made in the draft. See the note in Draft of the Federal Constitution: Report of Committee of Style, 12 Sept., printed below.

From Charles Willson Peale

Dr Sir   Augt 6 1787

Some Ladies & Gentlemen from Virginia having desired an Exhibition at ½ past 4 oclock in the afternoon of tomorrow gives me an opportunity of requesting the favour of your Company to partake of such Amusement as some of my labours may afford.[1] I am with the highest respect Dr Sir your Obl[i]ged Hbe Servt

C.W. Peale

LB, PPAmP: Charles Willson Peale Papers.

1. GW does not record in his diary attending Peale's exhibition on that day, but on 27 Sept. Peale in a letter to GW refers to GW's having visited "my Room."

To Clement Biddle

Dear Sir   August 7th 1787.

In addition to the articles contained in the Memo. given to you some time since,[1] I pray you to procure, and send by Captn Steward the following.

A Wimble bit—compleat.

Pickled Walnuts & India Mangoes none were sent before.

Thompsons Seasons and Gutheries Geography and the Art of Speaking.[2]

Some Pamphlets which have been sent to me since I came to Town; and Books purchased for my amusement whilst in it, I now send to be packed up, and sent round.[3]

The Top of the Cupolo (from Mr Rakestraw)—The Venetian blind from Mr Davis. A hogshead of Plaister of Paris, & a coob with two or three fowls, from Mr Barge; and the Chair—I mean shall take the opportunity afforded by the Dolphin of going to Mount Vernon.[4] and I pray you to recommend them to the particular care of the Captn.

I have bought one and mean to buy another, piece of fine linnen which I shall send to you.[5] I am—Dear Sir Yr Obedt Servt

Go: Washington

ALS, PHi: Washington-Biddle Correspondence.

1. GW's memorandum has not been identified, but it was not the one referred to in GW to Biddle, 22 Aug., n.1. See GW to George Augustine Washington, 12 August.

2. The books were James Thomson's *The Seasons* (London, 1787), William Guthrie's *A New System of Modern Geography* (London, 1786), and James Burgh's *The Art of Speaking* (Philadelphia, 1786). Entries in GW's cash accounts for 10 Sept. show charges for the books and for, among other things, a bottle of East Indian mangoes and 200 pickled walnuts (Ledger B, 261).

3. For other books purchased, see Philadelphia Cash Accounts, 9 May–22 Sept., printed above.

4. Jacob Barge was an established merchant in Philadelphia at 191 High Street.

5. See GW's record of his purchase of linen from John Waggener (Wagener, Wagner) entered on 27 July and 10 Aug. in Philadelphia Cash Accounts, 9 May–22 Sept. 1787, printed above.

Letter not found: from Edward Newenham, 10 Aug. 1787. GW wrote Newenham on 24 Feb. 1788: "I have been favoured with your letter of the 10th of Augt."[1]

1. A portion of this letter is quoted in GW to Charles Carter, 5 Feb. 1788.

From Pierre Roussilles

Sir,   Bordeaux [France] 12th Augt 1787.

Permit me to address the enclosed memorial to you, which will show the justice of my complaints & demands, your great heart will not be insensible to it & on you alone have I placed my hope.[1] I am respectfully Sir, Yr most Hble & obedt Servt

P. Roussilles.

Translation, in Tobias Lear's hand, DLC:GW; ALS, in French, DLC:GW. At the end of his letter Roussilles (Roussille) wrote: "Mon adresse maison de Mme Lamontagne V[euv]e Renart, rue Bragart Psse St Eloi à Bordeaux."

1. See enclosure. GW responded from Mount Vernon on 8 Jan. 1788: "Sir, I have received your letter & memorial of the 12 of Augt and in answer to them can only say, that however just & reasonable your demands may be, and however desireous I am to assist the injured in obtaining justice, it is not in my power to do any thing more than appea[r]s, by your memorial, to have been already done, that is, to refer you to the boards and offices which take cognizance of matters of that nature—As I have, long since, lain aside all publick business and live 300 miles from New york where the Congress sits and the publick Offices are established, I cannot, with any degree of propriety, interfere in your case. I am Sir Yr Most Obedt Hble Sert G. Washington.

P.S. I return your original documents which you may have occasion for" (LB, DLC:GW).

Enclosure
Memorial

[Bordeaux, c.12 August 1787]

The Memorial of Pierre Roussilles sheweth—That he is the son of a merchant of Bordeaux; and that he entered as a volunteer on board the Boston Frigate commanded by Captn Tucker on the 22d of may 1778—on the 19th June they took a prize on board of which the memorialist embarked to sail for Boston; but on their way thither they were retaken by a British frigate & carried to Portsmouth in Engld where he was detained a prisoner for two years, during which time he hear'd nothing of the frigate.[1]

On his return to France he learnt that the frigate had been very successful in taking a number of prizes which were sold in Nantz & their proceeds remitted to Captn Tucker, as he can prove by letters.

He thinks he ought to be entitled to a share of the prizes as well as those who remained on board, & it was particularly agreed upon between him & Captn Tucker before he left the Frigate that it should be so. He thinks a Citizen of France should be as much attended to in this case by the board of Admiralty as a Citizen of America.

He has written frequently to Captn Tucker & to the board of Admiralty, but could never obtain answers from either.

He laid his situation before the Marechal de Castries, who referred him to Doctor Franklin (then at Paris) who referred him to the marine department of the United States through the channel of the French Consul in America.

He accordingly wrote to Monsr de L'etombe the Consul at Boston who wrote him an answer in July 1784 informing him that Captn Tucker was dead. This however is a mistake, for I beleive Capt. Tucker is living at this time. & that he had laid his case before the marine board at Boston who could do nothing in the matter.[2]

He has likewise made application through Monsr de Marbois but has recd no satisfaction.

He therefore begs your recommendations of his case to the consideration of Congress not doubting but that it will have sufficient weight to obtain for him his wages & prize money.

The letters are, one from the Secretary of the marine department to Mr Jay informing him that if Captn Tucker was Agent for the Captors he, the memorialist, must apply there for his prize-money & if wages are due that he must apply to Joseph Pennell Esquire who settles accts in the marine department. One from Mr Jay to Mr Marbois enclosing the secretary's letter, not doubting but it would prove satisfactory. One from Doctor Franklin advising him to lay his compla[i]nts before the board of admiralty. Two respecting the Prizes which the Frigate took & informing the memorialist that Captn Tucker had recd the Captors share of them.[3]

Translation, DLC:GW; AD, in French, DLC:GW. This translation made for GW is in fact a summary of the French original. It is incomplete and, in part, inaccurate. The French original is in CD-ROM:GW.

1. Samuel Tucker (1747–1833) of Marblehead, Mass., in 1777 was made a captain in the Continental navy and was given command of the frigate *Boston*, which was captured at Charleston, S.C., in 1780.

2. In his *mémoire* Roussilles indicates that his letter from Castries (Charles-Eugène-Gabriel de La Croix, marquis de Castries; 1727–1801), the French ministre de la Marine, was dated 20 Aug. 1786 and the one from Benjamin Franklin, 12 Sept. 1786, whereas both Roussilles's letter to the French consul in Boston, Philippe-André-Joseph de Létombe (b. 1733), and Létombe's response were written in 1784.

3. Copies of most of these letters as well as other letters and reports regarding Roussilles's claims are in DNA:PCC. James Read (1743–1822) was the secretary to the agent of the Marine department.

To George Augustine Washington

Dear George,   Philadelphia 12th Augt 1787
    This letter is in acknowledgement of yours of the 5th Instt[1]— and painful indeed it is to find that the drought should continue with such unremitting violence with you, when from other parts (and indeed in your own Neighbourhd) by acct, it is seasonable; and is as much so here as could be wished.

    By the Dolphin, Captn Steward, I have sent some Goods, and other articles round; which I hope will arrive safe. Among them, is a top for the Cupulo of the House, which has been left so long unfinished.[2] I do not suppose there would have been any difficulty in fixing it without directions; but I requested the maker to give them; and they are sent accordingly. The sooner it is put up the better; but before it is done, the wood part (of what is sent) must receive a Coat of white paint. The spire (if it is not the case already) must have that of black; the bill of the bird is to be black. and the Olive branch in the mouth of it, must be green; these two last are otherwise by mistake—Great pains (and Mr Lear understands the Compass) must be taken to fix the points truly; otherwise they will deceive rather than direct— (if they vary from the North, South, East, and West)—one way of doing this may be by my Compass being *placed* in a *direct* North line on the ground at some distance from the House by means of which and a plumb line, the point may be exactly placed—that is by having the point in a true line between the plumb line and the Spire—So with respect to the other 3 points. What the paper means by cutting of the top of the present Cupulo, is no more than the small octagon at the very top, so as that the work of the *old* & *New* may fit well together; and this, if the sizes of the two do not exactly accord, must be so ordered as to do it. Let particular care be used to putty, or put copper on all the joints to prevent the leaking, & rotting of the wood as it will be difficult, & expensive to repair it hereafter.[3]

Your letter came too late for me to get & send the Mortice locks by the Vessel, but they shall go by the first conveyance that offers as they are already purchased agreeably to Mathews directions. The hinges you will receive in a bundle with the wimble bit agreeable to your Aunts request in a former letter. If the wimble bit (which is a complete one) is given to Mathew take a Memo. of the number and quality of the pieces & make him sign it for I have suspicions that many of my tools are converted after a while to the uses of themselves & called their own.

At your Aunts request a Coach Dog has been purchased and sent for the convenience, & benefit of Madame Moose; her amorous fits should therefore be attended to, that the end for which he is sent, may not be defeated by her acceptance of the services of any other dog.[4]

With respect to the money which has been called for by the

Directors of the Potomk Company, the treasurer must wait till I return; and this cannot be considered as any great indulgence as I have always been punctual hitherto in my payments. As I did not advert to the annual meeting of the Compy myself & did not receive your intimation of it till it was too late I could not appoint a substitute in time & must for these reasons be excused.[5]

If Fairfax does not chuse to stay on his present lay, he must go. I like him very well, but I do not chuse to give away my substance to overlookers; who I am sure cannot make so much in any other way. He cannot I should think have forgot, that his Wages were only £30 a year, & that it was my own act to add ten pounds more, long after the Bargain was made, merely on acct of the trouble he wd have with the fishery.[6]

If Mr Lund Washington wants Dows money he must have it; but really I see no more than the man in the moon, where I am to get money to pay my Taxes &ca &ca &ca if I have made no Crop, & shall have to buy Corn for my people.[7]

You must endeavour to get stuff for the Venitian blinds—one ready made goes by the Vessel which will be more satisfactory than directions in writing, for the proper kind of materials which the rest are to be made.[8]

I have sent the bust of Commodore Paul Jones (given to me by himself) which I request may be placed opposite to my own, in my study on a similar bracket, with that of the latter.[9] I have also sent 14 bushels of prepared Plaister of Paris with which I mean to make another experiment but desire nothing more may be done with it than to have it preserved in a dry & safe place.

I will make enquiry for Gudgeons & let you know the result.[10] Does your Turnip Seed come up? You have frequently in the reports, and in your letters, mentioned preparing ground for, & sowing them, but I do not recollect that in any one you have informed me of the coming up of a single Seed, and I should suppose not a Seed has come up, from the Acct you have given of the weather. It is now sometime since I wrote to Mr Marsteller to know whether there is any probability of his purchasing any of the articles mentioned in my Invoice to him, particularly Blankets—without receivg any answer—I wish you would make this enquiry & let me know[11]—Give my love to Fanny—tell Mr

Lear I have recd & forwarded his letter to Young Mr Lincoln. I am with sincere regard Yr Affectionate Uncle

Go: Washington

ALS, DLC:GW. George Augustine Washington noted on the cover of the letter that enclosed were "directions for fixing the top of the Cupula."

1. Letter not found.

2. See GW to Biddle, 7 August.

3. For other correspondence regarding the weathervane, see GW to George Augustine Washington, 3 June 1787, n. 4. See also GW to Joseph Rakestraw, 20 July 1787.

4. An entry for 14 Aug. in GW's Philadelphia Cash Accounts, 9 May–22 Sept. 1787, printed above, indicates that he paid 15 shillings for the dog.

5. See GW to William Hartshorne, 30 August.

6. See GW to George Augustine Washington, 29 July, n.5.

7. See GW to Lund Washington, 7 May, n.3.

8. See GW to George Augustine Washington, 10 June, n.11.

9. The bust of Jones, as well as the mortise locks, hinges, wimble bit, venetian blind, and "2 Boxes & other things for the Cupola" were among items placed in the Mount Vernon storehouse on 23 Aug. (Mount Vernon store book, 1787, ViMtV).

10. For GW's order of gudgeons for his mills, see GW to Clement Biddle, 22 August.

11. GW wrote to Philip Marsteller on 25 July.

From David Humphreys

Hartford [Conn.] Augst 13th 1787

I would not trespass upon your time, while I knew you was occupied in such momentuous affairs, as the revisal of the Confederation: but now that common Report says the principles are settled & the business, on which the Convenn assembled, nearly compleated, I take the liberty of addressing myself again to my dear General. And the rather as I do not know whether the letter I wrote from N. H., in which was enclosed the sketch of an answer to Mr Jefferson, has ever come to hand.[1]

It gives all the friends of good Government much pleasure to be advised that so great candour & unanimity have prevailed in the Deliberations of your national Assembly. Nor have the well affected been wanting in efforts to prepare the minds of the Citizens for adopting whatever may be the Result of your Proceedings. In case that every thing turns out in the best manner,

I shall certainly be among the first to rejoice in finding that our apprehensions & predictions were not verified, as well as to felicitate you upon having contributed your assistance on so important an occasion.

Since I had the honor of seeing you, in Philadelphia, I have made the tour of the N. England States as far as Portsmouth. I was happy to find in Massachusetts the spirit of Insurrection pretty generally subsided, and an impression left on the minds of people in most of the States that something energetic must [be] adopted respecting the national Government, or we shall be a ruined People.

From speaking of the general tendency of our old Government, I may be allowed to descend with propriety to speak of its influence on Individuals. Republics have commonly been noted for ingratitude, and I fear we shall not be found an honorable exception.

I was unhappy to find from but too good authority that our friend Cobb (I did not see him, tho' I previously wrote to have an interview in Boston) is not only in circumstances of indigence, but almost of distress. Would to God his Country might do somewhat for him.

ADf, CtY: Humphreys-Marvin-Olmstead Collection.
  1. Humphreys' letter is dated 28 May.

From Thomas Jefferson

Dear Sir   Paris Aug. 14[–15] 1787.
  I was happy to find by the letter of Aug. 1 1786 which you did me the honour to write me, that the modern dress for your statue would meet your approbation. I found it strongly the sentiment of West, Copeley, Trumbul & Brown in London, after which it would be ridiculous to add that it was my own. I think a modern in an antique dress as *just* an object of ridicule as an Hercules or Marius with a periwig & chapeau bras.

  I remember having written to you while Congress sat at Annapolis on the water communications between ours & the Western country,[1] and to have mentioned particularly the information I had received of the plain face of the country between the sources of Big beaver & Cayohoga, which made me hope that a canal of no great expence might unite the navigations of L. Erie & the Ohio. you must since have had occasion of getting better information on this subject &, if you have, you would oblige me by a communication of it. I consider this canal, if practicable, as a very important work.

I remain in hopes of great & good effects from the decisions of the assembly over which you are presiding. to make our states one as to all foreign concerns, preserve them several as to all merely domestic, to give to the federal head some peaceable mode of enforcing their just authority, to organise that head into Legislative, Executive, & Judiciary departments are great desiderata in our federal constitution. yet with all it's defects, & with all those of our particular governments, the inconveniencies resulting from them are as light in comparison with those existing in every other government on earth, that our citizens may certainly be considered as in the happiest political situation which exists. the assemblée des Notables has been productive of much good in this country. the reformation of some of the most oppressive laws has taken place & is taking place. the allotment of the state into subordinate governments, the administration of which is committed to persons chosen by the people, will work in time a very beneficial change in their constitution. the expence of the trappings of monarchy too are lightening. many of the useless officers, high & low, of the king, queen, & princes are struck off. notwithstanding all this the discovery of the abominable abuses of public money by the late comptroller general, some new expences of the court, not of a peice with the projects of reformation, & the imposition of new taxes, have in the course of a few weeks raised a spirit of discontent in this nation, so great & so general, as to threaten serious consequences. the Parliaments in general, & particularly that of Paris put themselves at the head of this effervescence, and direct it's object to the calling the states general, who have not been assembled since 1614. The object is to fix a constitution, and to limit expences. the king has been obliged to hold a bed of justice to enforce the registering the new taxes: the parliament on their side propose to issue a prohibition against their execution. very possibly this may bring on their exile. the mild & patriotic character of the new ministry is the principal dependance against this extremity.

The turn which the affairs of Europe will take is not yet decided. the Emperor on his return to Vienna, disavowed the retro-cessions made by his governors general in the low countries. he at the same time called for deputies to consult on their affairs. this, which would have been the sole measure of a wise sovereign, was spoiled by contrary indications resulting from his Thrasonic character. the people at first refused to send deputies. at last however they sent them without powers, & go on arming. I think there is little doubt but the Emperor will avail himself of these deputies to tread back his steps. he will do this the rather that he may be in readiness to take part in the war likely to be produced by the Dutch differences. the kings of England & Prussia were abetting the cause of the Stadholder, France that of the Patriots: but negotiations were going on to settle them amicably, when all of a sudden, the Princess of Orange, undertaking a secret journey to the Hague to incite an insurrection of the people there, is stopped on the road, writes an inflammatory letter to her brother, he without consulting England, or even his own council, or any thing else but his own pride, orders 20,000 men to march into the neighborhood of Holland.[2] this has been followed by the sailing of the English squadron somewhere Westwardly, & that will be followed by a squadron from Brest, & an army to the confines of Holland from this country. appearances therefore are within a few days past more like war than they had been. still however the negotiations are going on, & the finances both of France & England are so notoriously incompetent to war, that the arrest of hostile movements and an amicable adjustment are not yet altogether despaired of. a war, wherein France, Holland & England should be parties, seems primâ facie to promise much advantage to us. but in the first place no war can be safe for us which threatens France with an unfavourable issue. and in the next, it will probably embark us again into the ocean of speculation, engage us to overtrade ourselves, convert us into Sea-rovers under French & Dutch colours, divert us from agriculture which is our wisest pursuit, because it will in the end contribute most to real wealth, good morals & happiness. the wealth acquired by speculation & plunder is fugacious in it's nature and fills society with the spirit of gambling. the moderate & sure income of husbandry begets permanent improvement, quiet life, and orderly conduct both public and private. we have no occasion for more commerce than to take off our superfluous produce, & tho people complain that some restrictions prevent this, yet the price of articles with us in general shew the contrary. tobacco indeed is low, not because we cannot carry it where we please, but because we make more than the consumption requires. upon the whole I think peace advantageous to us, necessary for Europe, & desireable for humanity. a few days will decide probably whether all these considerations are to give way to the bad passions of kings & those who would be kings. I have the honour to be with very sincere esteem & respect dear Sir your most obedient & most humble servant

Th: Jefferson

P.S. Aug. 15. the Parliament is exiled to Troyes this morning.

ALS, DLC:GW.

1. See Jefferson to GW, 15 Mar., 6 April 1784, and GW to Jefferson, 29 Mar. 1784. See also GW to Jefferson, 1 Jan. 1788.

2. The Princess of Orange was the sister of Frederick William II of Prussia.

From Henry Knox

New York 14 August 1787

Influenced by motives of delicacy I have hitherto forborne the pleasure my dear Sir of writing to you since my return from Philadelphia.

I have been apprehensive that the stages of the business of the convention might leak out, and be made an ill use of, by some people. I have therefore been anxious that you should escape the possibility of imputation. But as the objects seem now to be brought to a point, I take the liberty to indulge myself in communicating with you.

Although I frankly confess that the existence of the State governments is an insuperable evil in a national point of view, yet I do not well see how in this stage of the business they could be annihilated—and perhaps while they continue the frame of government could not with propriety be much higher toned than the one proposed. It is so infinitely preferable to the present constitution, and gives such a bias to a proper line of conduct in future ⟨that⟩ I think all men anxious for a national government should zealously embrace it.

The education, genius, and habits of men on this continent are so various even at this moment, and of consequence their views of the same subject so different, that I am satisfied with the result of the convention, although it is short of my wishes and of my judgement.

But when I find men of the purest intentions concur in embracing a system which on the highest deliberation, seems to be the best which can be obtained, under present circumstances, I am convinced of the propriety of its being strenuously supported by all those who have wished for a national republic of higher and more durable powers.

I am persuaded that the address of the convention to accompany their proposition will be couched in the most persuasive terms.

I feel anxious that there should be the fullest representation in Congress, in order that the propositions should receive their warmest concurrence and strongest impulse.

Mrs Knox and myself have recently sustained the severe affliction of losing our youngest child of about eleven months old, who died on the 11th instant of a disease incident to children cutting their teeth in the summer season.[1] This is the third time that Mrs Knox has had her tenderest affections lacerated by the rigid hand of death.

Although her present grief is sharp indeed we hope it will [be] assuaged by the lenient hand of time. I am my dear Sir with the most perfect respect and affection Your sincere friend & humble Servant

H. Knox

ALS, DLC:GW.
    1. The little girl was named Caroline.

To Lafayette

My dear Marqs,   Philadelphia August 15th 1787
    Altho' the business of the Fœderal Convention is not yet clos'd, nor I, thereby, enabled to give you an account of its pro-

ceedings; yet, the opportunity afforded by Commodore Paul Jones' Return to France is too favourable for me to omit informing you, that the present expectation of the members is, that it will end about the first of next month; when, or as soon after as it shall be in my power, I will communicate the result of our long deliberation to you.[1]

News paper acct inform us that the Session of the Assembly of Notables is ended. and you have had the goodness (in your letter of the 5th of May) to communicate some of the proceedings to me, among which is that of the interesting motion made by yourself respecting the expenditure of public money by Monsr de Callonne, and the consequence thereof. The patriotism with which this Nation[2] was dictated throws a lustre on the action which cannot fail to dignify the Author, and I sincerely hope with you, that much good will result from the deliberations of so respectable a Council, I am not less ardent in my wish that you may suceed in your plan of toleration in religeous matters. Being no bigot myself to any mode of worship, I am disposed to endulge the professors of Christianity in the church, that road to heaven which to them shall seem the most direct plainest easiest and least liable to exception.

Had not the account of your recovery accompanied that of your indisposition I should have felt many anxious and painful moments from the recital of the former. but let the first admonish you, my dear Marquis, against application too intense. This may disqualify you for the laudable pursuits to which zeal for the good of your Country and the honor of human nature may prompt you, and which may prove injurious both to yourself and it.

The politicians of this Country hardly know what to make of the present situation of European affairs. If serious consequences do not follow the blood which has been shed in the United Netherlands these people will certainly have acted differently from the rest of Mankind; and in another quarter one would think their could hardly be so much Smoke without some fire between the Russian and Turk. Should these disputes kindle the flame of war it is not easy to prescribe bounds to its extention or effect. The disturbances in Massachusetts have subsided; but there are seeds of discontent in every part of this Union; ready to produce other disorders if the wisdom of the present Convention should not be able to devise, and the good sense of the people be found ready to adopt a more vigerious, and energetic government, than the one under which we now live—for the present, from experience, has been found too feeble, and inadequate to give that security which our liberties and property render absolutely assential, and which the fulfilment of public faith loudly requires. Vain is it to look for respect from a broad, or tranquillity at home—vain is it to murmur at the detention of our Western Posts—or complain of the restriction of our commerce—vain are the attempts to remedy the evil complained of by Mr Dumas to discharge the interest due on foreign loans, or satisfy the claims of foreign officers, the neglect of doing which is a high impeachment of our National character, and is hurtful to the feelings of every well wisher to this Country—in and out of it—vain is it to talk of chastising the Algirenes, or doing ourselves Justice in any other respect, till the wisdom and force of the Union can be more concentred[3] & better applied.

In what accountable terms, My dear Marquis, shall I express or convey to you, my thanks for the Malteses asses. Believe me, however, when I assure you, that your friendship in this respect has embarrassed me not a little for with much truth I can declare that nothing was further from my thoughts than to make you more then the medium of application or to saddle you with more than the first advance in obtaining them thro' you alone, I was enabled to accomplish this matter, and the desire of introducing animals of so much use into this Country prompted me to accept of your influence with admiral de Suffran, to whom, If I am under obligation, you would do me a singular favour to make my acknowledgments acceptable.[4] With sentiments of the highest respect, and most perfect regard for Madam de la Fayette and the rest of your family and with the most Affecte attachment to you. I am ever, yours—

G. Washington.

LB, DLC:GW.

1. See GW to John Paul Jones, 22 July, n. 1. GW wrote to Lafayette on 18 Sept., sending him a copy of the new federal Constitution.

2. The copyist, who displays his carelessness and inaccuracy throughout this letter, wrote "Nation"; Fitzpatrick in his edition of Washington's *Writings* changed the word to "motion," which presumably was the word used in the letter sent to Lafayette (Fitzpatrick, *Writings of Washington*, 29:258–61).

3. Jared Sparks changed this word to "concentrated," but GW may just as well have written "concentred." For comments on Sparks's corrections in GW's letter book, see GW to Charles Washington, 14 Feb. 1787, source note.

4. In his letter to GW of 6 Feb. 1786, Lafayette mentioned that he was enlisting the aid of Suffren (Pierre-André de Suffren-Saint-Tropez; 1726–1788) to obtain jackasses for GW. For GW's reception of the jacks, see James McHenry to GW, 5 Nov. 1786, and references in note 1 of that document.

To Henry Knox

My dear Sir,   Philadelphia 19th Augt 1787.

By slow, I wish I could add & sure, movements, the business of the Convention progresses; but to say when it will end, or what will be the result, is more than I can venture to do; and therefore shall hazard no opinion thereon. If however, *some* good does not proceed from the Session, the defects cannot, with propriety, be charged to the hurry with which the business has been conducted: yet many things may be forgot—some of them not well digested—and others become a mere nullity. Notwithstanding which I wish a disposition may be found in Congress—the several States Legislatures—and the community at large to adopt the Government which may be agreed on in Convention; because I am fully persuaded it is the best that can be obtained at the present moment, under such diversity of ideas as prevail.

I should have had great pleasure in a visit to New York during the adjournment of the Convention; but not foreseeing the precise period at which it would take place, or the length of it; I had, previously thereto, put my carriage into the hands of a workman to repair, and had not the means of going.

I condole very sincerely with Mrs Knox & yourself on your late misfortune; but am sure, however severe the trial, each of you have fortitude enough to meet it. Nature, no doubt, must feel severely before *calm* resignation will overcome it. I offer my best respects to Mrs Knox, and every good wish for the family—with great regard & unfeigned Affect. I am Yours

Go: Washington

ALS, NNGL: Knox Papers; LB, DLC:GW.

From William McIntosh

Avignon [France] 20th August 1787.

The Founder of the Common-wealth of America has established such a reputation in the World, as to render an apology unnecessary, upon any subject applicable to the great object which he has achieved, or the rights of Humanity, and the laws of well regulated Societies.

After having, from an early period, followed active lines in Legislature, Finance, Colonization, & the study of Commerce, an impaired Constitution, & heavy losses by the Capture of the West India Islands in the late war, have created in my mind a contempt of ambition; excursions over most parts of our Terrestrial Globe, have given birth to sentiments, not unworthy of a Citizen of the world; and these principles, have seduced me to seek better health, & more contentment, in a simple retreat, under a milder Climate, & in a purer air, than belong to my own Country. The air which I have imbibed for three Years in the place from whence this is dated, is excellent; but the climate is intemperate, because it is inconstant, frequently partaking of extremes; and the *liberty* transfused under church Domination, breathes more Licentiousness, & tolerates more immorality, than my ideas can reconcile, in any Government.

In this retirement, a mind habituated to activity, & possessing its natural vigour, has often found entertainment in the political machinations of the cabinets of Europe; and very often has it been occupied by the unsettled state of the American republic: An event which I foresaw at a remote distance. I have lately perceived, with pleasure, that the formation of a more decided System, was agitated as an indispensable measure, which is probably, now under deliberation: The great Outlines; & the minute police, adapted to so extensive a field, and the discordant dispositions of the provincials, having been the subject of much private reflection, I have within these few hours, ventured to select some of my thoughts, & to commit them to paper. They are contained within the small compass of three pages, and are, with proper deference, submitted, for your perusal, Sir, without presuming to hope, that they approach to perfection; but, in perfect confidence, that if they do convey to your patriotic mind, some useful hints, they will be well received, and applied with effect.[1]

It may seem strange, Sir, that a British Subject should feel an interest in the affairs of a Country, apparently disaffected to his. That conjecture may require some explanation. It is thus—Before the troubles broke out in America, I had prepared, and begun a plan for realizing a part of my fortune, & finishing the career of life in that Country, because I approved the Climates, & admired the temperance, industry, & prudence of the people. The petulance & false pride of the British Cabinet, obstructed that object. I thought that the Colonists were justified in their resistance; but, abstracted from the natural effects of Passions raised & warmed by injustice, I thought also, that in prudence, an accommodation, upon equal and equitable principles, would have been equally convenient to them. No wise man would wantonly thrust himself, & his means, into a Country, ravaged & disolated by a Civil War; After the restoration of peace, it did not appear to me that good order was also restored; as the measure of my means was also reduced to a smaller scale, it was incumbent on me to practice Circumspection; therefore, I could not hazard the application of a *Remnant,* before I could see a clear pavement to walk over. More over, my principles tell me, that when a *political* contest is finally adjusted, the ⟨ties⟩ of Consanguinity, and the obligations of personal friendship, should resume their former Stations in the mind; that a Similarity of manners, customs, Rights, Language, & religion, possess attractive qualities, & attach insensibly, and that the exercise of Commerce, should compose a new Cement, by that Confidence & Liberality, which neither the practice, nor the wealth of other manufactures, can Communicate.

This short account, will suffice, Sir, to satisfy your known candour and justice, that the author of the accompanying Sheet is actuated by good Sentiments; and will, likewise, induce you to believe, that no man entertains more lively Sentiments of true respect & Esteem for the person & virtues of General Washington than—

W. Macintosh

ALS, DLC:GW.

William McIntosh published in London in 1782 *Travels in Europe, Asia, and Africa: Describing Characters, Customs, Manners, Laws, and Productions of Nature and Art; Containing Various Remarks on the Political and Commercial Interests of Great Britain; and Delineating in Particular, a New System for the Government and Improve-*

ment of the British Settlements in the East Indies; Begun in the Year 1777, and Finished in 1781. When Thomas Jefferson in 1786 ordered from London a copy of the two-volume work for his library, he found that it was "entirely out of print" (John Stockdale to Jefferson, 8 Aug. 1786, in Boyd, *Jefferson Papers,* 10:201–2).

1. McIntosh's plan of "how to constitute a Government, which will embrace such a mixture in its composition, as to *Legislate, administer,* and *Execute,* without *democracy, Aristocracy,* or *Monarchy*" is in CD-ROM:GW. GW did not receive McIntosh's plan until after the new Constitution had been drafted. Months later, on 8 Jan. 1788, GW acknowledged from Mount Vernon the receipt of McIntosh's letter with its enclosure in these terms: "Sir, I have received your letter of the 28th [20th] of August enclosing your plan of Government suggested for the United States of America. As a Citizen of these States I return you my best thanks for the interest which you take in their happiness and prosperity; and as an individual, you will please to accept of my acknowledgments for your polite attention in sending me your sentiments upon so important a subject.

"The want of an efficient General Government in this Country is universally felt and acknowledged. The Convention which met at Philadelphia in may last for the purpose of forming a Constitution for the United States have handed to the People one (of which I now enclose you a copy) for their consideration and acceptance—it is to be submitted to conventions chosen by the people in the several States and by them approved or rejected. Two [three] States only have as ye[t] decided upon it, two of which accepted it unanimou[s]ly and the other by a majority of 2 to 1. Similar dispositions seem to preval in the other States and there is no doubt but that they will give it a determination equally favorable.

"When a Government is established in America that can give energy to its laws and security to property, it is not to be doubted but that many persons of respectibility and interest from the old world will make a valuable addition to the citizens of the new. I am Sir Yr Most Obedt Hble Sert G. Washington" (LB, DLC:GW). See also McIntosh's letter to GW of 12 June 1788, in which he comments on the new federal Constitution.

To Clement Biddle

Dear Sir,   [Philadelphia] 22d Augt 1787.

Since I came to this City, if I recollect rightly, you asked me if I now had, or could put up, a quantity of Herrings next season, for Sale.

Having revolved the matter in my mind, I wish in turn to be informed, if there is any responsible character who would enter into a contract for a number, to be delivered next Season? What number of Barrls he would contract for?—and at what price; to be paid on delivery—or on a credit to be agreed on? Answers to these questions would enable me to determine with respect to the propriety of entering into such a Contract, and in case of it, to prepare accordingly.

Be so good as to inform me whether you have engaged the gudgeons for my Mill, or not, and when they will be ready? also with respect to the price of window glass 9 by 11.[1] I shall want near 300 lights or squares—I am Dr Sr Yr Obt Ser.

Go: Washington

ALS, PHi: Washington-Biddle Correspondence.

1. An undated memorandum in GW's hand in the Washington-Biddle Correspondence (PHi) reads: "Gudgeons for two Mill Wheels—to be exactly of the following dimensions and of the fittest Iron for them viz. 23 Inches long; by 3¼—The neck 3¼ long, by 2¾ diameter.

"Did you ever enquire what price paints are? What is the price of glass 9 by 11 by the box. What is the price of Linseed oil."

From Walter Minto

Sir   Erasmus-Hall near New York 24th Aug. 1787

The reverend Doctor Mason my friend will present to you a small Tract on the Theory of the Planets. Its chief merit consists in the discovery of a mathematical truth—that the circular orbit of a planet may be determined by two observations only—which had not been thought of before. I beg you will do me the favor of receiving it as a small testimony of the esteem & veneration I have for the Man who has done so much for the rights & happiness of humankind.[1] I have the Honor to be, Sir, Your most humble Servt

Walter Minto

ALS, PHi: Gratz Collection; Sprague transcript, DLC:GW.

Walter Minto (1753–1796), a Scottish mathematician, arrived in New York in 1786 and became principal of Erasmus Hall in Flatbush on Long Island. In 1787 John Witherspoon called him to Princeton to succeed Ashbel Green as professor of mathematics at the College of New Jersey, where Minto remained until his death.

1. After the discovery of the planet Uranus in 1781, Minto wrote and published his *Researches into Some Parts of the Theory of Planets; In Which Is Solved the Problem to Determine the Circular Orbit of a Planet by Two Observations* (London, 1783). "The reverend Doctor Mason" is probably John Mason, from 1761 until his death in 1792 pastor of the Scotch Presbyterian Church (Associate Reformed Church), on the south side of Little Queen (Cedar) Street in New York.

During the Revolution he was an ardent Patriot and served as chaplain to the garrisons on Hudson River.

Letter not found: from George Augustine Washington, 20 Aug. 1787. On 26 Aug. GW wrote George Augustine: "your letter of the 20th . . . came by the Post yesterday evening."

To Alexander Spotswood

Dear Sir,   Philadelphia August 26 1787

Having heard nothing from you, in reply to a letter I wrote you in answer to yours of the 25th of June, respecting your wishes to enter your Son on[1] board the French Navy, I am led to apprehend a miscarriage, or that the letter to or from you may be lying in some of the Post Offices (a thing not very unusual) I therefore address you again on the subject.[2]

The purport of my former letter was to ask, whether you had been encouraged to hope, or to expect much (from any Gentleman competent to advise you) from such a project, if not, whether it would not be better to delay your decisions on this point till enquiry could be first made and that, under the impression[3] of the propriety of it, I would detain your letter for france till I could hear further from you on this subject among others for the Following reasons.

1. Because I think your Sons going into the French Navy would be attended with greater expence than you apprehend.

2. That the highest rank he could expect to meet at entrance would be that of Midshipman.

3. That for want of an interest always at hand his prospect of rising would be very unpromising.

4. That from a difference of Country, language, religeon and manners, the Service would soon become irksome and disagreeable to him and in the last place.

Because I do not think they are such good Seaman as the British or Americans.

Friendship and regard for you and your Son, induced me to make these observations before I parted with your letters (supposing a small delay could make no great difference in your plan) but if you have been well advised in the matter and will write me again I will immediately forward your letters with one

of my own to the Marqs de la Fayette. as the delay of your answer has far exceeded any thing that could have been expected,
I shall be concerned if any inconvenianc⟨e⟩ should have resulted
from it having every disposition to comply with your wishes in
this, or any other respect wherein I can do it consistently—My
love to Mrs Spotswood. I am &ca

G. Washington

LB, DLC:GW.

1. The copyist from time to time, as he did here, wrote "or" for "on."
2. Neither Spotswood's letter of 25 June nor GW's response has been
found.
3. The copyist wrote "impressur."

To George Augustine Washington

Dear George,   Philadelphia Augt 26th 1787.
    Not having received any letter from you last Week (by the Post
which arrives here on Thursdays) I have, of course, nothing to
reply to; but request to be informed of the depth of the Well (by
the Kitchen door) from the level of the Brick pavement, which
surrds it, to the surface of the Water within; and the depth of
the Water. To be clear, if I am not so already, I want the whole
depth from the surface & level of the pavement to the bottom
of the Well; with the depth of Water therein—I have some intention of placing a pump in it, instead of drawing the Water up in
a Bucket as at present, and for this purpose the enquiry is made.
I also request that you wd send me the dimensions (in the same
way you did the former one) of the Chimneys in the Parlour,
common dining room, and your Aunts bed Chamber; and let
me know if the present back and sides of the one in the dining
room can be fitted to any other chimney that has no plates, and
which is in common use.[1] The Mill Irons will go by the next
Vessel and I would send glass for the green house also but it
appears to me that the price here is equally high with that
in Alexandria—here it is 100/ by the box, wch is equal to 80/
with you; and the frieght, duty & Comn would be to be added.
I go on the presumption that each box contains 12 doz., or 144
panes; of this, inform me how the case is at Alexandria. or how
many square feet a box is said to contain there.

If the top for the Cupulo, & the directions which accompanied it, are well understood, I would (supposing every thing is on the spot necessary for it) have it put up immediately, whilst the weather is mild, still, and warm.

I have promised Mr Morris an exact pattern, made of wood, of Mr Youngs Iron Plow—when I speak of wood, I mean such parts of it as *Nat* cannot make *true* and *perfect* such as the beam— &ca—You will readily perceive that as this is intended for a model to make others by, that the whole of it ought to be as exact as it can be made—for this reason & knowing that Nat is a clumsey fellow, and supposing that Mathew wd do it in wood, more correctly, that I have mentioned wood; but as you know the intention, it may either be of wood, or Iron, or partly of both as shall be judged best on consulting Mathew & Nat. all I want is, that the Model may be a perfect representation in all its parts, and the putting of them together likewise of the original. The direction for fixing or setting you have in Mr Youngs letter.[2]

You may make enquiry for a fit person to supply the place of Fairfax at the Ferry, but do not engage any before I return or you shall hear from me because I do not know but I may find it convenient to put both that and Frenchs under the care of the Farmer, or some one man.[3]

I had written thus far when your letter of the 20th (which came by the Post yesterday evening) was delivered to me. I am happy to find by it that you have, at length, had a good rain.[4] The Young Corn, Buck Wheat, Grain newly sown—and vegitables of every kind will undoubtedly be benefitted by it and may undergo a considerable change if the weather should continue to be seasonable.

If I am to form an opinion of the last harvest of Wheat & Rye, from the produce of the fields of lay Wheat & Rye at Muddy hole, it must be miserable indeed. The first containing 10 acres, yielding only 32½ Bushl⟨s⟩; and the other, containing 13 Acres, but 47½ of Rye—In neither case 4 bushels to the acre—If all turns out like these my prospect is indeed poor—not a moment therefore should be lost (if the Fly is among the Wheat to get it ground up before the little that is made be injured by this destructive insec⟨t⟩)—I beg therefore that this matter may be closely attended to. If Merchantable flour can not be made of the old Wheat, it had undoubtedly better be given to the Negroes—And if necessity obliges you to resort to the Potatoes and Pease for their support I desire that the quantity used by them may be (of both) measured that I may not only know what they use, but what I make—without which my experiments will be inconclusive.

I am very well satisfied with the disposition of the stock agreeably to the list inclosed to me—but it would be very well to compare this list with the one taken sometime ago (in the Winter, I believe it was or fall) and make the Overseers if there is a difference acct for it—unless this is done no valuable end is answered by taking such lists; and they may sell, kill, or otherwise dispose of any part thereof with impunity.[5]

How does your grass Seeds come on? particularly the clover; What sort of Clover is that in the Neck of the last years sowing? In short how does it look at all the places—old as well as new? Your Aunt informs me that there is a probability Mr B. Bassett will be Married soon; and that should it take place before I return, you do not Incline to carry Fanny down; thinking it may be improper to leave home while I am absent; but should the event happen I desire that this may be no bar to your accompanying her, as I see no inconvenience that can happen by so doing.[6] Give my love to Fanny, and best wishes to Mr Lear. I am dear George Yr Affecte Uncle

Go: Washington

ALS, ViLxW.

1. See GW to Charles Pettit, 7 Sept., and note 1 of that document.

2. Arthur Young to GW, 1 Feb. 1787. Nat was a slave carpenter; Mathew Baldridge was the white joiner.

3. See GW to George Augustine Washington, 29 July, n.5.

4. George Augustine Washington's letter of 20 Aug. has not been found.

5. The enclosed list of farm animals has not been found, but see the lists made by GW in November 1785 and October 1787 printed in *Diaries*, 4:223–31, 5:194–202.

6. The marriage of Burwell Bassett, Jr. (1764–1841), of Eltham to Elizabeth McCarty, daughter of Daniel McCarty of Popes Creek, Westmoreland County, did not take place until 10 Jan. 1788. George Augustine and Fanny Bassett Washington left Mount Vernon on 5 Jan. to attend the wedding and then to visit Eltham (*Diaries*, 5:262).

Letter not found: from George Augustine Washington, 27 Aug. 1787. On 2 Sept. GW wrote George Augustine: "Your last letter of the 27th Ulto came in due course."

To William Hartshorne

Sir,   Philadelphia August 30th 1787
    The Gentleman who will present this letter to you is Major Baylies of Massachusetts—Son in Law to Genl Lincoln. He is on business to Virginia, and at his request, I give you the trouble of receiving it as introductory of him, believing him to be a man of character and worth.[1]
    I understand, that the subscribers to the Potomack Navigation has been called upon for another advance, my proportion of which shall be paid so soon as I return, which cannot, now, be at a distant period.[2] with great esteem I am—Dr Sir Yr Most Obedt Servant

G. Washington

LB, DLC:GW.
    1. Maj. Hodijah Baylies (1756–1842) was one of GW's aides-de-camp in 1782 and 1783. GW in 1789 made Baylies collector of the customs for Dighton, Massachusetts.
    2. See GW to George Augustine Washington, 12 August.

To Elizabeth Powel

[Philadelphia] Friday Morning [31 August 1787]
    Genl Washington presents respectful compliments to Mrs Powell. The afternoons being short, it is proposed, to set off for Mr Pen's precisely at 4 Oclock; for this purpose the Generals horses & Servts will be at Mr Powells a quarter before that hour; & the General will be ready for Mr Powells call at it.[1]

AL, ViMtV.
    1. On Friday, 31 Aug., after dining at Robert Morris's, GW "with a Party went to Lansdale [Landsdowne] & drank Tea with Mr. & Mrs. [John and Ann Allen] Penn" (*Diaries*, 5:182).

From James K. Tobine

May it please Your Excellency   [August 1787]
   With the most profound humility I beg leave to approach
You, in order to implore You, Sir, that You would be pleased to
permit Your Excellency's most illustrious Name to be prefixed
to a Subscription, which I am about to solicit towards the enabling me to print, & publish a certain dramatic Work, calld
Americania & Seraphina, or the Immortal Friendship, An ale-
gorical, musical Masque.
   If this very Great (and to me most important) Favour, without
Sir your knowing the tendency or Design of the Work, be inadmissible: I am ready to lay my poor Manuscript at Your Excellency's Feet,[1] and beg leave to Subscribe myself, Your Excellencys Most devoted Most humble and most faithful Servt
                                                James K. Tobine

ALS, DLC:GW. The letter is undated, but GW dockets it "Augt 1787."
   A Mr. Tobine played Ali in the tragedy of *Mahomet the Imposter* in Baltimore
in 1782 and Sir John Millamour in *Know Your Own Mind* in Richmond in 1790
(Seilhamer, *American Theatre*, 2:73, 328–29).
   1. No response to this letter and no record of the publication of Tobine's
"Americania & Seraphina" have been found.

To John Jay

Dear Sir,   Philadelphia 2d Septr 1787.
   I avail myself of the polite assurance of your last, to trouble
you with the enclosed. If the Commodore should have left New
York, you would oblige me by forwarding it.[1]
   I regretted exceedingly, not having had it in my power to visit
New York during the adjournment of the Convention, last
Month. Not foreseeing with any precision the period at which
it was likely to take place, nor the length of it, I had put my
Carriage into the hands of a Workman to be repaired;[2] and had
not the means of moving during the recess but with, or on the
curtesy of, others.
   I thank you for the hints contained in your letter,[3] and with
best wishes for Mrs Jay, and great affection for yourself I am—
Dear Sir Yr Most Obedt Servt
                                                Go: Washington

ALS (photocopy), Stan Henkels Catalog no. 1372 (1925); LB, DLC:GW.

1. See GW to John Paul Jones, this date. See also GW to Jones, 22 July, n.1.

2. For the refurbishing of GW's carriage, see GW to Samuel Powel, 25 July, n.1.

3. See Jay to GW, 25 July.

To John Paul Jones

Sir,   Philadelphia Sept. 2d 1787

Should this letter reach you in time, the purport of it is, to beg your care of the enclosed to the Marqs de la Fayette;[1] and to inform you that all the letters, Memorials, and Papers of every kind which had been transmitted to me as President General of the Society of the Cincinnati, were forwarded (not expecting to attend it myself) to the last General meeting holden in this City but how they were acted upon is not in my power to inform you, not being at it.[2]

I have received, and have forwarded to my house the Bust you did me the honor to present me with, and shall place it with my own.[3] wishing you every possible felicity I have the honor to be—Sir Yr Most Hble & Obed. Sert

G. Washington

LB, DLC:GW.

1. GW's letter to Lafayette is dated in his letter book 15 August.

2. See Jones to GW, 25 July, and note 3 of that document.

3. See Jones to GW, 25 July, and note 1 of that document.

From William Roberts

Dear Sir   Fredricks Burge 2d of Septr 1787

This is to inform You that I am at My Brotherinlaws Alfords at Colo. Pages Mill From Whome I Am informd by, that You Send Some Time Ago to Intemate as Much as if I was To Seeke Your Imploy Once More it Mite be Possable To be Reinstated once More at home.[1] for Living As Long in Your Imploy as I Did it became as Natral to Me as Altho I had been Raisd on the Place. thare Fore if Your Exsellency has A Mind To Imploy Me I am Ready & Willing To Serve You as Fathefull as I alwais have Dun on previsers Youl Give My £80 ⅌ Year & My Old Preveledges. & in Regard to Poltery Wold Desier to Rase No More then for our own use—My Brother Alford Informs Me of An Action in Alexandria Cort Which has Been Gavin Against Me to the Amount of £12 Which I am Liable to be Executed for Which has Detaind Me from Coming on the Besoness my Self if you See proper to Imploy Me & Settle the Sute thats Gaven Against Me that I Shant be Destrest I will Come & Enter Into a Contract for a Term of Years or My Life time was it to be Ended as Happy As Formaly. the first place I Am Not in a Compasety to Move My Self Without Selling a Neg⟨ro⟩ Boy Whome I Shold be Sorry to part from thare fore if youd Move Me up As You have a Good Teem & Lend Me £10 it Shold be paid in My first Qrs pay.

I Shold be Raley Glad to be once More in Your Good & Honast Imploy For Whare I have Livd Last I have been Yousd with De⟨frau⟩d & Rail Arbitery Purposess of thare own which I Am Determend to Fly From As Soon As Possable From Sir Your Most Obediant And Humble Servant

Wm Roberts

N.B. Pray Sir Be So Kind as To favour Me With your answer By Mr Taylor.[2]

ALS, DLC:GW.

GW reluctantly discharged the skilled miller in 1785 after Roberts had "become such an intolerable sot, and when drunk so great a madman" that GW could not bring himself to "bear with him any longer" (GW to Robert Lewis & Sons, 1 Feb. 1785). GW and Roberts corresponded as late as the summer of 1799 about the possibility of Roberts's returning to Mount Vernon.

1. Mann Page, Jr., of Mannsfield near Fredericksburg, visited Mount Vernon as recently as 12–14 July 1786 (*Diaries*, 5:7–8). Alford is probably Thomas Alford (Alfred), formerly William Roberts's apprentice at Mount Vernon.

2. Mr. Taylor may be Alexandria merchant Jesse Taylor who dined at Mount Vernon on 23 Sept., the day after GW returned from Philadelphia (ibid., 188).

To George Augustine Washington

Dear George,   Philadelphia 2d Septr 1787.

Your last letter of the 27th ulto came in due course of Post, and gave me the pleasure to hear that you had had a continuance of rain.[1] Seasonable weather may bring on young Corn, & help that which was not too far gone. At any rate the Buck Wheat, and vegitables of every kind, must receive benefit.

When I expressed a wish to have the race widened from the mill upwards, it was on a supposition that the Water had not been turned into it; had I believed this was the case I should not have requested it; tho' I shall not be at all dissatisfied at the delay occasioned by it, provided the work is well done; for to accomplish this was all I had in view.

The Acct you have given of the present State of the different species of Crops, is very satisfactory; a similar one, weekly, would give me a precise idea of them; but I trust I shall not remain here more than a fortnight longer to receive these accts, or any thing else.

By your Aunts letter to me, I find that Mr Hanson has applied to, and received payment from Mr Porter for the board of George & Lawrence Washington. I beg you will request (Mr Hanson) never to do the like again. Mr Porter must conceive very strangely of this; I am sure I do; & cannot acct for the application[2]—And I further beg that you will, in my name, let your father know, in explicit terms, that if he will not keep me furnished with the means to defray the expences of these boys that he must take the whole of their affairs on himself. The demands upon me for money are too numerous & heavy to answer the calls I have on their acct. He seems not to consider that the calls on me for their schooling, board, cloathing &ca encrease with time, but on the contrary when a sum is once paid, that the matter is done with—Another quarter I suppose must be due, or nearly so, by this time, besides the Schooling—the Cloathing from Mr Porter &ca &ca—all of which I shall, I expect to be saluted by, as soon as I return. He ought to put the produce of their Estates (if they have any, and if they have not, I know what to depend upon) as fast as it is raised into my hands. this certainly would be as proper as to be keeping me constantly in advance, & exposed to Duns on their acct when I know not which way to turn, to obtain money to pay the pressing calls for Cash I own on my own Acct.

I am sorry to find that the Green paint which was got to give the dining room another Coat, should have turned out so bad; such impositions (besides the disappointment) are really shameful. I did not know that any part of the Boston leather was black, consequently could have no particular design in view at the time it was sent—but as it is so—and good—it may be appropriated for shoes for the House Servants—Overseers &ca.[3]

In my last I wrote to you for an exact model of Youngs Plough—to be made of Wood or Iron, or partly of both as Mathew and Nat might agree, for Mr Robt Morris; what I meant by a model was that it should be exactly of the size in all its parts, and as truely put together as Mr Young's is; that the representation may be perfect for others to be made, & fixed by. Send it by the first Vessel after it is ready. and send with it also, a peck of what you conceive to be Youngs spring wheat; which, unquestionably, is the most indifferent looking of the two red kinds.[4] accompany the Plow & Wheat with a line to Mr Morris.

I am well satisfied from the account given of the New ground, in your last letter, (in front of the House) that the Succours and Sprts together with the Huckleberry shrubs &ca, are not sufficiently destroyed to sow grain in, and therefore if you have not begun to do it desire that it may be delayed untill I return home.

Fairfax's Terms, I suppose must be agreed to, though he seems disposed to make hay (or in other words Cloaths) whilst the Sun shines.[5] Hardly any weekly report comes to hand by which it does not appear that Thos Greene is absent one or more days. I desire you will tell him that this custom is a bad one—contrary to any ideas I entertained when he was bargained with, and that it must be broke.[6]

I desire you will send me the number of New blankets your Aunt has in her Store room. They are not to be had here but on high terms, and yet this is the year that *all* my people are entitled to receive them, except the Women who have had Children and been supplied on that occasion. do you know the Alexandria price for the large striped dutch blanketing? (15 I believe are in a piece)—If you do not, pray enquire & let me know when you next write. Also the price of Bills of Exchange drawn on London, at 30 days sight? that I may know whether it is best to sell here, or there.

Miss Allan's letter has been given to Mr Rutlidge who has promised to forward, or carry it safe to Major Read.[7] My love to Fanny, & best wishes to Mr Lear—With sentiments of great regard I am—Dr George—Yr Affecte Uncle

Go: Washington

ALS, Sulgrave Manor, England.

1. Letter not found.
2. See Samuel Hanson to GW, 23 Sept., and notes.
3. For the "Boston Leather," see Nathaniel Ingraham to GW, 31 May 1787.
4. "Indifferent" is used in the obsolete sense meaning of a medium quality.
5. See GW to George Augustine Washington, 29 July, n.5.
6. See GW to George Augustine Washington, 1 July, n.2.
7. "Miss Allan" may have been Sarah Allen who lived at the Calverts' Mount Airy in Maryland and often visited Eleanor Calvert Custis Stuart at Abingdon. John Rutledge was soon to leave Philadelphia for Charleston, South Carolina. Jacob Read (1752–1816), a lawyer in Charleston who was an important political figure in South Carolina and an officer in the state's militia, was married in October 1785 to Catherine Van Horne of New York.

Letter not found: from George Augustine Washington, 2 Sept. 1787. On 9 Sept. GW acknowledged George Augustine's "letter of the 2d of this month."

From Robert Fenning

September 5th 1787
Sir   No. 25 St martens Le Grand London
    I hope your Excellence will excuse the freeness of a strainger troubleing you with a Letter, as he had no other way to make himself known, or aquaint your Excellency, that he was about three years ago examind by Mr Laurence, and Mr Chase in London; Mr Laurence, of Charles Town, South Caralione and Mr Samuel Chase, of Maryland in Ameraca.[1]
    I must now beg Leave to aquaint your Excellence, that I was borought up in the Practical part of Husbandry, have Lived in the most Principal Corn Countys, in England and Ireland with Nobleman and Gentleman to Improve thare Estates, and have had a Quantity of Land, under my Care, Laid out for Regular Courses of experiments, to find out the mystrys, and Errors in Husbandry, and have made, some great discoverys, perticular in Wheat, Turnips, Rape, and Coleseed, Wheat, why so much is destroyd, by Insects, when first sown, and why so much is destroy'd by wet, and frost; Turnups, why they are so much distroy'd by flies, and Insects, in it's infant state; and why so much Rape, and Coleseed is destroy'd by frost; and a many Other

Mystrys in Husbandry, to teadous here to mention; and not only why it [is] so; but means to prevent it's being so, and having a Machanical turn of mind, have made Imploments of Husbandry my study, thinking that a princapal, Consideration, to Reduce the great expense on Labour; have made great emprovements on many, and have Invented several, that has Lesend the expense, in several Cultures in Agriculture—all this I mention'd to Mr Laurence, and to Mr Chase, and told them; Gentleman to Refer too; Mr Laurence told me he thought I should be very useful in Ameraca, and should do well thare, but upon a point of delicacy, woud not Intice a useful subject from England, but woud give me a Line or two, to Mr Chase in Dover Street, who prehap woud hire me; I was with Mr Chase several times, till he could get a Letter from a Gentleman, in Ireland, of Large Landed property, who I had serv'd, to attest my abilities, honesty and sobriety; after that came; he told me, from that, and several other Letters, and discharges that I showd him, he woud give me a Letter of Recommendation to your Excellence, and to Major General Smallwood, (which I have by me,) that if, I did not meet with Imployment by one of you Honourable Gentleman, (which he has no douts of) he, and Brother, had Land in Maryland, and woud Let me have some, near a Town; that woud pay me well, for growing vegetables and that himself was going soon to Ameraca—but my friends preswaded me not to come, as the distance was so great, with out I Could get a sure agreement, worth excepting, before I Left England—since I see Mr Chase I have been Imploy'd by a gentleman of the London Society of Agriculture, who may be Refer'd too; by any Merchant, or gentleman, if your Excellence thought proper—I Have had a great deal of stock of all kinds under my Care, Breeding, and fatting Stock; if from the above account I have given of my self; your Excellence could think I Could be useful to you, or to any Gentleman in Ameraca, I do in this offer my ⟨*mutilated*⟩ if your Excellence woud be please to give me a Letter ⟨outl⟩ining your Terms, what Sallery ⅌ year, and what you'd be pleasd to allow me, for my Pasage; should Like to come directly to any healththy part of Ameraca, I beg your Excellence's pardon, in asking, the Honour of a Letter from you; as probable I might be preswaded to trouble your Excellence with the secant, thinking this might miscarry, or [be] Lost in the Passage—thinking your Excellence woud wish to know my age, its 45 years.[2] I am your Excellence's most Obedient & Humble Servant

Robert Fenning

P.S. I have measured amany hundred Acres of Land and amany hundred Load of Timber.

ALS, DLC:GW.

1. Henry Laurens was taken to London in 1780 as a prisoner of war and remained in England until 1784. Samuel Chase was sent to London by the governor of Maryland in 1783 and was there for one year.

2. GW responded from Mount Vernon on 8 Jan. 1788: "Sir, I have received your letters of the 5th of Septr In answer to which I can only say that I am not at present in want of a person of your description, but if you are desireous of settling in this country, and will let me know precisely what your terms and expectations are, I think it is very probable I shall hear of some Gentleman who would be willing to engage you for the purpose of superintending thir farms, provided your knowledge and experience in husbandry &c. is such as you have mentioned & you can bring authentic testimonials thereof and your terms are not extravagant. I am Sir Yr Obedt Hble Servant G. Washington" (LB, DLC:GW).

From William Gordon

My dear Sir　　　　　　　　　　London Sepr 6. 1787

I rejoice to find that your Lady has of late been troubled less than formerly with the bilious cholick. May She be wholly freed from it, & all prescriptions become unnecessary!

Thank you for your kind wishes, they are still needful. No settlement has yet offered. I am going on with my History, & toward the latter end of next month shall begin printing. Health & strength permitting, shall continue it till the work is published.

The bill upon Salem has been duly honored, & the money remitted & received. Had no apprehension on my own part, but that the publications alluded to were equally false with foregoing ones. Am sorry that the conduct of the Bay-men & Rhode Islanders has been so disgraceful, & given so much ground for reproaches.[1]

Holland at present takes up the attention of the public. Am fearful it will terminate in a war. Should the ministry, alias the king, involve this nation afresh in that dreadful judgment, may they succeed only in proportion to the equity of their conduct.

How far the seeds already sent, may have answered my good intentions must be learnt from future letters. Have sent you three quarters of a pound of larkspur to make the garden gay. They consist of equal shares of the double rose—the tall double rocket—& the dwarf double ditto. You have been engaged with others in a very arduous business. Shall exult upon finding that your united labours have provided a safe, efficacious, & permanent remedy, for the evils which have so long existed & diffused themselves so extensively. 'Tis mortifying that the advantages gained by the late glorious contest for that so fine a country should not be better improved. It is to be feared, that the scenes of blood which have taken place in this old world, will be repeated in the new, in some distant period; & that America in its turn will become the Aceldama,[2] while Europe possibly may sink again into barbarism. These events however are so distant, that our happiness need not be much impaired with the thought of them.

Mrs Gordon joins in most affectionate regards to Self, Lady, the rest of the family, & Mr & Mrs Lund Washington, with my dear Sir Your sincere friend & most humble servant

William Gordon

ALS, DLC:GW.
   1. See GW to Gordon, 10 April 1787.
   2. Aceldama is a field of blood, a scene of slaughter.

From John Jay

Dr Sir   N. York 6 Septr 1787

I was yesterday honored with your Letter of the 2d Inst., inclosing one for Commodore Jones, which was immediately conveyed to him.

New York entertained Hopes of seeing you here, and wishd for such an occasion of giving you fresh Proofs of Esteem & attachment, for your consenting to take a Seat in the Convention has given your Country fresh Reasons for both.

You will oblige me by putting it in my power to do you any services which occasions may render convenient to you, and be assured of the constant & perfect Respect & Regard with wh. I am Dr Sr your most obt & very hble Servt.

ADf, NNC. The ALS was offered for sale and printed in Henkels Catalog no. 738, item 1120, 1895. Except for the signature the draft and printed copy are identical.

To Charles Pettit

Sir   Philadelphia Sept. 7th 1787

Having received the dimensions of three more of my Chimneys for which I want castings, I have to request them as follows.

3. 6½ high in front
1. 6½ deep   } First
3. 3 Wide at the back
3. 2½ high in front
1. 6½ Deep   } Second
3. 5 Wide at the back
3. 1 high in front
1.10 Deep   } third
3. 5 Wide at the back

The above being the exact size of the Chimneys (already built and in use) it is not to be forgotten that the thickness of the *back* plate is to be deducted from the width of those on the sides or vica versa as shall be adjudged best.

The mould already made, may subserve for the above Casting reducing it first to the largest of the above Chimneys—then to the second size—and lastly to the smallest—the crest and Cypher to each.[1]

I should be glad to receive them as soon as possible and the money shall be immediately paid for them. I am yrs &ca

G. Washington

LB, DLC:GW.

Charles Pettit (1736–1806), who was trained as a lawyer, was an import merchant in Philadelphia and a member of Congress. For details of his career, see the editors' note in Pettit to GW, 24 May 1789. See also the note in Pettit to GW, 5 Aug. 1788.

1. GW wrote George Augustine Washington on 3 June asking him to secure the measurements of the fireplace in the chimney in the New Room at Mount Vernon, and it was probably in a missing letter of 24 June to Pettit that GW ordered the firebacks for that chimney. He wrote George Augustine Washington on 26 Aug. for the dimensions of the fireplace in the chimneys referred to

here. For further correspondence regarding these firebacks, see GW to Pettit, 2, 14 Oct., 3 Dec. 1787, and Pettit to GW, 1, 6 Nov. 1787, 22 April 1788.

From Jonas Phillips

Sirs　　　　　Philadelphia 24th Ellul 5547 or Sepr 7th 1787

With leave and Submission I address my Self To those in whome there is wisdom understanding and knowledge. they are the honorable personages appointed and Made overseers of a part of the terrestrial globe of the Earth, Namely the 13 united states of america in Convention Assembled, the Lord preserve them amen.

I the subscriber being one of the people called Jews of the City of Philadelphia, a people scattered and despersed among all nations do behold with Concern that among the laws in the Constitution of Pennsylvania their is a Clause Sect 10 to viz.—I do belive in one God the Creator and governour of the universe the Rewarder of the good and the punisher of the wicked—and I do acknowledge the scriptures of the old and New testement to be given by devine inspiration—To Swear and belive that the new testement was given by devine inspiration is absolutly against the Religious principle of a Jew and is against his conscience to take any such oath. By the above law a Jew is deprived of holding any public office or place of Government which is a Contradectory to the bill of Right Sect. 2 viz.—[1]

That all men have a natural and inalienable Right To worship almighty God according to the dictates of their own Conscience and understanding, and that no man aught or of Right can be compelled to attend any Religious Worship or Erect or support any place of worship or Maintain any minister contrary to or against his own free will and Consent nor can any man who acknowledges the being of a God be Justly deprived or abridged of any Civil Right as a Citizen on account of his Religious Sentiments or peculiar mode of Religious Worship and that no authority can or aught to be vested in or assumed by any power what Ever that shall in any Case interfere or in any manner Controul the Right of Conscince in the free Exercise of Religious Worship.

It is well Known among all the Citizens of the 13 united states

that the Jews have been true and faithfull whigs; and during the
late contest with England they have been foremost in aiding and
assisting the states with their lifes and fortunes, they have supported the cause, have bravely fought and bleed for Liberty
which they can not Enjoy.

Therefore if the honourable Convention shall in their Wisdom think fit and alter the said oath and leave out the words to
viz.—and I do acknowledge the scriptures of the new testement
to be given by devine inspiration, then the Israelites will think
themself happy to live under a government where all Religious
societys are on an Eaquel footing. I solecet this favour for my
Self my Children and posterity and for the benefit of all the
Israelites through the 13 united States of america.

My prayer is unto the Lord—May the people of this states
Rise up as a great and young lion, May they prevail against their
Enemies, May the degrees of honour of his Exceellency the pres-
ident of the Convention George Washington, be ⟨Extolled⟩ and
Raise up, May Everyone speak of his glorious Exploits—May
God prolong his days among us in this land of Liberty—May he
lead the armies against his Enemys as he has done hereuntofore,
May God Extend peace unto the united States—May they get
up to the highest Prosperitys—May God Extend peace to them
and their Seed after them so long as the Sun and moon En-
dureth—and May the almighty God of our father Abraham
Isaac and Jacob endue this Noble Assembly with wisdom Judgement and unamity in their Councills, and may they have the
Satisfaction to see that their present toil and labour for the well-
fair of the united States may be approved of Through all the
world and perticular by the united States of america, is the ardent prayer of Sires Your Most devoted obed. Servant

Jonas Phillips

ALS, DNA: RG 360, Records of the Federal Convention. The letter was directed to GW and the other members of the Convention.

Jonas Phillips (1736–1803) emigrated from Hesse to London and from
there in 1756 first to Charleston, S.C., then to New York. After his marriage
to Rebecca Mendez Machado in Philadelphia in 1762, she bore him twenty-
one children. He moved from New York to Philadelphia in 1773 and during
the Revolution became one of the leaders of the Jewish community in the city.
He went back to New York to live in 1786 but remained only a short time
before returning to Philadelphia (N. Taylor Phillips, "Family History of the
Reverend David Mendez Machado," *Publications of the American Jewish Historical*

Society, 2[1893], 45–61). The Convention had already, on 20 Aug., adopted the provision that appeared in Article VI of the Constitution: "No religious test or qualification shall ever be annexed to any oath of office under the authority of the United States" (Madison's Notes in Farrand, *Records of the Federal Convention,* 2:335).

1. Phillips also petitioned the Pennsylvania state constitutional convention in 1789 to remove the religious oath. The Pennsylvania constitution of 1790 provided "That no person who acknowledges the being of a God, and a future state of rewards and punishments, shall, on account of his religious sentiments be disqualified to hold any office or place of trust or profit under this commonwealth" (Wolf and Whiteman, *Jews of Philadelphia,* 151–52).

To Elizabeth Powel

[Philadelphia] Friday 7th Sep. 1787

Genl Washington presents his respectful compliments to Mrs Powell. He has, with much pleasure, perused the enclosed. He finds the sentiments perfectly just—the advice good, and he is persuaded of the favourable reception, and efficacy of them in the mind of his Nephew.[1]

AL, ViMtV.

1. The "enclosed" has not been identified.

From Elizabeth Powel

Dear Sir   [Philadelphia] ⟨Septem⟩ber 8 1787

I have taken the Liberty to send you a reflecting Lamp for your Hall. I well know your Delicacy on the Subject of accepting the smallest Present even from your best Friend; but I as well know your Patriotism, & that when it has come in Competition with your own Feelings the latter have ever yielded. That Light is an Object of immense Consequence no one will venture to deny, & that the Importation of Tallow takes off a great deal of Money I believe is very certain. Your Example will, I flatter myself, be always sufficient to reccommend & establish the Use of any Articles in America.

After the fullest & fairest Experiment it has been found that one of these Lamps gives more Light than Three Spermaceti or Six Tallow Candles. Three spermaceti Candles cost 2/6 & the Tallow 1/6 Two Gills of spermaceti Oil at Five Shillings pr Gallon, which is the highest retail Price, will not cost quite Four-pence and will burn as long as the Candles. This is an immense saving in any one Article of Family Use; & tho' I suppose & believe this would be no Object with you, in your own particular Instance, yet, as you are so happily formed as to step out of yourself & consult the Circumstances & Situation of others, I think you will be struck with the Propriety & Utility of bringing them into general Use in Virginia, where I am told they have not gained sufficient Credit to be generally imported. An attempt has been made here to make them but they are so badly & clumsily executed as to be totaly unfit for gentlemens Use; but I hope we shall soon make them equal to the english ones. The One sent is not of the ornamental Kind, but simple & neat; but, with your Temperance & Aversion to Ostentation, that will be no objection. I have sent half a Dozen spare Glasses in case of accidents, & Wick sufficient for Two or Three Years The Mandril is to fix the Wick on with.

The Lamp is put up in a Box with the Wick &Ca very safely I think and the Directions are also in it[1]—I am with great Sincerity dear Sir Your affectionate Friend and very humble Servt

Eliza. Powel

ALS, DLC:GW.

1. In reply on "Saturday Morng 8th Sepr 1787," GW wrote: "Dear Madam, The reflecting lamp, with which you have been so obliging as to present me, I shall highly esteem. The benefits which will flow from the general use of such Lamps, are too apparent for the light of them to be long hid from the American World. Neat simplicity, is among the most desirable properties of the one you have sent me, but that which stamps the highest value thereon, is the hand from which it comes. I have the honor to be wth Affecte regard Dr Madam" (AL, owned [1991] by Mr. Joseph Rubinfine, West Palm Beach, Florida). GW had the lamp, which, he wrote, "could not have cost 20/," shipped to Virginia (GW to Clement Biddle, 10 September).

From John Paul Jones

Sir,   New-York Septr 9th 1787.

It gives me pain to inform you that the same cause that prevented me from returning to France in the July Packet, precludes me from embarking in the one that is to sail to Morrow. I have been every day expecting my Business here to be concluded; and, if Congress had met any day since the beginning of last Month, my matters would have been immediately determined. As Mr Jay does not think it expedient to commit his Dispatches, either to the Mail or to any of the Passengers, I have not thought myself authorized to forward the Packets you did me the honor to entrust to my care. But I have written to the Marquis de la Fayette, mentioning your Packets, and that, in my opinion, the one for the Marquis de Bouillé may, perhaps, contain his Diploma of the Cincinnati.[1]

Your determination to *"place my Bust with your own"* confers on me a greater Honor than I ever before received—An Honor which I shall ever be ambitious to merit—But, what Man can hope to vie with the Talents—the virtuous perseverance and exertions of a General Washington! I shall leave you, Sir, to imagin my extreme sensibillity on this occasion, for, I feel, it would be impossible for me to communicate it in words.

May you long enjoy perfect Health, and perfect Happiness! and may you have the satisfaction to see the new Constitution, over which you Preside, become the means of our National Honor, Dignity, and Felicity! I am, with profound Respect, Sir, Your most obliged and most humble Servant

Paul Jones

ALS, DLC:GW.

1. GW wrote to Jones on 2 September. See also GW to Jones, 22 July, n.1, and GW to Bouillé, 1 June.

To George Augustine Washington

Dear George, Philadelphia Septr 9th 1787.

This, in acknowledgment of your letter of the 2d of this Month,[1] is probably the last letter I shall write you from this place; as the probability is, that the Convention will have compleated the business which brought the delegates together, in the course of this Week. God grant I may not be disappointed in this expectation, as I am quite homesick.

As Mr McPhearson's glass (if good) is cheaper than the first cost here of that article, independently of the Comn, freight, &ca; I request that you will get what may be necessary for the Green house, from him, that the building may be finished.[2]

I had no idea, nor can I now see the necessity, for stripping the Shingling from the Cupulo, in order to fix on the top which was sent from this place; As nothing more than the Iron spire is to pass through it, surely taking away the laths & plaistering on the inside would have been sufficient for the purpose of fixing the foot thereof—and this, instead of requiring a fortnight, would scarcely have been the business of a day; but it is too late now, I expect, to offer this opinion, as the work (some way or another) will have been nearly, if not altogether, compleated before this letter will have reached Mt Vernon.

I am very glad to hear of the interruptions your field work has met with from the Rains which have lately fallen. If the weather should be warm, and the fall fine, they may facilitate the growth of every thing—the new meadow, so abundantly productive of weeds, ought to have been mown, as well for the sake of the young grass, as to prevent the seeds of the weeds from maturing and stocking the ground. I have but little expectation however, I must confess, that the latter Corn will come to *much;* and less that Pumpkin, which are *now* only in blossom, can come to *any thing.* Of the Pease, from your acct of them much may be expected; but I should be glad to know whether the Vines cover the ground well (those in broad cast I mean) and whether they bear well? What is the general height of the Buck wheat, how the ground is covered with it, & whether it is generally in blossom? If the Potatoes are so slow in forming, I fear not much is to be expected from the yield of them neither. I had expected, till your letter held up the contrary idea, that there would have been more than a sufficiency of old rails at Morris's to have enclosed the fallow field, especially as they were aided, or to be aided, by a ditch. There is not a right understanding with respect to doors opening to the right or left⟨,⟩ for sure I am that the hinges I last sent were, according to the conception *here* for a door opening to the left—however I will get another pair contrary, if I can, to those last sent.

Inclosed I send a letter (to whom I offer best wishes) to Mr Lear. It came under cover to me from the Eastward. I hope Mathews model will be exact,[3] and arrive soon; accompanied by the spring wheat I wrote for (I believe) in my last. My love to Fanny, & with affectionate regard I am Yours

Go: Washington

P.S. If the Flax has not been spread to rot, it is time it should be—It ought to be turned, well watched, & taken up as soon as it is sufficiently rotted and this can only be known by frequent examination after turning.

ALS, John Rylands Library, Manchester, England.

1. Letter not found.

2. Isaac and Daniel McPherson were merchants in Alexandria.

3. GW is referring to Arthur Young's plow. See GW to George Augustine Washington, 3 June 1787.

To Clement Biddle

Dear Sir, [Philadelphia] Monday 10th Septr 1787.

I have received both your Notes of this Morning, and thank you for Notice of the Vessels sailing. The Books, I perceive, are only small treatises upon education, referred to by Doctr Rush, which I can get, & carry in my Trunk.[1] remember the clothes baskets. I send a small box containing a Lamp—it is a present, but could not have cost 20/.[2] If the hounds presented to me by Captn Morris are not provided for, will it not be necessary to lay something in for them?[3] I think of nothing else at this time; therefore, if you will let me know how the acct stands between us I would wish to square it.

AL, PHi: Washington-Biddle Correspondence.

1. Biddle's notes have not been found. The "small treatises" may have been two pamphlets written by Benjamin Rush himself. In 1786 he had published in Philadelphia *A Plan for the Establishment of Public Schools and the Diffusion of Knowledge in Pennsylvania,* and on 28 July 1787 he addressed to the Female Academy in Philadelphia his *Thoughts upon Female Education, Accommodated to the Present State of Society, Manners, and Government of the United States of America,* which was then published during the same year. The latter is known to have been in GW's library at the time of his death.

2. See Elizabeth Powel to GW, 8 September.

3. See GW to Biddle, 19 Sept., Biddle to GW, 23 Sept., and Samuel Morris to GW, 21 September.

Draft of the Federal Constitution: Report of Committee of Style

[12 September 1787]. GW (or, in a few instances, the secretary of the convention William Jackson) entered on his printed copy of the draft of the Constitution presented to the Convention on 12 Sept. by the committee of style, all of the various changes in form and content adopted by the Convention between 12 and 15 Sept. when the Constitution took its final form.

D, DLC:GW.

On 8 Sept. the Convention chose William Samuel Johnson, Alexander Hamilton, Gouverneur Morris, James Madison, and Rufus King "to revise the stile of and arrange the articles which had been agreed to by the House" (Madison's Notes in Farrand, *Records of the Federal Convention,* 2:553). On 12 Sept. Johnson, "from the Committee of revision," reported "the Constitution as revised and arranged"; it was "ordered that the Members be furnished with printed copies thereof" (Madison's Notes, ibid., 582). For the next three days the Convention went through the document, and GW entered each of the deletions, additions, or other changes that the Convention adopted between 5 and 12 Sept., all of which appear in the Constitution.

From Henry Knox

My dear Sir   New York 14 September 1787
    presuming that you will not set out from Philadelphia untill Monday the 17th I write you a line to congratulate you on the termination of your arduous business & to wish you a happy sight of Mrs Washington and your family.
    In every event respecting the reception of the propositions of the convention you will enjoy the high satisfaction of having performed every thing that could possibly be expected of you— But I flatter myself that You will see the government proposed adopted fully by the people.
    Mrs Knox unites with me in presenting our respectful affections to Mrs Washington. With the most ardent wish for your perfect felicity, in every stage of your existence I am my dear Sir Your sincere & truly affectionate friend and Humble Servt
                                                                    H. Knox

ALS, DLC:GW.

To Clement Biddle

[Philadelphia] Saturday Morng 15th Septr [1787]
Genl Washington prests his Compliments to Colo. Biddle & would be glad to know if the Vessel for Alexandria is gone. The lowest price the best dutch (striped) Blankets sell at, by the piece. and how his acct stands since the late purchases made by him as he has expectations that the business of the Convention will be brought to a close, or nearly so this day.

AL, PHi: Washington-Biddle Correspondence.

To John Cannon

Sir,   Philadelphia Sept. 16th 1787
I was suprized to find by your letter of the 8th of may, dated in this City (received after I came to it) that you had not got the letter I wrote to you sometime before under cover to Colo. Bayard of Pittsburg especially as the Colonel has acknowledged the receipt of it, and promised that it should be carefully forwarded to your house.[1]

In that letter, to the best of my recollection, I requested that you would take charge of all my concerns—as well as those in Fayette, as Washington Counties & act for me as you would do for yourself. To this, if my memory serves me, your powers already extend—if not, I now give them to you by this letter.

I cannot consent to take two dollars a acre for the Land in Washington County. If the Government of this Country gets well toned, and property perfectly secured, I have no doubt of obtaining the price I have fixed on the land, and that in a short time, in the mean while, I had rather rent it from year to year than give leases for a term of years as the latter will certainly impede the Sale.

For the Land in Fayette County, I have been offered the price I had fixed on it—viz. Forty Shillings pr Acre—by a number of New Jersey people but we have differed with respect to the mode of payment and perhaps shall never agree I would not therefore have you Slip an opportunity of disposing of that Tract, if that price and the payment thereof is well secured. I would, as I thi[n]k you have already been informed; be content with one fourth of the money paid down—the remainder in four annual payments with interest.

I am willing to take usual allowance of the Crops which were on the ground and hope you have taken your measures accordingly less than this, the Tenants cannot I should conceive think of giving—as the whole of them might have been demanded. I am Sir Yr Most Obed. Servant

G. Washington

LB, DLC:GW.

1. Cannon's letter of 8 May 1787 has not been found. GW's letter to Cannon is dated 13 April 1787. Neither GW's covering letter to Stephen Bayard nor Bayard's response has been found, but on 26 April Clement Biddle wrote that he was forwarding GW's letter to "Col. Ste[phen] Bayard at Pittsburgh."

To Chastellux

My Dr Marqs   Philadelphia Sept. 16th 1787

Mr Pinkney will do me the favor of presenting this letter to you[1]—He is a Gentleman of fortune, family & character in South Carolina—A member of Congress, and delegate to the Fœderal Convention, now sitting in this City. As he proposes to visit your Country I take this liberty of introducing him to your acquaintance and attentions—and this I do with pleasure⟨.⟩ I persuade myself that you will in him find, abilities and information. I am &ca

G. Washington

LB, DLC:GW.

1. GW on this day also wrote to Lafayette and Rochambeau on behalf of Charles Pinckney (1757–1824). He wrote Lafayette: "My dear Marqs, Permit me to introduce Mr Pickney to you the bearer of this. He is a Gentleman of Fortune, family and Character in South Carolina—a member of Congress and at present a delegate in the Fœderal Convention.

"Having a desire to travel I take the liberty of introducing him to your civilities & attention as a Gentleman of information and one with whome you will be well pleased. I am &ca G. Washington" (LB, DLC:GW).

The letter-book copy of his letter to Rochambeau reads: "My dear Count, The Gentleman who will do me the honor of presenting this letter to you is Mr Peckney of So. Carolina—a member of Congress, and deligate to the Fœderal Convention from that State. Having an inclination to travel I take the liberty of giving him this letter of introduction to your acquaintance and civilities as a Gentleman of Information and worth. I am &ca G. Washington" (LB,

DLC:GW). Pinckney did not go to Europe in 1787; he returned to Charleston and served as a delegate in the South Carolina Ratifying Convention in 1788.

To Richard Noble

Sir, Philadelphia Sept. 16th 1787

By a letter which I have received from Major Thomas Freeman since I came to this City I am informed that he has lodged some money of mine in your hands, as also a receipt from Thomas Smith Esqr. for £533.19.0 with sundry other papers.[1] I shall be obliged by your forwarding the money to me by the First good conveyance; the papers I beg you to place in the hands of Colo. Cannon of Washington County to whose care I had committed my business in that County long before I had any knowledge or information from Major Freeman of his having committed these matters to you.[2] If no shure and safe conveyance should offer for sending the money immediately to me I request in that case that you would be so obliging as to deliver it to Thomas Smith Esqr. Attorney at Law who will apply it to the uses, and agreeable to the advice I have given. I am Sir Yr Most Obed. Sert

G. Washington

LB, DLC:GW.

Richard Noble (b. 1749), originally from Charles County, Md., settled about 1772 with his family on a large grant of land in what is now South Fayette Township in Allegheny County, Pa., establishing a trading post and town.

1. Neither Thomas Freeman's letter nor Thomas Smith's receipt has been found, but see GW to Smith, this date.

2. See GW to John Cannon, 13 April and 16 Sept. 1787.

To Thomas Smith

Sir, Philadelphia 16th Septr 1787.

You will be puzzled to acct for my long silence. The truth is, before I came to this City I resolved to Postpone writing till I should have arrived at, and should have met with, a direct conveyance from it; and after I came here the variety of matters which occurred and pressed upon me has in some measure put it out of my power to do it at an earlier period.[1]

I wish sincerely that you had been so obliging as to have designated the Sum with which you would have been satisfied for your services in conducting my Ejectments—I still wish that you would do this and receive it out of the money which—by Majr Freemans report to me—you must be on the point of recovering—and permit me to add moreover that I wish yet more ardently I had it in my power to pay you in a more agreeable manner than this, but the fact is, my expences in this City have been so much greater than I expected that it has deprived me of the means.

Major Freemans letter to me contains this paragraph. "at March term I delivered Mr Smith sundry obligations and took his receipt for them, which with the one in his hands before, amounts to £533.19.0—I make no doubt he will soon recover the money and transmit it to you" he adds "I have lodged with Mr Richard Noble near redstone old Fort £38.1.3"—This sum I have requested Mr Noble to pay you if it has not been forwarded to me through some other channel—and I hope measures has been, or will be taken to obtain from my opponants the legal fees and other costs which they burdened me to prosecute my right.[2]

Mr Smiley handed me a letter some time after my arrival at this place accompanied by £12.10 recovered from one Cunningham.[3]

For the anxiety you express to have undergone during the prosecution of the Ejectments, I feel myself exceedingly obliged, and pray you to accept my thanks for this proof of your zeal as well as for the good wishes you are pleased to express for me. I am Sir Yr Most Obedt & obliged Hble Servt

Go: Washington

ALS, PWacD: Sol Feinstone Collection, on deposit PPAmP; LB, DLC:GW.

1. No letter from GW to Smith written since the ejectment trials were held in October 1786 has been found. Smith wrote GW about the trials on 7 Nov. 1786; he wrote again on 17 Feb. and 22 May (missing) 1787.

2. Thomas Freeman's letter has not been found. See GW's letter to Richard Noble, this date. See also GW to Smith, 3 Dec. 1787, 5 Mar. 1788, and 3 April 1788.

3. Smith's letter has not been found. See GW to Bushrod Washington, 29 Dec. 1787, and GW to Thomas Smith, 22 Feb. 1788. Mr. Smiley may be John Smilie of Fayette County, Pa., who became one of the leaders of the Anti-

federalists in the Pennsylvania Ratifying Convention. On 13 June GW entered £12.10 in his accounts "To Thomas Smith Esqr. recd of him a suit ag. Cunningham in Washington C[oun]ty" (Philadelphia Cash Accounts, 9 May–22 Sept. 1787). Cunningham was one of the defendants in GW's ejectment suits prosecuted for him in Washington County, Pa., by Smith (see Thomas Smith to GW, 9 Feb. 1785).

From William Jackson

[Philadelphia] Monday evening [17 September 1787]
Major Jackson presents his most respectful compliments to General Washington—He begs leave to request his signature to forty Diplomas intended for the Rhode Island Society of the Cincinnati.

Major Jackson, after burning all the loose scraps of paper which belong to the Convention, will this evening wait upon the General with the Journals and other papers which their vote directs to be delivered to His Excellency.[1]

AL, DLC:GW.

1. In his "Notes" for 17 Sept., James Madison wrote: "The President having asked what the Convention meant should be done with the Journals &c, whether copies were to be allowed to the members if applied for. It was Resolved nem: con: 'that he retain the Journal and other papers, subject to the order of Congress, if ever formed under the Constitution'" (Farrand, *Records of the Federal Convention*, 2:648). During the controversy over Jay's treaty in 1796, GW deposited the journal of the Convention and other papers with the secretary of state (see GW's message to the House of Representatives, 30 Mar. 1796, in *Annals of Congress*, 4th Cong., 1st sess., 759–61).

From Robert Edge Pine

Philadelphia. 17 Sep. 1787
This Work was Executed, by Order of his late Royal Highness William Duke of Cumberland and a few Setts given to the most Illustrious Millitary Characters in Europe—after which, the Plates were distroyed His R. H. having been pleased to give this Sett to the late John Pine, who Engrav'd it—his Son, Robt Edge Pine, has now the honour of presenting it to his Excellency General Washington.[1]

AL (photocopy), ViMtV.

1. Pine's father, John Pine (1690–1756), was a prominent engraver in London. William Augustus, duke of Cumberland (1721–1765), George II's third son, was the victor in the Battle of Culloden (1746) over the Stuart pretender to the throne.

To the President of Congress

[Philadelphia, 17 September 1787]

We have now the Honor to submit to the Consideration of the United States in Congress assembled that Constitution which has appeared to us the most advisable.[1]

The Friends of our Country have long seen and desired that the Power of making War Peace and Treaties, that of levying Money & regulating Commerce and the correspondent executive and judicial Authorities should be fully and effectually[2] vested in the general Government of the Union. But the Impropriety of delegating such extensive Trust to one Body of Men is evident[3]—Hence results the Necessity of a different Organization.

It is obviously impracticable[4] in the fœderal Government Of these States to secure all Rights of independent Sovereignty to each and yet provide for the Interest and Safety of all—Individuals entering into Society must give up a Share of Liberty to preserve the Rest. The Magnitude of the Sacrifice must depend as well on Situations and Circumstances as on the Object to be obtained. It is at all Times difficult to draw with Precision the Lines between those Rights which must be surrendered and those which may be reserved⟨.⟩ And on the present Occasion this Difficulty was encreased by a Difference among the several States as to their Situation Extent Habits and particular Interests.

In all our Deliberations on this Subject we kept steadily in our View that which appears to us the greatest Interest of every true american the Consolidation of our Union in which is involved our Prosperity Felicity Safety perhaps our national Existence. this important Consideration seriously and deeply impressed on our Minds led each State in the Convention to be less rigid on Points of inferior Magnitude than might have been otherwise expected. And thus the Constitution which we now present is the Result of a Spirit of Amity and of that mutual Deference & Concession which the Peculiarity of our political Situation rendered indispensible.

That it will meet the full and entire[5] Approbation of every[6] State is not perhaps to be expected. But each will doubtless consider that had her Interests been alone consulted the Consequences might have been particularly disagreable or injurious to others. That it is liable to as few Exceptions as could reasonably have been expected we hope and believe That it may promote the lasting Welfare of that Country so dear to us all and secure her Freedom and Happiness is our most ardent wish.[7]

Df, DNA: RG 360, Records of the Federal Convention; copy, Nc-Ar: Governor's Letter Book, Thomas Burke, G.L.B. 7; *JCC*, 33:502–3. Except for variations in capitalization and punctuation, and in the spelling of "welfare," the body of the two texts are identical. The draft is in the hand of Gouverneur Morris, one of the members of the committee of style which was charged with preparing the letter, and it is one of the documents that GW turned over to the secretary of state in March 1796 (see Draft of the Federal Constitution: Report of Committee of Detail, 6 Aug., note). The copy in the printed *Journals of the Continental Congress* was taken from Benjamin Bankson, *Ratifications of the Constitutions*, 71–73 (*JCC*, 33:502). The bracketed heading and closing of the letter are taken from the Burke copy; the wording is the same in *JCC*.

The Convention on 10 Sept. voted to instruct "the Committee for revising the stile and arrangement of the articles agreed on, to prepare an Address to the people, to accompany the present Constitution, and to be laid with the same before the U— States in Congress" (Madison's Notes in Farrand, *Records of the Federal Convention*, 2:564). When the committee of style reported the draft of the Constitution on 12 Sept., it also reported the "draught of a letter to Congress," which "was read once throughout, and afterwards agreed to by paragraphs" (ibid., 582).

1. On Saturday, 15 Sept., "on the question to agree to the Constitution. as amended. All the States ay." On Monday, 17 Sept., after Benjamin Franklin's plea for "every member of the Convention who may still have objections to it" to "put his name to this instrument," Nathaniel Gorham moved to change the clause declaring "the number of Representatives shall not exceed one for every forty thousand" to every "thirty thousand" in order to remove some of the objections to the Constitution (ibid., 633, 643, 644). It was at this point that GW spoke for the first time in the Convention. "When the President rose, for the purpose of putting the question, he said that although his situation had hitherto restrained him from offering his sentiments on questions depending in the House, and it might be thought, ought now to impose silence on him, yet he could not forbear expressing his wish that the alteration proposed might take place. It was much to be desired that the objections to the

plan recommended might be made as few as possible—The smallness of the proportion of Representatives had been considered by many members of the Convention, an insufficient security for the rights & interests of the people. He acknowledged that it had always appeared to himself among the exceptionable parts of the plan; and late as the present moment was for admitting amendments, he thought this of so much consequence that it would give much satisfaction to see it adopted" (ibid., 644). In the first sentence after "putting the question" Madison wrote and struck out "he made a few observations"; and he substituted the second clause of the last sentence for "of such peculiar importance was its amendments, he could not therefore suppress his approbation of them" (DLC: Madison Papers). Gorham's motion "was agreed to unanimously."

2. Gouverneur Morris struck out "exclusively" and inserted "effectually."

3. Morris wrote "self evident" and struck out "self."

4. Morris made a false start at the beginning of this paragraph.

5. Morris struck out a more lengthy insertion before inserting "and entire."

6. Morris first wrote "any one" and then substituted "every."

7. Transmitted to Congress along with GW's letter and the signed copy of the Constitution was a resolution signed by GW and headed "In Convention Monday September 17th 1787": "Present The States of New Hampshire, Massachusetts, Connecticut, Mr Hamilton from New York, New Jersey, Pennsylvania, Delaware, Maryland, Virginia, North Carolina, South Carolina and Georgia.

"Resolved, That the preceeding Constitution be laid before the United States in Congress assembled, and that it is the Opinion of this Convention, that it should afterwards be submitted to a Convention of Delegates, chosen in each State by the People thereof, under the Recommendation of its Legislature, for their Assent and Ratification; and that each Convention assenting to, and ratifying the Same, should give Notice thereof to the United States in Congress assembled.

"Resolved, That it is the Opinion of this Convention, that as soon as the Conventions of nine States shall have ratified this Constitution, the United States in Congress assembled should fix a Day on which Electors should be appointed by the States which shall have ratified the same, and a Day on which the Electors should assemble to vote for the President, and the Time and Place for commencing Proceedings under this Constitution. That after such Publication the Electors should be appointed, and the Senators and Representatives elected: That the Electors should meet on the Day fixed for the Election of the President, and should transmit their Votes certified, signed, sealed and directed, as the Constitution requires, to the Secretary of the United States in Congress assembled, that the Senators and Representatives should convene at the Time and Place assigned; that the Senators should appoint a President of the Senate, for the sole Purpose of receiving, opening and counting the Votes for President; and, that after he shall be chosen, the Congress, together with the President, should, without Delay, proceed to execute this Constitution. By the unanimous Order of the Convention Go: Washington Presidt"

(DLC: U.S. Constitution Collection). For the Convention's discussion of this resolution on 10 Sept. when it was tabled "for a day or two," see Farrand, *Records of the Federal Convention*, 2:555–64.

To William Washington

Dear Sir, Phil[adelphi]a Sept. 17th 1787

The Coachmaker who have furnished me with the enclosed Card have done work for me and having executed it well—and promising to work as cheap [as] any others in the City, I do their request, recommend them, that if you, or any of your friends should have occasion for Carriages you may if you think proper apply to them. with affectionate regard I am &c.

G. Washington

LB, DLC:GW.

The addressee probably is GW's cousin William Washington of Sandy Hill, South Carolina. For GW's dealings with the carriage maker, see GW to Samuel Powel, 25 July 1787, n.1.

To Thomas Jefferson

Dear Sir, Philadelphia Sept. 18th 1787

Yesterday put an end to the business of the Fœderal Convention. Inclosed is a copy of the Constitution, by it agreed to, not doubting but that you have participated in the general anxiety which has agitated the minds of your Countrymen on this interesting occasion, I shall be excused I am certain for this endeavor to relieve you from it[1]—especially when I assure you of the sincere regard and esteem with which I have the honor to be, Dr Sir Yr Most Obedt and Very Hble Servant

G. Washington

LB, DLC:GW.

1. To GW's distress, this letter was long delayed. See GW to Jefferson, 1 Jan. 1788.

To Lafayette

My dear Marqs,   Philadelphia Sept. 18th 1787

In the midst of hurry, and in the moment of my departure from this City I address this letter to you. The principal, indeed the only design of it is, to fulfil the promise I made that I would send you the proceedings of the Fœderal Convention as soon as the business of it was closed. More than this, circumstanced as I am at present is not in my power to do. nor am I inclined to attempt it, as the enclosure, must speak for itself & will occupy your thoughts for sometime.

It is the production of four months deliberation. It is now a Child of fortune, to be fostered by some and buffited by others. what will be the General opinion on, or the reception of it, is not for me to, decide, nor shall I say any thing for or against it—if it be good I suppose it will work its way good—if bad it will recoil on the Framers.[1] my best wishes attend you, and yours— and with the sincerest friendship and most Affectionate regard I am ever yours

G. Washington

LB, DLC:GW.

1. For Lafayette's opinion of the new Constitution, see his letter to GW of 1 Jan. 1788.

Letter not found: GW to Samuel Morris, 18 Sept. 1787. GW wrote Clement Biddle on 19 Sept.: "Yesterday before I left the City, I wrote to Captn Morris."

To Ann Allen Penn

[Philadelphia] Tuesday 18th Sepr 1787.

Genl Washington takes the liberty of offering his respectful compliments to Mrs Penn—and the Vision of Columbus. It is one of several Copies for which he subscribed some years ago and received since he came to this City. To the merit, or demerit of the performance the General can say nothing—not having had time to read it.[1]

AL (photocopy), DLC:GW.

1. GW notes in his cash accounts for 18 May that he had "p[ai]d into the h[an]ds of Colo. [David] Humphreys [£10] my Subs[criptio]n for 20 Vols. of

his [Joel Barlow's] Poem entitled the Visions of Columbus @ 1⅓ Dol. each"
(Philadelphia Cash Accounts, 9 May–22 Sept. 1787, printed above). Two other
of GW's letters of 18 Sept. presenting copies of Barlow's poem have been
found. The one to Benjamin Franklin's daughter, Sarah Bache (1743–1808),
reads: "Genl Washington presents his respectful Compliments to Mrs Bache
and prays her acceptance of Barlows Vision of Columbus. It is one of several
copies for which he subscribed some years ago and has received since his
arrival in this City" (AL, NjMoNP). The almost identical note to the wife of
George Clymer (1739–1813), Elizabeth Meredith Clymer, reads: "Genl Washington offers Compliments and best wishes to Mrs Clymer, and begs her acceptance of Barlows Vision of Columbus—It is one of several Copies for which he
subscribed some years since and received in this City" (ALS, owned [1992] by
Mr. Gary Hendershott). According to the list of subscribers printed at the end
of the volume, only Louis XVI of France subscribed to more copies than GW.
The king received twenty-five copies and Lafayette, ten.

To Clement Biddle

Dear Sir,   Head of Elk [Md.] 19th Septr 1787.
    Yesterday before I left the City, I wrote to Captn Morris re-
questing the favor of him to furnish me with a description of the
hounds he was so good as to give me, that I might know how to
apply the names contained in the list you sent me; for without,
though I had eight names, I might not apply one right; Whether
Captn Morris sent the discription, or not, I will not say, but it
did not come to my hands, and without it, I shall find myself at
a loss. I asked some other questions also; answers to which
would be satisfactory, and I would thank you for obtaining &
forwarding them to me by the first Post after this letter shall
have reached you; my letter to him, will remind him of them,
on your application.[1] I am Dear Sir Yr Obedt & Obliged Servt
                                              Go: Washington

ALS, PHi: Washington-Biddle Correspondence.
    1. GW's letter to Samuel Morris has not been found, but see Samuel Morris
to GW, 21 September.

From Samuel Morris

Dear Sir   Philad[elphi]a Septemr 21st 1787
    Mr Clement Biddle has just shewn me your Letter to him of
the 19th by which I Observe I had been favour'd with a Note

from you for a description of the Dogs sent by Capt. Ellwood. I never Receiv'd it, or would have immediately Answer'd it. The Names & descriptions follow

    Droner, a black & white dog with spotts
    Doxy—black or rather dark brown & white
    Dutchess—mostly White & large
    Hearkwell—a younger dog than either of the foregoing
                with a long Tail & Spotted
    These four are heavy dogs with long Ears
    Shingas—nearly black
    Pluto—mostly white
a little grey about their heads, shorter Ears than the others & lighter dogs, but these Six dogs have been thought of, as being as good as any in the Country.
    Dublin—a young dog brown & white
    Rover—ditto—with a black Spott on his Rump
    These two were too young to Enter last Season, but from their make & breed I think will be slow & good.
    I wish them safe to hand & that they may Afford you & your Friends as much pleasure as they often have to Your Sincere Friend & Obedt Servant

Saml Morris

ALS, DLC:GW.

From Clement Biddle

Sep. 23d 87

    On rect of your favour from the head of Elk I waited on Capt. Morris who informed me he had not recd your note respecting the Hounds but he has now wrote you fully on that subject as far as your Queries went in my Letter—if there is any thing omitted he begs you to inform him[1]—Mr Haines from whom I had the seed Barley for you informs me that there has been most extraordinary great Crops of that Article here & that a Sloop load just arrived from Rhode Island will not sell I mention this for your Government as there may be a Demand at Baltimore, if not at Alexandria. Mr Haines wishes to know how it succeeded as it has not been so fairly tried to the southward before[2]—Mrs Biddle gives her &c.

C. Biddle

ADfS, ViMtV: Clement Biddle Letter Book.

1. GW's letter to Biddle is dated 19 Sept.; GW's note to Samuel Morris has not been found. Morris's letter to GW is dated 21 September.

2. See Biddle to GW, 5 Nov. 1786, 20 Feb. 1787.

From Samuel Hanson

Sir   Alexandria, 23d Sepr 1787

I embrace the earliest Opportunity, after notice of your return to Mount Vernon, to address you on a Subject that has given me no small share of disquiet.

A few days ago I received a Letter from Majr Washington; informing me that "You had been made acquainted with my draught on You in favour of Mr Porter; That you were unable to account for my applying to any Person for what was due from you; and that you requested I might not repeat the Act of drawing in favour of Mr Porter."

In answer to a charge so unexpected I replied to the Major, and "denied that I ever applied to Mr Porter for money on your Acct as that Gentleman will assure you. I acknowledged that I had drawn on you in favour of Mr Porter, but conceived that, in doing so, I had not acted improperly, nor out of the customary mode of business." I also informed the Majr that I had no doubt of explaining to yourself, immediately on your arrival, the propriety of my Conduct.

To proceed then, Sir, with the utmost candour, I admit that Mr Porter furnished me, at sundry times, with repeated Sums of money, and several Articles of goods, previous to my draught on you. But that Gentleman will declare to you that both the Money and Goods were furnished, on his part, & received on mine, purely on the Score of our private friendship; and that your name was never mentioned, nor your Account alluded to, at those times, by either of us. At the time of my first draught, I perfectly recollect that my reason for making it payable to *him* was, that, as your Servants generally call on him, when in town, it might have the readier Conveyance—Before the second payment became due, I had become indebted (in the manner mentioned) to Mr Porter, and really conceived it to be totally immaterial to you whether the Money were paid to Mr Porter or myself.

Thus, Sir, have I endeavoured to explain to your Satisfaction a part of my Conduct which, I have good reason to apprehend, has (from misrepresentation, I trust) incurred your displeasure. If I shall be so unfortunate as not to have succeeded in this attempt, I must, in justice to myself, beg you to furnish me with the particulars of the charge against me, that I may have an Opportunity of vindicating myself hereafter.

When you placed your Nephews under my Care, you were pleased to express a Confidence in my good intentions towards them. Believe me, Sir, I was more flattered by some obliging passages in your Letters than you would choose me to express. You may easily, then, conceive the proportional Chagrin I suffer, under the Apprehension of forfeiting your good Opinion at a time when I was in hopes that my Conduct towards your Nephews would have a tendency to confirm you in it.[1] With the utmost respect & Esteem, I remain, Sir, your most obedt and most humble Servant

S. Hanson of Saml

P.S. It may be easily conceived that the employment of accommodating Boys is, of itself, sufficiently unpleasant, without the adventitious mortifications arising from the present Subject. With respect to myself, I confess it is not a business of *choice*. Upon *you*, Sir, I am persuaded that this declaration will have the effect of inclining you to diminish, rather than encrease, the irksomeness of the Task I have engaged in. While on this Head, it is necessary to repeat, what I have already mentioned both to Mr McWhir[2] & Mr Porter (*before* the receipt of the Major's Letter) viz. That, should I remain here (which is uncertain) and you should incline to continue the Boys with me, I would, in consequence of the fall of House Rent, take them at a less price than the present one. I am &c. &c.

S.H. of Saml

ALS, DLC:GW.

1. Tobias Lear wrote Gideon Snow from Mount Vernon on 9 July 1787:

"Mr Hanson's last bill in favor of Messrs P[orter] & I[ngraham] I gave to the General, & I suppose Mr Porter has charged him accordingly, or if he has not, he ought to have done it—tho' the Genl told me at the time, that he beleived Mr Porter must think it a little strange that Mr Hanson should take up money from him on his Acct—I told Mr Porter so—but he said—he did not think it strange—Mr Hanson wanted the money, was a very clever fellow &c.—& he advanced it to him very willingly. I am not sure that it was the General's agreement with Mr Hanson to advance him the money for the Boys board before it became due, tho' I think if there was not something mentioned respecting the matter he would not take it up beforehand" (ViMtV). See GW's complaint about Hanson in his letter to George Augustine Washington of 2 September. GW wrote Hanson on 27 Sept. accepting Hanson's explanation.

2. William McWhir, mistakenly identified in *Papers, Confederation Series*, 2:62, as Alexander McWhir, ran the academy in Alexandria where GW's two nephews were at school.

To Benjamin Harrison

Dear Sir,   Mount Vernon Sept. 24th 1787

In the first moments after my return I take the liberty of sending you a copy of the Constitution which the Fœderal Convention has submitted to the People of these States.[1]

I accompany it with no observations—your own Judgment will at once descover the good, and the exceptionable parts of it. and your experience of the difficulty's which have ever arisen when attempts have been made to reconcile such variety of interests, and local prejudices as pervade the severeal States will render explanation unnecessary. I wish the Constitution which is offered had been made more perfect, but I sincerely believe it is the best that could be obtained at this time—and as a constitutional door is op[e]ned for amendment hereafter—the adoption of it under present circumstances of the Union is in my opinion desirable.

From a variety of concurring accounts it appears to me that the political concerns of this Country are, in a manner, suspended by a thread. That the Convention has been looked up to by the reflecting part of the community with a Sollicitude which is hardly to be conceived, and that, if nothing had been agreed on by that body, anarchy would soon have ensued—the seeds being reiply sown in every soil. I am &c.

G. Washington

LB, DLC:GW. The copyist's heading, "To Patrick Henry Esqr. Benj: Harrison Esqr. & Genl Nelson," indicates that the same letter was sent to both Henry and Nelson. See note 1. The letter to Henry is quoted in the *New York Times*, 2 April 1919.

1. GW also sent copies of the new Constitution to Lafayette, on 16 Sept., and to Thomas Jefferson, on 18 September. Harrison on 4 Oct. and Henry on 19 Oct. each wrote GW to express his misgivings about the document. Thomas Nelson, who also disapproved of the Constitution, responded only after Virginia had ratified it, in a letter dated 19 July 1788, which has not been found (see GW to Nelson, 3 Aug. 1788).

To Johnzee Sellman

Sir,   Mount Vernon Sept. 25th 1787

As I observe by the Baltimore advertiser that you are Administrator of the late Mr John Rawlins I take the liberty to mention to you an error which happened in the payment of an order drawn by Rawlins upon me during my late absence from home, and which was not discovered till I pointed it out since my return from Philadelphia.

Some time last fall I agreed with Mr Rawlins to furnish me with a number of friezes and mouldings, for which I was to pay forty three pounds twelve Shillings Virginia Currency, but in consequence of some defect in the work, he afterwards wrote (which letter I have now by me) to me informing me that he should charge but forty five pounds Maryland currency, he furnished them accordingly; and in July last sent one Thomas Hammond to wash some stucco work, which was done by himself & Mr Thorp, and gave him an order for the above forty five pounds, but not mention in the order, whether it was Maryland or Virginia Currency. The person who paid the money (not recuring to Mr Rawlines's agreement which was in the house) paid it in Virginia currency and took Mr Hammonds receipt for the same, specifying virginia currency in the receipt.[1]

I must therefore request Sir, that you will investigate the matter and have the difference of exchange in the above sum (which will be thirty dollars) returned. I am Sir, Yr Obed. Hble Servant

G. Washington

LB, DLC:GW.

A man named Johnzee Sellman was married to Sarah Rawlins in 1792 in Baltimore County.

1. For GW's negotiations with John Rawlins to complete the New Room at Mount Vernon, see GW to Rawlins, 29 Aug. 1785, and the references in note 1 of that document. For the articles of agreement between GW and Rawlins, dated 25 Feb. 1786, see Tench Tilghman to GW, 1 Mar. 1786. Rawlins's letter regarding his charges of £45 in Maryland currency is dated 10 Mar. 1787, and GW's letter to Rawlins withholding payment until Thomas Hammond and Richard Tharpe had completed their work is dated 13 April 1787. For the payment of Rawlins's charges by John Augustine Washington in July 1787 during GW's absence in Philadelphia, see GW to George Augustine Washington, 1 July, and 29 July, n.3. An advertisement for the sale of Rawlins's estate appears in the *Maryland Journal, and Baltimore Advertiser,* 24 Aug. 1787. Rawlins's widow, Mary Rawlins, advertised on 1 April 1788 that she "carries on the COMPOSITION-WORK, in all its Branches, (such as MOULDING, and ORNAMENTS for DOORS, WINDOWS, and for WOOD CORNICES, and particularly CHIMNEY-PIECES, in the neatest and newest Fashion) which was carried on by her late Husband JOHN RAWLINS, and at the same Place, on St. Paul's Lane. . . ."

To Samuel Hanson

Sir, Mount Vernon Sept. 27. 1787

By your letter of the 23d, with which I have been favoured since my return home, I perceive there has been a misconception on my part of the transaction between you and Mr Porter respecting payment for the board of my Nephews. it thus arose—in the enumeration of monies which remained for me to pay according to the account transmitted, I found the sum of £17.10 due to Mr Porter on your account, this, and the recollection (I believe I am not mistaken therein) finding the like sum paid by that Gentleman before any application had been made to me for it, led me to suppose (as I had requested you to apply to that Gentleman for such articles of Clothing as the boys really wanted) that application had been made to him for their board also which as no deposit was made in his hands to answer such demands, would had the case really been so have given him cause to think strangely of me, this idea of mine was the cause of the letter you recd from my nephew.

A draugh in favor of Mr Porter, or in behalf of any other Gentleman, is, unquestionably as proper as any other mode of application and will be equally agreeable to me.

For any particular care or attention which you have shewn, or may shew my Nephews I shall always think myself obliged and thinking as I certainly have done, that the board was high

I receive with pleasure the information of your intention of reducing it, for without intending a compliment I repeat the satisfaction I feel from the consideration of their being under the eye of a Gentleman so capable as you are of advising and exacting a proper conduct from them. I am &c.

G. Washington

LB, DLC:GW.

From Charles Willson Peale

Dr Sir   Phila[delphi]a Sep. 27th 1787

By this Post I take the liberty of sending a few Prints for your acceptance. I have not been able to Execute a greater number of Plates as yet, but am prepairing some others, which I hope will be published some time in the ensuing fall and Winter.[1]

Since you did me the favor of Visiting my Room, several natural Productions have been added, but the most Valuable are a pair of Panthers, male & female of full groath—most Terrifick Animals.[2]

With my best respects to your Lady, I am with the highest Esteem your obliged Friend and Humble Servant

C.W. Peale

ALS, DLC:GW; LB, PPAmP: Charles Willson Peale Papers.

1. Peale refers to a mezzotint print of Benjamin Franklin in his letter of 27 Feb. 1787 to GW, and by April Peale had completed a mezzotint of Lafayette. While at the Constitutional Convention, GW sat for Peale, who wished to produce a mezzotint of GW (see Peale to GW, 29 May 1787). Peale advertised in the *Pennsylvania Packet* (Philadelphia) on 20 Aug. the sale within two weeks of his prints of Washington. GW hung at Mount Vernon the print of himself alongside those of Lafayette and Franklin (Wick, *Graphic Portraits of Washington*, 95–96).

2. One of the mountain lions, Peale wrote, was "eight feet in length, and the other seven and a half" (Miller, *Peale Papers*, 1:490, n.2).

From David Humphreys

My dear General   New Haven Septr 28th 1787

I would not trespass on your attention, while you was occupied in such momentuous affairs as the revisal of the confederation: the last time I had the honor of addressing a letter to you, was, I believe, in the beginning of June, from this place—in that letter was enclosed the sketch of an Answer to Mr Jefferson. I hope it came safe to your hands.[1]

We have been, a few days since, gratified with the publication of the Proceedings of the Convention. I must acknowledge myself to have been favorably disappointed & highly pleased with the general tenor of them. Altho' it is impossible in so short a time to collect the sentiments of the Public with certainty, and altho attempts to prevent the adoption must be expected, yet, I cannot but hope, from what I hear, that the opposition will be less than was apprehended. All the different Classes in the liberal professions will be in favor of the proposed Constitution. The Clergy, Lawyers, Physicians & Merchants will have considerable influence on Society. Nor will the Officers of the late Army be backward in expressing their approbation. Indeed the well affected have not been wanting in efforts to prepare the minds of the Citizens for the favorable reception of whatever might be the result of your Proceedings. I have had no inconsiderable agency in the superintendence of two Presses, from which more News Papers are circulated, I imagine, than from any others in New England. Judicious & well-timed publications have great efficacy in ripening the judgment of men in this quarter of the Continent. In case that every thing succeeds in the best manner, I shall certainly be the first to rejoice in finding that my apprehensions were not verified; as well as to felicitate you upon having contributed your assistance on so interesting & important an occasion. Your good Angel, I am persuaded, will not desert you. What will tend, perhaps, more than any thing to the adoption of the new System, will be an universal opinion of your being elected President of the United States, and an expectation that you will accept it for a while.

Since I had the honor of seeing you, in Philadelphia, I have made the tour of the New England States as far as Portsmouth. I was happy to find in Massachusetts the spirit of Insurrection pretty generally subsided, and an impression left on the minds of People, in most of the States, that something energetic must be adopted respecting the national Government or we shall be a ruined Nation.

I have lately lost both my Father and Mother, in a good old

age. The former was upwards of eighty, the latter Seventy six years old. They had lived in circumstances of more happiness than commonly falls to the lot of mortality. They were the best of Parents. I feel myself less attached to this particular part of the Country than formerly.

And now, my dear General, I know not of any thing that will prevent me, very soon, from paying a visit to Mount Vernon—and a visit for the winter—I propose coming with my Servant & Horses. I should have been apprehensive of occasioning too much trouble, had I not believed your unequivocal & warm expressions of kindness & friendship were the indications of a cordial reception. Let the Ship of the Public float towards the harbour of tranquility & safety, or let her be in danger of being stranded on the rocks of discord & anarchy; we shall be conscious that some individuals have done their duty; and, I flatter myself, we shall enjoy in the bosom of your family, such hours of domestic satisfaction, as I recollect to have experienced formerly at Mount Vernon. I am in full hopes of being on the spot this year to do ample justice to the Christmas Pye.

I beg that every sentiment of affectionate regard may be presented, on my part, to Mrs Washington & the good family under your roof—With the sincerest friendship I am, my dear General, Your most obedient & Most humble Servant

D. Humphreys

ALS, DLC:GW.

1. Humphreys wrote a letter to GW on 28 May, in which he enclosed the "sketch." See note 2 of that document.

To Richard Sprigg

Dear Sir,   Mount Vernon 28th Septr 1787.

I have this moment been favoured with your letter without date from Prince George County, and have ordered the Jennies to be delivered to Mr Dove—hoping both will prove with foal. Royal Gift never fails—the other is a young hand, but I hope will be equally sure.[1]

I am glad to hear that the Jenny you sent to R. G. last year has produced a Jack[2]—and that you have been so successful in your importation of Deer. My Country Does have brought Fawns, &

I have a buck and doe of those given me by Mr Ogle; yet if you shd be successful, I would thank you for a pair (male or female) of yours.[3]

My best respects, if you please to Mrs Sprigg, and thanks for your kind congratulations on my safe return home, after a long absence from it. I am Dear Sir Yr Most Obedt Servt

Go: Washington

ALS (photocopy), DLC:GW. GW wrote on the cover of the letter: "By Mr Dove."

1. Sprigg's letter has not been found. Samuel Dove and Richard Dove both lived in Prince Georges County at this time. GW's bill, dated 8 Sept. 1787, shows charges of £10 for "2 Jennis covered by Royal Gift & the Knight of Malta at 5£ each" and £2.14 for "pasturage of the above Jennies from the 6th of June to the 8th of September, 9 weeks @ 3/ each per week" (DLC:GW). Tobias Lear's receipt on behalf of GW for the payment of £12.14 is dated 27 Sept. (DLC:GW; see also Ledger B, 248).

2. Sprigg sent two jennies to Mount Vernon in May 1786 to be mated with Royal Gift, the jackass sent to GW by the king of Spain (Sprigg to GW, 1 June 1786; GW to Sprigg, 28 June 1786). On 1 April 1787 GW wrote Sprigg that a jenny of his seemed to be with foal and asked that Sprigg remove her from Mount Vernon.

3. See Benjamin Ogle to GW, 12 July 1786.

From James Madison

Dear Sir   N. York Sepr 30 1787

I found on my arrival here that certain ideas unfavorable to the Act of the Convention which had created difficulties in that body, had made their way into Congress. They were patronised cheifly by Mr R.H.L. and Mr Dane of Massts.[1] It was first urged that as the new Constitution was more than an Alteration of the Articles of Confederation under which Congress acted, and even subverted these articles altogether, there was a Constitutional impropriety in their taking any positive agency in the work. The answer given was that the Resolution of Congress in Feby had recommended the Convention as the best mean of obtaining a firm *national Government*; that as the powers of the Convention were defined by their Commissions in nearly the same terms with the powers of Congress given by the Confederation on the subject of alterations, Congress were not more restrained from acceding to the new plan, than the Convention were from proposing it. If the plan was within the powers of the Convention it was within those of Congress; if beyond those powers, the same necessity which justified the Convention would justify Congress; and a failure of Congress to Concur in what was done, would imply either that the Convention had done wrong in exceeding their powers, or that the Government proposed was in itself liable to insuperable objections; that such an inference would be the more natural, as Congress had never scrupled to recommend measures foreign to their Constitutional functions, whenever the Public good seemed to require it; and had in several instances, particularly in the establishment of the new Western Governments, exercised assumed powers of a very high & delicate nature, under motives infinitely less urgent than the present state of our affairs, if any faith were due to the representations made by Congress themselves, ecchoed by 12 States in the Union, and confirmed by the general voice of the People. An attempt was made in the next place by R.H.L. to amend the Act of the Convention before it should go forth from Congress. He proposed a bill of Rights—provision for juries in civil cases & several other things corresponding with the ideas of Col. M. He was supported by Mr Me—— Smith of this State.[2] It was contended that Congress had an undoubted right to insert amendments, and that it was their duty to make use of it in a case where the essential guards of liberty had been omitted. On the other side the right of Congress was not denied, but the inexpediency of exerting it was urged on the following grounds. 1. that every circumstance indicated that the introduction of Congress as a party to the reform, was intended by the States merely as a matter of form and respect. 2. that it was evident from the contradictory objections which had been expressed by the different members who had animadverted on the plan, that a discussion of its merits would consume much time, without producing agreement even among its adversaries. 3. that it was clearly the intention of the States that the plan to be proposed should be the act of the Convention with the assent of Congress, which could not be the case, if alterations were made, the Convention being no longer in existence to adopt them. 4. that as the Act of the Convention, when altered would instantly become the mere act of Congress, and must be proposed by them as such, and of course be addressed to the Legislatures, not conventions of the States, and require the ratification of thirteen instead of nine States, and as the unaltered act would go forth to the States directly from the Convention under the auspices of that Body— Some States might ratify one & some the other of the plans, and confusion & disappointment be the least evils that could ensue. These difficulties which at one time threatened a serious division in Cong[res]s and popular alterations with the yeas & nays on the journals, were at length fortunately terminated by the following Resolution—"Congress having recd the Report of the Convention lately assembled in Philada, Resol[ve]d *unanimously* that the said Report, with the Resolutions & letter accompanying the same, be transmitted to the several Legislatures, in order to be submitted to a Convention of Delegates chosen in each State by the people thereof, in conformity to the Resolves of the Convention made & provided in that case." Eleven States were present, the absent ones R.I. & Maryland. A more direct approbation would have been of advantage in this & some other States, where stress will be laid on the agency of Congress in the matter, and a handle taken by adversaries of any ambiguity on the subject. With regard to Virginia & some other States, reserve on the part of Congress will do no injury. The circumstance of unanimity must be favorable every where.[3]

The general voice of this City seems to espouse the new Constitution. It is supposed nevertheless that the party in power is strongly opposed to it. The Country must finally decide, the sense of which is as yet wholly unknown. As far as Boston & Connecticut has been heard from, the first impression seems to be auspicious. I am waiting with anxiety for the eccho from Virginia but with very faint hopes of its corresponding with my wishes. With every sentiment of respect & esteem, & every wish for your health & happiness, I am Dear Sir, Your Obedient, humble servt

Js Madison Jr

P.S. A small packet of the size of 2 Vol. 8° addressed to you, lately came to my hands with books of my own from France. Genl Pinkney has been so good as to take charge of them. He set out yesterday for S. Carolina & means to call at Mount Vernon.[4]

ALS, DLC:GW; copy, in Madison's hand, DLC: Madison Papers.

1. Nathan Dane (1752–1835) represented Massachusetts in the Continental Congress. An opponent of the new Constitution, he was an unsuccessful candidate for the state ratifying convention.

2. Melancton Smith (1744–1798) of New York served in the Continental Congress from 1785 to 1788.

3. See *JCC*, 33:540–44, 549, and the editors' note in Kaminski and Saladino, *Documentary History of the Ratification of the Constitution*, 8:20–21.

4. Charles Cotesworth Pinckney and his wife, Mary Stead Pinckney, spent the night of 11 Oct. at Mount Vernon. When Madison wrote Thomas Jefferson on 24 Oct. 1787, he thanked him for the shipment of books from Paris and informed him that the items intended "for the two Universities and for General Washington have been forwarded" (Rutland and Hobson, *Madison Papers*, 10:205–18). For a possible identification of the two volumes sent to GW from France, see Essarts to GW, 1 May 1787, and note 1 of that document.

From La Luzerne

Sir,   Paris [c. September 1787]

Monsieur le Cte du Moutier will have the honor to transmit this to your Excellency; he is desireous (as every good Frenchman is) to be acquainted with a man whose virtue & great talents have secured the independence of his Country, & established the happiness of a great part of the Universe. He is destined to fill my place as minister Plenipotentiary from his Majesty to the United States; he will think himself extreemly happy if, during the time of his Mission, he can be able to obtain the esteem & confidence of your Excellency, and I dare assure you before hand that he will render himself worthy of it.[1]

I cannot express to you, Sir, how unhappy I am that particular circumstances prevent me from returning to America—I passed near six years there, & have been a witness of the great events, which, under the wise direction of your Excellency, have terminated to the happiness of your Country.

I know all those great Patriots who have successively composed the Congress. I have been connected with Citizens of the most distinguished eminence, and I venture to assure you that from inclination & affection I had myself become a Citizen of the United States—and whatever Mission the King may honor me with I shall always regret that of America.

The Gazettes & publick papers have undoubtedly long since

informed your Excellency of the seeds of discussion which divide the Courts of Europe. The unhappy situation of affairs in Holland will, it is feared, bring on a war between England, Prussia & France. War also appears inevitable on the side of the Levant. The Turks have made a bustle which nobody thinks anything of; they have unexpectedly declared war against Russia without having the means of offending or defending: The Emperor is obliged, by treaty, to assist Russia when attacked—One of these powers will alone be sufficient to overthrow the Ottoman Empire. In this State of the things it is difficult to say what will be the event, and those who conduct the different Cabinets have enough to do to guard & attend to their interests. I see with pleasure that the Americans take no part in these disputes. I hope they will seize this moment of peace & tranquility to consolidate their Government.

I put great faith in the Convention over which your Excellency presides, & all Europe expects that the doings of that body will put a finishing stroke to that great work which has been thus far advanced by the military & patriotic virtue of your Excellency.

I assure you I offer my sincerest prayers for the welfare of the United States in General, & more particularly & tenderly for that of your Excellency. I beg you to accept the sentiments of Respect & veneration with which I have the honor to be Yr very Humble & Obedient Servt

Chevlr de la Luzerne

Translation, by Tobias Lear, DLC:GW; ALS, in French, DLC:GW.

1. Eléanor-François-Elie, comte de Moustier (1751–1817), wrote to GW on 24 Jan. 1788 shortly after he arrived in New York to become the French minister to the United States. See the editors' identification of Moustier in Moustier to GW, 5 Oct. 1788.

From John Rutledge

Dr Sir   Philadelphia octr 1. 1787.

I recd the inclosed by the last Packet, from my Son, at Paris— He requests me, to present, to you, his very particular Thanks, for the Letters of Introduction with which you were pleased to honour him—permit me to add mine.[1]

I returned, Yesterday, from New York, where, I think, the new Constitution will be very generally approved—It is, here, almost universally—to Morrow, I shall embark for Charleston, where it would give me pleasure to pay Attention to any of your Friends, who may make that Tour. I have the Honour to be, with the greatest Esteem & respect, dr Sir yr most obedt Servt

J: Rutledge

ALS, DLC:GW.

1. The enclosure has not been identified. For GW's letters of introduction for John Rutledge, Jr., see GW to Chastellux, 6 June 1787, and note 3 of that document.

To Robert Morris

Dear Sir, Mount Vernon October 2d 1787

By the charming Polly Capt. Ellwood I forward you a perfect model of the plough which was sent to me by Mr Young with the direction of that Gentleman for setting it for use, from the character I have received of its performance surpasses any that has ever been tried before, on my Farms.[1] I also send you a part of the summer wheat with which Mr Young has furnished me as springing from seed sent by the Empress of Russia to his Britanic Majesty for the advantage it may have over other wheat I shall not vouch; to vary the seed time of this grain must, I conceive be its best recommendation, you will likewise receive part of the Sainfoin Seed I had come in—sufficient I think to sow a quarter of an acre in broad Cast if good—and much more in drills. It is held in high estimation in England. the grass delights in dry soil. if it be stoney so much the better; Sow it without delay with wheat or Rye or very early in the spring with Barley or oats.

My mind will ever retain warm impressed of, and feel very sensibly the polite & friendly attentions I received from Mrs Morris and yourself whilst I was in Philadelphia, to have opportunities of proving sincerity of this declaration would give me much pleasure but in no place to the same degree as under this roof.

Mrs Washington begs that you and Mrs Morris will accept her respectful compliments and best wishes; mine in a particular, and affectionate manner are added not only to you both but to all the young folks of the Family and to Govr Morris Esqr. I am &c.

G. Washington

P.S. Will you be so obliging as to give me your process for preparing the Duck wheat straw for fodder. The effects of the drought with me has exceeded any thing I could have conceived and has driven me to ever[y] substitute for Hay, It is possible I may avail myself of your kind offer of sending for India Paper for my new Room but presuming there is no opportunity to do it soon; I shall not, at this time give you the dimenscions of it. G.W.

LB, DLC:GW.

1. GW wrote George Augustine Washington on 26 Aug. that he had promised Morris a model of the plow that Arthur Young had sent him from England on 1 Feb., and he instructed George Augustine to have the plow made for Morris. See also GW to George Augustine Washington, 2 September.

To Charles Pettit

Sir,   Mount Vernon October 2d 1787

By the charming Polly Capt. Ellwood I send you patterns for the hearths of Chimneys which I beg may be cast and sent to me by the first conveyance to Alexandria—the cost you will please to annex to the other plates, bespoke before I left the City, and the amount shall be paid when it is maid known to[1]—Sir—Yr Obedt Hble Servant

G. Washington.

LB, DLC:GW.

1. See GW to Pettit, 7 Sept., and note 1 of that document.

From Henry Knox

New York 3 October 1787

By this time my dear Sir, you will have again renewed your attention to your domestic affairs, after the long absence occasioned by the convention. I flatter myself with the hope that you found Mrs Washington and your family in perfect health.

Every point of view in which I have been able to place the subject induces me to believe, that the moment in which the convention assembled, and the result thereof, are to be estimated among those fortunate circumstances in the affairs of men, which give a decided influence to the happiness of society for a long period of time.

Hitherto every thing promises well. The new constitution is received with great joy by all the commercial part of the community. The people of Boston are in raptures with it as it is, but would have liked it still better had it been higher toned.

The people of Jersey and Connecticut who are not commercial embrace it with ardor. There has not yet elapsed sufficient time to hear from the interior parts of the other States excepting this, which however does not seem to have decided on its plan of conduct. It will not probably be among the first which shall adopt it, but I presume the powerful circumstance of interest will ultimately induce it to comply.

As the information now appears Virginia probably will give the new plan, the most formidable opposition.

The unanimous resolve of Congress to transmit it to the respective States will not lessen the general disposition to receive it.

But notwithstanding my strong persuasion that it will be adopted generally, and in a much shorter time than I some time ago beleived, yet it will be opposed more or less in most of the States.

The germ of opposition originated in the convention itself. The gentlemen who refused signing it will most probably conceive themselves obliged to state their reasons publickly. The presses will groan with melancholy forebodings, and a party of some strength will be created. This is an evil, but it is an infinitely lesser evil than that we should have crumbled to peices by mere imbecillity.

I trust in God, that the foundation of a good national government is layed. A Way is opened to such alterations and amendments from time to time as shall be judged necessary. and the government being subjected to a revision by the people will not be so liable to abuse. The first Legislature ought to the be ablest & most disinterested men of the community—Every well founded objection which shall be started in the course of the discussions on the subject should be fairly considered, and such fundamental Laws enacted as would tend to obviate them.

Mrs Knox unites with me in presenting our most affectionate respects to Mrs Washington. I am my dear Sir with the sincerest & most respectful friendship Your most humble Servant

H. Knox

ALS, DLC:GW.

From Benjamin Harrison

My dear Sir   Berkley Octr 4th 1787

Your favor of the 28th Ulto[1] got to me two days ago: I am particularly oblig'd to you for this additional mark of your friendship, and attention, than which, there are very few things indeed, that can be more acceptable: I feel my self deeply interested in every thing that you have had a hand in, or that comes from you, and am so well assured of the solidity of your judgment, and the rectitude of your intentions, that I shall never stick at trifles to conform my self to your opinions; in the present instance, I am so totally uninform'd as to the general situation of America, that I can form no judgment of the necessity the convention was under to give us such a constitution as it has done; If our condition is not very desperate, I have my fears that the remedy will prove worse than the disease. Age makes men often over cautious; I am willing to attribute my fears to that cause, but from whatever source they spring, I can not divest my self of an opinion, that the seeds of civil discord are plentifully sown, in very many of the powers given both to the president and congress, and that if the constitution is carried into effect, the States south of potowmac, will be little more than appendages to those to the northward of it. You will say that general charges, are things without force, they are so, but in the present instance, I do not withhold particular observations, because I want them, but that I would not tire your patience, by entering deeply into a subject, before I had heard the reasons which operated in favor of the measures taken. After the meeting of the assembly and hearing from those who had a hand in the work, the reasons that operated with them, in favor of their measures, I will then more at large give you my sentiments, in the interim, I shall only say, that my objections chiefly lay, agst the unlimited powers of taxation, and the regulations of trade, and the jurisdictions that are to be established in every State, altogether independent of their laws. The sword, and such powers will; nay in the nature of things they must sooner or later, establish a tyrany, not inferiour to the triumvirate, or centum viri of Rome.[2] But enough of this, till another opportunity, in the mean time I have only to add, that I am with the most unfeigned attaćhment, and perfect esteem Dear Sir your most obedient and affectionate servant

Benj. Harrison

ALS, DLC:GW.

    1. GW's letter-book copy of the letter that he sent not only to Harrison but also to Patrick Henry and Thomas Nelson is dated 24 September.

    2. Benjamin Harrison was a delegate to the Virginia convention in June 1788 and opposed the ratification of the new Constitution.

To William Smallwood

Dear Sir,   Mount Vernon 6th Octr 1787.

When I had the pleasure of being at your house last fall, you gave me reason to believe that you would become the purchaser of my land adjoining yours, in Charles County—And if I recollect rightly, was to have written me on that subject from Annapolis.

I am still disposed to part with this tract; and wish you could make it convenient to be the purchaser thereof.[1]

I told you in the conversation we had on this subject before, that I would endeavor to make the payments as easy as my own circumstances would admit—I now repeat it—and if you have corn to dispose of, at a moderate price, I would take at least 500 Barrls in payment; also Wheat (if good, clean, & free from the Fly) delivered at my Mill, to which Boats can come, at the cash price in Alexandria. Your answer by the bearer would much oblige Dear Sir Your most Obedt Hble Servt

Go: Washington

ALS, NjP: deCoppet Collection; LB, DLC:GW. The ALS is addressed "By Mr Jno. Fairfax."

    1. Smallwood did not buy from GW the 552½-acre tract in Charles County, Md., which GW acquired from Daniel Jenifer Adams in December 1775. See

Smallwood to GW, 6 April 1784, and notes. Before he went to Philadelphia, GW wrote and signed this statement: "On Monday the 12th day of Septr 1785 A Mr Caywood, or some person in his behalf, presented an acct of Taxes, or the claims of the public for some Land I have in Charles County Maryland, which was the first application ever made to me, for the same. Whether previously, or subsequent to, that period any demand was ever made of Mr Lund Washington who had charge of my business till the close of that year for them is more than I can determine—but, no doubt, can be resolved by him. Given under my hand at Mount Vernon this 30th day of March 1787. Go: Washington" (ADS, DLC:GW).

To George Mason

Dear Sir,   Mount Vernon October 7th 1787

Doctr Stu[a]rt whom I have seen since his return from Gunston informs me (of what indeed you had done before) that your Crop of Corn is very short—and that you had it in contemplation to draw a supply from No. Carolina might be had cheap.

My crop is much below what I had conceived, even from the distressing accounts which were handed to me. I much doubt whether the aid of 800 Barriels will be more than sufficient to carry me thro' the year. If therefore you have matured any plan by which my adding 500 barriels would be the means of facilitating, I shold be glad to be informed of it. In that case, if I can see my way to obtain the money (necessary for the payment) I would gladly join you.[1]

I am sorry to hear you met with an accident on your return. I hope you experience no ill effect from it. The family here join me in compliments and good wishes to you, Mrs Mason and Family. I am Dr Sir, Yr Most Obed. & Affecte Hble Servant

                                G. Washington

LB, DLC:GW.

1. See Mason to GW, this date, and note 1 of that document.

From George Mason

Dear Sir   Gunston Hall Octor 7th 1787.

Upon examining my Fields in this Neck, I think they will not produce more than about one third of my usual Crops; at my other plantations they are something better, & may turn out about two thirds of the usual Crop. I think I shall be obliged to buy two hundred Barrells of Corn at least; and have lately written to a Gentlemen in Maryland (who owes me a Sum of Money) to know if he can supply me with that Quantity; I have not received his Answer, and have no great Dependence from that Quarter. When on the Convention, Dr Williamson & Colo. Davie shewed me several Letters from North Carolina, mentioning the great Crops of Corn there, and that some of the principal Crop-Masters were then offering to contract for their Corn at a Dollar ℔ Barrel; it was this gave me the Idea of supplying myself from thence; as soon as I get down to Richmond, I intend to write to Dr Williamson (who lives in Edenton) to know, with certainty, upon what Terms a Quantity can be engaged, to be delivered in all March, for ready Money; & as soon as I recieve his Answer, will advise you thereof. If I can be of any Service to You in making such a Contract as You approve, it will give me a great deal of pleasure.[1]

I got very much hurt in my Neck & Head, by the unlucky Accident on the Road; it is now wearing off; tho' at times still uneasy to me.[2]

I take the Liberty to enclose You my Objections to the new Constitution of Government; which a little Moderation & Temper, in the latter End of the Convention, might have removed. I am however most decidedly of Opinion, that it ought to be submitted to a Convention chosen by the people, for that special purpose; and shou'd any Attempt be made to prevent the calling such a Convention here, such a Measure shall have every Opposition in my power to give it.

You will readily observe, that my Objections are not numerous (the greater part of the inclosed paper containing reasonings upon the probable Effects of the exceptionable parts) tho' in my mind, some of them are capital ones.[3]

Mrs Mason, & the Family, here join in their Compliments to your Lady and Family, with dear Sir Your affecte & obdt Sert

G. Mason

ALS, DLC:GW.

1. No further reference to obtaining corn in North Carolina or to correspondence with Hugh Williamson (1735–1819) has been found in Mason's or GW's papers. William Richardson Davie (1756–1820) practiced law in North Carolina and was a political leader and later governor of the state.

2. Daniel Carroll (1730–1796) of Montgomery County, Md., wrote to James Madison on 28 Oct. and reported that after leaving Philadelphia he overtook Mason and James McHenry "on the road: By the time they had reachd within 9 Miles of Baltimore, they had exhausted all the stories of their youth &ca. and had enterd into a discusn. of the rights to the Western World. You know they are champions on opposite sides of this question. The Majr. having pushd the Col. hard on the Charters of Virginia the latter had just wax'd warm, when his Char[i]oteer put an end to the dispute, by jumbling their Honors together by an oversett. I came up soon after. They were both hurt—the Col. most so— he lost blood at Baltimore, & is well" (Rutland and Hobson, *Madison Papers,* 10:226–27).

3. Mason's enclosure, his Objections to the Constitution of Government Formed by the Convention (DLC:GW), is included in CD-ROM:GW and is printed in Rutland, *Mason Papers,* 3:991–94. For the text of Mason's statement and its publication beginning in November, see George Mason: Objections to the Constitution, in Kaminski and Saladino, *Documentary History of the Ratification of the Constitution,* 8:41–46. GW made an abstract of Mason's statement, c.7 Oct. 1787, on the cover. It reads:

"Declaration of Rights.

In the lower Ho.—only the Shadow of representn.

The Senate have the power of altering all Money Bills—and of originating appropriations of Money & the Sallary of the officers of their own appoint[-men]t in conjunction with the Presidt.

Their great Powers—viz.—Makg treaties—Trying impeachments— appointing ambassadors and all other public Officers—Influence on the Executive—Duration in Office.

Judiciaries so constructed as to absorb all power & to destroy the Judiciaries of the sevl States. and to render law tedious, expensive &ca.

President no Constitutional Council—dangers arising therefrom.

Ditto—Granting Pardons. Consequences of it.

By declaring all treaties supreme laws of the Land the Executive & the Senate in many cases have an exclusive power of Legislation. this might have been avoided—by &ca.

A Majority to make Commercial regulations and Navigation Laws ruinous to the 5 Southern States because &ca.

Construction of the general clause at the end of the enumerated powers— will admit Monopolies—Constitute new crimes—inflict unusual punishments—& leave no power in the State governments. or secure the people in their rights.

Liberty of the press—No declaration to secure it or the Tryal by Jury in civil causes—Nor against the Danger of Standing armies in time of Peace.

The State Legislatures are restraind ⟨*illegible*⟩ from laying export Duties on their own produce.

The general legislature is restrained from prohibiting the further importation of Slaves for the term of 20 odd years—tho' &ca.

Ex post facto Laws

This Governt &ca." (AD, DLC:GW).

For the reaction of GW and James Madison to Mason's criticism of the Constitution, see GW to Madison, 10 Oct., and Madison to GW, 18 October. It was through the agency of GW's secretary Tobias Lear that Mason's "Objections to the Constitution" first appeared in print on 22 Nov. in the *Virginia Journal, and Alexandria Advertiser.* Lear wrote John Langdon on 3 Dec. that George Mason had given his objections "in manuscript to persons in all parts of the country where he supposed they would make an impression, but avoided publishing them.—I waited for a long time in expectation that they would appear in the publick papers, but finding they did not, I conveyed a copy of them to the printer of the Virginia Journal who published them, this has had a good effect as the futility of them strikes every unprejudiced person who reads them.—I have answered some of them & am now answering the rest, but as it is under an assumed signature, it is not known, even to the General, by whom it is done" (Kaminski and Saladino, *Documentary History of the Ratification of the Constitution,* 8:196–98). Lear's attack on Mason's "Objections" under the name of "Brutus" appeared in the *Virginia Journal, and Alexandria Advertiser;* Mason's "Objections" were printed in newspapers throughout the country.

From Lafayette

My dear General   Paris october the 9th 1787

I Hope the time is drawing Near, when I will Receive the letter You Have Announced to Me, and while I Have the Unspeackable Satisfaction to Hear from my beloved General, I will also Gratify my Heartfelt Curiosity to know the proceedings of the Convention[1]—May it Have devised proposals, and found in the people a disposition which Can insure the Happiness, prosperity, and dignity of the United states! I Confess that My pride, with Respect to America, Can Bear No Mortification—and Yet I Feel Every day that she does Not Enjoy that Consequence which ought to be Hers—I hope to God this Opportunity May be Made Use of, so as to Give solidity and Energy to the Union, without Receding However from the principles of democraty— for Any thing that is Monarchichal, or of the Aristocratical kind is Big with Evils. I am sometimes affraid least the ill effects of a democratic Relaxation Be the Cause of leaning too much on the other side. But We are to Expect that so Many Enlightened, Experienced, and Virtuous Senators, will Have Hit the Very point where the people will Remain in possession of their Natural Rights, of that perfect Equality Among fellow citizens, and Yet Governement, with the powers freely and frequently invested in them, will be able to provide with Efficacy and act with Vigour.

The Conduct of Rhode Island is strange indeed. Has England some personal Views to Answer on that spot?

The affairs of france are still in an Unsettled Situation—a large deficiency is to be filled up with taxes, and the Nation are tired to pay what they Have not Voted. The ideas of liberty Have Been, since the American Revolution, spreading very fast. The Combustible Materials Have been kindled by the Assembly of Notables. After they Had got Rid of us, there were the Parliaments to fight with, and Altho' they are only Courts of judicature, they Have Made use of their Right of Registering, to deny their Sanction to Any taxes, Unconsented by the Nation. Some of them were exiled, some others were Not. they Made arrêts which were Broken by the King's Council—and a paper war insued. Count d'artois, while He Came to Carry the King's orders, was Hissed by the Mob.[2] Some Ministers have Been Burnt in Effigy. At last the Parliament of Paris Very foolishly Agreed to An Arrangement which was to take back the two proposed taxes, provided they would Register an Augmentation of the old ones. The provincial Assemblies Have Held their first Meetings. Regulations were Given to them by the King whereby they were entirely submitted to His Majesty's intendants in Each province. We made loud Complaints, and the Regulations Are Mending. You see that the King is often obliged to step Back, and Yet the people at large are Unsatisfied. So Great is the discontent that the Queen dares not come to Paris for fear of Being ill Received. And from the proceedings that have taken place these six Months past, we shall at least obtain the infusion of this idea into Every Body's Head, Viz. that the King Has no Right to tax the Nation, and Nothing in that Way Can be stipulated But By an Assembly of the Nation.

The King in France is all mighty. He Has all the Means to Enforce, to punish, and to Corrupt. His Ministers Have the inclination, and think it their duty to preserve despotism. There are swarms of low and effeminate Courtiers. The influence of women, and love of pleasure Have Abated the spirits of the Nation, and the inferior Classes are ignorant. But on the other Hand the Genius of the french is lively, enterprising and inclined to Contempt of their Rulers. Their Minds are getting Enlightened by the works of philosophers, and the Example of other Nations. They are lately Actuated By a Becoming sense of

Honour, and altho' they are slaves dont like to Confess that it is the Case. The inhabitants of the Remote provinces are disgusted with the despotism, and the Expences of Court. So that there is a strange Contrast Betwen the Turkish power of the King, the Regard of the Ministry to preserved it untouched, the intrigues and servility of a set of Courtiers on the one Hand, and on the other the General freedom of thinking, speaking, and writing in spite of the spies, the Bastille, and the library laws, the spirit of Criticism, and patriotism in the first Class of the Nation, many of them personally servants to the King, mixed with a fear to loose their stations and pensions, the frolicking insolence of the Mob in the City ever Ready to Give way to a detachement of the Guards, and the More serious discontents of the Country people, all which ingredients Mixed together will By little and little, without Great Convulsions, Bring on an independant Representation of the people, an of Course a diminution of Regal Authority. But it is an Affair of time, and will be the slower on its way, as the Crass interets of powerfull people will put Bars in the Wheels.

There have been Great Changes in Administration. The Arch Bishop of toulouse is prime Minister. He is Honest, Sensible, and Enlightned. I Confess He Has Committed Errors since He is in place. Yet do I think Him a Man of the first Rate. He Has Been twisted of in the two storms of interior and foreign politics. But should a more Calm weather Come on, I am sure He would be able, and disposed to do Great things. Marechals de Castries and Segur Have Resigned. The former is still Much Consulted. it is a great loss to the Council. You know I am Much Connected in friendship with Him. The two New Ministers are for the War Count de brienne Brother to the Arch Bishop, and Count de la Luzerne, the chevalier's Brother for the Navy. He Has Been sent for to Hispaniola where He Now Commands.[3] I think this one May be usefully disposed towards American Concerns. You know that My friend Mr de Malesherbes is Again one of the Council.[4] Upon the whole this New Administration Are Composed of very Honest Men—some of whom Very sensible. it is a great thing to Have a prime Minister who Acts the King's part. I wish they Had some Men Among them of Military Experience. it is much to be feared we shall Have a War.

The ottoman Empire has been long threatened—france supported it against its Ennemies, while she Advised the Turks Against Bringing upon themselves a fatal war with the two imperial Courts. But through the intrigues of England, the Grand Signor Has Been driven into Hostilities Against the Russians, and Now the Turkish Empire in Europe must probably fall. it has been a March stolen of us, and it is still doubtfull wether france will Support the Turks, Unfaithfull, and Mad as they are, or Occupy some interesting posts in the Mediterrean, on which the English Have long Had an Eye—such as Candia, the Morée, and perhaps Ægipt.

You will also Hear, My dear General, of the dismal Event that took place in Holland. The indecision of our Ministry, the Blunders of M. de Verac the french Ambassador, the Rascality of a Cowardly Advanturer, the Rhingrave de Salm, are No doubt much to blame. Verac knew nothing of what was doing, said Nothing of what was to be said. Mr de Salm who Had infatuated this Court spoke great wonders, and did Nothing But to Run a way[5]—and the ministers were slow in their preparations, dilatory in Recalling their Ambassador, and Compleatly deceived in their Negotiations. But it Must Be said on the other Hand that the Patriotic Party in Holland Could Never Agre in Any plan, and were Almost as Much opposed to Each other as they were to the State Holder. and the Entrance of the King of Prussia's troops was Equally Contrary to the laws of Honour since there was a Negotiation on foot, and to those of politics since He throws us into an Austrian Alliance Very disadvantageous to Him. We Have been Surprised, He Mislead, the dutch Ruined, and England is the only one that Gained in the Bargain.

it is Unknown wether Great Britain will be satisfied with Keeping a very advantageous treaty of Commerce with us, and Having Regained Her influence in Holland or wether she will take this opportunity to Revenge for the American war. The later is the British King's wish, and is probable Enough. These Alliances will then probably be formed—france, the Emperor, Russia, and Spain, Against England, prussia, and an Army of Hanoverians, Hessians, and Brunswickers Helped with the Stateholderian influence in Holland—Unless we find Means to Enter it with an Army, and Raise up again the Republican party, which Now is pretty difficult. I Have been thinking what part America ought to take, and this is My Humble opinion. There is No doubt But what the United States will either join france or Remain Neutral. in the first supposition, they will Recover the forts, and Canada will probably Be an Addition to the Confederacy. But How far is it to Be Expected that the Southern, and Part of the Eastern States will like a war that would deprive them of a portion of their trade, and is America so situated a[s] to support a war without great inconvenience to Herself? I Would think that a Neutrality suits Better Her interests, But such A Neutrality as will Actually Help Her Allies, and increase Her own Wealth. You know that By the treaty the possessions of Each other in America are Mutually garanteed. france Must Be induced Not to insist upon a litteral Compliance with this point, while she Enjoys the full Advantage of an other Article that Empowers Her to introduce and Refit Her fleets, and to sell Her prizes within the Harbours of the United States. france would there By find a shelter, a Magazine, a Repairing Yard whereEver she pleases and the United States Would Have the profit of the sale. at the same time, Some letters of Marque Could be Given to American privateers, mixed with french who would Bring in under french colours a part of the west india English produce. in the Mean While the American Merchants will Go on trading with Both. and the United States Cannot Be quarrelled with By England, since on one Hand they strickly Comply with their treaty, and on the other they Cannot prevent the french from purchasing and fitting out Vessels Where ever they please. I would Not Have A fear of Appearing timid or Ungrateful to Carry the United States farther than such a friendly, Helping Neutrality as I Have described—which if well Managed May Enable us to Get france to insist on the Restoration of the forts in the treaty of peace. But I would be afraid of a war, on account of the expense.

You know, My dear General, that the letter to M. jefferson Has Been attended with Embarassements and Misunderstandings, owing Not to Any change of disposition in the Ministry, But to the subterraneous Chicanes of the farm, which the Hurry and Crisis of internal Business, and the frequent Ups and downs of the several Ministers, prevented Administration to set to Rights. The Work Has Been lately finished By my friend Mr jefferson and Myself as well as we Could settle it for the present. and Considering the intricate difficulties, of fiscal laws and Exclusive privileges Under which this Country still labours, I Hope You will find that the trade from the United States Receives as much favour as it was possible to obtain Untill the present state of things is changed for the Better.[6]

I shall Now, my dear General, tell You some thing of Myself, a part in My Gazettes that I know is Not Uninteresting to You. after the Assembly of Notables Has Been Ended (wherein I Had the Misfortune to displease their Majesties, Royal family, and a set of powerfull men and Courtiers, while that Conduct of Mine, Much Criticized there, Made me very popular Among the Nation at large, and was Countenanced By the Parliaments Who Repeated What I Had said) I turned My thoughts towards the provincial Assembly in Auvergne. the presidency was not Given to me, and I did Not wish for it. that I previously Had declared, Because the president, Being Named By the King, is Not so free in His Motions as a private Member. I Even wished to Be Named By the Assembly a Member at the County Meetings, altho' I Could not Attend on Account of the American Commercial Business which Have Called me Back and keep me Here. The first session of the Assembly was only to Compleat its Members, Because the system of deputation is only to take place in three Years time, and the first Nomination was made Half By the King and the other Half By ourselves, who also Named one Half of the subordinate Assemblies, they to Compleat themselves By their own choice. I Made a tour through the province, wherein I was Received By all Classes of the inhabitants with the Most Affecting Marks of love and Confidence. in the Mean while there was something Going on in Holland Much to My wishes and advantage, Had it Not Been spoiled By the Very Men who ought to Have Supported it. the dutch Had long ago thought of introducing me into their Affairs, and it was lately Much Agitated to put me at the Head of the twenty thousand embodied Volonteers, in Case they did Agree to Meet, a Measure which the interest of the Cause, and the opinion of the Most sensible Among them Called for very Earnestly—I Could also, and Would no doubt as soon as affairs grew serious, Have Been put at the Head of the Whole Military forces in the Republican provinces. While that Plan was Arranging, Much to the satisfaction of the Arch Bishop of toulouse and Marechal de Castries (for altho' I am Not on Very Good terms with the Crowned Heads, it does not in the least lessen My influence with the Ministers some of whom I am very friendly with, particularly the prime Minister) and While *ternant*[7] who Has Acted a Noble and important part in the dutch service did Expect the proposal Would immediately Be Made, the Rhingrave de Salm, and His friend the french Ambassador did put a stop to the whole transaction By persuading the Leaders that such a proposition would Not please the Court of france. and as the Matter originated with the dutch, not With the Ministry, who Had Nothing to do in the Business, it was Abandonned, or at least procrastinated. and they Now say that they Have in this, as well as in other things Been deceived By the absurdity of the french Ambassador and the knavery of the Rhingrave.

Amsterdam Had a little fight the other day with the Prussians. But they Have Since Capitulated.

Mr de Moustiers sends me word that He is just Going. I shall Have time and probably a safe Opportunity to write Before He sails. But as this letter is of a very Confidential Nature, and is not fit for post offices, particularly in this Country, I think it safer to lodge it into that Gentleman's Hands, and will Continue it in a few days.[8] Adieu, My dear General, with filial tenderness and Respect I Have the Honour to be Your devoted and loving friend

Lafayette

ALS, PEL; copy, MH.

1. GW wrote his "Announced" letter on 18 September. See also GW to Lafayette, 15 August. After reading the proposed Constitution "with an unspeakable eagerness and attention," Lafayette wrote to GW on 1 Jan. 1788, giving a generally hearty approval.

2. Charles-Philippe, comte d'Artois (1757–1836), was the younger brother of Louis XVI and a leader of the reactionary party at court. He became king of France as Charles X in 1824.

3. The archbishop of Toulouse gave way to Jacques Necker in the summer of 1788. The archbishop's brother who became minister of war was Athanase-Louis-Marie de Loménie, comte de Brienne (1730–1794). The chevalier de La Luzerne's older brother, César-Henri, comte de La Luzerne (1737–1799), wrote to GW from Port au Prince in Hispaniola (Haiti) on 12 Nov. 1787 shortly before returning to Paris to become minister of marine.

4. Chrétien-Guillaume de Lamoignon de Malesherbes, with whom GW had some indirect dealings in 1784, remained a *conseil du roi* until 1789. He was guillotined in 1794 at the age of 72. See GW to George Clinton, 25 Nov. 1784, n.5.

5. Charles-Olivier de St. George, marquis de Vérac (1743–1828), had been French ambassador to Holland since 1784. The Rhinegrave de Salm (Frédéric, prince de Salm-Kyrbourg; b. 1746) was guillotined in 1794.

6. The "letter to M. jefferson" is that from Calonne of 22 Oct. 1786 granting the French ministry's approval of the agreement reached in May 1786 regarding the farmers-general's management of the tobacco trade. For the difficulties Jefferson and Lafayette were encountering in getting the farmers-general to live up to the terms of the agreement, see Documents on the American Trade in Boyd, *Jefferson Papers*, 12:76–93.

7. Jean-Baptiste, chevalier de Ternant (1751–1816), served as lieutenant colonel and later colonel of Armand's corps in the American Revolution. From 1785 to 1788 he was a colonel in Maillebois's legion. In 1791 he was named France's minister plenipotentiary to the United States.

8. Moustier, who did not sail for New York until November, enclosed this letter and one of Lafayette's two letters of 15 Oct. in his own letter to GW of 24 Jan. 1788.

To David Humphreys

My dear Humphreys,   Mount Vernon Octr 10th 1787.

Your favor of the 28th Ult. came duly to hand, as did the other of June.[1] With great pleasure I received the intimation of your spending the Winter under this roof. The invitation was not less sincere than the reception will be cordial. The convention shall be, that in all things you shall do as you please—I will do the same—No ceremony shall be observed—nor any restraint be imposed on any one.

The Constitution that is submitted, is not free from imperfections; but there are as few radical defects in it as could well be expected, considering the heterogenious mass of which the Convention was composed—and the diversity of interests which were to be reconciled. A Constitutional door being opened, for future alterations and amendments, I think it would be wise in the People to adopt what is offered to them; and I wish it may be by as great a majority of them as in the body that decided on it; but this is hardly to be expected, because the importance, and sinister views of too many characters will be affected by the change. Much will depend however on literary abilities, & the recommendation of it by good pens, should it be openly, I mean publicly attacked in the Gazettes. Go matters however as they may, I shall have the consolation to reflect, that no objects but the public good, and that peace & harmony which I wished to see prevail in the Convention, ever obtruded, even for a moment, in my mind, during the whole session lengthy as it was. What reception this State will give to the proceedings (thro' the great territorial extent of it) I am unable to inform you. In these parts of it, it is advocated beyond my expectation. The great opposition, if great is given, will come from the Counties Southward and Westward; from whence I have not, as yet, heard much that can be depended on.

I condole with you on the loss of your parents, but as they lived to a good old age you could not be unprepared for the shock; tho' there is something painful in bidding an adieu to those we love, or revere, when we know it is a final one. Reason, religion & Philosophy may soften the anguish, but time *alone* can irradicate it.

As I am beginning to look for you, I shall add no more at present, but the best wishes of the family, and the affecte regards of your Sincere friend and Obedt Hble Servt

Go: Washington

ALS, NIC; LB, DLC:GW.
  1. Humphreys' letter "of June" is dated 28 May.

To James Madison

My dear Sir,   Mount Vernon Octr 10th 1787.
  I thank you for your letter of the 30th Ult. It came by the last Post. I am better pleased that the proceedings of the Convention is handed from Congress by a unanimous vote (feeble as it is) than if it had appeared under stronger marks of approbation without it. This apparent unanimity will have its effect. Not every one has opportunities to peep behind the curtain; and as the multitude often judge from externals, the appearance of unanimity in that body, on this occasn, will be of great importance.

  The political tenets of Colo. M. & Colo. R.H.L. are always in unison—It may be asked which of them gives the tone? Without hesitation, I answer the latter;[1] because the latter, I believe, will receive it from no one. He has, I am informed, rendered himself obnoxious in Philadelphia by the pains he took to dissiminate his objections amongst some [of] the leaders of the seceding members of the legislature of that State.[2] His conduct is not less reprobated in this County.[3] How it will be relished, *generally*, is yet to be learnt, by me. As far as accts have been received from the Southern & Western Counties, the Sentiment with respect to the proceedings of the Convention is favourable—Whether the knowledge of this, or conviction of the impropriety of withholding the Constitution from State Conventions has worked most in the breast of Col. M. I will not decide; but the fact is, he has declared unequivocally (in a letter to me) for its going to the people.[4] Had his sentiments however been opposed to the measure, Instructions which are given by the freeholders of this County to their representatives, would have secured his vote for it. Yet, I have no doubt but that this assent will be accompanied by the most tremendous apprehensions, and highest colourings to his objections. To alarm the people, seems to be the ground work of his plan. The want of a qualified Navigation Act, is already declared to be a mean by which the produce of the Southern States will be reduced to nothing, & will become a monopoly of the Northern & Eastern States. To enumerate all his objections, is unnecessary; because they are detailed in the address of the seceding members of the Assembly of Pensylvania; which, no doubt you have seen.

I scarcely think that any powerful opposition will be made to the Constitution's being submitted to a Convention of the people of this State. If it is given, it will be at that meeting—In which I hope you will make it convenient to attend; explanations will be wanting—none can give them with more *precision* and accuracy than yourself.

The Sentiments of Mr Henry with respect to the Constitution which is submitted, are not known in these parts. Mr Jos[ep]h Jones (who it seems was in Alexanda a few days before my return home) was of opinion that they would not be inemical to it—others however conceive, that as the advocate of a paper emission, he cannot be friendly to a Constn wch is an effectual bar.[5]

From circumstances which have been related, it is conjectured that the Governor wishes he had been among the subscribing members,[6] but time will disclose more than we know at present with respect to the whole of this business; and when I hear more, I will write to you again. In the mean while I pray you to

be assured of the sincere regard and affection with which I am—
My dear Sir Yr Most Obedt & Very Hble Servt

Go: Washington

P.S. Having received (in a letter) from Colo. Mason, a detail of his objections to the proposed Constitution I enclose you a copy of them.[7]

ALS, MA; LB, DLC:GW.

1. GW meant the former, not the latter; Madison recognized that GW was referring to George Mason and not to Richard Henry Lee (Rutland and Hobson, *Madison Papers*, 10:191, n.2). For the grounds on which Lee opposed the Constitution, see Lee to GW, 11 October.

2. The Antifederal members of the Pennsylvania legislature who withdrew on 28 Sept. in an attempt to prevent the calling of a state ratifying convention issued the next day a statement defending their actions and attacking the Constitution. An extract of the statement, which was printed widely in 1787, appears in Kaminski and Saladino, *Documentary History of the Ratification of the Constitution*, 13:293–97. Mason's statement of his objections to the Constitution, which he drew up before the end of the Convention, was being circulated as early as 18 Sept. (ibid., 346–48).

3. At a meeting in Fairfax County on 2 Oct., the assembled freeholders instructed their delegates to the legislature, George Mason and David Stuart, to support the calling of a convention of the people to ratify the Constitution. The resolutions of the Fairfax meeting are reprinted ibid., 8:23–25.

4. See George Mason to GW, 7 Oct., n.3.

5. Five days later GW alluded to Patrick Henry's intentions to oppose ratification of the Constitution (GW to Henry Knox, 15 October). See also GW to Madison, 22 Oct., and Henry to GW, 19 October.

6. Edmund Randolph did not make public his reasons for not signing the Constitution until 27 Dec. 1787. See Randolph to GW, 27 December.

7. See note 4.

From Alexander Hamilton

D. Sir, [c.11 October 1787]

You probably saw some time since some animadversions on certain expressions of Governor Clinton respecting the Convention—You may have seen a piece signed a Republican, attempting to bring the fact into question and endeavouring to controvert the conclusions drawn from it, if true—My answer you will find in the inclosed. I trouble you with it merely from that anxiety which is natural to every man to have his veracity at least stand in a fair light[1]—The matter seems to be given up by the Governor and the fact with the inferences from it stand against him in full force, and operate as they ought to do.

It is however, of some importance to the party to diminish whatever credit or influence I may possess; and to effect this they stick at nothing. Among many contemptible artifices practiced by them, they have had recourse to an insinuation that I *palmed* myself upon you and that you *dismissed* me from your family—This I confess hurts my feelings, and if it obtains credit, will require a contradiction.[2]

You Sir will undoubtedly recollect the manner in which I came into your family and went out of it; and know how destitute of foundation such insinuations are. My confidence in your justice will not permit me to doubt your readiness to put the matter in its true light in your answer to this letter. It cannot be my wish to give any complexion to the affair which might excite the least scruple in you; but I confess it would mortify me to be under the imputation either of having obtruded myself into the family of a General or of having been turned out of it.

The New Constitution is as popular in this City as it is possible for any thing to be—and the prospect thus far is favourable to it throughout the state. But there is no saying what turn things may take when the full flood of official influence is let loose against it. This is to be expected, for, though the Governor has not publicly declared himself, his particular connections and confidential friends are loud against it. I remain with perfect esteem Yr Excellency's Obdt Servt

Alexander Hamilton

Mrs Hamilton joins in respectful compliments to Mrs Washington.

ALS, DLC:GW; ADfS, DLC: Hamilton Papers; copy, in the hand of Hamilton, DLC: Hamilton Papers.

1. Hamilton's anonymous attack on Gov. George Clinton for Clinton's opposition to the Federal Convention (New York *Daily Advertiser,* 21 July) and Hamilton's "response" to "Republican's" defense of Clinton (*New-York Journal,* 6 Sept.), which Hamilton printed in the *Daily Advertiser,* 15 Sept., are printed in Syrett, *Hamilton Papers,* 4:229–32, 248–53.

2. This item appeared in the *New-York Journal* on 20 Sept.: "I have also known an upstart attorney, palm himself upon a great and good man, for a youth of extraordinary genius, and under the shadow of such a patronage, make himself at once known and respected; but being sifted and bolted to the brann, he was at length found to be a superficial, self-conceited coxcomb, and

was of course turned off, and disregarded by his patron" (quoted in Hamilton to GW, 11–15 Oct. 1787, n.3, in Syrett, *Hamilton Papers*, 4:280–81).

From Richard Henry Lee

Dear Sir,   New York Octobr 11. 1787

I was unwilling to interrupt your attention to more important affairs at Phila. by sending there an acknowledgement of the letter that you were pleased to honor me with from that City;[1] especially as this place afforded nothing worthy of your notice. We have the pleasure to see the first Act of Congress for selling federal lands N.W. of Ohio becoming productive very fast—A large sum of public securities being already paid in upon the first sales: and a new Contract is ordered to be made with a company in N. Jersey for the lands between the two Miamis that will rid us of at least 2 millions more of the public debt. There is good reason to suppose that by the next spring we shall have reduced the domestic debt near six millions of dollars. And it seems clear that the lands yet to be disposed of, if well managed, will sink the whole 30 Millions that are due. The assiduity with which the Court of London is soli[ci]ting that of Spain for the conclusion of a Commercial treaty between those powers, renders it a signal misfortune that we have not been able to get a sufficient number of the States together to produce a conclusion of the Spanish Treaty. The state of Europe, with respect to the continuance of peace, still hangs in doubtful ballance. The finance weakness of France and G. Britain most strongly opposes war, yet the state of things is such as renders it very questionable, whether even that difficulty, great as it is, will secure the continuance of peace—It is under the strongest impressions of your goodness and candor that I venture to make the observations that follow in this letter, assuring you that I feel it among the first distresses that have happend to me in my life, that I find myself compelled by irresistible conviction of mind to doubt about the new System for federal government recommended by the late Convention.

It is Sir, in consequence of long reflection upon the nature of Man and of government, that I am led to fear the danger that will ensue to Civil Liberty from the adoption of the new system in its present form. I am fully sensible of the propriety of change in the present plan of confederation, and altho there may be difficulties, not inconsiderable, in procuring an adoption of such amendments to the Convention System as will give security to the just rights of human nature, and better secure from injury the discordant interests of the different parts of this Union; yet I hope that these difficulties are not insurmountable. Because we are happily uninterrupted by external war, or by such internal discords as can prevent peaceable and fair discussion, in another Convention, of those objections that are fundamentally strong against the new Constitution which abounds with useful regulations. As there is so great a part of the business well done already, I think that such alterations as must give very general content, could not long employ another Convention when provided with the sense of the different States upon those alterations.

I am much inclined to believe that the amendments generally thought to be necessary, will be found to be of such a nature, as tho they do not oppose the exercise of a very confident federal power; are yet such as the best Theories on Government, and the best practise upon those theories have found necessary. At the same time that they are such as the opinions of our people have for ages been fixed on. It would be unnecessary for me here to enumerate particulars as I expect the honor of waiting on you at Mount Vernon in my way home early in November.[2] In the mean time I have only to request that my best respects may be presented to your Lady and that I may be remembered to the rest of the good family of Mount Vernon. I have the honor to be dear Sir, with the most unfeigned respect, esteem, and affection, Your most obedient and very humble servant

Richard Henry Lee.

If the next Packets should bring us any important advices from Europe I will communicate them to you immediately.

ALS, DLC:GW.

1. GW wrote Richard Henry Lee on 19 July in answer to Lee's letter of 15 July.

2. Whether Lee gave GW a copy of his proposed amendments when he visited Mount Vernon on 11 and 12 Nov. is not known.

From Francis Mentges

Sir   Philadelphia the 12 8bre 1787.
     Some time ago I presented a memorial to the Honorable the
Congress respecting the Command I had from your Excellency
to superintend the Hospitals in the state of Virginia, and praying for a Compensation for Extra services. To support that
Claim, I inclosed your Excel. letter of the 28th March 1782, in
which your Excel. signified the highest approbation of my Conduct on that Duty—Congress has taken my Memorial into Consideration and appointed a Committee to report thereon, I am
now informed by a friend of mine in Congress, that it was necessary to produce to Congress a Certificate from your Excel., when
I was ordered and recalled from that Command, I believe that
your Excel. remembers that General St Clair marched with the
Pennsy. line from york town in Virginia the 4th of November
1781—and the 5th Novr your Excel. was pleased to order me
to superintend the Hospitals in the different parts of Virginia,
but the latter your Excel. can not ascertain unless your Excel.
will believe me that it was the 28th of March 1782, and previous
to your Excellencys orders from want of necessaries for the sicke
to support them, which I mentioned in my letter—I am sorry
to call your Excel. attention from busseness of greater moment,
necessity obliges me to request of your Excel. for a Certific⟨ate⟩
your Excel. will be the best judge wheter I am intitulled to a
Compensation[1]—certain I am that the Command not only in
superintending the Hospitals, but more in paying attention to
British ⟨illegible⟩ and collecting the prisoners in the Divers part
of Virginia, have been very expensive to me, and were executed
by me by an order from Count Rochambeau—I beg you will be
pleased to answer my Request, and I am with the highest Esteem
your Excel. Most Ob. humble Servt
                                                    F. Mentges

ALS, DLC:GW.

1. Mentges' memorial to Congress asking for compensation for extra service
while superintending the hospitals in Virginia in 1781–82 is dated 23 Feb.
1787 (DNA:PCC, item 41). On the recommendation of the Board of Treasury,
Congress on 18 April denied Mentges's petition (*JCC*, 32:211). GW replied
on 27 Oct.: "Sir, In answer to your favor of the 12th I shall inform you that
without unpacking my public Papers (which would be very troublesome to me
as they are volumenous and in a variety of [   ] I cannot ascertain with *preci-*

sion the commencement of your superintendance of the Hospital in Willimsburg—and if these ware to be unpacked I might not come at the date of your recall from this duty. I should suppose you acted under written orders in both cases—these therefore will go fully to the points you want to establish.

"That you must have taken charge of the Hospital in Wiliamsburg at the time you say—viz. the 5th of November 1781 cant I believe, admit of no doubt as all the distributions were then making and as far as the recollection of circumstances will aid me, I think you must have remained on that duty till the latter part of the spring following. If this testimoney of the matter, and a thorough persuation of your having discharged the trust reposed in you with intelligence and fidility can avail your cause this cirtificate may be adduced from. I am Sir &c. G. Washington" (LB, DLC:GW).

From James Madison

Dear Sir   New York Octr 14. 1787.

The letter herewith inclosed was put into my hands yesterday by Mr de Crœvecœr who belongs to the Consular establishment of France in this Country. I add to it a pamphlet which Mr Pinkney has submitted to the public, or rather as he professes, to the perusal of his friends; and a printed sheet containing his ideas on a very delicate subject; too delicate in my opinion to have been properly confided to the press. He conceives that his precautions against any farther circulation of the piece than he himself authorises, are so effectual as to justify the step. I wish he may not be disappointed. In communicating a copy to you I fulfil his wishes only.[1]

No decisive indications of the public mind in the Northn & Middle States can yet be collected. The Reports continue to be rather favorable to the Act of the Convention from every quarter; but its adversaries will naturally be latest in shewing themselves. Boston is certainly friendly. An opposition is known to be in petto[2] in Connecticut; but it is said not to be much dreaded by the other side. Rhode Island will be divided on this subject in the same manner as it has been on the question of paper money. The Newspapers here have contained sundry publications animadverting on the proposed Constitution & it is known that the Government party are hostile to it. There are on the other side so many able & weighty advocates, and the conduct of the Eastern States if favorable, will add so much force to their arguments, that there is at least as much ground for hope as for apprehension. I do not learn that any opposition is likely to be made in N. Jersey. The temper of Pennsylvania will be best known to you from the direct information which you cannot fail to receive through the Newspapers & other channels.

Congress have been of late employed chiefly in settling the requisition,·and in making some arrangements for the Western Country. The latter consist of the appointment of a Govr & Secretary, and the allotment of a sum of money for Indian Treaties if they should be found necessary. The Requisition so far as it varies our fiscal system, makes the proportion of indents receivable independently of specie—& those of different years indiscriminately receivable for any year, and does not as heretofore tie down the States to a particular mode of obtaining them. Mr Adams has been permitted to return home after Feby next, & Mr Jeffersons appointment continued for three years longer. With the most perfect esteem & most affectionate regard, I remain Dr Sir, Your Obedt friend & servant

Js Madison Jr

ALS, DLC:GW; copy, in Madison's hand, DLC: Madison Papers.
1. The letter forwarded by Crèvecoeur has not been identified. Charles Pinckney's *Observations on the Plan of Government Submitted to the Federal Convention, on the 28th of May, 1787* . . . (New York, 1787) was later to play a part in the controversy over the so-called Pinckney Plan. The broadside, or "printed sheet," which Madison also enclosed, was entitled *Mr. Charles Pinckney's Speech, in Answer to Mr. Jay . . . on the Question of a Treaty with Spain. Delivered in Congress, August 16, 1786* (New York, n.d.). For a discussion of these two publications and for other references, see notes 1 and 2 of the same letter printed in Rutland and Hobson, *Madison Papers,* 10:195.
2. GW occasionally used the Italian phrase *in petto,* meaning held in reserve.

Letter not found: to Robert Morris, 14 Oct. 1787. On 25 Oct. Morris acknowledged "the receipt of your obliging letter of the 14th Inst."

To Charles Pettit

Sir,   Mount Vernon October 14th 1787.
The enclosed ought to have accompanied the letter and the box by Capt. Ellwood. That it did not was an omission.[1]

In addition to the Plates there written for, let me request two others; th[r]ee feet nine each square, I want them for a Green house and would have quite plain and full as thick as they are *usually* cast for Chimney backs.[2] I am Sir, Yr Most Obed. Servant

G. Washington

LB, DLC:GW.

1. GW wrote Pettit on 2 Oct. that he was sending with the letter "patterns for the hearths of Chimneys." The patterns have not been found.

2. See Charles Pettit to GW, 1 November.

To Henry Knox

My dear Sir,   Mount Vernon October 15th 1787

Your favor of the 3d instt came duly to hand.

The fourth day after leaving Phila. I arrived at home, and found Mrs Washington and the family tolerably well, but the fruits of the Earth almost entirely destroyed by one of the severest droughts (in this neighbourhood) that ever was experienced. The Crops generally, below the Mountains are injured; but not to the degree that mine, & some of my Neighbours, are here.

The Constitution is now before the judgment seat. It has, as was expected, its adversaries, and its supporters; which will preponderate is yet to be decided. The former, it is probable, will be most active because the Major part of them it is to be feared, will be governed by sinester and self important considerations on which no arguments will work conviction—the opposition from another class of them (if they are men of reflection, information and candour) may perhaps subside in the solution of the following plain, but important questions. 1. Is the Constitution which is submitted by the Convention preferable to the government (if it can be called one) under which we now live? 2. Is it probable that more confidence will, at this time, be placed in another Convention (should the experiment be tried) than was given to the last? and is it likely that there would be a better agreement in it? Is there not a Constitutional door open for alterations and amendments, & is it not probable that real defects will be as readily discovered after, as before, trial? and will not posterity be as ready to apply the remedy as ourselves, if there is occasion for it, when the mode is provided? To think otherwise will, in my judgment, be ascribing more of the amor patria—more wisdom—and more foresight to ourselves, than I conceive we are entitled to.

It is highly probable that the refusal of our Govr and Colo. Mason to subscribe to the proceedings of the Convention will have a bad effect in this State; for as you well observe, they *must* not only assign reasons for the justification of their conduct, but it is highly probable these reasons will appear in terrific array, with a view to alarm the people—Some things are already addressed to their fears and will have their effect. As far however as the sense of *this* part of the Country has been taken it is strongly in favor of the proposed Constitution. further I cannot speak with precision—If a powerful opposition is given to it the weight thereof will, I apprehend, come from the Southward of James River, & from the Western Counties.

Mrs Washington & the family join me in every good wish for you and Mrs Knox—and with great and sincere regard I am, My dear Sir Yr Affecte

Go: Washington

ALS (photocopy), DLC:GW; copy, NNGL: Knox Papers; LB, DLC:GW.

From Lafayette

My dear General   Paris october the 15th 1787

This letter will Be delivered By Mr du Pont the Son of a Very Sensible and Honest Gentleman, who Has Been Much Emploied in Affairs of Administration, and is Now Very zealously Engaged in drawing Up A Report for our Commercial affairs. His Son Goes out for His instruction, and With a wiew to fit Himself for future Emploiement.[1] I Beg leave to Recommend Him to Your patronage and Advices, and am Happy, My Beloved General, in Every opportunity to Remind You of Your tenderest, and I am Bold to Say, Your dearest friend Who shall, as long as He lives, glory to Be Your adoptive son and most Respectfull Servant

lafayette

ALS, CSmH.

1. Victor Marie Du Pont (1767–1827), son of Pierre-Samuel Du Pont de Nemours (1739–1817), became an attaché to the French legation in New York and on 2 Nov. 1788 was one of the party of the French minister, Moustier, who dined at Mount Vernon (*Diaries*, 5:417–18).

From Lafayette

My dear General   Paris October the 15th 1787

I Have a few days Ago writen to You By M. de Moustier the New Minister from this Court. He is a Sensible and Honest man with whom I think that the people of America will be satisfied. He is Very desirous to be presented to you, and I Have invited Him in Your Name to Mount Vernon, as well as Madame de Brehan, a very agreable lady, His sister in law, who Goes out with Him.[1] inclosed is, my dear General, the Copy of an official letter to Congress wherein I Have Expressed My Sentiments on the present state of Affairs.[2] What is Become of the Happy Years, My Beloved General, when, before My Sentiments were formed, I Had time to model them after Your judgement! This Comfort at least Remains for me to Endeavour Guessing what Your Opinion will be on Every Case that Occurs. There is Nothing New since I wrote my last. Amsterdam Has Ended her Resistence—and there are Now States Generals, and Provincial States for each of the Seven provinces, Regularly Elected which are to a Man Bound to the State Holderian Party. it is one of the Vices of their Constitution, that the Voice of their Magistrates, Howsoever elected is mistaken for the Voice of the Nation. Mr Jefferson and Myself are now employed in Commercial affairs for the United States. Mr de Calonne's letter will Be framed into a arrêt of the Council, and additional favours will Be so adjusted as to take in every thing that is Consistent with this Governement. the disposition of the Ministers is as good as we Can wish. and I am Happy in the Good fortune America Had, that such a man as Mr Jefferson was Sent to this Country.[3]

Nothing as Yet is decided with Respect to war. if it Breacks out the fault will lie with England. The new Secretary at war Has Created a Board of eight general officers to Carry on the affairs of that departement whereof He is the president. Such a measure is very Meritorious, and Cannot fail to do him Great Honour. He is, as you know, the Brother of the Archbishop.

Adieu, My dear General, I Hope You think often of an adoptive son who loves you with all the powers of His Heart, and as long as it Has any life, shall Ever Be Your Most Gratefull, affectionate, and respectfull friend.

                                                                Lafayette

My Best and tenderest Respects wait on Mrs Washington. Remember me most respectfully to Your Mother and Relations, particularly to George. I pay my Compliments to all friends adieu, my dear General.

ALS, PEL.

1. Lafayette wrote GW at length on 9 October. The marquise de Bréhan, a favorite of Thomas Jefferson, was an artist who did not find New York or the United States to her liking.

2. Lafayette's letter to John Jay, dated 15 Oct. 1787, is in DNA:PCC, item 156.

3. See Lafayette to GW, 9 Oct., n.6.

From Battaile Muse

Honourable Sir,   Octr 15th 1787

By Dennis I Send you a Bay mare which I have Procured For your Advantage In the way of rent—Money is So Very Scearce that I cannot Procure it in Every Case nor Indeed at any rate. the Mare is now with Foal & is Six years old Last Spring the price Ten pounds Fifteen Shillngs ℔ Voucher in my hands Please To Send me a receipt For that Sum.[1]

your accts Stands in my Favour I do not Expect To have any money in my hands untill after christmast if I Should be so Fortunate as To Collect any You shall receive it. I expect To be In Alexandria about the 7th day of Next Month and if Possable will Call at Mount vernon—I wish you To Send by Dennis if agreeable about Eight Blank Leases Signed & witness For Some Lots in Fauquier—when I Bargain with a Tenant it's Best To Secure the Conditions by Lease Immediatly To Prevent disputes & Trouble.[2]

the disputed Lines in Fauquier County is not yet run and I cannot say with any certainty when it will be done.[3]

Mrs Lemert is Very much in arrears and Seem not To Lessen the Debt but Very Little also Henry Shover is much in arrears—Pray advise me whether I am To distress them.

John Thompson on goose creek Tract run of Last Spring Considerable in Debt I Sued Him He being Very Poor—I Drew the Suit at His Cost & have Procured Security For the Payment of Twenty Pounds in January Next.

charles Rector on the Same Tract Run a way Ninety odd pounds in your Debt He is Very Poor—I am a Fraid to Sue Him —Perhaps if He was Sued He would give Security To Pay Twenty Pounds at Some Future day.[4]

Colo. Kennday Cannot Pay In ⟨*mutilated*⟩ His assumsit For the Debt.[5]

Mr Rutherford Has Paid of His note not with Interest.[6] I have nearly Secured all other Debts only the above Mention'd—I have the Honour To Be your Obedient Humble Servant

Battaile Muse

ALS, DLC:GW.

1. See Muse to GW, 4 Feb. 1787, in which he refers to the availability of horses in payment of rent. The entry for 17 Oct. in GW's account with Muse shows the receipt of £10.15 for "a mare sent me" (Ledger B, 213).

2. Muse went to Alexandria in November but did not go out to Mount Vernon (Muse to GW, 7 November).

3. For the Hite case involving a dispute over land ownership in Fauquier County, see Thornton Washington to GW, 6 June 1786, n.2.

4. For Muse's dealings with these tenants, see particularly the notes in List of Tenants, 18 Sept. 1785.

5. See GW to Muse, 8 Mar. 1786, n.3.

6. See Robert Rutherford to GW, 28 Mar. 1786, source note.

Letter not found: from David Stuart, 16 Oct. 1787. On 5 Nov. GW wrote Stuart to thank him for his "letters of the 16th and 26th ulto." GW quotes Stuart's letter of 16 Oct. at length in his letter to James Madison of 22 October.

To David Stuart

Dear Sir,   Mount Vernon Octr 17th 1787.

As the enclosed Advertiser contains a speech of Mr Wilson's (as able, candid, & honest a member as any in Convention) which will place the most of Colo. Mason's objections in their true point of light, I send it to you. The re-publication (if you can get it done) will be of service at this juncture.[1] His ipso facto objection does not, I believe, require an answer—every mind must recoil at the idea. And with respect to the Navigation act, I am mistaken if any three men, bodies of men, or Countries, will enter into any compact or treaty if *one* of the three is to have a negative controul over the other two[2]—There must be reciprocity or no union, which is preferable will not become a question in the mind of any true patriot. But granting it to be an evil, it will infallibly work its own cure, and an ultimate advantage to the Southern States. Sincerely & Affect⟨*mutilated*⟩ I am Dear Sir Yr Obedt Servt

Go: Washington

ALS, ViLGU; LB, DLC:GW.

1. James Wilson, a leading member of the federal Convention, delivered his speech defending the Constitution on 6 Oct. at a public meeting assembled outside the Pennsylvania state house to nominate candidates to represent Philadelphia at the state ratifying convention. The speech was first printed in the *Pennsylvania Herald, and General Advertiser* (Philadelphia) on 9 Oct., a copy of which GW was sending to Stuart. It appeared on 24 Oct. in the *Virginia Independent Chronicle* (Richmond) and on 25 Oct. in the *Virginia Journal, and Alexandria Advertiser.* The text of the speech is printed in Kaminski and Saladino, *Documentary History of the Ratification of the Constitution,* 13:337–44.

2. See GW's extract of George Mason's statement of objections to the Constitution, printed in note 3, Mason to GW, 7 October.

Letter not found: from Noah Webster, 17 Oct. 1787. On 4 Nov. GW wrote: "I have received your letter of the 17th ulto."

To Alexander Hamilton

Dear Sir,   Mount Vernon Octr 18th 1787.

Your favor without date came to my hand by the last Post.[1] It is with unfeigned concern I perceive that a political dispute has arisen between Governor Clinton and yourself. For both of you I have the highest esteem and regard. But as you say it is insinuated by some of your political adversaries, and may obtain credit, "that you *palmed* yourself upon me, and was *dismissed* from my family"; and call upon me to do you justice by a recital of the facts. I do therefore, explicitly declare, that both charges are entirely unfounded. With respect to the first, I have no cause to believe that you took a single step to accomplish, or had the most distant ⟨ide⟩a of receiving, an appointment in my ⟨fam⟩ily 'till you were envited thereto. And ⟨with⟩ respect to the second, that your quitting ⟨it was⟩ altogether the effect of your own ⟨choic⟩e.

When the situation of this Country ⟨calls⟩ loudly for unanimity & vigor, it is to be lamented that Gentlemen of talents and character should disagree in their sentiments for promoting the public weal. but unfortunately, this ever has been, and more than probable, ever will be the case, in the affairs of man.

Having scarcely been from home since my return from Philadelphia, I can give but little information with respect to the *general* reception of the New Constitution in *this* State. In Alexandria however, and some of the adjacent Counties, it has been embraced with an enthusiastic warmth of which I had no conception. I expect notwithstanding, violent opposition will be given to it by *some* characters of weight & influence, in the State.

Mrs Washington unites with me in best wishes for Mrs Hamilton and yourself. I am—Dear Sir Yr Most Obedt & Affecte Hble Servt

Go: Washington

ALS, DLC: Hamilton Papers; LB, DLC:GW. Where the manuscript is mutilated, the letters and words in angle brackets are taken from the letter-book copy.

1. Hamilton's letter is printed under the date c.11 October.

From James Madison

Dear Sir   N. York Octr 18. 1787.

I have been this day honoured with your favor of the 10th instant, under the same cover with which is a copy of Col. Mason's objections to the Work of the Convention. As he persists in the temper which produced his dissent it is no small satisfaction to find him reduced to such distress for a proper gloss on it; for no other consideration surely could have led him to dwell on an objection which he acknowledged to have been in some degree removed by the Convention themselves—on the paltry right of the Senate to propose alterations in money bills—on the appointment of the vice President—President of the Senate instead of making the President of the Senate the vice president, which seemed to be the alternative—and on the *possibility*, that the Congress may misconstrue their powers & betray their trust so far as to grant monopolies in trade &c. If I do not forget too some of his other reasons were either not at all or very faintly urged at the time when alone they ought to have been urged; such as the power of the Senate in the case of treaties & of impeachments; and their duration in office. With respect to the latter point I recollect well that he more than once disclaimed opposition to it. My memory fails me also if he did not acquiesce in if not vote for, the term allowed for the further importation of slaves; and the prohibition of duties on exports by the States. What he means by the dangerous tendency of the Judiciary I am at some loss to comprehend. It never was intended, nor can it be supposed that in ordinary cases the inferior tribunals will not have final jurisdiction in order to prevent the evils of which he complains. The great mass of suits in every State lie between Citizen & Citizen, and relate to matters not of federal cognizance. Notwithstanding the stress laid on the necessity of a Council to the President I strongly suspect, tho I was a friend to the thing, that if such an one as Col. Mason proposed, had been established, and the power of the Senate in appointments to offices transferred to it, that as great a clamour would have been heard from some quarters which in general eccho his Objections. What can he mean by saying that the Common law is not secured by the new constitution, though it has been adopted by the State Constitutions. The common law is nothing more than the unwritten law, and is left by all the constitutions equally liable to legislative alterations. I am not sure that any notice is particularly taken of it in the Constitutions of the States. If there is, nothing more is provided than a general declaration that it shall continue along with other branches of law to be in force till legally changed. The Constitution of Virga drawn up by Col. Mason himself, is absolutely silent on the subject. An *ordinance* passed during the same Session, declared the Common law as heretofore & all Statutes of prior date to the 4 of James I, to be still the law of the land, merely to obviate pretexts that the separation from G. Britain threw us into a State of nature, and abolished all civil rights and Obligations. Since the Revolution every State has made great inroads & with great propriety in many instances on this *monarchical* code. The "revisal of the laws" by a Committee of wch Col. Mason was a member, though not an acting one, abounds with such innovations. The abolition of the *right of primogeniture*, which I am sure Col. Mason does not disapprove, falls under this head. What could the Convention have done? If they had in general terms declared the Common law to be in force, they would have broken in upon the legal

Code of every State in the most material points: they wd have done more, they would have brought over from G.B. a thousand heterogeneous & antirepublican doctrines, and even the *ecclesiastical Hierarchy itself,* for that is a part of the Common law. If they had undertaken a discrimination, they must have formed a digest of laws, instead of a Constitution. This objection surely was not brought forward in the Convention, or it wd have been placed in such a light that a repetition of it out of doors would scarcely have been hazarded. Were it allowed the weight which Col. M. may suppose it deserves, it would remain to be decided whether it be candid to arraign the Convention for omissions which were never suggested to them—or prudent to vindicate the dissent by reasons which either were not previously thought of, or must have been wilfully concealed—But I am running into a comment as prolix, as it is out of place.[1]

I find by a letter from the Chancellor (Mr Pendleton) that he views the act of the Convention in its true light, and gives it his unequivocal approbation.[2] His support will have great effect. The accounts we have here of some other respectable characters vary considerably. Much will depend on Mr Henry, and I am glad to find by your letter that his favorable decision on the subject may yet be hoped for.[3] The Newspapers here begin to teem with vehement & virulent calumniations of the proposed Govt. As they are cheifly borrowed from the Pensylvania papers, you see them of course. The reports however from different quarters continue to be rather flattering. With the highest respect & sincerest attachment I remain Dear Sir Yr Obedt & Affecte Servant

Js Madison Jr

ALS, DLC:GW.

1. Madison's points regarding Mason's stand on these issues are dealt with in Rutland and Hobson, *Madison Papers,* 10:196–98, and Kaminski and Saladino, *Documentary History of the Ratification of the Constitution,* 8:76–78.

2. An extract of Edmund Pendleton's letter of 18 Oct. is printed in Rutland and Hobson, *Madison Papers,* 10:188–89. Pendleton had been the chief judge or chancellor of Virginia's high court of chancery since its establishment in 1777.

3. Patrick Henry's letter to GW of 19 Oct. removed all doubt about his opposition to the new Constitution.

From Patrick Henry

Dear sir.   Richmond October 19th 1787

I was honor'd by the Rect of your Favor together with a Copy of the proposed fœderal constitution, a few Days ago, for which I beg you to accept my Thanks.[1] They are also due to you from me as a Citizen, on Account of the great Fatigue necessarily attending the arduous Business of the late Convention.

I have to lament that I cannot bring my Mind to accord with the proposed Constitution. The Concern I feel on this Account, is really greater than I am able to express. perhaps mature Reflection may furnish me Reasons to change my present Sentiments into a conformity with the opinion of those personages for whom I have the highest Reverence. Be that as it may, I beg you will be perswaded of the unalterable Regard & Attachment with which I ever shall be Dear sir your obliged & very humble Servant

                                        P. Henry

ALS, DLC:GW.

1. GW sent Henry a copy of the federal Constitution on 24 September.

Letter not found: from Bushrod Washington, 19 Oct. 1787. On 9 Nov. GW wrote Bushrod Washington: "I received your letters of the 19th & 26th Ult."

Letter not found: from James Wood, 20 Oct. 1787. On 29 Oct. GW wrote Wood about "your letter of the 20th Instt."

Letter not found: from Henry Banks, 21 Oct. 1787. On 22 Nov. GW thanked Banks "For the letter you did me the favor to write to me on the 21st Ult."

Letter not found: from Charles Carter, 21 Oct. 1787. On 14 Dec. GW wrote Carter apologizing for the delay in answering his "favor of the 21st of Octr."

To James Madison

My dear Sir,   Mount Vernon Octr 22d 1787.

When I last wrote to you, I was uninformed of the Sentiments of this State beyond the circle of Alexandria, with respect to the

New Constitution.[1] Since, a letter which I received by the last
Post, dated the 16th, from a member of the Assembly, contains
the following paragraphs.[2]

"I believe such an instance has not happened before, since the
revolution, that there should be a house on the first day of the
Session, and business immediately taken up. This was not only
the case on Monday, but there was a full house; when Mr Pren-
tice was called up to the Chair as Speaker, there being no opposition. Thus, the Session has commenced peaceably.[3]

"It gives me much pleasure to inform you that the sentiments
of the members are infinitely more favourable to the Constitution than the most zealous advocates for it could have expected.
I have not met with one in all my enquiries (and I have made
them with great diligence) opposed to it, except Mr Henry who
I have heard is so, but could only conjecture it, from a conversation with him on the subject. Other members who have also
been active in their enquiries tell me, that they have met with
none opposed to it. It is said however that old Mr Cabell of
Amherst disapproves of it—Mr Nicholas has declared himself a
warm friend to it.[4]

"The transmissory note of Congress was before us to day,
when Mr Henry declared that it transcended our powers to decide on the Constitution; that it must go before a Convention.
As it was insinuated he would aim at preventing this, much pleasure was discovered at the declaration. Thursday week (the
25th) is fixed upon for taking up the question of calling the Convention, and fixing the time of its meeting: In the meantime,
five thousand copies are ordered to be printed, to be dispersed
by the members in their respective Counties for the information
of the People. I cannot forbear mentioning that the Chancellor,
Pendleton, espouses the Constitution so warmly as to declare he
will give it his aid in the Convention, if his health will permit. As
there are few better judges of such subjects, this must be deemed
a fortunate circumstance."[5]

As the above quotations is the sum of my information, I shall
add nothing more in the subject of the proposed government,
at this time.

Mr C. Pinkney is unwilling (I perceive by the enclosures contained in your letter of the 13th)[6] to loose any fame that can be
acquired by the publication of his sentiments. If the discussion

of the navigation of the Mississipi *could* have remained as silent, & glided as gently down the Stream of time for a few years, as the waters do, that are contained within the banks of that river, it would, I confess, have comported more with my ideas of sound policy than any decision the case can obtain at this juncture. With sentiments the most Affecte and friendly I am— Dear Sir Yr most Obedt Servt.

AL, DLC: Madison Papers; LB, DLC:GW.

1. GW wrote on 10 October.

2. This is the missing letter of 16 Oct. from David Stuart, who with George Mason was in Richmond as a delegate to the house from Fairfax County. Daniel Carroll wrote Madison on 28 Oct.: "I have not been in the way of obtaining any intelligence to be depended on, untill last monday [22 Oct.] when I saw General Washington at a meeting of the Potomack Compy. The information from him was pleasing; Docr. Stuart, Representative for Fairfax, writes to him from Richmond, that their was a full House the 1st day; & that he did not find a Member, but what appeard to be in favor of the New Govt., except Patrick Henry, who was reserv'd, but express'd sentiments in favor of recommending a Convention" (Rutland and Hobson, *Madison Papers,* 10:226–27).

3. Joseph Prentis (1754–1809) represented York County in the Virginia house of delegates from 1782 and was speaker from 1786 until January 1788, when he was elected a judge of the General Court.

4. William Cabell, Sr. (1730–1798), represented Amherst County in the convention in 1788 and voted against ratification. George Nicholas (d. 1799) representing Albemarle County voted for ratification.

5. Edmund Pendleton (1721–1803) was made president of the state ratifying convention of 1788 and voted for ratification.

6. Madison's letter is dated 14, not 13, October.

From Jean Le Mayeur

Sir   charleston [S.C.] Octb. 24. 1787

I hope your Excellency by this time has recovered the fatigue of your Great work in the Convention which must afford the Greatest satisfaction when his Excellency hears as I have done for five hundred miles where the people seem so well satisfied of the new forms of Governement—principly in the Expectation to have at their head the *first legislature.*

I hope Lady washington to whom I prefers my profound respect as well as Major and Mrs washington.

I have been here a few days and intend to Continue till the midle of january from whence to st augustine to obtine a passage to havanah (as mentioned in my answer to your Excellencys last favour of the 5th of may)[1] and then to st domingo from where I intend to return in june upon the Continent at Baltimore or Alexendria if it is in my power Col. washington has not been well for some time past.[2] I have the honour to be with the most profound Respect and veneration Your Excellencys Most obdt & most hble serviteur

john Le Mayeur.

ALS, DLC:GW.

    1. In his letter to GW of 23 May 1787, Le Mayeur refers to a letter from GW of 5 May, which is missing.

    2. This is William Washington of Sandy Hill in South Carolina.

From Robert Morris

Dear Sir   Philad[elphi]a Octr 25th 1787

    That you may not think me guilty of Neglect, I acknowledge the receipt of your obliging letter of the 14th Inst. by Post, but that by the Charming Polly is not yet arrived, when it comes to hand I shall have the pleasure of addressing you again.[1] Mr G. Morris went to New York to stay Nine days, he has been gone near five Weeks & I wait his return before I can finally decide whether I can set out for Virginia or Not.[2]

    We rejoiced much to hear of your safe arrival at Home having been made very uneasy by the report of the accident at the Head of Elk[3] If you read our News Papers you see much altercation about the proposed Constitution the oponents are not Numerous altho they fill the News Papers every day.

    Mrs Morris & myself are much obliged by your & Mrs Washingtons good wishes We can truely say they are reciprocal & I am with great Sincerity Dear Sir Your most Obedient humble Servant

Robt Morris

ALS, DLC:GW.

    1. GW wrote to Morris by the *Charming Polly* on 2 Oct.; his letter of 14 Oct. has not been found.

    2. See Gouverneur Morris to GW, 30 October.

    3. The following story appeared in the *Delaware Gazette* (Wilmington) on 26 Sept.: "On Wednesday last, his Excellency General Washington passed through Wilmington, on his return from this city [Philadelphia] to his seat in

Mount Vernon—and on the same day, in crossing the bridge near the Head of Elk, the bridge gave way and his horse fell into the river. His Excellency had alighted in order to walk over the bridge, which fortunate circumstance probably saved a life so dear to his country" (quoted in Kaminski and Saladino, *Documentary History of the Ratification of the Constitution*, 13:243).

Letter not found: from Thomas Smith, 26 Oct. 1787. On 3 Dec. GW wrote Smith: "I have recd your letter of the 26th of Octr."

From Steuben

Sir   [October 26, 1787]

I have lately made a fresh application to Congress for a final settlement of my affairs on the ground of a contract made with that honorable body previous to my joining the American army.[1] The particulars and the evidence of that contract are stated in a printed pamphlet a copy of which Mr. Hamilton informs me he has transmitted to your Excellency.[2] I have been just informed that Congress intend making some inquiry of Your Excellency respecting a matter which they suppose will throw light upon the subject.[3] I am glad of this reference, because though I doubt that it will be in your power to elucidate the question of the contract, I have entire confidence in your justice and favourable sentiments towards me as to any collateral point which may arise in the inquiry.

The truth is my situation is peculiarly grievous. The manner in which the compensations, I have received from the public have been dealt out to me, has been such as to prevent their having been of any use to me beyond a momentary supply. I trust I shall not be necessitated to abandon a country to which I am attached by the strongest ties to return to Europe destitute of resources with no consolation for my services but the right of complaining of the unkindness of those to whom they were rendered. Surely it cannot redound to the Credit of America to drive me to so painful an extremity. I am persuaded Your Excellencys feelings will not approve of my experiencing so ill-deserved a lot. I have the honor to be With the most perfect respect and esteem Yr Excellencys Most Obed & hum servant

Syrett, *Hamilton Papers*, 4:286–87. This was a copy of a draft made by Alexander Hamilton; the letter sent to GW has not been found.

1. For a brief description of Steuben's efforts in 1782 and again in 1785 to secure from Congress what he considered adequate compensation for his voluntary services as a major general in the Continental army beginning in 1777, see GW to Thomas Jefferson, 15 Mar. 1784, n.1. Steuben's eight-page letter to Congress, October 1787, and a copy of his account, 1778–86, are both in DNA:PCC, item 19. See also James Duane to Steuben, 16 Oct. 1787, DNA:PCC, item 19.

2. See Alexander Hamilton to GW, 30 Oct., n.2.

3. See Charles Thomson to GW, 27 October.

Letter not found: from David Stuart, 26 Oct. 1787. On 5 Nov. GW thanked Stuart for his "letters of the 16th and 26th ulto." Stuart's letter of 26 Oct. is quoted at length in GW to James Madison, 5 November.

Letter not found: from Bushrod Washington, 26 Oct. 1787. On 9 Nov. GW wrote Bushrod Washington: "I received your letters of the 19th & 26th Ult."

From Thomas Marshall

Dear General   Frederick County 27th of Octr 1787
    I have brought with me from Kentuckey for you some of the different specias of wild rhye, a few of the Coffee nuts, Buckeye, the seeds of the Papaw-apple, a few acrons of an excellent Specias of the white oak, larger & finer timber than I ever before saw & different from any I have seen elsewhere. I have sent you also some of the natural grass seed of that country it is of a very luxurient growth and as far as I have tried it appears to be excellent for hay, but as I have only cultivated a small spot, sow'd last fall in my garden, I can as yet judge of it with no great certainty: it does not require a wet soil, but the ground it is sow'd in ought to be rich & made fine. Feby will be a good time, & sow it about as thick as Tobo seed. I have also sent you some petrefied shellfish of a specias I never saw but in that country; I came to a layer or stratum of them about 4 feet under the surface of the Earth as I was diging a seller & although many of them are seen in the branches I don't remember to have seen any of them alive. I thought to have sent you some of the seed of the Cucumber tree but could get none as they do not grow in that part of the country where I live; nor can I hear of any such shrub as the tulip-bearing laurel.[1]

Mr Colston has promisd to convey to you the seeds &c., together with this letter[2] which I shall only lengthen by adding that I have the honor to be with the most respectful esteem Dear General Your most obedient humble Servt

T. Marshall

ALS, DLC:GW.

1. Before Thomas Marshall left for Kentucky in the summer of 1785, GW asked him to secure seeds of plants in that region for the botanical garden of Louis XVI at Versailles. See Marshall to GW, 12 May 1785, n.1.

2. Rawleigh Colston was Marshall's brother-in-law.

From Charles Thomson

Sir,   [Philadelphia] Oct. 27, 1787

The enclosed order of the United States in Congress assembled will apologize for the trouble I give in requesting you to send me the copy of a paper enclosed in Mr President Lauren's letter of the 19 feby 1778 and marked "Committee's Conference with Baron Steuben."[1]

The Baron thinks himself entitled to an indemnification for an annuity of about £600 sterling for life which he relinquished upon coming to America.[2] To obtain this he has made application to Congress grounding his claim upon a verbal contract with a committee who conferred with him when he first came to York town. There is no mention of such a contract on the journal nor any trace of it on the files. But in the letter of the 19 feby 1778 which Mr Laurens wrote to you by the Baron there is a paragraph wherein he says that "upon the arrival of this illustrious stranger at York town, Congress ordered a committee consisting of Mr Witherspoon Mr McKean Mr F. L. Lee and Mr Henry to wait upon & confer with him to pay the necessary compliments on his appearance in America and *to learn explicitly his expectations from Congress*" and then proceeds to say "the committee were directed to deliver him the substance of their conference in writing to be transmitted for your excellency's information—& that all he received or knew on this head will be seen in an enclosed paper marked Committee's conference with Baron Steuben to which he begs leave to refer your Excellency."[3] As it is expected that this paper will throw light on the subject and remove all doubts, I have to request the favour of you to send me a copy of it to be communicated to Congress.[4] I embrace the present occasion to assure you that I am with the most sincere esteem & respect Sir Your most obedt & most humble servt.

Copy, DNA:PCC, item 18B. The copy, or draft, is headed "Office of Secretary of Congress."

1. See GW to Thomson, 10 Nov., n.1.

2. See Steuben to GW, 26 Oct., and note 1 of that document, and Hamilton to GW, 30 October.

3. Henry Laurens's letter is in DNA:PCC, item 13.

4. See note 1.

From James Madison

Dear Sir   New York Octr 28 1787.

The mail of yesterday brought me your favor of the 22d instant. The communications from Richmond give me as much pleasure, as they exceed my expectations. As I find by a letter from a member of the Assembly, however, that Col. Mason had not got down, and it appears that Mr Henry is not at bottom a friend,[1] I am not without fears that their combined influence and management may yet create difficulties. There is one consideration which I think ought to have some weight in the case, over and above the intrinsic inducements to embrace the Constitution, and which I have suggested to some of my correspondents. There is at present a very strong probability that nine States at least will pretty speedily concur in establishing it. What will become of the tardy remainder? They must be either left as outcasts from the Society to shift for themselves, or be compelled to come in, or must come in of themselves when they will be allowed no credit for it. Can either of these situations be as eligible as a prompt and manly determination to support the Union, and share its common fortunes?

My last stated pretty fully the information which had arrived here from different quarters, concerning the proposed Constitution. I recollect nothing that is now to be added farther than that the Assembly of Massachusetts now sitting certainly gives it a friendly reception. I inclose a Boston paper by which it appears that Governour Hancock has ushered it to them in as propitious a manner as could have been required.

Mr P.'s Character is as you observe well marked by the publications which I inclosed. His printing the secret paper at this time could have no motive but the appetite for expected praise: for the subject to which it relates has been dormant a considerable time, and seems likely to remain so.[2]

A foreign gentleman of merit, and who besides this general title, brings me a letter which gives him a particular claim, to my civilities, is very anxious to obtain a sketch of the Potowmac and the route from the highest navigable part of it, to the western waters which are to be connected with the potowmac by the portage; together with a sketch of the works which are going on, and a memorandum of the progress made in them.[3] Knowing of no other channel through which I could enable myself to gratify this gentleman, I am seduced into the liberty of resorting to your kindness; and of requesting that if you have such a draught by you, your amanuensis may be permitted to take a *very rough copy* of it for me. In making this request I beseech you Sir to understand that I do it with not more confidence in your goodness than with the sincerest desire that it may be disregarded if it cannot be fulfilled with the most perfect conveniency. With sentiments of the most perfect esteem & the most Affecte regard I remain Dear Sir, your Obedt friend & hble servt

Js Madison Jr

The British Packet has arrived but I do not learn that any news comes by her. Her passage has been a tedious one.

ALS, DLC:GW; copy, in Madison's hand, DLC: Madison Papers.

1. John Dawson, delegate from Spotsylvania County, wrote Madison on 19 Oct.: "I enclose you a paper in which you will find a piece said, with truth I believe, to be written by Colo Mason. He is not yet arriv'd, but is hourly expected. . . . The freeholders of Fairfax have, in the most pointed terms directed Colo Mason to vote for a convention, and have as pointedly assur'd him he shall not be in it" (Rutland and Hobson, *Madison Papers*, 10:198–99). See also GW to Madison, 10 Oct., n.2. The paper that Dawson enclosed may have been the letter from *Cato Uticensis* printed in the *Virginia Independent Chronicle* (Richmond) on 17 October. It has been reprinted in Kaminski and Saladino, *Documentary History of the Ratification of the Constitution*, 8:70–76.

2. "Mr P." is Charles Pinckney. See Madison to GW, 14 Oct., n.1.

3. The "foreign gentleman of merit" has not been identified. Madison wrote to Thomas Jefferson on 20 Dec.: "I subjoin an extract from a letter from Genl. Washington dated Decr. 7th which contains the best information I can give you as to the progress of the works on the Potowmack" (Rutland and Hobson, *Madison Papers*, 10:331–33). The extract was from GW's letter of 7 Dec. written

in answer to Madison's of 28 Oct., and on 20 Dec. Madison thanks GW for the information about the Potomac River Company and tells him "that you will not consider it as an object of any further attention."

To Mathew Carey

Sir, Mount Vernon October 29th 1787

The last post brought me your letter of the 22d[1]—your application to me for the loan of £100 is an evidence of your unacquaintedness with my inability to lend money. To be candid—my expenditures are never behind my income—and this year (occasioned by the severest drought that ever was known in this neighbourhood) instead of selling grain which heretofore has been my principal source of revenue it is not £500 that will purchase enough for the support of my family—after this disclosure of my Situation you will be readily persuaded that inclination to serve without the means of accomplishing it, is of little avail. This however is the fact so far as it respects the point in question.

As you seem anxious that the contents of your letter should not be known I put it in your own power to distroy it by returning it under the same cover with this. I wish success to your Museum and am Sir, yr &c.

G. Washington

LB, DLC:GW.

1. Letter not found. On 4 Sept. in his Philadelphia Cash Accounts, 9 May–22 Sept., printed above, GW records paying Carey nine shillings for his subscription to the second volume, or issue, of Carey's *American Museum* (Philadelphia).

From Gardoqui

New york 29th Ocbre 1787.

Permitt me my dear Sir to intrude upon your rural repose once more with a subjectt that from the moment that I became acquainted with the United States I have exerted myself with unabated zeal to establish a permanent & sincere amity between our two countrys on the principles of mutual interest.

No two nations in the world in my opinion apply so exactly to each other.

On such solid bassis I hoped to have founded a national connexion which wou'd have dayly acquair'd strength from the experience of it's advontages & did not doubt but the objectt of my wishes wou'd have been acomplish'd with facility.

The generous conductt & views of my Royal Master shine highly with the most sincere freindship & had I mett with a consonant temper in all the states, the great work wou'd have long ago been compleated & our Countrys wou'd have been now in the actual enjoyment of the Conforts & adventages of a freindly intercourse. But the oppossition of Virginia express'd by the published instructions of the last Assembly to her Delegates in Congress has perhaps obstructted the conclussion of the negociation.[1]

These instructions I doubt not must have reach'd the Courts of Madrid & London.

By the publick prints from the last of those places it is assur'd that one of their most ablest politicians has been order'd to the former, & I think we must give it for granted that he will indubitaby avail himself of the above mention'd opossition & instructions.

I leave to your superior penetration to judge of what the consequences may be & whether some thing ought not to be done immidiatly, beleiving it from my heart to be highly essencial to the true interest of the United States, before it is too latte.

I cannot refrain from making this candid communication to you convinced that your constant attachment to the publick good will prompt you to take into consideration these truths & that your Knowledge of my conductt will induce you to attribute this confidence to my sincere desire to promote the harmony & interest of the two nations & to the reluctance which I feel in the prospectt of being obliged to abandon an objectt which has so long held the first place in my heart & which I beleive to be essential to the interest & prosspectt of our two Countries.

Give me leave to congratulate you & to express my sincere joy on the happy escape you made in a Bridge in the way home.[2]

May the Allmighty continue preserving you for many years for the good of this country & of mankind in general & permitt me to conclude with my most humble respectts to your worthy Lady & with unfeighned assurances that I have the honor to be with the highest consideration & respectt Dear Sir Your most obedt & very humble servt

James Gardoqui

ALS, DLC:GW.

1. On 29 Nov. 1786, the Virginia house of delegates adopted a series of resolutions declaring that whereas "the right of navigating the Mississippi" was "the bountiful gift of nature to the United States" and any sacrifice of that right would be "a flagrant violation of justice, [and] a direct contravention of the end for which the Federal Government was instituted," Virginia's delegates in Congress would be instructed to oppose any move on the part of Congress to surrender "the free and common Use of the river" by citizens of the United States (*House of Delegates Journal, 1786–1790*).

2. See Robert Morris to GW, 25 Oct., n.3.

To James Wood

Dr Sir, Mount Vernon October 29th 1787

I beg you to accept my thanks for the friendly information contained in your letter of the 20th Instt[1] but from an entire unacquaintedness with business of the land office, since the Alterations which have taken place consequent of the Revolution,[2] I really know not how to avail myself of it. The case you allude to is—on the 2d of April 1752—I surveyed for one Thomas Mullen (under authority of the Proprs Office) a tract of waste land in Frederick County, lying on the timber ridge near great Cacapen head of Smiths run—400 acres Extending So. Wt 320 to 3 hic[kor]ys in a hollow near a drain. No. Wt 200 poles to 3 black Oaks on a ridge No. Et 320 poles to a black Oak and 2 White Oaks on a ridge—So. Et 200 poles to the beginning, containing as above 400 Acres—for making this Survey I received no compensation. indeed at *that* time it was done, the Land was (by others) thougt inadequate to the Fee—and that Mullen was a madman. soon after this Mullen, who was a single man, and I believe without connections, ran away and finding no prospect of getting paid by him I caveated the Land intending if no near[3] or better claiment should appear to obtain a patent in my own name—In this situation I *presume* it lay till I was called from home in the year 1775 afterwards, and till you had the goodness to remind me of the transaction never once occurred to my recollection—If under this statement which I believe is canded and accurate, it shall be thought that my right to the land is preferable or equal to that of any other, I should be glad to Obtn it—if not I shall rest contented[4]—your advice and assistance (if proper) would be esteemed a further mark of your Friendship. With great regard I am Dr Sir, &c.

G. Washington

LB, DLC:GW.

1. The letter from James Wood of Frederick County has not been found.
2. The copyist wrote "Resolution."
3. Howell Lewis, the copyist, wrote "hear."
4. For GW's survey of the Mullin (Mullen) tract, see *Papers, Colonial Series*, 1:31. Mullin showed up and on 8 Nov. 1790 assigned his rights to the land to Michael Capper, whose grant is dated 6 Dec. 1791 (ibid., 31, 35). See also Wood to GW, 8 July 1790.

From Alexander Hamilton

Dr Sir October 30. 1787

I am much obliged to Your Excellency for the explicit manner in which you contradict the insinuations mentioned in my last letter—The only use I shall make of your answer will be to put it into the hands of a few friends.[1]

The constitution proposed has in this state warm friends and warm enemies. The first impressions every where are in its favour; but the artillery of its opponents makes some impression. The event cannot yet be foreseen. The inclosed is the first number of a series of papers to be written in its defence.

I send you also at the request of the Baron De Steuben a printed pamplet containing the grounds of an application lately made to Congress. He tells me there is some referrence to you, the object of which he does not himself seem clearly to understand—But imagines it may be in your power to be of service to him.[2]

There are public considerations that induce me to be somewhat anxious for his success. He is fortified with materials which in Europe could not fail to establish the belief of the contract he alleges—The documents of service he possesses are of a nature to convey an exalted idea of them—The compensations he has received though considerable, if compared with those which have been received by American officers, will according to European ideas be very scanty in application to a *stranger* who is acknowleged to have rendered essential services. Our reputation abroad is not at present too high—To dismiss an old soldier empty and hungry—to seek the bounty of those on whose justice he has no claims & to complain of unkind returns and violated engagements will certainly not tend to raise it. I confess too there is something in my feelings which would incline me in this case to go farther than might be strictly necessary rather than drive a man at the Baron's time of life, who has been a faithful servant, to extremities. And this is unavoidable if he does not succeed in his present attempt.

What he asks would, all calculations made, terminate in this—an allowance of his Five hundred and Eighty guineas a year. He only wishes a recognition of the contract—He knows that until affairs mend no money can be produced. I do not know how far it may be in your power to do him any good; but I shall be mistaken, if the considerations I have mentioned do not appear to Your Excellency to have some weight.[3] I remain with the great Respect and esteem Yr Excellys Obed. serv.

A. Hamilton

ALS, DLC:GW; copy, in Hamilton's hand, DLC: Hamilton Papers.

1. See GW to Hamilton, 18 October.

2. The 32-page undated pamphlet containing a statement of Steuben's claims on the United States is in DNA:PCC, item 19.

3. See Steuben to GW, 26 Oct., Charles Thomson to GW, 27 Oct., and GW to Steuben, to Thomson, and to Hamilton, all 10 November.

From Archibald Johnston

Dear Sir   30th Octr 1787

Some time past I saw your Advertisement forbidding all persons from hunting on your lands without leave first being obtain'd from you[1]—Should esteem it a singular favour if you wou'd grant me the indulgence of hunting from the Tumbling Dam to your Mill, some Ponds in the White Oak Swamp and a small part of your River Shores such as you shall think proper, the strictest attention shall be paid to all orders you shall think proper to give me respecting the same the above favour shall allways be acknowledged[2] by dear Sir Your Obt H. Servt

Archibald Johnston

P.S. My three brothers join in the above request. A.J.

ALS, DLC:GW.

Capt. Archibald Johnston, son of George Johnston (d. 1766) of Belvale, lived on the Colchester Road downstream from Mount Vernon on property adjoining Wilfrid Johnston's.

1. On 10 Aug. 1786 GW placed this notice in the *Virginia Journal, and Alexandria Advertiser:* "THE subscriber does, in explicit terms, forbid every person who has not permission in writing (which is to be shewn to the nearest overseer) from taking wood or stone, from his shore. Under this pretext continual depredation is made on his sheep, hogs, &c. In like manner all persons are forewarned not to hunt or fowl on his land; for besides depriving him of the advantages which are to be derived from these sources, his fences (which are erected at considerable expence) are thrown down, and his pastures made a common.

"It would be painful to prosecute any person for trespasses of this sort; but after this public notice, he is determined to proceed with the utmost rigor against any one, who in violation thereof, shall invade his property. G. WASHINGTON."

2. GW responded from Mount Vernon on the same day in these terms: "Sir, My fixed determination is, that no person whatever shall hunt upon my grounds or warters. To grant leave to one, and refuse another, would not only be drawing a line of discrimination which would be offensive, but would subject me to great inconvenience—for my strict, and positive orders to all my people are—if they hear a Gun fired upon my Land to go immediately in pursuit of it—Permission therefore to any one would keep them either always in pursuit—or make them inattentive to my orders under the supposition of its belonging to a licensed person by which means I should be obtruded upon by others who to my cost I find had other objects in view[.] Besides, as I have not lost my relish for this sport when I can find time to endulge myself in it and Gentlemen who come to the House are pleased with it, it is my wish not to have the game within my Jurisdiction disturbed. For these reasons I beg you will not take my refusal amiss because I would give the same to my brother if he lived off my land. I am Sir Yr Very Hble Servant G. Washington" (LB, DLC:GW).

From Gouverneur Morris

Dear Sir   Philadelphia 30 October 1787

Shortly after your Departure from this Place, I went to my Farm and returned hither last Sunday Evening. Living out of the busy World, I had Nothing to say worth your Attention, or I would earlier have given you the Trouble you now experience. Altho not very inquisitive about political opinions I have not been quite inattentive. The States Eastward of New York appear to be almost unanimous in favor of the new Constitution; for I make no Account of the Dissentients in Rhode Isld. Their Preachers are Advocates for the Adoption, and this Circumstance coinciding with the steady support of the Property and other Abilities of the Country makes the Current set strongly, and I trust, irresistibly that Way. Jersey is so near Unanimity in her favorable Opinion, that we may count with Certainty on something more than Votes should the state of Affairs hereafter require the Application of pointed Arguments. New York, hemmed in between the warm Friends of the Constitution could not easily (unless supported by powerful States) make any important Struggle, even tho her Citizens were unanimous, which is by no Means the case. Parties there are nearly balanced. If the Assent or Dissent of the New York Legislature were to decide on the Fate of America there would still be a chance, tho I believe the Force of Government would preponderate and effect a Rejection. But the Legislature cannot assign to the People any good Reason for not trusting them with a Decision on their own Affairs, and must therefore agree to a Convention—In the Choice of a Convention it is not improbable that the fœderal Party will prove strongest, for Persons of very distinct and opposite Interests have joined on this subject. With Respect to this State I am far from being decided in my Opinion that they will consent. True it is that the City and its neighbourhood are enthusiastic in the Cause: but I dread the cold and sour Temper of the back Counties, and still more the wicked Industry of those who have long habituated themselves to live on the Public, and cannot bear the Idea of being removed from the Power and Profit of State Government, which has been and still is the Means of supporting themselves, their Families and Dependents; And (which perhaps is more grateful) of depressing and humbling their political adversaries. What opinions prevail more Southward I cannot guess. You are in Condition better than any other Person to judge of a great and important Part of that Country.

I have observed that your Name to the new Constitution has

been of infinite Service. Indeed I am convinced that if you had not attended the Convention, and the same Paper had been handed out to the World, it would have met with a colder Reception, with fewer and weaker Advocates, and with more and more strenuous opponents. As it is, should the Idea prevail that you would not accept of the Presidency it would prove fatal in many Parts. Truth is, that your great and decided Superiority leads Men willingly to put you in a Place which will not add to your personal Dignity, nor raise you higher than you already stand: but they would not willingly put any other Person in the same Situation because they feel the Elevation of others as operating (by Comparison) the Degradation of themselves. And however absurd this Idea, you will agree with me that Men must be treated as Men and not as Machines, much less as Philosophers, & least of all Beings as reasonable Creatures; seeing that in Effect they reason not to direct but to excuse their Conduct.

Thus much for the public Opinion on these Subjects, which must not be neglected in a Country where opinion is every thing. I will add my Conviction that of all Men you are best fitted to fill that Office. Your cool steady Temper is *indispensibly necessary* to give a firm and manly Tone to the new Government. To constitute a well poised political Machine is the Task of us common Workmen; but to set it in Motion requires still greater Qualities. When once agoing, it will proceed a long time from the original Impulse. Time gives to primary Institutions the mighty Power of Habit and Custom, the Law both of wise Men and Fools serves as the great Commentator of human Establishments, and like other Commentators as frequently obscures as it explains the Text. No Constitution is the same on Paper and in Life. The Exercise of Authority depends on personal Character; and the Whips and Reins by which an able Character governs unruly steeds will only hurl the unskilful Presumer with more speedy & headlong Violence to the Earth. The Horses once trained may be managed by a Woman or a Child; not so when they first feel the Bit. And indeed among these thirteen Horses now about to be coupled together there are some of every Race and Character. They will listen to your Voice, and submit to your Control; you therefore must I say *must* mount this Seat. That the Result may be as pleasing to you as it will be useful to them I wish but do not expect. You will however on this, as

on other Occasions, feel that interior Satisfaction & Self Approbation which the World cannot give; and you will have in every
possible Event the Applause of those who know you enough to
respect you properly.[1] Indulge ⟨*illegible*⟩ so far as to place in that
Number Dr Genl Yours

Gouv. Morris

ALS, DLC:GW; ADfS, NNC: Gouverneur Morris Papers. Written on the cover:
"Alexandria 29th Octr 1787. The Northern Stage arrived at half past 7.
OClock P.M. Jas. M. McRea."

1. Morris was not the first of GW's correspondents to allude to the likeli-
hood of his being elected president under the new Constitution, but perhaps
he was the first to confront him with an argument for his acceptance.

From Charles Pettit

Sir, Philadelphia 1st Novemr 1787

I had the Honor to receive your Letter of the 14th ult. by Post
some Time before that of the 3d by Capt. Elwood. The latter
arrived but just in Time to get the Patterns on board a Vessel
going round to the Iron Works. The Castings ordered in these
two Letters cannot be expected to be in this Town in less than
two or three weeks & shall be forwarded by the first Opportunity afterwards. The four Backs with side plates formerly ordered are now ready to go on board of Capt. Elwood when he
shall be ready to receive them which may be in a day or two.[1]
They are executed as well as we could get our Workmen to do
them, but with less Elegance than I wished considering the
Crest & Cypher they bear; but they are nevertheless far from
bad. After scrubbing the Faces with a hard Brush, a Coat of black
Lead mixed with Whites of Eggs & a little Sugar & Water will
embellish their Appearance.

Some of the Backs are rather longer than a proportion to the
side Plates; this was unavoidable without the Expences of more
Patterns. It may easily be remedied by inserting so much of the
Back below the level of the Hearth as to bring the Top to the
proper Line with the Side plates. Some little Allowance is also
made in the width of the Plates for occasional swelling by Heat.
The workman who made the Patterns thought this necessary &
that any Vacancy that might happen on this Account between
the Plate & the Wall should be filled up with thin Mortar so as

to form a solid Bed for the Plate. He also recommends a small, tho' very small space to be left between the front Edge of the side Plate and the Marble Facing, lest the former on swelling should urge the latter out of Place. With perfect Respect & Esteem, I am, Sir Your most obedient & most hume Servant

Chas Pettit

ALS, DLC:GW.

1. For the shipping and the charges for the firebacks that GW ordered from Pettit in the summer, see Pettit to GW, 6 Nov., and note 1 of that document; see also GW to George Augustine Washington, 3 June 1787, n.3. The additional plates that GW ordered on 3 and 14 Oct. are referred to in Pettit's letter of 6 Nov. 1787 and again on 22 April 1788 when Pettit wrote that Clement Biddle was forwarding them to GW.

To Arthur Young

Sir   Mount Vernon Novr 1st 1787.

Your favor of the 1st of Feby came to hand about the middle of May last. An absence of more than four months from home, will be the best apology I can make for my silence 'till this time.

The Grain, Grass-seeds, Ploughs &ca arrived at the sametime agreeable to the list; but some of the former were injured (as will always be the case) by being put into the hold of the Vessel; however, upon the whole they were in much better order than those things are generally found to be, when brought across the Atlantic.

I am at a loss, Sir, how to express the sense which I have of your particular attention to my commissions; and the very obliging manner in which you offer me your Services in any matters relating to Agriculture, that I may have to transact in England. If my warmest thanks will in any measure compensate for these favors, I must beg you to accept of them. I shall always be exceedingly happy to hear from you, and shall very readily & chearfully give you any information relative to the state of Agriculture in this Country, that I am able.

I did myself the honor to hand the set of Annals to the Agriculture Society in Philadelphia, which you sent to that body, through me. The President wrote a letter to you expressive of the sense they entertained of the favor which you did them; and mentioned therein the effects of some experiments which had been made with Plaster of Paris, as a manure;[1] I intended to have given you an acct of it my self, as I find the subject is touched upon in your Annals, but this letter has precluded the necessity of it.[2]

The 5th volume of the Annals wch was committed to the care of Mr Athawes for me, did not come to hand till some time after I had received the 6th.[3]

The quantity of Sainfoin which you sent me was fully sufficient to answer my purpose; I have sown part of it, but find that it comes up very thin, which is likewise the case with the Winter Wheat, & some other Seeds which I have sown.

I have a high opinion of Beans as a preparation for wheat, and shall enter as largely upon the cultivation of them next year, as the quantity of seed I can procure, will admit.

I am very glad that you did not engage a ploughman for me at the high wages which you mention, for I agree with you, that that single circumstance, exclusive of the others which you enumerate, is sufficiently objectionable. I have tried the Ploughs which you sent me and find that they answer the description which you gave me of them; this is contrary to the opinion of almost every one who saw them before they were used, for it was thought their great weight would be an insuperable objection to their being drawn by two Horses.

I am now preparing materials to build a Barn precisely agreeable to your plan, which I think an excellent one.

Before I undertake to give the information you request respecting the arrangements of farms in this neighbourhood &ca I must observe that there is, perhaps, scarcely any part of America where farming has been less attended to than in this State. The cultivation of Tobacco has been almost the sole object with men of landed property, and consequently a regular course of Crops have never been in view. The general custom has been, first to raise a Crop of Indian Corn (maize), which, according to the mode of cultivation, is a good preparation for wheat; then a crop of wheat, after which the ground is respited (except from weeds, & every trash that can contribute to its foulness) for about eighteen months; and so on, alternately, with out any dressing; till the land is exhausted; when it is turned out without being sown with grass seeds, or any method taken to restore it; and another piece is ruined in the same manner. No more cattle is raised than can be supported by low land meadows, swamps, &ca; and the tops & blades of Indian Corn; as very few persons have attended to sowing grasses, & connecting cattle with their Crops. The Indian corn is the chief support of the labourers & horses. Our lands, as I mentioned in my first letter to you, were originally very good; but use, & abuse, have made them quite otherwise. The above is the mode of cultivation wch has been generally pursued here, but the System of husbandry which has been found so beneficial in England, and which must be greatly promoted by your valuable Annals, is now gaining ground; There are several (among which I may class myself) who are endeavouring to get into your regular & systematic course of cropping as fast as the nature of the business will admit; so that I hope in the course of a few years, we shall make a more respectable figure as farmers than we have hitherto done.

I will, agreeable to your desire, give you the prices of our products as nearly as I am able, but you will readily conceive from the foregoing acct, that they cannot be given with any precision. Wheat for the four last years will average about 4/ sterlg pr Bushl of 8 Gallns—Rye abt 2/4—Oats 1/6—Beans, Pease &ca have not been sold in any quantities. Barley is not made here, from a prevailing opinion that the climate is not adapted to it, I, however, in opposition to prejudice, sowed about 50 Bushls last Spring & found that it yielded a proportionate quantity with any other kind of grain which I sowed; I might add more. Cows may be bought at abt £3 Sterlg per head—Cattle for the slaughter vary from 2¼ to 4½ Sterlg pr lb.—the former being the currt price in summer, the latter in the winter or Spring. Sheep @ 12/ Sterg pr head, and wool at abt 1/ Sterlg pr lb. I am not able to give you the price of labour as the land is cultivated here wholly by Slaves, and the price of labour in the Towns is fluctuating, & governed altogether by circumstances.

Give me leave to repeat my thanks for your attention to me, and your polite offer to execute any business relating to husbandry, which I may have in England; and to assure you that I shall not fail to apply to you for whatever I may have occasion for in that line. I am—Sir With very great esteem Yr most Obedt Hble Servt

Go: Washington

P.S. I observe in the 6th Volume of your Annals, there is a plate & description of Mr Winlaws Mill for seperating the grain from the heads of Corn. Its utility or inutility has, undoubtedly, been reduced to a certainty before this time; if it possesses all the properties & advantages mentioned in the description, & you can, from your own knowledge, or such information as you *entirely* rely on, recommend it as a useful machine, where labourers are scarce, I should be much obliged to you to procure one for me (to be paid for, & forwarded by Mr Welch[)], provided it is so simple in its construction as to be worked by ignorant persens without danger of being spoiled (for such only will manage it here) & the price of it, does not exceed £15 as mentioned in the Annals, or thereabouts.[4]

ALS, PPRF; LB, DLC:GW.

1. See GW to Samuel Powel, 30 June 1787, and note 2 of that document.

2. GW "extracted from H. Wynkoop Esqr. Letter to the Phila. Agricultural Society dated 13th Aug. 1787" a one-page account of the good effects Wynkoop had discovered in spreading in March "8 bushels of the Plaister of Paris upon 2½ acres of Wheat stubble ground" (DLC:GW).

3. See Young to GW, 7 Jan. 1786, n.2.

4. Young wrote GW on 1 July 1788 that the accounts he had received of "the merit of Winlaws threshing machine" were "too vague to be satisfactory." In 1790 GW witnessed a demonstration of the Winlaw thresher at Baron von Poellnitz's farm on Manhattan Island. He described the use of the machine and at that time concluded that "it appears to be an easier, more expeditious and much cleaner way of getting out Grain than by the usual mode of threshing; and vastly to be preferred to treading . . ." (*Diaries*, 6:12). The article on the thresher, written by Winlaw himself and entitled "A Description of William Winlaw's Mill, for Separating the Grain from the Corn, in Place of Threshing," was printed in Young's *Annals of Agriculture*, 6(1786), 152–55.

From William Deakins, Jr.

Sir   Geo:Town [Md.] Novr 2d 1787

The bearer Peter felix Mauger, has been Informed that a Horse he has is an Exact Match for one of your's, he has not yet paid the Amount of his Bond to Mrs Kirk, but is now Anxious to do it, if he can make Sale of his Horse,[1] I beleive he finds it difficult to raise the Cash, I have pressed him hard to get this debt paid—& I hope he will soon Accomplish it—I am Very Respectfully Your Obt Servt

Will. Deakins Junr

ALS, DLC:GW.

1. Mrs. Kirk was the widow of James Kirk, a merchant in Alexandria whose house was across the river in Maryland. See GW to Bridget Kirk, 20 Feb. 1787, and note 1 of that document. Peter Felix Mauger in June 1794 was a member of the Independent Volunteer Company of Infantry formed in Dumfries.

From Henry Knox

My dear Sir   New-York 2 November 1787
    The bearer the Marquis de Chappedelaine has been made known to me by my old friend Colo. Mauduit duplessi. The Marquis who is an officer in the service of his most christian Majesty thinks that he should have come to America to little purpose were he to depart without having seen your Excellency, I therefore take the liberty of introducing him to your attention.[1] I am with the most perfect respect my dear Sir Your Most obedient humble Servant

                                                        H. Knox

ALS, DLC:GW.

1. Chappedelaine and several men from Alexandria were among those who dined with GW at Mount Vernon on 13 Feb. 1788. For the possible identity of Chappedelaine, see the editors' note, *Diaries,* 5:276.

To George Mason and David Stuart

Gentn   Mount Vernon Novr 4th 1787.
    In consequence of a resolution which passed at the last meeting of the Potomk company, and in behalf of the Directors, I transmit the enclosed Petition to you, for the consideration of your Honble House.
    The Petition is short. We therefore rely on you, if the sentiment shall meet your approbation, for argument in support of it; begging at the sametime (as the *sole* end is to obtain a more summary mode of recovering the dividends) that you would make such alterations (keeping the object in view) as will entitle it to a favourable reception.
    It is, I believe, almost needless to add, that unless some relief is afforded by the Assembly in this instance, that the work will soon stop. The delinquencies are great, & the legal process to

enforce payment so slow, that it seems *almost* endless and un-availing to attempt it by the mode prescribed by the Act of incor-poration. Under these circumstances the *willing* members are discouraged; and too good a pretext is afforded to a third class, who are neither punctual in their payments, nor yet *very great* delinquents, to with-hold the dividends which have already been required—and to oppose fresh calls, till the old arrearages are paid up. The consequences of all this is easily to be foreseen, if no redress can be had from the quarter it is sollicited.[1]

Whatever may be the fate of the Petition, I do, in behalf of the board pray, that you would give me the earliest advice of it; be-cause a similar application must be made (but at present it is suspended) to the Assembly of Maryland, when I shall have heard from you on this subject, that the Acts may be in unison.[2] With very great esteem & regard I am—Gentn Yr Most Obedt Servt

Go: Washington

ALS, PHi: Dreer Collection; LB, DLC:GW.

1. The president and directors of the Potomac River Company met in Alex-andria on 1 Nov. and adopted the petition that GW was sending to the Fairfax County delegates in the Virginia general assembly. GW enclosed this letter addressed to the delegates Mason and Stuart along with a copy of the petition in a letter to Stuart on 5 November. On 17 Nov., "A petition of the President and Directors of the Potomac River Company, was presented to the House and read; praying that an act may pass, enabling them to recover by motion in the courts of the counties where the proprietors respectively reside, such sum or sums of money as are now in arrear, or hereafter may become due from the respective proprietors of shares in the said company." This petition and a petition of the James River Company "to the same effect" were simulta-neously referred to the house's committee of proposition and grievances (*House of Delegates Journal, 1786–1790*). The committee reported its approval of the petitions on 23 Nov. and was ordered by the house to bring in an appro-priate bill. On 3 Dec. the senate reported it had passed "the bill 'giving a more speedy remedy against delinquent subscribers to the Potomac and James River Companies'" (ibid.). The act provided that the directors of the company could secure payment from subscribers by order of the General Court rather than relying on the individual county courts. No copy of the petition itself has been found, but for the text of the act, see 12 Hening 508–9.

2. On 9 Dec. GW sent a copy of the act of the Virginia assembly to the two Maryland directors of the Potomac River Company, Thomas Johnson and Thomas Sim Lee. Johnson wrote GW on 11 Dec. that the copy of the Virginia act arrived in the nick of time with the Maryland assembly scheduled to ad-journ on 15 December. Johnson had received leave from the Maryland house

to bring in an act with the same title as the Virginia act, "An act giving a more speedy remedy against delinquent subscribers to the Potowmack and James river companies," but he would provide in his bill for the directors of the Potomac Company to choose in Maryland between the general and county courts in its suits against delinquent investors. See Thomas Johnson to GW, 11 December.

To Noah Webster

Sir,   Mount Vernon 4th Novr 1787.

I have received your letter of the 17th ulto, together with your remarks on the proposed Constitution;[1] for which you will please to accept my best acknowledgments—and the assurance of being Sir

AL[S], NN: Washington Collection.

1. Letter not found. Webster published in Philadelphia on 17 Oct. his 55-page pamphlet entitled *An Examination into the Leading Principles of the Federal Constitution Proposed by the Late Convention Held at Philadelphia. With Answers to the Principal Objections That Have Been Raised against the System.*

To Thomas Digges

Revd Sir,   Mount Vernon Novr 5th 1787.

If this letter should be put into your hands, it will be delivered by Mr Powell a Gentleman of character from Philadelphia; who with his Lady are returning from a visit to Mrs Byrd (Sister to Mrs Powell) in this State.[1]

As I am sure it will afford pleasure to Mrs Digges and yourself to shew them civility, I will make no apology for the liberty I take in introducing them to your acquaintance but with respectful compliments to that Lady, in which Mrs Washington's are united, beg leave to assure you of the respect and regard with which I have the honr to be Revd Sir, Yr Most Obedt Hble Ser.

                                                        Go: Washington

ALS, ViMtV. GW addresses the letter to "The Revd Mr Digges Mellwood Honored by Mr Powell."

After the death of his brother Ignatius Digges in 1785, the Rev. Thomas Digges, a Roman Catholic priest, continued to live at Melwood in Prince Georges County, Md., with his brother's widow, Mary Carroll Digges (d. 1825).

1. Samuel and Elizabeth Willing Powel arrived at Mount Vernon on Sunday

evening, 4 Nov., and on the following Tuesday crossed "the river to Mr. Digges a little after Sunrise" (*Diaries*, 5:211–12). Mary Willing Byrd was the widow of William Byrd III. Powel wrote to GW from Philadelphia on 13 November.

To James Madison

My dear Sir,   Mount Vernon Novr 5th 1787.

Your favor of the 18th Ulto came duly to hand. As no subject is more interesting, and seems so much to engross the attention of every one as the proposed Constitution, I shall, (tho' it is probable your communications from Richmond are regular and full with respect to this, and other matters, which employ the consideration of the Assembly) give you the extract of a letter from Doctr Stuart, which follows—

"Yesterday (the 26th[1] of Octr) according to appointment, the calling of a Convention of the people was discussed. Though no one doubted a pretty general unanimity on this question ultimately, yet, it was feared from the avowed opposition of Mr Henry and Mr Harrison, that an attempt would be made, to do it in a manner that would convey to the people an unfavourable impression of the opinion of the House, with respect to the Constitution: And this was accordingly attempted. It was however soon baffled. The motion was to this effect; that a Convention should be called to adopt—reject—or amend—the proposed Constitution. As this conveyed an idea that the House conceived an amendment necessary, it was rejected as improper. It now stands recommended to them, on (I think) unexceptionable ground, for 'their full and free consideration.' My collegue[2] arrived here on the evening before this question was taken up: I am apt to think that the opponants to the Constitution were much disappointed in their expectations of support from him, as he not only declared himself in the fullest manner for a Convention, but also, that notwithstanding his objections, so federal was he, that he would adopt it, if nothing better could be obtained. The time at which the Convention is to meet, is fixed to the first of June next. The variety of sentiments on this subject was almost infinite; neither friends or foes agreeing in any one period. There is to be no exclusion of persons on acct of their Offices.

["]Notwithstanding this decision, the accounts of the prevailing sentiments without, especially on James River and Westwardly, are various; nothing decisive, I believe, can be drawn. As far as I can form an opinion however, from different persons, it should seem as if Men judged of others, by their own affection, or disaffection to the proposed government. In the Northern Neck the sentiment I believe, is very generally for it. I think it will be found such thro the State.["]

The Doctor further adds—"The subject of British debts was taken up the other day when Mr Henry, reflected in a very warm declamatory manner, on the circular letter of Congress, on that subject.[3] It is a great and important matter and I hope will be determined as it should be notwithstanding his opposition."

So far as the sentiments of Maryland, with respect to the proposed Constitution, have come to my knowledge, they are strongly in favor of it; but as this is the day on which the Assembly of that State *ought* to meet, I will say nothing in anticipation of the opinion of it. Mr Carroll of Carrollton, and Mr Thos Johnson, are declared friends to it. With sincere regard and Affecte. I am—My dear Sir Yr sincere frd & Obedt Ser.

Go: Washington

ALS, NN: Emmet Collection.

1. This should be 25*th*; the actions described here by David Stuart took place on 25, not 26, October. Furthermore, in his letter to Stuart of 5 Nov., GW refers to Stuart's letter of 26 October. Stuart's letter of 26 Oct. has not been found.

2. James Madison drew an asterisk here and wrote, at the bottom of the letter, "Col: Mason."

3. The draft of the letter was presented to Congress and agreed to on 13 April (*JCC*, 32:177). A broadside copy is in DNA:PCC, item 49.

To John Francis Mercer

Sir,   Mount Vernon November 5th 1787.

Presuming that it may have been from the want of your knowing of a safe conveyance that I am not furnished with the sum promised me by you at Philadelphia, I shall be glad to know by return of the Post when I may send for it.

Had you been so good as [to] have favoured me with it by Genl Peckney or Mr Houston who stopped at annapolis and took this in their way to the Southward—or by any of the many opportunities to Alexa. it would have saved me the expence of a special messenger—the cost of which will, it is proba[b]le, sink the Interest of the sum which shall be received if not larger than was promised, but this the exigency of my calls will oblige me to submit to.[1] I am &c.

G. Washington

LB, DLC:GW.

1. Mercer seems to have been up to his usual tricks with regard to the debt of his father's estate to GW. See particularly GW to Mercer, 12 Aug. 1786, n. 3. Charles Cotesworth Pinckney and his wife spent the night of 11 Oct. at Mount Vernon en route to South Carolina from Philadelphia (*Diaries*, 5:193). William Houstoun and his future wife, Mary Bayard, stopped on 18 Oct. on their way to Savannah (ibid., 204).

To David Stuart

Dear Sir,   Mount Vernon Novr 5th 1787.

I thank you for the communications in your letters of the 16th and 26th ulto both of which came safe.[1] It gives me pleasure to hear that the Assembly has sent the Constitution to a Convention by an unanimous vote, unstamped with marks of disapprobation. If Mr Charles Lee however, has been able to form a just opinion of the sentiments of the Country with respect to it; it is, that the major voice is opposed to it—particularly in the Southern & Western parts of the State. Is this your opinion, from what you have seen—heard—and understood?

Maryland, tho' the Assembly has not yet met (from which source any thing can have been drawn) is, we are told, exceedingly well disposed to the adoption of it. Nay further, that Mr Chase is become a convert to it. The accts from the States Northward & Eastward speak the same language, though the papers team with declamation against it, by a few—A paper in favor of it, written as I am informed by, or under the auspices of Mr Wilson, in numbers, I here with send you.[2]

With respect to the payment of British debts, I would fain hope (lett the eloquence or abilities of any man, or set of men in opposition be they what they may) that the good sense of this Country will never suffer a violation of a public treaty, nor pass

Acts of injustice to Individuals. Honesty in States, as well as in Individuals, will ever be found the soundest policy.

We have nothing new in this quarter. The Constitution which is submitted seems to have absorbed all lesser matters. Mrs Stuart (who had got very well) and your two little girls went from this on tuesday last, for Chotank, under the escort of your brother; and the wind being high, kept the Potomack on their left to ensure their journey.[3]

I must engage, *absolutely*, Six hundred barrels of Corn. Less, I am sure will not carry me through the year. Had I the money, or was I certain of getting it in time (but this is not to be depended upon) I might, as I am informed through different channels, engage my quantity on very moderate terms on the Eastern shore of Maryland. But as I dare leave nothing to chance I must take it from Mr Henly. The price, as it is ready money to me, will, I expect, be proportioned thereto. It will not be safe to remove the Corn till after January, as it does not get sufficiently dry to lye in bulk sooner. The last I had from York river got damaged in spite of every exertion in my power to save it. And I must entreat as I shall give Mr Henly timely notice of my sending, that it may be beat out on plank floors, and in a dry house; otherwise it will contract dampness which will render its preservation precarious, even at that Season. I beg also that he may be clear and ⟨decide⟩ with respect to his furnishing me with ⟨the⟩ quantity I want—viz. Six hundred Barrels, for I must meet with no disappointment ⟨of⟩ what is engaged.[4]

Herewith is a letter jointly to ⟨Colo.⟩ Mason & yourself, on the business of the ⟨Po⟩tk Company.[5] With great esteem & sincere r⟨eg⟩d I am—Dear Sir Yr Most Obedt & Affecte Servt

Go: Washington

ALS, ViU; LB, DLC:GW.

1. Neither of these letters has been found, but GW quotes both at length: the one dated 16 Oct. in his letter to Madison of 22 Oct., the one dated 26 Oct. in his letter to Madison of 5 November.

2. GW on 17 Oct. had already sent to Stuart James Wilson's speech of 6 Oct. defending the Constitution. What he now was sending probably was "An American Citizen," written by Tench Coxe at the behest of James Wilson and others, originally published as a broadside and, beginning on 24 Oct., reprinted in the Philadelphia newspapers and eventually throughout the country. For the text of the piece, see Kaminski and Saladino, *Documentary History of the Ratification of the Constitution*, 13:431–37.

3. Mrs. Stuart left Mount Vernon with her two youngest children on the morning of 30 Oct. accompanied by her brother-in-law William Stuart (b. 1761). David Stuart's father, the Rev. William Stuart (1723–1798), lived at Cedar Grove in the Chotank area of King George County. The Stuarts were pursuing their journey all the way through Virginia instead of taking the easier route across the Potomac to Maryland and crossing the Potomac again at Hooe's ferry to King George County, Virginia.

4. David Henley, the manager of the Custis plantations on the York River, did not disappoint GW, for on 4 June 1788 GW recorded in Ledger B, 272, receiving 600 barrels of corn at 15 shillings a barrel. See also GW to William Thompson, 12 Jan. 1788, and notes 1 and 3 of that document. The material in mutilated parts of the manuscript is taken from the letter-book copy and inserted in angle brackets.

5. See GW to George Mason and David Stuart, 4 November.

From George Mason

Dear Sir   Richmond Novemr 6th 1787.

On Saturday last, in a Committee of the whole House upon the State of the Commonwealth, to whom was referred sundry Petitions, some praying for an Emission of Paper Money, & others for making Property, at an appraised value, a Tender in Discharge of Debts, I moved & carryed the Resolutions of which I inclose a Copy.[1] During the Discussion of the Subject, after treating the Petitions as founded upon Fraud & Knavery, I called upon any of the Members of the House, who were Advocates for such Measures, if any such there were, to come boldly forward, & explain their real Motives; but they declined entering into the Debate, & the Resolutions passed unanimously—I hope they have given this iniquitous Measure a mortal Stab, & that we shall not again be troubled with it.

A Resolution this Day passed for an absolute P[r]ohibition of all imported Spirits, with some others, in my Opinion almost equally impolitic, & calculated to subject the Eastern Part of the State to the arbitrary Impositions of the western: the Prohibition of the single Article of Rum wou'd cut off a nett Revenue of eleven thousand pounds ℔ annum. When the Bill is brought in I think they will find such insuperable Difficultys in the Mode of carrying it into Execution, as will oblige them to abandon the Project.[2]

I take the Liberty of enclosing a Copy of the Resolutions upon the proposed federal Government; by which it will appear that the Assembly have given time for full Examination & Discussion of the Subject, and have avoided giving any Opinion of their own upon the Subject.[3]

I beg to be presented to Your Lady & Family; and am, with the greatest Respect & Regard, dear Sir Your affecte & obdt Servt

G. Mason

P.S. A Plan is before the House for a three Years Installment of all Debts; tho' in my Opinion very exceptionable, it is better than the Plans of that kind heretofore proposed, & I believe will be adopted, in Spight of every Opposition that can be made to it, I shall therefore, instead of pointing the little Opposition I can make, against the whole, endeavour to change the plan, by making the Consent of the Creditor necessary, & the Instalments voluntary, & in such Cases giving the Force of Judgements to the Instalment-Bonds.[4]

ALS, DLC:GW.

1. Mason's enclosed Resolutions Condemning the Use of Paper Money, 3 Nov. 1787, is printed in Rutland, *Mason Papers*, 3:1008–9.

2. Instead of prohibiting the importing of spirits, the Virginia legislature imposed a heavy tax on wine, porter, ale, beer, and imported rum (12 Hening 412–32). For Mason's description of the failed bill, see his letter to GW of 27 November.

3. After deciding that the proposed constitution should "be submitted to a Convention of the people for their full and free investigation and discussion," the house of delegates on 25 Oct. provided for the election of delegates in March and for their meeting in convention at the state house in Richmond on the fourth Monday in May, later changed to 1 June (*House of Delegates Journal, 1786–1790*). Mason enclosed a printed copy of these resolutions of 25 October. See also The General Assembly Calls a State Convention 25–31 October in Kaminski and Saladino, *Documentary History of the Ratification of the Constitution*, 8:110–20.

4. The legislature rejected any installment plan for the collection of debts, but it passed "An act directing the mode of proceeding under certain executions," which gave debtors additional protection (12 Hening 457–67).

From Charles Pettit

Sir   Philadelphia 6th Novr 1787

I have the Honor to inclose herewith an Invoice & Bill of Lading for 4 Chimney Backs & 8 side Plates or Jambs to correspond therewith, on board of the Sloop Charming Polly, Capt. Elwood pursuant to your Excellency's Order. The Charges for Patterns are the Sums actually paid to the Workmen who made them in this Town. The Carriage to the Works & the alterations made there to accomodate them to the different Sizes successively, are not charged.[1] The Plates since ordered are not yet come to Hand, but shall be forwarded by the first Opportunity after they arrive.[2]

Col. Biddle has been so obliging as to offer, on Behalf of your Excellency, to pay for these Articles & to take the Trouble of forwarding them; which offer I declined accepting, not knowing how far it might be agreeable to your Arrangements. If, however, such mode of Payment should be as much or more convenient to you than another, it will be at least equally so to me. With perfect Respect, I have the Honor to be Your Excellency's most obedt Servant

Chas Pettit

The Captain has a Certificate of the Plates being American Manufacture, to guard against Difficulties at the Custom House.

ALS, DLC:GW.

1. See Pettit to GW, 1 November. Pettit's "Invoice of 4 Setts of Cast Iron Backs & Jambs ship'd by Charles & Andrew Pettit on Board the Sloop charming Polly John Ellwood Ju[nio]r Master bound for Virginia" was dated 6 Nov. and sent from Philadelphia (DLC:GW). The charge for four cast-iron backs and eight jambs was £15.5.7 with the additional charges of £1 for "making a Sett of Patterns," 0.2.0 for "Porterage to the Sloop," and £1.17.6 for "the Carvers Bill for Crest & Cypher," bringing the total to £18.5.1. GW wrote Pettit from Mount Vernon on 3 Dec.: "Sir, I have received your letter of the 6 Ulto— the Backs and Jambs mentioned in it arrived safe. I have requested Colo. Biddle to pay you the amount of your account sent to me which he will undoubtedly comply with. I am Sir, Yr most Obedt Hble Servant G. Washington" (LB, DLC:GW). GW's letter to Clement Biddle in which he instructed him to pay Pettit is also dated 3 December.

2. See Pettit to GW, 1 Nov., n.1.

From Battaile Muse

Sir, Alexandria Novr 7th 1787

My being detain'd two days Longer at Home on acct of two Trickey Tenants Ocations my business To Prevent my Seeing you as I intended[1]—I am oblige to Leave Alexandria on Satterday next in order to be ready For Loudoun Court. I doubt not but that you always want money, if you Can make it Convenient to Send to Mr A. Waleses on Friday Evening—I will Endeavour to raise Thirty Pounds—your accts are now in my Debt Twenty odd pounds—Your Tenants in Genl are not much in arrears unless the runaways—From them nothing Can be Expected—Mrs Lemert and Henry Shover is Considerable in Debt, and I am unneasy about it, I do not want any blame or charge against me. They are Poor and I beleave never will be Richer—I know its to your Interest to distress them I do not Like to do it without orders, as It's Very distressing to me to Breake them up, altho I know it must be the case if they Are made Ever to Pay.[2] Many of the accts are Still in Confusion, I expect by next Spring (at which Time I Shall make return) the accts will be Known, altho Impossable under the Scarcity of Produce as well money, and worse than all, the Execution of our Laws, to Collect the full amount; I Shall Collect as Fare as I can; and advize the Tenants to Comply with the Covenants of their Leases—as but Little regard is Paid to them and indeed any other Obligation at this Time in this Country.

My Servant will deliver a mare on acct of Majr Geo. Washington whome I expect will be at Mountvernon Thursday the 8th Instant.

My Servant has a Horse I obtaind by Law From one Bradwell who run away, to Prevent Imposition by the Sheriff I Priced this Horse among others things at £4.10.0 if you chuos to Take the Horse I will Contrive Him after my return Home to any Person you will apoint in Alexandria, if not I Shall Keep Him, altho I am not in much need—but money Can not be had at this Time for Horses—He will make a good Horse to go of arrents as a Drudge or for a Small Boy to ride the major mentiond that He would answer for Master Custis to ride[3]—their is some Poor Lots in Fauquier that I want Leases for to Fix the Tenants on a Certainty—to Prevent any Misunderstanding Between Land Lord & Tenant—Some few Lots will not bear the Improvements I can Scarcely get a Tenant at any rate to Live on them—if you chews to Send me Six Leases Sign'd I will Promise to do for you as my Self in Executing them—under my Present Sittuation I

Expect you will Excuse my not Visiting you and Look over any Imperfectness in this Scrawl as I write in a hurry—I am Sir your Obedient Humble Servant

Battaile M⟨use⟩

N.B. I can Lodge the Horse some Time at Mr Andrew Wales if you chews to Take him.

ALS, DLC:GW.
    1. Muse referred to his intended visit in his letter of 15 October.
    2. See List of Tenants, 18 Sept. 1785, nn.12, 19. See also GW's reply of 8 Nov. 1787.
    3. Under the date of 8 Nov. in GW's account with Muse, GW entered £4.10 for "a Horse sent to me" (Ledger B, 213). Jessie Bradwell (Breadwell) was a tenant in Fauquier County. Battaile Muse's account book details efforts by Muse from 1786 to 1788 to force some sort of payment from Bradwell.

To Battaile Muse

Sir: Mount Vernon, November 8, 1787.
    Your letter of yesterday was handed me by your Servant—I shall agreeable to your advice, Send to Mr Waless on Friday evening for the thirty pounds.
    I do not wish to have Lemert & Shover so far distressed as to break them up, but I should think they might find some method of paying a part, at least, of what they owe, or of securing the debt to me.
    If the Tenants do not comply with Covenants of their Leases, they cannot expect that I shall sit quietly under it, for the sole motive of leasing the land at the low rents which they give, was in expectation of having such improvements made thereon as are mentioned in the leases, if that is not done a great end for which they were leased are defeated.
    I send, agreeable to your desire, six leases signed, I hope you will be cautious in filling them up.
    I am sorry to find that there is any difficulty on procuring tenants for any of my Lots—Mr Bushrod Washington, informed me that he had leased out his land at £17 per hundred & could have disposed of a million of acres at that rate if he had them.[1]
I am Sir Your Obedt Hble Servt

G. Washington

Toner Transcript, DLC:GW; ALS was advertised in Thomas Birch's catalog 683, item 16, April 1892.

1. Bushrod Washington visited Mount Vernon in early October, and thereafter he wrote three letters to GW, all of which are missing (*Diaries*, 5:191, 192; GW to Bushrod Washington, 9 November).

Report of the Potomac Company Directors

Alexandria Novr 8th 1787

The President & Directors of the Potowmack Company beg leave to report that they have call'd for one Dividend of six ℔ Cent since their Communication of August 7th 1786, of which a small part only, has been received, & there are still considerable Ballances due of the sums formerly call'd for, the particulars of which being too tedious for this report, will appear by reference to the Books of the Treasurer.

The several Expenditures have appear'd by the Accots this day laid before you by which a Ballance of 64.7.0 is due to the treasurer.

For the Several orders in conducting the Business entrusted to our care we beg leave to refer you to the Books of the Secretary—in consequence of which the Work has been carried on at the Great falls where the Canal is extended down to the place at which the Locks must begin, the whole of which Canal is nearly Compleated—One of the most difficult passes, also, between the Great Falls & Seneca is open'd & a good Tow path made. The River continued high throughout the summer & Fall of 1786 which greatly retarded the Operations intended[.] A part of the Hands were sent to Seneca in July last, & hopes were entertain'd from the report of Mr Smith, that the River would be pass'd by loaded Boats in the approaching Spring but the bad State of Health experienced by the people there will prevent its being effected as soon as was reasonably Supposed.

At Shenandoah the work has been carried on at the most difficult & Expensive part, which promises the Success wished for, although in appearance so much has not been done as if the Hands had been employed on the more easy parts.

It appears to us by the Books of the Treasury which you have had before you, that the Sums paid into his hands since our last report amount to Four Thousand Seven Hundred Eighty Nine Pounds Sixteen Shillings & four pence Sterling which added to the former sum received makes Ten Thousand Seven Hundred & twenty Nine Pounds Sixteen Shillings & four pence Sterling in which are to be consider'd the Servants, Utensils &Ca on hand belonging to the Company agreeable to the Lists herewith Submitted to you.[1] In behalf of the Directors

Go: Washington P.

DS, NIC.

1. GW and the directors of the Potomac River Company met in Alexandria on 8 Nov. (*Diaries,* 5:213).

From Gardoqui

My dear Sir   New York 9th Novre 1787.

Under the 29th Octre I did myself the honor to write you candidly upon a subjectt to which beg your reference.[1]

Since that time nothing new has occurr'd upon it, but haveing the wish'd for oportunity to renew my respectts by my good freind Colln. H. Lee, I gladly embrace it requesting you wou'd accept & give a place in your Library to the last Spanish Edition of Don Quixote which I recolectt to have hear'd you say at Dr Franklin's that you had never seen it.

I cou'd have wish'd it was in English for your particular entertainment, but it being reckoned the very best Edition of that celebrated work & one in which every thing has been manufactur'd in Spain induces me to request your acceptance.[2]

Permitt me to repeatt my humble respectts to your worthy Lady & to conclude with my sincere wishes for the pleasure of haveing you nearer subscriving myself in the mean time My Dear General Your most obedt & very humble servt

James Gardoqui

ALS, CtY: Knollenberg Collection; Sprague transcript, DLC:GW.

1. Gardoqui is referring to the stand the Virginia legislature took on the negotiations regarding navigation of the Mississippi River (Gardoqui to GW, 29 Oct., n.1).

2. GW while in Philadelphia bought Thomas Smollett's four-volume translation of *Don Quixote.* Two four-volume editions of the work were listed in the inventory of the library at Mount Vernon. The Smollett edition is known to

have been sold later; the other set may have been this Spanish edition given to GW by Gardoqui (Philadelphia Cash Accounts, 9 May–22 Sept. 1787, n.50; Griffin, *Boston Athenæum Collection,* 482–83).

From John Paul Jones

Sir,   New-York Novr 9. 1787.

Accounts having arrived and being credited here, that the British Fleet was out, and had been seen steering to the Westward, and that a British Squadron was cruising in the north Sea, I was advised by my Friends not to embark in the French Packet that sailed hence the 25. Ult. I am sorry to have lost that opportunity as those accounts are now contradicted.

I shall embark to morrow, in an American Ship bound for Amsterdam, and have bargained to be landed in France. I shall go directly to Paris, and deliver the two Packets you sent to my care immediately on my arrival, with two others from you that have been since put into my Hands for Mr Jefferson and the Marquis de la Fayette.[1]

I am exceedingly sorry for the long detention of your Letters; but Colonel Carrington, who does me the honor to carry this, can inform you, that it has not depended on me to forward them sooner, and that Mr Jay has had no opportunity till now of sending his dispatches to Europe since the month of June.[2] I am, Sir, with profound respect and perfect esteem, Your most obedient & most humble Servant

Paul Jones

ALS, DLC:GW.

1. For the two packets of GW's letters being conveyed to France by Jones, see GW to Jones, 22 July 1787, and notes. The more recent letters to Lafayette and Thomas Jefferson, enclosing copies of the Constitution, are dated 18 September.

2. GW does not record in his *Diaries* (5:263) a visit from Edward Carrington until 9 Jan. 1788, by which time GW had already received Jones's letter.

To Bushrod Washington

Dear Bushrod,   Mount Vernon Novr 9th 1787.

In due course of Post, I received your letters of the 19th & 26th Ult.; and since, the one which you committed to the care of Mr Powell.[1] I thank you for the communications therein, & for a continuation, in matters of importance, I shall be obliged to you.

That the Assembly would afford the people an opportunity of deciding on the proposed Constitution I had hardly a doubt; the only question with me was, whether it would go forth under favourable auspices, or be branded with the mark of disapprobation. The opponents, I expected, (for it has ever been, that the adversaries to a measure are more active than its friends) would endeavour to give it an unfavourable complexion, with a view to biass the public mind. This, evidently, is the case with the writers in opposition; for their objections are better calculated to alarm the fears, than to convince the judgment of their readers. They build them upon principles which do not exist in the Constitution—which the known & litteral sense of it, does not support them in; and this too, after being flatly told that they are treading on untenable ground and after an appeal has been made to the letter, & spirit thereof, for proof: and then, as if the doctrine was uncontrovertable, draw such consequences as are necessary to rouse the apprehensions of the ignorant, & unthinking. It is not the interest of the major part of these characters to be convinced; nor will their local views yield to arguments which do not accord with their present, or future prospects; and yet, a candid solution of a single question, to which the understanding of almost every man is competent, must decide the point in dispute—namely—is it best for the States to unite, or not to unite?

If there are men who prefer the latter, then, unquestionably, the Constitution which is offered, must, in their estimation, be inadmissible from the first Word to the last signature, inclusively. But those who may think differently, and yet object to parts of it, would do well to consider, that it does not lye with *one* State, nor with a *minority* of the States, to superstruct a Constitution for the *whole*. The seperate interests, as far as it is practicable, must be consolidated—and local views as far as the general good will admit, must be attended to. Hence it is that *every* state has some objection to the *proposed* form; and that these objections are directed to different points. That which is most pleasing to one, is obnoxious to another, and vice versa. If then the Union of the whole is a desirable object, the parts which

compose it, must yield a little in order to accomplish it; for without the latter, the former is unattainable. For I again repeat it,
that not a single state nor a minority of the States, can force a
Constitution on the majority. But admitting they had (from their
importance) the power to do it, will it not be granted that the
attempt would be followed by civil commotions of a very serious
nature? But to sum up the whole, let the opponants of the proposed Constitution, *in this State,* be asked—it is a question they
ought certainly to have asked themselves; What line of conduct
they would advise it to adopt, if nine other States should accede
to it, of which I think there is little doubt? Would they recommend that it should stand on its own basis—seperate & distinct
from the rest? Or would they connect it with Rhode Island, or
even say two others, checkerwise, & remain with them as outcasts from the Society, to shift for themselves? or will they advise
a return to our former dependence on Great Britain for their
protection & support? or lastly would they prefer the mortification of comg in, when they will have no credit there from? I
am sorry to add in this place that Virginians entertain *too* high
an opinion of the importance of their own Country. In extent
of territory—In number of Inhabitants (*of all descriptions*) & In
wealth I will readily grant that it certainly stands first in the
Union; but in point of *strength,* it is, comparitively, weak. To this
point, my opportunities authorise me to speak, decidedly; and
sure I am, in every point of view, in which the subject can be
placed, it is not (considering also the Geographical situation of
the State) more the interest of any one of them to confederate,
than it is the one in which we live.

The warmest friends to and the best supporters of the Constitution, do not contend that it is free from imperfections; but
these were not to be avoided, and they are convinced if evils are
likely to flow from them, that the remedy must come thereafter;
because, in the *present moment* it is not to be obtained. And as
there is a Constitutional door open for it, I think the people (for
it is with them to judge) can, as they will have the aid of experience on their side, decide with as much propriety on the alterations and amendments wch shall be found necessary, as ourselves; for I do not conceive that we are more inspired—have
more wisdom—or possess more virtue than those who will come
after us. The power under the Constitution will always be with

the people. It is entrusted for certain defined purposes and for a certain limited period to representatives of their own chusing; and whenever it is exercised contrary to their interests, or not according to their wishes, their Servants can, and undoubtedly will be, recalled. There will not be wanting those who will bring forward complaints of mal-administration whensoever they occur. To say that the Constitution *may be strained,* and an *improper* interpretation given to some of the clauses or articles of it, will apply to any that can be framed—in a word renders any one nugatory—for not one, more than another, can be binding, if the spirit and letter of the expression is disregarded. It is agreed on all hands that no government can be well administred without powers; and yet, the instant these are delegated, altho those who are entrusted with the Administration are taken from the people—return shortly to them again—and must feel the bad effect of oppressive measures—the persons holding them, as if their natures were immediately metamorphosed, are denominated tyrants and no disposition is allowed them, but to do wrong. Of these things in a government so constituted and guarded as the proposed one is, I can have no idea; and do firmly believe that whilst many ostensible reasons are held out against the adoption of it the true ones are yet behind the Curtain; not being of a nature to appear in open day. I believe further, supposing these objections to be founded in purity itself that as great evils result from too much jealousy, as from the want of it. And I adduce several of the Constitutions of these States, as proof thereof. No man is a warmer advocate for *proper* restraints, and *wholesome* checks in every department of government than I am; but neither my reasoning, nor my experience, has yet been able to discover the propriety of preventing men from doing good, because there is a possibility of their doing evil.

If Mr Ronald can place the finances of this Country upon so respectable a footing as he has intimated, he will deserve its warmest, and most grateful thanks. In the attempt, my best wishes—which is all I have to offer—will accompany him.[2]

I hope there remains virtue enough in the Assembly of this State, to preserve inviolate public treaties, and private contracts. If these are infringed, farewell to respectability, and safety in the Government.

I never possessed a doubt, but if any had ever existed in my breast, re-iterated proofs would have convinced me of the impolicy, of all commutable taxes. If wisdom is not to be acquired from experience, where is it to be found? But why ask the question? Is it not believed by every one that *these* are time-serving jobs by which a few are enriched, at the public expence! but whether the plan originates for this purpose, or is the child of ignorance, oppression is the result.

You have, I find, broke the ice (as the saying is). one piece of advice only I will give you on the occasion (if you mean to be a respectable member, and to entitle yourself to the Ear of the House)—and that is—except in local matters which respect your Constituants and to which you are obliged, by duty, to speak, rise but seldom—let this be on important matters—and then make yourself thoroughly acquainted with the subject. Never be agitated by *more than* a decent *warmth*, & offer your sentiments with modest diffidence—opinions thus given, are listened to with more attention than when delivered in a dictatorial stile. The latter, if attended to at all, altho they may *force* conviction, is sure to convey disgust also.[3]

Your aunt, and the family here join me in every good wish for you. and I am with sentiments of great regd and Affecte—Yours

Go: Washington

P.S. The letter you sent by Mr Powell for Nancy was forwarded next day to Doctr Brown, for the best conveyance that should offer from alexandria.[4]

ALS (photocopy), ViMtV; LB (dated 10 Nov.), DLC:GW.

1. None of the three letters has been found. When on 4 Nov. Bushrod Washington sent to Robert Carter (1728–1804) of Nomini Hall, Westmoreland County, copies of the federal Constitution and the Virginia assembly's resolutions calling a state convention, he wrote: "I have no doubt but that you will discover some imperfections in it [the Constitution], but when it is considered that it is the child of mutual concessions between States different in Situation and Interest, and that without some efficient Government we must shortly be involved in Anarchy that certain road to Despotism . . . we should not hesitate concerning its adoption" (quoted in Kaminski and Saladino, *Documentary History of the Ratification of the Constitution*, 8:143–44).

2. William Ronald was a delegate from Powhatan County, which he had represented in the house of delegates since 1781; but it almost certainly was Alexander Donald, a Richmond merchant engaged in foreign trade, to whom Bushrod Washington had referred. Donald wrote Thomas Jefferson on 12

Nov.: "At the request of Colo. George Mason, I have drawn up a Plan for a new Bill, which will more effectually secure the Revenue than the former [a rejected paper money bill], and will remove the many objections that Mercantile People had to the last [the repealed Port Bill]" (Boyd, *Jefferson Papers*, 12:345–48). Perhaps Donald provided the original draft of the revenue bill that passed on 1 Jan. 1788, entitled "An act to amend the laws of revenue, to provide for the support of civil government, and the gradual redemption of all the debts due by this commonwealth" (12 Hening 412–32). In his letter to Jefferson, Donald also wrote: "I staid two days with General Washington at Mount Vernon about Six weeks ago [5–6 Oct.]. He is in perfect good health, and looks almost as well as he did Twenty years ago. I never saw him so keen for any thing in my life, as he is for the adoption of the new Form of Government. As the eyes of all America are turned towards this truly Great and Good Man, for the First President, I took the liberty of sounding him upon it. He appears to be greatly against going into Publick Life again, Pleads in Excuse for himself His Love of Retirement, and his advanced Age, but notwithstanding of these, I am fully of opinion he may be induced to appear once more on the Publick Stage of Life. I form my opinion from what passed between us in a very long and serious conversation as well as from what I could gather from Mrs. Washington on same subject" (Boyd, *Jefferson Papers*, 12:345–48).

3. Bushrod Washington had been elected for the first time to the house of delegates, where he represented Westmoreland County. The county also elected him to the ratifying convention in 1788.

4. Bushrod Washington married Nancy Blackburn in October 1785. Samuel and Elizabeth Willing Powel arrived at Mount Vernon on 4 Nov. en route to Philadelphia after visiting Mary Willing Byrd at Westover on the James River. Dr. William Brown (c.1732–c.1792) practiced medicine in Alexandria.

To Warner Washington

Dear Sir,   Mount Vernon 9th Novr 1787.

Having received an Official acct (from Mr Athawes) of the death of Colo. Geo: Wm Fairfax, together with the enclosed letter, I take the safe conveyance afforded by Mr Muse, of forwarding them to you.[1]

On this occasion I sincerely condole with Mrs Washington and yourself. Colo. Fairfax has appointed me an Executor of his Will in this Country; but the multiplicity, & perplexed state of my own affairs, and of those with which I have been concerned, (occasioned by a long absence from home, and continual interruptions since my return) render acceptance of the trust altogether inadmissible, however well disposed I otherwise should have been to pay this last tribute of respect to his Memory. The

Letter which is enclosed does, I presume, give information of the bequest to your lady, but in case it shd not the following is the only mention which is made of either of you, in the Will.

"I give devise & bequeath unto my Sister in law Hannah Washington (wife of Warner Washington Esqr.) the sum of five hundred pounds currt money of the said state of Virga besides the lands I gave her Husband."[2]

The Will being very long I have sent it to the other Executors in this Country—viz.—Wilson Cary, and George Nicholas Esqrs. without taking a copy of it. The principal part of his Estate (at the decease of Mrs Fairfax) is given to his Nephew, Ferdinand, Son of Mr Bryan Fairfax, as appears by some extracts I have taken from the Will.[3] Mrs Washington joins me in best wishes for your Lady & family, and I am—Dear Sir Your Affecte & Obedt Hble Servt

Go: Washington

ALS, NHi: George and Martha Washington Papers. Written on the cover: "By favour of Mr [Battaile] Muse."

1. Athawes wrote GW on 20 July 1787.

2. Warner Washington, Sr. (1722–1790), GW's first cousin, was living with his wife Hannah Fairfax Washington, George William Fairfax's half sister, at Fairfield in Frederick County.

3. For Bryan Fairfax's reaction to the terms of his brother's will, see Bryan Fairfax to GW, 16 November.

To Alexander Hamilton

Dear Sir,   Mount Vernon Novr 10th 1787.

I thank you for the Pamphlet, and for the Gazette contained in your letter of the 30th Ult. For the remaining numbers of Publius, I shall acknowledge myself obliged, as I am persuaded the subject will be well handled by the Author.[1]

The new Constitution has, as the public prints will have informed you, been handed to the people of this state by an unanimous vote of the Assembly; but it is not to be inferred from hence that its opponants are silenced; on the contrary, there are many, and some powerful ones—Some of whom, it is said by *overshooting* the mark, have lessened their weight: be this as it may, their assiduity stands unrivalled, whilst the friends to the Constitution content themselves with barely avowing their approbation of it. Thus stands the matter with *us,* at present; yet, my opinion is, that the Major voice is favourable.

Application has been made to me by Mr Secretary Thompson (by order of Congress) for a copy of the report, of a Committee, which was appointed to confer with the Baron de Steuben, on his first arrival in this Country—forwarded to me by Mr President Laurens. This I have accordingly sent. It throws no other light on the Subject than such as are to be derived from the disinterested conduct of the Baron. No terms are made by him "nor will he accept of any thing but with general approbation"— I have however, in my letter enclosing this report to the Secretary, taken occasion, to express an unequivocal wish, that Congress would reward the Baron for his Services, sacrafices and merits, to his entire satisfaction. It is the only way in which I could bring my sentiments before that honble body, as it has been an established principle with me, to ask nothing from it.[2] With very great esteem & regard I am—Dear Sir Yr Most Obedt Servt

Go: Washington

ALS, DLC: Hamilton Papers; LB, DLC:GW.

1. James Madison on 18 Nov. began sending to GW copies of the papers of the *Federalist* as they came out.

2. See GW to Steuben and to Charles Thomson, both this date.

To Steuben

Sir,   Mount Vernon Novr 10th 1787

The letter with which you were pleased to honor me, dated the 26th Ult., came duly to hand. By the same Post, I received a letter from Mr Secretary Thompson (by order of Congress) requesting a copy of the report of a Committee which was transmitted to me by Mr President Laurens, in Feby 1778. This is accordingly sent, and is the counterpart of the paper I herewith enclose, for your own information.[1]

As I do not recollect ever to have had any further knowledge of the contract which is alluded to, than what is therein contained, it is not in my power to speak more fully to the point; but in my letter to the Secretary, I have expressed, in unequivocal terms, a wish, that your merits and sacrafices may be recompensed to your entire satisfaction. If they should not, and it proves the mean of your with-drawing from the United States, I shall be among the number of those who will regret the event; as it would give me pleasure, that you shd continue in a Country, the liberties of which, owe much to your Services. I have the honor to be Sir Yr Most Obedt and Most Hble Servt

Go: Washington

ALS, DNA: RG 46; LB, DLC:GW; copy, DNA:PCC, item 19.

1. Charles Thomson's letter is dated 27 October. See GW to Thomson, this date, n.1.

To Charles Thomson

Sir,	Mount Vernon Novr 10th 1787.

In compliance with the resolve of Congress—contained in your letter of the 25th Ult.—I have the honor of sending you a copy of the paper enclosed in Mr Presidt Laurenss letter to me, of the 19th of Febry 1778, endorsed "Committees report."[1]

It would, I confess, give me great pleasure to hear that the importt Services of the Baron de Steuben could meet with a reward adequate to his merits & sacrafices. What may have been his verbal, or other engagements with Congress, is not for me to say, further than is contained in the paper herewith enclosed but certain it is, he hazarded his life and fortune at a critical period of our affairs, without those obligations on his part, which impelled Americans to the measure; and from that moment to the close of the War, rendered essential Services to the cause in which we were engaged. I embrace this, as I shall do every occasion, of expressing to you the esteem & regard with which I am—Sir, Your Most Obedt Hble Servt

Go: Washington

ALS, DNA:PCC, item 19; LB, DLC:GW; copy, DNA: RG 46.

1. The enclosed copy of the certificate, endorsed "Copy—Examined Go: Washington," is in DNA:PCC, item 19: "The Baron Stuben who was a Leiutenant General and Aide de Camp to the King of Prussia—desires no rank—is willing to attend General Washington, and be subject to his orders—does not require or desire any command of a particular Corps or Division, but will serve occasionally as directed by his General—expects to be of use in planning Encampments &c. and promoting the discipline of the Army—he heard, before he left France, of the dissatisfaction of the Americans with the promotion

of foreign officers, therefore makes no terms, nor will accept of any thing but with general approbation and particularly that of General Washington. Signed by Mr Wetherspoon, Mr F. L. Lee[,] Mr McKean[,] Mr Henry." See also the report of Congress on Steuben, 23 Jan. 1788, in *JCC,* 34:13.

Letter not found: to Richard Bland Lee, 11 Nov. 1787. On 23 Nov. Lee wrote GW that he had "recieved your Excellency's letter of the 11th Instant."

From William Morris

Dear Sir   Philadelphia 11th November 1787
I take this opportunity of returning you my most sincere thanks for the fusee you were so obliging as to send me & I shall allways remember with pleasure the time when I recieved a present from that Patriotick Chief, who at the head of a raw & undisciplined army defended his Country from the invasion of a Veteran band of Soldiers who were sent by one of the most powerfull Kingdoms of Europe to enslave us, but thanks to Heaven & to you Sir they were disappointed. Be assured Sir its being of American manufacture so far from lessening its value in my eyes heightens its value in them; as I am sure it would in those of any lover of his Country for a People who depend upon any Nation for the articles they consume can not be called entirely independant.

I dare say Sir it will give you some pleasure to hear that this State is likely to conform with the opinion of the Fœderal Convention in chusing a State Convention.

By the New con[s]titution Foreign Princes may see that the American chiefs are not only Warriors in the field but also (if I may be allowed the expression) Warriors in the Cabinet. Mama desires me to offer you & Mrs Washington her most respectfull compliments. Sir, I remain with the greatest respect Your obedient Servant

Wm Morris

ALS, DLC:GW.
William Morris, the third son of Robert and Mary White Morris, was 16 years old in 1787. He died in October 1798.

From César-Henri de La Luzerne

Sire   Port au Prince [Haiti] 12th Novr 1787.

The assembly which ought to have been held in France in order to particularize the number & quality of French Officers, who, having Served the last war in America, would be admitted into the respectable Society of the Cincinnati, having not been yet convened; I am solicited by Monsieur de Saqui des Toures, Commander of a Ship, with whom I am particularly acquainted and very desireous of obliging, to obtain, for him, permission to wear the Insignia of the Order. I am doubtful whether the French branch of this Society will ever convene, and I thought it right to consult you upon the hopes & wishes of Monsr de Saqui.[1]

This Officer embarked on board the Languedoc in quality of Leiutenant, having served a cruize with the Count d'Estaing and being badly wounded was obliged to return to Fran[c]e. Among the favors with which he was recompensed at that time,[2] he was not at hand to solicit this decoration which was granted to others less deserving of it. He was entitled to it on account of his wounds, as well as many other officers who had absolutly no other recommendation for it. He is more eligible than ever since he has become Commander of a Ship. He claims it as having been one of the first Frenchmen who bore arms in defence of American Liberty.

I beg your Excellency to inform me if you think this officer, whose merits are known to me, will be permitted to carry the Insignia by which this respectable society are distinguished. For my own part I should wish that my recommendation may obtain the favor which he desires, and of which I can assure you he is worthy.

I know the attachment which my Brother has to you, & I also know the friendship with which you honor him. I am persuaded that he would willingly join me in favor of Monsr de Saqui, if he was at hand.

I am glad, Sir, that this circumstance has given me an occasion of renewing the assurances of my sincere atttachment, and the high consideration with which I have the honor to be Yr Excellency's Most Hble & Obedt Servt

La Luzerne

Translation, by Tobias Lear, DLC:GW; ALS, in French, DLC:GW; ALS, in French, DSoCi, enclosed in a letter of 30 Nov. 1787 from Barbé-Marbois.

The comte de La Luzerne was at the point of leaving his post as governor of Hispaniola to return to Paris to become the minister of Marine. His brother, the chevalier de La Luzerne, whom GW knew as France's first minister to the United States, was soon to become France's ambassador in London.

1. In his letter to GW of 30 Nov., Barbé-Marbois supports La Luzerne's petition. See GW's reply to Barbé-Marbois, 4 April 1788. Louis-Chrétien-Hilarion, chevalier de Saqui des Tourès, was made an honorary member of the French Society of the Cincinnati (Contenson, *La Société des Cincinnati de France*, 258).

2. This is the translator's rendition of "Parmis les graces qui furent à cette epoque Sa recompense."

From Joseph Lewis, Jr.

Sir,   Alexandria 12th November 1787

Being in company with a Party of young Gentlemen last sunday morning it was proposed taking a Sail, accordingly we procured a Sailing Boat and some of the company mentioning that 2 or 3 Guns wou'd be very entertaining as we shou'd probably meet with chances at Ducks in the course of our Sailing and at their request I borrowed of Mr R. W. Ashton a Gun & Mr Charles Ashton took another belonging to Colo. R. Hooe with whom we both live[1] and as the Wind & Tide were both setting down the River, consequently it obliged us to sail that course, and chanced (unfortunately for us; without your favour) to land at a noted Place called *Johnston's Spring*,[2] and of course took the Guns on shore, to prevent negroes or others from Stealing them, for I assure you it was not our intention to land for the purpose of Gunning on your, (or any other Gentlemans) Property—however we had not been there but a few minutes before three Negroes came up to us, one of which had a Gun, they presently espied a Squirrell and insisted much on Mr Ashtons shooting it, which he accordingly did (not supposing he was doing wrong) they then told Mr Ashton & myself that if we wou'd go a little farther into a small piece of Woods, that we cou'd find a large Quantity of Squirrells promp'd by their earnest sollicitations we accordingly went about 200 yards from our company and the negroes still following us very near, we began to return, and as we were getting over a fence they altogether instantly seized us in the most Violent manner Knocked us from off the fence & snatching up the Guns they all ran off declaring that they had gained ⟨10£⟩, and that they wou'd instantly carry them before you—in short they treated us with more Barbarity than any Highwayman wou'd have done, (finding that we were small)—I never shot once on shore, and Mr Ashton but once— from the above declaration (which I am ready to swear to) shou'd your Excellency think it Injurious to your property for that small trespass, (Tho' by us innocently done) we are willing to give any satisfaction your Excellency shall think Proper,[3] but we must beg that you will send the Guns by L'Amour, the bearer hereof, as they are borrowed one's and must confess that I am really asham'd that the Owners shoud Know that we suffered Negroes to take them from us[4]—I am your Excellencies most Obt & very Humble Servt

Joseph Lewis Junr

ALS, DLC:GW.

1. Charles Ashton, son of John and Mary Watts Ashton of Westmoreland County, was the younger brother of Richard Watts Ashton, who was a lieutenant in the Fairfax County militia and, like Robert Townsend Hooe, a merchant in Alexandria. Joseph Lewis, Jr., witnessed a deed with Hooe in 1786 and was probably the Joseph Lewis who witnessed legal documents for Hooe and his business partner, Richard Harrison, on 21 Sept. 1789 and 19 July 1790.

2. Johnston's Spring was near Clifton's ferry and a short distance north of GW's River farm on a part of the Clifton's Neck land that GW had acquired in 1760.

3. See Archibald Johnston to GW, 30 Oct. 1787, n.1.

4. L'Amour was the name of a slave who was freed by Richard Harrison in 1791.

To Samuel Vaughan

Dear Sir,   Mount Vernon November 12th 1787
The letter without date, with which you were pleased to honor me, accompanied by a plan of this Seat, came to my hands by the last Post—for both I pray you to accept my sincere and hearty thanks.[1]

The plan describes with accuracy the houses, walks, shrubs beries &ca except in the front of the Lawn—west of the Ct yard. There the plan differs from the original—in the former, you have closed the prospect with trees along the walk to the gate—whereas in the latter the trees terminate with two mounds of earth one on each side on which grow Weeping Willows leaving an open and full view of the distant woods—the mounds are at 6o yards apart. I mention this because it is the only departure from the origl.[2]

Altho' I can have little doubt of the pleasure you must feel at the prospect of being soon reunited to your lady and family in England, I do not scruple to confess that I shall be among those who will view your departure from this Country with regret. at the same time I beg leave to add that I shall reflect with pleasure on the friendship with which you have honored me. The testimonies you have left of this, could my mind be so ungrateful as to forget it, would be constant remembrancers. For your kind offer of Services in England I shall feel my self ever obliged and should occasion require it I shall avail myself of your kindness.

I am sorry it was not in my power to take you by the hand the day I left Philadelphia—I called once and as you were not within I did not leave my name intending to have called again but circumstance preventing it I requested Mr Gouvr Morris to offer you my apology and best wishes. should your Son who is lately arrived from England be promted by business or inclination to travel into this State it would give me much pleasure to shew him every civility in my power—the same to any branch of your family—or any of your friends—In wishing you (whenever it shall be undertaken) a pleasent and prosperous voyage, and a happy meeting with Mrs Vaughan and the other parts of your family and friends in England; I am with great cordiallity and sincerity Joined by Mrs Washington the Major and Fanny. and with sentiments of the most perfect esteem and regard—I am—Dr Sir—&c.

G. Washington.

LB, DLC:GW.

1. Vaughan's letter has not been found.

2. Vaughan visited Mount Vernon for nearly a week in August 1787 during GW's absence in Philadelphia. While there, he took extensive notes on the layout at Mount Vernon and made a sketch of the house itself and its environs. From the sketch and notes he developed the "plan" that he sent to GW. Vaughan's notebook and plan are now at Mount Vernon.

From Samuel Powel

Dear Sir   Philadelphia 13 Novr 1787

As I am sure it will afford Pleasure to Mrs Washington and yourself to hear of our safe Arrival in Philadelphia, I embrace this early Opportunity of informing you that we had the Satisfaction of seeing our Friends in good Health on Saturday Evening last.

At Annapolis we had the Pleasure of seeing General Smallwood from whom we experienced the most polite & obliging Treatment. Indeed our Reception and Treatment, throughout our whole Journey, were such as were highly acceptable. The friendly and cordial Attentions we received at Mount Vernon have left an Impression which cannot be easily obliterated from gratefull Minds.

Our good Friends Messrs Robert & Gouverneur Morris left this City Yesterday & will probably be with you before the Arrival of this Letter. They will be able to give you a full and ample Detail of all Matters relative to our grand Question, I mean the Acceptation of the fœderal Constitution. For this Reason I shall say no more upon this Subject than just to observe that there appears to be no Cause to doubt of its Reception in Pennsylvania—All the eastern States, New York, New Jersey and Delaware are esteemed to be decided for it, In Maryland there is a secret Opposition from a Member of the Assembly; but it is believed that his Politics will not succeed. I have not heard a Doubt relative to the States to the Southward of Virginia, & even there I hope & believe there is Virtue & good Sense enough to overbalance the Arts of interested, designing &, I had almost said, dishonest Men.[1]

It is said that R. H. Lee escaped the resentment of the People at Chester by his short Stay there, which he employed in fixing up & distributing printed Papers against the proposed Constitution. At Wilmington he harangued the Populace and cautioned them against hastily adopting it, assuring them that a powerfull Opposition was forming against it in Philadelphia and, in Confirmation of his Assertions distributed many of his inflammatory Papers. On such Conduct there can be but one Comment made.

Our Passage across the Chesapeak was tedious tho' smooth. We embarked at Eleven in the Morning and landed at Eight at Night. Mrs Powel bore the Voyage admirably well & without Apprehensions of Danger. She begs Leave to join me in affectionate Comps. to Mrs Washington, your good self, Major & Mrs Washington, the young Ladies, & our Friend the young Squire. She will execute Mrs Washington's Commands, relative to the young Ladies Collars, by the first Opportunity.[2]

I return you, dear Sir, my best Thanks for the chestnuts and Saintfoin, which I have received. The Nuts are injured by the Voyage, & some of them sprouted. They are so acceptable to my Friends, that I am tempted to request the Favor of you to send me a few more, if it will not be giving you too much Trouble.

If it is in my Power to be of Service to you here, I beg that you will, with all Freedom, honor me with your Commands—and be assured that the Recollection of the Time spent under your hospitable & friendly Roof ever affords real Satisfaction to dear Sir Your affectionate Friend & most obedt humble Servt

Samuel Powel

Mrs Morris & Family were well at Noon this Day.

ALS, DLC:GW.
1. The Powels left Mount Vernon on 6 Nov.; Richard Henry Lee arrived at Mount Vernon on 11 Nov. and left the next day; Robert and Gouverneur Morris came for a two-day visit on 19 Nov. on their way to Richmond.
2. For "the young Ladies Collars," see Powel to GW, 12 December, n.2.

From Robert Lawson

Sir, Richmond Novr 14th 1787

It is with great diffidence that I address you on a subject, which concerns my private Interest only; the motive, I must entreat you, Sir, to consider, & suffer it to plead my apology.

I have due me in the two States of South Carolina, & Georgia, about five hundred pounds, in the hands of two Gentlemen; and I have made several attempts (through a person empowered as my Attorney in fact) to have it collected; but owing to the scarcity of specie, I have as yet been disappointed.

This sum is too considerable to me to suffer longer to lie dormant. I shall therefore after the adjournment of this Session go to Charles Town, & from thence to Augusta in Georgia, at which places my Debtors reside. But being almost an entire Stranger in

Charles Town especially (except in a few instances of Gentlemen formerly in the military line) I will esteem, Sir, a singular obligation, if you would honor me with a Letter, or Letters Introductory.

Doctor Steward is so polite as to forward this for me; and should any mistake in Judgment have made me sollicit an improper thing, I must beg once again that it may be pardon'd.[1] I have the honor to be with every sentiment of respect, Sir Your mo. obedt Servt

Ro: Lawson

ALS, DLC:GW.

Robert Lawson, a lawyer and planter, at this time was representing Prince Edward County in the house of delegates.

1. GW wrote Lawson from Mount Vernon on 25 Nov.: "Sir, Herewith enclosed you will please to receive two letters of Introduction—The one to the Govr of South Carolina—the other to the Chief Justice, or Chancellor (I forget now wch) of that State. I wish you a pleasant Journey when it shall be commenced, and the accomplishment of your business—and with esteem & regard am Dr Sir Yr Most Obedt Hble Serv⟨t⟩ Go: Washington" (ALS, CSmH). The letters of the same date enclosed in GW's letter to Lawson were directed to Thomas Pinckney and John Rutledge. The letter to Pinckney reads: "Genl Lawson who will do me the honor of presenting this letter to your Excellency, and whom I take the liberty of introducing to your civilities, is called by business to Charleston & Georgia. He is a Gentleman of character & merit in this State; having been a Colonel in the Continental Army and is now a Member of our Assembly. I have the honor to be Sir Yr Most Obedt & Most Hble Servt Go: Washington" (ALS, CSmH). The text of the letter to Rutledge is: "Dear Sir, Permit me to introduce Genl Lawson, the bearer of this letter, to your civilities. Genl Lawson was a Colonel in the Continental Army—is now a representative in the Assembly of this State—and is called by business to Charleston & Georgia. My best respects attend Mrs Rutledge, in which I am joined by Mrs Washington. With very great esteem & regard. I am—Dear Sir Yr Most Obedt & Very Hble Servt Go: Washington" (ALS, LNCD). Lawson wrote from Richmond on 21 Dec.: "The great honor you have done me, by the polite attention paid to my request, for Letters of Introduction to the State of South Carolina, impresses my mind with the most lively gratitude; and I entreat, Sir, that you will be pleas'd to accept my cordial & respectfull acknowledgments. In whatevr situation Fortune may place me in future, it shall continue to be the ardent wish of my Soul, that you may live long to be, the Father, and Protector, of Americas dearest rights" (DLC:GW). "Doctor Steward" is David Stuart, whose letter of 14 Nov. is missing.

Letter not found: from David Stuart, 14 Nov. 1787. On 30 Nov. GW wrote Stuart: "Your favor of the 14th came duly to hand."

Letter not found: from Clement Biddle, 15 Nov. 1787. On 3 Dec. GW wrote Biddle: "Your letters of the 23d of Septr & 15th of Novr came duly to hand."

To Wilson Miles Cary and George Nicholas

Gentn   Mount Vernon November 15th 1787

A few days ago, the letter herewith sent from Mr Athawes, accompanying the will of our much esteemed and greatly to be lamented friend, the Honble George Wm Fairfax Esqr. came to my hands—on which melancholy occasion I sincerely condole with you.

The small package containing the watch (which is mentioned in the Will) and the two letters spoken of in Mr Athawes letter (one for Thomas Fairfax Esqr. and the other for Colo. Warner Washington) I have (presuming it would be your wish) forwarded to their respective addresses by safe conveyances.[1]

However desirous I may be of giving unequivocal proofs of my respect for the deceased, and of my regard for, and attachment to the amiable lady he has left behind; yet, such is the peculiar situation of my own concerns so much are they deranged—and so much more attention is due to them occasioned by nine years absence and bad management than in my power to give them that it would be folly in the extreme in me, to undertake a fresh trust which I am Confident is not in my power to discharge agreeable either to the intention of the testator, or to the dictates of my own Judgment. In a word, from a variety of causes with the enumeration of which I shall not trouble you, I have not leizure to recover my own affairs (and some others which are involved with them) from that disordered state into which they have fallen. But if there are any friendly Offices in this part of the Country & within my reach in the discharge of which I can be useful, I shall have great pleasure in rendering them.

Having said thus much, it is unnecessary for me to add that the le[g]acy bequeathed me by the Will becomes a nullity.

Permit me to remind Mr Nicholas that there is an escruitore with many Papers belonging to the deceased in my possession many of them of great Value. They might be packed in a Trunk and sent by the Stage to Richmond but a careful and responsible person ought to take charge of them.[2] With the greatest esteem and regard. I am Gentn Yrs &c.

G. Washington

LB, DLC:GW.

1. Samuel Athawes's letter is dated 20 July 1787, and GW's letter to Warner Washington is dated 9 Nov. 1787. GW probably enclosed Fairfax's letter to Thomas Fairfax, Bryan Fairfax's son, in a letter that he wrote to Bryan Fairfax (see Bryan Fairfax to GW, 16 November).

2. GW refers to the papers in George William Fairfax's escritoire in his letters to Fairfax of 10–15 June 1774 and 30 June 1786.

Letter not found: to George Mason, 15 Nov. 1787. On 27 Nov. Mason wrote GW: "I this Morning received your Favour of the 15th."

From Stephen Sayre

Sir   London 15th novr 1787

Some particular circumstances prevented my sending your Excellency the inclosed papers sooner.[1] I am happy in being able to congratulate you on the change of Constitution, so wisely plan'd.

I could have wish'd, there had been more Members of the House of delegates for the present, & that their doors should be open to the public—great assemblies dare not do wrong, while on their natural Basis—when a man speaks to a nation, he feels himself on high & commanding ground—the people feel themselves interested in his Character—they communicate mutual aid, that leads to greatness, to honor, & to safety—an assembly of men secluded from the Ears & Eyes of their fellow Citizens (call them what you please) are but an Inquisition, just in proportion, to their seclusion, or seperation; in which, bad men will intregue, without detection, & where good men, may contend without effect.

Nothing has preserved this Country from convultion, under their intolerable weight of Taxes, but the satisfaction of knowing the causes & having, by their most favorite delegates opposed their increase. The reason why this public assembly have gone too far, is not because they are a public Body, but because they are not the real delegates of the people—they have committed many enormities, but corruption has its limits and ceases to be destructive, where it becomes known. There is another reason why a more numerous Assembly should have now taken place—you would thereby, have taken into it, all those ambitious, or interested men, who may, to preserve their own consequence, oppose the new Constitution—for I fear there are too many members of this stamp, who compose the respective Assemblies of the 13 States. If great, & effective opposition is made—which I fear will be the Case—there will remain no remedy but that of admitting every Member, duly elected, to take his Seat in one General Assembly, or Congress, instead of siting in 13 Assemblies—the Senators forming one Senate &c. &c. But I hope the Constitution, as it is, will take place, & command the respect of those Nations, who now, virtually insult us—Since my arrival in this Country I have been drawn into an expensive Lawsuit—have given Security to bring it to issue, therefore am compel'd to remain some time Longer, either in England, or near it.[2]

But wherever I am, your excellency may believe, I feel every sentiment of veneration, that can fill the heart of man, and am, with sincere wishes, that you may live long, & happy, to enjoy those solid honors, the world are compel'd to grant you. Yours. &c. &c.

Stephen Sayre

P.S. If I can render you any Service while I stay in this Country, write, under cover to Messrs Newnham & Co. Bankers. London.

ALS, MnHi.

1. The enclosed papers have not been identified.

2. The adventurer Stephen Sayre, with whom GW corresponded in 1784 about opening up the upper Potomac to navigation, was in prison in London for debt, where he had been for eleven months and remained until his release in the fall of 1788 (Alden, *Sayre*, 150–54; see also William Duer to GW, 5 June 1784, n.1, Sayre to GW, 20 Aug., 15 Oct. 1784, and GW to Sayre, 1 Sept. 1784).

From Bryan Fairfax

Dear Sir   Towlston Novr the 16th 1787

This is to acknowledge Your Favor in sending me an Accot of my Brother's Will and also the Receipt of the Watch by Mr Muse.[1] It can't be expected that You should act as an Executor upon this Occasion amidst that multiplicity of Business you are engaged in. In a few Instances I was so circumstanced that I could not comply with Ld Fx's desire as well as my Brother's tho' I had a great Regard for them both yet they both treated me afterwards in a loving manner: I suppose they entered into some hasty Resolutions with respect to myself and my Son Thomas who was innocent with respect to them and has behaved to me wth dutifulness as well as a proper Fortitude under difficulties which my own Negligence as well as misfortunes have exposed him to.[2]

Mrs Fairfax joins me in respectful Compliments to Mrs Washington & I am Dr Sir with great Regard & Esteem Yr most obedt & obliged humble Servt

Bryan Fairfax

ALS, DLC:GW.

1. GW's letter to Fairfax has not been found, but see GW to Warner Washington, 9 Nov., GW to Wilson Miles Cary and George Nicholas, 15 Nov., and Battaile Muse to GW, 19 November.

2. By George William Fairfax's will, the bulk of his fortune was to go to Bryan Fairfax's third son, Ferdinando (1769–1820), rather than to Bryan Fairfax's oldest son, Thomas (1762–1846).

To Catharine Sawbridge Macaulay Graham

Madam,   Mount Vernon Novr 16th 1787.

Your favor of the 10th of Octr 1786 came duly to hand, and should have had a much earlier acknowledgment, had not the business of the public (in which I have been, in a manner, compelled to engage again) engrossed the whole of my time for several months past; and my own private concerns required my unremitted attention, since my return home.

I do not know to what cause I shall impute your not receiving my letter of the 10th of Jany 1786 till the last of June; it went by the common rout—subject to the common incidents.

Mr Pines Historical paintings does not appear to go on very rapidly. He informed me, when I was in Philadelphia, that he had been collecting materials to enable him to proceed with it, but that it must be a work of time to accomplish it.

You will undoubtedly, before you receive this, have an opportunity of seeing the plan of Government proposed by the Fœderal Convention for the United States. You will very readily conceive, Madam, the difficulties which the Convention had to struggle against. The various & opposite interests which were to be conciliated. The local prejudices which were to be subdued. The diversity of opinions & sentiments which were to be reconciled. And in fine, the sacrafices wch were necessary to be made on all sides, for the general welfare, combined to make it a work of so intricate & difficult a nature, that I think it is much to be wondered at, that any thing could have been produced with such unanimity as the Constitution proposed.

It is now submitted to the consideration of the People, & waits their decision. The legislatures of the several States which have been convened since the Constitution was offered, have readily agreed to the calling a Convention in their respective States— some by an unanimous vote, and others by a large Majority, but whether it will be adopted by the People or not, remains yet to be determined. Mrs Washington & the rest of the family join me in Compliments and best wishes for you and Mr Graham. I have the honor to be Madam—Yr Most Obedt & Very Hble Servant

Go: Washington

ALS, Leicester City Museum and Art Gallery, England; LB, DLC:GW.

From Thomas Johnson

Sir   Annapolis 16 November 1787.

I happen to be one of a Committee to report on the petition of Mr John Fitch of Pennsylvania for an exclusive Privilege in this State, similar to what he has obtaind in Virginia and several others, to propel vessells through the water by the Force of Steam Engines—I have found a Necessity to mention to the Committee a Conversation I had with Mr Rumsay in the Month of October, I think, in 1785 on the principle he expected to effect his boat Navigation when he told me that he was to gain his first power by Steam—It was so different from what I conjectured and had been led some how to beleive that I remarked he had treated you with indelicacy by exhibiting his Model and Experiment before you on a false principle and obtaining your Certificate he told me that although he exhibited on a different

principle to prevent his being traced he mentioned and explained to you alone that he relied on the Force of Steam to gain
his first power[.] I remarked that it was well he did since there
might be no other way of protecting his exclusive Right but by
recurring to you—In the present Situation of the Committee
and with the strongest Desire to do Justice between Mr Rumsay
and Mr Fitch the Committee request, if that is consistent with
your Situation, that you will be pleased to inform me by a Line
whether Mr Rumsay disclosed to you any Idea of gaining his
first power by Steam as he asserted to me or not.[1] I am sir, with
great Respect Your most obedient & most humble Servant

                                            Th. Johnson

ALS, DLC:GW.
   1. See GW's response of 22 Nov. and James Rumsey to GW, 17 December.
See also GW to Rumsey, 31 Jan. 1786, and note 1 of that document.

From Samuel Hanson

Sir,   Alexandria, Novr 18th 1787
    The last time I did myself the honour to address you, I prom-
ised to take your Nephews, if it were agreeable to you, another
Year.[1] You will, I fear, suspect me of being whimsical in requesting the favour of you to release me from the obligation of
that promise. I have lately engaged with some Gentlemen to
dine with me by the year: and I find that the accommodating
of these will clash with the attention necessary to the Boys. As
the Boys must dine early, in order to attend School, we shall be
under the necessity of keeping for them a separate Table. The
trouble of doing this, would exceed any profits which so small a
number could afford. I, therefore, hope you will not think my
request unreasonable.
    I make it with less reluctance, as I have been with Mr McWhir
to know if he would take them, and have reason to believe that
he would. I am very sincere in declaring that, from the course
of my observations on boys in general, there is no situation for
them so eligible as the immediate inspection of their Teacher. I
should, Sir, be unjust to the confidence you have reposed in me,
if I did not add that, with respect to your Nephews, they ought

to be placed under some person willing, & capable, to controul them. The difficulty of doing this appears to be encreased by a particular Circumstance which, from restraints of respect, I can but hint at—I have often had cause to suspect that your Kinsmen arrogate to themselves no Small degree of Self-Estimation from those high & distinguished Offices to which you have been appointed. It has been my endeavour to discourage any pretensions arising in them from Considerations foreign to their own merit: but not, as I conceive, with entire effect.[2]

I beg you not to impute the freedom of this remark to any asperity remaining from some occasional disagreement with the Boys, nor to any other unworthy motive. They have, indeed, my hearty good-wishes for their wellfare and advancement in Learning; but I am persuaded their progress will be best facilitated under Some one invested with a proper Authority to controu⟨l and⟩ if necessary, to correct, the⟨m⟩. I remain, with perfect resp⟨ect⟩ and Esteem, Sir Your most obedt Servt

S. Hanson of Saml

ALS, DLC:GW.

1. Hanson wrote GW on 23 September.

2. The brothers George Steptoe Washington and Lawrence Augustine Washington had been studying at William McWhir's academy in Alexandria since November 1785 and living in Hanson's house since January 1787. GW replied from Mount Vernon on 24 Nov.: "Sir, I am sorry it is not convenient for you to board my Nephews any longer—Mr Lear is desired to see what can be done with them—For the advice you have given them I feel myself obliged & wish they had sense & prudence enough to be governed by it. I am &c. G. Washington" (LB, DLC:GW). After leaving Hanson's house GW's nephews boarded at Mr. McWhir's for only a few months. On 16 Mar. 1788 Hanson wrote GW that as McWhir could not "accomodate your Nephews any longer," he was applying to GW "to let me have them again." By 4 May Hanson once more was complaining to GW about the conduct of George Steptoe Washington. In view of Hanson's fairly constant flow of criticism of the two boys, GW must have taken some satisfaction when he attended the school exams earlier in November and learned that "in the Second [class], examined in Latin and ancient Geography, George Washington and Charles Alexander were deemed the best scholars" (*Virginia Journal, and Alexandria Advertiser,* 8 Nov. 1787).

From James Madison

Dear Sir　　　　　　　　　　　　　　New York Novr 18. 1787.

Your favor of the 5th instant found me in Philada whither I had proceeded, under arrangements for proceeding to Virginia or returning to this place, as I might there decide. I did not acknowledge it in Philada because I had nothing to communicate, which you would not receive more fully and correctly from the Mr Morris's who were setting out for Virginia.

All my informations from Richmond concur in representing the enthusiasm in favor of the new Constitution as subsiding, and giving place to a spirit of criticism. I was fearful of such an event from the influence and co-operation of some of the adversaries. I do not learn however that the cause has lost its majority in the Legislature, and still less among the people at large.

I have nothing to add to the information heretofore given concerning the progress of the Constitution in other States. Mr Gerry has presented his objections to the Legislature in a letter addressed to them, and signified his readiness if desired to give the particular reasons on which they were founded.[1] The Legislature it seems decline the explanation, either from a supposition that they have nothing further to do in the business, having handed it over to the Convention; or from an unwillingness to countenance Mr Gerry's conduct; or from both these considerations. It is supposed that the promulgation of this letter will shake the confidence of some, and embolden the opposition of others in that State; but I cannot discover any ground for distrusting the prompt & decided concurrence of a large majority.

I inclose herewith the 7 first numbers of the federalist, a paper addressed to the people of this State. They relate entirely to the importance of the Union. If the whole plan should be executed, it will present to the public a full discussion of the merits of the proposed Constitution in all its relations. From the opinion I have formed of the views of a party in Virginia I am inclined to think that the observations on the first branch of the subject may not be superfluous antidotes in that State, any more than in this. If you concur with me, perhaps the papers may be put into the hand of some of your confidential correspondents at Richmond who would have them reprinted there.[2] I will not conceal *from you* that I am likely to have such *a degree* of connection with the publication here, as to afford a restraint of delicacy from interesting myself directly in the republication elsewhere. You will recognize one of the pens concerned in the task. There are three in the whole. A fourth may possibly bear a part.

The intelligence by the packet as far as I have collected it, is contained in the gazette of yesterday.

Virginia is the only State represented as yet. When a Congress will be formed is altogether uncertain. It is not very improbable I think that the interregnum may continue throughout the winter. With every sentiment of respect & attachment I remain dear Sir, yr Affect. hble servant

Js Madison Jr

ALS, DLC:GW; copy, DLC: Madison Papers.

1. Elbridge Gerry's letter to the Massachusetts General Court, dated 18 Oct. 1787, is reprinted in Farrand, *Records of the Federal Convention*, 3:128–29, and in Kaminski and Saladino, *Documentary History of the Ratification of the Constitution*, 13:548–50.

2. On 30 Nov. GW sent these seven papers of the *Federalist* to David Stuart in Richmond for republication. The *Virginia Independent Chronicle* (Richmond) reprinted the first three papers, in succession, on 12, 19, and 26 December. Madison sent GW numbers 8 through 14 of the *Federalist* papers on 30 Nov., and he sent copies of subsequent papers on 7, 14, and 20 December. Alexander Hamilton sent GW the first paper of the *Federalist* on 30 Oct. (GW to Hamilton, 10 November).

From Battaile Muse

Honorable Sir,   Novr 19th 1787

The Letters Put into my Care to Mr B. Fairfax and Colo. Warner Washington is delivered.[1]

at my arrival home I Found a Letter From you dated the 7th Instant[2] Enclosed one From Mr W. Weathers that He Thought Mr Clymount a Tenant of yours was hard & unjustly Dealt by— I Know of no Foundation for Such a Suspicion—unless Mr Weathers Judges me to be Like His Brother E. Weathers who over charged in Taxes and Kept and Execution of yours in [h]is hands Twelve month I was a Bout To Bring Him before the Court and did notify the High Sheriff on the Ocation the Day For appearance He Setled—that Matter and all Knowing that I will not Let the Guilty go unnoticed has ocationd these People To Put it into the Tenants mines that they are hard and unjustly Dealt By in their accts.[3] I have been Told by the Insolent a suspicion of the Kind before. I have Indulged them near Two years under the Law and have always Limited the Sheriff in all Cases So as not To Take advantages or be oppressive. The old Man mentiond I have been Very attentive to and indeed all the rest in Setling their acct Perfectly as Fare as Circumstances would permit, and gave Such Indulgences From Time To Time as the stages of Law and Compation dictated. Indulgences I have Ever Found gave Time For deception—I Set out this day to Fauquier Court and Shall Enquire Into what may be necessary. I have the Honor To be your obedient Humble Servant

Battaile Muse

ALS, DLC:GW.

1. See GW to Warner Washington, 9 Nov., GW to Wilson Miles Cary and George Nicholas, 15 Nov., n.1, and Bryan Fairfax to GW, 16 November.

2. No letter from GW to Muse of 7 Nov. has been found, but it is likely that Muse was referring to GW's letter of 8 Nov., written in response to Muse's letter of 7 November.

3. For Muse's dealings with GW's tenant Deel Clymer, see List of Tenants, 18 Sept. 1785, n.26. "W. Weathers" and "His Brother E. Weathers" are probably William and Enoch Withers, sons of Thomas Withers (d. 1794), all of Fauquier County where Clymer was a tenant.

To Henry Banks

Sir,   Mount Vernon November 22d 1787

For the letter you did me the favor to write to me on the 21st Ult: I offer you my thanks.[1] no application has ever been made to *me* or to any person on *my* account that has ever come to my knowledge, for the taxes of my land in Greenbrier and totally ignorant am I of the amount of them—If you can inform me, I would thank you.[2]

I have no objection to the settlement of my Lands on the Great Kankawa,[3] or on the Ohio above it, provided it could be done to the reciprocal benefit Landlord and tenant. Every advantage of situation and Soil is possessed by these lands in a superlative degree—full conviction of this fact—a firm belief that I can obtain no rent *now* which will be adequate a few years hence to the value of the land, by which to be induced to lease it. and having thoughts of selling some, if not the whole, If I can get what I conceive to be the worth have been the means of its lying in a dormant State till this time, but if it is likely to be pressed with taxes, something must be done with it and soon—it not being convenient for me to pay these without some return—preparative therefore to this I should have no objection in the first instance to let as many families as may incline, live on it three years Rent free—on condition of their making certain Improvements which may be stipulated. but what agreement (under the circumstances I have mentioned) to make with them afterwards is a difficulty which weighs powerfully in my mind—If leases are given for money Rents, they must either commence high or rise proportionately to the increasing value of the land, otherwise I shall not receive a compensation. To let the land for ⅓ of the produce may do well for the Landlord whose eye is always on the tenant; but would not I conceive, be very productive to him who lives 3 or 400 Miles distant from them unless he should happen to hit upon a faithful and attentive agent. Some thing however as I observed before must be done, and 3 years Rent free, any families may be upon a certainty of holding it and a preference given to them at the end thereof *on* the *terms* which may be offered by others. I have none of my printed advertisements left, or I would trouble you with one of them—They offered the Land to best of my recollection, in three ways—first for 21 years at five pd ℔ Hundred Acres—2d for ever at an anual rent of £10—and 3d for 999 years the rent to commence at £5 and encrease in a certain Ratio every ⟨100⟩ years—In each case an exemption from Rent was allowed for the 3 first years and in all of them certain buildings and other improvements were required.

Your having mentioned that you hold land at the mouth of Coal River, I would beg leave to observe that I have one tract of 2000 Acres in the point of fork between that River and the Kankawa running up the 1st about 2 Miles (from the point) and up the latter more than 4—and on the opposit 2 Miles above the fork a nother of my tracts for 3000 Acres begins, and runs upwards 6 Miles bordering on the River for quantity. as these tracts are in the vicinity of yours it is possible you may have been on them in which case I would thank you for your opinion of them.

From the mouth of Pokitellica on the East side the river for 13 Miles down the Kankawa I hold the land—and on the other side, from within 2 or 3 miles of the mouth I have a tract which runs near 20 Miles along the River equal to any and I have ever seen all of which may be Seated as hath been mentioned, together with that on the Ohio above.[4] I am &c.

G. Washington.

LB, DLC:GW.

1. Letter not found. In a letter to Bushrod Washington on 3 Dec., GW describes Banks's letter of 21 Oct. and asks Bushrod to make inquiries about his fellow delegate Banks. Banks was a member of the house from Greenbrier County.

2. For the taxes that GW owed and in 1788 paid on his land on the Great Kanawha River in Greenbrier County, see Charles Lee to GW, 17 April 1788, GW to John Hopkins, 27 April 1788, and Hopkins to GW, 14 May 1788.

3. The copyist usually misspelled Kanawha in this way.

4. For GW's landholdings on the Ohio and the Great Kanawha, which GW describes a number of times in his previous correspondence, see GW to Samuel Lewis and to Thomas Lewis, both 1 Feb. 1784, and notes. For a brief description of these tracts by GW, see his letter to David Stuart of 15 Jan. 1788.

To Thomas Johnson

Sir,   Mount Vernon Novr 22d 1787

The letter with which you have been pleased to honor me —dated the 16th Instt, came to my hands the day before yesterday; by the Post of tomorrow, this answer will be forwarded to you.

Mr Rumsey has given you an uncandid acct of his explanation *to me,* of the principle on which his Boat was to be propelled against stream. At the time he exhibited his model, and obtained my certificate, I had no reason to believe that the use of steam was contemplated by him—sure I am it was not mentioned; and equally certain am I, that it would not apply to the project he *then* had in view; the first communication of which, *to me,* was made in Septr 1784 at the Springs in Berkley. The November following, in Richmond, I again met Mr Rumsey, who at that time was applying to the Assembly of this State for an exclusive Act.[1] He then, it is true, spoke of the effect of steam, and of the conviction he was under of the usefulness of its application for the purposes of inland Navigation; but I did not conceive, nor have I done so at any moment since, that it was suggested as part of his original plan, but rather as the ebullition of his genius. It is proper for me howev[e]r to add, that sometime *after this,* Mr Fitch called upon me on his way to Richmond, and explaining his scheme, wanted a letter from me introductory of it to the Assembly of this State—the giving of wch I declined; and went so far as to inform him that tho' I was enjoined not to disclose the principles of Mr Rumseys discovery, yet I would venture to assure him that the thought of applying steam for the purpose he designed it, was not original; but had been mentioned to me by Mr Rumsey. This I conceived incumbent on me to say; that, which ever (if either) of them was the discoverer, might derive the benefit of the invention.[2]

To the best of my recollection, the foregoing is an impartial recital of what has passed between Mr Rumsey and me, on the subject of his Boat Navigation.

Permit me to ask you, my good Sir, if a letter which I wrote to you during the sitting of your last Assembly, enclosing one from Mr Willm Wilson to me, respecting the confiscated property of (I thk) Messrs Dunlap & Co. of Glasgow, ever reached your hands? and if it did, whether any thing was, or can be done, in that business? As an Executor of the Will of Colo. Thos Colvill it behoves me to know precisely what is to be expected from that quarter, as a large sum is due from that Compy to his Estate. I am the more anxious to obtain this information immediately, as Mr Wilson who is concernd in that House, is about to leave the Country.[3] With great esteem & regard I am—Sir Your Most Obedt Hble Servt

Go: Washington

ALS, anonymous donor; LB, DLC:GW.

1. See Certificate for James Rumsey, 7 Sept. 1784 (printed above), James Rumsey to GW, 19 Oct. 1784, 10 Mar. 1785, Hugh Williamson to GW, 19 Feb. 1785, and GW to Hugh Williamson, 15 Mar. 1785.

2. See GW to James Rumsey, 31 Jan. 1786. See also Rumsey to GW, 17 Dec. 1787.

3. GW sent Johnson the letter from the Scottish merchant in Alexandria William Wilson on 28 Dec. 1786. Colin Dunlap & Sons was one of the great Glasgow mercantile firms. GW's involvement in the settlement of Thomas Colvill's estate dated back to 1767 and was not yet near an end. For an introduction to the complexities of the Colvill estate, see Thomas Montgomerie to GW,

24 Oct. 1788, and notes. Wilson had dined at Mount Vernon on Sunday, 18 November.

From Richard Bland Lee

Sir   Alexandria Novr 23 1787

I recieved your Excellency's letter of the 11th Instant to day inclosing one guinea & an half on account of the ram Lamb[1]— As no expence was incurred by me in having him brought to this town permit me to return the half guinea which has been sent on account of charges & beleive me to be with the highest esteem—Your Excellency's most Ob. & hum. Servant

Richard Bland Lee

ALS, PHi: Gratz Collection; Sprague transcript, DLC:GW.

Richard Bland Lee (1761–1827), younger brother of Charles and Henry, Jr., at this time was living in Loudoun County.

1. Letter not found. In the entry in his cash accounts of 15 Nov., GW notes paying Lee £2.2 "for a Cape of Good Hope Lamb" (Ledger B, 256).

Letter not found: from George Weedon, 25 Nov. 1787. On 3 Dec. GW wrote Weedon: "I have received your letter of the 25th Ulto."

From James Jemima Jacobina Douglas

Dr sir   Eden[burgh, Scotland] new Town 1787 nov. 26

I sit down to adres you as father of your Country and as one who his the pour to redres the injur'd one of your subjects Mr Glass Strahcan in virg⟨i⟩nia richmond town James river phychiuns ⟨then owse⟩ to my father andrwe Douglas in 74 6 hundre pound which with the interest upon must near double the sum[.][1] my fath⟨er⟩ dying sudingly with out neading up his affairs his been hard on ⟨me⟩ I am lauffaly proclaimd heir as I am all that reamains of my father if you my Dr sir will be so good as use your pour for me and write a line to me please direct to Shakespeare square new Town Edenburgh I am Dr Sir your humble servant[2]

James Jemima Jacobina Douglas

sir inclosd is a letter to Mr Glas Strahcan which I take upon me to trouble you with as it is hard for a young woman to want that part of my fortune which was gaind with honnour I mea say my father was a genrall freind to all whatever part they Came from excuse my freedom it is only on you I relly for the recovry of it.[3]

ALS, DLC:GW. Miss Douglas addressed the letter to "His Excellency General Washington North America."

1. Dr. Alexander Glas Strachan (b. 1749), a Scot trained at the University in Edinburgh, came to Virginia before the Revolution and settled in Petersburg. There he practiced medicine and established an apothecary business, Alexander G. Strachan & Co. Strachan was also a well-to-do planter.

2. In DLC:GW there is another version of this letter, dated 15 Nov. and in the docket marked "Duplicate." Headed "Eden. new town bak of the theatre," it reads: "I adrese you as the father of your Country you will se by the hand it is a woman that writes for help to Call in a debt due to me by alecxsender Glass Strahcan suregeon in virginia he stays on James river richmond town my father andrwe Douglas sent out the goods to him it was six hundre poun⟨ds⟩ at his death which was in the year seventafour so you will se the interest Can near double the sum if you sir of your Clemency will be so good as use your pour to recover that part that is mine in virginia it will much oblige your humble servant James Jemima Jacobina Douaglas. if you sir will honour with a line it will greatly oblige me."

3. GW answered Miss Douglas from Mount Vernon on 12 May 1788: "Miss, I have received your letter of the 26th of November and have lately had an opportunity, (by a Gentleman of this neighbourhood who was in Richmond) of making the enquieries which you desired. He informs me that he saw the Gentleman mentioned in your letter who acknowledges there is a balance in his hands due to your father but says the sum is not so large as you mention, some part of it having been already paid.

"It will readily occur to you that the only method of recovering the money will be to invest some person on the spot with proper power to act on your behalf and receive it for you. The necessity of appointing some person living in the neighbourhood of the Gentleman from whom the money is due is so obvious that you cannot but be sensible of it. and permit me to observe here that my agency in this business thus far has been no ways inconvenient or disagreeable to me, but my various avocations which require a constant and unremitting attention would compel me to do an injury [to] my feelings by declining to take any part in recovering or receiving the money if it should be proposed. I am Madam, Yr most Obedt Hble Servant Go. Washington" (LB, DLC:GW). The letter to Strachan enclosed by Miss Douglas in her letter to GW has not been found.

From George Mason

Dear Sir   Richmond Novemr 27th 1787.

I this Morning received your Favour of the 15th[1] and shall do myself the Honour of communicating such of our Proceedings as are important; tho' very little Business of that kind, has yet been compleated. The Installment Plan, after being presented to the Committee of the Whole House upon the State of the Commonwealth, & some Hours Debate upon the Subject, has been postponed from time to time; from the best Information I can collect, I fear there is a Majority for it; I shall therefore, whenever the Committee proceed upon the Consideration, endeavour to substitute the Resolve, of which I inclose a Copy; and upon which I wish to be favour'd with your Sentiments.[2]

The performance of the Treaty, with respect to British Debts, has taken up three Days of warm debate; Mr Henry Genl Lawson & Merriweather Smith on one Side; & Colo. Geo. Nicholas (who is improved into a very useful Member) & myself on the other; the Yeas & Nays were demanded upon three Questions on this Subject; first upon an Amendment proposed by Mr Henry, for suspending the Operation until the Treaty shou'd be fully perform'd on the Part of Great Britain; which was rejected by a Majority of 33—secondly upon an Amendment proposed by Mr Ronald, tantamount to an Instalment of British Debts; knowing that Instalments were calculated to please a strong Party, we avoided going into the Subject at large, & confined ourselves to the Impropriety of instaling British Debts, before we cou'd know the Sense of the Legislature upon a general Instalment of all Debts; as any Discrimination wou'd be a palpable Infraction of the Treaty. The Amendment was rejected by a Majority of 22; the main Question was then put upon the Resolve for repealing all Laws which prevented the Recovery of British Debts, with a clause suspending the operation of the Repeal until the other States shall also pass Laws to enable British Subjects to recover Debts, & carried by a Majority of 40; a Bill has been brought in, in Consequence of the said Resolve, once read, & committed to a Committee of the Whole House on Friday next; some of the most respectable Characters in the House were nominated a Committee to prepare the Bill; but Mr C———n with the Vanity so natural to a Young Man, took upon himself to draw it without the other Gentlemen having time to consider it, and has drawn it so very injudiciously, that in it's present Shape, it wou'd infallibly be thrown out on the third Reading— however we will take care to regenerate it in Committee; & I make no Doubt of it's passing the House of Delegates; there will be a strong, but I trust a fruitless Opposition in the Senate;[3] so soon as the Treaty Bill is secured, we will bring forward the Sequestration Business; 275,000£ Paper Curry of the average Value of about 14d. in the pound, having been paid into the Treasury, in Discharge of British Debts; In the Discussion of this Subject, I expect we shall see some long Faces. A Bill for receiving Tobo in Discharge of Taxes will certainly pass; it is in my Opinion a foolish & injurious Project; & as such it was opposed; but to no Purpose; after finding their Strength, the first Step was to raise the last Year's Price of the James River Tobo we had then nothing left, but to endeavour to bring up the Price of our Tobo in Proportion, in which we, with some Difficulty, succeeded, & got our Tobo fixed at 28/ the James River Tobo having been previously setted at 30/.

Little Progress has yet been made on the Subject of Revenue. I shall use my best Endeavours to prevent the rect of public Securitys of any kind in Taxes, (as the only effectual Means of digging up Speculation by the Roots) and appropriating a good Fund for purchasing them up at the Market Price; by way of Experiment, & to shew the Members the Utility of such a Plan, we have this Day, against a strong Opposition, ordered about £6000 now in the Treasury, to be immediately applyed to that Purpose; which I hope will have a good Effect upon the Minds of the Members; yet I fear the Interest of the Speculators is too powerful, to suffer any regular extensive System upon this Subject.

The Bill for prohibiting the Importation of Spirits stands committed to a Committee of the Whole House, the Day after to-morrow. Dr Stuart tells me he has sent you one of the printed Bills; you will find it fraught with such Absurdities as render it perfectly ridiculous; yet I much doubt their finding them out, so as to amend the Bill in the Committee; the opposers ought to let them go on their own Way, & reserve their Attack to the passage on the third reading—as the Bill now stands, according to the strict grammatical Construction, Spirits are subject to Forfeiture after they have been swallowed, & the Informer will be equally subject to the penalty with the persons he informs against—but besides the Nonsense of the Bill, the very Principle of it is impolitic as it will affect our Commerce, & Revenue; partial & unjust in sacrificing the Interest of one part of the Community to the other. I am afraid this Scrawl is hardly legible; being obliged, as I am, to write with bad Spectacles, bad Light, & bad Ink. I beg my Compliments to your Lady, and the Family at Mount Vernon; and am, with the most sincere Respect & Esteem dear Sir, Your affectionate & obdt Sert

G. Mason

ALS, DLC:GW.

1. Letter not found.

2. The debt installment plan, to which Mason alludes in his letter of 6 Nov., was rejected. The resolution Mason enclosed regarding this plan is in CD-ROM:GW and is printed in Rutland, *Mason Papers*, 3:1021–22.

3. Patrick Henry and Robert Lawson were the two delegates from Prince Edward County; Meriwether Smith represented Essex County, and George Nicholas, Albemarle. The three votes were taken in the house of delegates on Saturday, 17 November. Francis Corbin (1759–1821), the "Young Man" who was first elected to the house of delegates in 1784 to represent Middlesex County, was chairman of a committee of ten, including both Mason and Nicholas, to bring in a bill for repealing provisions of state laws contravening the Treaty of Peace of 1783. An act "to repeal so much of all and every act or acts of Assembly, as prohibits the recovery of British debts" received final passage on 12 December.

To Gardoqui

Dear Sir, Mount Vernon November 28th 1787

I have received your letters of the 29th of October & 9th of Novr. The latter was handed to me by Colo. H. Lee, together with 4 Vols. of Don Quixote which you did me the honor to send to me. I consider them as a mark of your esteem which is highly pleasing to me, and which merits my warmest acknowledgment, I must therefore beg, my dear Sir, that you will accept of my best thanks for them.

You[r] wish to establish a permanent and sincere amity between these States and the Court of Spain is highly meritorious; and if, as you observe, no two nations apply more exactly to each other, a connexion between them upon the basis of reciprocal interest must be a very desireable event.

Altho no man could feel more pleasure and satisfaction than myself in seeing this Country form such connexions as would render it happy and flourishing, yet my being totally detached from all matters of government, entirely prevents my interfering, with any degree of propriety, in an affair of this nature. I am far removed from, and have as little to do in the publick transactions of this State as any citizen in it; and in matters which come under the cognizance of the United States I have been careful not to have any concern, unless when called upon for information respecting any subject which was connected with my publick employment during the war.

I shall be exceedingly sorry to see you obliged to abandon an object which has in view the interest and advantage of both our countries, and I cannot yet despair of their being connected in such a manner as to ensure a mutual benefit. With Sentiments of the Most perfect consideration And respect I have the Honor to be, Dear Sir—Yr Most Obedt and very Hble Servant

G. Washington

LB, DLC:GW.

From Barbé-Marbois

Sir.   Port au Prince November the 30th 1787
I have so many times experienced your Excellency's Favour that I hope you'll forgive me for an application which I could not refuse to a brave officer who at the same time is a friend of mine. you will see by a letter of Count de la Luzerne which accompagnies this that he takes a particular interest in knowing whether Mr de Saqui des Tourets can or not wear the insignia of the Cincinnati. I heartily wish your opinion may be in his favor & I shall regard it as one conferred on myself If I am ennabled to tell him he is thougt by you, Sir, a Fit Subject for that Society. I know you cannot positively determine the question: but your opinion would considerably assist us in forming one.[1]

Mrs Marbois who received some marks of Friendship from your Excellency has made me a very happy husband, She has given me two fine daughters half french half american. I wish I may at a future day introduce them to you, sir they may be a specimen of the good effect of the union of the two nations.[2]

You know Count de la Luzerne has been appointed a Minister of the Navy and Sailed for France on the 13th Instant to take possession of that Department.

The Chevalier is very likely to go to London as an ambassador *in case circumstances will admit of his displaying that character.*[3] With great respect I am Sir, Your Excellency's Most humble obedient Servant

Demarbois

LS, DLC:GW; LS, DLC:GW; LS, DSoCi. GW mistakenly docketed the second LS at DLC "1788" instead of "1787." The assistant secretary general of the Society of the Cincinnati, George Turner, wrote on the cover of the LS in DSoCi: "Produced in Extra-Meetg May 1788."

1. See César-Henri de La Luzerne to GW, 12 Nov., n.1. See also GW to Barbé-Marbois, 4 April 1788.

2. François Barbé de Marbois (Barbé-Marbois) married Elizabeth Moore of Philadelphia in 1784 (Barbé-Marbois to GW, 8 June 1784, n.2).

3. "The Chevalier" is Anne-César de La Luzerne de Beuzeville, chevalier de La Luzerne. See note 1.

From Richard Butler

Excellent Sir   Carlisle [Pa.] 30th Novr 1787

To know at any time that it is your Excellencys wish that any thing within my power should be done, will always be a Sufficient motive with me to do it. But when you were pleased to inform me that it had been required by the August Empress Sovereign of all the Russias, Through the medium of that Excellent Character the Right Honorable Major General The Marquis de La Fayette, it was an additional excitement to the completion of this work, And I only regret the difficulty of Obtaining more, which if wished for must be the work of time there being so few of our people or Uropeans Among the Indian tribes who have perseverence and understand a Sufficiency of their own tongue to be able to Translate the Indian into it— Should this be an Object of future Attention nothing will give me greater pleasure than to add my endeavours to its promotion.

With the greatest Respect I have the Sattisfaction to transmit this to your hand, and to Assure your Excellency That I am at all times and all places, Your Excellencys most Obedient Hbl. St

Richd Butler

ALS, DLC:GW. This letter is bound with: (1) Shawnee and Delaware Indian vocabularies, or word lists, running to forty pages in all, prepared by Butler, along with a copy of a two-page Cherokee and Choctaw vocabulary prepared by Benjamin Hawkins (see Enclosure I); and (2) an abstract of a letter from Butler to GW containing his observations on the life and culture of the Ohio Valley Indians (printed as Enclosure II). These bound manuscript pages are encased in a wallpaper cover. A notation by Jared Sparks indicates that the manuscripts, bound in this fashion, were a part of GW's papers when he examined them early in the nineteenth century. The letter printed here is inserted after the seventh page of Butler's vocabulary (see source note, Enclosure I). Butler also at this time returned to GW the printed vocabulary that Lafayette had sent to have the Indian words inserted.

Lafayette wrote GW the year before on 10 Feb. 1786, that he was enclosing "a Vocabulary which the Empress of Russia Has Requested me to Have filled up with indian Names as she has ordered an Universal dictionary to be made of all languages—it would greatly oblige Her to collect the words she sends translated into the several idioms of the Nations on the Banks of the Oyho." GW replied on 10 May 1786 that he would do his best to have Catherine's vocabulary "compleated" but warned that she must be patient, for "the Indian tribes on the Ohio are numerous, dispersed & distant from those who are most likely to do the business properly."

On 20 Aug. 1786 GW wrote to Thomas Hutchins, the geographer of the United States, who was supervising the survey of the Ohio territory for Congress. He sent to Hutchins Lafayette's letter of 10 Feb. with "a specimen of the vocabulary" and urged him to "extend the vocabulary as far as, with the aid of your friends, you conveniently can." Presumably the "specimen" was Lafayette's list of words, and by asking him to "extend the vocabulary" GW apparently meant that Hutchins should include as many tribal languages or dialects as he could. Hutchins wrote in reply on 8 Nov. 1786 that he would try to "make the Vocabulary as extensive and perfect" as possible.

Before receiving Hutchins's reply, having learned that the Indian agent Richard Butler (1743–1791) had been made superintendent of Indian affairs for the northern department, GW wrote to Butler, on 27 Nov. 1786, to request him "also" to assist with the Indian vocabulary. "If Capt. Hutchins is on the Ohio," he told Butler, "he will shew you the paper which was transmitted to me by the Marquis, and which I forwarded to him. If he is not, it may be sufficient to inform you that it was no more than to insert English words & the name of things in one column—& the Indian therefor [thereof] in others on the same line, under the different heads of Delaware, Shawnees, Wiendots &c. &c." In his introduction to the Shawnee-Delaware vocabulary (see Enclosure I), Butler speaks of "the words which were sent me to be translated," indicating that he received from Hutchins Lafayette's list of English words for which Indian equivalents were to be supplied. (On 3 April 1788 GW responded to a letter from Butler dated 13 Mar., which has not been found: "My not acknowledging the reception of the printed Vocabulary must have been an omission, for it came safely to hand with the manuscript one.") On 10 Jan. 1788 GW sent to Lafayette the Indian vocabulary that Butler enclosed in this letter, the vocabulary treated here in Enclosure I being a copy of the one sent to Lafayette or possibly Butler's expanded version of it.

GW at the same time sent Lafayette "a shorter specimen of the language of the Southern Indians" prepared by Benjamin Hawkins (see the note for Enclosure I) and "The Delaware Indian & English spelling Book by Mr [David] Zeisberger."

Hutchins failed to send his vocabulary to GW before his death in April 1789 (see George Morgan to GW, 1 Sept. 1789).

Enclosure I
Richard Butler's Indian Vocabulary

[c.30 November 1787]

The following Seven pages to the word Ten markd thus #, are the words which were sent me to be translated, The Shawano I have done myself which are Spelled as nearly as possible to the real Sound of the Indian word. The Lenoppea, or Delaware, was done by a Young man Called John Killbuck, an Indian of that nation who has been Educated at Princetown College at the Expence of the U.S. & patronage of Congress, and is Spelled according to his own Idea of the Idiom[1]—The residue of the 7th page I have filled up in Shawano to Shew their maner of counting from one, to ten thousand—Note—*A* in the Shawano tongue is to be Sounded broad as in *All, Wall* &c. Except where it follows *E* in the middle or at the end of a word, it is then Sounded soft as in the English. Marks, Thus (__) under a Syllable denotes that the letters are to be expressed, or Sounded, as conjunctly as possible. Thus, (,) below & between the letters, denote the division of the Syllables. The Emphasis must be placed agreeable to the combination of Sound attached to, or attendant on, the Same letters in the English, being obliged to Spell to the sound of the Indian word *Ie* at the beginning of a word, & *ie* at the end, is to be sounded like double *ee*[2]—and *Ia* when composing a Syllable at the begining of a word is Sounded like *double ee, and a broad yained,* or like *ya.* And *eh* after *u, e* or *o,* in the same syllable to be Sounded gutterally as *gh in aught.* And *chi, cha, che* are to be sounded as ch in change, che in *cherry* or ch in *child,* &c. which are the chief directions which appears to me necessary for Reading this vocabulary.

R. Butler

Indian Vocabulary

English	Shawano	Lenoppea, or Delaware
God	Wos,sa-Mon,nit,ta	Keeshalamscocup
Father	Noo,tha	Nuha
Mother	Nie,kea	Awnah
Child	Nie,chan	Memendid
Me	Nie, or Nie,la	Nee
Yes	Scea,la or Ah! Ah![3]	Cohan
No	Mot,ta	Matta
Cold	Wea,pie	Taha
Name	Os,se,tho, or Os,se,tho,tchie	Lowasowocan
Circle	Wa,wa,we,a,kie	Toquahaso
Is	Ie,nie, or Ee,nie	Nancy
Mind	Ish,itte,he[4]	Letohaocon
Animal	Mie,ken,whe	Anasus
Stake	Ap,pas,sie	Hetook, or Nebatoke
Word	Pec,ki,cot,to,[5]	Lewaogan
River	Mis,sie Thee,pee	Seapo
Work	Hosto,[6]	Mekomosoogan
Death	Nep,poa	Ankaluogan
Water	Nip,pee	Nappie
Sea	Chie,kam,mi,kie	Hequepie
Hill	Wat,chi,wie	
Mountain	Missie Wat,chi,wie	Keytatennunk
Pain	Och,quot,ka	Wanamatamen
Laziness	Mel,la,wat,ti,thie	Nulatawoogan
Summer	Mel,loock,com,mie	Neppan
Salt	Nip,pee-Pim,mie	Seakaha
Year	Cuch,cut,too	Couten
Ox	Me,tho,tho Ki,chilsi,we	Oxzon
Light	Wap,po,ne	Ohaack
Heart	Ot,to,hie	Weyta
Strength	Wis,sa,cut,tawie	Gitinasogen
Health	We,wos,sa,kie	Weylamulsoogan
Well	Kie,kea	Welamulsoe
Ill	Och,quil,loo,kie	Mattamulsoe
Handsome	Wil,li,thie	Waylosoe
Hand	Let,chie	Naark
Foot	Kus,sie	Waseed
Eyes	Kis,kees,si,qua	Wisking
Ear	Och,to,wa,ka	Weytaoak
Nose	Chas, or Chas,sie	Wekeyon
Mouth	Ton,nie	Wayt
Head	Wee,sie	Wile
Forehead	Kis,keesqua	Lawokalaa
Teeth	Peet,tal,lie	Weepitald

D, DLC:GW. The document includes a copy, in Butler's hand, of the Shawnee-Delaware word list, or vocabulary, prepared by Butler "entirely myself," and a copy, also in Butler's hand, of a shorter Cherokee-Choctaw vocabulary made independently by Benjamin Hawkins. Both are in DLC:GW bound with Butler's letter to GW of 30 Nov. and Butler's copy of an extract of another letter from him to GW, undated but written at the same time. See the source note, Butler to GW, 30 November. Butler's Shawnee-Delaware vocabulary in DLC:GW is a copy of, or an expansion of the one that he sent to GW on 30 Nov., which GW in turn forwarded to Lafayette for Catherine on 10 Jan. 1788. It runs to thirty-seven pages of forty to forty-five lines each. The first six pages and a part of the seventh are a listing of the English words that were to be translated for Catherine with the Shawnee and Delaware equivalents entered in parallel columns. At this point, on page seven, Butler inserted his letter to GW of 30 November. And thereafter, for the rest of the vocabulary, he first listed Shawnee, not English, words and groups of words and gave their English equivalent—one or more words, phrases, or expressions—in the opposite column. (For insight into why Butler saw this as a better approach for attaining some understanding and appreciation of the language of the Shawnee, see the passage taken from Butler's draft of a letter to GW and printed in Enclosure II, source note). On the last four pages of his vocabulary, Butler constructs a dialogue, in Shawnee and English, in which a Shawnee who has recently returned after a long absence in the white man's world, converses first with a messenger, then with a conductor, and, finally, with a chief, to demonstrate the differences between the ordinary and the formal speech of the Shawnee. He ends his vocabulary with the Lord's Prayer in Shawnee with its English translation. Only Butler's introduction of his vocabulary and the first page of the vocabulary are printed here.

None of Hawkins's Cherokee-Choctaw vocabulary, which begins with the words *god, good, bad,* and *body,* has been printed here. James Madison, having heard of GW's intended efforts to secure Indian vocabularies for Catherine the Great, obtained from Benjamin Hawkins the Cherokee-Choctaw word list and on 18 Mar. 1787 sent it to GW.

1. In the spring of 1779, at the behest of Congress, Delaware chiefs brought three boys to George Morgan's farm adjoining the college campus at Princeton and left them there to be educated. One of these was 16-year-old John Killbuck, who along with Thomas Killbuck, his father's half brother, returned to Ohio in 1785 (Ruth L. Woodward and Wesley Frank Craven, *Princetonians, 1784–1790: A Biographical Dictionary* [Princeton, N.J., 1991], 442–52).

2. Butler's signature appears here in the middle of the sentence, and at the end of the document he signed his initials. The signature has been moved to the end of the document.

3. Butler inserted: "sounded from the Stomach Sharp & broad."

4. Butler added here: "Thought."

5. Butler added the meaning: "to Speak."

6. Butler added: "to do, or make."

Enclosure II
Extract of letter from Richard Butler

[c.30 November 1787]
Extract of a Letter from General Butler to General Washington (accompanying this Vocabulary).

The little which I have been able to collect of the history of the Shawanoes from oral tradition & their old men, with some observations of my own may not be unacceptable, & may probably assist, or open a door to more able Inquirers. They say they were originally from an Island, and that they came to the country of the Ohio & Susquehana (which is the most easterly point I can trace of their having resided in a body) from the Seacoast of So. Carolina & Georgia, or Florida, and I know that there are yet the remains of a tribe of Shawanoes called the ⟨Tha,wic, kel,loo⟩ among the Cherokees, who still retain the tongue in its perfection, and in my time among the Shawanoes many families came from thence to the Shawano country & found Relations in their Towns. These circumstances have led me to suspect that they were originally from the Island of Cuba & had probably fled from thence to the main from the severity of the Spanish Settlers there. And the great extent westward which this language is *partly understood* & is still useful in traveling, leads me to suppose that many of our western tribes are from the same, or other Islands in the Mexican Gulph & that quarter of the world, and altho' their languages are not the Same (as was the case on those Islands when first discovered) yet there is some affinity as has been already mentioned. And it is found that the Indians & Languages from the Lakes Southward to the sea, differ very considerably from those nations which inhabit Northward & Eastward to the Sea, which has also led me to form an idea, that this *certain* difference of people has been the cause of the latter, as well as the former wars which have once depopulated the Ohio & other parts of the Western Country of its ancient Inhabitants; as that country was long a waste & kind of *war* or disputed hunting ground between the Northe[r]n & Southern tribes, even to our time, and I have it also (as a corroborant to this opinion) from Oral tradition that a very numerous people called the *Spil,les* did certainly inhabit the Ohio & its waters from whom it derived the name of *Spil,le,wi-Thee,pie* or *Mis,spil,le,wi-Thee,pie,* which signifies the Spille-River, or the great River of the *Spil,les:* and who are supposed by the present inhabiting Indians to be the authors of all the works yet to be seen in that Country. This name for the Ohio has been generally mistaken by the Traders, who construed it into the great River of the Turkeys from the amazing plenty of that fowl wild on its banks, and the near resemblance of the names in the Shawano language, A Turkey being called (*Pel,le,wa*)—A River *Thee,pie,* & the word *Missi,* big, which words being combined would be *Mis,si-Pel,le,wa Thee,pie*—Englished—The *great Turkey River* and abreviated into the Indian manner of expressing it, would make it sound nearly as above *Mis,spil,le,wi-Thee,pie,* and their want of the information which I have had, is the force from whence this mistake arose.

These wars which I have mentioned, and the traces of antiquity, such as the large Cones or Mounds of Earth filled generally with human bones, and the Fortifications which appear on many parts of the Ohio & the Western Country, have led me to look back & think, whether the people, whose numbers agreeable to the magnitude of those works must have been very great, might not be those expelled from these waters by the ancient Iroquois, (as the same Indian tradition says they went off in a body & crossed the Mississippi westward) and afterwards the very formers of the Mexican Empire. For we find, from the historical accounts of the discovery of that Country, that such mounds were frequent & were sometimes the alters of sacrifice, which being admitted, may account for these being filled with human bones, many of which appear to have undergone the action of fire. We also find that the Fortifications bear some resemblance in both Countries, and that some of the stone Hatchets, spears & arrow points of flint &c. bear a great likeness. It is also said that some rude hyerogliphicks have been discovered on peices of stone; some very curious articles I have lately seen of stone— but their use I cannot devise; one is about three inches diameter circular & about half an inch thick, with a hole of an inch diameter in the Center, and hollowed out on the two flat sides to the center as if it had been countersunk, being thin in the middle and thick at the outside; The other is a cylindrical piece of marble about an inch & one eighth diameter, the hollow part or caliber is about as wide at one end as a musket, and tapers or narrows at the other which terminates in a small hole as if designed to have been hung with a string; the inside evinces its having been bored or ground out with another stone or some hard substance which proves it not to be a petrefaction. There have been also discovered some rude kinds of monumental architecture such as graves or repositories for dead bodies formed by rude stones, some in the natural shape & some broken or jointed by some such instrument as the stone hatchet or hammer. The pottery is also another proof or support to the supposition that, that species of manufacture was in similar perfection and composed of the same ingredients in the Ohio & Mexican Countries.

We also find that the Indians called by the historian *Iroquois* (the remains of whom the five Northern nations at present claim to be) are from the East & North part of this Continent, & that they were a very warlike people, and Conquerors of all the Indian Nations from the Lakes to the Mississippi and on all the waters of the Ohio long since the arrival of the first settlers from Europe; and that they may be of Tarter Origins or descent I think not improbable, as they may have come from the Northern parts of Asia across to our Continent, and streached, some along the Seacoast by Hudson's Bay, & others by the way of the Lakes from the high north Latitudes where the Asiatic & American Continents approach each other and their language differs exceedingly from all the Southern Indians.[1]

AL (incomplete), DLC:GW. Butler extracted this from his draft of a letter dated 30 Nov. 1787 in the Draper Papers: Frontier Wars (WHi). Butler omits the first, long paragraph of the draft in which he provides considerable insight into his thoughtful and sophisticated approach to preparing his Indian vocabulary. The omitted paragraph reads: "The Sattisfaction⟨s⟩ I have had, & shall always enjoy in obeying evrey command of your Illustrious s⟨elf⟩—The honor of gratifying in this ⟨instance⟩ the curiosity of the August Empress Sovereign of Russia—and the pleasure of puting it [in] your power to comply with the requisition made for that purpose by that most Amiable ⟨Ch⟩aracter the Rt Honble Majr Genl The Marquis De La Fayette (who will ⟨ever be⟩ thot of with gratitude by Americans). I concieve as the highest ⟨in⟩ducements to Such an undertaking—Accept then great Sir the ⟨labour⟩ of Some painful hours caused by A broken leg⟨,⟩ which has been the means of procrastinating this work & keeping it so long from your Excellencies hand—This circumstance Sir Should not have been mentioned did I not think it proper your Excellency should know that something of more than common import had interfered between me & the execution of any thing required by your Exc⟨e⟩llency & the Sattisfaction I a⟨m⟩ confident it will ⟨*mutilated*⟩ am again ⟨*mutilated*⟩ was led to attempt its completion in the Shawano tongue as early as Strength of body & mind would ⟨per⟩mit—& only regret I have not as yet been Able to Obtain from any other quarter vocabularys of any other than the delaware tongue—To say that the Shawano vocabulary (which I have done intirely myself) is as well done as it could be would be Saying too much but that it is done with as much precision or exactness as the maner & time would admit of is certain—The words translated from the English to the Shawano—& from the Shawano to the English hath given the full Sence, & in many instances are as nearly litteral as possible *adhering to the Idiom* but it must be Observed, that to reduce or combine Single words to the form of⟨,⟩ or to Answer in general conversations from this kind of Vocabulary is nearly impossible and I believe it is beyond a doubt that the most lerned in the Oriental languages (which have been reduced to form or meathod) have found this difficulty and were consequently obliged to go deep into the Spirit of any of these languages in order to obtain a Sufficient knowledge of the Strength of expression & a proper Idea of the Sence Attending both Single & compound words to come at or gain that point—This difficulty is I suppose not less in the languages of our modern Indians as I find a great difference between *their council* or bussiness language⟨,⟩ & that of their Dialogue & common conversation, The former being Strong & impressive—full of Rhetorical flowers & fine Allegory—the latter, plain, to the point & Simple in the mode of Expression Consequently to form A grammer, or book with Sattisfactory Specimens of these Different Species of one language must take a considerable time to compleat in form—This I have not ventured to attempt for the two following reasons first It was your Excellencies wish that Specimens Should be Sent forward as Soon as possible—Secondly, I did not know whether it is an Object to go so deep into A matter which does not promise to give much light into the Origin or Antient history of A people who have no records & whose Oral tradition is both poor & Shallow & (as this will) could only Serve to compare with the languages of the ⟨*illegible*⟩ world—in order to form Some Idea of their Origin from Any Similarity or Affinity which may be found in these languages, or Some expressions of them."

1. In the draft of this letter, Butler concluded with this passage: "many other Observations might be yet made upon this extensive Subject, but I fear the length of this epistle is already too great an intrusion on your Excellencys ⟨patence⟩ therefore will close with mentioning that I have Submited the vocabulary to the Observation of the Revd Doctor Chars Nesbit Presidt of Dickenson College who is acknowledged to be A gentleman of great learning & an ⟨extensive⟩ judge of the Oriental & other languages."

From James Madison

Dear Sir   N. York Novr [c.30] 1787.

My last inclosed the seven first numbers of the paper of which I gave you some account. I now add the seven following numbers, which close the first branch of the subject, the importance of the Union. The succeeding papers shall be forwarded from time to time as they come out.[1]

The latest authentic information from Europe, places the Dutch in a wretched situation. The patriots will probably depend in the event on external politics for the degree of security and power that may be left them. The Turks & Russians have begun a war in that quarter. And a general one is not improbable.

I have heard nothing of consequence lately concerning the progress of the New Constitution. The Pennsylvania Convention has probably by this time come to a decision; but it is not known here.

Not more than two or three States are yet convened. The prospect of a quorum during the winter continues precarious. With every sentiment of respect & attachment I remain Dear Sir yr Affect. humble servt

Js Madison Jr

ALS, DLC:GW; copy, DLC: Madison Papers. Madison dated this letter 20 Nov., but as the editors of the *Madison Papers* demonstrate, it could not have been written before 30 Nov. and probably was written on that date. See Rutland and Hobson, *Madison Papers*, 10:284, n.1.

1. Madison enclosed the first seven papers of the *Federalist* in his letter of 18 November. See note 2 of that document.

To Samuel Powel

Dear Sir,   Mount Vernon Novr 30th 1787.

With much pleasure we received the acct of the safe arrival of Mrs Powell & yourself at Philadelphia; and that your journey was unattended by accidents, and less delayed than might have been expected.[1]

The Mr Morris's gave us the pleasure of their company two days & nights on their way to Richmond, & did not leave us without hope of their pursuing this rout back.

By this evenings Post (for the papers brot by which I am now sending to Alexanda) we expect to know the decision of your State Convention on the Fœderal Government. In this State, matters remain, I believe, nearly in statu quo.

I would with great pleasure have sent you more of the Spanish Chesnuts had not the few which I saved for my own use been planted before your letter came to hand. Next year, if the Trees bear, I will save as many as you or your friends may have occasion for—and lest I should forget it, I beg you to remind me abt the first of October.[2]

Mrs Washington and the family join me in affectionate regards for Mrs Powell and yourself and we join in requesting you to accept our grateful thanks for the tender of kind offices you have respectively made us. With great esteem & regard I am Dear Sir Yr Most Obedt Hble Servt

Go: Washington

ALS, ViMtV; LB, DLC:GW.

1. Powel wrote on 13 November.

2. Powel on 9 Sept. 1788 reminded GW of his promise to send him chestnuts.

To David Stuart

Dear Sir,   Mount Vernon 30th Novr 1787.

Your favor of the 14th came duly to hand.[1] I am sorry to find by it that the opposition is gaining strength. At this however I do not wonder. The adversaries to a measure are generally, if not always, more active & violent than the advocates; and frequently employ means which the others do not, to accomplish their ends.

I have seen no publication yet, that ought, in my judgment, to shake the proposed Government in the mind of an impartial public. In a word, I have hardly seen any that is not addressed to the passions of the people; and obviously calculated to rouse their fears. Every attempt to amend the Constitution at this time, is, in my opinion, idly vain. If there are characters who prefer disunion, or seperate Confederacies to the general Government which is offered to them, their opposition may, for ought I know, proceed from principle; but as nothing in my conception is more to be depricated than a disunion, or these seperate Confederacies, my voice, as far as it will extend, shall be offered in favor of the latter.

That there are some writers (and others perhaps who may not

have written) who wish to see these States divided into several confederacies is pretty evident. As an antidote to these opinions, and in order to investigate the ground of objections to the Constitution which is submitted to the People, the Fœderalist, under the signature of Publius, is written. The numbers which have been published I send you. If there is a Printer in Richmond who is really well disposed to support the New Constitution he would do well to give them a place in his Paper. They are (I think I may venture to say) written by able men; and before they are finished, will, if I mistake not, place matters in a true point of light. Altho' I am acquainted with some of the writers who are concerned in this work, I am not at liberty to disclose their names, nor would I have it known that they are sent by *me* to *you* for promulgation.[2]

You will recollect that the business of the Potomack Company is withheld from the Assembly of Maryland until it is acted upon in this State—That the sitting of that Assembly is expected to be short—And that our operations may be suspended if no other recourse is to be had than to common law processes to obtain the dividends which are called for by the Directors, & not paid by the Subscribers.[3]

Certificate & Commutation taxes I hope will be done away by this Assembly. And that it will not interfere either with public treaties, or private contracts. Bad indeed must the situation of that Country be, when this is the case. With great pleasure I received the information respecting the commencement of my Nephews political course—I hope he will not be so buoyed up by the favourable impression it has made as to become a babbler.[4]

If the Convention *was* such a tumultuous, & disorderly body as a certain Gentleman has represented it to be, it may be ascribed, in a great degree to some dissatisfied characters who would not submit to the decisions of a majority thereof.[5]

I shall depend upon the Corn from Mr Henley—all here are well & join me in good wishes for you—I am Dr Sir Yrs Affectionately

Go: Washington

ALS, MiU-C: Schoff Collection; LB, DLC:GW.
1. Letter not found.
2. See James Madison to GW, 18 Nov. 1787, n.2.

3. See GW to George Mason and Stuart, 4 Nov., GW to Thomas Johnson and Thomas Sim Lee, 9 Dec., and Johnson to GW, 11 December.

4. See GW to Bushrod Washington, 9 November.

5. GW undoubtedly was referring to George Mason. Mason wrote GW on 7 Oct. complaining about the lack of "Moderation & Temper, in the latter end of the Convention."

To Clement Biddle

Dear Sir,   Mount Vernon Decr 3d 1787.

Your letters of the 23d of Septr & 15th of Novr came duly to hand.[1] You may inform Mr Haines that my Barley, this year, shared the same fate with my other crops. The drought during the summer was so excessive that I cannot form any just opinion of what it might produce in a seasonable year; it yielded about 14 bushls to the acre which was a proportionate crop to any other kind of Grain which I sowed; and if I judge of its success from this circumstance it must be favourable. This information I would have given you sooner had I been able to have ascertained the quantity of Barley that was made.[2]

I have requested Thomas Smith Esqr. of Carlyle, who, I expect, has, or will recover some money which is due to me in the Western Country, to put it into your hands, unless he has an opportunity of forwarding it directly to Alexandria; if you should receive it I will thank you to deposit it in the bank for me, & send me the notes that I may negociate them here as I have occasion for the Money.

I enclose to you a letter to Mr Smith which I will thank you to forward in as safe & expeditious a manner as you can.[3]

As I imagine you have, by this time, recd the interest due on my warrant in your hands, or if you have not, Mr Smith will, upon receiving the enclosed letter, forward some money to you, I must request you to pay Mr Charles Pettit's bill for 4 Backs & 8 Jambs sent to me, which amounts to £18.5.1.[4]

I will thank you to inform me the lowest prices for which good fresh Clover, Timothy & Orchard Grass seed can be purchased with you. I am Dear Sir, Yr most Obedt Hbe Servt

Go: Washington

P.S. The Leopard skin sent by Captn Steward arrived safe.[5]

LS, PHi: Washington-Biddle Correspondence; LS ("duplicate"), PHi: Washington-Biddle Correspondence; LB, DLC:GW. Both LS's are in the hand of Tobias Lear and were docketed by Biddle. GW enclosed the duplicate in his letter to Biddle of 24 Jan. 1788.

    1. Biddle's letter of 15 Nov. 1787 has not been found.

    2. See Biddle to GW, 23 Sept., and note 2 of that document.

    3. See GW to Thomas Smith, this date.

    4. For Charles Pettit's charges for these items, see Pettit to GW, 6 Nov., n.1.

    5. Steward may be the ship captain Aaron Steward, who as the master of the *Dolphin* had brought goods to GW from Biddle in the past.

To Embree & Shotwell

Gentn   Mount Vernon Decr 3d 1787

    Colo. Henry Lee (who called upon me as he returned home from New York)[1] informed me that you dealt largely in grass seeds (saved in this Country)—that you sold none but what was good—and those on the most moderate terms.

    Under this information I beg leave to ask the price of the following, and whether an opportunity could be depended upon for sending them by water to Alexandria before the month of March next.

    Red Clover   Seed
    Timothy   Do
    Orchard grass   Do

He told me that he had bought some of the first from you and he thinks at 4 dollars pr Bushl but not having the Bill at hand could not be positive. Imported Seeds or the Seeds of this Country if not of the last years growth I would not purchase. the first, unless brot in the Cabbin is always injured and the latter is not to be depended upon.[2] Your answer to this letter by the Post will oblige Gentn Yr Most Obedt Sert

                             G. Washington

LB, DLC:GW.

    Embree & Shotwell (Lawrence Embree and William Shotwell) of 24 Queen Street, New York, specialized in the sale of grass seeds.

    1. On 7 Dec. Henry Lee, Jr., wrote to James Madison of his visit to Mount Vernon on 24–26 Nov.: "I saw Genl. Washington on my return, he continues firm as a rock" (Rutland and Hobson, *Madison Papers,* 10:295–96; see *Diaries,* 5:220).

2. Embree & Shotwell replied from New York on 14 Dec.: "Respected Friend Thy Esteemed Favour of 3d Inst. was duly Recd. We now have the pleasure of replying thereto, And wish it was in our power to give thee Assurances, of supplying thee with ⟨all⟩ the kinds of Grass Seeds thou mentions; but the Orchard Grass is not at present to be procured, and we are something doubtfull whether we shall be able to obtain any, timely to ship for Alexandria; As to Clover and Timothy, we are at present selling of the Growth of this Country; The former @ 1od. ℔ lb. & the latter @ 22/ ℔ Bushel, of unquestionable Quality. Imported Seeds we decline dealing in, they being so uncertain that we dare not recommend them. Should have but little doubts of meeting with a Conveyance for Alexandria, tho at present know of none. Should thou incline to Order any Seed, will thank thee for thy Instructions as early as Convenient" (DLC:GW).

After receiving this response GW wrote on 30 Dec. from Mount Vernon: "Gentn Your letter of the 14th came duly to hand. Colo. Lee either did not comprehend the price of your Seeds or I have misunderstood him for they are higher than I was led to conceive. However as I want seeds on which I can depend. I will, provided they can be got to me by the end of March *at farthest* and as much sooner as you please—take ten Bushels of red clover seed, and 8 Bushels of Timothy seed; both of the last years growth, clean and good.

"If in consideration of the quantity, and the prospect of my dealing with you every year for a large supply of these articles (if I find my interest in it) you should be disposed to lower the retale prices mentioned in your letter to me, it may prove Mutually advantage to you, (if the Seed is sent) to whom, or in what manner the cost of them shall be remitted.

"Be so good, upon the receipt of this letter as to inform me if there be a moral certainty of a supply from you in the abovementioned time for should I depend there on and be disapointed it will be very injurious to me as the whole is for my own sowing and the ground will be prepared for it. I am Gntn Yr Most Obedt & very Hble Servant G. Washington" (LB, DLC:GW).

GW acknowledged the arrival of the seed in a letter from Mount Vernon of 22 Feb. 1788: "Gentlemen, I have received your letter of the 28th Ulto enclosing an Invoice of the Seeds shipped on board the Sloop Molly Beverly on my account which have since safely arrived.

"The amount of your bill will be paid you by the House of Murray Mountford & Bowen at New York.

"The quality of the seeds cannot be determined till I have an opportunity of trying them, but let them turn out as they may, I dare say there has been nothing wanting on your part to procure those of the best quality for me. I am Gentlemen Yr Most Obedt Hble Servant Go. Washington" (LB, DLC:GW). GW again bought seed from Embree & Shotwell in the winter of 1788–89 (see GW to Embree & Shotwell, 3 Oct., 26 Dec. 1788, 28 Jan., 15 Mar. 1789, Embree & Shotwell to GW, 17 Oct., 3 Dec. 1788, 19 Jan. 1789, and GW to William Shotwell, 7 April 1789). For GW's payment to Embree & Shotwell through the New York firm of Murray, Mumford & Bowen for the seed that he received in February 1788, see GW to Embree & Shotwell, 3 Oct. 1788, and Embree & Shotwell to GW, 17 Oct. 1788, and note 1 of that document.

To John Langdon

Sir, Mount Vernon Decr 3d 1787

I have received your letter of the 6th Ulto and am much obliged to you for the information contained in it.[1] I am happy to find that the dispositions in your part of the Continent are so favourable to the proposed plan of Government; if the true interest of the United States was consulted I think there could be but little opposition to it in any part of the Country.

The publick papers have undoubtedly announced to you, before this, the proceedings of the legislature of this State upon the business; they have appointed the convention to meet on the first monday in June; whether putting it off to so late a period will be favourable or otherwise must be determined by circumstances, for if those States, whose conventions are to meet sooner, should adopt the plan, I think there is no doubt but they will be followed by this, and if some of them should reject it, it is very probable that the opposers of it here will exert themselves to add this to the number.[2] I am Sir, Yr Most Obedt Hble Servt

Go. Washington

LS, in Tobias Lear's hand, NhSB: John Langdon Collection; LB, DLC:GW.

1. Langdon's letter from Portsmouth, N.H., of 6 Nov. reads: "Sir Your Excellency will permit me to congratulate you on the prospect that appears in this part of the Continent of speedily establishing the National plan of Government in the formation of which you took so laborious a part I have not heard a single person object to the plan & very few find fault even with a single sentence, but all express their greatest desire to have it establish'd as soon as may be. Our General Court unfortunately adjourn'd a few days before the official plan came to hand but will meet again next month & no doubt will call the Convention early for the purpose of accepting the National plan of Government. I have the Honour to be With the highest sentiments of Esteem and Respect Your Excellency's Mo. Obdt St John Langdon" (DLC:GW).

2. On the same day (3 Dec.) GW's secretary Tobias Lear wrote Langdon, who was his patron: "since the Genls. return from Philadelphia his correspondents from all parts of Europe & America have poured their letters upon him so fast that it requires my constant & unremitting attention to them, and to be candid with you, my dear Sir, you are more obliged to him for the trouble of this letter than to me, for as he was about to write to you himself he asked me if I should answer your letter at this time, I told him I did not think I should be able to do it, he replied 'that it should be done'—I was therefore obliged to obey—tho' it will cost him half an hour of his own time to do what I should have been doing for him" (printed in Kaminski and Saladino, *Documentary History of the Ratification of the Constitution,* 8:196–98).

To Thomas Smith

Sir,   Mount Vernon Decr 3d 1787.

I have recd your letter of the 26th of Octr[1] and am much surprised to find that my letters to the Western Country so often miscarry. I enclose a duplicate of a letter which I wrote to you from Philadelphia, and committed to the care of Captn Bradley who informed me that he lived at the Court House in Washington County, should pass through Carlyle, & promised to deliver it himself.[2]

I have written to Mr Smith of Baltimore requesting him to forward to me the money which you informed me you had lodged in his hands for me.[3]

The money which you recover on my acct may be put into the hands of Clement Biddle Esqr. of Philadelphia, who will be so good as to give me information thereof: but if a safe opportunity should offer to Alexandria I would prefer having it lodged there in the hands of Mr William Hunter Junr.[4]

Permit me Sir to repeat my thanks to you for your attention to my business, and once more to request that you, and Mr Ross, would mention the sum with which you will be satisfied for conducting my Ejectmts &c. and receive it out of the money which you may recover on my acct.[5] I am Sir, Yr most Obedt Hbe Servt

                                        Go: Washington

LS, in the hand of Tobias Lear, PWacD: Sol Feinstone Collection, on deposit in PPAmP; LB, DLC:GW. Written on the cover: "Philad. Decr 12th 1787 Received & forwarded by Yr very hume Sevt Clement Biddle."

1. Letter not found.

2. GW wrote to Smith on 16 September. Captain Bradley has not been identified.

3. GW's letter, probably to the Baltimore merchant William Smith (1728–1814), has not been found.

4. Smith sent £200 to Clement Biddle (Smith to GW, 5 Feb. 1788; Biddle to GW, 5 Mar. 1788).

5. GW agreed to Smith's proposal that he and James Ross should each receive £50 (Smith to GW, 5 Feb. 1788; GW to Smith, 22 Feb., 5 Mar. 1788).

To Bushrod Washington

Dear Sir, Mount Vernon December 3d 1787

A Mr H. Banks, of your Assembly is disposed to be kind to me or has some view of being so to himself. Charity leads to the first—suspicion to the latter opinion. He has informed me that the Sherif of Greenbrier has a considerable demand upon me for the taxes of my land on the Great Kankawa, in that Country—but has forborne (through *his* means) from proceeding to extremities till *he* could advice me thereof.[1] This is the first intimation directly or indirectly I have had of these taxes. He thinks I might settle these lands immediately, if an exemption from Rent was allowed for a term—moderate Rents agreed for hereafter—and these to be in specific Articles proportionate to the Crop. After naming one Hines, or Stines as his Agent in that Country, and a Capt. William L. Lovely, whose continuance there he says is doubtful he offers any services in his power to facilitate any plan I may adopt for seating—He also wants to buy some of the Land but is not able.[2] Under this Statement let me ask, *confidentially,* the Character and circumstance of this Banks[3]—and I would thank you for obtaining the most satisfactory answers, from the Representatives of Greenbrier, Montgomery, Bottetourt or other Counties in that quarter to the following questions.

1st The distance from Stanton to Green Court House?

2d From thence to the Mouth of Coal River, a branch of the Great Kankawa?

3d Whether there is a direct Road from G. K. Court Ho. to the last mentioned place, or whether this road crosses or comes to the Kankawa above, or below the Mouth of Coal River?

4th What sort of a road it is—to wit—Mountainous, or tolerably level, and what kind of a Country does it pass thro', and how Settled?

5th Whether there is any road leading—from the mouth of Coal River, or that part of the Kankawa to which the Greenbrier road strikes into the mouth.

6th The distance and what kind of a road, if any?

7th Whether Colo. Lewis (the Son of Genl Andw Lewis) lives at the mouth of the Kankawa?[4]

8th And what Settlement there is at that place whether by the

Roads above enumerated is his rout, or is the most direct road from Staunton to the mouth of the Great Kankawa, and whether the distances from place to place a description thereof?

9th What are the *rich* bottom lands on the Kankawa supposed to be worth? and for what would they Sell, credit being given.

10th For what would the[y] Rent?

11th The most advantageous and practicable mode of doing this?

12th Is there any person of character living on the Kankawa from the mouth of Coal River to the confluence of it with the Ohio, in whom confidence could be placed to Rent my lands there? and transact business for me?

13th How are the Counties of Greenbrier Botetourt and Montgomery divided? or in what County is the lands on the East of the Kankawa from the mouth of Coal to the Ohio. and in what County or Counties are the lands *on* the Ohio between the mouths of the two Kankawas?

14th Supposing a person was to undertake a Journey from Alexandria to the Great Kankawa which would be his best rout and what the distance from place to place exclusive of the way by Fort Pitt?

Necessity will compel me to do something, and soon, with these lands. It will not do to pay taxes and receive nothing in return for them. Knowing that the quality and Situation of them is exceeded by none in the western Counties, I may have held them in high estimation to obtain Tenants on the terms which have been advertised by me and it is difficult to fix rents on land encresing evry day in value that will be an equivolent some years hence. unless on the terms sugested by Mr Banks that is to receive ⅓ of the Crops to this however elegable it may be to a landlord on the spot. many reasons may be opposed by one at a distance viz. Idleness and want of honesty in the tenant—Want of Care, attention and integrity in the agent. and want of a market if the other two could be obviated. Yet something must be done, and by getting them seated, and in some degree improved it would enable me to rent them more advantageously hereafter.

I wish you would let me know (if you can come at the means of doing it) what taxes these lands of mine are subject to—Tho' I requested, in answer to Mr Banks's letter to me, (to which I have received a reply)[5] to be informed of this, he has passed it over in silence.

Write to me on all the points here submitted, as soon as you can obtain information, as I shall postpone a second letter to Mr Banks till I hear from you. My land on the Ohio lyes between the Mouths of the two Kankawas—and on the great Kankawa in 4 tracts from within two Miles of the mouth to and above the Mouth of Coal River. I am &c.

G. Washington

LB, DLC:GW.

1. See GW to Henry Banks, 22 Nov., n.3. The copyist wrote "Kankawa" for Kanawha throughout this letter.

2. After further correspondence GW in April 1788 paid to the sheriff of Greenbrier County a total of £203.6.3 in taxes on his Great Kanawha lands for 1785 and 1786, and in June 1788, a total of £71.14.6 (Ledger B, 268). Hines or Stines may be Henry Haines who along with Henry Banks was among those who in September 1782 claimed tracts along the Great Kanawha surveyed by John Madison. William Lewis Loveley had served throughout the Revolution, ending up as a captain in the 4th Virginia Regiment.

3. Bushrod Washington's answer to this query has not been found, but on 10 Nov. 1788 GW wrote David Stuart that he had "no idea of committing my business to his [Banks's] management, or recommendation."

4. See GW to Thomas Lewis, 25 Dec., in which he asks Lewis to act as his agent in managing his lands on the Great Kanawha and Ohio rivers.

5. Banks's reply to GW's letter of 22 Nov. has not been found.

To George Weedon

Dear Sir,   Mount Vernon December 3d 1787

I have received your letter of the 25th Ulto enclosing the proceedings of the Cincinnati of this State, which I am much obliged to you for forwarding to me.[1]

I will, agreeable to your request, send some cuttings of the Golden willow to Alexandria to be forwarded to you, but I imagine this is an improper season to put them out, for as they are to be propagated from the slip the spring seems to be the most suitable time for setting them; should these fail I will send you more in the spring if you will remind me of it.[2] I am Dr Sir—Yr Most Obedt Hble Servant

G. Washington

LB, DLC:GW.

1. Letter not found. The Virginia Society of the Cincinnati met at Anderson's tavern in Richmond on 10 and 12 Nov. (Edgar Erskine Hume, *Sesquicentennial History and Roster of the Society of the Cincinnati in the State of Virginia, 1783–1933* [Richmond, 1934], 83).

2. GW again wrote Weedon from Mount Vernon on 17 Dec.: "Dear Sir, This letter is accompanied by a bundle (containing 50 cuttings) of the yellow, or golden Willow. As I observed to you in my last, I do not conceive the season so favourable as the Spring—yet there can be little doubt of their succeeding—Should they [not] do it however you can at any time get more as I have an abundance of them. I am Dear [Sir] Yr Most Obedt Servt Go: Washington" (ALS, ViMtV).

From Battaile Muse

Honorable Sir, Berkeley County Decr 4th 1787

I was in Fauquier County Last week among the Tenaments, and have Tenants Engaged For all the Lots Excepting one which is a wood Lot on goos creek, Part of the Lot that Tompson Lived on,[1] no one will have it on any Terms; and many of the Lots on the upper Tract are Setled with Very Poor Tenants on accot of the Poorness of the Land—on those Poor Lots I cannot get a Tenant to stay Two years. as I had Promises From Mrs Lemert and Shover To raise Some money by Christmast I thought it best not To distress at this Time if they run away the Lots will rent as they are not So bad.

the disputed Line between you and Scott I could not get run as Scott wants the Line Setled by Colo. Leven Powell. Capn Moffet & Mo⟨y⟩e who is to Fix Burgues Line To Terminate a Suit He has with one Flory—I am To have notice when these Gentn go on that Business—as Colo. Powell is at the Assembly I do not Expect the Business will do done untill next spring—their is apart of that Land not under Lease, I have not Engag'd it—nor Shall not untill the Lines are Established—and then on Such Terms as for all the Leases To Fall at once[2] the Fauquier Tenants are Still in arrears—not a Large Sums, only Lemert & Shover. I demanded of Mr Weathers His Authority For writeing To you as He did, His asswer was that He was Sorry for it & will be more Carefull in Future.[3]

I enclose and order on Scoth Wm Hunter Esqr. for Fifty pounds your acct When that is Paid will Stand in Debted To me upard of Thirty pounds I do not Expect you will receive any more money From me untill next spring as the Present years rents will not be Collected before, if then.

I wish Mr Lear To Compair the Inclosed Acct with your Books. I shall be anxious to hear whether Mr Hunter pays the money[4]—I have the Honour To be your Obedient Humble Servant

Battaile Muse

ALS, DLC:GW. Written on the cover: "Mr [Thomas] Porter in Alexandria will P⟨le⟩ase To Convey this Letter with Care & oblige B. Muse."

1. This is William Thompson. See List of Tenants, 18 Sept. 1785, n.16.

2. For GW's dispute with Robert Scott, see GW to Muse, 5 Jan. 1786, and note 1 of that document. John Moffet (born c.1747), a longtime member of the Fauquier County court, was a surveyor. To whom Muse is referring to as "Mo⟨y⟩e" has not been determined, and Flory has not been identified. In 1731 Col. Charles Burgess surveyed and claimed more than 23,000 acres in six parcels in what had become Fauquier and Loudoun counties.

3. For William Withers's (Weathers) accusations, see Muse to GW, 19 November.

4. Muse enclosed the accounts of GW's tenant Anthony Gholson (Gholston), which are in DLC:GW. GW responded on 16 Dec. and this portion of his letter was printed in John Heise Catalog no. 4561, item 31, 1926: "Your two letters of the 19th. Nov. & 4th. inst. have come to hand, the latter enclosing a bill upon William Hunter, Esq. in my favor, which he has accepted and will pay at the time mentioned in it.—Mr. (Tobias) Lear has compared [Anthony] Golston's account with my Books & tells me that it stands there as you have stated it.—I am much obliged to you for your attention to, & delivering of the letters committed to your care for Mr. Brian Fairfax & Col. Warner Washington. . . ." See also Muse to GW, 26 Dec., n.1.

Letter not found: from David Stuart, 4 Dec. 1787. GW wrote Stuart on 11 Dec. "to acknowledge the receipt of your favor dated the 4th Instt."

Letter not found: to John Lewis, 7 Dec. 1787. Lewis wrote GW on 15 Dec. that he did not receive his "favor of the 7th Inst. till yesterday."

To James Madison

My dear Sir,   Mount Vernon Decr 7th 1787.

Since my last to you, I have been favored with your letters of the 28th of Octr & 18th of Novr—With the last came 7 numbers of the Fœderalist under the signature of Publius. For these I thank you. They are forwarded to a Gentleman in Richmond for re-publication.[1] The doing of which, in this State, will, I am persuaded, have a good effect; as there are certainly characters in it who are no friends to a general government—perhaps I might go further, & add, who would have no great objection to the introduction of anarchy & confusion.

The sollicitude, to know what the several State Legislatures would do with the Constitution, is now transferred to the several Conventions thereof; the decisions of which being more interesting & conclusive, is consequently more anxiously expected than the other. What Pensylvania & Delaware have done, or will do, must soon be known: Other Conventions are treading closely on their heels—but what the three Southern States have done, or in what light the New Constitution is viewed by them, I have not been able to learn. North Carolina it is said (by some Accts from Richmond) will be governed in a great measure by the conduct of Virga. The pride of South Carolina will not, I conceive, suffer this influence to operate in her Councils; and the disturbances in Georgia will, or at least ought to shew the people of it, the propriety of a strict union, and the necessity there is for a general government.

If these, with the States Eastward and Northward of us, should accede to the proposed plan, I think the Citizens of this State will have no cause to bless the opponents of it here, if they should carry their point.

A Paragraph in the Baltimore Paper has announced a change in the Sentiments of Mr Jay on this subject; and adds, that from being an admirer of it, he is become a bitter enemy. This relation, without knowing Mr Jays opinion, I discredit, from a conviction that he would consider the matter well before he would pass judgment, and having done so, would not change his opinion, *almost* in the same breath. I am anxious however to know, on what ground this report originates, expecially the indelicacy of the expresn.[2]

It would have given me great pleasure to have complied with your request in behalf of your foreign Acquaintance—at *present* I am unable to do it.[3] The Survey of the Country between the Eastern and Western Waters is not yet reported by the Commissioners, tho' promised to be made very shortly—the Survey being compleated. No draught that can convey an adequate idea of the Work, on this river, has been yet taken. Much of the labour, except at the great falls, has been bestowed in the bed of the river; in a removal of rocks, and deepning the Water. At the great falls, the labour has indeed been great. The Water there (a sufficiency I mean) is taken into a Canal about 200 yards above the Cataract, & conveyed by a level cut (thro' a solid rock in some places, and much stone everywhere) more than a mile to the lock seats; five in number; by means of which, when compleated, the craft will be let into the river below the falls (which together amount to 76 feet). At the Seneca falls, Six miles above the great Falls, a channel which has been formed by the river when inundated, is under improvement for the Navigation. The same, *in part* at Shanondah. At the lower falls, where nothing has yet been done, a level cut and locks are proposed. These constitute the principal difficulties & will [be] the great expence of this undertaking; The parts of the river between requiring loose stones only to be removed, in order to deepen the water where it is too shallow in dry seasons. With very great esteem & regard I am—My dear Sir Yr Most Obedt & Affece Ser.

Go: Washington

P.S. Since writing the foregoing, I have received a letter from a member of our Assembly at Richmond, dated the 4th instt giving the following information.[4]

"I am sorry to inform you that the Constitution has lost ground so considerably that it is doubtful whether it has any longer a majority in its favor. From a vote which took place the other day this would appear certain, tho' I cannot think it so decisive as the enemies to it consider it. It marks however the inconsistency of some of its opponants. At the time the resolutions calling a Convention were entered into Colo. M——n sided with the friends to the Constitution, and opposed any hint being given, expressive of the sentiments of the House as to amendments. But as it was unfortunately omitted at that time to make provision for the subsistence of the Convention, it became necessary to pass some resolutions for that purpose; among these is one providing for any expence which may attend an attempt to make amendments. As M—— had on the former occasion declared that it would be improper to make any discovery of the sentiments of the House on the subject, and that we had no right to suggest any thing to a body paramount to us, his advocating such a resolution was matter of astonishment: It is true he declared it was not declaratory of our opinion; but the contrary must be very obvious. As I have heard many declare themselves friends to the Constitution since the vote, I do not consider it as altogether decisive of the opinion of the House with respect to it.[5]

"In a debating society here, which meets once a week, this subject has been canvassed at two successive meetings, and is to be finally decided on tomorrow evening. As the whole Assembly almost has attended on these occasions, their opinion will then be pretty well ascertained. And as the opinion on this occasion will have much influence, some of Colo. Innis's friends have obtained a promise from him to enter the lists.[6]

"I am informed both by Genl Wilkinson (who is just arrived from New Orleans by way of No. Carolina) and Mr Ross, that North Carolina is almost unanimous for adopting it. The latter received a letter from a member of that Assembly now sitting.[7]

"The Bill respecting British debts has passed our house, but with such a clause as I think makes it worse than a rejection."

The letter of which I enclose you a printed Copy—from Colo. R. H. Lee to the Govr has been circulated with great industry in manuscript, four weeks before it went to press, and is said to have had a bad influence.[8] The enemies to the Constitution leave no stone unturned to encrease the opposition to it. Yrs &ca

G. W——n

ALS, MA; LB, DLC:GW.

1. GW sent these papers of the *Federalist* to David Stuart in Richmond on 30 November.

2. In the story reprinted in the Baltimore *Maryland Journal* from the Philadelphia *Independent Gazeteer* on 30 Nov., Jay was quoted as describing the Constitution as "a wicked conspiracy" against the people. Madison wrote to GW on 20 Dec. that GW "did not judge amiss," that the letter was "an arrant forgery."

3. See Madison to GW, 28 October. Madison extracted the rest of this paragraph for inclusion in his letter to Thomas Jefferson, 20 Dec. (Rutland and Hobson, *Madison Papers*, 10:331–33).

4. GW extracted this passage from the missing letter from David Stuart of 4 Dec. which on 11 Dec. GW acknowledges.

5. The house resolutions of 30 Nov. calling for defraying the expenses of the delegates to the ratifying convention to be held in Richmond on 1 June 1788 included a provision for paying the expenses of attendance at a second federal convention if one should be held. A bill to this effect was passed by the

General Assembly on 12 December. See Kaminski and Saladino, *Documentary History of the Ratification of the Constitution*, 8:183–93, for an account of the bill's passage and for the proceedings of the legislature.

6. The Union Society, or Political Society, at its meeting in Richmond on 21 and 28 Nov. undertook "A full consideration of the Foederal Government lately recommended by the Convention." At its meeting on 13 Dec. the society voted 128 to 15 in favor of the Constitution (ibid., 170–72).

7. After the Revolution Gen. James Wilkinson (1757–1825) went from Pennsylvania to Kentucky to live and began his long career of intrigue in local and international politics. His visit to Richmond in November 1787 came when he was returning by way of Charleston, S.C., from his trip down the Mississippi to Spanish New Orleans. There, in the summer of 1787, he had negotiated with Spanish authorities, holding out to them the prospect of Kentucky's separating itself from the American Union in return for trade concessions from which Wilkinson himself would profit. For a fuller and more circumstantial account of Wilkinson's activities at this time, see Thomas Marshall to GW, 12 Feb. 1789, n.1. David Ross was a prominent merchant in Petersburg and a planter in Southside Virginia.

8. This is Richard Henry Lee's letter to Edmund Randolph of 16 Oct. setting forth his objections to the Constitution with his proposed amendments appended. See Kaminski and Saladino, *Documentary History of the Ratification of the Constitution*, 8:59–67, for the text of the letter with the proposed amendments and a history of its publication.

From James Madison

Dear Sir   New York Decr 7. 1787

My last inclosed a continuation of the Fœderalist to number 14 inclusive. I now add the numbers which have succeeded.

No authentic information has yet arrived concerning the posture of Europe. Reports, with some less doubtful symtoms, countenance the suspicions of war.

I understand that the Constitution will certainly be adopted in Connecticut; the returns of the deputies being now known, and a very great majority found to be its declared and firm friends. There will be more opposition in Massachusetts, but its friends there continue to be very sanguine of victory. N. Hampshire, as far as I can learn, may be set down, on the right list. I remain Dear Sir, with the highest respect and the most unfeigned attachment Your Obedient humble servant

                                                            Js Madison Jr

ALS, PHi: Gratz Collection; copy, DLC: Madison Papers.

To Thomas Johnson and Thomas Sim Lee

Sir,   Mount Vernon December 9th 1787

Presuming that Colo. Fitzgerald according to his promise has communicated to you the vote of the Potomack Co. passed at the last general Meeting, held at George Town, and the measures consequent of it, taken by the directors, I shall trouble you with no more than the result which you will find in the enclosed authenticated Act of the Assembly of this State.[1]

It is scarcely necessary to observe to you, Gentlemen, that unless a similar one is obtained from your Assembly, during its present Session that the work of navigation will soon be at a stand. You know what steps have been taken, & how ineffectually, to collect the dividends from the tardy members. The others think it hard to be further called on and some indeed have advance they will no more until the arrearages are paid up. To recover these will be a work of immense time under the existing law.

You know best under what form to bring this matter before your Assembly—If by way of Pitition you will Please to have one drawn—and if it is necessary the name of the President should be affixed thereto I hereby authorise you to give it my signature[.][2] with great esteem I am Gentlemen—Yr Most Obedt & very Hble Servant

Go. Washington

LB, DLC:GW.

1. See GW to George Mason and David Stuart, 4 Nov., and note 1 of that document.

2. See Johnson to GW, 11 December.

Letter not found: from Frederick Weissenfels, 10 Dec. 1787. GW wrote Weissenfels on 10 Jan. 1788: "I have received your letter of the 10th of December."

From Thomas Johnson

Sir,   Annapolis [Md.] 11 December 1787.

Your Favor of the 9th directed to Mr Lee and myself and it's Inclosure came to Hand today very opportunely—The Gentlemen of the Assembly purpose to rise next Saturday and prepa-

ratory to it resolved in the Morning to receive no new Business
after this day this Circumstance precluded all Formality and Mr
Lee being absent I moved for Leave to bring in a Bill under the
same Title as the Act passed in Virginia—Leave was granted and
I expect there will be no Opposition in any Stage of it—I think
at present to make a small Deviation by giving the president and
Directors their Choice to prosecute in the County Courts, which
will generally be speedier, or in the Genl Court.

Our Affairs are so embarrassed with a diversity of paper
Money and paper Securities a sparing Imposition and an infa-
mous Collection and payment or rather non-payment of Taxes
that Mr Hartshorns repeated Applications to our Treasury have
proved fruitless nor can I say when there will be Money in Hand
to answer the 300£ Sterl. due[1]—Some of our Debts are so pressing that a good many of us Delegates feel very uneasy and I yet
hope a serious Attempt for an immediate provision for them
and that the potomack Demand may be included—The present
Circumstances with respect to the future Seat of Congress in
my Opinion call for vigorous Exertions to perfect the Naviga. of
potomack speedily and it is truly mortifying to see so little prospect of being supplied with the essensial Means—surely 5 or 600
Miles of inland Navigation added to the Central Situation and
other Advantages would decide in favor of Potomack for the
permanent Seat of Congress.

Colo. Fitzgerald wrote Mr Lee and myself to mention the
Time we could meet at Shannadoah to enquire into Complaints
against Mr Steward in his Absence—I could only write him that
I would attend at any Time that might be agreeable to you
and the other Gent. after my Return home which will probably
be the last of next Week—I wish sir your Convenience to be
consultd and that it may be convenient and agreeable to you to
make my House, in your Way very little Notice of the Time to
meet will be sufficient for me and I dare say for Mr Lee.[2]

Late in the last Session I received your Letter relative to Mr
Wilsons Application to our Assembly it was next to impossible
then to draw any Attention to that or to investigate any Subject
in a proper Manner we had grown Impatient in the Extream—
On the most diligent and repeated Searches since my Receit of
your Favor of the 22d of Novemr his papers cannot be found
though Mr Digges and some of the other Members have it on

Memory that on reading in the House the Business was referred—My own Diligence and that of a Gent. or two besides has been exerted to prevent the Necessity of informing you that so little Care is taken of our Papers.[3]

The Leson of your State is working in ours—the Scale of power which I always sugested would be the most difficult to settle between the great and small States, as such, was in my Opinion very properly adjusted any necessary Guards for personal Liberty is the common Interest of all the Citizens of America. and if it is imagined that a defined power which does not comprehend the Interference with personal Rights needs negative Declarations I presume such may be added by the fœderal Legislature with equal Efficacy & more propriety than might have been done by the Convention—Strongly and long impressed with an Idea that no Governmt can make a people happy unless they very generally entertain an Opinion that it is good in Form and well administered I am much disposed to give up a good deal in the ⟨form⟩ the least essential part[.] But those who are clamorous seem to me to be really more afraid of being restrained from doing what they ought not to do and being compelled to do what they ought to do than of being obliged to do what there is no Moral Obligation on them to do—I believe there is no American of Observation Reflection and Candour but will acknowledge *Men* unhappily need more Government than he imagined—I flatter myself that the plan recommended will be adopted in twelve of the thirteen States without Conditions sine qua non—but let the Event be as it may I shall think myself with America in general greatly indebted to the Convention and possibly we may confess it when it may be too late to avail ourselves of their Moderation & Wisdom—You will pardon me my good Sir the Effusions which I cannot restrain when on this Subject and believe me to be with very great Respect Your most obedt Servt

Th. Johnson

ALS, DLC:GW.

1. By the acts of the Maryland and Virginia legislatures creating the Potomac River Company, the treasurer of each state was "to become subscribers to the Amount of Fifty Shares," at £100 a share (GW and Horatio Gates to the Virginia Legislature, 28 Dec. 1784, Enclosure I).

2. The meeting of the officers of the Potomac River Company was sched-

uled for 14 Jan. 1788 at the falls of the Shenandoah River, but bad weather forced its cancellation (*Diaries*, 5:264–65).

3. See note 3 in GW to Johnson, 22 November.

From Henry Knox

My dear Sir   New York 11th December 1787.
    I thank you for your kind favor of the 15th October which was duly received.

Notwithstanding the opposition and writings of the enemies of the new constitution it is now pretty apparent that it will be received by considerable majorities in New Hampshire, Massachusetts Connecticut New Jersey, Pennsylvania, and Delaware.

The information from Maryland is defective, but Virginia it is said will powerfully oppose it. North Carolina will be materially influenced by the conduct of Virginia[.] In South Carolina and Georgia it is presumed that it will be adopted.

Respecting this state it is difficult to determine with any precision. The City, and the enlightened and independent men of the Country are generally for it—The warm friends of the new constitution say that the majority of the people are in its favor while its adversaries assert roundly that the majority is with them. The paper money people both in this State and Rhode Island are against it.

But as a War between France and England seems inevitable, and a general War in Europe probable, the result may be highly beneficial to this Country—1st By preventing the European intrigues against our being a respectable nation, which would most probably be the case were their agents instructed by their courts on the subject—The war will find them other employment—2dly The War will impress on the fears of the people of the United States the necessity of a general government to defend them against the insults and invasions of the Europeans[.] Feeble as the powers of the federal government are in this moment, it would be difficult, if not impracticable to prevent our own people from improperly interfering in the dispute by taking one side or the other—Reprisals would be made on our commerce, and a war ensue, without a hope of success on our side[.] This subject being forcibly impressed on the public mind will have its full effect unless we are devoted to destruction.

Mrs Knox a few days ago was delivered of her eighth child a son, who with his mother are perfectly well—As an evidence of our respect and affection for you which we hope will survive ourselves, we have done him the honor of giving him your name.[1] Mrs Knox joins me in presenting our sincere and affectionate respects to Mrs Washington and I am my dear sir with the most perfect attachment Your very humble Servant

H. Knox

If Colonel Humphreys is with you please to present my love to him—He has grown so big, that I feel quite small in comparison with him—I hope he *lives solely* on water gruel.

ALS, DLC:GW.

1. George Washington Knox, "a fine black eyed black hair'd boy," born on 27 Nov. (Knox to Hannah Urquhart, 5 Dec., NNGL: Knox Papers), died before he reached the age of two.

Letter not found: to Peterson & Taylor, 11 Dec. 1787. Peterson & Taylor wrote GW on this date: "yours ℔ the boy came safe to hand."

From Peterson & Taylor

Sir   Alexa[ndri]a 11 Decr 1787.

yours ℔ the boy came safe to hand and observe its contents,[1] we can in answer, deliver at the Genl Landing pine Scantling of any dimentions that may be wanting, but no Oak. the Price of Scantling 6/ reduced to plank Measure, the Common Kind of 18 Inch Shingles Called ½ Inch d[itt]o 13/6 M. Bald Cyprus— 3 feet B. Cypress do, 54/ ℔ th[ousan]d these are the Common prices we Sell at daily, your fish we will give the common price of the Season, and Shall want at Considerable quantity, we have only to add if the above prices are Approved off, in order to accomodate an agreement will be to determine, the quantity of each—as well when to be delivd &c. &c.[2] Your Obt Servts

Peterson & Taylor

ALS, DLC:GW.

1. Letter not found.

2. For GW's purchase of planking and framing from the Alexandria firm, see GW to Peterson & Taylor, 5 Jan. 1788.

To David Stuart

Dear Sir   Mount Vernon 11th Decr 1787

Not recollecting till this moment, the Winter regulation of the Post; & being desirous of getting the Loan Office certificates (herewith enclosed) to you before you shall have left richmond; I have scarcely time to acknowledge the receipt of your favor dated the 4th Instt,[1] much less to write more fully on the subject of my Back Lands. I now pray, if it is in your power, to obtain the Interest on my Certificates that you would do it—for I can truly say that at no period of my life have I ever felt the want of money so sensibly as now—among other demands upon me, I have no means of paying my Taxes—the Certificate for the Executed Negro ought to be discharged, I should think—this I also send.[2] And let me beg of you to enquire in what manner, and by what certain Channel, I could open a correspondence with Mr Lewis (his Chn name I know not) on the Kanhawa; and whether it is likely he would act as an Agent for me in the Renting of my Lands on the Kanhawa & Ohio above it.[3] I have not time to add more; hardly expecting this letter will get to the Post Office in time. Yrs Sincerely

Go: Washington

ALS, PHi: Dreer Collection.

1. Letter not found, but see GW to James Madison, 7 Dec., where Stuart's letter is quoted at length.

2. Stuart gave the certificate for a slave executed in 1781 to the state auditor, John Pendleton, nephew of Judge Edmund Pendleton, for payment of the interest due on the certificate (GW to John Pendleton, 1 Mar. 1788). Pendleton on 6 Mar. 1788 returned the certificate, explaining that Edmund Randolph as attorney general had ruled that interest on a certificate of an executed slave would begin no earlier than the passage of the appropriation act of 1784. GW then wrote his attorney Charles Lee on 4 April 1788: "As you are now in Richmond I take the liberty of enclosing to you (in a letter from Mr Pendleton) a Certificate for a negro executed in the year 1781 Amounting to £69 which I will thank you to negociate for me there upon the best terms you can, and pay the proceeds thereof in behalf of what is due from me to the James River Company—The principal for the negro, and three years interest thereon (which is all that was allowed) amounted to £138 which was divided into two Cirtificates, one receivable in the taxes now due, which I retain, to discharge part of my taxes for the year 1787 and the other you have with this." In the postscript of the letter, GW instructs Lee to use the £69 to pay taxes instead. GW records payment of £65 on 21 June 1788 to the James River Company

(Ledger B, 354). See also Charles Lee to GW, 11, 14 April 1788, and GW to Charles Lee, 27 April 1788.

3. See GW to Thomas Lewis, 25 December.

From Samuel Powel

Dear Sir   Philadelphia Decr 12. 1787

I had, this Day, the Pleasure of your very obliging Letter, for which I return you my best Thanks.[1]

The important Question is at length decided and Pennsylvania has had Virtue enough to adopt the proposed fœderal Constitution by a Majority of Forty Six against Twenty Three. On this Event I sincerely felicitate my Country, & trust that her Example will be followed by the other States. So fœderal are we that an Invitation has been handed to the Convention, signed by the Landholders of Philadelphia County, offering the said County as the Seat of the future Government. This Measure was taken at a very respectable Meeting.

All Ranks of People here rejoice in the Event of this Evenings Deliberations, which was proclaimed thro' the City by repeated Shouts & Huzzas. The Convention will sign the Ratification To-morrow Morning.

New Jersey will, probably adopt the Constitution this Week, & Massachusetts next Month. I think & hope it will be generally accepted.

Mrs Powel did herself the Honor of writing to Mrs Washington Yesterday, & also sent her little Commission to the Care of Col. Fitzgerald at Alexandria.[2] I beg the Favor of you to present me, most respectfully to all the good Family, & to believe that I am, unfeignedly, dear Sir Your very affect. humble Servt

Samuel Powel

ALS, DLC:GW.

1. GW wrote Samuel Powel on 30 November.

2. Elizabeth Willing Powel wrote to Martha Washington on 30 Nov. 1787 to thank her for her hospitality, saying that "a Desire to accompany my Letter with Collars for the young Ladies [the Custis girls], has, alone, prevented an earlier Acknowledgement of my sense of the elegant Hospitality exercised at Mount Vernon; where the good Order of the Master's Mind, seconded by your excellent Abilities, pervades every Thing around you, & renders it a most

delightful Residence to your Friends. . . . I hope the Collars will meet your Approbation. The Cost runs three Dollars. . . . Those I have sent may be raised by means of the Screw. I have made a little Ornament of Ribband, which may be worn over them as a Disguise when the young Ladies are dressed or go without a Vandike. It is a Pity that a fine Form should be spoiled by a Childs not holding herself erect." She also sent "our little Favorite, Master [George Washington Parke] Custis, the Work I promised him" and to Mrs. Washington, "a Morrocco Thread Case" like the one of her own that Mrs. Washington had admired (ViMtV).

To Charles Carter

Dear Sir,   Mount Vernon December 14th 1787
Your favor of the 21st of Octr would not have remained so long unacknowledged could I with any degree of precision have answered your quæries sooner.[1] I wish it was in my power to do it satisfactorily now. The drought of last Summer in *this* neighbourhood was so unconsionably severe, that the experiments I contemplated were by no means conclusive—the result such as it is—I will give you.

In level ground, as equal in quality as I could obtain it, I laid of 10 squares; each square containing by exact measurement, half an acre. half of each of these I manured at the rate of 200 bushls of well rolled farm yard dung to the Acre to ascertain the difference between slight manuring such as we might have it in our power to give the land, and no manure. The whole of this ground received the first plowing in the winter; and each square previous to sowing, or planting was worked exactly alike afterwards: Two of these were sown with Oats (of different sorts) on the [   ] of [   ]—Two with Barley (of different sorts) on the [   ] of [   ]. One with Buck wheat on the [   ] day of [   ]. another with Jerusalem Artichokes on the [   ] day of [   ]. another with Irish Potatoes on the [   ] day of [   ] another with sweet (or Country) Ditto on the [   ] day of [   ]. another that is to say ⅓ with the *common* sort of homony bean—⅓ with the bunch homony bean and the other one third with very small, and round black eyed Pease called the Gentlemans Pea—The two squares was sown half in Carrots, and half in Turnips both in Broad Cast.

Yield as Follow.

		Acres of Land.	Dung	undung	Total.
The 9 squares of oats makg togethr		1	14½	11	25½
2 of Barley not worth dividg for the same reason }		1	2	1⅝	3⅝
1 Do	Jerm Artichoke	½	29½	29	58½
1 Do	Buck Wheat	½	2¼	1⅓	4
1 Do	Irish Potatoes	½	19¼	9½	28¾
1 Do	Sweet Do	½ {	6½ la[rge] 5 la.		
			5½ Seed 5½ Sd 22½²		
1 Do	½ Carrots	¼	12	12	24
	½ Turnips	¼			
1 Square—@ ⅓ in Comn homony beans		⅙			
	⅓ in Bunch Do Do	⅙			
	⅓ in sml rd bla. eyed Pease	⅙			

I have already observed, that the drougth was too intense to authorize any just conclusion from this experiments; for besides occasioning many of the seeds and plants to come up badly, the growth of all was so much retarded as to leave little hope at one time that any thing would be produced from some of them.

The Barley was exceedingly *thin;* in some parts of the ground hardly any. of the Buck Wheat ¼ of the square (undunged parts) had not a plant—of the Jerusalem Artichoke out of 442 hills 417 were Missing—both kinds of Potatoes were a good deal missing; and the Irish sort had not roots as big as a Pea the first of Septr when in a commonly seasonable year they would at that time have been fit for use. The Carrots and Turnips were thin— as were the Pease and Beans.

Adjoining to these squares I laid of exactly 10 Acres in an ob- long form and drilled them with Corn in rows 10 feet a part, and 18 Inches asunder in the rows, between these rows Irish Potatoes Carrots, Turnips, and the common bla. eyed Pease were alternately planted and sown (that no advantage of soil or situation should be more in favore of one than the other)—By this mode you will perceive that *half* the Rows were in Corn, an ⅛ in Potatoes, an ⅛ in Carrots an ⅛ in Pease and the remaining ⅛ in Turnips (or I ought rather to have said were intended for them but they could not be got to grow).

The Corn yielded only	443 Bushels of sound
Potatoes	47¾
Carrots	22

> Pease these by mistake got mixed with others and the quantity could not be ascertained but did not yield much.

The Potatoes were missing, The Carrots much more so. from this experiment which is not more conclusive than the other, it appears that the Potatoe rows, though but a fourth of the Corn Rows, yielded nearly as many bushels; and that the Carrots also but a fourth of the Corn rows amounted to nearly half—Had the Potatoes stood as well as the Corn, the number of bushels wold have been more than that of Corn—and had the Carrots stood as well as the Potatoes, the quantity of bushels it is supposed would not have fallen short of the Potatoes. From the quantity of Corn (but a barriels to the Acre which in a moderately seasonable year would have yielded 2 or 2 and an half to the Acre) you may form some conception of the severity of the drought, as the ground was well tilled and especially when I add that all my grass seeds were destroyed by it. The Potatoes, ultimately, grew to a good size, and the Carrots were *remarkably* large—few smaller than the wrist—and numbers larger than the small of the leg. Inconclusive as these trials have been I am nevertheless clearly of opinion that Corn in Drills 3 feet apart and the plants 18 Inches asunder in the rows, with Carrots or Potatoes or both (for the Seasons to put them in the ground and taking them up differing, the farmer is less hurried) in his operations will be found a most profitable husbandry. I have no doubt that an Acre of Corn planted in this manner will yield as much as an Acre of the same quality in the usual mode of planting—If this be true (and I have very little doubt of it) the Potatoes and Carrots are nearly clear profit as very little more labour is required in this mode of cultivating of them than the Corn would need, and receive if nothing was between it. The only consideration then is, whether the production is too much for the Land? The books say *generally,* that neither Carrots nor Potatoes are exhausters. But as the cultivation of them, with me, is new, I shall decide nothing on this point but shall practice the mode untill I meet with discouragements.

I do not know that the Agricultural Society of Philadelphia have adopted any regular mode of communicating the information they receive to the Public—good would certainly result from such communications and I presume after it has got a little better established this will be the case. That I have not received any answer to my letter respecting the Wolf dogs is matter of surprize to me—when I do, the result shall be communicated to you.[3]

I thank you for your Congratulations on my return from the Convention and with what you add respecting the Constitution. My decided opinion of the matter is that there is no alternative between the adoption of it and anarchy. If one State however important it may conceive itself to be should suppose, or a minority of the States, that they can dictate a Constitution to the Majority unless they have the power of administring to good effect, administering the Ultema ratio they will find themselves deceived. All the opposition to it, that I have yet seen, is I must confess addressed more to the passions than to the reason—and clear I am if another Fœderal Convention is attempted the sentiments of the members will be more discordent or less Conciliator than the last—in fine, that they will agree upon no genl plan. General Government is now suspended by a thread I might go farther and say it is really at an end, and what will be the consequence of a fruitless attempt to amend the one which is offered, before it is tried—or of the delay from the attempt, does not in my Judgment need the gift of prophecy to predict. I am not a blind admirer (for I saw the imperfections) of the Constitution to which I have assisted to give birth—but I am fully persuaded it is the best that can be obtained at *this* day and that it or disunion is before us—if the first is our choice when the defects of it are experenced a Constitutional door is open for amendments and may be adopted in a peaceable maner without tumult or disorder.[4] I am &ca

G. Washington.

LB, DLC:GW; copy, Austria: Osterreichishen Staatsarchivs.

1. Letter not found.

2. It is not clear what the copyist, Howell Lewis, intended here.

3. GW's letter to Sir Edward Newenham inquiring about wolf dogs in Ireland has not been found, but see GW to Carter, 5 Feb. 1788.

4. These remarks on the Constitution were, to GW's distress, published and received wide circulation. See James Madison to GW, 20 Dec., n.5, GW to Carter, 12 Jan., n.1, 20, 22 Jan. 1788, GW to Benjamin Lincoln, 31 Jan. 1788, and GW to Madison, 5 Feb. 1788.

From James Madison

Dear Sir New York Decr 14. 1787.

Along with this are inclosed a few of the latest gazettes containing the additional papers in favor of the federal Constitution.

I find by letters from Richmond that the proceedings of the Assembly, are as usual, rapidly degenerating with the progress of the Session: and particularly that the force opposed to the Act of the Convention has gained the ascendance.[1] There is still nevertheless a hope left that different characters and a different spirit may prevail in their successors who are to make the final decision. In one point of view the present Assembly may perhaps be regarded as pleading most powerfully the cause of the new Government, for it is impossible for stronger proofs to be found than in their conduct, of the necessity of some such anchor against the fluctuations which threaten shipwreck to our liberty. I am Dear [Sir] with the most sincere & perfect Esteem, Your affecte & obedt humble servt

Js Madison Jr

ALS, PHi: Gratz Collection; copy, DLC: Madison Papers.

1. See particularly Archibald Stuart to Madison, 2 Dec., in Rutland and Hobson, *Madison Papers,* 10:290–93.

From Joseph Davenport

Sr Mill [Mount Vernon] Decemr 15 1787

Major Washington tells me that you will not Concent for me to keep a horse—but Sir if I pay you What is reasonable and Customary Your Excelency Can not think hard of it—farr be it from me to ask aney thing out of reason—Sir you know to Sell him at this Season of the year. I Cannot Get the worth of him. to winter him out I may as well have none—Sir I Did not Get this horse because I thought You had a right to keep him for me—I ment to pay for his keeping from the first—but Sir Plese to favour me with an answer and your Commands Shall be Obayed by your Friend[1]

Jos. Davenport

ALS, DLC:GW.
  1. What answer GW gave to his miller has not been determined.

From John Lewis

Dear Sir,   15 Decr 1787
  Being at Richmond for some time past did not get your favor
of the 7th Inst. till yesterday.[1] I have inclosd a Coppy of the
Account you requested, the articles you stand Charged with
⟨not⟩ extended I will get the accot of from Mr Payne & send
you.[2] I think I have seen amg my Fathers papers a list of money
he was to receive & pay away for you at one of the General
Courts I have looked for it but as yet have not found it. I have
some papers in Culpeper (where I some time since lived) which
it perhaps may be among I shall go to Culpeper in the course
of a few days when I will look for it. and if I can find it I will
send it you.[3] I wish the Lands in which you were interested with
my Father sold. provided a tolerable price can be had for them
wou'd you undertake the disposal of them I shoud be exceedingly glad you wou'd[.] I am satisfied any Sale you might make
of them wou'd be agreeable to the Executors[4] I believe I shall
go to the Westward this next Summer if not sooner if possible
wou'd wish the Lands sold before I go, yet as tis a very bad time
for the Sale of property owing to the Scarcety of money will be
guided in the sales of the land by yr better Judgment. There is
also the Share my Father held in the Dismal Swamp Company
lands for Sale what do you suppose it worth I have been apply'd
to for it but am not able to say what price to ask. As well as I
recollect my Father valued it at £2000 I doubt whether the one
half of that sum cou'd be had for it at present. Colo. Jameson
informs me some Gentlemen are desirous of draining the lands
for a share of them If I can with propriety agree to such a proposition I would do it Chearfully as I think it woud greatly inhance
the value of the Shares. have you heard of any such proposition.[5] Please to give my Compts to Mrs Washington. I am Dr Sir
Your Most Obedt Servt

                                                         John Lewis

ALS, ViMtV.
  1. Letter not found.
  2. The account has not been identified. Mr. Payne may be Daniel Payne of

Stafford County who was a merchant in partnership with Charles Yates of Fredericksburg in 1787 (William Crozier, *Virginia County Records: Spotsylvania County, 1721–1800* [New York, 1905], 406). John Lewis was living in Fredericksburg.

3. John Lewis's father, Fielding Lewis, who died in 1781, attended to some of GW's business for him at the beginning of the Revolution. See GW's Memorandum to Fielding Lewis, and its enclosure, 30 April 1775, and notes.

4. For the two tracts of land, one in Nansemond County, Va., the other in Gates County, N.C., which GW and his brother-in-law Fielding Lewis purchased jointly before the Revolution and for the sale of the tracts, see GW to Thomas Walker, 10 April 1784, n.3; see also GW to John Cowper, 25 May 1788, GW to John Lewis, 16 Sept., 8 Dec. 1788, and John Lewis to GW, 7 Dec., n.1, 13 Dec. 1788.

5. GW and Fielding Lewis were among the founding members of the Dismal Swamp Land Company in 1763 (*Papers, Colonial Series,* 7:269–74). Colo. Jameson was undoubtedly John Jameson who served as an officer throughout the Revolution, reaching the rank of lieutenant colonel in the 2d Continental Dragoons in 1779.

From James Rumsey

Sir,   Annapolis Decr 17th 1787

Inclosed you have Coppies of two Certificates of what the Boat performed at Sum tryals we have been making I have a number more but as they are the Same in Substance I thought it not nessasary to Coppy them, we Enhibeted under many disadvantages and Should not have Come forth publicly untill Spring if it had not been for Mr Fitches *Stealing* a march on me in Virgine[1] I have Sent Down a number of certificates to the asemblely of the first Days performance the Second was not then made[2] I also Inclose you a Contrast Drew by Capt Bedinger Between Mr Fitches Boat and mine.[3] I met with Govenor Johnson He toald me of a Letter he had wrote you respecting Sum Conversation that him and me had about my applying Steam to work the Boat[4] as well as I Rembar it happened in octer 1785, when I Informd him of my Entention of applying Steam and Spoke to him for to Cast Cillinders for me, he Said that from what Little he Could gather on the Subject he Suposed it to be quite an other kind of a machine I toald him that the modle which I Showed to you was, he then Said he thought I had used you— the[n] I Toald him I beleived not for that I had Informed you of my Intention, to try Steam, I Can Recolect no more that was Said upon that Subject But it Seems that govenor Johnson has taken Up a Rong Idiea of the matter and Supposed that I had Informed you, of my Intention to apply Steam at the time I obtained your Certifycate[5] nor did I know untill now that he Veiwed my Information in that Light, nor did I Ever Conceive that I had gave you any information Respecting it only that I had Such a thing in Ideia, untill the Letter that I wrote you on the 10th of march 1785,[6] nor had I before near about that time Reduced it To any form Sufisantly promising to determin me to make the Tryal I was then det[e]rmened, as I wrote you as follows—"I have taken the greatest pains to afect an other kind of Boat, upon the principles I was mentioning to you at Richmond I have the plasure to Inform you That I have broght it to great perfection it is true it will Cost Sum more than the other way but when done is more mannageable and Can be worked by as few hands the power is amence and I have quite Convinced myself that Boats of pasage may be made to go against the Corrent of missippa or ohio River or in the gulf Stream from the Leward to the windward Isllands from Sixty to one hundred miles per day["]—this was Certainly an Information And was what I aluded to when I toald govenor Johnson that I had Informed you of it, a Little farther on in the Same Letter is the following paragraff—"the plan I intend to persue is to build the Boat with boath the powers on Board on a Large Scale["]—As you did not make anny objection to the plann proposed when you wrote me an answer to that Letter[7] I Considered myself at Liberty to go on upon the Steam plan Conected with the other nor did I Drop the Idea of Doing So untill Long after I had the Honor of Seeing [you] Last But not Being able to accomplish the Building of an Other Boat and finding by the Little Experiments I made that one Boat would not do alone I was at a great Loss to know how to act and if it had not been on account of your Certificate I Would then have Quit it, being under To many Embarrasments and nearly a new mecheine to be made before any thing Could be done as my new Constructed Boiler made Such hot Steam as to melt all the Soft Solder and news Comeing frequently that Mr Fitch would Soon Come forth,[8] ad to this that the Ice Carryed away my Boat and Broke thirty feet out of Her middle, a Large family to Support no Business going On, In debted, and what Little money I Could Rake together Expended, a gentleman has Since assisted me to whome I have Mortgaged a few family negroes which must Soon go if I do not Rais the money for him before Long. my present plan is So Simple Cheap and powerfull that I think it would be Rong to attemt the former plan, I would wish to Say Sumthing to the public about it, on your account.[9] But doubt my own Abelityes to give that Satisfaction I would wish. It has gave me much uneaseyness Especially as I have By a train of unforeseen Events So often apeared to you as a person acting Inconsistantly and I Can Say in truth hower unfortunate I have been in the attempt that my greatest ambetion is & has been to Deserve your Esteem—I intend to philidelphia Before my Return, and in January I will (if in my power) go to South Carelino & gergia—your Letter to govenor Johnson prevented Mr Fitch from geting an act here[10] You have Sir my Sincerest thank for the many favors you Conferred on me—I am your much Obliged Hbe hbe Servt

James Rumsey

P.S. the original papers from which These are Coppyed was acknowledged bef⟨ore⟩ Magestretes and the County Seal affixe⟨d to⟩ them, which I Did not think nessesary to Copy I am with great Esteem—J. Rumsey

ALS, DLC:GW.

1. The first of the two certificates, both copies made by Rumsey, is that of Horatio Gates, "Late Majr General of the Continental army," who gives an account of the first experiment: "On Monday December the 3d 1787 I was Requested to See an Experiment on potomack River made by—James Rumseys Steam Boat and had no Small pleasure to See her g⟨e⟩t on her way with near half her Burthen on Board and move against the Current at the Rate of three miles per hour by the force of Steam without any External applycation whatever, I am well Informed and Verily believe that the Mechine at present is Very Imperfect and by no meanes Capeble of performing what it would Do if Compleated. I have not the Least Doubt but it may be broght Into Common Use and be of great advantage to navegation, as the Mechine Is Simple, Light, and Cheap, and will be Exceedingly Durable, and Does not occupy a Space of more than four feet by two and a half" (DLC:GW). The account of the second experiment, with the names of Charles Morrow, the Rev. Robert Stubbs, Henry Bedinger, the lawyer Thomas White, and Abraham Shepherd affixed, reads: "Being Requested to See an Experiment made by—James Rumseys Steam Boat on potomack River on Tuesday the 11th of December 1787 it was with great pleasure that we Saw her get on her way with upwards of three tons on board And move against the Current at the Rate of about four miles an hour by the force of Steam, without any External application whatever. we are well Informed and beleive That the Mecheinery is at present Very Imperfect

and by no meanes Capeble of performing what it would Do if Compleated. We are perswaded that it may be broght Into Common Use, and be of great advantage to navegation; as the mecheinery is Simple, Light, and Cheap, and Does not Occupy a Space of more than four f⟨oo⟩t by two and a half" (DLC:GW).

A public notice, dated 16 Dec. 1787, of the trial of Rumsey's boat made on 11 Dec. 1787 appeared in the *Virginia Gazette, and Winchester Advertiser* on 11 Jan. 1788: "On the eleventh day of this month, Mr. Rumsey's steam boat, with more than half her loading (which was upwards of three tons) and a number of people on board, made a progress of four miles in one hour against the current of the Potomac river, by the force of steam, without any external application whatsoever, impelled by a machine that will not cost more than twenty guineas for a ten-ton boat, and that will not consume more than four bushels of coals, or the equivalent of wood, in twelve hours. It is thought that if some pipes of the machine had not been ruptured by the freezing of the water, which had been left in them a night or two before, and which ruptures were only secured by rags tied round them, that the boat's way would have been at the rate of seven or eight miles in an hour. As this invention is easily applied to boats or ships of all dimensions, to smooth, shallow and rapid rivers, or the deepest and roughest seas, freightage of all kinds will be reduced to one-third of its present expense" (quoted in Beltzhoover, *Rumsey*, 19).

According to an account given many years later by Maj. Henry Bedinger, Rumsey's brother-in-law took the helm and Dr. James McMechen was aboard to help Rumsey with the machinery when the boat moved up the river as the inhabitants of Shepherdstown watched from the Potomac's banks. "After going for a half mile or more," Bedinger is quoted as saying, "to a point opposite what is known as Swearingen's Spring, she rounded to and returned, going for some little distance. . . . Thus she continued to go to and fro, up and down the river, for about the space of two hours, in full view of many hundreds of spectators" (ibid., 18).

2. The Virginia Assembly took no notice of Rumsey's certificates before its session ended on 8 Jan. 1788.

3. The statement by Henry Bedinger has not been found.

4. See Thomas Johnson's letter to GW of 16 Nov. in which he reports that Rumsey had claimed that he had informed him of giving up his original efforts to use the force of the river's current to move his boat and was attempting instead to harness steam for that purpose.

5. GW's certificate stating that he had witnessed James Rumsey's boat moving upstream propelled by mechanical means, dated 7 Sept. 1784, is printed above.

6. See Rumsey's letter, printed above.

7. See GW's letter to Rumsey of 5 June 1785.

8. See, for example, GW's letter of 31 Jan. 1786 urging Rumsey to get on with the development of his mechanical boat. GW wrote after learning of John Fitch's plans to develop a steam-driven boat.

9. In a pamphlet that he published in 1788 after he had gone to Philadelphia (see Rumsey to GW, 24 Mar. 1788, n.1), Rumsey wrote: "My machine with

all its misfortunes upon its head, is abundantly sufficient to prove my position, which was that a boat might be so constructed as to be propelled through the water at the rate of ten miles an hour, by the force of steam, and that the machinery employed for that purpose might be so simple and cheap as to reduce the price of freight at least one-half in common navigation;—likewise that it might be forced by the same machinery, with considerable velocity, against the constant stream of long and rapid rivers. Such machinery I promised to prepare, and such a boat to exhibit; this I have now so far performed in the presence of so many witnesses, and to the satisfaction of so many disinterested gentlemen, as to convince the unprejudiced, and to deprive even the sceptic of his doubts, &c." (quoted in Beltzhoover, *Rumsey,* 20).

10. GW to Thomas Johnson, 22 Nov. 1787.

From James Madison

Dear Sir   New York Decr 20. 1787.

I was favoured on Saturday with your letter of the 7th instant, along with which was covered the printed letter of Col. R. H. Lee to the Governour. It does not appear to me to be a very formidable attack on the new Constitution; unless it should derive an influence from the names of the correspondents, which its intrinsic merits do not entitle it to. He is certainly not perfectly accurate in the statement of all his facts; and I should infer from the tenor of the objections in Virginia that his plan of an Executive would hardly be viewed as an amendment of that of the Convention. It is a little singular that three of the most distinguished Advocates for amendments; and who expect to unite the thirteen States in their project, appear to be pointedly at variance with each other on one of the capital articles of the System. Col. Lee proposes that the President should chuse a Council of Eleven and with their advice have the absolute appointment of all Officers[.] Col: Mason's proposition is that a Council of six should be appointed by the Congress. What degree of power he would confide to it I do not know. The idea of the Governour is that there should be a plurality of co-equal heads, distinguished probably by other peculiarities in the organization. It is pretty certain that some others who make a common cause with them in the general attempt to bring about alterations differ still more from them, than they do from each other; and that they themselves differ as much on some other great points as on the Constitution of the Executive.

You did not judge amiss of Mr Jay. The paragraph affirming a change in His opinion of the plan of the Convention, was an arrant forgery. He has contradicted it in a letter to Mr J. Vaughan which has been printed in the Philadelphia Gazettes.[1] Tricks of this sort are not uncommon with the Enemies of the new Constitution. Col. Mason's objections were as I am told published in Boston mutilated of that which pointed at the regulation of Commerce.[2] Docr Franklin's concluding speech which you will meet with in one of the papers herewith inclosed, is both mutilated & adulterated so as to change both the form & the spirit of it.[3]

I am extremely obliged by the notice you take of my request concerning the Potowmack. I must insist that you will not consider it as an object of any further attention.

The Philada papers will have informed you of the result of the Convention of that State. N. Jersey is now in Convention, & has probably by this time adopted the Constitution. Genl Irvine of the Pena Delegation who is just arrived here, and who conversed with some of the members at Trenton tells me that great unanimity reigns in the Convention.[4]

Connecticut it is pretty certain will decide also in the affirmative by a large majority. So it is presumed will N. Hampshire; though her Convention will be a little later than could be wished. There are not enough of the returns in Massts known for a final judgment of the probable event in that State. As far as the returns are known they are extremely favorable; but as they are cheifly from the maritime parts of the State, they are a precarious index of the public sentiment. I have good reason to believe that if you are in correspondence with any gentlemen in that quarter, and a proper occasion offered for an explicit communication of your good wishes for the plan, so as barely to warrant an explicit assertion of the fact, that it would be attended with valuable effects. I barely drop the idea. The circumstances on which the propriety of it depends, are best known to, as they will be best judged of, by yourself[5]—The information from N. Carolina gave us great pleasure. We hear nothing from the States South of it. With the most perfect esteem & regard I am Dear Sir your affecte friend & obedt servt.

Js Madison Jr

ALS, DLC:GW; copy, in Madison's hand, DLC: Madison Papers.

1. See note 2 in GW's letter to Madison of 7 December. John Jay's letter to John Vaughan, 1 Dec. 1787, was printed in the *Pennsylvania Packet* (Philadelphia), 7 December.

2. The version of George Mason's "Objections to the Constitution" appearing in the *Massachusetts Centinel* (Boston) on 21 Nov., and frequently reprinted, omitted Mason's objection to having navigation acts adopted by a simple majority of Congress (Kaminski and Saladino, *Documentary History of the Ratification of the Constitution*, 8:42).

3. The editors of the *Madison Papers* (10:335) suggest that Madison sent GW a printed commentary on the speech that Benjamin Franklin made at the end of the Convention, which used quotations from the speech in a way to make it appear that Franklin was unenthusiastic about the Constitution. The commentary appeared in the *New York Journal* on 17 December.

4. William Irvine (1741–1804), an Irishman who served as a brigadier general during the Revolution and was a member of Congress from 1786 to 1788, lived at Carlisle, Pennsylvania. GW wrote to him on 11 Jan. 1788 to secure information about western navigation.

5. The unauthorized publication of an excerpt from GW's private letter to Charles Carter of Ludlow, 14 Dec. 1787, seems to have served the purpose. See GW to Madison, 5 Feb. 1788, and Madison to GW, 20 Feb. 1788. But see also GW to Benjamin Lincoln, 31 Jan. 1788.

Letter not found: from Charles Carter (of Ludlow), 21 Dec. 1787. On 20 Jan. 1788 GW wrote Carter that his "favor of the 21st of last month" had come to hand.

Letter not found: from Chastellux, 21 Dec. 1787. On 25 April 1788 GW wrote to Chastellux: "In reading your very friendly and acceptable letter of the 21st of December 1787...."

To David Stuart

Dear Sir,   Mount Vernon Decr 22d 1787.

To the best of my recollection I have sent you Seven numbers of the Fœderalist, under the signature of Publius. The subsequent numbers that have come to my hands, I herewith enclose.

Have you received a letter from me, enclosing one for my Nephew Bushrod Washington; containing queries respecting my lands in the Western Country?[1] It is sometime since it was dispatched from this, & having received no acknowledgment of it, I apprehend a miscarriage.

From your acct this letter will hardly find you in Richmond, from that of others the Assembly will set till Feby. Under this uncertainty I only add the Compliments & good wishes of this family to you; and the assurance of the regard with which I am—Dr Sir Yr Obedt & Affecte Servt

Go: Washington

P.S. A number of Certificates were sent to you a few days ago—have these been received by you from me?

ALS, PHi: Dreer Collection.

1. GW's letter to Bushrod Washington is dated 3 December. Unless GW sent the letter to Bushrod with his letter to Stuart of 11 Dec., the letter to Stuart referred to here is missing.

From Michael Ryan

Sir   Fredricksburg Decr 23rd 1787

Having had the honor of being known to your Excelly in the Army I make bold to adress you, on a subject extremely interesting to me and perhaps not indifferent to your Excellency.

A Mr Whitcroft of Annapolis and myself have lately by purchase become joint proprietors of Two Hundred thousand Acres of Land on the Western Waters of Virginia, Eighty thousand Acres of which lie contiguous to your Excellency's Land on the great Kanawa, it being too large a tract of Land for men in our circumstances to hold unimprov'd we have laid a plan for the improvement of the same the outline of which plan I beg leave to lay before your Excellency.

We will lay off two towns in the most convenient parts of Said Lands and divide the remaining Land into farms of Five Hundred Acres each. we intend to encourage European Farmers by giving every Farmer a Farm rent free for 7 years from the time of the Settling thereon and one Lott in a Town for himself and one Lott for each of his Children for ever. Three Hundred Mechanics who shall first settle in the Towns shall be each intitled to one Lott for ever.

This being too arduous an undertaking for us unconnected we propose forming a Company of twenty Shares each Share to consist of an undivided Ten thousand Acres which we will Sell at the rate of two Shillings ℔ acre and demand only One Hundred Guineas ℔ Share when the Patents Issue in the Companys Name

One Hundred Guineas twelve Months thereafter and the residue in three years.

When the Company is form'd they May at their joint expence Send two Gentlemen of the Company to Europe with Ample powers to dispose of part of Said Lands and encourage Settlers[.] a Sale of an undivided One Hundred thousand Acres would undoubtedly throw a considerable balance into the hands of the Company and perhaps be effected before the Second payment becomes due.

Admit it sold as Low as 4/6 Sterling ℔ Acre The company would have after paying us and other expences—£11000—197 Farms of 500 Acres each—And about 4500 Town Lotts Half an Acre each.

It is needless to point out to a gentleman of your Excellencys information the probable advantages that may result from this Mode of Settlement not only to individuals but to the whole Western Country I will therefore only remark from my own observation this Summer at Greenbrier and from the Opinion of intelligent inhabitants of that Country that it bids fair to be one of the richest Settlements in the United States.[1]

Should your Excellency approve of our plan and think it deserving your encouragement I shall be happy in attending at any place that may be appointed to give a fuller explanation thereof and receive Such advice as your Excellency May please to honor me with. I am Sir With every sentiment of respect Your Excellencys Devoted Humble Servt

M. Ryan

ALS, DLC:GW.

1. GW responded from Mount Vernon on 9 Jan. 1788: "Sir, I have received your letter of the 23d of December wherein you express a wish that I would become a joint proprietor with yourself and some other Gentlemen in a large tract of Land which you have upon the Western waters of Virginia. I am much obliged to you, Sir, for your politeness in making the proposal to me and submitting the plan of settleing the land &c. to my consideration. But I must decline taking any part in it, however advantageous the terms may be, and however desirious I am to promote any laudable plan for the settlement of the Country; for the lands which I already possess in those parts are untenanted, and I am at preasent endeavouring to have them seated, this will engage me as extensively in business of this nature as I wish to be, and operates as one strong reason against my embarking any further in it; another, still more weighty, is the constant and unremitting attention which the arrangment and cultivation of my estate here requires. I am Sir Yr Most, Obedt Hble Sert G.

Washington" (LB, DLC:GW). Michael Ryan, an officer in both the 4th and 5th Pennsylvania regiments during the Revolution, and his partner William Whitcroft of Annapolis, met with failure in their scheme. See Ryan to GW, 12 Mar. 1790.

From William McWhir

Your Excellencie's   Alexandria Decr 24th [1787]
Patronage and Bounty has so very essentially contributed to the growth and respectability of our school, that it would be highly blamable and imprudent in me, who am supported by it, to think of undertaking any thing which might have the smallest probability of injuring it, without taking the liberty of consulting you. Especially as your approbation or disapprobation of the measure, would render it injurious or the contrary. And upon this principle shall either put my design in execution or not, as Your Excellency shall think proper to advise.

From several letter[s] which I have lately had from my Father it appears to be highly necessary both to my interest and happiness that I should visit my Native country in the course of the ensuing year. The nature of my present employment however is such that I should scarcely have thought it practicable had I not received a letter a few weeks ago from a Young Gentleman who informs me that he will be in Alexandria next Spring. He is a young man of liberal education, and unexceptionable Moral Character and would no doubt give satisfaction to the Trustees, if I can persuade him to supply my place for a few months. I should not propose being absent more than six, or at most, eight months; during which time I design to visit some of the principal towns both in Ireland and Scotland and should make it my business to enquire particularly after a Good Mathematician (a person much wanted in our School), A good Writer is also much wanted. I should also establish a connection by which I could have a constant supply of such books as we want, which at present cannot be got in N. York, Baltimore, or Philada. The People whom I have consulted upon this matter willingly agree to my going if I will promise to come back. This I am fully determined to do. And if I can only meet with Your Excellencies approbation I shall go with a cheerful heart looking upon my interest as secure.[1] Please to pardon the liberty I take in troubling you with my private affairs and believe me to be Your Excellencies Most Obedt Hble Servt

W. McWhir

ALS, DLC:GW.

1. GW responded from Mount Vernon the next day: "Sir, I have recd your letter of yesterday & in answer to it must observe that however desireous I may be to comply with your request and gratifying your wishes I do not consider myself at liberty to give an opinion on the subject, for altho' I was appointed a visitor or Trustee yet having never acted in that capacity or taken any part in the management of the Acadamy I should not wish to interfere on this occasion, but will readily and cheerfully agree to whatever may be done by the Trustees on the subject.

"I am very glad to find that you have agreed to take my Nephews to board with you—I shall feel myself under less apprehension of any irregular and improper conduct on their parts while they are under your immediate inspection, than if they were to be placed with a person to whose advice or direction they would not consider themselves obliged to pay any attention. I am Sir— Yr Most Obedt Hbl. Servant G. Washington" (LB, DLC:GW). The Rev. William McWhir (1759–1851) did not return to Alexandria in 1788 from a visit to his native northern Ireland.

Letter not found: GW to Bushrod Washington, 24 Dec. 1787. Letter listed in *American Book Prices Current*, 27 (1921), 1021.

To Thomas Lewis

Sir,   Mount Vernon December 25th 1787.

It is my desire, and I am told it is the wish of many—and sure I am policy requires it—that the uncultivated tracts of land on the Great Kankawa and Ohio belonging to the military should be setled.[1] The difficulty with me respecting mine has been, how to draw the line of mutual advantage for Landlord and Tenant, with respect to the terms; and where to find a confidential person on, or near the spot who would act for me a[s] Agent.

Two reasons, hitherto, have restrained me from making application to you, on this head. first, the uncertainty I was under of your having become an actual resident in those parts—and second, a doubt whether it might be agreeable to you to accept this trust on account of the trouble, and little profit that would derive from the agency; at least for some time.

The first cause being removed, (having understood by means

of some Members in Assembly that you live at Point Pleasant)—
I shall take the liberty of trying you on the second; under a
hope, that more from the desire of seeing the Country settled
the neighborhood strengthened and property thereby secured;
and the value of it encreased; than from any pecuniary considerations at the present moment, you may be induced to aid me in
seating my lands on the great Kanakawa and on the Ohio between the mouths of the two Rivers bearing that name.

If you accept the trust this letter shall be your authority—
fully—and amply given and binding upon me and my heirs for
the following purposes.

First. To place as many Tenants on the several tracts of Lands
(Plats of which with my signature annexed to them shall accompany this Power) as you can obtain consistently with your Judgment, and suggestions hereafter mentioned.

Second. That an exemption from the payment of Rents for
the term of three years shall be allowed them provided certain
reasonable improvements such as you shall stipulate for—and
which I think (but leave the matter to you) ought to be comfortable houses [   ] Acres of Arable—and [   ] Acres of Meadow
Land—and a certain number of frute Trees planted.

Third, That for the fourth year, Rents shall become due, and
shall consist (as I am told the custom of the Country is) of a
third of whatever is raised on the premises, which rents shall be
annually paid thereafter to you, or my Agent for the tirm being
in that Country.

Fourth, That under this tenure they may be assured of the
places (if they incline to remain, and will go on to improve them)
for the term of [   ] years; were these not to exceed ten, it
would be more pleasing to me than any extension beyond that
number; but if this limitation will not be exceded to on the part
of the Tenant, I must leave it to your discretion to augment
them, making the term definite, and not for lives, which is not
only uncertain, but often introductory of disputes to ascertain,
the termination of them. Instances of which have happened to
me. All mines and Minerals will be reserved for the landlord—
and where there are valuable streams for water works, the Rent
must bear some proportion to the advantages which are likely
to result from them.

Fifth, Whether custom authorizes, or justice requires that the tenant should pay the land tax of what he agrees to hold before the rent becomes due; or afterwards, in whole, or part, must be governed by the practice which prevails, and consequently is left to your decision.

Sixth. I do not conceive it necessary, nor should I incline to go into much, or indeed any expence in laying the Land off into Lots till it begins to be thick settled and productive. The first comers will of course have the first choice—but they and all others are to be informed that their lotts (be the quantity little or much) will be bounded by water courses, or (where this is not the case) by convenient and regular forms. And as most of my Tracts (as you will see by the plats) have extensive boundaries on the rivers running but a little ways back it is my wish indeed, it naturally follows that back part of the land should be considered as the support of that which will be first settled and cleared on the margins of the Rivers and a sufficiency of it reserved for the purpose.

Seventh, For your trouble in negotiating this business, I am very willing to allow the usual Commission for collecting—converting into Cash—and transmitting to me, the rents after they shall commence and whatever you may think proper to charge me (in reason) for your trouble till this shall happen. I will chearfully agree to pay.

Whether you accept this trust or not, you will do me a favor in the communication of your sentiments on the subject—there are two ways by which letters will come safe. Viz. thrown into the Post Office at Philadelphia or into that at Richmond. Colo. Bayard an acquaintance of mine, or any acquaintance you may have at Fort Pitt, will forward them to the first place—and the means of doing it to the latter you must be a better Judge of then myself—If the letters once get into the Post Office I shall be sure of them—On private conveyances there is no reliance— they are tossed about and neglected so as rarely to reach their intended distination when sent in this manner.

If you should incline to act under this power your own good sense and Judgment will at once dictate the propriety, indeed necessity of promulgating it as extensively as you can by Advertisements to those parts from whence Setlers are most likely to be drawn over and above the opportunities which your situation gives you of communicating the matter to travellers by water on the Ohio.

On the other hand if you do not incline to act I would thank you for returning me the papers herewith enclosed as it will save me the trouble of making other copies.[2]

Whether the improvements which I had made on the Lands (of which you have herewith the draughts) in the years 1774 and 5 will be of use to Settlers at this day, or not—you are on the spot can best determin—they cost me, or were valued to between £1500 and 2000. if they are useful the ex[e]mption from rent should be shorter—I thought it necessary to bring the matter into view tho' my expecttations from it are small. I am Sir—Yr Most Obedt Sir

Go. Washington

P.S. I have a small tract called the round bottom containing abt 600 Acres, which I would also let. It lyes on the Ohio, opposite to pipe Creek, and a little above Capteening.[3]

LB, DLC:GW.

Thomas Lewis (1754–1824), son of Gen. Andrew Lewis (1720–1781), had settled at Point Pleasant near the junction of the Great Kanawha and Ohio rivers. Lewis wrote GW in August 1788 saying that he had not been able to secure settlers for his own land located in the same area as GW's.

1. For references to these bounty lands on the Great Kanawha and Ohio belonging to GW, see GW to Samuel Lewis, 1 Feb. 1784, source note.

2. Lewis wrote to GW, 27 Aug. 1788, refusing to act as his agent.

3. For references to GW's Round Bottom tract, see GW to Thomas Freeman, 11 April 1785, and note 2 of that document.

To Edward Newenham

Dear Sir,   Mount Vernon December 25th 1787

I have recd your letters of the 9th of Decr 1786—27th of Feby and 2d of march 1787.[1] They should have had an earlier & more regular acknowledgment had not the publick business in which I was, in a manner, compeled to engage the last summer, joined to the unremitting attention which my own private affairs require rendered it almost impossible to observe that punctuallity with my correspondents that I could wish.

I thank you, my dear Sir, for the information which you gave me in your several letters, relative to the state of publick affairs in your Country. I hope the exertions of good men and a concurrence of circumstances will finally produce that tranquility, concord and happiness among you which you so earnestly wish for.

The publick attention here is at present wholly employed in considering and animadverting upon the form of Government proposed by the late convention for these States. The inefficacy of our present general system is acknowledged on all hands, and the proposed one has its opponents but they bear so small a proportion to its friends that there is little or no doubt of its taking place, Three States have already decided in its favor— two unanimously and the other by a majority of two to one; these are the only States whose conventions have as yet determined upon the subject, but from every information, the others will be found pretty fully in sentiment with them. The establishment of an enerjetic general Government will disappoint the hopes and expectations of those who are unfriendly to this Country—give us a national respectibility—and enable us to improve those commercial and political advantages which Nature and situation have placed within our reach.

I wrote to you sometime since and enclosed a letter from Doctor Franklin to me in answer to one which I had written respecting your Sons being appointed Consul at Marseilles; he applied to Mr Jay, Minister of foreign Affairs, (whose answer to him I likewise forwarded to you;)—the result of the application was that it could not be granted because there existed a resolution of Congress declaring that none but an American citizen should be appointed to that Office.[2]

Mrs Washington joins me in the Compliments of the season to Lady Newenham & yourself, and in wishing you many happy returns of it. I am Dr Sir—Yr Most Obedt Hble Servant

G. Washington

LB, DLC:GW.

1. None of these letters has been found.

2. GW's letters are dated 10 Mar. and 20 April 1787. The copyist wrote "relsolution."

Letter not found: from David Stuart, 25 Dec. 1787. On 29 Dec. GW wrote Stuart: "your letter of the 25th is come to hand."

From James Madison

Dear Sir   New York Decr 26. 1787.

I am just informed by a Delegate from New Hamshire that he has a letter from President Sullivan which tells him that the Legislature had unanimously agreed to call a convention as recommended, to meet in February. The second wednesday is the day if I have not mistaken it.[1] We have no further information of much importance from Massachusetts. It appears that Cambridge the residence of Mr Gerry has left him out of the choice for the Convention, and put in Mr Dana formerly a Minister of the U. States in Europe, and another Gentleman, both of them firmly opposed to Mr Gerry's Politics.[2] I observe too in a Massts paper that the omission of Col. Mason's objection with regard to commerce, in the first publication of his Objections, has been supplied. This will more than undo the effect of the mutilated view of them.[3] New Jersey the newspapers tell us has adopted the Constitution unanimously. Our European intelligence remains perfectly as it stood at the date of my last. With the most affectionate esteem & attachment I am Dear [Sir], Your Obedient & very hble Servt

Js Madison Jr

ALS, DLC:GW; copy, DLC: Madison Papers.

1. Gen. John Sullivan (1740–1795) was president of New Hampshire. The ratifying convention met in Exeter in February and on the twenty-second, without taking action, adjourned until June.

2. Elbridge Gerry, who had declined to sign the Constitution at Philadelphia, was invited to attend the ratifying convention in Boston in January to answer questions, but he stalked out on 19 Jan. after engaging in a shouting match with Francis Dana (1743–1811), who was presiding. See Rufus King to Madison, 20 Jan. 1788, in Rutland and Hobson, *Madison Papers*, 10:400–401. The second member of the Cambridge delegation was Stephen Dana, who voted for ratification on 5 February.

3. See Madison to GW, 20 Dec., n.2.

From Battaile Muse

Honorable Sir   Decr 26th 1787

I have only Time as the Post is waiting To Say I have Enclosed and Order on Mr Willim Hunter for £50—altho I am not in your Debt[1]—I Shall write To you Very Fully by First opportunity. I have the Honour to be your Faithfull Servant

                                                                Battaile Muse

Please To inform me whether my orders are accepted To Ennable me To do what may be wright.

ALS, DLC:GW. Written on the cover: "Mr [Thomas] Po[r]ter will much oblige To Forward this Letter with dispatch & Care B. Muse."

1. The entry of 5 Jan. 1788 in GW's account with Muse records £100 received in "two Drafts on William Hunter Junr Esqr. in my favor for £50 each" (Ledger B, 213). For the second £50 draft, see Muse to GW, 4 Dec., n.4.

From Edmund Randolph

Dear sir   Richmond Decr 27. 1787.

The inclosed pamphlet speaks so fully for itself, that any explanation of it from me would be useless.[1] I send it to you, because I know your friendship for the writer, and because I take pleasure in subscribing myself at all times, with unfeigned truth my dear sir Yr obliged friend & serv.

                                                              Edm: Randolph

ALS, DLC:GW.

1. The pamphlet contained Randolph's letter to the speaker of the house of delegates, dated 10 Oct., giving his reasons for not signing the Constitution. It is reprinted in Kaminski and Saladino, *Documentary History of the Ratification of the Constitution,* 8:260–75. Randolph also sent a copy of the pamphlet to James Madison. For the differing reactions of the two to the publication of Randolph's statement, see GW to Randolph, 8 Jan. 1788, and Madison to Randolph, 10 Jan. 1788, in Rutland and Hobson, *Madison Papers,* 10:354–57.

To David Stuart

Dear Sir   Mount Vernon, Dec. 29th 1787

In more fear that this letter will not find you in Richmond than of expectation that it will, it goes from me by the Post of this day. The sole intent therefore of it is to request the favor of you to give the packet enclosed with it the safest conveyance that offers, to Colo. Thos Lewis of Point Pleasant in Greenbrier County—to whom I have delagated a power to let my lands on the Great Kanhawa & the Ohio above it.[1]

I forgot in my last, and suppose it is too late in this letter to inform you that I have never received, or heard more of the White Deer abt which you say Mr Lewis was enquiring, than what was mentioned in your letter—the Buffalo Bull mentioned by him I should [like] to receive—and doubly glad if a mate could be obtained for him—But whether the Deer, or Buffalo gets to hand or not, I feel the obligation this Gentleman intended to confer on me very sensibly.[2]

Will interest be allowed on the Certificate for my Executed Negro? I have been out of the money 6 years, or nearly.[3] I ought to have told you long ago, but in my hurried situation forgot it, that I do not believe there was the least foundation for M——s report, about which you enquired; [   ] Acct I have received, I believe no state in the Union will adopt the Constitution with more unanimity than Maryland.

I Am glad to hear that the District bill has passed—And should like, I must confess, to see the statement of the Govr's objection to the constitution they ought to appear [   ], & no [   ], he has taken abundant time to digest them—But what can he, or you mean by saying "He thinks it would be of service to the Constitution"? If it was for this purpose he wrote, why did he oppose the Constitution? If not, why does he write in such terms as to injure the cause he means to support? This is a paradox I am not able to comprehend! A person will sometimes say & do things that, in their operatives, make against them— but when this is previously expected by them it becomes an enigma.[4]

Mrs Stuart, your little girls, and Sister Nancy are here, and all well.[5] I am—Dear Sir with great Esteem Yr Affecte

G. Washington

P.S. Since writing the above, your letter of the 25th is come to hand.[6] I have also (since my last to you) received one from my Nephew containing answers to my querries[7]—I shall this day give the Governor's letter a reading.[8] put [   ] as have come to my hand I send you—If my memory serves me you ⟨have⟩ had [   ] to the 18th inclusive[9]—Mrs Stuart puts a letter under this cover to you.

G.W.

Mrs Washington begs you would bring her an almanac for the ensuing year.

Copy, owned (1985) by Mr. Lonsdale F. Stowell, New York City. The person who made this relatively recent copy was unable to read some words and clearly misread others.

1. See GW to Thomas Lewis, 25 December.

2. GW later wrote Andrew Lewis, Jr., on 1 Feb. 1788, thanking him for the white doe and asking him about the buffalo calf that Stuart had reported he "had it in contemplation [to] offer me." No evidence has been found that GW ever owned a buffalo.

3. See GW to Stuart, 11 Dec., n.2.

4. See Edmund Randolph to GW, 27 December.

5. David Stuart's sister Ann (Nancy) Stuart was living at Abingdon with her brother and sister-in-law. She later married George Mason's son William Mason.

6. Letter not found.

7. The letter from Bushrod Washington has not been found, but see GW to Bushrod Washington, 29 December.

8. See note 4.

9. GW is referring to the numbers of the papers of the *Federalist* that he has sent Stuart. See James Madison to GW, 18 Nov., n.2.

To Bushrod Washington

Dear Bushrod   Mount Vernon Decr 29th 1787.

Altho' I have little expectation that this letter will find you in Richmond I still send it thither. Under this persuasion, I shall add no more than to acct for the enclosure being so long in my possession.

The truth of the case is, with a letter for myself, from Mr Smith, it was enclosed with the Papers with which he was furnished for prosecuting the ejectments of the People living on my lands on Shurtee; & these being accompanied by *another* letter from that Gentleman, I took it for granted that the bundle (which was sealed) contained only the Papers which related to my land and therefore never opened it till the day before yesterday. If it is of consequence I am sorry for its detention, if that will avail any thing. Mr Smiths letter to me, under the same predicament, would, had I have opened it in time relieved me from a suspence respecting some matters which I was unable to acct

for.[1] You have my best wishes & I am Dr Bushrod with sentiments of very gt regd Yr Affecte Uncle

Go: Washington

ALS (photocopy), owned (1990) by Mr. Joseph M. Maddalena, *Profiles in History,* Santa Monica, California.

1. The "letter for myself, from Mr Smith," is the one that GW refers to in
his letter to Thomas Smith of 16 Sept. 1787. The letter from Smith that had
been enclosed which GW had recently discovered was dated 22 May 1787.
Neither letter has been found. See GW to Thomas Smith, 22 Feb. 1788.

Letter not found: from James Wilkinson, 30 Dec. 1787. GW wrote
Wilkinson on 20 Feb. 1788: "I have received your letter of the 30th
of December."

Comments on David Humphreys' Biography of George Washington

Editorial Note

David Humphreys wrote GW from France on 30 Sept. 1784 about the
utility of having a biography of George Washington, particularly one
written by GW himself. In early 1785 Humphreys began suggesting
himself as a possible biographer, to which GW agreed (Humphreys
to GW, 15 Jan. 1785, GW to Humphreys, 25 July 1785). Humphreys
apparently started work on the biography when he visited Mount Vernon in the late summer of 1786 (Zagarri, *Humphreys' Life,* xix); but
he must have written most of it after his return to Mount Vernon in
November 1787, where he remained until GW traveled to New York
in April 1789 to assume the presidency. It also was during this time
that GW must have made the notations that are printed here. Humphreys' manuscript, which was broken up and dispersed, at best was
the draft of a biographical sketch. Rosemarie Zagarri has reassembled
its parts and rendered it intelligible in the publication cited above. At
the end of the notes that GW made for Humphreys, GW wrote: "The
information given in these sheets—tho related from Memory, It is I
believe to be depended upon. It is hastily and incorrectly related—but
not so much for the⟨se⟩ reasons, as some others, it is earnest⟨ly⟩ re-
questd that after Col. Humphreys has extracted what he shall judge
necessary, and given it in his own language, that the *whole* of what Is
here contained may be returned to G. W., or committed to the flames.

some of the enumerations are trifling; and perhaps more important circumstances omitted; but just as they occurred to the memory, they were committed—If there are any grains among them Col. H. can easily seperate them from the chaff."

Remarks

AD, New York: *Forbes Magazine* Collection. The page numbers in the notes refer to Zagarri, *Humphreys' Life*.

[1787–88]

It was rather the wish of my eldest brother (on whom the general concerns of the family devolved) that this shd take place & the matter was contemplated by him—My father died when I was only 10 years old.[1]

He was not appointed Adjutant General of the Militia of Virginia untill after his return from the expedition to Carthagena. Nor did he Command the Colonial troops on that occasion. these were under the Orders of Sir Wm Gooch Lt Govr of Virginia—He was no more than the Senior Officer of those which were raised in this Colony & wch with those of the other Colonies formed what was called the American Brigade—under Sir William Gouch—he was scarcely of age when he went on this expedn.[2]

and from whom he had received many distinguished marks of patronage & favor.[3]

Not all—for the second Son (Augustine) left many childn, sevl of whom are now living; and inherit a very large portion of his Fathers Estate. perhaps the best part.[4]

1. This is GW's comment on: "It was the design of his Father that he should be bred for an Officer in the British navy" (7–8).

2. GW's comment on: "After having been appointed Adjutant General of the Militia of Virginia, [Lawrence Washington] commanded the Colonial Troops in the expedition against Carthagena" (8).

3. GW's comment on: "On his return [from Cartagena, Lawrence Washington] called his patrimonial Mansion, Mount Vernon, in honour of the Admiral of that name with whom he had contracted a particular intimacy" (8).

4. GW's comment on: "On the death of all the children by the first marriage, General Washington acceded to a large landed property" (8). GW may have noted that his three full brothers shared in the inheritance from his father.

Before he was 20 years of age.[5]

He was then more than 21 years—as will appear from dates.[6]

at a most inclement Season, for he travelled over the Apalachean Mountains, and passed 250 miles thro an uninhabited wilderness Country (except by a few tribes of Indians settled on the Banks of the Ohio) to Presque Isle within 15 Miles of Lake Erie in the depth of winter when the whole face of the Earth was covered with snow and the waters covered with Ice; The whole dist[anc]e from Wmsburgh the then seat of Governmt at least 500 miles.[7]

It was on this occasion he was named by the half-King (as he was called) and the tribes of Nations with whom he treated— Caunotaucarius (in English) the Town taker; which name being registered in their Manner & communicated to other Nations of Indians, has been remembered by them ever since in all their transactions with him during the late war.[8]

This is a task to which G. W. feels himself very incompetent (with any degree of accuracy)[9] from the badness of his mem-

5. GW added this to: "the future hero of America began his military career by a principal appointment in that Department [adjutant general], with the rank of Major" (8).

6. GW's comment on: "When he was little more than twenty one years of age . . . Young Mr Washington . . . was sent [to Forks of the Ohio in 1754] with plenary powers to ascertain the facts, to treat with the Savages, and to warn the French to desist from their aggressions" (9).

7. GW's comment on: He "performed the duties of his Mission [to the Ohio in 1754] with singular industry, intelligence & address" (9).

8. GW's comment on: "But it was deemed by some an extraordinary circumstance that so young and inexperienced a Person should have been employed on a negotiation [in 1754], with which subjects of the greatest importance were involved" (9–10).

9. The "task" that he set for GW as described by Humphreys was: "to give, in brief, some few of the most interesting facts relative to this [mission] & the subsequent campaigns, viz., the actions at the great Meadows—the siege & surrender of fort Necessity—with other occurences until Braddock's death— and indeed to annex similar accounts after Braddock's defeat untill his own leaving the service; if there should be any thing particularly worthy of preservation; according to the minute scale, on which this specimen of biography is intended" (10). The surviving public record of these events as collected and printed in volumes 1 through 6 of *Papers, Colonial Series* does, with perhaps two notable exceptions, confirm the rather high "degree of accuracy" with which GW was able to recall these experiences from the war he fought as a young man in the 1750s.

ory—loss of Papers—mutilated state, in which those of that date were preserved—and the derangement of them by frequent removals in the late war & want of time to collect and methodize them since. However accordg to the best of his ⟨recollection:⟩ by the indefatigable Industry of the Lt Colo. and the Officers who seconded his measures the Regiment was in great forwardness at Alexandria (the place of general rendezvous) early in the spring of 1754 and without waiting till the whole should be compleated—or for a detachment from the Independant Companies of regulars in the Southern Provences (which had been ⟨reqsd⟩ by the Executive of Virginia for this Service) or for troops which were raising in North Carolina and destined in conjunction to oppose the Incroachment of the French on our Western frontiers—He began his March in the Month of May in order to open the Road, and this he had to do almost the whole distance *from Winchester* (in the County of Frederick not more than 80 miles from Alexandria to the Ohio)—⟨For⟩ deposits—&ca—and for the especiall purpose of siezing, if possible, before the French shd arrive at it, the important Post at the conflux of the Alligany and Monongahela; with the advantages of which he was forcibly struck the preceeding year; and earnestly advised the securing of with Militia, or some other temporary force—But notwithstanding all his exertions, the New, and uncommon difficulties he had to encounter (made more intolerable by incessant Rains and swelled waters of which he had many to cross) he had but just ascended the Lawrel Hill 50 M: short of his object: after a March of 230 Miles from Alexa. when he received information from his Scouts that the French had in force, siezed the Post he was pushing to obtain; having descended from Presque Isle by the Rivers Le beouf and Alligany to this Place by water with artillery &ca &ca—The object of his precipitate advance being thus defeated—The detachmt of regulars, wch had arrived at Alexa. (by water) and under his orders being far in his rear—and no Acct of the Troops from No. Carolina—it was thought advisable to fall back a few miles, to a place—known by the name of the great meadows—abounding in Forage more convenient for the purpose of forming a Magazine & bringing up the rear—and to advance from (if we should ever be in ⟨force⟩ to do it) to the attack of the Post which the enemy now occupied; and had called Du Quesne—At this place, some days after, we were joined by the above detachment of regulars; consisting (before they were reduced on the March by desertion, Sickness &ca) of a Captn (McKay a brave & worthy Officer)— three Subalterns—and 100 Rank & file. But previous to this junction the French sent a detachment to reconnoitre our Camp to obtain intelligence of our strength & position; notice of which being given by the Scouts G. W. marched at the head of a party, attacked, killed 9 or 10; & captured 20 odd. This, as soon as the enemy had assembled their Indian allies, brought their whole force upon him; consisting, according to their own compared with the ⟨best accts⟩ that could be obtained from others of about 1500 Men. His force consisted of the detachment above mentioned, and between two and 300 Virginians; for the few Indians which till now had attended ⟨him,⟩ and who by reconnoitering the enemy in their March had got terrified at their numbers and resolved to retreat as they advised us to do also but which was impracticable without abandoning our Stores—Baggage—&ca as the horses which had brought them to this place had returned for Provision & had left us previous to the Attack. About 9 Oclock on the 3d of July the Enemy advanced with Shouts, and dismal Indian yells to our Intrenchments, but was opposed by so warm, spirited, & constant a fire, that to force the works in *that way* was abandoned by them—they then, from every little rising—tree—Stump—Stone—and bush kept up a constant galding fire upon us; which was returned in the best manner we could till late in the afternn when their fell the most tremendous rain that can be conceived—filled our trenches with water— wet, not only the ammunition in boxes and firelocks, but that which was in a small temporary Stockade in the middle of the Intrenchment called Fort Necessity erected for the sole purpose of its security, and that of the few stores we had; and left us nothing but a few (for all were not provided with them) Bayonets for defence. In this situation & *no* prosp⟨ect⟩ of bettering it[,] terms of capitulation were offered to us by the ene⟨my⟩ wch with some alterations that were insisted upon were the more readily acceded to, as we had no Salt provisions, & but indifferently supplied with fresh; which, from the heat of the weather, would not keep; and because a full third of our numbers Officers as well as privates were, by this time, killed or wounded— The next Morning we marched out with the honors of War, but were soon plundered contrary to the articles of capitulation of great part of our Baggage by the Savages. Our Sick and wounded were left with a detachment under the care, and command of the worthy Doctr Craik (for he was not only Surgeon to the Regiment but a lieutt therein[)] with such necessaries as we could collect and the Remains of the Regimt, and the detachment of Regulars, took up their line for the interior Country.[10] And at Winchester met 2 Companies from No. Carolina on their March to join them—These being fresh, & properly provided, were ordered to proceed to Wills's Creek & establish a post (⟨afterwards⟩ called Fort Cumberland) for the purpose of covering the Frontiers⟨,⟩ Where they were joined by a Company from Maryland, which, about this time, had been raized—Captn McKay with his detachment remd at Winchester; & the Virginia Regiment proceedd to Alexandria in order to recruit, & get supplied with cloathing & necessarys of which they stood much in need. In this manner the Winter was employed, when advice was recd of the force destined for this Service under the ordrs of G. B. and the arrival of Sir Jno. St Clair the Q: Mastr Genl with some new arrangement of Rank by which no officer who did not *immediately* derive his Comn from the *King* could command one *who did*—This was too degrading for G. W. to submit to; accordingly, he resigned his Military employment; determining to serve the next campaign as a Volunteer; but upon the arrival of Genl Braddock he was very particularly noticed by that General—taken into his family as an extra-Aid—offered a Captns Comn by *brevet* (which was the highest Grade he had it in his power to bestow⟨)⟩) and had the compliment of several blank Ensigncies given him to dispose of to the Young Gentlemen of his acqe to supply the vacancies in the 44 and 48 Regts which had arrived from Ireland.

In this capacity he commenced his second Campaign and used every proper occasion till he was taken Sick & left behind in the vicinity of Fort Cumberland to impress the Genl, & the principal Officers around him, with the necessity of opposing the nature of his defence, to the mode of attack which, more

10. GW's account of his first campaign ending in his capitulation at Fort Necessity is neither a complete nor an impartial one. See The Capitulation of Fort Necessity, 3 July 1754, in *Papers, Colonial Series*, 1:159–73.

than probably, he would experience from the *Canadian* French, and their Indians on his March through the Mountains & covered Country but so prepossed were they in favr of *regularity* & *discipline* and in such absolute contemp⟨t⟩ were *these people held,* that the admonition was suggested in vain.

About the middle of June, this Armament consisting of the two Regiments from Ireland—some Independant Companies and the Provincial troops of Virga Maryld & North Carolina, began to move from Fort Cumberland whither they had assembled—after several days March; and difficulties to which they had never been accustomed in regular Service, in Champaign Countries; and of whh they seemed to have had very little idea—the Genl resolved to divide his force, and at the head of the first division which was composed of the flower of his Army, to advance; and leave Colo. Dunbar with the second division & the heavy Baggage & Stores, to follow after. By so doing, the first division approached the Monongahela 10 miles short of Fort Duquesne the 8th of July; at which time and place having so far recovered from a severe fever and delerium from which he had been rescued by James's powder, administed by the positive order of the Genl as to travel in a covered Waggon, he joined him and the next day tho' much reduced and very weak mounted his horse on cushions, & attended as one of his aids.

About 10 Oclock on the 9th, after the Van had crossed the Monongahela the *second time,* to avoid an ugly defile (the season being very dry & waters low) and the rear yet in the River the front was attacked; and by the unusual Hallooing and whooping of the enemy, whom they could not see, were so disconcerted and confused as soon to fall into irretrievable disorder. The rear was forced forward to support them, but seeing no enemy, and themselves falling every moment from the fire, a general panic took place among the Troops from which no exertions of the Officers could recover them—In the early part of the Action some of the Irregulars (as they were called) *without direc⟨t⟩ns* advanced to the right, in loose order, to attack; but this *unhappily* from the unusual appearance of the movement being mistaken for cowardice and a running away was discountenanced—and before it was *too late,* & the confusion became general an offer was made by G. W. to head the Provincials, & engage the enemy in their own way; but the propriety of it was not seen into until it was too late for execution[.] after this, many attempts were made to dislod⟨ge⟩ the enemy from an eminence on the Right but they all proved eneffectual; and fatal to the Officers who by great exertions and good examples endeavourd to accomplish it. In one of these the Genl recd the Wd of which he died; but previous to it, had several horses killed & disabled under him. Captns Orme & Morris his two Aids de Camp having received wounds which rendered them unable to attd G. W. remained the sole aid through the day, to the Genl; he also had one horse killed, and two wounded under him—A ball through his hat—and several through his clothes, but escaped unhurt—Sir Peter Halket (secd in Command) being early killed—Lieutt Colo. Burton & Sir Jno. St Clair (who had the Rank of Lt Colo. in the Army) being badly wounded—Lieutt Colo. Gage (afterwards Genl Gage) having recd a contusion—No person knowing in the disordered State things were who the Surviving Senr Officer was & the Troops by degrees going off in confusion; without a ray of hope left of further opposition from those that remained G. W. placed the Genl in a small covered Cart, which carried some of his most essential equipage, and in the best order he could, with the ⟨last⟩ Troops (who only contind to be fired at) brought him over the *first* ford of the Monongahela; where they were formed in the best order circumstances would admit on a piece of rising ground; after wch, by the Genls order, he rode forward to halt those which had been earlier in the retreat: Accordingly, after crossing the Monongahela the *second time* and ascending the heights, he found Lieutt Colo. Gage engaged in this business to whom he delivered the Genls order and then returned to report the situation he found them in—When he was again requested by the Genl whom he met coming on, in his litter with the first halted troops, to proceed (it then being after sundown) to the second division under the command of Colo. Dunbar, to make arrangements for covering the retreat, and forwarding on provisions & refreshments to the retreating & wounded Soldiery—To accomplish this, for the 2d division was 40 odd miles in the rear it took up the whole night & part of the next morning—which from the weak state in which he was, and the fatigues and anxiety of the last 24 hours, rendered him in a manner wholly unfit for the execution of the duty he was sent upon when he arrived at Dunbars Camp—To the best of his power however, he discharged it, and remained with the secd division till the other joined it. The shocking Scenes which presented themselves in this Nights March are not to be described—The dead—the dying—the groans—lamentation—and crys along the Road of the wounded for help (for those under the latter descriptions endeavoured from the first commencement of the action—or rather confusion to escape to the 2d divn) were enough to pierce a heart of adamant. the gloom & horror of which was not a little encreased by the impervious darkness occasioned by the close shade of thick woods which in places rendered it impossible for the two guides which attended to know when they were in, or out of the track but by groping on the ground with their hands.

Happy was it for him, and the remains of the first division that they left such a quantity of valuable and enticing baggage on the field as to occasion a scramble and contention in the seizure & distribution of it among the enemy for had a pursuit taken place—by passing the defile which we had avoided; and they had got into our rear, the whole, except a few woodsmen, would have fallen victims to the merciless Savages—Of about 12 or 13 hundred which were in this action eight or 9 hundd were either killed or wounded; among whom a large proportion of brave & valuable Officers were included—The folly & consequence of opposing compact bodies to the sparse manner of Indian fighting, in woods, which had in a manner been predicted, was now so clearly verified that from hence forward another mode obtained in all future operations.

As soon as the two divisions united, the whole retreated towards Fort Cumberland; and at an Incampment near the Great Meadows the brave, but unfortunate Genl Braddock breathed his last. He was interred with the honors of war, and as it was left to G. W. to see this performed, & to mark out the spot for the reception of his remains—to guard against a savage triumph, if the place should be discovered—they were deposited in the Road over which the Army, Waggons &ca passed to hide every trace by which the entombment could be discovered. thus died a man, whose good & bad qualities were intimately blended. He was brave even to a fault and in regular Service would have done honor to his profession—His attachments were warm—his enmities were strong—and having no disguise about him, both ap-

·

peared in full force. He was generous & disinterested—but plain and blunt in his manner even to rudeness—After this event, the Troops continued their March for, and soon arrived at Fort Cumberland without molestation: and all except the P[rovincia]ls immediately resolved to proceed to Philadelphia; by which means the Frontiers of *that* State but *more especially* those of Virginia and Maryland were laid *entirely* open by the *very avenue* which had been prepared. Of the direful consequences of this measure G. W., in a visit wch he immediately made to Williamsburgh for the purpose brought the Govr & Council of Virga acquainted—But In vain did they remonstrate against the March of the B. Troops to that place to the Officer comdg them. They proceeded to augment their own: the command of which under a very enlarged & dignified Commission, to Command *all* the Troops now raised, or to be raised in the Colony, was given to him with very extensive powers, and blank Commissions to appoint all New Officers. About this time also or soon after it the discontents and clamours of the Provincial Officers, and the remonstrance of G. W. in person, to Genl Shirley, the then Comr in chief of the British Forces in America and through the Govr & Council to the Kings Minister with respect to the degrading Situation in which they were placed[,] a new arrangement took place by the Kings order, by which every Provincial Officer was to rank according to the Comn he bore, but to be junr to those of the same grade in the established Corps.[11]

As G. W. foresaw, so it happened, the frontiers were continually harrassed—but not having force enough to carry the war to the gates of Du Quesne, he could do no more than distribute the Troops along the Frontiers in Stockaded Forts; more with a view to quiet the fears of the Inhabitants than from any expectation of giving security on so extensive a line to the settlements. During this interval in one of his tours along the frontier posts—he narrowly escaped, according to the acc. afterwards given by some of our People who were Prisoners with them, and eyewitness at the time ⟨*illegible* falling⟩ by an Indian party who had waylaid (for another purpose) the communication along which

11. GW took command of the new Virginia Regiment at the end of the summer of 1755, and he traveled to Boston to see Gen. William Shirley in February 1756. See Adam Stephen to GW, 4 Oct. 1755, n.6, and GW to Robert Dinwiddie, 14 Jan. 1756.

with a small party of horse only he was passing—the road in this place formed a curve—and the prey they were in weight for being expected at the reverse part, the Captn of the party had gone across to observe the number [and] manner of their move-mt &ca in order that he might make his disposition accordingly leaving orders for the party not to take notice of any passengers the other ⟨way⟩ till he returned to them—in the mean time in the opposite direction I passed & escaped almt certain destruction for the weather was raining and the few Carbines unfit for use if we had escaped the first fire—This happened near Fort Vass. Never ceasing in the mean time in his attempts, to demonstrate to the Legislature of Virga—to Lord Loudoun —&ca that the only means of preventing the devastations to which the middle states were exposed, was to remove the cause. But the war by this time raging in another quarter of the Continent all applications were unheeded till the year 1758 when an Expedition against Fort Du Quesne was concerted, and undertaken under the conduct of Genl Forbes; who tho a brave & good Officer, was so much debilitated by bad health, and so illy supplied with the means to carry on the expedition, that it was November before the Troops got to Loyal hanning: 50 or 60 miles short of Duquesne & even then was on the very point of abandoning the Exhibition when some seasonable supplies arriving the Army was formed into three Brigades took up its March—and moved forward; the Brigade Commanded by G. W. being the leading one.

Previus to this, and during the time the Army lay at Loyal haning a circumstance occurred wch involved the life of G. W. in as much jeopardy as it had ever been before or since[.][12] the enemy sent out a large detachment to reconnoitre our Camp, and to ascertain our strength; in consequence of Intelligence that they were within 2 Miles of the Camp a party commanded by Lt Colo. Mercer of the Virga line (a gallant & good Officer)

12. GW's interruption of his brief narrative of the Forbes expedition in 1758 to revert to an account of the skirmish in the darkening Pennsylvania woods between two contingents of the Virginia troops, his and Col. George Mercer's, is the only place in his writings that GW alludes to this incident. It does not appear even in his formal reports at the time. Reference to contemporary and other accounts of what happened on that day suggests that the passage of time had erased from GW's memory some of the painful truth. See Orderly Book, 12 Nov. 1758, n.1.

was sent to dislodge them between whom a Severe conflict & hot firing ensued which lasting some time & appearing to approach the Camp it was conceived that our party was yielding the ground upon which G. W. with permission of the Genl called (for dispatch) for Volunteers and immediately marched at their head to sustain, as was conjectured the retiring troops. led on by the firing till he came within less than half a mile, & it ceasing, he detached Scouts to investigate the cause & to communicate his approach to his friend Colo. Mercer advancing slowly in the meantime—But it being near dusk and the intelligence not having been fully dissiminated among Colo. Mercers Corps, and they taking us, for the enemy who had retreated approaching in another direction commenced a heavy fire upon the releiving party which drew fire in return in spite of all the exertions of the Officers one of whom & several privates were killed and many wounded before a stop could be put to it. to accomplish which G. W. never was in more imminent danger by being between two fires, knocking up with his sword the presented pieces.

When the Army had got within about 12 or 15 miles of the Fort the enemy dispairing of its defence, blew it up—having first embarked their Artillery Stores & Troops—and retreated by water down the Ohio to their Settlements below—thus ended that Campaign, a little before Christmas in very inclement weather; and the last one made during that War by G. W. whose health by this time (as it had been declining for many months before occasioned by an inveterate disorder in his Bowels) became so precarious as to induce him (having seen quiet restored by this event to the Frontiers of his own Country which was the principal inducement to his taking arms) to resign his Military appointments—The sollicitation of the Troops which he commanded to Continue—their Affecte farewell address to him, when they found the Situation of his health and other circumstances would not allow it affected him exceedingly and in grateful sensibility he expressed the warmth of his attachmt to them on that, and his inclination to serve them on every other future occasion.

I beleive about 7,000 Bushls of Wheat and 10,000 bushels of Indn Corn which was more the staple of the farm.[13]

13. GW's comment on: "Before the war he raised [   ] bushels of wheat, in one year" (24).

Whether it be necessary to mention that my time & services were given to the public without compensation, and that every direct, and indirect attempt afterwards, to reward them (as appeared by the Letter of G. Mifflin—and the vote of 50 shares in each of the Navigations of Potomack & James River by the State of Virga who knew that I would refuse any thing that should carry with it the appearance of reward[)]—you can best judge.[14]

(1). once a week is his fixed hunts tho sometimes he goes oftner.[15]

(2) and many others in this Country[16]

(3) remarking the state of the Weather—nature of the Soil &ca[17]

14. GW makes this note after Humphreys tells of GW's return to Mount Vernon at the end of the war (33).

15. GW's comment on: "He keeps a pack of hounds, & in the season indulges himself with hunting once in a week" (37).

16. GW adds this to: "To acquire practical knowledge [of agriculture], he corresponds with Mr Arthur Young who has written so sensibly on the subject" (37).

17. Humphreys wrote: "He also makes copious Notes in writing relative to his own experiments the state of the seasons, nature of soils, effect of different kinds of manure & everything that can throw light on the farming business" (37). For GW's instructions regarding his notes, see the editorial note.

Index

NOTE: Identifications of persons, places, and things in previous volumes of the *Confederation Series* are noted within parentheses.